W9-CXK-196

EARLY MEDIEVAL
ENGLAND

EXPLICIVNT·CAPITVLA·
INCIPIT·LIBER·PRIMVS
MACHABEORVM·

regnauit in grecia. egreffus de terra
cethim darij regem pfarum & medo
conftituit plia multa. & omium ob

EARLY MEDIEVAL ENGLAND

❖

M. T. CLANCHY

LONDON
THE FOLIO
SOCIETY
1997

A HISTORY OF ENGLAND

General Editor: FELIPE FERNÁNDEZ-ARMESTO

England and its Rulers 1066–1272 was first published by Fontana in 1983. The text of this edition follows that of the first edition with minor emendations and the inclusion of the author's revised Further Reading list. This edition is published by arrangement with HarperCollins Publishers Ltd.

The Written Word in the Middle Ages comprises extracts from *From Memory to Written Record*. This title was first published in 1979 by Edward Arnold Ltd in the UK and by Harvard University Press in the USA; a revised second edition was published by Blackwell Publishers in 1993. The text of *The Written Word in the Middle Ages* is based on that of the second edition of *From Memory to Written Record*. This edition is published by arrangement with Blackwell Publishers.

General Preface © The Folio Society Ltd 1997
Introduction © M. T. Clanchy 1997
Maps drawn by Reginald Piggott

Second printing 1997

Typeset at The Folio Society and printed by
St Edmundsbury Press, Bury St Edmunds
on Caxton Laid paper, and bound by
Hunter & Foulis, Edinburgh
in full cloth

Designed by Bernard Roberts

Frontispiece, PLATE I: *The battle of the Maccabees.
Detail from the Bible given to Durham Cathedral
by Bishop Puiset, c. 1175*

❄ CONTENTS ❄

THE WRITTEN WORD IN THE MIDDLE AGES

❈ ILLUSTRATIONS ❈

❈ GENERAL EDITOR'S PREFACE ❈

For the Folio History of England we have sought classic works by historians eminent in their day and influential since—books still worth reading for their status as literature or their contribution to historiography. Where no properly classic volume is available, recent works have been adopted—well written, impactful at their first appearance and likely to endure. All the volumes are intended to represent important strands in the fabric of English historical writing during the last hundred years. They have been chosen for variety. They are not meant to be consistent or even compatible. They were written from a diversity of perspectives, with a diversity of methods, at widely separated moments from the first decade of the twentieth century to the last. Readers with appropriate sensibilities may fancy that they can detect between them, as they lie on the shelf, the kind of friction which generates energy. The truth of English history—if we could get at it—would consist of the totality of all possible perspectives: by shifting in and out of different viewpoints, the Folio History will therefore get closer to the truth than would a conventionally planned series, unified by a very limited set of guidelines and shared assumptions.

None of the works in this series is meant to be unexceptionable. The prejudices and speculations of the writers—even when at variance with evidence which is currently given great weight—are treated as part of the picture of the past, enhancing or enriching the reader's experience. Controversial works, which would not necessarily command mainstream assent or approval today, are, for purposes of this series, deemed virtuous. The introductions by experts are meant to set the volumes in their peculiar contexts and to prevent the reader from being misled. In each case, the last edition of the work revised by the author provides the text of the Folio edition. Some volumes incorporate new material specially prepared by the author. The series begins to appear as the Folio Society prepares to celebrate its fiftieth year. It ought to reflect the goal of the entire fifty years of effort: outstanding volumes in a unique combination.*

FELIPE FERNÁNDEZ-ARMESTO

---

* For the full version of the General Editor's Preface, please see Peter Hunter Blair's *Anglo-Saxon England*.

❀ INTRODUCTION ❀

The title of the first section, *England and its Rulers 1066–1272*, emphasises that this book describes England after the Norman Conquest from the viewpoint of its new rulers. Over the twelfth and thirteenth centuries the Anglo-Norman lords, who were the heirs of the victors at Hastings in 1066, formed a tight-knit élite. They succeeded in holding on to power by adapting to new conditions as they arose, while drawing at the same time on the Norman and French culture in which they had their roots. French remained the principal language of the aristocracy down to the fourteenth century and the shared ideals of an international crusading knighthood sustained them in their frequent wars. So confident and successful was this Anglo-Norman élite within the British Isles that it spread beyond the Anglo-Saxon boundaries of England into Wales, Scotland and Ireland. William the Marshal, who started his career in war in 1152 as a hostage offered to King Stephen (at the age of four or five) and concluded it in 1219 as the regent defending England from the French, is the best example of such an Anglo-Norman lord with estates in Normandy, England, Wales and Ireland. Castles, culminating in the majestic fortresses built by Edward I in north Wales, are the most conspicuous monuments today to Anglo-Norman power.

Militarily the Anglo-Normans were successful within the British Isles, but they sustained a series of defeats in France from the death of Richard I in 1199 onwards. His new castle of Château-Gaillard failed to protect Normandy in 1204, when King Philip Augustus of France marched in. All that remained of the Anglo-Norman duchy was the lordship of the Channel Islands. In retrospect we can see that the so-called Angevin Empire, comprising the king of England's overlordship across northern and western France down to the Pyrenees, was irrevocably compromised by the loss of Normandy; but it took years for the kings of England and the aristocracy to accept this, as they had formed loyalties and interests on both sides of the Channel. The baronial rebellion against Henry III in 1258 was led by a Frenchman whom the king had introduced to England, Simon de Montfort. The castles of Edward I in Wales were designed by a Savoyard, Master James of St George, just as many Savoyards had been involved in government under Henry III.

The Anglo-Norman lords never had been a mere warband of adventurers collecting booty and tribute in England, as their Anglo-Saxon opponents alleged in the aftermath of the victory at Hastings. Over the years, the Anglo-Normans became increasingly proud of their English heritage:

probably in Lincolnshire in 1140, the historian Gaimar used the *Anglo-Saxon Chronicle* to write his *Estoire des Engleis*, one of the first books anywhere to be written in the French language. The newcomers invested their wealth in England by becoming the developers of agriculture and towns and patrons of churches and monasteries. Nearly all the English cathedrals were rebuilt in the century after the Norman Conquest. Today, in Durham above all, with its magnificent cathedral and castle and its precious charters and books, the achievements of the Norman incomers can best be appreciated. In their work at Durham the Normans were very conscious that they were restoring the prestige of Northumbrian culture reaching back to St Cuthbert and the Venerable Bede four centuries earlier. Similarly at Canterbury William the Conqueror's archbishop, Lanfranc, aimed to revive the triumphs of St Augustine's conversion of the English under Pope Gregory the Great. Lanfranc claimed primacy over the whole of Britain including the Orkney Islands, just as the Romans had done. William the Conqueror claimed to be the lawful heir of Edward the Confessor and Anglo-Saxon greatness. England made William into a king; until then he had been a duke theoretically subject to the king of France.

The Anglo-Normans prided themselves on restoring past majesty by being innovative. The spiral piers and rib-vaults in the nave of Durham cathedral have parallels in France and St Peter's, Rome; but nowhere else had these elements been combined with such force and clarity. Durham symbolised the enduring greatness of England's ancient saints and the mastery exercised by its new rulers in every sphere of endeavour. The illuminated manuscripts produced by Anglo-Norman monks are among the greatest works of art in the world: the Carilef and Puiset Bibles at Durham, the Winchester Bible and Psalter made for Bishop Henry of Blois (King Stephen's brother), and the Bury St Edmunds Bible painted by Master Hugh. At Canterbury the inscription framing the full-page portrait of the scribe Eadwine declares: *Scriptorum princeps ego*— 'I am the prince of writers: my praise and fame will never die.' Judging by his name, Eadwine was an Englishman, or a Frenchman who had taken an English name on becoming a monk of Canterbury. Either way, his art epitomises the amalgam which Anglo-Norman lordship produced. In the thirteenth century the skills of monks, clerics and builders rose to new triumphs in the Gothic cathedrals of Lincoln and Salisbury and in the choir of Henry III's Westminster Abbey. They are French in style, but English in interpretation. When Henry III first saw the Sainte Chapelle, on a visit to St Louis in Paris, he wanted to take it back to London in a cart.

It cannot be emphasised too strongly that the king and his lords, who dominated England with such style, were an aristocracy numbering no more than a few thousands (in a population estimated at a million and a half in 1066 and three or four million by 1300). The Anglo-Normans created a cultured world of art and literature thanks to the daily labour of hundreds of thousands of peasants. In the chronicle of John of Worcester Henry I is illustrated having a series of nightmares in which each of the three orders of medieval society—knights, churchmen and peasants— threaten him with their weapons: knights with swords, bishops with croziers and the peasants with scythes and cudgels. Peasants have left no written records of their lives because they were given no opportunities to do so. The stone castles and the iron-mailed knights of the Normans were intended to intimidate the workers on the surrounding land as much as rival aristocrats. War in twelfth-century England, as in twentieth-century Vietnam or anywhere in the Third World, consisted principally of killing peasant families and burning their crops and houses of thatch and wood.

The monks and clergy were the brothers and cousins of the lords and knights. The monastic virtues of poverty, chastity and obedience made no sense except to the aristocracy. For the rest of the population, poverty and obedience were facts of everyday life and chastity was inadvisable, as too many children and future workers died in infancy. The clergy used their superior education to justify their privileged status as men of God and to raise funds from their military patrons for their monasteries and cathedrals. The threefold ordering of duties was an accurate model of medieval society. The knights, the *bellatores* (warriors), made war in the name of Holy Church: whether on the battlefields at Hastings, Lewes and Evesham, or on crusade, or on their neighbours in England itself. Secondly came the churchmen, the *oratores* (the men of prayer), who interceded for the salvation of their benefactors and made wonderful buildings and books for the glory of God and their patrons—and for their own glory too, as Eadwine's inscription makes clear.

Thirdly came the great majority, the *arratores* (the diggers), who provided a living for everybody else as best they could in good years and bad. In the general opinion of the knights and clergy, the peasants who produced the wealth of England were dirty, crude 'rustics' (*rustici* literally meant 'country people'). Their names were not inscribed in illuminated letters in the *LiberVitae*, the 'Book of Life' kept on the high altar at Durham Cathedral and other churches, as the profits from their labour were insufficient to make anything over to the Church—and hence to God. Nevertheless, the message of the Christian Gospel promising salvation to all good men, regardless of poverty or riches, filtered down to the peasants, who struggled with their sick to the shrines of local saints and perhaps got some comfort from the prospect of heavenly salvation. In the century after the Norman Conquest the lot of the peasants temporarily found a voice in the *Anglo-Saxon Chronicle*, with its doleful annual record of bad harvests, arbitrary taxes and cruel lords, including the alien kings who had made new forests and fenced enclosures (the Normans introduced warrens for their imported French rabbits). By Henry II's reign, however, when the tradition of Anglo-Saxon monasticism had been absorbed into the mainstream of Anglo-Norman lordship, the voice of the rustic majority ceased to be recorded. The *Anglo-Saxon Chronicle* and the Old English written language petered out in the fenlands round Peterborough Abbey, where Hereward the Wake had led his rebellion against William the Conqueror a century earlier. The draining and exploitation of these East Anglian wetlands is another example of Anglo-Norman initiative.

The voice of women, of any social class, is almost as hard to hear in the records as the voice of peasants. At Durham Cathedral women were not admitted to the shrine of St Cuthbert because the monks argued, perhaps correctly, that the ascetic saint had never approved of them. With its celibate male clergy, medieval Christianity was an overtly patriarchal religion, though women could find a place in it as the mothers of monks and holy men, just as the Virgin Mary had a growingly revered place in the devotions of the Catholic Church as a whole because she had been the mother of Jesus. Even so, Mary was entirely exceptional, not least in being both a virgin and a mother. The best thing earthly women could do was to imitate the monks by becoming nuns, though generally only women with property were accepted in convents and some of the reforming monks, notably the Cistercians, were suspicious of religious women altogether. The life of Christina of Markyate from the twelfth century poignantly describes the battles that one aristocratic woman fought to resist the marriage which had been planned for her, and equally to resist sexual harassment from the clergy who were intended to protect her, including Ranulf Flambard, bishop of Durham and guardian of the shrine of St Cuthbert. Christina triumphed, however, and the illustrated Psalter which she owned is one of the most beautiful books from the twelfth century.

Despite the relative scarcity of records from the Middle Ages, its ways of doing things are more accessible to readers today than some later periods of history because medieval authors wrote so vividly. Most of the principal sources from the twelfth and thirteenth centuries are available in modern English translations, notably in the two volumes of 'English Historical Documents' (edited by D. C. Douglas and H. Rothwell respectively) and in the thirty or so volumes of 'Oxford Medieval Texts'. The life of Christina of Markyate is one of a number of biographies and memoirs, which have great immediacy through their apparent naïvety and directness. (Such naïvety was a consummate skill in the writing of saints' lives, which are not as simple as they look.) Letters too were an art-form, taken to the highest point of sophistication and charm in the correspondence of John of Salisbury, who was Thomas Becket's secretary. The chronicles of Jocelin of Brakelond (a monk of Bury St Edmunds in the reign of Henry II) and Matthew Paris (a monk of St Albans in the reign of Henry III) have rightly always been famed for their readability. Despite being monks, the best chroniclers wrote in a very worldly and anecdotal way as if they were journalists. In a *Courtier's Trifles* Walter Map, who was not a monk but a highly educated cleric, constructed a kind of *Finnegans Wake* of miscellaneous anecdote and scandalous comments, ostensibly arising from his experiences at the court of Henry II. His contemporary, Gerald of Wales, wrote with similar verve and acerbity.

The most immediately appealing record from this period must be the Bayeux Tapestry. Its apparently naïve account, in pictures and Latin captions, of the battle of Hastings and its causes conceals all kinds of subtleties. The tapestry is so powerful that it is impossible to think of the Normans without it. It has been reproduced in reduced size in numerous facsimiles and the whole tapestry (203 feet in length) is now on permanent exhibition at Bayeux. The viewer can move along its length, slowing down or speeding up the action from frame to frame, as if the tapestry were a video. Its mysteries will probably never all be solved, but in confronting them, a new eye has an advantage over a scholarly expert, however experienced he or she may be. Much the same applies to the monastic chronicles and histories now accessible in English translations. Anyone living in or visiting England, who has an eye for detail and an ability to ask unexpected questions, has the medieval past all around him: in the shape of landscape and town plans, churches large and small, castles (whether in ruins or engulfed in later restorations), and the books and documents now conserved in museums, libraries and archives. As with other remote periods of history, archaeology still produces surprises, as well as being an illuminating guide to material culture. (The Museum of London is one of the best introductions to medieval archaeology.)

The documents of the king's government kept in the Public Record Office, from Domesday Book and the pipe rolls of the twefth-century Exchequer onwards, are an inexhaustible source of information about medieval England and an extraordinary monument to the government which made them. For the period up to 1300 they constitute millions of items of information on thousands of lengths of parchment, handwritten in Latin. Much of this is still unpublished and uncomputerised; so numerous new discoveries are likely to be made in the coming decades. The contents of the Public Records is primarily legal and financial, but they are not all boring or routine because the makers of these documents were still experimenting with doing the task. Walter Map, who acted as a royal judge, was presumably one of their creators. A remarkably lively description of how the Exchequer worked in the 1180s is given by Richard Fitz Nigel in the *Dialogue of the Exchequer*. This book, which was kept with the records of government, facetiously imitates a Platonic dialogue between a master and his untutored pupil. The master points out that information about how the king's money is obtained and kept will prove a good deal more useful than all the scholarly writing about the liberal arts and philosophy. Between them, master and pupil reveal the king's secrets: how tally-sticks were cut, the silver pennies assayed, and the accounts written in permanent ink on specially prepared sheepskins (the pipe rolls).

The second section, *The Written Word in the Middle Ages*, surveys all writing in England between the Norman Conquest and the reign of Edward I (1066–1307). It puts the records in a wider social context of increasing literacy. The argument is that literacy diffused downwards from the royal government. The king sent out written orders concerning law enforcement and taxation to officers in the counties and they responded by giving further written instructions of their own. By Edward I's reign even peasants were required to have seals to authenticate documents. This kind of public governmental literacy was obviously of more concern to men than women, who were largely confined to the household. But, at the same time, within their houses ladies were encouraging literacy for religious purposes. Because the woman of the house was responsible for the upbringing of children, initiating them into prayer and Scripture—and hence into literacy—was her duty. From these dual roots of bureaucratic demands and religious obligations, literacy began to increase markedly. By the thirteenth century lay landowners have archives and history books of their own and their wives have prayer-books. Books of Hours, which are illuminated liturgical books for the laity, have their origin at this time. Most of them were made for women and they came from the same workshops, in Oxford notably, as the scholastic texts made for students and their masters. In the long term, the growth of all forms of writing and education was the most significant development in this period.

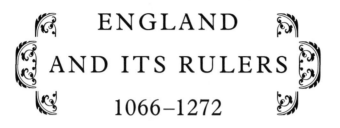

ENGLAND
AND ITS RULERS
1066–1272

Foreign Lordship
and National Identity

❁ PREFACE ❁

This book is intended both as an outline narrative of political history for students and as a new interpretation of the period. Within a necessarily limited format I have been able to give references for all quotations but not for every statement made. However, in the bibliography I list the principal sources available in English translation as well as some suggestions for further reading. I have aimed throughout to keep the reader in contact with the sources (particularly the monastic chroniclers) and to provide a commentary on the views of historians since the time of William Stubbs a century ago. His Constitutional History remains the best single work on this period despite its faults.

I wish to thank Mrs M. Sword for her expert typing, my colleague Mr C. P. Wormald for commenting on the book in draft, and Professor G. R. Elton for his encouragement throughout.

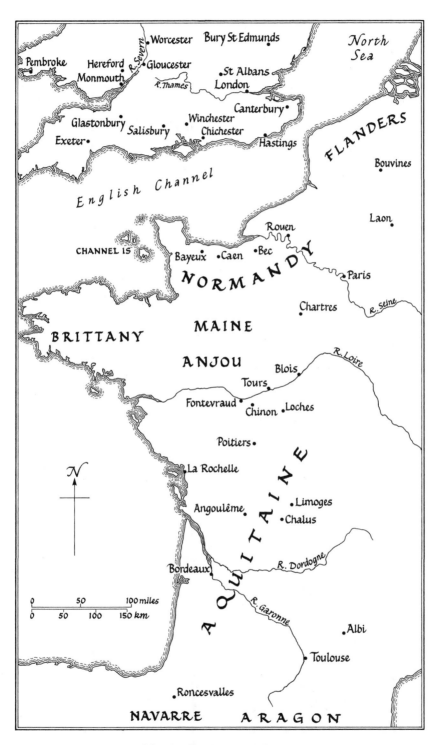

Map 1. England and France

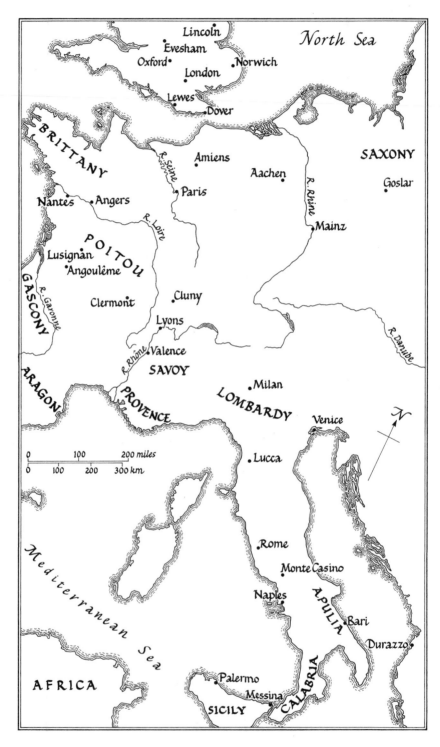

Map 2. England and the Mediterranean

✠ I ✠

ENGLAND'S PLACE IN MEDIEVAL EUROPE

This book concerns the rulers of England and their aspirations in the period between the Norman Conquest of 1066 and the death of Henry III in 1272. During these two centuries England was dominated by men from overseas. This trend had begun before 1066 with the rule of the Danish king Cnut (1016–35) and of the half-Norman Edward the Confessor (1042–66), and it lingered on after 1272 in the French-speaking court of Edward I (1272–1307) and his successors. Nevertheless the most significant period of overseas domination of political and cultural life in the English kingdom followed the Norman Conquest and continued into the twelfth century and beyond. When the Norman dynasty failed in the male line with the death of Henry I in 1135, England became the battleground between two of William the Conqueror's grandchildren, Stephen and the Empress Matilda. On Stephen's death the kingdom was inherited by Henry II (1154–89), who was count of Anjou in his own right and duke of Aquitaine by marriage. The area of the king of England's political concern had therefore widened beyond William the Conqueror's Normandy to include Anjou and the huge lands of Aquitaine and Poitou south of the Loire. This extension of power is described by historians—though never by contemporaries—as the 'Angevin Empire', implying an overlordship by the dynasty of Anjou over England and half of modern France. According to Gerald of Wales, Henry hoped to extend his rule beyond France to Rome and the empire of Frederick Barbarossa. In leading Christendom in the crusade against Saladin, Richard I (1189–99) was following in the footsteps of the Angevin kings of Jerusalem as well as fulfilling promises made by Henry II. His death in the struggle with Philip Augustus of France and King John's subsequent loss of Normandy to Philip did not bring an end either to overseas influence in England or to the ambitions of its kings, as John hoped to regain Normandy from his base in Poitou and Aquitaine. He established the strategy, which was vigorously pursued by his successor Henry III (1216–72), of using Poitevins as administrators and war captains in England. Through them and the support of the papacy Henry hoped to construct a system of alliances which would win his family the huge inheritance in Italy and Germany of the greatest of the medieval emperors, Frederick II, and thus surpass the achievements of Henry II and Richard I. 'We wish', wrote Pope Alexander

IV in 1255, 'to exalt the royal family of England, which we view with special affection, above the other kings and princes of the world.'[1]

The rebellion of 1258 against Henry's Poitevins and papal ambitions
compelled both king and barons to recognise the separateness of England: the king by conceding the Norman and Angevin lands to Louis IX of
France in 1259, and the barons by forming their revolutionary commune
of England. As if to emphasise the persistence of overseas influence, that
commune was led by a Frenchman, Simon de Montfort. This period of
rebellion and civil war marked a turning-point in the definition of English
identity. Its rulers thereafter continued to pursue overseas ambitions, first
in France in the Hundred Years War and then as a worldwide maritime
power, but they did so now as heads of an English nation and not as alien
warlords like William the Conqueror and Henry II. In order to emphasise
the influence of outsiders and at the same time to provide a chronological
framework, this book is divided into parts comprising three periods each
of about seventy years' duration: the Normans (comprising the reigns of
William the Conqueror, William Rufus and Henry I); the Angevins (the
reigns of Stephen, Henry II and Richard I); the Poitevins (the reigns of
John and Henry III). The titles 'Normans', 'Angevins' and 'Poitevins' are
not intended to suggest that the rulers came exclusively from these
regions, but that the king of England's predominant overseas connections
shifted from Normandy in the eleventh century through Anjou in the
twelfth to Poitou in the thirteenth.

England and its conquerors

The English had developed a settled identity precociously early among
the European powers. The Anglo-Saxon kings of the tenth century, building on the achievements of Offa in Mercia and Alfred in Wessex, had created a single kingdom. At its best, a sacrosanct king headed a well-defined
structure of authority (consisting of shires, hundreds and boroughs),
which used a uniform system of taxation and coinage and a common written language in the Anglo-Saxon of writs and charters. Even the fragility
of these achievements, in the face of the Danish and Norman invasions of
the eleventh century, encouraged a sense of common identity in adversity,
as the kingdom's misfortunes were attributed in such works as Wulfstan's
Sermon of the Wolf to the English to the sinfulness of the people rather than
to the shortcomings of the political system. Monastic writers were therefore able to transmit to their successors the hope that the English kingdom would emerge intact from foreign domination. Thus Orderic Vitalis,
who was sent to Normandy when still a child to become a monk, never-

theless identified fiercely with England's woes. Describing Norman atrocities after the rebellion of Edwin and Morcar, he upbraids the Normans
who 'did not ponder contritely in their hearts that they had conquered not
by their own strength but by the will of almighty God, and had subdued a
people that was greater, richer and older than they were'.[2] This sense of
Englishness, transmitted like the English language as a mother tongue
despite its disappearance in official circles, persisted as a powerful under-
current throughout the twelfth century to emerge as a political force in
the thirteenth. The isolated monks who continued with the *Anglo-Saxon
Chronicle* after the Norman Conquest, noting for example that the year
1107 was the 'forty-first of French rule in this country', and the gregarious
mothers and wet-nurses who naturally spoke to their infants in English
had together saved the nation's identity.

The unity of the English kingdom at the time of the Conquest was
a sign not of its modernity by eleventh-century standards but of its antiquity. Its centralised government was based on the models of imperial
Rome and the Carolingian empire, whereas the tendency of the tenth and
eleventh centuries had been away from royal centralisation and towards
aristocratic feudalism. Power had shifted from kings and their hierarchies
of officials towards self-sufficient knights in their castles. Similarly the
clergy were beginning to question the value of sanctified kings as their
protectors and were demanding instead to be free from lay domination.
'Who does not know', asked Pope Gregory VII in 1081, 'that kings and
dukes originated from those who, being ignorant of God, strove with
blind greed and insufferable presumption to dominate their equals, that is
their fellow men, by pride, violence, treachery and murder? And when
they try to force the priests of the Lord to follow them, can kings not best
be compared to him who is the head over all the children of pride? The
devil.'[3] With the Norman Conquest and the civil wars of Stephen's and
Henry II's reigns, England was therefore brought into the mainstream of
European politics, where knights waged war from stone fortresses and
clergy, educated at reformed monasteries and the new universities,
claimed to be above royal power. The values and style of life of the two
most admired Englishmen of the twelfth century, William the Marshal,
the model of the new knighthood, and Thomas Becket, the martyr of the
reformed clergy, would scarcely have been comprehensible to an Anglo-
Saxon thane or bishop of a century earlier.

Such was the power of the new knights and clergy that they reshaped
the traditional order of Europe in the eleventh and twelfth centuries. England was not unique in experiencing foreign conquest. At the same time

as William the Conqueror was establishing Norman rule in England, other Normans led by Robert Guiscard were forming a new lordship in southern Italy and Sicily by overawing the pope and the abbot of Monte Cassino and defeating the Byzantines and the Moslems. Similarly in 1085 Alfonso VI of Castile and León entered Toledo as conqueror of the Moslems and in 1099 the army of the First Crusade triumphantly entered Jerusalem. Although these conquests were not directly related to each other, they were due—whether in England, Italy, Spain or Palestine—to the superiority of mounted knights when inspired by a militant clergy.

In the opinion of the conquered people such invaders were no better than a rabble of robbers. This is how at first the English saw their Norman conquerors, how the Byzantines and the popes saw Robert Guiscard, and how the Moslems saw the Cid in Spain and the crusaders in the East. But in each case the invaders demonstrated that they were more than raiders and looters, as they established strong and resilient forms of government which, while depending on the use of force, tempered and directed it through the disciplines of feudalism and the idealism of the reformed clergy. Feudal values, as enunciated in the *Song of Roland* (which is contemporary with the Norman Conquest and may have been sung at the battle of Hastings), gave knights a sense of hierarchy and of loyalty to their lords as well as an irrepressible pride and delight in their war-horses, armour and other instruments of bloodshed. Clerical idealism, as enunciated by Pope Urban II in his sermons launching the First Crusade (and before him by Gregory VII), acknowledged the savagery of knights but aimed to point them in a similar direction to the *Song of Roland*: they would be a *militia* fighting for Christ instead of a *malitia*, the servants of the devil and the embodiment of malice. Although the knights' new sense of righteousness brought only misfortune to those whom they killed, maimed and ransomed, it did make them a sufficiently disciplined and motivated force to build on the ruins of war. Often, too, their sense of realism as fighting men encouraged them to learn from those they conquered. The Normans in England took over and strengthened the Anglo-Saxon taxation and writ system, just as their counterparts in the Moslem lands of Sicily, Palestine and Spain benefited from the superior civilisations over which they ruled.

This book concentrates on the rulers of England and not on the peasants, or 'natives' as the lords called them. The peasants were 'natives' in the sense both of belonging to a subjugated nation, the English, and of being tied by their inferior birth to the land on which they lived and worked. They are the subject of Professor Hallam's volume *Rural England 1066–1348*. The lords, on the other hand, exhibited their superior status by moving freely on horseback from place to place, as their life was spent in hunting and collecting levies of money and produce from their tenants. They exercised their power not only through physical force as knights but through intellectual superiority as clergy. The ideology and resources of the church were as essential to lordship as the skills and equipment of knighthood. The local bishop or abbot was often the brother or kinsman of the lord of the land. King Stephen, for example, depended frequently on his brother, Henry of Blois, who was bishop of Winchester for more than forty years (1129–71). This book therefore includes the higher clergy within its purview because they were worldly lords and rulers despite the insistence of ecclesiastical reformers on being a caste apart.

The power and aspirations of lordship, both clerical and lay, were manifested in buildings and works of art as well as through the personal presence of the knight on horseback and the cleric with his sacred scripture. Much of what most impressed people at the time has disappeared: the burnished war helmets and jewel-encrusted reliquaries, the robes and hangings of silk and ermine, the iron strong-boxes filled with gold. Nevertheless enough remains, particularly in the outer forms of castles and churches, to recall this lost way of life. Above all, illuminated manuscripts, many of which are almost perfectly preserved, radiate from their pages not only the colour and brilliance of Romanesque and Gothic art but the thought-worlds of their medieval creators. These works were the supreme products of lordship, the legacy which was deliberately left to posterity as a tribute to divine power from men who recognised their own skills. 'I am the prince of writers,' the inscription in the frame around Eadwine of Canterbury's portrait declares in c. 1150, 'neither my praise nor my fame will die hereafter . . . The beauty of this book displays my genius; God accept it as a gift pleasing to him.'[4] The book which this portrait accompanies is a text of the psalms with three variant Latin texts (Gallican, Roman and Hebrew) and English and French translations. It illustrates very well the mastery of the rulers and the way they were part of the civilisation of western Christendom as well as building on English traditions.

Europe and the world

Knowledge of England's place in space and time was the speciality of monks and other clerical writers who inspired the men of action to their pilgrimages and crusades and recorded their deeds in chronicles and histories. Although much of this knowledge was inaccurate and some of it was fictitious, like Geoffrey of Monmouth's popular *History of the Kings of*

Britain which elaborated the story of King Arthur, it nevertheless gave the rulers a yardstick by which to measure their endeavours and achievements. Varying Voltaire's epigram, if Arthur did not exist it would be necessary to invent him. The monks of Glastonbury recognised this in 1191 when they discovered and exhumed the alleged bodies of Arthur and Guinevere. Arthur or no Arthur, it is a mistake to underestimate the range of knowledge which medieval writers claimed to have or to dismiss altogether the existence of now lost books such as the one which Geoffrey of Monmouth said he had used. His contemporary, the historian William of Malmesbury, assumed a wide knowledge in his reading public. Defending in 1125 his decision to produce a history of the English bishops, he wrote: 'It was certainly slothful and degrading not to know the names of the principal men of our province when our knowledge otherwise extends as far as the tracts of India and whatever lies beyond, open to the boundless ocean.'[5]

In William's time the world was pictured schematically in *mappae mundi* as a circle with Jerusalem at the centre and the three continents of Asia, Africa and Europe placed around it. Asia occupies the top half of the circle while Africa and Europe are placed in the bottom right- and left-hand quarters respectively. (Neither medieval Europeans, nor the Romans and Greeks who preceded them, had any certain knowledge of Africa south of the equator or of America and Australasia.) The whole circular landmass is surrounded by the 'boundless ocean' to which William of Malmesbury refers. What he meant by saying that our knowledge extends to India is that the conventional representation of three continents had been handed down from ancient geographers via the encyclopedist Isidore of Seville. William and his fellow western Christians had no knowledge from experience of either Asia or Africa, although that was beginning to change now that crusaders and Italian merchants were establishing themselves all around the Mediterranean. Representations of the earth in the form of Jerusalem-centred world maps were a step back rather than forwards from the point of view of geographical science. Thus the large circular wall-map at Hereford Cathedral, attributed to Richard of Haldingham and drawn in the late thirteenth century, is less accurate in its representation of Britain, though it is more detailed, than the square map in the British Museum (MS Tiberius B.v) which dates from about AD 1000.

Jerusalem-centred maps showed the world as planned by God rather than according to what was known about it by physical scientists. Sometimes God, as the creator of heaven and earth, is depicted hovering protectively above the map with his angels in the star-filled universe. Such maps represent with accuracy not the relationships of places as measured by fallible men but the words of scripture: 'Thus saith the Lord God; this is Jerusalem: I have set it in the midst of the nations and countries that are round about her.' St Jerome comments on this passage from Ezechiel (5 : 5) that Jerusalem is sited in the centre of the world because it is the umbilical cord which connects divine life with earthly life. Jerusalem-centred maps, which become the standard form in the twelfth century, also represent contemporary aspirations. In William of Malmesbury's account of Urban II's speech at Clermont launching the First Crusade the pope uses the image of the *mappa mundi* of three continents, with Asia occupying half the circle and Europe only a quarter. He describes how the Moslems are threatening to take over the whole world, as they already have Asia, which was the cradle of Christianity, and Africa, which produced so many of the fathers of the church. 'The learned will know what I am talking about,' the pope assures his audience: 'thirdly there is the remaining region of the world, Europe, of which we Christians inhabit only a small part'.[6] The pope's comment is strange at first sight, as the Moslems in 1095 possessed only the southern half of Spain together with the Balearic islands and Sicily. But it becomes explicable in the light of his next statement: 'For who will say that all those barbarians who live in the remote islands of the glacial ocean are Christians, as they lead a monstrous life?' Northern Europeans, some of whom in Norway and Sweden had indeed not been converted to Christianity at the time of Urban's speech, are therefore equated by the Mediterranean pope with the sea monsters who live at the world's end.

According to the Jerusalem-centred world view, England bordered the remote islands in the glacial ocean such as Iceland and the Orkneys. England was on the perimeter of the circle, 'the outer edge of the earth's extent' as the Anglo-Saxon Ælfric had described it.[7] Wales and Ireland were consequently on the furthest borders of the world (according to Gerald of Wales), and beyond Scotland there was no habitation (in the words of the Declaration of Arbroath). In the thirteenth century the schoolman Robert the Englishman was obliged to acknowledge in his lectures on cosmology that England was too far north to be included in the recognised climes or regions of geographers. 'But the reason for this', Robert explains, 'is not because it is unfit to live in, as some will have it, but because it was not inhabited at the time of the division into climes.'[8] This slur on England's good name leads Robert, like other medieval writers, to launch into a paean praising the country's fertility and climate.

The elements of such patriotic descriptions had remained much the same since Bede (himself drawing on the works of Nennius and Gildas) set the pattern for them in the opening chapter of his *Ecclesiastical History of the English People* in the early eighth century. Indeed just as Jerusalem-centred maps of the twelfth and thirteenth centuries were less accurate than those of the earlier Middle Ages, so descriptions of England's geographical characteristics show a decline in precision. This is because even those learned in astronomy and the physical science of the time, like Robert the Englishman, preferred Geoffrey of Monmouth's exaggerations to the circumstantial work of Bede. Geoffrey, describing Britain rather than England as such, calls it 'the best of islands'.[9] It provides in unfailing plenty everything that is needed: all sorts of minerals, all kinds of crops from the rich soil, every variety of game in its forests; there are fat cattle on its pastures and green meadows, bees gathering honey from its beautiful flowers, plentiful fish in its rivers and lakes, and people lulled happily to sleep on the banks of its babbling brooks. (Geoffrey borrowed this last image from Gildas, who had written in the sixth century.) Britain also — and this is Geoffrey's main subject—has an extraordinarily distinguished history, beginning with its formation by the Trojan Brutus and progressing through Lear and Cymbeline to Arthur who had dominated Europe.

All this is of course exaggerated and some of it is absurd. Nevertheless such optimism was echoed by other writers. For example Richard of Devizes in the 1190s describes a French Jew persuading a fellow Frenchman to go to England, that land flowing with milk and honey where no one who strives to make an honest living dies poor. Although by modern European and American standards life in the Middle Ages was poor, nasty, brutish and short, that was not the universal opinion of those who experienced it. They veered between extremes of delight in the bountifulness of the earth and its seasons, like William the Conqueror's fellow ruler the troubadour William IX of Aquitaine, and by contrast deep awareness, among reforming monks like St Bernard in particular, of the transitoriness of life and the immediacy of divine retribution. Over the centuries patriotic historians and writers developed Geoffrey of Monmouth's ideal of the best of islands into the famous description in Shakespeare's *Richard II* of:

> This blessed plot, this earth, this realm, this England,
> This nurse, this teeming womb of royal kings . . .

In one way at least England actually was pleasanter in the twelfth century than now, and that was in its climate. In his description of the Vale of Gloucester, William of Malmesbury comments that 'the frequency of vines there is more concentrated, their produce more fruitful, and their

PLATE II. The Hereford world map *c.* 1290. Jerusalem is at the centre
and the British Isles are shown at bottom left, at the edge of the world

taste sweeter than in any other area of England'.[10] This implies, and there is other evidence to support it, that viticulture was quite common in twelfth-century England. Even the *Anglo-Saxon Chronicle's* pessimistic account of how things went from bad to worse during the nineteen years of Stephen's reign concludes with a description of the Norman abbot of Peterborough, Martin of Bec, planting a vineyard as part of his improvements to the abbey. William of Malmesbury adds that the wines from the Gloucester area could bear comparison with French ones, whereas by implication those from less favoured areas could not. He wrote this in the 1120s when northern Europe was still enjoying a relatively warm period before cold and rain began to predominate in the latter half of the thirteenth century. At the time therefore when England was ruled by incomers from France, its climate (in the south at least) would not have made such a strong contrast with their own. Nevertheless England never was a large wine-producing country. Medieval Englishmen characteristically drank beer and they were notorious abroad for consuming too much (see page 178 below).

England's destiny

England's place in the medieval world could be viewed in different lights. Certainly England was physically remote from the centre and seemed to those who had only theoretical knowledge of it to be on the outer periphery of civilisation. On the other hand it was reputed to be rich, in both minerals and agricultural produce, and its climate was benign. Although the wealth of England was probably exaggerated both at home and abroad, it served as a strong inducement to conquerors and adventurers. Eadmer of Canterbury tells a story of how in the reign of Cnut the bishop of Benevento in central Italy went on a fund-raising tour on behalf of his church, which claimed to possess the body of the apostle St Bartholomew: the bishop was offering for sale an arm from this precious relic. Passing through Italy and France he decided to proceed to England when he heard talk of its wealth and of how he was likely to get a better price there than anywhere else. In this the bishop succeeded, selling the arm to Queen Emma for several pounds of silver. Eadmer uses this story to illustrate how in those days, before the coming of Lanfranc and the Norman reformers, the English valued relics above everything. For us the story illustrates England's reputation for wealth, which Eadmer thought a commonplace as he was writing in the reigns of William Rufus and Henry I when the treasures of England and the loot amassed by its Norman conquerors were the talk of Europe.

Throughout the twelfth century the kings of England were reputed to be wealthier than the Capetian kings of France. William Rufus, writes Abbot Suger of St Denis, was 'opulent, a spender of the treasures of the English and a marvellous dealer in and payer of knights', whereas his own king, Louis VI, was short of money.[11] To display their wealth and power the Norman kings built on an unprecedented scale. The Tower of London, completed by Rufus in 1097, was the greatest stone keep yet built in western Europe. Similarly Westminster Hall, which was also the achievement of Rufus, was the largest roofed space (238 ft. × 68 ft.), being more than twice the size of the emperor's hall at Goslar. Yet Rufus is reported to have commented that it was only 'half as big as it should have been'.[12] The new cathedral at Winchester (533 ft. long), where Rufus was brought for burial after being killed in the New Forest, was surpassed in length only by the third abbey church of Cluny which was nearing completion at the same time.

Such displays of power gave a sense of reality to beliefs that the kings of England were destined to play a dominant role in European politics. William of Malmesbury states that, if belief in the transmigration of souls were permitted, the soul of Julius Caesar had entered Rufus. 'He had huge ambitions,' writes William, 'and he would have achieved them if he could have spun out the tissue of the Fates, or broken through and escaped from the violence of fortune. Such was his force of mind that he was audacious enough to promise himself any kingdom whatsoever.'[13] The best monastic historians like William enjoyed composing obituaries of this sort which evoked the antique world of pagan heroes striving against the gods. Such writing in a classical idiom was as Romanesque as the sculpture and painting of the time; it used classical motifs but the essentials were medieval. The image of Rufus as a conquering Caesar, cut off in his prime, was taken further by Gaimar in his romantic history of the English, which was written in c. 1140 in French rhyming couplets and is here translated into prose: 'On account of his great nobleness all his neighbours were subject to him, and if he could have reigned longer he would have gone to Rome to claim the ancient right to that country which Brennius and Belinus had.'[14] Gaimar here associates the career of Rufus with Geoffrey of Monmouth's History of the Kings of Britain which had just been published. Brennius and Belinus, the sackers of Rome in 390 BC, were (in Geoffrey's version) British kings who had first conquered the Gauls and the Germans before uniting against Rome. The fantastic achievements of this pair, like those of Arthur himself, fulfilled (in Geoffrey's story) the prophecy of the goddess Diana, who had told the

Trojan Brutus to seek an island in the ocean beyond the setting of the sun and the realms of Gaul; there he would found a second Troy and from him would descend a line of kings who would make subject the 'circle of the whole earth'.[15]

Geoffrey's prophecy of Diana is a myth which explains the ambivalent position of Britain. It is an island which lies on the periphery of the earth, beyond the setting of the sun as seen from the centre, but its rulers originate from the centre and are destined to return there to rule. It is impossible to know how much of this myth Geoffrey made up and how much of it derived from oral traditions or writings in books now lost. What is not in doubt, however, is the popularity of Geoffrey's work: it is extant in over two hundred medieval manuscripts (more than Bede's *History*), fifty of which date from the twelfth century. It was translated from Geoffrey's Latin into French, English and Welsh and one-third of the total number of manuscripts are in continental Europe. These facts make Geoffrey's history the most popular work emanating from medieval Britain and perhaps the most popular of all medieval histories.

As significant as Geoffrey's popularity is the credence he was given by reputable and scholarly writers. Thus Robert the Englishman includes Geoffrey's prophecy of Diana in his lectures as an explanation of why England is prosperous despite its lying beyond the climes. By his time Geoffrey's history had been incorporated into numerous English chronicles, along with the Old Testament and miscellaneous late Roman sources, in narratives of the seven ages of the world from its creation up to the Christian era. This illustrates the medieval scribal tendency to add new information to old rather than to evaluate it critically. The acceptance of Geoffrey is the more remarkable considering that William of Newburgh in the latter half of the twelfth century had put forward the objections which modern critics repeat. William compares Geoffrey's narratives with Bede's and concludes that Geoffrey 'has dressed up in colourful Latin style under the honest name of history tales of Arthur taken from old British legends and augmented by his own inventions'.[16] Geoffrey's history triumphantly survived such criticism because William's comments had a very limited circulation (a problem for any critic of a popular work before the invention of printing) and also perhaps because Geoffrey told people what they wanted to hear. He put the history of Britain into a grand and dynamic context which fed the ambitions of the Anglo-Norman conquerors. Although Geoffrey's book concerned Britain rather than England and might have been interpreted as Celtic propaganda against the Normans, it was dedicated to Robert earl of Gloucester,

Henry I's distinguished bastard son. Indeed Geoffrey went further and wished to attribute the work not to his humble self but to Earl Robert, so that it too would be the offspring of the illustrious king.

The best illustration of how Geoffrey's history inflated Englishmen's sense of their own importance is William Fitz Stephen's description of London in the time of Becket. It is the most famous city in the world according to William. To it merchants bring gold from Arabia, oil from Babylon, gems from the Nile, silk from China, wines from France, and furs from the Baltic lands and Russia. The references to gold from Arabia and gems from the Nile were certainly clichés of the time rather than a factual description of trade goods. On the other hand French wines and a variety of northern furs were imported. As in Geoffrey's work, fact, fiction and classical allusions are inextricably mixed together in William's account. He reveals his debt to Geoffrey by stating, 'on the good faith of chroniclers', that London is far older than Rome because it was founded by the Trojan Brutus.[17] William likewise cites the prophecy of Diana concerning Brutus, though he ascribes it to the oracle of Apollo. In this version the second Troy of the prophecy is London, and the ruler from Britain in particular who subjected the world is Constantine, the greatest of the emperors from a Christian point of view.

A modern scientist rightly dismisses as nonsense medieval *mappae mundi* which make Jerusalem the centre of the world and histories which claim that London was founded by the Trojans. Nevertheless appreciation of such ideas is essential to a historian because they gave twelfth-century people, however erroneously, a concept of their place in space and time. England's rulers believed that they lived on the edge of the world and increasingly in the twelfth century they aspired to reach the centre, that Jerusalem which was both a real place and a symbol of contact with the divine, the umbilical cord of the earth. Viewed in this way, the aims of Richard I in particular can be seen in their medieval perspective. His ten-year reign (1189–99), of which only six months were spent in England, was not an aberration from the practice of his predecessors but a progression from it. The Norman kings (William the Conqueror, William Rufus and Henry I) had spent less than half their time in England and Richard's father, Henry II, did likewise. Richard was not much criticised by chroniclers for going on crusade and taxing England so heavily. On the contrary, his exactions were blamed on his counsellors and he himself was written about as a hero who had raised England's name by fighting for Jerusalem. His successors, King John and Henry III, spent much more of their time in England but that was not from choice. Rather it was because they were being driven out of their continental lands and out of Mediterranean politics by their rivals, the great French kings, Philip Augustus and St Louis.

The ambitions of England's rulers were fed by a variety of historical myths and chance circumstances. Paradoxically they were given literary shape during Stephen's reign (1135–54) when the kingdom was torn by civil war. This is the time of Geoffrey of Monmouth's *History of the Kings of Britain*, of Gaimar's *Estoire des Engleis*, and of the speech made at the battle of the Standard in 1138 which celebrated the defeat of the Scots. In the earliest report of this speech, which is attributed to the bishop of the Orkneys, the 'great men of England and the distinguished men of Normandy' are reminded of their pre-eminence: 'No one resists you with impunity; brave France has tried and taken shelter; fierce England lay captive; rich Apulia flourished anew under your rule; renowned Jerusalem and noble Antioch both submitted themselves to you.'[18] This is one of the few sources which explicitly links the Normans who conquered England with the achievements of Robert Guiscard in Italy and of his son, Bohemond, who became prince of Antioch during the First Crusade. If this speech were made by the bishop of the Orkneys (in another version it is attributed to the Yorkshire baron Walter Espec), it would have served also to link these islands on the edge of the world with the centre in Jerusalem, as the Normans had reached both. In the versions in which it has come down to us this speech, like Urban II's at Clermont before the First Crusade, is too literary and learned to have directly inspired knights on the battlefield. What it does indicate, however, is the way the Norman victories of the eleventh century had developed into a mythology of conquest in the twelfth which united English and Norman ambitions. All the people of England, according to the chronicler Henry of Huntingdon, replied 'Amen! Amen!' to this speech.

Interpretations of English history

Historians of the nineteenth and twentieth centuries, like their medieval counterparts, have reacted ambivalently to the fact that England was placed on the edge of the medieval world. Some Victorians proudly emphasised England's splendid isolation, while others welcomed the Norman Conquest. Thomas Carlyle's approach was as extravagant as anything in Geoffrey of Monmouth. Without the Normans and Plantagenets, he asked, what would England have been? He trenchantly replied: 'A gluttonous race of Jutes and Angles, capable of no great combinations; lumbering about in potbellied equanimity; not dreaming of heroic toil and silence and endurance, such as leads to the high places of the

Universe and the golden mountain-tops where dwell the Spirits of the Dawn.'[19] Edward Freeman, on the other hand, with prejudices almost as explicit, saw the strength of England coming not from the forceful drilling of the Normans but from its endurance of this fiery trial. For Freeman England belonged to the Teutonic north; indeed it is a more purely Teutonic country than Germany itself. 'We Englishmen', he wrote, 'live in an island and have always moved in a sort of world of our own.'[20] This gave the natives the strength to resist and absorb the incomers: first the Normans, then the accession of the Angevins 'which was almost equivalent to a second conquest', and finally the 'fresh swarms of foreigners under Henry III'. Where Carlyle and Freeman agree is in crediting the conquerors with encouraging English unity.

Popular Victorian historians like Carlyle and Freeman could not avoid a polemical style when discussing England's medieval identity because they wrote for an audience imbued with national feeling. Historians of all the European powers in the nineteenth century laboured to produce scholarly editions of the records of their peoples and to explain their national significance to the public. The problem was that the facts of medieval history were often at variance with the pattern of nineteenth-century national states. Who did Charlemagne belong to, for example, France or Germany? And how did the most powerful government of the twelfth and thirteenth centuries, the papacy, fit into this nationalist scheme? French and German scholars coped with the overlap in their record sources sometimes by agreement but more often by printing the same documents in the *Recueil des Historiens des Gaules et de la France* and in the *Monumenta Germaniae Historica*. English historians faced a more manageable task, as the Anglo-Saxon kingdom had developed a distinct identity precociously early and some medieval writers had believed (with Freeman) that Englishmen moved in a sort of world of their own. The special problem for English national history came with the Norman Conquest, as it appeared at a stroke to destroy the distinctiveness of England and subject it to continental domination in military, ecclesiastical and cultural terms. Furthermore, as Freeman points out, this domination persisted beyond the Normans through the Angevins and into the reign of Henry III.

The most influential Victorian historian to tackle the problem of England's medieval identity was William Stubbs in his authoritative *Select Charters*, first published in 1870, and in the three-volume *Constitutional History* which followed between 1873 and 1878. These works were overtly nationalist, as their purpose was to make English students understand their own institutions as well as those of ancient Greece and Rome on which they had been reared. These institutions, Stubbs argued, 'possess a living interest for every nation that realises its identity, and [they] have exercised on the wellbeing of the civilised world an influence not inferior certainly to that of the classical nations'.[21] In other words, English national consciousness was to be identified and nurtured by studying the origins of its monarchy, law courts and parliament. At his most ambitious Stubbs was proposing an alternative curriculum for higher education in which the future rulers of England at Oxford and Cambridge would read their Latin in Magna Carta and Matthew Paris instead of Cicero and Livy. This would serve to make history respectable as a subject for academic study and it would also be a better preparation for governing because (in Stubbs's opinion at least) English history was more relevant than that of Greece and Rome.

Stubbs was too knowledgeable and intelligent a scholar not to know that the flaw in his approach was that in the period on which he concentrated, between the Norman Conquest and the reign of Edward I (much the same period as this book concerns), many English institutions were similar to continental ones in their outward forms and nomenclature. Royal courts of justice, fiefs, ecclesiastical councils, parliaments, communes and liberties were not unique to England. Although Stubbs admitted the deep and wide basis which medieval England shared with the Continent, he argued that it was a mistake to think that customs 'are borrowed or derived in their matured form by one national system from another'.[22] Taking his metaphor from the railways, which were such a prominent feature of Victorian England, he argued instead that 'the history of institutions, as of nations, runs through occasional tunnels'.[23] These hide the continuous line by which for example medieval boroughs grew out of Anglo-Saxon burhs, or parliament out of the witan. Twelfth- and thirteenth-century institutions were of course connected with their Anglo-Saxon predecessors. Stubbs was mistaken not in this assertion but in his insistence that institutional practice could not be derived by one system from another. Boroughs and parliament in his view had to progress in a single line from their Anglo-Saxon beginnings, even if parts of the line were concealed from view. They could not be significantly influenced by Flemish towns or the French *parlement*, however close the similarities and nomenclature might appear to be, because it was an axiom that each national system created its own institutions and gave to its people a unique and inimitable character. This axiom derived from the fashionable Hegelian philosophy of the time and it also justified Stubbs's hope that English students would realise their identity by studying their history. If that identity were confused with that of France, Germany or Spain, the wrong conclusions might be drawn.

To ensure that only the right message reached his readers Stubbs avoided expressions which belonged in his opinion 'more properly to French and German history'.[24] He disliked the word 'commune', for example, as a description of an association because it was French. Consequently when the rebel barons of 1258 formed 'le commun de Engleterre' Stubbs translated this as 'the commonalty of England'. Whereas 'commune' had associations with revolution and France, both in the thirteenth century and in the nineteenth, 'commonalty' was an archaic English term for a corporation (the mayor and 'commonalty' of a borough) and also for the common people (the commons as distinct from the lords). These usages suited Stubbs's purpose, as 'commonalty' sounded distinctively English and its archaism suggested something conservative rather than revolutionary. Nevertheless this translation was misleading, as the 'commune' of 1258 was in origin a conspiratorial association of barons associated in particular with the Frenchman Simon de Montfort (as explained in chapter 11 below). Its antecedents were in revolutions in continental towns in the twelfth century rather than in the common folk of England.

Although the materials for medieval English history have not substantially changed since the Victorian period, attitudes to it have. The medieval past no longer has to bear the burden which Stubbs imposed on it of justifying England's imperial mission and demonstrating the unique value of its constitutional arrangements. Instead of insisting on a linear growth of institutions from Anglo-Saxon roots, this book emphasises how England's rulers were influenced by movements of power and ideas from overseas. These influences would have been felt even without the Norman Conquest and the Angevin kings, as they were transmitted by clergy and scholars as much as by knights. Nevertheless the fact that England, like southern Italy and the kingdom of Jerusalem, was conquered by aliens helped to accelerate and reinforce change. Highlighting foreign rule in this way does not obscure England's identity. On the contrary, it clarifies and accentuates it by viewing it as far as possible through medieval eyes. In that Jerusalem-centred world England stood on the outer rim of Europe and its rulers were drawn towards the centre. They knew the world was round, but they viewed it not as a mere fact of modern cartography but as an image of faith and hope. Like the rose windows and circular mazes found in the great Gothic cathedrals, or the round table of King Arthur, the Jerusalem-centred world radiated supernatural power and mystery.

PART ONE

The Normans
(1066–1135)

THE NORMANS took their name from the 'Northmen', the Viking pirates who had attacked both England and France in the ninth century. In the same way as King Alfred acknowledged Viking settlement in the northern part of England, the Frankish king, Charles the Simple, ceded his northern territory at the mouth of the Seine in 911 to Rollo, whom the Normans recognised as their first duke. Norman history in the next century is very obscure. By the time William the Conqueror was born, however (in 1027 or 1028), the Normans had created a distinct identity for themselves. Their earliest historian Dudo of St Quentin recorded a story about the homage done by Rollo to Charles the Simple. The Frankish bishops insisted that Rollo should kneel down and kiss the king's foot. Rollo refused, although he permitted one of his warriors to approach the king. This man indeed kissed the royal foot, but he did so without kneeling down by tipping the king backwards off his throne amidst the laughter of the Normans.

This story reveals more about the Normans of William the Conqueror's time than the events of 911. They were proud and ferocious warriors without respect for rank or tradition other than their own. It was as a typical Norman that Robert Guiscard took the pope prisoner at Civitate in 1053 and went on to become duke of Apulia and Calabria ostensibly by the grace of God and St Peter. His son Bohemond impressed himself similarly on the memory of Anna Comnena, the daughter of the Byzantine emperor Alexius, when he towered above both crusaders and Greeks in the imperial tent inspiring admiration and terror: 'A certain charm hung about the man but it was marred by a general sense of the horrible. For in the whole of his body he showed himself implacable and savage both in his size and glance. He was no man's slave, subject to none of all the world; for such are great natures, people say, even if they are of humble origin.'[1] These Mediterranean Normans, the descendants or followers of Tancred of Hauteville, were only remotely connected with the conquerors of England. Nevertheless there were contacts between them. When William the Conqueror's half-brother, Odo of Bayeux earl of Kent, was arrested in 1082, he was believed to have been planning an expedition to Italy to make himself pope which would have linked up the Normans in England with those in Italy. The similarities between the two groups moreover were noticed by medieval writers, even if only as wishful thinking. William of Poitiers in his account of the conquest of England (written within a decade of the battle of Hastings) mentions Norman triumphs in Italy and Byzantium, and the author of *The Song of the Battle of Hastings* (which may not be strictly contemporary) has William the Conqueror exhort his men before the battle as: 'Apulian and Calabrian, Sicilian, whose darts fly in swarms; Normans, ripe for incomparable achievements!'[2]

The Normans had a mixture of contradictory qualities which chroniclers delighted to describe. In Italy Geoffrey Malaterra (who may have been of Norman origin himself) commented on their passion for wealth and power, though they despised what they had and were always looking for more. Another contradiction was their love of flamboyant dress and their impulsiveness; and yet, when necessity demanded, they could endure all the rigours of a disciplined military life. In England William of Malmesbury, independently of Geoffrey, described similar contradictions: 'The Normans were—and still are [William was writing in about 1125]—proudly apparelled and delicate about their food, though not excessively. They are a race inured to war and scarcely know how to live without it . . . They live in huge houses with moderation. They envy their equals and wish to excel their superiors. They plunder their subjects, though they defend them from others. They are faithful to their lords, though a slight offence makes them perfidious. They measure treachery by its chance of success.'[3] Such contradictions were resolved by the logic of war. The Normans were so formidable because they were warlords operating in a Europe that was beginning to be more settled and prosperous. As descendants of the Vikings they were the last barbarian invaders. But they had learned a great deal since the time of Rollo's legendary act of insubordination to the Frankish king. The art of war, like the art of building in stone or the 'liberal arts' of the schoolmen, had become more sophisticated in the eleventh century, and Norman knights were its chief exponents.

The best monument to Norman military methods is the Bayeux Tapestry, though it was probably made by English artists. Its most striking and recurrent feature is the groups of knights in chain-mail, equipped with long shields and lances, charging on their war-horses. They give the same impression of vigour and ferocity which Anna Comnena observed in Bohemond. The 'general sense of the horrible' is conveyed too in the Tapestry in its lower border where the dead are depicted in terrible postures lying amid a litter of abandoned shields, broken swords and wounded horses. The importance of eating well, which William of Malmesbury had commented on, is also graphically illustrated in the Tapestry. The first action the Normans take on landing on English soil is to seize livestock, slaughter it with their battleaxes, roast it on spits and serve it up at a banquet presided over by the warrior bishop, Odo of

Bayeux. From there the Normans move on to building a castle at Hastings and burning villages. The Tapestry's emphasis on the practicalities and daily routines of war indicates the Normans' professionalism. Duke William, like the duke of Wellington, knew that battles are won by attention to details of supply. A large section of the Tapestry shows the Normans' thorough preparation for the invasion: trees being cut down and made into planks; ships being specially built and launched; the loading of supplies (coats of mail, swords, lances, helmets); and finally the putting into the ships of the Norman knights' most precious possession, their highly trained war-horses. Almost as many horses as men are shown in the ships crossing the Channel and Duke William's own charger is individually depicted at the start of the battle.

In the Bayeux Tapestry the invaders are not described as 'Normans' but as 'Franci', that is 'Franks' or 'Frenchmen'. Similarly the *Anglo-Saxon Chronicle* describes them as 'Frencyscan'. In its account of the events of 1066 King Harold defeated the Normans (the 'Normen', that is, the Norwegians) at Stamford Bridge, before himself being killed by the French at Hastings. Similarly the Norman kings of England invariably addressed their people in charters as 'French and English' and not as 'Normans and English'. These usages raise doubts about the cohesion of Norman identity, despite Norman and other chroniclers' descriptions of themselves. The solution lies in the relative position of the observer. The Normans were generally described as Frenchmen in England to distinguish them from the Northmen and because they came from France (Francia). Furthermore a fair number of the 'French' who fought at Hastings were not Normans anyway, but men from Brittany, Maine, Picardy and Flanders. In France itself, on the other hand, they were described as Normans to distinguish them from Angevins, Poitevins, Gascons and so on. Although the Normans are called a 'race' (*gens*) by some contemporaries (Orderic Vitalis, for example), their cohesion lay essentially in their beliefs about themselves rather than in genealogy or blood relationships. Scarcely any Norman family could reliably trace its descent back before the year AD 1000, and their greatest duke was generally known in the Middle Ages not as the Conqueror but as William the Bastard.

Their lack of distinguished ancestry made the Normans' ideology of war and power all the more important to them. They had to fight all the harder to dominate the oldest institutions in Europe (the papacy, the Byzantine Empire and the Anglo-Saxon kingdom) and they were ready to absorb men and ideas from any quarter which would help them. In military terms they embodied the greatness of the barbarian Franks who had conquered Roman Gaul and created the Carolingian empire. But they reflected too the new French knighthood whose prowess was enshrined in the *Song of Roland*. By the twelfth century, as a consequence rather than a cause of their success, the victors of Hastings were: 'You whom France famed for nobility has bred, chivalrous warriors, renowned young men whom God chooses and favours!'[4]

Although the Normans were essentially war-lords, they were a force much more complex than mere barbarians or brigands. A contradiction at first sight is the way they succeeded in attracting the two greatest church-men and intellectuals of their time, Lanfranc and Anselm from south of the Alps, to their cause. These two men built up the new monastery at Bec in William the Conqueror's time into one of the most famous and enter-prising schools in Europe, and they became in succession archbishops of Canterbury. This paradox between the Normans' love of war and their advancement of religion did not escape the notice of William of Malmes-bury. He says, exaggerating the contrast between the old and the new, that 'by their arrival in England they revived the observance of religion which had grown lifeless. Everywhere you see churches in villages, and monas-teries in towns and cities, erected in a new style of architecture.'[5]

The great Norman churches, epitomised by Durham Cathedral above all, are now the best memorial to the aspirations of the Normans. Their ambition and love of display are seen in the massive proportions of the nave; their blend of the traditional and the new in its Romanesque arches and cylindrical pillars on which is imposed the first rib-vault to roof a European cathedral; the demands of war dictate the choice of site on a precipitous peninsula, which is further defended by the bishop's huge castle alongside the cathedral. The Normans built their churches and castles beside each other on fortified hills, as if the surrounding popula-tion were pagan hordes instead of native Christians of long standing. Building stone had never before been massed on such a scale to symbolise both man's mastery of his environment and the individual's puniness in the face of power. In a brilliant and ultimately inexplicable interlude the Normans commanded the forces of their time and identified divine authority with themselves.

The Norman Conquest (1066–87)

In the centuries before 1066 England had experienced numerous over-seas invasions and it was ruled by the Danish dynasty of Cnut between 1016 and 1042. William the Conqueror's invasion was the second of the year. A few days before William crossed the Channel in September 1066, Harold of England had defeated at Stamford Bridge in Yorkshire as for-midable an invasion force led by the Norwegian king Harold Hardrada and Earl Tostig, who was Harold of England's brother. Duke William moreover came ostensibly not as a foreign conqueror but as the recog-nised heir of Edward the Confessor. Nor as a Norman was he entirely a stranger. Edward the Confessor, whose mother was a Norman, had intro-duced Normans into high places, most notably by making Robert of Jumièges bishop of London and archbishop of Canterbury. According to Edward's biography men from France became his most secret counsellors and the controllers of business in the royal palace. Seen from this view-point, Harold's death at the battle of Hastings was simply the elimination of a usurper and Duke William was crowned king of the English in West-minster Abbey on Christmas Day 1066 as the lawful successor of Edward the Confessor. William described Edward as his kinsman and he claimed to rule over the 'country [*patrie*] of the English by hereditary right'.[1]

Immediately after the Conquest

If these were the circumstances, it is surprising that the battle of Hastings became so memorable and that William of Malmesbury and other English writers of the twelfth century looked back on it as 'that fatal day for Eng-land, the sad destruction of our dear country [*dulcis patrie*]'.[2] The change of attitude is best accounted for by the events of the decade following William's coronation. In the Normans' opinion the English were disloyal to their lawful king and betrayed him by rebelling. The *Anglo-Saxon Chronicle* on the other hand maintains that William did not behave like an English king, as he let his foreigners oppress the people. The coronation itself had not gone smoothly and it was a presage of what was to come. The Normans had introduced a new element into the ceremony whereby the congregation were asked, as in France, whether it was their wish that William should be crowned as their lord. But this acclamation of the new king only emphasised the division between the English and the Normans, as the question had to be put twice: first by the archbishop of York in English and then by the bishop of Coutances in French. Furthermore the shouting within the church sounded so sinister that the Norman guards outside took fright and started setting fire to London.

Much of the Normans' oppressive conduct in the next decade can be explained by nervousness of this sort. They found they were unwelcome and so they took steps to defend themselves. This 'primitive state of the kingdom after the conquest' is graphically recalled by Richard Fitz Nigel in the twelfth century: 'What were left of the conquered English lay in ambush for the suspected and hated race of Normans and murdered them secretly in woods and unfrequented places as opportunity offered.'[3] Such killers subsequently became the heroes of folk legend, like Hereward the Wake, and then merged into the Robin Hood tradition of free Englishmen lying in wait under the greenwood tree for cruel Norman sheriffs and fat prelates. The Normans themselves reacted by punishing whole districts with murder fines when one of their men was killed. The crime of murder now meant killing Normans. In these early years the Normans were obliged to behave as an army of occupation, fortified in their new castles and sallying out in groups to interrogate people and cow them into submission. The *Anglo-Saxon Chronicle* concludes its annal for 1066 with the comment that the Norman regents, Odo of Bayeux and William Fitz Osbern, 'built castles far and wide throughout the land, oppressing the wretched people, and things went continually from bad to worse'.[4]

Immediately after the Conquest things went from bad to worse for the Normans as much as for the English. William was in a most hazardous position. His rule in England was threatened not only by sporadic native rebellions but by the Scots and the Welsh and much more seriously by the Danes. Furthermore in the long term he was far from secure in Normandy where his own family, the outlying areas of Norman rule and the French monarchy were all potential threats. After 1073 William spent most of his time in Normandy, not peacefully at home enjoying his triumphs but in wars with the men of Maine (1073), the Bretons (1076), the Angevins (1077–8 and 1081) and the French (1087). In the years 1067–72 he had spent more time in England but this too was primarily in order to suppress rebellions. The earliest of these occurred in 1067–8 and were directed against Odo of Bayeux in Kent and William Fitz Osbern, and then in 1068 Exeter rebelled. In 1069–70 there were larger risings which looked in retrospect like a national rebellion. The Northumbrians joined forces with a Danish fleet and with the English claimant to the throne, the

PLATE IIIa. Wine was made in the south and west of England until the import of French wine superseded it; this scene of grape pressing is from the Holkham Bible Picture Book of *c.* 1320–30

IIIb. A detail from the Bayeux Tapestry showing the charge of the Norman knights in the battle of Hastings

Atheling ('prince') Edgar, and captured York where they killed 'many hundreds of Frenchmen' (according to the *Anglo-Saxon Chronicle*).

This led to the notorious 'Harrying of the North', when King William in the winter of 1069–70 systematically burned the countryside and destroyed villages so that Danish or Norwegian fleets in future would find nothing to live off. How permanent such damage was and whether the numerous deaths of men and livestock from disease were directly caused by William's policy are matters for debate. Certainly wastelands were prominent in the north in Domesday Book fifteen years later. Although William showed himself ruthless towards the peasants of the north, he was lenient towards the English earls, Gospatric and Waltheof, who had taken part in the revolt. This proved a mistake, as they both subsequently betrayed William and in 1069 two other English earls, Edwin and Morcar, also rose in rebellion. From 1070, the year in which William suppressed these rebellions and appointed Lanfranc (a Lombard by origin and a Norman monk by adoption) as archbishop of Canterbury, government in England became more ruthless and more closely identified with Norman rather than native interests. This is the time too when English was superseded by Latin as the written language of government, presumably because Lanfranc and other foreign clerics found it uncouth and could not understand it anyway. William's most impressive achievement was to march up into Scotland as far as the Tay in 1072 and compel King Malcolm to submit to him. This action was essential for controlling Northumbria and it also helped Lanfranc's claim to be primate of all Britain.

In retrospect in the twelfth century these rebellions against William and his suppression of them were seen in nationalistic terms. For example, Orderic Vitalis described the beheading of Earl Waltheof for treason in 1076 as if he were a martyr. The execution was held at dawn to prevent the English rescuing 'so noble a compatriot' and Waltheof was venerated as a saint at Crowland Abbey where he was buried.[5] His head was miraculously restored to his body and in a vision this man who had been an earl on earth appeared as a king in heaven. Orderic himself composed an epitaph stating that Waltheof had been done to death by Norman judges. Despite Orderic's enthusiasm Waltheof was not a simple English patriot. His father was a Dane, he himself had supported the Danish invasion of 1069, and he was suspected of doing the same in 1075. He had twice been pardoned and reinstated by William, once after the battle of Hastings and again after the rising of 1069–70. The opposition William faced from earls like Waltheof was not necessarily directed against him as a Norman oppressor but as an English king. Edward the Confessor had experienced similar rebellions. The difference was that William suppressed them with such vigour and ruthlessness that his methods were felt in retrospect to be un-English.

Debates about the Conquest

No event in English history has been more continually or fiercely debated than the Norman Conquest. Disagreement started at the time of the Conquest itself in the contrast between the eulogy of William the Conqueror by William of Poitiers and the harsh verse obituary given him in the *Anglo-Saxon Chronicle*. Many of the essential facts, let alone interpretations, are in dispute and the truth is now impossible to establish. Did William have a legitimate claim to the throne, for example? William of Poitiers, the Bayeux Tapestry and other Norman sources imply that William had been promised the kingdom by Edward the Confessor, whereas the *Anglo-Saxon Chronicle* and Florence of Worcester make no mention of this. Did the English chroniclers suppress this information, or not know about it, or did they fail to mention it simply because Edward never made such a promise? The right answer is anybody's guess and any answer implies that someone was a liar. The Normans themselves overcame this problem in the end by arguing that they ruled by right of conquest anyway. They were accustomed to testing disputed evidence by appealing to the supernatural through an ordeal. God would allow the just man to be unharmed by hot iron or water or to triumph in trial by combat. The ordeal of the battle of Hastings was the supreme trial and the result proved who had the better right.

In the twelfth century, however, such appeals to the supernatural began to be distrusted and schoolmen argued that it was better to enquire into things by human reason. Thenceforward debating about the Norman Conquest became a matter for academics and there it has remained. Commentators in the twentieth century have been less concerned with the rightness or wrongness of William's claim than with the effects of the Conquest. This discussion gives scope to the most diverse points of view. As with the succession question, it is more useful to state the problems than to attempt to resolve them. The following contradictory statements by professional historians illustrate how opinions can differ. 'At the level of literate and aristocratic society,' Sir Richard Southern says in a presidential address to the Royal Historical Society, 'no country in Europe, between the rise of the barbarian kingdoms and the twentieth century, has undergone so radical a change in so short a time as England experienced after 1066.'[6] On the other hand H. G. Richardson and G. O. Sayles in *The*

Governance of Medieval England state that 'if the Conqueror's will had prevailed and the dukedom of Normandy had gone to his eldest son (Robert) and his line and the kingdom of England to his second son (William Rufus) and his line, the Norman Conquest would have been a transitory episode and the foreign element it had introduced would, we make bold to say, have been absorbed into English society almost without trace'.[7]

Such diversity is possible because opinions differ about what made society distinctively English or Norman. If castles, feudalism, bureaucratic government, foreigners in high places, monastic reform and an active urban life were all characteristics of Anglo-Saxon England (as is argued by some), then the Normans cannot have been responsible for cataclysmic change because these were already features of their own society and indeed of all advanced European states of their time. The significant time of change, it can be argued, was not 1066 but the rule earlier in the century of Cnut and his Danes, or the period earlier still when Alfred and his successors organised a unified kingdom in reaction to the first Danish invasions. Just as plausibly on the other hand it can be argued that the significant period of change reflecting overseas movements came in the twelfth century with the government of Henry I, the civil wars of Stephen's reign and the reorganisation of the kingdom by the Angevin Henry II. The first Norman conquerors could be absorbed (Richardson and Sayles argue) 'almost without trace', just as the Danes had been absorbed before them, whereas the cross-Channel monarchy of the twelfth century made greater demands and transformed English society.

Southern and others who argue the case for radical change as an immediate consequence of 1066 marshal equally attractive arguments. The Old English aristocracy was eliminated by William the Conqueror. Although this was not an immediate consequence of the battle of Hastings, by the time of the Domesday survey in 1086 only two Englishmen, Thurkill of Arden and Colswein of Lincoln, held tenancies of the first order under the king himself. Some aristocrats had been killed, many dispossessed, and others were exiles: in Scotland and Denmark, and even in Russia and in the imperial guard in Byzantium. In 1081 English exiles defended the Byzantine territory of Durazzo against Robert Guiscard and his Normans. Similarly nearly all bishops and abbots were foreigners by 1086 and as a consequence the English language ceased to be used as the written language of government and of the religious life. The few who persisted with English, like the writers of the *Anglo-Saxon Chronicle*, were therefore making a deliberate effort to preserve their culture in the face of foreign hostility. Such a cataclysmic and pessimistic view of the consequences of the Conquest also reflects medieval opinion. For William of Malmesbury the day of Hastings was that *dies fatalis* for England.

But even William of Malmesbury's words can be interpreted in another way. The day was fatal, he says, because of the change-over to new lords. Historians have argued that the new Norman lords had neither the wish nor the ability to change everything. On the contrary, they readily stepped into the places of their predecessors and they did their best to maintain and strengthen Anglo-Saxon institutions because they had no governmental ideology of their own. The fact, for example, that the royal Chancery used Latin instead of English for its writs from the 1070s onwards was simply a change in the medium of communication. The form and meaning of the writs, with their stark instructions, continued to reflect the authoritarianism of Anglo-Saxon royal government. Similarly the basic institutions of counties and hundreds, with their officers and courts, remained essentially unchanged. The Norman rulers simply called earls 'counts' and sheriffs 'viscounts'; such well-established royal offices were too useful to abolish. Above all, William the Conqueror continued with the English taxation and coinage systems because from a king's point of view these were the best in Europe. They gave England its reputation for huge wealth and allowed the Norman kings to pay their armies.

If this line of thought is pursued very far, however, it raises the question of how the Normans overcame a kingdom that was so well organised. The answer often given is to argue that, once William had become king, he could use the strength of the royal administration to advance the Conquest. At the regular meetings of county and hundred courts, for example, he and his men could discover who the property-owners were and who opposed the Normans. Domesday Book on this line of argument is the greatest monument to the efficiency of Anglo-Saxon government and it underlined continuity by asking how things stood on the day that Edward the Confessor had died. It may even have been based on Anglo-Saxon documents which were simply translated into Latin by the Normans. William's success therefore arose from his initial victory at Hastings and not from superior Norman administrative talents. It is not even necessary to argue that the Normans were superior warriors, as their success at Hastings can be attributed to luck. Harold and his men were exhausted and unprepared because they had just rushed down from the battle against the Norwegians at Stamford Bridge.

The argument that William was lucky comes back to the medieval notion that his victory was a divine judgement, either to punish the Anglo-

Saxons for their sinfulness or to demonstrate William's righteousness, or both. The concept of the Anglo-Saxons' sinfulness which was expounded by William of Malmesbury (for example, he says that the nobility had been drunken and lustful, while the clergy enjoyed food and fancy vestments) has been developed by some historians into the larger idea that the Anglo-Saxons were politically decadent. Thus D. C. Douglas, the greatest authority on the Norman Conquest, put forward as an agreed proposition that 'there can be little doubt that England was politically decadent in 1066' and that this explained why it was unable to defend its civilisation.[8] As Douglas knew, this notion went back to Carlyle's 'gluttonous race of Jutes and Angles' (see page 15 above) and this in its turn (via Milton and others) back to William of Malmesbury. As a foil to the decadent Anglo-Saxons, the Normans have sometimes been seen as supermen (either admirable or vicious according to taste) and this view too can be found in medieval sources in the Normans' opinion of themselves: Orderic Vitalis describes them as a warlike race, who continually struggle for mastery, and in the battle speeches recorded by their chroniclers Norman leaders insist on their superiority.

The Norman Conquest supplies a point of interest and identification for almost any point of view and this explains the variety of the problems and the difficulty of resolving them. Those who believe that battles can decisively alter history point to Hastings, while those who think change comes slowly and imperceptibly can argue that the battle by itself had little effect. Similarly those who favour authority and military discipline can recognise these traits in the Normans, while liberals and democrats (particularly in the nineteenth century and earlier) feel some kinship for the Anglo-Saxons. (In fact both Normandy and Anglo-Saxon England were warrior societies and all medieval groups had consultative assemblies.) Nationalist sentiments can likewise be used in a variety of guises. The Normans are either the oppressors of the English nation and language or its revivifiers. Although the Normans might not have recognised themselves in some of these guises, they would no doubt have been pleased that an interest was still being taken in them a thousand years later, as they liked to be noticed and intended to be remembered.

English feelings about the Normans

Judging from the evidence of the *Anglo-Saxon Chronicle* and of twelfth-century monastic writers, the Norman Conquest caused bitter resentment. The difficulty is to gauge how long this continued and to evaluate the testimony of monks who themselves lived under Norman rule.

Orderic Vitalis, for example, describes England as being 'subjected' to William as a conqueror and to the foreign 'robbers' who were his supporters. Orderic's most recent editor, Dr Chibnall, finds this too inflammatory a statement and translates the Latin *praedonibus* not as 'robbers' but as 'invaders'.[9] Nevertheless it was probably robbery that Orderic meant, as later on in his book he reports that the Norman monk Guitmund refused preferment in England and told William the Conqueror to his face that 'the whole of England was like the hugest robbery [*praedam*]'.[10] According to Orderic, the words of this monk who had called the Norman acquisition of England 'robbery' were repeated all over the country. The distinction between plunder and legitimate spoils of war was a fine one. The Normans made no secret of the spoils they took. William of Poitiers says that English treasures were distributed to churches up and down France as well as in Normandy itself. King Harold's banner, which was woven of the purest gold, was sent as a thank-offering to Rome. The penances which were imposed by the Norman bishops on the invaders— for war of any sort was recognised to be a lapse from Christian perfection —are realistic about the conditions which prevailed at the time of the invasion. Not only are those who killed or wounded men in the battle itself to do penance but also those who killed resisters when foraging through the countryside or plundering.

Like the distinction between plunder and legitimate spoils, the difference between lawful taxation and theft depended on one's point of view. In its verse obituary of William the Conqueror the *Anglo-Saxon Chronicle* makes avarice his besetting sin and accuses him of piling up gold and silver taken from his subjects without justice or need. The arbitrariness of taxation is one of the *Chronicle*'s continual themes, as is injustice. But the writer's tone is rhetorical rather than specific and inconsistencies are self-evident. Under the year 1086, for example, the collapse of law and order is castigated (the more just laws were talked about, the more unlawful things were done), whereas the entry for the next year admires the harshness of William's rule which instilled such fear that an honest man could travel throughout the country with his pockets full of gold. Considering how much the king and his Normans coveted gold and silver in the *Chronicle*'s opinion, it is surprising that there was anything left for honest travellers. The voice of the *Anglo-Saxon Chronicle*, which had always been pessimistic because it had started at the time of the Danish invasions in Alfred's reign and was composed by monks who looked forward to a better life in heaven, reached new depths of depression after 1066. The writer frequently concludes his record of the misfortunes of the year (storms, famine, disease, oppression) with an invocation to God to relieve the wretched people.

Such misfortunes were not necessarily new and neither were they all caused by the Normans, though William the Conqueror did use destruction of the countryside as a defensive tactic, not only in his Harrying of the North in 1070 but also in reaction to the threatened Danish invasion of 1085. The peculiar circumstances of the Norman Conquest, which made the lords of the land into an alien people as well as a ruling class, give this part of the *Anglo-Saxon Chronicle* its distinctive tone. Although it was written by monks who normally identified with the rulers, alienation after 1066 caused them to enunciate something which came close to a peasant or popular voice. The writer describes the sufferings of the people in the countryside and castigates the robber barons, most notably in the description of the troubles of Stephen's reign. This unusual tone disappears from English writing later in the twelfth century, once Norman and English ecclesiastics had begun to co-operate, and it does not reappear until the fourteenth century with the Peasants' Revolt and Piers Plowman. The *Anglo-Saxon Chronicle* therefore articulates a feeling which may have been deeper and more widespread than national sentiment. It voices the bitter helplessness of the labourers in the fields, who contended with the arbitrariness of nature exacerbated by the demands of lords.

A particular point of resentment against William the Conqueror was his introduction of the forest laws. The *Chronicle*'s verse obituary devoted its principal attention to this. William protected deer and wild boar and let the hares run free by contrast with his meanness to people. In fact both Cnut and Edward the Confessor had maintained royal forests. Nevertheless the strict regulation of areas like the New Forest was undoubtedly Norman. The purpose may have been governmental as much as protective of royal prerogatives and pleasures. William was certainly not a modern conservationist, as his ravaging of the countryside makes clear; but the forests were the refuge of the patriots and outlaws, in both legend and fact, who carried on a guerrilla war against Norman rule and lordship. By the end of the twelfth century the royal forests covered about a quarter of England and they can therefore be seen as the most important Norman innovation. They gave the king revenue and recreation as well as jurisdiction over dangerous terrain. Furthermore, as head of a hunting band, the Anglo-Norman king represented the most ancient form of authority known to man.

Given the significance of the forest, it was appropriate that the destiny

of England in 1066 should have been symbolised by a green tree. The
earliest biographer of Edward the Confessor, who wrote at the time of
the Norman Conquest, described how when the king lay dying he had
a vision in which God cursed the English kingdom for its sinfulness.
Edward asked when there would be a remission of God's anger and
received the reply that the troubles would continue until a green tree,
which has been cut down, is restored to its trunk and begins once more to
bear fruit. The green tree was understood to symbolise the English nation,
which had been cut down by the battle of Hastings. The interest of the
dream lay in the conditions it required for a restoration between the
ancient trunk and the severed top. William of Malmesbury interpreted
the dream to mean that the tree would never be restored: 'We now experience', he wrote in 1125, 'the truth of this prophecy, as England today is
made the home of foreigners and the domain of aliens.'[11] Nevertheless
when Ailred of Rievaulx came to consider the same dream in his new life
of Edward the Confessor (written in the 1160s), he found in it the symbolism of reconciliation and pride in being English: 'The tree signifies the
kingdom of the English, adorned in glory, fertile in riches and delights,
excelling in the sublimity of royal dignity.'[12] The green top had been
restored to its trunk by the marriage of Henry I to Matilda, who was
descended from the English royal family, and it had borne fruit in Henry
II. 'He, rising as the light of morning,' wrote Ailred changing his metaphors, 'is like a cornerstone joining the two peoples. Now certainly England has a king of the English race.' This was special pleading, as few of
Henry's roots were in England. Nevertheless Ailred's interpretation fits
other comments of the latter half of the twelfth century which suggest that
the distinction between Normans and English no longer mattered. Thus
Richard Fitz Nigel explained that 'nowadays, when English and Normans
live together and intermarry, the nations are so mixed that it can scarcely
be decided who is English by birth and who is Norman'.[13] Fitz Nigel made
the significant proviso, however, that he was speaking of freemen only.
Serfs, *Anglicani* (English) or *nativi* (natives) as they were called, were still
a living reminder of how lords were essentially Norman and peasants were
English.

Names and languages

One reason why it was difficult to decide who was Norman and who was
English by Fitz Nigel's time was that most freemen by then used non-
English personal names like 'Richard' and 'Robert'. Striking evidence of
this comes from Winchester, where information is available from the years

1066, 1110, 1148 and 1207. At the time of the Norman Conquest 29 per cent of property-owners in Winchester had foreign names. This proportion increased to 62 per cent by 1110, 66 per cent by 1148 and 82 per cent by 1207. Comparable rates of increase occur at Canterbury, where about 75 per cent of the names listed in the rent surveys of the 1160s are non-English and this increases to about 90 per cent by 1206. Greater foreign influence would of course be felt in Winchester and Canterbury than elsewhere, as these two cities were respectively the governmental and ecclesiastical centres of the Anglo-Norman lordship. What is most significant in these figures is the increase in the twelfth century. Evidently each new generation gave a larger proportion of its children foreign names, as Norman rule and French fashions became more normal, until by 1200 the great majority of freemen in southern England at least had ceased to bear English names. This information, because it is derived from a large number of individuals, is a better indicator of attitudes to foreign rule than are isolated statements in chronicles. A fact of comparable significance is that 'William' became and remained the single most common recorded name in the twelfth century, which suggests that William the Conqueror and William Rufus were not as unpopular as the *Anglo-Saxon Chronicle* made out. Peasant families in the countryside (most of whose names are unrecorded), as distinct from householders in cities like Winchester and Canterbury, were presumably much slower to adopt foreign names, although they can be found doing so by the thirteenth century.

The increasing use of foreign names by the upper classes has a parallel in the way the English language lost status in the century after 1066. As with other changes in the wake of the Conquest, there is considerable room for debate as to how quickly and how profoundly the language was affected. Because William the Conqueror claimed to be the legitimate heir of Edward the Confessor, he at first issued his written instructions in English just like his Anglo-Saxon predecessors. But in the 1070s, after the numerous rebellions had caused William to rely more on foreigners (as already discussed at page 27 above), English ceased to be the written language of government, although a few royal charters for Canterbury continue to be recorded bilingually (in Latin and English) until Henry II's reign in 1155. Simultaneously the use of English sharply declined for literary purposes. Some Old English works continued to be copied (indeed some texts only survive in twelfth-century copies) in monastic houses and there was a little new composition, of which the most striking example is the *Anglo-Saxon Chronicle* which continued to be compiled at Peterborough until 1154. Nevertheless the text of the *Chronicle* proves the rule that the status of English was changing. Up to the year 1121 it is written in standard Old English, but thereafter it displays local east midlands variants whose spelling and script depart further from standard forms as the years advance. The problem for the *Chronicle*'s later writers, isolated in the fens of Peterborough, was that they no longer had a consistent standard on which to model their prose. Before 1066 Old English in its principal written form had been a uniform language whose quality was maintained by the royal government and the Church. The effect of the changes of the 1070s was to remove—for better or worse—these constraints on written English. As it was no longer an official centralising language, its forms proliferated into a wealth of local variations. Latin (which had already been very influential before 1066) replaced English as the standard language of government records and literature and remained dominant for two centuries.

In the long term it can be argued that the Norman Conquest, so far from damaging the English language, gave it new life: first by releasing it from official constraints and then by enriching its vocabulary with numerous words derived from French and Latin. The latter phenomenon is brilliantly illustrated by F. W. Maitland in his history of English law, where he shows how modern legal vocabulary is primarily of French origin (*agreement, burglary, court, debt, evidence* and so on): 'In the province of *justice* and *police* with its *fines*, its *gaols* and its *prisons*, its *constables*, its *arrests*, we must—now that *outlawry* is a thing of the past—go as far as the *gallows* if we would find an English institution.'[14] In the short term, in the century after 1066, the English language suffered a setback, measured by its written extant output. But such a measure takes no account of literary works which have been lost, and furthermore the written use of a language is an inadequate indicator of total use. The amount and variety of English being spoken (as distinct from written) probably increased in the twelfth century, because the population was larger and the incomers intermarried and learned some English.

It is a mistake to assume that French replaced English as the common language of people in England. It cannot even be proved that the Norman conquerors in the second and subsequent generations spoke French as their mother tongue, although there is no doubt that French had great status as a social and literary language in England in the thirteenth century (see chapter X, page 183 below). The chronicler Orderic Vitalis, who was born near Shrewsbury in 1075 and was the son of a priest from Orléans and an English mother, never learned French in England. He remarks that when he was sent to Normandy to become a monk at the age of ten he felt an exile, like Joseph in Egypt, because he heard a language which he could not understand. Orderic's ignorance of French before he went to Normandy is the more remarkable considering that his father was a counsellor of Roger Montgomery and special pains had been taken with his basic education. He had been put in the charge of an English priest at the age of five who taught him Latin. The neglect of French in Orderic's early education suggests that instruction in it was not thought a matter of importance by his father, as French (unlike Latin and English) had not yet developed as a literary language. Furthermore, as Orderic remarks, the Normans until the time of William the Conqueror had devoted themselves to war and not to reading and writing. By 1200 every educated man needed to know French, but that was not so in 1066. The literary language to which the Norman Conquest gave new life and discipline was not French but Latin, primarily through the influence of the archbishops of Canterbury, Lanfranc and Anselm, who were northern Italians in origin.

The effects of the Norman Conquest on language in England are therefore rich in paradoxes. English declined in the short term as a literary language and yet it gained new life as the spoken language of the people and re-emerged, enormously enriched, two centuries later. French, from being a despised vernacular in 1066, became in the twelfth century a literary language of high status. Its use by both the Norman and Angevin rulers of England may have contributed to this. For example, the earliest and best text of the *Song of Roland* is English (Bodley MS Digby 23), although its language is French, and other early French texts emerge first in English contexts. As for Latin, the consequence of its revival was that authors of English origin were again appreciated abroad, which they had not been since the days of Bede or Alcuin. Such Latinists as John of Salisbury and the rhetorician Geoffrey de Vinsauf (an Englishman despite his name) sought an international and predominantly clerical audience and therefore had no wish to restrict themselves to an English or French vernacular. To what extent these changes were caused by Norman actions, or were a reaction to them, remains a matter primarily for speculation, as language is shaped by many diverse influences.

Domesday Book

The greatest single achievement of William the Conqueror was his making of Domesday Book in 1086, a year before he died. This survey of the land, county by county, was done with such thoroughness that the *Anglo-Saxon Chronicle* commented with pardonable exaggeration that there was not one ox nor one cow nor one pig which was left off the record. Such detailed and consistent information was achieved by requiring jurors representing each hundred to answer a battery of questions such as: what is this manor called, how many villeins are there, how many freemen, how much woodland is there, how much meadow, how many mills, what is the estate worth, how much does each freeman have? These and many other details were to be answered for at three different dates: when Edward the Confessor was alive (1065), when William the Conqueror granted the estate (depending on when that was), and at present (1086).

Such an unprecedented and searching inquisition gave the book its name *Domesday* because it reminded the natives (according to Richard Fitz Nigel) of 'Doomsday', that Last Judgement when Christ in majesty would judge the living and the dead. This was an appropriate comparison, as the Domesday survey sought information about the dead (the Anglo-Saxon landowners who had been killed or died between 1065 and 1085), as well as the living, and its text was meant to serve as a final judgement about every disputed property. Fitz Nigel in the twelfth century recorded a tradition emanating from Winchester, where Domesday Book had been compiled, that it was intended as the finishing touch to William the Conqueror's plan 'to bring the subjected people under the rule of written law', so that each person in future would be content with his own rights and not encroach unpunished on those of others.[15]

Whether Domesday Book had any more immediate purpose than a general though extraordinarily detailed survey of the land has been much debated. In 1085 William the Conqueror's rule was threatened by a joint invasion from Denmark and Flanders, and he brought over from Normandy the largest army which had ever been seen in England. It has therefore been argued that the purpose of the Domesday survey was to reassess the Anglo-Saxon tax of Danegeld to pay for defence. But this hypothesis does not have clear contemporary support and furthermore much of the information in Domesday Book is irrelevant to such a purpose. Although the *Anglo-Saxon Chronicle* reports the billeting of William's army and the planning of the Domesday survey as successive events, it does not explicitly link the two and neither does it mention Danegeld in this context. Such an elaborate survey was certainly intended to raise money but not necessarily from traditional Anglo-Saxon sources. A recent hypothesis (by Dr Sally Harvey) questions the originality of the survey. So far from being unique, Domesday Book was the last in a series of Anglo-Saxon royal land surveys, representing a practice which may have extended back to the time of King Alfred. These earlier surveys have been lost because they were in Old English and became obsolete once

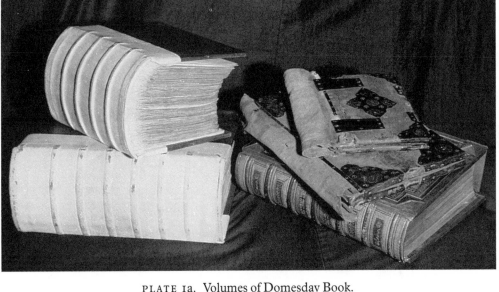

PLATE 1a. Volumes of Domesday Book.
1b. Text describing the county of Suffolk. The book was produced *c.* 1085–6

Domesday Book was made. The problem with this hypothesis is that it is difficult to distinguish between records which are an ancillary product of the Domesday survey (those describing the state of particular properties in 1065, for example) and those which were actually made in the Anglo-Saxon period.

To acknowledge that the making of Domesday Book was the special achievement of William the Conqueror is not to assume that the Normans were efficient and energetic administrators, whereas Anglo-Saxon government had been decadent and illiterate. Domesday Book could not have been made without the Anglo-Saxon organisation of shires and hundreds and the habit of settling property disputes at meetings of the county court in the presence of royal officers. The most interesting fact about Domesday Book is that William the Conqueror delayed twenty years before having it made. Why was it necessary in 1086? The best explanation, though this again is a modern hypothesis (by R. H. C. Davis), is that William needed the Domesday survey because the process of the conquest and redistribution of lands had been chaotic. The impression is often given in school textbooks that after the battle of Hastings William distributed the conquered land among his followers in an orderly and peaceful manner, giving so much to each and requiring specific services from them. But he cannot have done this in 1066 or 1067 because his hold on the country was still insecure and he and his men would have had only the haziest notion of how big England was or of who owned what. Orderic Vitalis (who wrote in the twelfth century) attributes the systematic redistribution of the land not to the years 1066–7 but to 1071–2 after the defeat of Edwin and Morcar.

Orderic's statement suggests that it was as a consequence of the rebellions of 1067–71, and not of the battle of Hastings, that William decided that he was entitled to dispossess English landholders on a massive scale. Even then the dispossession cannot have been an orderly process. Scarcely any charters or writs are known in which William grants English lands to laymen. The redistribution depended on verbal instructions. Typically the property of a dispossessed Anglo-Saxon magnate would be granted as a whole to one of William's magnates, such as Roger Montgomery or Hugh of Avranches. Such a man would often have already been in possession of some of the property, and it was now up to him and his knights to identify and occupy the rest of it. This would be done by going in force to the county court and then to specific villages extorting information. In the words of R. H. C. Davis, 'a Norman could not very well ride round an English shire "alone and palely loitering" asking in every village if Ulf or Tovi had held any land there'[16] because he would have been cheated or murdered. This primitive state of the kingdom, when the 'English lay in ambush for the suspected and hated race of Normans', is vouched for by Fitz Nigel (see page 26 above).

The purpose and achievement of the Domesday survey was to bring order out of the inevitable chaos caused by the Norman Conquest. The survey was a model of efficiency, but of efficiency imposed after the event and necessitated by the unprecedented disorganisation caused by the Conquest. The purpose of asking for precise details of each estate and at three different times (before, during, and since the Conquest) was to find out who now possessed what, and what title they claimed other than force. Domesday Book declared the results of the Conquest like the results of a cricket match. It showed that the royal family possessed about one fifth of the land, the Church about a quarter, and ten or eleven lay magnates another quarter. Althogether it is estimated that by 1086 there were about 2,000 foreign knights (or 10,000 new settlers in total) in a population of about one and a half million. The obvious points here are how small a proportion the incomers were, when compared with the total population, and how wealth was concentrated in very few hands: the king's family, a handful of lay magnates (men such as Roger Montgomery, Hugh of Avranches, William de Warenne and Geoffrey de Mandeville), less than 50 prelates, and another 170 persons with estates worth more than £100 per year. In other words the land was controlled by about 250 individuals. This concentration of power did not differ much from the situation in Edward the Confessor's reign. The difference was that nearly every one of these 250 by 1086 was an incomer. Controversy about the effects of the Norman Conquest turns ultimately upon how much, or how little, can be achieved by such a tiny ruling élite.

The Conquest, in all its savagery at Hastings and in the Harrying of the North, proved the Normans' power. Domesday Book entitled them to rule, literally in the sense that it recorded the titles to their lands and symbolically in the sense that it demonstrated their capacity to organise. Legally, if not in reality, the Conquest marked a new start; for no one except the king now possessed a title to property from earlier than 1066 and everyone's rights stemmed from the Conquest. In the twelfth century, when a dispute arose about the charters of Battle Abbey (which had been built as a war memorial on the field of Hastings), the chief justiciar told Henry II that even if all documents perished, 'we should all ourselves be its charters, for we are the feoffees from that conquest made at Battle'.[17] The Norman Conquest left a memory which has never been erased.

❧ III ❧

Norman Government (1087–1135)

By the time he died in 1087 William the Conqueror had firmly established his rule in England, as Domesday Book clearly demonstrated. Nevertheless the continuance of strong government was far from certain. William left three surviving sons: Robert, William Rufus and Henry. Robert, the eldest, claimed Normandy as his paternal inheritance and he had also perhaps been designated duke of Normandy by his father. William Rufus was left the symbols of English royalty by William the Conqueror on his deathbed and he legally acquired Normandy when Robert pawned it to him in 1096 on his departure for the First Crusade. Henry succeeded Rufus as king in 1100 when Rufus was killed. But Robert was still alive and returned from the Mediterranean to defend his inheritance. He was captured by Henry I in 1106 and imprisoned until his death in 1134. These events suggest that the union of England and Normandy was preserved largely by accident and that from the first it had to be defended by almost continual warfare. Both William Rufus and Henry I, once they had acquired Normandy (in 1096 and 1106 respectively), spent much more of their time there than in England, and this fact suggests an order of priority or necessity.

Each of the three sons aspired to follow his father in being both king and duke, because neither the practice of primogeniture (which would have given everything to Robert) nor that of division of the property between the children was firmly established. In this confusion the royal family was no different from any other aristocratic family of the time. The feeling was that all a man's children, but particularly boys of legitimate birth, shared the inheritance of their father. After his death they came to what arrangements they could by compromise or war. According to Norman sources, William the Conqueror left England only to God, because he had acquired it through God's help at Hastings, but he hoped God would give it to Rufus. The future Henry I was also intended to get something, and William of Malmesbury (who was writing with the advantage of hindsight) reports that William the Conqueror said to the boy when he was being bullied by one of his elder brothers: 'Don't cry, you too will be a king!'[1] William of Malmesbury also comments that the kingdom seemed particularly to pertain to Henry because he was the only son of William the Conqueror to have been born after 1066. He had therefore inherited royal blood, sanctified by the ceremony of coronation and anointing, whereas his brothers had not. These differing opinions show how far contemporaries were from the concept of automatic inheritance by the eldest son.

Rivalry between the three sons of William the Conqueror might easily have led to chaos in England and incessant civil war. That this did not occur was partly a matter of chance (Robert had gone off to the crusade), but also a consequence of the exceptional ability of the younger sons, William Rufus and Henry I. They as much as their father were responsible for establishing strong government in England. This was a matter of necessity for them, for in order to survive in Normandy they had to exploit English sources of wealth and power to their uttermost. Each depended on a Norman chief minister: Rufus on Ranulf Flambard, and Henry on Roger bishop of Salisbury. As a consequence, in the half century between 1087 and 1135 the financial system centred on the Exchequer was created, and the legal system was strengthened through the Chancery. These institutions combined Anglo-Saxon governmental traditions with the most modern administrative expertise from the French schools. William the Conqueror had won a kingdom for his sons. They consolidated the Norman hold on England and developed institutions which have survived in name until the present day.

William Rufus and Henry I

These two kings have conventionally been presented as opposites. In the opinion of the *Anglo-Saxon Chronicle* Rufus was wicked and came to a fitting end by being killed without time to repent, as he was an oppressor of the Church and of the poor. Henry on the other hand was a good man, who made peace for man and beast, and no one dared injure another in his time. Other contemporary sources similarly contrast the two rulers, but they draw a more subtle picture. What the clergy saw as vices in Rufus were the virtues of knighthood: he was generous to his men and let them make war. Henry by contrast was the clergy's idea of a king. Although the name *Beauclerk* was not given him until later, he had been educated in Latin and (unlike Rufus) did not relish fighting in person, defending himself with the Latin tag that 'My mother bore me to be a commander not a soldier.'[2]

Rufus is described by William of Malmesbury as a model knight, whose promise was spoiled by the impetuousness of youth and the corruption of power. His early death meant that he had no time to live down his mistakes. He was of outstanding physical strength and had been trained in the knightly skills of riding with a lance. He always wanted to be the foremost in any fight and the first to challenge an adversary. Archbishop Lanfranc had made him a knight and to Lanfranc too he owed his throne. At the siege of Rochester in 1088 (when Odo of Bayeux rebelled), he taunted the English that they would be judged as *nithing*, 'worthless', if they did not aid their king. Similarly at the siege of Mont St Michel, Rufus (fighting the future Henry I) rewarded the man who unhorsed him saying: 'By the Holy Face of Lucca, henceforth you shall be mine and, included in my roll of honour, you shall receive the rewards of knighthood!'[3] William of Malmesbury compares Rufus on this occasion to Alexander the Great, and on another occasion, when he released a prisoner so that he could fight another day, Rufus is compared to Julius Caesar.

All this would have reminded twelfth-century readers of the heroes of chivalrous epic as in the *Song of Roland*. Such knights were loyal to their lords (as Rufus was consistently loyal to his father, according to William of Malmesbury), they were of superhuman strength and endurance (Rufus was dragged by a horse which died under him but leapt on to another one without assistance), and they were motivated in battle by honour rather than caution (Rufus returned to the siege of Le Mans without assembling all his troops, knowing that his young men would follow him). Above all, Rufus was famed for his generosity to his men, so that his reputation extended throughout the west and knights came to join him from many provinces. He was, as the chronicler of Battle Abbey (which was necessarily committed to the Norman cause) called him, that *vir preclarus militiaque strenuus*, 'that celebrated man, vigorous in knighthood'.[4]

This early generation of knights to which Rufus belonged was only on the threshold of being converted, in the opinion of church propagandists, from *malitia* (wickedness) into a Christian *militia*. Rufus did not respond to the pope's appeal for the crusade in 1095; instead he took advantage of it to acquire Normandy from Robert. Because knighthood had not yet been sanctified, clerical writers of the time could acknowledge that Rufus was a great knight by secular standards while condemning his conduct. Thus Orderic Vitalis joined William of Malmesbury in disapproving of the extravagant fashions of Rufus's courtiers (particularly their long hair and pointed shoes with curled-up ends), but he also recorded that Rufus was a masterful and brave man who delighted in the honours of knighthood. Rufus's generosity to his knights is likewise consistent with the *Anglo-Saxon Chronicle*'s image of him as an oppressor of the Church and the poor, as chivalrous standards were applied by knights to their own class only and not to peasants.

The ruler with whom Rufus is most comparable is his contemporary William IX count of Poitou and duke of Aquitaine. Indeed, according to William of Malmesbury, Rufus said the day before he was killed that he intended to spend Christmas in Poitou, which William IX was going to pledge to him before going on crusade. Like Rufus, William IX had a reputation as a freethinker, maintaining that events were governed by chance and not by divine providence, and he too was an anti-clerical. He was the first of the troubadours, the knightly poets who voiced an alternative ethic to the Church's teaching. He sang of his delight in worldly things: in physical love, horses, furs and the changing seasons. There could be no greater contrast between the joyous yet fragile aristocratic spirit of William IX's songs and the lugubrious moralising tone of the *Anglo-Saxon Chronicle*. With his exotic oath ('by the Holy Face of Lucca') and large ambitions, Rufus looked out into a wider world than either England or Normandy. Like William IX, he loved *cavalaria et orgueill* ('chivalry and pride'), and he too could say:

> *De proeza et de joi fui*
> *Mais ara partem ambedui.*

> [I have lived in prowess and joy
> but now we both part company.][5]

Rufus was brought down at the height of his power in 1100 when he was killed while hunting in the New Forest. Whether his death was an accident, and who was really responsible for it, cannot now be established. What is certain is that the future Henry I, who was also hunting in the forest, moved fast and that the death came at an opportune moment for him, as his elder brother Robert was on the way back from the crusade. Henry took control of the treasury at Winchester within hours of Rufus's death and he was crowned king at Westminster three days later.

From a legal point of view Henry was in a weaker position than Rufus had been on his accession, as he could not claim that his predecessor had designated him king, and furthermore he had been crowned neither by the archbishop of Canterbury (as Rufus had been) nor by York (as William the Conqueror had been) but by the bishop of London. Anselm of Canterbury had been exiled by Rufus, and Henry was obliged to send him a submissive letter claiming that he had been chosen (*electus*) king by the clergy and people of England. At the same time Henry sent a circular letter around the counties stating similarly that he had been crowned king by the common counsel of the barons of the whole kingdom. This document, which subsequently became known as Henry's 'coronation charter', made a series of promises in its bid to win support. It therefore indicates the sort of complaints which property-owners had against the government of Rufus. The principal points were that Henry undertook not to tax vacant churches, whereas Rufus had derived up to one fifth of his revenues from this source, and not to make arbitrary charges on the inheritances and marriages of his barons. This was a move towards acknowledging that inheritance was a right and not a privilege. To the lesser royal tenants, the knights, Henry made the large concession that they should be exempt from taxation (the geld) and other non-military burdens. As a pledge of good traditional government Henry granted the so-called 'laws of Edward the Confessor', subject to the emendations made by William the Conqueror. To give substance to these promises Henry dismissed Rufus's minister Ranulf Flambard and imprisoned him in the recently completed Tower of London. Only on one point did Henry explicitly make no concessions: the royal forests were to be retained as in the time of William the Conqueror. To the New Forest Henry owed his kingdom.

These concessions, taken together with the cost of winning the compliance of Robert duke of Normandy and of the count of Flanders, probably lost Henry one third of Rufus's annual revenue. He could not afford to act with the cheerful abandon of Rufus and he had learned caution in his brother's reign, when he had stood awkwardly between the rivalry of Robert and Rufus. Although the capture of Robert at Tinchebrai in 1106 won Henry Normandy, it soon led to further strife with Robert's son and heir William Clito, with Fulk count of Anjou who claimed Maine, with Flanders and with Louis VI of France. In many years (notably in 1112, 1117–19, 1124 and 1128) the *Anglo-Saxon Chronicle* recorded that Henry remained the whole year in Normandy. A characteristic annal is that for 1118:

All this year King Henry stayed in Normandy because of the war with the king of France and the count of Anjou and the count of Flanders. Because of these hostilities the king was very much distressed and lost a great deal both in money and also in land. But those who troubled him most were his own men, who frequently deserted and betrayed him and went over to his enemies and surrendered their castles to them to injure and betray the king. England paid dear for all this because of the various taxes, which never ceased in the course of all this year.[6]

The annal illustrates three constant themes of Henry's reign. First, he was never strong enough to defeat decisively his rivals in France despite successes like his victory over Louis VI at Brémule in 1119. Secondly, rebellions both in Normandy and England were common among the barons, as they manoeuvred for new positions in case Henry's power collapsed. This problem was made more acute after 1120 by the drowning of Henry's only legitimate son in the White Ship disaster off the coast of Normandy. Thirdly, the alienness of Norman rule in England was reinforced in Henry's reign by the feeling that the heavy taxes were being used to fight foreign wars. William of Malmesbury was unique in viewing the battle of Tinchebrai as an English victory and a tit-for-tat for the battle of Hastings forty years before. Henry's new men raised 'from the dust' were not native English but Normans (from the Cotentin and the west in particular), like Roger bishop of Salisbury, Geoffrey of Clinton, and Ralph and Richard Basset. Richard Basset is described returning to his native village in Normandy 'bursting with the wealth of England'.[7]

Although in retrospect the *Anglo-Saxon Chronicle* and other clerical sources (notably Henry of Huntingdon) saw Henry's reign as a time of peace and order compared with the civil wars which followed, Henry seemed to many of his contemporaries to be avaricious and cruel. Most chroniclers comment on the gruesome penalties which he used to instil fear. Thus he blinded the count of Mortain, who had fought against him at Tinchebrai, and thieves were likewise blinded and castrated. In 1125 all the moneyers (minters of coin) in England were sentenced to have their right hands cut off and be castrated. Although such penalties were characteristic of the Middle Ages, Henry's application of them must have been unusually severe to have merited comment. He was believed to live in fear. Abbot Suger of St Denis reports that Henry was so frightened of plots that he frequently changed the position of his bed and had his sword and shield hung near to hand. In this he was like his contemporary and kinsman, Vladimir prince of Kiev, who advised his sons never to lie down to sleep without first looking behind them. Henry's fears are strikingly depicted in drawings in John of Worcester's chronicle, where his nightmare of a rebellion by all three orders of society (peasants, knights and clergy) is described. Each order complains of oppressive taxation and towers above the bedside of the sleeping king wielding instruments appropriate to their class. The peasants carry a scythe, a two-pronged fork and a spade, the knights their arms and armour, and the bishops and abbots their croziers.

The positive side of Henry's fearful severity was the reputation he acquired as a maintainer of law and order, despite the concessions he made at the beginning of his reign and the rebellions which continued until the end. He was the 'Lion of Justice', as John of Salisbury and others called him. Nevertheless even this epithet is double-edged, as it derives from the prophecies of Merlin in Geoffrey of Monmouth's Arthurian history. The characteristics of this lion, according to the prophecy, do not refer to law and order but to its shaking of the towers of Gaul and the squeezing of gold from the lily and silver from cattle. In other words Henry was identified as the 'Lion of Justice' because he fought the French and extracted money from his subjects. The image was the more appropriate because after the Lion would follow a time of bloodshed which could be identified with Stephen's reign. Rather better evidence of Henry's authority is the attribution to him, in the legal text called the *Laws of Henry I*, of *tremendum regie majestatis imperium*, 'the tremendous power of the royal majesty'.[8] To compensate for his insecurity Henry developed from the traditions of William the Conqueror and the Anglo-Saxon past a commanding tone in his letters which became the characteristic tone of the English Chancery henceforward. This is best heard in an often quoted instruction which Henry addressed to the authorities in Worcestershire in *c.* 1110. Even when it is weakened by translation from Latin, the emphasis on personal authority remains: 'I order my county and hundred courts to sit where and when they sat in King Edward's time. I forbid my sheriff to make them sit anywhere else to suit some need of his. But I myself, whenever I wish, may have these courts summoned for my lordly needs at my will.'[9] Henry needed to insist that the courts and their officers were his, and that his prerogative was superior to their customs, in order to counteract the strong pulls of localism and seignorial power.

The development of institutions

Although contemporaries tended to contrast Rufus and Henry I, the long-term consequences of their combined reigns were much the same. Both kings were plagued by rebellions and had to spend huge sums on holding Normandy. They succeeded by giving away crown lands in exchange for support. Thus Rufus created the earldom of Surrey for William de Warenne during Odo of Bayeux's rebellion in 1088, and among the new men rewarded by Henry was Richard de Redvers who was given lands which became the earldom of Devon. To compensate for loss of revenue from land, which had been such a prominent part of royal wealth in Domesday Book, Rufus and Henry had to exploit the Crown's rights from such sources as the county farms, feudal dues, profits of justice, and incomes from vacant churches. To do this required detailed and continuous records of who had paid how much for what and when. Domesday Book was insufficient for this purpose, as it went out of date almost before it was made. Instead, lists needed to be compiled and kept from year to year.

In addition to better record-keeping the governments of Rufus and Henry had also to ensure that sheriffs really acted as royal officers in each county and not as local barons. Hence the tone of Henry's letter to Worcestershire insisting on *my* courts and *my* sheriff. That letter was witnessed by 'Roger the bishop'. The man who was well known enough to be described in this way, without specifying where he was bishop of, was Henry's chief minister Roger bishop of Salisbury. He had been in origin a poor Norman priest whom, according to one story, Henry first of all made a chaplain to his soldiers because he could say Mass so fast. Through such practical applications of clerical skills to secular life Roger became indispensable to Henry and was described as his *procurator* or 'manager'. His main function was to call the sheriffs and other royal officers to account and to ensure that every possible source of revenue was tapped. This job was judicial as much as administrative because the Crown's demands were repeatedly challenged by prelates and lay barons who claimed exemption by custom or charter. Rufus's chief minister Ranulf Flambard had likewise been described as *procurator*, and also as *judex* and *justiciarius*, meaning 'judge'.[10] Although Henry made a great show of dismissing Ranulf on his accession, he in fact governed in the same way through Roger, and furthermore Henry restored Ranulf to his bishopric at Durham in 1101. Like Roger, Ranulf was of humble origin. He had first been known as 'Passeflambard', meaning a 'torch-bearer' or 'link-boy'. Like Roger too, he was a Norman.

The government of England was administered by these two Norman clerics for half a century. Nevertheless Ranulf and Roger were not irresponsible favourites who squandered the king's resources but managers and guardians, as the term *procurator* implied. In Richard I's reign, when Hubert Walter exercised similar powers, he was known as the 'chief justiciar' and the origins of this office can be traced back to Ranulf and Roger. Their greatest achievement was to expand the sources of royal revenue and bring them under strict control through the Exchequer. As England was renowned especially for its wealth, it is appropriate that the most elaborate financial instrument in Europe should have been created there. But this was not intended to benefit the English, as it was devised by the

Normans. Where the first generation of conquerors had taken wealth from the country in the form of looted treasure, Rufus's and Henry I's more sophisticated ministers did it through bureaucracy.

The Exchequer

In origin the Exchequer was not a government department but an object. 'It is', says Richard Fitz Nigel, 'a rectangular table measuring 10 feet by 5 feet.'[11] Similarly Gerald of Wales describes it as 'a sort of square table in London where royal dues are collected and accounted for'.[12] The table was covered with a cloth on which lines were ruled, giving it the appearance of a section of a huge chessboard (hence the Latin name *scaccarium* meaning chess or chequers). At one end of the table sat the king's highest officials (the justiciar, the chancellor, the constable, the marshal and so on) and at the opposite end by himself, or at best with the support of a clerk, sat the sheriff whose accounts were being examined. The strange appearance of the table and the high rank of those around it should have been enough to impress upon most sheriffs the hazard of defrauding the king of his revenues. The table served as a simplified gigantic abacus on which the king's *calculator* or accountant, who stood at one of the wider sides of the table, did sums by moving counters from square to square like a croupier. As the accountant set out the counters he called out the numbers, so that everyone could understand what was going on. The great officials sat round the table to resolve disputes about the accounts as they arose. As Fitz Nigel explains, 'The highest skill at the Exchequer does not lie in calculations but in judgments of all kinds, for it is easy to set down the sum due and to set underneath for comparison the sums paid and to find by subtraction if anything is still due.'[13] The way it worked is best illustrated by a diagram:

	£1000	£100	£20	£1
Sum due £2381	• •	• • •	• • • •	•
Sum received £2160	• •	•	• • •	

The accountant first of all set out on the table in counters the sum due from the sheriff in columns representing tens of thousands of pounds, thousands, hundreds, scores, single pounds and shillings and pence. (For simplicity's sake tens of thousands and shillings and pence have been omitted in the example in the diagram.) Beneath the sum due, the accountant set out a similar representation of the sum so far received, and a glance at the difference between the top set of counters and the lower one told him that £221 were still owing. In essence the Exchequer was a way of doing elementary addition and subtraction. If that is the case, why was it such an important step forward in financial administration? The answer is twofold. First, elementary arithmetic was harder to do with Roman numerals than modern ones. The calculation in the example above is very simple but anything involving shillings and pence was made easier by moving counters from one column to another. The abacus also converted sums into convenient multiples of ten and used a nought by leaving a space blank. Secondly, the Exchequer table ensured that accounts were not only done but seen to be done, step by step, by all those who sat round the table.

As important as doing the calculations in the presence of witnesses was converting the results into a lasting form of record, since the counters on the Exchequer table were impermanent. The principal records were of two sorts, tallies and pipe rolls. Tallies were pieces of wood (rather like a ruler) which served as receipts. Sums were represented on them by incisions of different sizes and shapes using the same notation of units, scores and hundreds as on the Exchequer table. The pipe rolls were sheets of parchment, looking like pipes when rolled up, on which the treasurer's scribe recorded the accounts in detail. Both tallies and pipe rolls were written records. Tallies were only useful if they had inscribed on them the name of the county and the date and purpose of the payment. The sums of money were recorded by incisions with a knife instead of pen and ink in order to prevent fraud, as the incisions were made before the stick was split down its length, one part being retained by the treasury and the other given to the sheriff as his receipt. Receipts could of course have been produced in a purely parchment form from the start. The wooden format of the tally may have been preferred because sheriffs on the threshold of literacy found them easier to hold on to and store and they seemed foolproof. Tallies were in keeping with the basic purpose of the Exchequer to make accountancy visible and tangible. The pipe rolls on the other hand were for the treasury's own use and could therefore be in a more elaborate written form. Both the tally cutter and the treasurer's scribe sat at the Exchequer table to make the record on the spot.

The Exchequer therefore involved interlocking techniques which were simple enough for people with limited education to operate and which could be repeated and expanded. It had three essential components: a method of making calculations (the Exchequer table), a standard form of receipt for payers-in of revenue (the tally sticks), and a more detailed form of record for the treasury (the pipe rolls). In being simple, interlocking and expandable the Exchequer system was the foundation of bureaucracy in medieval England. When Fitz Nigel came to write the *Dialogue of the Exchequer* in the 1170s he described the system with pride. Bureaucratic procedure was a peculiar subject for a medieval author to have chosen to write about, instead of theology or history, for example. Fitz Nigel knew this and in his prologue he justifies himself in the face of Aristotelian and Christian traditions: 'We are of course aware that kingdoms are governed and laws maintained primarily by prudence, fortitude, temperance, justice and the other virtues, for which reasons the rulers of the world must practise them with all their might. But there are occasions on which sound and wise policies take effect rather quicker through the agency of money.'[14] The Exchequer ensured that the king's money was duly collected and spent in the right place, at the right time by the right people. There was no value, in Fitz Nigel's opinion, in hoarding up treasure for its own sake; money is not piles of gold and silver but a commodity which smooths over difficulties in both peace and war.

Although he had a great respect for custom and an interest in tradition, Fitz Nigel was unsure about the origins of the Exchequer. Some said it had been imported from Normandy by William the Conqueror, while others believed it had existed under the Anglo-Saxon kings because the rates of county taxes were known from before 1066. 'But', as Fitz Nigel observes, 'this is a cogent proof of the payment of the farm but not of the session of the Exchequer.'[15] Although tally sticks and the abacus may well have been used in Anglo-Saxon administration, the 'session of the Exchequer' (that is, the practice of making financial judgements at its table) was a post-Conquest development which can be proved to have existed in Henry I's reign but no earlier. The 'lords of the Exchequer' (*barones de scaccario*) are first mentioned in a writ dating from 1110 and the earliest pipe roll dates from 1130.[16] An attractive hypothesis for the Exchequer's beginnings was put forward by R. L. Poole. He pointed out that at Laon in northern France there taught in the first decade of the twelfth century Master Anselm (he is a different Anselm from the archbishop of Canterbury) and his brother Ralph. These two ran the most successful school of their time, Anselm being famed for his biblical teaching and Ralph for arithmetic. Many clerics from England went to this school, among them Adelard of Bath, who wrote a treatise on the abacus, and two nephews of Roger bishop of Salisbury. One of these nephews, Nigel bishop of Ely, subsequently became treasurer and his son wrote the *Dialogue of the Exchequer*. These and other connections with Laon led Poole to the conclusion that 'the Exchequer is a system of account rendered possible by a simple mathematical apparatus which Englishmen learned in France' in the first decade of Henry I's reign.[17] Although this is an over-simplification, it perhaps was Roger bishop of Salisbury, on the advice of masters from Laon, who combined the techniques of abacus, tallies and pipe rolls into the sessions of the Exchequer and thus created a new institution.

Sir Richard Southern has argued that 'Henry I was not a creator of institutions; he contributed nothing to the theory of kingship or to the philosophy of government; he created men.'[18] The contrasts between men and institutions and theory and practice in this statement are difficult to substantiate. Certainly Henry brought in new men, both as barons and as clerks, but it is also likely that the greatest of England's medieval institutions, the Exchequer, was created in his reign. Furthermore Chancery writs for litigation likewise begin to take a set form at this time. Their peremptory tone—'Unless you do this, my sheriff shall have it done so that I hear no further complaint for lack of justice'—may echo Henry's own voice and is certainly consistent with his reputation for stern justice. Although bureaucracy covered up all sorts of weaknesses, both the Exchequer and the Chancery contributed to the theory of kingship and the philosophy of government by making royal orders accountable, repeatable and widespread. Such orders moreover went out in the form of personal letters from the king to his men. Although the king would not have known the contents of every writ sent out in his name, each one bore his seal as a token of his approval. As the number of such writs increased (annual output probably doubled between the reigns of Rufus and Henry I), the king's commands began to reach every village. Henry was certainly no philosopher but through his ministers like Roger bishop of Salisbury, on the foundations already laid by Ranulf Flambard, he put the monarchy's theoretical claims into practice.

Medieval rulers had no difficulty in elaborating political theories, as the controversy between the papacy and the empire which was raging at this time demonstrates. Their problem lay in giving substance to their claims. Being ordained by God and the heir to ancient Rome did not cause either the pope or the emperor to ride any faster around his domains. The Norman kings of England overcame this disability by establishing bureaucratic procedures which automated royal commands and kept checks on those who disobeyed. In this light Fitz Nigel's *Dialogue of the Exchequer*, with its emphasis on the efficacy of money rather than virtue, looks like the first work by a British empiricist.

Feudalism

The concept of feudalism has been left to the last in this discussion because many of its problems disappear once the bureaucratic and empirical tradition in Anglo-Norman government is understood. For a century or more controversy has raged among historians about whether the Normans introduced feudalism into England and, if they did, whether this demonstrates their superiority over the Anglo-Saxons. Difficulties arise because feudalism is used in different senses. Roughly there is a wide definition favoured by French and German historians and a narrow one preferred by some historians of the Norman Conquest. The classic formulation of the wide definition is Marc Bloch's in *Feudal Society*: 'A subject peasantry; widespread use of the service tenement instead of a salary; the supremacy of a class of specialised warriors; ties of obedience and protection which bind man to man . . . and in the midst of all this the survival of other forms of association, family and state; such then seem to be the fundamental features of European feudalism.'[19] Feudalism in this wide sense thus embraces all medieval societies between the ninth century and the twelfth, as Bloch intended. Consequently late Anglo-Saxon society is broadly feudal, as F. W. Maitland pointed out long ago in *Domesday Book and Beyond* when discussing Oswald of Worcester's memorandum to King Edgar about riding duties and other services owed for land. F. M. Stenton's criticism of Maitland in *The First Century of English Feudalism 1066–1166* is the best introduction to the narrow definition. Stenton's title itself, implying that there was no English feudalism before 1066, is significant. He compared Oswald of Worcester's memorandum (dating from the 960s) with twelfth-century charters of feoffment and argued that the differences between them represent 'the habits of thought of two races, and to suggest, as Maitland suggested, that the services described in the memorandum are all the more feudal because they are miscellaneous and indefinite is to give "feudalism" so wide an extension that the word becomes almost meaningless'.[20] In Stenton's view services must be exactly defined in order to be feudal and 'this new precision which governed relationships throughout the higher ranks of post-Conquest society is the most obvious illustration of the difference between the Old English social order and the feudalism which replaced it'.[21] Feudal precision in Stenton's opinion was a product of the habits of thought of the Norman 'race'.

A sufficient explanation for the greater precision found in twelfth-century charters is that more was being written down in 1150 than 950. Theories about race and even about feudalism are irrelevant in this context. Norman charters of the twelfth century are no more nor less precise on average than those from other parts of western Europe. The move towards greater precision in charters was associated with an increase in the number of people who could read and write and a more professional interest in legal documents. The 'Twelfth-century Renaissance' is a more appropriate general term for this development than 'feudalism'. Nor in the eleventh century can it be convincingly shown that the Normans defined relationships more precisely than the Anglo-Saxons. Norman charters dating from before 1066 do not usually specify the services for which land is held and they rarely even call the land in question a fief. There is insufficient evidence for J. H. Round's thesis that William the Conqueror introduced knight service into England by specifying quotas of knights from each tenant in accordance with Norman practice. Certainly such quotas existed in the twelfth century but they were probably made the rule in both England and Normandy by Henry I rather than William the Conqueror. The quotas being in multiples of five and ten suggests an association with the Exchequer's practice of decimal computing, although there was a precedent in a writ of William the Conqueror to the abbot of Evesham concerning five knights. The kind of precision involved in fixing numbers of knights and in specifying their services is characteristically twelfth-century rather than characteristically Norman.

Where a narrow definition of feudalism does make sense in the context of the Norman Conquest is in the proposition that knights and castles were introduced by the Normans, provided these words are restrictively defined. The Normans did not introduce the 'knight' by that name as the Anglo-Saxon 'cniht' already existed, nor did they introduce the concept of noble service as the 'thegn' was an honoured retainer. If, however, a knight is defined as 'a warrior trained to fight on horseback with a lance', then it can be argued that the phalanxes of such men depicted in the Bayeux Tapestry were a novelty at the battle of Hastings. Nevertheless knights did not invariably fight on horseback (Henry I's barons were on foot when they won the battle of Tinchebrai) and their training and equipment underwent large changes in the twelfth century (most knights in the Bayeux Tapestry do not hold their lances steady at the hip but brandish them around their heads like light spears).

A comparable case can be made for the Norman introduction of castles, provided castle is restrictively defined to mean 'a fort designed to overawe the surrounding town or countryside'. Orderic Vitalis comments that the type of fortifications which the French called *castella* were uncommon in England and that is why the English were weakened in their resistance to the Normans despite being warlike and brave. Similarly the first words of the *Anglo-Saxon Chronicle*'s obituary for William the Conqueror are that 'he had castles built and poor men hard oppressed'.[22] Such castles were built in county towns in particular as strongholds for the first Norman garrisons and then as centres of government. Houses were cleared away and the local population organised into piling up a great mass of earth, the 'motte', on top of which a wooden stockade was constructed. Mottes like this can still be seen in Oxford and at Clifford's Tower in York. The building of stone keeps on the top of such earthworks took a longer time, although William the Conqueror had established the pattern for them in the Tower of London. The Anglo-Saxons had boroughs and fortified camps to defend the population but not these strongholds garrisoned by knights, which were designed as concentrations of power in a hostile land. The four or five castles recorded in England before 1066 were the work of the 'Frenchmen' introduced by Edward the Confessor, as the *Anglo-Saxon Chronicle* complained.

If knights and castles (as restrictively defined as in the preceding paragraph) are the essential characteristics of feudalism, then it would be true to say that feudalism was introduced by the Norman Conquest. But such a statement comes near to being a tautology, since knights and castles were the necessary instruments of conquest and appear in this clear-cut form only in those countries which were subjected to conquest. In this sense the Norman kingdoms of England and Sicily and the crusading lands in Spain, the Mediterranean and eastern Germany are the perfect feudal states. Feudal society is best exemplified in these places because the process of conquest provided a need and an opportunity to sharpen and reinforce relationships. This occurred in the physical sense that the natives faced the sharp end of the knight's lance and the force of his castle and also in the theoretical sense that the rights of lords and the duties of their men were defined and fixed in written surveys, of which the most ambitious is Domesday Book. Definition was essential because war had inevitably destroyed trust and customary practice. Specifying services was an attempt to hold the process of conquest at a fixed point and it might therefore be a sign of weakness rather than strength. The stipulation, for example, that a vassal owed his lord one and a half knights or that he would serve for only forty days does not express the generous spirit in which the heroes of the *chansons des gestes* serve their lords and companions until death.

Feudalism is an all-embracing term, which includes the large world of knightly heroes as well as the restrictive legalism of twelfth-century charters. In English history the different definitions can be built up on top of each other to mark chronological stages. Before 1066 England was a feudal society in the broad terms used by Marc Bloch. As a consequence of the Norman Conquest it became more rigorously militarised by the building of castles and the introduction of specialised knights. With William Rufus, 'that celebrated man, vigorous in knighthood', chivalric values are displayed for the first time. Then in the reign of Henry I the king's clerks and other drafters of documents begin to define services more exactly. This is when the term *feodum* meaning a 'fief' is first used in England. As a consequence feudalism became institutionalised in the twelfth century as a system of holding property and raising revenue. Building on the powerful traditions of the Anglo-Saxon monarchy, the Norman kings thus consolidated their hold on England by heading a hierarchy of lords controlling knights and castles. Nevertheless even this was a fragile edifice, as the civil wars of Stephen's reign were to show. Despite the development of institutions, the king still needed the personal loyalty which a knight pledged to his lord.

❦ IV ❧

CHURCH REFORM

The Anglo-Saxon Church

Through its church a medieval community expressed both its own identity and its relationship with other communities. This was as true of the village centred on its little structure of wood or occasionally of rough-hewn stone as it was of the English people as a whole, whose Church as a spiritual entity was headed by the archbishops of Canterbury and York. Ever since Bede had written his *Ecclesiastical History of the 'English People'* (the *gentis Anglorum* in Latin, the 'race of the English'), Christianity in England had been the strongest agent of national identity. Because they transcended local rivalries, Christian missionaries and the bishops and reforming abbots who followed them contributed to making England one kingdom. (Following William the Conqueror's Harrying of the North, Lanfranc took this tendency further and claimed to be primate of all Britain, citing Bede to the pope as his authority.) Ideally all Englishmen, regardless of class or regional differences, were united in leading a Christian life which distinguished them from pagan invaders. The Anglo-Saxon kings from Alfred to Cnut in unison with the bishops had promulgated decrees regulating the Christian life down to the requirement (in Wulfstan's redaction of Cnut's laws) that everyone should learn the Lord's Prayer and the Creed. It is impossible to know whether everyone did, as the lives of peasants are unrecorded. Nevertheless in the unique biography of Godric of Finchale, who was born of poor parents in Norfolk at the time of the Norman Conquest, the writer mentions in passing as a commonplace that Godric had learned the Lord's Prayer and Creed from the cradle and often pondered them.

The best evidence of popular piety comes from the building of churches. Although very few Anglo-Saxon churches survive to the present day, as they have been rebuilt, both archaeological evidence and contemporary comment agree that they were numerous. In 1050 Bishop Herman of Ramsbury (who was not English by origin but Lotharingian) boasted in Rome that England was replete with churches and that new ones were being added in new places every day. These churches were in towns as well as in the countryside. At the time of the Domesday survey Norwich had nearly fifty churches, and a similar number has been estimated for Winchester. Such churches were tiny and architecturally unimpressive, but they can be viewed as better evidence of Christian values at the grass roots than the great basilicas built by the Normans. Liturgical practices in these room-sized churches were presumably as unelaborate, if not crude, as their construction. But a priest who preached in English and could expound the gospel from a stock of traditional homilies might have a more profound effect on his community than a foreign bishop who was learned in Latin and canon law.

It is a mistake, however, to regard the Anglo-Saxon Church as having purely vernacular and peasant virtues. Its links with the papacy were direct and of long standing. Bede's *Ecclesiastical History* had shown the superiority of Gregory the Great and Roman practice, through Augustine of Canterbury's mission in 597, over the Celtic traditions of the west and north. The special relationship of England with the papacy was brought to everyone's attention each year on St Peter's day by the payment of Peter's Pence. No other kingdom paid such a tax to the papacy. Its names, 'Rome penny' and 'hearth penny', emphasise its purpose and how widely it was levied. There were many other ties with Rome and Italy, as well as with the monasteries of France and Lorraine. Although the best documented links are the formal ones (archbishops going to the pope to receive the pallium, bishops going to ecclesiastical councils, monks experiencing the discipline of other monasteries), the majority of those treading the roads were pilgrims journeying to points as distant as Rome, Santiago and Jerusalem. Even those who never went abroad were made aware of the larger Christian community through relics and images of the saints. The great miracle-working crucifix over the altar of St Peter at Bury St Edmunds was said to be exactly modelled on the Holy Face of Lucca, which Abbot Leofstan had venerated on his journey to Rome. William Rufus later adopted 'By the Holy Face of Lucca' as his distinctive personal oath; his knowledge of this may have derived from Bury rather than Italy.

Like the Anglo-Saxons, William the Conqueror had strong ties with the papacy. Indeed, because they were more recent and personal, they proved to be more effective. Lanfranc, who had been prior of Bec and was abbot of Caen in 1066, was known personally to the pope, Alexander II, and had taught the pope's relatives if not Alexander himself at the school of Bec. Anselm, another immigrant to Normandy and scholar of international reputation, had succeeded Lanfranc as prior of Bec in 1063. The Normans thus possessed the two most influential scholars of their day, who in turn became archbishops of Canterbury. They had perhaps been attracted to Normandy because of its previous generosity to Italian clerics like William of Volpiano and John of Ravenna. Normandy was an open and adventurous society for clergy as well as knights. The pope also knew of the Normans through the exploits of Robert Guiscard, who was well established by the 1060s as the 'vassal of St Peter' and the military protector of the Holy See. Through this network of connections William won papal approval for his invasion of England and was presented by the pope with a banner, which headed his troops at the battle of Hastings and is depicted in the Bayeux Tapestry. The pope may have understood this banner to signify that William was now a vassal of St Peter like Robert Guiscard and that he too was to conduct a holy war. For William the banner was perhaps no more than a sign of approval which everyone could see. From his experience of Guiscard the pope may also have estimated on a worldly level that William would win because he was a Norman. The pope's credit would have suffered if his banner had been captured, just as English credit suffered by Harold's banner being sent as a thank-offering to Rome by William.

Although William came to England as the pope's crusader, he took no immediate steps to reform the Church. Archbishop Stigand of Canterbury, of whom successive popes had complained for nearly twenty years, was recognised as metropolitan (chief bishop) and assisted at William's coronation, although the archbishop of York anointed the king. Stigand and two other bishops were deposed in 1070 after the spate of rebellions had made William nervous of their loyalty. Stigand was condemned on ecclesiastical charges which were correct in canon law: his appointment to Canterbury had been irregular and he held it in plurality with Winchester. Nevertheless these charges could have been made in 1066, or even in 1062 when the same papal legate, Ermenfrid of Sion, had been on a mission to England. The facts that nothing was done until 1070, that Ermenfrid had already removed an archbishop of Rouen for Duke William in similar circumstances, and that the only prelates to be deposed were those suspected of disloyalty, all suggest that the depositions were primarily political. Henceforward William chose only foreigners to be bishops in England. It may have been at this time that he asked Hugh abbot of Cluny, the most prestigious monastery in Christendom, to send him half a dozen monks to make into bishops and abbots. Hugh refused despite, or perhaps because of, William's offer of £100 of silver per monk per year.

Lanfranc and Norman control

William's instrument for controlling the Church in England was a prestigious monk of his own, Lanfranc, who was appointed archbishop of Canterbury in 1070 by papal authority. Superficially he did not look a promising choice for this crucial post upon which the future of Norman rule depended. He was an elderly scholar, wishing to retire from the world, and he was not a Norman. About two years after his appointment he wrote to Alexander II begging to be allowed to return to the monastic life. He explained that there was so much unrest and distress in England that things seemed to be going from bad to worse: 'While the king lives we have peace of a kind, but after his death we expect to have neither peace nor any other benefit.'[1] Nevertheless Lanfranc overcame his understandable nervousness about the future of Norman rule and up until his death in 1089 he set about enforcing discipline among the clergy. His strength came from his grounding in law and logic and his integrity as a monk. Although he was unworldly he had years of political and administrative experience behind him, as he had been responsible for building up the school at Bec and then, as head of the Abbaye-aux-Hommes at Caen, he was William's family counsellor.

Lanfranc's opponents were as often his fellow Norman prelates as English ones. Thus he wrote to Herfast bishop of Thetford, who had been William the Conqueror's chaplain: 'Give up dicing (to mention nothing worse) and the world's amusements, in which you are said to idle away the entire day; read holy scripture and above all set yourself to master the decretals of the Roman pontiffs and the sacred canons.'[2] Enforcement of canon law was the key to Lanfranc's approach. First it was necessary to ensure that the clergy possessed correct and up-to-date copies of the laws. The book of decretals which Lanfranc purchased from Bec and presented to the library at Christ Church Canterbury still exists. His lawyerly approach to problems is best illustrated by the decrees of the council of London in 1075, which removed bishoprics to the cities of Salisbury, Chichester and Chester among other acts. Each decree cites an authority or precedent for the action from the early Church; thus the councils of Sardis and Laodicaea prohibited bishoprics in villages. The revival of canon law in this learned way was intended to restore the Roman church to its pristine perfection in the days of Sts Benedict and Gregory the Great.

The same aim of reviving the splendour of the early Church through Roman order and uniformity is displayed in the basilicas which the Normans built in place of Anglo-Saxon cathedrals and abbeys. The size and number of these buildings together with the speed with which they were erected is extraordinary. As William of Malmesbury commented on Lanfranc's rebuilding of Canterbury: 'You do not know which to admire more, the beauty or the speed.'[3] The cathedrals of Canterbury and York,

Lincoln, Old St Paul's, Old Sarum, Rochester, Winchester and Worcester were all rebuilt (though not necessarily completed) during Lanfranc's pontificate; as were the abbey churches of Battle, Bury St Edmunds, St Albans, St Augustine's at Canterbury, and Tewkesbury. In the next generation in the 1090s the work continued with the abbeys of Gloucester, St Mary's York and the cathedrals of Chester, Chichester, Durham and Ely. Of the bishops only Osbern of Exeter had not remodelled his cathedral. These buildings were the achievement of numerous and mostly anonymous men and they were not entirely a consequence of the Conquest, as Westminster Abbey had been rebuilt in the same style by Norman architects in Edward the Confessor's last years. Nevertheless the common features of the great churches (both abbeys and cathedrals) built in Normandy and England between about 1060 and 1100 suggest common values. In their starkness, repetitiveness and huge proportions they can be seen as buildings typical of conquerors in a hurry to make their mark. The north transept of Winchester Cathedral, for example, may be felt to lack the intimate prayerfulness which can be sensed in the Anglo-Saxon church at Bradford-on-Avon. But this is not comparing like with like and furthermore Norman interiors now look stark only because they have lost their paint and metalwork and are no longer lit by lamps and candles. Even so, it is probably right to see a uniform ideology reflected in the design of these buildings. They demonstrate not so much the conquest of England as the triumph of the stonemason and of the clarity and order which the Rome of the Christian emperors and Gregory the Great evoked.

This style of building is appropriately described as Romanesque and in its most rigorous and monumental form is distinctively Norman. Although Lanfranc was not its originator, he was responsible for building the Abbaye-aux-Hommes at Caen in the 1060s which, in its proportions and method of construction, became the model for the great Norman churches in England starting with Lanfranc's own cathedral at Canterbury. For some of these churches the building stone itself was brought from Caen. In accommodating hundreds of worshippers in one congregation, these huge basilicas proclaimed the power of one faith and one liturgy by contrast with local cults and little parish churches. At the dedication of the new cathedral at Canterbury in 1077 there was no ceremonial translation of the church's relics, as was customary on such an occasion, but a procession of the consecrated Eucharist. Christ himself was to be the cult and treasure of the church and not some local bones. Such Roman unity and uniformity was presumably Lanfranc's. His abbey church at Caen and cathedral at Canterbury may have evoked for him the imperial splendour of the sacred palace of Theodoric and Otto III at Pavia, where he had first practised as a lawyer and a Christian. Lanfranc came from a larger and older world than his fellow Norman prelates.

Lanfranc's revival of canon law and Roman idealism was characteristic of the movement which is now called 'Gregorian reform' after Gregory VII, who was pope from 1073 to 1085 throughout the greater part of Lanfranc's time at Canterbury. He did not, however, get his ideas direct from Gregory, as they both shared ideals which had been developing for fifty years or more in France and Italy. Lanfranc was more 'Gregorian' in his devotion to Pope Gregory the Great, the last of the fathers of the Church who had been responsible for the conversion of England, than to Gregory VII. Indeed Gregory VII in 1080 accused Lanfranc of disloyalty to the Roman Church because he did not succeed in persuading William the Conqueror that he owed fealty to the pope. The demand for fealty from William, on the grounds that he rendered the service of Peter's Pence (and perhaps also because of the papal banner given him in 1066), was characteristic of Gregory VII's methods rather than those of the reformers in general. Lanfranc was able to reconcile the deference he owed the Holy See, in accordance with canon law, with the fealty he owed the king. He demonstrated this in Rufus's reign when William of St Carilef bishop of Durham was suspected of treason. When the bishop in accordance with strict 'Gregorian' principles claimed that his trial by laymen violated canon law and was a disgrace to the Church, Lanfranc rejected his plea. 'Well spoken, old bloodhound!' a Norman baron shouted.[4]

Lanfranc was the Normans' bloodhound not only in the pursuit of disloyal vassals but in his attitude to English sentiment. The most generous comments were Eadmer's (Anselm's biographer) who described him as 'somewhat unfinished as an Englishman' and 'a novice citizen of England'.[5] In this context he described Lanfranc's attitude to the English hero Archbishop Elphege, who had been killed by the Danes and was venerated as a martyr at Canterbury. Lanfranc had his feast day, together with St Dunstan's, removed from the calendar, although he later relented when Anselm persuaded him that Elphege might be said to have died for truth and justice if not explicitly for Christ. Lanfranc was not gratuitously anti-English like some Normans, but he would not at first allow local sentiment to stand in the way of canonical regulations and the emphasis reformers were putting on the unity of the faith. Furthermore, although he described himself in 1071 as a 'novice Englishman', he was too old and isolated by his office to adopt England in the way he had adopted Nor-

mandy thirty years before. This sense of alienation is suggested by Eadmer's record of Lanfranc telling Anselm how 'these Englishmen among
whom we spend our time' have set up saints for themselves.[6] Lanfranc
had not come to England by choice and he could not be other than the
Norman kings' faithful hound. The fact that no Englishman was made
a bishop during Lanfranc's time at Canterbury shows that he at least
approved of this policy, even if he were not its initiator. Not every Englishman was removed, as Wulfstan II lived on as bishop of Worcester until
1095, but further appointments were excluded not only in Lanfranc's
time but throughout the period of Norman rule. J. Le Patourel has
demonstrated that between 1070 and 1140 only one cleric who was definitely English, Aethelwulf of Carlisle, was appointed to an English see,
and Carlisle was as much Scottish as English. Not all the bishops were
Norman, as some like Lanfranc came from elsewhere in Europe, but they
were all aliens in England.

Not only bishops but many abbots and even some of the monks (at
Christ Church Canterbury, for example) were brought in from abroad. At
Glastonbury Thurstan, a monk from Lanfranc's former abbey of Caen,
was appointed abbot and brought bowmen into the church to compel the
monks to abandon their English tradition of chant. Although Lanfranc
disapproved of this violence, Thurstan was not deposed and the aim of
making English monastic practice conform with foreign models had Lanfranc's support, as he based his reformed rule for Christ Church on Cluniac customs. He provoked comparable violence in 1088 in Canterbury
itself at St Augustine's when he, together with Odo of Bayeux, imposed a
second Norman abbot on the monks. The English prior of the abbey had
to be removed to Christ Church, other monks were imprisoned in chains
in the castle, and one was made an example of by being publicly flogged at
the abbey's gates. 'Thus did Lanfranc enforce obedience by terror' is the
contemporary comment of his colleagues on this.[7]

These events reveal the ugly side of Norman rule, which was as real
and ever-present as the spaciousness of the new churches and the elegance of Lanfranc's manuscripts. Ideals of reform were inevitably distorted by the violence of the time, and this was compounded in England
by the Normans being alien conquerors. Although Lanfranc laid down
regulations for his monks at Canterbury as well as for the English clergy
as a whole, he did not necessarily benefit the Church in the larger sense
of the Christian community. Normanisation isolated the higher clergy
from the rest of the population. This was in a way a 'Gregorian' ideal, as
the leaders were to be kept pure and separate. But, when combined with

Normanisation, 'Gregorian reform' primarily meant that the higher clergy became a privileged class for whom the scriptures and canon law were titles to privilege. Like Gregory VII's dispute with the Emperor Henry IV, the long-term effect of Lanfranc's pontificate in England was to engender scandalous and uncontrollable disputes about clerical jurisdiction. This occurred on a national scale in the dispute about the primacy of Canterbury over York, which Lanfranc started, and locally in the rivalry between St Augustine's Canterbury and Lanfranc's new foundation of St Gregory's. In each case the participants forged documents and publicly abused each other.

By focusing on rights and law, Norman monks and bishops lost much of the evangelical fervour which had once inspired Anglo-Saxon missionaries and lived on through the episcopates of Wulfstan II of Worcester (1062–95). No new collections of vernacular prayers, homilies or penitential manuals were made by Lanfranc or other Norman prelates because there was too large a gulf in language and culture between them and the native English. A bishop's duty as pastor of his flock was not effectively revived in England until the episcopate of Robert Grosseteste of Lincoln 150 years later. Lanfranc was most effective over the things he could control and best understood. Thus his achievement in assembling good texts of the Latin Church fathers and of canon law for the library at Christ Church, as distinct from more popular works in English, cannot be questioned. Likewise the encouragement he gave to the building and furnishing of churches and monastic buildings made its mark. His example in both book collecting and building was followed most spectacularly at Durham by Bishop William of St Carilef. But in the more amorphous area of inspiring parish priests, as distinct from promulgating regulations about them, and reaching down to the mass of believers, Lanfranc cannot be shown to have achieved much because he had to rule through fear. 'He was a good shepherd to everyone, insofar as he was allowed to be' is how Eadmer sums up his career.[8]

Anselm and religious perfection

Anselm's career before his appointment to Canterbury in 1093 was remarkably similar to Lanfranc's and it might have been expected to continue to follow a similar course. He was an immigrant to Normandy, from Aosta on the Italian side of the Alps, who had succeeded Lanfranc as prior of Bec and then became abbot in 1078. Like Lanfranc he was a scholar and a devoted monk. As he had been prior and abbot at Bec for thirty years before he came to Canterbury, he was accustomed to worldly business and effective at it. Eadmer, his biographer, describes how at meetings he would refuse to intrigue but discoursed on the scriptures instead and, if no one listened, he went to sleep but would wake up and demolish his opponents' arguments in a moment. Anselm was the most intelligent and high-minded prelate of his time and this set him apart from his clerical colleagues as much as from the king and his barons. When he went into exile in 1097 to seek Pope Urban II's advice in his dispute with William Rufus, the bishops chided him (according to Eadmer at least) for not coming down to their level: they had their family and material interests to consider, whereas he already dwelt in heaven. 'If you choose to continue to hold fast to God and to him alone, then, so far as we are concerned, you will have to travel alone. We will not withdraw the fealty we owe the king.'⁹

Anselm's stance differed from Lanfranc's over the crucial question of obedience. At the trial of William of St Carilef, Lanfranc had insisted that the bishop answer Rufus's accusations and not shield himself behind canon law (see page 62 above). At Rockingham in 1095 the roles were reversed. William of St Carilef spoke on Rufus's behalf against Anselm's claim that his first loyalty was to Urban II as pope. Anselm uncompromisingly spelt out the logic of his position. The pope was the successor of St Peter, to whom Christ had given the keys of the kingdom of heaven. This divine charge had been given to the pope and not to any emperor, king, duke or earl whatsoever. As none of the assembled prelates dared repeat Anselm's words to the king, he went and told Rufus this himself. This meeting at Rockingham marks the point where 'Gregorian reform', in the strict sense of the ideology of Gregory VII himself, enters England. Anselm's argument accorded with Gregory's claim against the Emperor Henry IV in 1081 that the authority of kings and dukes, so far from being divinely ordained, originated from the devil and was based on greed, pride, violence, treachery and murder. Moreover Rufus, in the opinion of his clerical opponents, lived up to this image of the prince of darkness by his seizure of Church property and the arrogance of his knights.

At the time of his appointment to Canterbury Anselm had likened the attempt to co-operate with Rufus to yoking together a wild bull with a feeble old sheep. This evoked the traditional image of archbishop and king (Church and State in later parlance) working together at the plough of God's husbandry. There had never been in the Anglo-Saxon Church or in Lanfranc's time fundamental dispute between the king and the bishops because they shared the same ideas about government. But Anselm's image of the plough team failed to mention that there had been a change of driver. In place of the quiescent popes of the tenth century there had been Gregory VII, who tried to destroy the Emperor Henry IV, and now Urban II (1088–99), who took over the leadership of Europe by launching the First Crusade in 1095, the same year as the meeting at Rockingham. By going into exile in 1097 and being in daily contact with Urban II, Anselm was in the forefront of the new papal idealism and a powerful figure in his own right. It was he, for example, who argued the case for the Roman Church against the Greeks at the council of Bari in 1098. He was mentally as active as ever. During his disputes with Rufus, which would have distracted any lesser man, he began his *Cur Deus Homo* ('Why was God made Man?'), which revolutionised the theology of the redemption, and he followed this in the last decade of his life with works on original sin, free will and the trinity. Unlike later medieval thinkers, Anselm combined profundity with a clear and attractive style.

Because of Anselm's reputation and the insecurity of his own position, Henry I had no option but to recall him from exile in 1100, although he proved to be more uncompromising than ever. The dispute now centred on the question of royal investiture of bishops with the crozier and ring, symbolising their pastoral and apostolic office, and the homage which they did to the king. In 1093 Anselm had been invested by Rufus in the traditional manner and had probably also done him homage. Nevertheless, on Henry I's accession Anselm refused to receive investiture from him or to do homage because Urban II's council of Rome in 1099 had prohibited these practices. This is another example of Anselm belatedly introducing 'Gregorian reform' in the strict sense into England, as Gregory VII had banned royal investiture in his struggle with Henry IV in order to clarify the difference between the spiritual eminence of a bishop and the worldly rule of a layman. From a royal point of view the problem was that a bishop, too, exercised worldly rule, as he was a landlord, who in England owed knight-service to the king. At one point in the investiture controversy Pope Paschal II (1099–1118) proposed to follow Gregory VII's logic to the point of divesting the church of all its property, so that it would be truly spiritual, but his clerical colleagues took fright. In England, as elsewhere in Europe, the controversy was settled by uneasy compromises, which kept Anselm once more in exile between 1101 and 1107. Henry I surrendered the right of investiture but bishops continued to do homage.

Superficially Anselm's pontificate achieved less than Lanfranc's, as it was torn by disputes and he was in exile half the time. Real power remained with the king and with the worldly clergy who had told Anselm in 1097 that he must travel alone on his high-minded road. After his death in 1109 contact with the papacy almost ceased and no new archbishop of Canterbury was appointed until 1114. Henry I seems to have decided to have only one archbishop at a time and he was content with Thomas II archbishop of York. He came from a more traditional ecclesiastical milieu than Lanfranc or Anselm, being the son of Samson bishop of Worcester (who had succeeded Wulfstan in 1096), the brother of Richard bishop of Bayeux, and the nephew of Thomas I archbishop of York (1070–1100). This family of clergy were all associated with the church of Bayeux, of which William the Conqueror's half-brother, the warrior prelate Odo, had been bishop. When Thomas II of York died of overeating in 1114, Henry I wanted to appoint Faricius, the reforming abbot of Abingdon (a native of Arezzo and Henry's physician), as archbishop of Canterbury, but he agreed after protests from the other bishops to have a Norman instead. Thurstan, another clerk with Bayeux connections, succeeded as archbishop of York. His father was a canon of St Paul's, who had settled in London with his wife, and his brother was a bishop. These Norman prelates were not reformers in their attitude to clerical celibacy. Eadmer's allegation that they told Anselm that they had their family and material interests to consider rings true.

As archbishop, Anselm had taken an increasingly strict 'Gregorian reform' view of clerical marriage as of his other duties. At the council of London in 1102 priests, deacons and canons were ordered to put away their wives; priests living with women were forbidden to celebrate Mass and their Masses were not to be heard by the faithful; the sons of priests were not to inherit the churches of their fathers. Similar legislation was repeated in 1108 after Anselm had returned from exile. The ban on clerical marriage was intended to reduce simony (the buying and selling of ecclesiastical offices) and it also emphasised that the clergy were the *kleros* (the elect) by contrast with the laity or *laos* (the crowd). Furthermore Gregory VII had emphasised the sacramental function of celibacy: just as Christ had been born of a virgin, so the Eucharist must be consecrated at Mass by a priest dedicated to chastity.

There was nothing new in principle in the idea that the clergy should be chaste. Anglo-Saxon bishops had legislated and preached against clerical marriage, as had Lanfranc. Anselm's legislation differed only in its uncompromising nature. As with the questions of obedience to the pope and investiture, he took his stand on absolute principles, whereas his colleagues acknowledged the world as they found it. The total prohibition of the marriage of priests might cause the collapse of parish life, Herbert Losinga bishop of Norwich warned Anselm, because most priests lived with women and many aimed to pass on their churches to their children or at least to provide for them within the clerical order. The children of priests were not necessarily corrupt. Some of the most distinguished monks of the twelfth century were the sons of priests, like Orderic Vitalis and Ailred of Rievaulx, and they owed their education to that fact. Heredity and family interest had the same advantages and disadvantages for churchmen as for knights. The gains of stability and continuity were counterbalanced by the risks of complacency and incompetence. In the opinion of moderate churchmen celibacy was a counsel of perfection. It was for the truly religious, for monks like Anselm who already dwelt in heaven, and not for the secular clergy who lived in the world. To be 'converted to religion' in the twelfth century meant to become a monk.

Monastic expansion

Strict 'Gregorian reform' aimed to make the life of religious perfection led by monks into the norm for all the clergy. As a whole this policy failed, since the clergy remained predominantly worldly throughout the Middle Ages, though some learned to be more discreet about their women if not their wealth. Nevertheless failure was not total. Although Anselm's and Lanfranc's legislation had little effect, the monastic ideals by which they lived gave an example to both clergy and laity. In the period 1066–1135 the number of religious of all sorts (both monks and nuns), as distinct from the secular clergy, is estimated to have increased from about 1,000 persons at the time of the Norman Conquest to 4,000 or 5,000. Similarly the number of religious houses increased from about 60 to 250 or 300. (The figures are imprecise because the number of inmates is not exactly recorded and the dates of foundation and separate status of some houses is in doubt.) This four- or fivefold increase in the number of religious in seventy years shows that the ideals of the reformers took root among an élite at least. On the other hand even 5,000 people 'converted to religion' was pitifully few in a population of about one and a half million.

Monks were the aristocracy of the church just as knights were of the state. The number of religious in this period was approximately the same as the number of knights. If 2,000 or so knights could effect the Norman Conquest (see page 40 above), a similar cohort of monks through prayer and example might overcome the devil. 'In your country there is a prize of my Lord's and yours,' Bernard of Clairvaux wrote to Henry I in 1132 in support of the Cistercian monks who brought Fountains Abbey into their order, 'which I am resolved to seize by sending our force of knights. For this purpose I have sent forward these men to reconnoitre. Assist them therefore as officers of your Lord and fulfil through them your feudal service.'[10] Bernard was doing more here than adapting his language to Norman feudalism and Henry I's military fame, as monastic life itself was becoming increasingly military in its organisation through religious orders like the Cistercians.

In Anglo-Saxon England as elsewhere in Europe the great monasteries (like Bury St Edmunds, Glastonbury, or St Albans) had been independent of each other and followed their own customs, although they all subscribed to the Rule of St Benedict and were subject to outside reforming movements. Instead of these individual houses, monasteries in the period 1066–1135 were being organised into orders, which took directions from the mother house and followed a common rule in every detail. The Burgundian abbey of Cluny had been the forerunner of such huge and tight organisation under its abbot, Hugh the Great (1049–1109), at the time of the Norman Conquest. Although he had refused to send monks to William the Conqueror, even for £100 each (see page 59 above), and was reluctant to extend his jurisdiction across the English Channel, the first Cluniac house was founded at Lewes in 1077 by the Norman baron William de Warenne, and by 1135 there were twenty-four such houses including dependencies. A significant influence here was William the Conqueror's daughter Adela countess of Blois, who became a Cluniac nun in her widowhood. She encouraged her brother, Henry I, to found Reading Abbey in 1121 and had her son, Henry of Blois (King Stephen's brother), educated at Cluny. In 1130 Cluny penetrated into the heartland of English nationalism when its abbot, Peter the Venerable, visited Peterborough with a view to bringing it under his rule. 'May God Almighty destroy these wicked plans,' prayed the *Anglo-Saxon Chronicle*, 'for the wretched monks of Peterborough stand in need of the help of Christ and of all Christian people!'[11] What was reforming severity to Peter the Venerable seemed religious persecution to the Peterborough monks.

The monastic order which made the greatest impact was the Cistercians through the voice of Bernard, who was abbot of Clairvaux from 1115 to 1153. Nevertheless the Cistercian rule, which gave them such an effective organisation, may have been the work of an Englishman, Stephen Harding, who became abbot of Cîteaux in 1110. Despite Harding, however, the Cistercians were essentially Burgundians like the Cluniacs who were their rivals. To distinguish themselves from the Cluniacs, they wore white habits instead of black, and Bernard spread it about with effective exaggeration that the Cluniacs were worldly whereas they were pure. The powerful draw of the Cistercians is well described in the account of how

Ailred of Rievaulx first heard of them in 1134. He was told by a friend of some wonderful monks who had come to Yorkshire from across the sea. Their habits of undyed wool symbolised their angelic purity. They were all subject to one rule and 'for them everything is fixed by weight, measure and number'.[12] Their house at Rievaulx was set in a wooded valley which seemed like a new Garden of Eden. Ailred accordingly rushed to join. By the time Bernard of Clairvaux died in 1153 there were at least three hundred Cistercian houses in Europe and fifty of these were in England.

The Cluniac and Cistercian orders were as much an aristocracy, in both an ecclesiastical and a social sense, as the traditional Benedictines (or Black monks) whom they claimed to reform. Their leaders, like Peter the Venerable and Bernard of Clairvaux, came from Burgundian noble families and their patrons were magnates, like William de Warenne at Lewes and Walter Espec at Rievaulx. The monastic virtues of poverty, chastity and obedience were attractive only to aristocrats. Peasants already lived in poverty, they could not afford chastity (children were needed to assist their labours and support them in old age), and they already owed obedience to their lords. Walter Daniel, the biographer of Ailred of Rievaulx, is careful to explain that the Cistercians cultivate poverty and not the penury of the negligent and idle. This divine poverty is a *voluntaria necessitas* ('voluntary necessity').[13] In this paradox the biographer identifies the contradiction at the root of monastic life, which undid the work of every reformer from St Benedict to St Francis, as real or involuntary poverty was not a virtue in medieval eyes but a common disgrace. Hence the poor could not be fully fledged monks, although the Cistercians did take the unusual step of giving them a place as 'converts' or 'lay' brothers who volunteered their labour. These 'converts' in place of serfs were the gardeners of Eden, who first made Rievaulx, Fountains and Tintern Abbeys into the earthly paradises they are today.

Less spectacular but more numerous than Cluniac and Cistercian monasteries were the houses which began to describe themselves as Augustinian in Henry I's reign. About sixty English houses recognised the Augustinian rule by 1135. They were not a centralised organisation, taking their instructions from Burgundy, like the Cluniacs and Cistercians. Nor was their rule, for which they claimed the authority of St Augustine, standardised and detailed like that of the other religious orders. Augustinians described themselves as 'canons', who led the communal and celibate life laid down for the clergy by canon law and the fathers of the Church. The title 'Augustinian canon' gave a respected name and an air of legality to a variety of usually small groups of monks and nuns. Many, though not all of them, were concerned with pastoral work in teaching, caring for the sick, and preaching. They were 'Gregorian reform' in action, as the canonical life provided a way for clergy to be celibate and yet continue with a pastoral ministry. Whereas the Cistercians claimed to be poor and humble while being collectively rich and powerful, some Augustinian groups really were poor, as they demanded less from their founders. Instead of withdrawing to huge estates like Fountains and Rievaulx, the Augustinians brought the religious life to the laity.

The risk run by Augustinian canons was that they would be contaminated by the world in which they worked. This is why monks in the Benedictine tradition, like Cluniacs and Cistercians, insisted on vast lands to make them independent of the laity. They withdrew from the world and prayed for themselves and their noble patrons because there was no hope of salvation in daily life. A good example of a house of canons being contaminated almost as soon as it started is Lanfranc's own foundation of St Gregory's at Canterbury in 1087. This community acknowledged the Augustinian rule by the 1120s and was typical in its size and purpose. Lanfranc had provided for six priests and twelve clerks, who would conduct a grammar and music school and look after the poor in a hospital. As he had little wealth of his own with which to endow this foundation, Lanfranc transferred to it bits and pieces of Canterbury property within his jurisdiction. Among these was the miracle-working corpse of St Mildred. Lanfranc's disapproval of Anglo-Saxon saints was well known, but he may have softened in his attitude to English superstitions in his old age and St Mildred would be useful to his canons, as her cult brought in money from offerings. The dedication of the church to Pope Gregory the Great, 'patron of us and of all England' (as Lanfranc called him in the foundation charter), was too idealistic for the average churchgoer and so Lanfranc had also provided the more immediate attractions of the relics of St Mildred and two other Anglo-Saxon ladies, Sts Eadburga and Ethelburga.[14]

The flaw in Lanfranc's endowment was that the neighbouring abbey of St Augustine's, whose monks Lanfranc had imprisoned and flogged in 1088 (see page 63 above), also claimed to have the corpse of St Mildred and they commissioned the hagiographer and polemicist Goscelin of St Bertin in the 1090s to write 'against the inane usurpers of St Mildred the Virgin'.[15] Goscelin's arguments reveal more about ordinary beliefs at the time than the idealism of Lanfranc and other reformers. He starts with some strong arguments to a modern ear: St Gregory's is insolently encouraging superstition among the masses and its historical evidence is shaky. But these rational arguments are given less emphasis than the miracles which Goscelin uses to prove his case. He tells how St Mildred once stood up in her tomb at St Augustine's and hit the abbey's janitor, because he was asleep; and on another occasion she hit a man who fell asleep while praying at her tomb. Moreover, when the rival claimants used the ordeal of water to establish the truth, the trussed-up child they used would not sink into the consecrated water, even when the canons of St Gregory's pushed him. Goscelin's most recent evidence was that on St Mildred's last feast day one of the young monks at St Augustine's had foretold rain, because Mildred brought them annual fertility, and it had duly rained.

Remote as fertility cults, sacrificial children and animated corpses are from modern Anglicanism, they were all familiar parts of Lanfranc's and Anselm's world. The gulf which separated Anselm's theology from daily religious life was huge. He even had to reprove Eadmer, his biographer, for wanting a larger piece of the skull of St Prisca than the bishop of Paris had given him. (The bishop had allowed Eadmer as much of the bone as he could break off at one try.) Nevertheless the intellectuals and reformers, although they were a minute group, exercised a disproportionate influence because they were at the top of the ecclesiastical hierarchy at Canterbury as much as at Rome. The Normans reinforced the already strong links between the English Church and the papacy, and in Lanfranc and Anselm, who were not Normans, they gave England the greatest spiritual lords of their day. At the bottom of the ecclesiastical pyramid, however, among the English-speaking village priests, nothing perhaps changed for better or worse.

PART TWO

The Angevins
(1135–99)

THE CONNECTION between England and Anjou originated in 1128 with the marriage of Matilda, Henry I's daughter and heiress, to Geoffrey Plantagenet, heir of the count of Anjou. Through this alliance Henry hoped to bring Norman and Angevin rivalries to an end and to leave Matilda with a stronger power-base than he had had on his accession. As events turned out, however, the Angevin alliance was a disaster for Matilda because it caused twenty years of civil war in England and bitter campaigns at the same time in France between Angevins and Normans. In the longer term Henry II (1154–89) succeeded in holding together his diverse possessions by his own determination, and Richard I (1189–99) pursued the logic of his great inheritance in the crusade against Saladin (Richard had a claim to the kingdom of Jerusalem through his great-grandfather, Fulk of Anjou) and in war against Philip Augustus of France. Nevertheless the Angevin connection had overstretched the capacities of even these energetic rulers, as they never succeeded in giving a sense of common purpose to their diverse lands. In the words of J. C. Holt:

> The Plantagenet lands were not designed as an 'empire', as a great centralised administrative structure, which was ultimately broken down by rebellion and French attack. On the contrary these lands were simply cobbled together. They were founded, and continued to survive, on an unholy combination of princely greed and genealogical accident.[1]

Historians since the nineteenth century have for convenience described these lands as the Angevin Empire. Contemporaries, on the other hand, although they acknowledged that Henry II's dominions stretched from the Northern Ocean (that is, from Scotland) to the Pyrenees, never used the term 'Angevin Empire' because they looked on Henry's lands as the lucky acquisition of a quarrelsome family and not as an institution.

Henry II's father, Geoffrey count of Anjou, had neither the ability nor the inclination to unite England and Normandy with Anjou. Although his marriage to Matilda designated him as king on Henry I's death, he never set foot in England and Henry I even obstructed him from obtaining the castles in Normandy which were Matilda's dower. Geoffrey's conduct contrasts with that of his father, Fulk, who likewise married the heiress to a kingdom, Melisende of Jerusalem, in 1129. Fulk immediately went to Palestine and ruled there as king from 1131 to 1143, whereas Geoffrey in 1131 forfeited his chance to be king of England by allowing Matilda to cross the Channel without him and accept the oath of allegiance of the English barons at Northampton on her own. Geoffrey had only succeeded to Anjou in 1129 and he may have felt that he could not abandon it, as his father had just done, by crossing over to his wife's kingdom. Furthermore he would probably not have been welcome, either in England or in Normandy.

Contemporaries give no satisfactory explanation for Geoffrey's indifferent career. The chronicler of Anjou, Jean de Marmoutier, characterises him in much the same way as his son Henry II would later be eulogised as 'admirable in probity, outstanding in justice, dedicated to acts of knighthood, and excellently educated'.[2] Orderic Vitalis in Normandy, on the other hand, describes the failure of Geoffrey's four successive invasions between 1135 and 1138 and records that the Angevins made themselves hated by their brutality, although Geoffrey did get himself accepted as duke of Normandy in 1144. He had also faced rebellions in his native Anjou which obstructed effective action in Normandy. As for England, it was entirely foreign to him and he had problems with Matilda as well. She was the widow of the Emperor Henry V and persisted in calling herself 'Empress' throughout her life, as if her marriage to Geoffrey was of no significance. Geoffrey retaliated by staying put in France. William of Malmesbury reports that when in 1142 Matilda appealed to Geoffrey to do his duty by coming to defend his wife's and his children's inheritance in England, he replied that he knew none of her ambassadors and would deal only with Robert earl of Gloucester. When Robert crossed the Channel at considerable personal risk, Geoffrey made excuses but, as a great favour, he did allow the future Henry II (who was then aged nine) to be taken to England as the rallying point for Matilda's cause. In this oblique way the Angevins came to England.

Geoffrey's lack of success in the decade following his marriage to Matilda contrasts with the future Henry II's vigour in his early years. In 1149 he was knighted at the age of sixteen by David I of Scotland. In that year or in 1150 he was inaugurated as duke of Normandy. In 1151 he succeeded his father as count of Anjou and in 1152 he married Eleanor of Aquitaine. 'It is astonishing', comments a contemporary, 'how such great good fortune came to him so fast and so suddenly that within a short time without expecting it, he was called duke of Normandy and count of Anjou.'[3] Although Henry owed his sudden elevation to the unexpected death of his father (at the age of forty) and to his father's belated pacification of Anjou and Normandy, he managed—by contrast with his father—to establish his authority immediately in his new dominions. Furthermore in 1153, by the treaty of Winchester, Henry's title to the kingdom of England was recognised by Stephen, who disinherited his own surviving son. Henry was now twenty years old, the same age as Geoffrey had been in 1131 when he had first forfeited his chance to be king of England.

Henry II's success, when compared with his father's career, suggests that his dominance depended on personal qualities rather than on luck or on inherited institutions. He created the illusion of an Angevin Empire by grasping opportunities and by hard riding. Herbert of Bosham (one of Becket's biographers) likened government to a human chariot, of which the king is both driver and marksman, dragging everyone along in fear and excitement. Walter Map recorded that Henry was constantly travelling, 'moving by intolerable stages like a courier . . . Impatient of repose, he did not hesitate to disturb almost half Christendom.'[4] There was little that was specifically Angevin in all this. It is true that Henry's methods were similar to those of his ancestors, Fulk the Black and Geoffrey Martel who had made Anjou into a distinct and great lordship, but the dukes of Normandy and the counts of Poitou—indeed all successful feudal lords —had done likewise. Henry looks more Angevin in the circumstances of his birth and death, as he was born at Le Mans (the counts of Anjou had recently tightened their hold on the county of Maine) and he died at Chinon. He also visited these two towns more frequently than any others in his Angevin lands because Le Mans stood at the pivot of Brittany, Normandy and Anjou, and at Chinon was the treasury of the region. Nevertheless, if Henry's long reign from 1154 to 1189 is looked at as a whole, the more striking fact is that he spent only half as long in Anjou as he did in England or in Normandy. All in all London, Winchester and Woodstock—and Rouen, Caen and other towns in Normandy—were more frequently and regularly visited than Henry's patrimony in Anjou.

Henry II could not—and perhaps did not wish to—prevent his continental possessions from centring on France. 'Five duchies has the French Crown and, if you count them up, there are three of them missing,' wrote the troubadour Bertran de Born.[5] He meant that Normandy, Brittany and his own Aquitaine were under the lordship of Henry II and his sons, and he exhorted King Philip of France not to make a dishonourable peace with the English king. It is significant also in this context that Bertran calls Henry il reis engles (the English king) who bribes those in France with English money. To a Poitevin chronicler similarly Henry seemed an alien and cruel figure: 'the king of the North'. The French kingdom, on the other hand, through its associations with Charlemagne and heroes of epic like Roland and Raoul de Cambrai, was a stronger centre of unity than the Angevin Empire which modern historians have reconstructed out of theories of feudalism. 'The Angevin Empire', writes Jacques Boussard, 'was conceived as an extremely strong state, but within the framework of the feudal system.'⁶ This feudal proviso fundamentally weakens the concept of a strong Angevin state. Certainly Henry II strengthened government within his various lordships both in Britain and in France, but the unity of his French lands could be no more than personal because each of their components already owed allegiance to the French Crown.

Ironically Henry's energetic rule strengthened the French monarchy rather than his own in the long term. Thus when he distributed his lands among his sons in his will in 1170, he allowed them to do homage to the French king. Moreover in 1183 Henry himself did liege homage to King Philip for all his continental lands. Previous dukes of Normandy had acknowledged the French king's overlordship but they had never humbled themselves to the point of doing liege homage (by which a vassal became the loyal man of his lord). Duke Rollo's warriors had allegedly tipped the French king off his throne for demanding as much (see page 21 above).

England was not dominated by Angevins in the twelfth century in the way that Normans had mastered it in the eleventh or Poitevins were prominent at court in the thirteenth. Contemporary chroniclers do not complain of Angevins in the way that the *Anglo-Saxon Chronicle* laments the Norman Conquest or Matthew Paris attacks Poitevins. Nor was Henry II seen as an Angevin interloper. His paternal inheritance from the counts of Anjou was played down in England, while his descent through Matilda from the Anglo-Saxon kings was emphasised. Nor had Matilda described herself as countess of Anjou: on her seal she is 'Queen of the Romans' and in charters she is 'Empress' and 'Lady of the English'. Only her opponents called her 'countess of Anjou' or 'Lady of the Angevins' to emphasise that she was an alien interloper. She had become Empress through her marriage to the Holy Roman Emperor Henry V who had died in 1125. Henry II's imperial associations derived from being Matilda's son, and hence 'Fitz Empress', rather than from the lordship of a hypothetical Angevin Empire. Nevertheless 'Angevin' is useful as a general rather than specific term for the widening circle of the king of England's interests and influence which stemmed from the Angevin marriage of 1128. England's rulers were no longer narrowly Norman: Stephen came from the house of Blois; Matilda called herself Empress; of Henry II's eight great-grandparents only one (William the Conqueror) was a Norman; Richard I ruled his mother's lands of Poitou and Aquitaine, which were two or three times the size of Normandy, and his troubadour ancestor William IX (who died in 1127) had proudly declared that he had never had a Norman or a Frenchman in his house.

The style of government and culture in the years 1135–99 was therefore cosmopolitan rather than being exclusively English, Norman or Angevin. It is typified by King Stephen's brother, Henry of Blois bishop of Winchester (1129–71), who commissioned the Winchester Bible and bought antique statues in Rome for his episcopal palace, or by John of Salisbury, the greatest Latinist of his age, who (as he tells us) in the year of Henry I's death was beginning his studies with Abelard in Paris. John became bishop of Chartres and his compatriot Nicholas Breakspear was elected pope as Adrian IV (1154–9). How shocked John was when Walkelin archdeacon of Suffolk named his bastard son Adrian in honour of the only English pope and proposed to call a daughter Adriana. There was now a two-way traffic in talent between England and the Continent instead of the Normans importing experts, like Lanfranc and Roger bishop of Salisbury, as they had done in the period 1066–1135. In increasing numbers in Henry II's reign in particular, men who had been born in England began to hold high office, but they were not little Englanders or the vanguard of an Anglo-Saxon revival. On the contrary they were the products of a competitive and cosmopolitan education, exemplifying the ideals of French chivalry like William the Marshal or the clerical superiority of the schools of Paris and Bologna like Thomas Becket. Latin and French were therefore the languages in which they excelled, and not English. The two most prolific and original writers moreover, Walter Map and Gerald of Wales, drew their inspiration (as Geoffrey of Monmouth did likewise) from Celtic Britain rather than Anglo-Saxon England. Furthermore, although Marshal and Becket were Englishmen in the sense that they had been born in England, they were the descendants of Normans.

On Becket's suggestion Henry II recalled Englishmen who had been living in France as clerics or masters in the schools and gave them offices. Henry also invited Master Thomas Brown to return from the kingdom of Sicily, where he had been Roger II's secretary, to a seat at the Exchequer to watch over the king's special interests. London, as the seat of Henry II's government as well as of commerce, was becoming a cosmopolitan capital; it was the most famous city in the world in the opinion of William Fitz Stephen (see page 14 above). Looking down over the Thames from his turret window in the Tower of London in the 1170s, Richard Fitz Nigel conceived a new sort of book which epitomises the distinctive style of Henry II's court. Although his *Dialogue of the Exchequer* is in the classical form of a didactic dialogue, it concerns (as he explains) not the scholastic technicalities (*subtilia*) of Aristotle and Plato but useful information (*utilia*) about government. The law book attributed to Henry II's justiciar

Ranulf Glanvill is a similar amalgam of a classical form (recalling Justinian's *Institutes*) and practical modern information. Taking pride in their classical education, these authors flatter Henry by describing his power in terms of a Roman and not of an Angevin empire. Fitz Nigel writes that 'he has extended his power [*imperium*] over large tracts of land in victorious triumph', and Glanvill says that the praise of Henry's victories 'has gone out to all the earth and his mighty works to all the borders of the world'.[7]

These authors did not consider Henry's *imperium* to be particularly Angevin but neither was it distinctively English, because it extended so far over the medieval world. For lack of any better term to describe this distinctive but passing phenomenon, the 'Angevin Empire' stands as a necessary historical convenience rather than a precise twelfth-century reality. Nevertheless, although there was no 'empire' in the sense of uniform institutions, the power of the Angevin family of Henry II was real enough. Through it educated Englishmen, Anglo-Normans and Welshmen extended their horizons and made, most notably through their Latin writings, a considerable and distinctive contribution to the Europe of the Twelfth-century Renaissance.

✣ V ✣

STRUGGLES FOR THE KINGDOM

(1135–99)

The death of Henry I in 1135 was seen by contemporaries as a calamity. With the wisdom of hindsight they looked back on his reign as a time of tranquillity: 'England, once the seat of justice, the home of peace, the height of piety, the mirror of religion, became thereafter a place of perversity, a haunt of strife, a school of disorder, and the teacher of every kind of rebellion,' wrote the author of the *Gesta Stephani* ('The Deeds of King Stephen').[1] What was most surprising in the opinion of this author was that even wild animals suffered. Formerly huge herds of them (deer are presumably meant) overflowed the whole land, whereas henceforward a man was lucky to see even one because they had been indiscriminately killed. The miseries caused by robber barons are described in such similar terms by different chroniclers that the catalogue of atrocities becomes trite. Both William of Malmesbury and the *Anglo-Saxon Chronicle* describe the building of castles and how knights went out from them to plunder the countryside, dragging off anyone with money to their dungeons. What particularly shocked monastic writers was the lack of respect for churches and churchyards. Because they were vulnerable, these writers looked at war from the point of view of those who suffered from it, particularly peasants (the 'men of the land') in the case of the *Anglo-Saxon Chronicle*. The knights who committed these atrocities considered themselves entitled to booty and they used arson and robbery as weapons against their opponents. Thus the author of *Gesta Stephani* describes how in 1149 King Stephen and his counsellors decided that the only way to compel their opponents to surrender was to burn crops and destroy all means of sustaining life. Consequently Stephen's son Eustace, who is described elsewhere in the book as a gentle and affable knight, went to Devizes with his men and killed everyone they came across, 'committing indiscriminately every cruelty they could think of'.[2] By having to generalise, chroniclers exaggerated both the state of peace which had existed before 1135 and the chaos which followed. The idea of England and its ancient institutions—'the noblest nurse of peace, the special home of tranquillity' (in William of Malmesbury's words)—survived the nineteen winters of Stephen's reign, so that Henry II on his accession could ignore them and claim that he was returning directly to the good rule of his grandfather, Henry I. The chroniclers' contrast between the good old days and the present thus became enshrined in Henry II's propaganda and reinforced in further chroniclers' narratives like that of William of Newburgh.

Property and inheritance

The barons of Stephen's reign can be seen as family men ensuring their own property, rather than as robbers. Because central authority was in dispute, they had to reinforce their local power in order to survive against their rivals. The Norman Conquest had temporarily weakened regional lordships, but they had begun to re-establish themselves in Henry I's reign. Stephen and Matilda were coming to terms with realities in recognising local principalities. The number of earldoms trebled between 1135 and 1154 and furthermore the earls looked upon the counties from which they took their titles as their family property; sheriffs therefore became earls' deputies rather than royal officers answerable directly to the king. In Latin charters earls are described as *comites* (that is, 'counts' or heads of counties) and sheriffs are *vicecomites* ('viscounts'). As R. H. C. Davis has demonstrated, there were only five counties which had no earl in Stephen's reign and (apart from Shropshire) the omissions can be explained by special circumstances, such as Henry of Blois's jurisdiction as bishop of Winchester in Hampshire or Geoffrey de Mandeville's authority in Middlesex as keeper of the Tower of London.

Royal offices had a strong tendency to become hereditary and the extension of the idea of family property to them could be seen as a force making for stability rather than disorder. As kingship was hereditary (though not necessarily by strict primogeniture), why should not earldoms and sheriffdoms likewise be inherited? Counts and viscounts were hereditary in France; why not in England? The political importance of the reigns of Stephen and Henry II is that they established which offices should be hereditary in England and which should not. The outcome was a compromise. Earldoms, baronies and knights' fees were acknowledged to be hereditary, whereas sheriffdoms and justiceships were not (except in isolated cases like the Beauchamp sheriffdom of Worcestershire). Earldoms, baronies and knights' fees had thus started on the road which would make them titles of honour rather than governmental jurisdictions. Nevertheless, because Henry II successfully reversed the tendencies of Stephen's reign, England never developed a nobility with powers of life and death over their tenants, and neither did the privileges of noble birth extend equally to all members of a family.

There was so much strife in twelfth-century England because this out-come was essentially contradictory. Stephen, with a poor hereditary claim to the throne, granted away royal offices as inheritances whereas Henry II, who insisted on his own hereditary right, deprived the barons of these inheritances. The most revealing of Stephen's grants is his charter to Geoffrey de Mandeville, made in 1141 after Stephen had been humiliated by being captured at the battle of Lincoln. He concedes to Geoffrey the keepership of the Tower of London and the offices of justice and sheriff in London, Middlesex, Essex and Hertfordshire, 'wherefore', Stephen's charter declares, 'I wish and firmly order that he *and his heirs after him* shall have and hold all such holdings and grants as freely and quietly and honourably as any earl in the whole of England'.³ In reality no earl at this time did hold his lands 'freely and quietly', and Geoffrey would have to fight to maintain his privileges. Nevertheless, if the English monarchy had permanently lost the Tower and the counties immediately north of London, it would have ceased to exist as an effective government. Barons like Geoffrey de Mandeville, who had been granted financial power as sheriffs, judicial power as justices and military power as castellans (in Geoffrey's case with the right to build and maintain castles wherever he wished), would have become independent rulers like the nobility in France and Germany.

In resisting this tendency Henry II was opposing the normal form of aristocratic government in his time, going against the precedents estab-lished by his mother the Empress Matilda (like Stephen she had made grants of hereditary sheriffdoms), and contradicting the hereditary principle upon which his own claim to rule depended. Henry described himself even before he came to England in 1142 as the 'rightful heir of England and Normandy' and he attempted to reinforce the principle of hereditary monarchy by copying French and imperial practice in having his eldest son, Henry the Young King, crowned in 1170. In the same year as this coronation attempted to buttress his own family's hold on Eng-land, Henry launched the Inquest of Sheriffs which challenged the hered-itary and traditional rights of everyone else. This inquiry extended beyond the conduct of sheriffs themselves to 'archbishops, bishops, abbots, earls, barons, sub-tenants, knights, citizens and burgesses, and their stewards and officers'.⁴ As the surviving records from Norfolk and Suffolk show, a detailed scrutiny was made of baronial and bishops' officials as well as the king's. The assumption behind the Inquest was that all authority stemmed from the king. In 1170 the challenge to the clergy was the most provoc-ative part of the Inquest (the king's justices were to inquire into the conduct of archdeacons and deans) and the year ended with the murder of Becket. Under his leadership the clergy had proved more obdurate than the lay nobility in surrendering the privileges which they had gained during Stephen's reign, when Henry of Blois bishop of Winchester had for a time held the balance of power.

Because of the contradictions in his attitude to hereditary and traditional jurisdictions Henry II could not develop a coherent ideology justifying his rule. To his opponents he appeared capricious and tyrannical. Consequently he and his sons, Richard I and John, had to insist on their own will-power as the ultimate justification for their actions. *Vis et voluntas* (force and will) and *ira et malevolentia* (anger and prejudice) were the keynotes of Angevin kingship. As J. E. A. Jolliffe has argued: 'The king rules by his passions more than by his kingship, and is ready to advance them, if not as a moral or political, at least as a natural justification.'[5] Henry II's wilful anger was seen at its most formidable on the occasion of Becket's murder. But, as the consequences of that crime and the rebellion of Henry's sons against him in 1173 showed, wilfulness was a double-edged weapon. On the other hand, lack of will-power brought worse consequences. Contemporaries were agreed that it was because King Stephen was a 'mild man who was soft and good' (in the words of the *Anglo-Saxon Chronicle*) that he did no justice.[6]

Stephen and Matilda

It is ironical that Stephen, the classic weak king of English history, should have won the throne by determined action whereas Henry II, the strong king, inherited it with less apparent effort. The author of the *Gesta Stephani* could see in Stephen's changing circumstances only the revolutions of Fortune's wheel; he and his opponents were engaged in 'doleful games of chance'.[7] The circumstances of his accession to the throne were not very different from those of William Rufus and Henry I, who had each excluded a nearer heir, their elder brother Robert. Like Rufus, Stephen claimed that he had been designated as successor by the king on his deathbed. Like Henry I, he rushed to seize the treasury on the death of his predecessor and then presented his rivals with a *fait accompli*, as he had been accepted as king by the Londoners, by his brother, Henry of Blois bishop of Winchester, and by Roger bishop of Salisbury who had headed Henry I's administration. Stephen could not have succeeded without the support of his brother who rallied the bishops behind him.

Stephen became king for lack of any better candidate. Although Matilda had been designated as Henry I's heiress in 1126 and Stephen had been prominent in swearing loyalty to her, her position had been compromised in 1128 by her marriage to Geoffrey of Anjou. He was not acceptable to the Norman barons and therefore was rejected by their fellows in England. Conversely the Norman barons favoured Theobald count of Blois and Chartres, who was Stephen's elder brother and the closest legitimate male heir, but he seems to have had no wish to add Normandy and England to his considerable domains, which extended from Blois through Chartres to Reims and Champagne. The Normans therefore shifted their allegiance to Stephen. If Theobald had accepted the English crown, historians might have written of a Chartrean empire instead of an Angevin one. Another candidate for the throne (who subsequently became Matilda's principal supporter) was Robert earl of Gloucester, Henry I's bastard son. Bastards might become kings and there could be no stronger precedent than William the Conqueror, the bastard duke of Normandy. But Robert was compromised, like Stephen, by having sworn loyalty to Matilda and furthermore the Church was beginning to disapprove of bastards as it developed its laws about Christian marriage. By moving fast and by default Stephen thus came out as the winner and, once he had been crowned, he should have been very difficult to budge. As he declared in his charter of 1136, he had been elected into the kingdom by the clergy and people, consecrated by the archbishop of Canterbury, and confirmed by the pope. Furthermore his rival, Robert earl of Gloucester, was among the magnates who witnessed this charter at Oxford and therefore acknowledged Stephen as king.

Having acquired the throne with dazzling assurance and with as much legality as any of his predecessors, particularly the three Norman kings, Stephen began to lose his hold. Why this happened is a matter of opinion. Contemporary opponents attributed Stephen's lack of success to his failure to support the Church; his disasters demonstrated that he was a usurper and a perjurer. His supporters, on the other hand, saw blind chance and his kindness as the causes of his misfortunes; his enemies took advantage of his sense of honour. For example, the author of the *Gesta Stephani* recounts how in 1147, when the future Henry II could no longer pay his troops in England and neither Matilda nor Robert earl of Gloucester would help him, Stephen who 'was always full of pity and compassion' sent him money because he was his kinsman.[8] Thus Stephen 'childishly' helped his most formidable opponent to power. The problem with all such retrospective assessments, whether they are made by twelfth-century chroniclers or modern historians, is that they are no more than wisdom after the event. Whether it was Stephen's 'weak' acts or his 'strong' ones which brought him down is debatable. By the 'weak' act of aiding the future Henry II in 1147 he may have won his goodwill, which was an advantage to Stephen when he came to negotiate the treaty of Winchester with Henry in 1153. Certainly the author of *Gesta Stephani* thought that Stephen had acted sensibly in this. His 'weakness' or kindness is most vividly illustrated in the biography of William the Marshal. As a child William had been handed over as a hostage to Stephen by his father who repudiated the boy, saying that he had the equipment to make more sons. Stephen should have hanged the boy, but instead he took him from the place of execution to his tent. There they were found playing 'knights' with plantain stalks; Stephen had given William the first turn in the game and he had cut off the head of the king's 'knight'. Stephen's kindness had, as so often, brought him a further humiliation instead of success.

On the other hand Stephen's 'strong' acts also had disastrous consequences. In 1138 Theobald of Bec and not Stephen's brother, Henry of Blois, was elected archbishop of Canterbury. Although the circumstances are obscure, there is little doubt that Henry expected to be elected and it is possible that Stephen excluded him because he thought he was getting too powerful. Nevertheless the principal effect of Stephen's action was not to weaken his brother, as he got a papal legateship instead, but to bring his own support into doubt. In 1139 Stephen took an even more radical action by arresting Roger bishop of Salisbury and his nephews, Alexander bishop of Lincoln and Nigel bishop of Ely. This should have won Stephen control of the administration, as Roger and his nephews had been the principal officers in the Exchequer and Chancery since Henry I's reign. But this resolute action merely enabled Henry of Blois to demonstrate his new powers as papal legate by summoning Stephen to Winchester to answer for the crime of imprisoning bishops. Henry reminded his brother that it was the favour of the Church and not the prowess of knights which had raised him to the throne.

These were the circumstances in which Robert earl of Gloucester brought Matilda to England to claim the throne in the autumn of 1139. William of Malmesbury, who favoured Matilda's cause though not the lady herself, compared Robert's arrival with Julius Caesar's crossing of the Rubicon, with this difference: that, where Caesar had only Fortune and his legions to support him, Robert had the strength of the Holy Spirit and the Virgin Mary. Certainly in each case this was the start of a long and bitter civil war. For the next fourteen years (1139–53) the fortunes of each side waxed and waned without much purpose or pattern until the future

Henry II, having gained military and political superiority (particularly through his acquisition of Normandy in 1150) and benefiting from the sudden death of Stephen's eldest son Eustace, was able to negotiate the treaty of Winchester: Stephen's second son William surrendered his claim to the English throne in exchange for the right to keep his lands; Stephen himself acknowledged Henry to be his heir and lawful successor.

Of the years of warfare the most important had been 1141. In February Stephen had been captured by Robert earl of Gloucester at the battle of Lincoln and the way was clear for Henry of Blois, as papal legate, to declare that his brother's capture was a judgement of God for his wrong-doing and that Matilda should be chosen in his place. But her supporters had not allowed for the attitude and power of the Londoners. They had formed themselves into what they called a 'commune', the first reference to this type of revolutionary association in England (see pages 96–7 below), and they demanded Stephen's release. Matilda underestimated their strength and, instead of being crowned in midsummer, she was chased out of Westminster by the Londoners. As in later years, the commune proved itself to be 'a tumult of the people and a terror of the realm'.[9] Henry of Blois changed back to supporting his imprisoned brother's cause and turned Matilda's attack on him at Winchester in September 1141 into a rout of her supporters. Robert earl of Gloucester was captured and this enabled the two sides to exchange their prisoners, Stephen being exchanged for Robert. In the years that followed Stephen was never able to overturn this balance of power. His contradictory qualities are best summed up by William of Malmesbury: 'He was a man of energy but little judgement; active in war, of extraordinary spirit in undertaking any difficult task, he was lenient to his enemies and easily appeased.'[10]

Henry II's ancestral rights

The coronation of Henry II in 1154 symbolised the return of peace. For the first few years everything went well. When Henry left England in the summer of 1158 he was at the height of his power, and he did not return until the beginning of the Becket dispute in 1163. His success enabled him to make a reality of the idea that Stephen was a usurper who had let anarchy loose on the land, and that now Henry II had arrived providentially to restore the good rule of Henry I. This was propaganda rather than simple fact because Henry II came to the throne as Stephen's lawful successor and heir (as negotiated by the treaty of Winchester), and Stephen likewise had been the lawful successor of Henry I (as he had been duly elected into the kingdom and consecrated). Nevertheless Henry's actions in the years

1154–8 made sense of his interpretation of history, as he demonstrated that he had restored the tranquillity of the kingdom which Stephen's contemporaries had described as disappearing on the death of Henry I. 'Stephen's manifest failure, no less than Henry I's excellence, was part of Henry II's title to rule,' as Edmund King had observed.[11] Henry II remained conscious of this role. 'When by God's favour I attained the kingdom of England,' he declared in a charter from the last years of his reign, 'I resumed many things which had been dispersed and alienated from the royal demesne in the time of Stephen my usurper.'[12] Some historians of the reign like Roger of Howden and Walter Map were Henry II's partisans, but even those who were more impartial, notably William of Newburgh, followed suit and described the king restoring order.

Henry's first action after his coronation was to banish William of Ypres and his Flemish mercenaries who had served as a standing army for Stephen. Next Henry ordered all castles which had been built during Stephen's reign to be demolished or surrendered. Similarly he revived the laws of his grandfather, Henry I, and appointed new judges. Most importantly he reclaimed Crown lands and restored the Exchequer to collect royal dues. The difference between Henry's attempt at strong government and Stephen's was that Henry's worked. He demonstrated his power in 1155 by taking Scarborough castle from William of Aumale, who had been the real king of northern England in Stephen's reign (William of Newburgh remarks), and by taking Bridgnorth from Hugh Mortimer. In 1157 Henry pursued his advantage by making Malcolm IV of Scotland surrender Northumberland, Cumberland and Westmorland, the northernmost counties which David I had held and which for geographical and cultural reasons might just as well have been incorporated into Scotland as into England. Henry had less success in his attempt in the same year to subjugate Wales, although his attack on Gwynedd and Anglesey reveals him as a forerunner of Edward I in his strategy.

Henry seems to have aimed from his accession at an overlordship over the whole British Isles, as he obtained in 1155 a papal bull authorising him to conquer Ireland. This was issued by the English pope, Adrian IV, and obtained by John of Salisbury. Even so it is surprising that the papacy, which had produced a scheme of reform for the Irish Church in 1152, should only three years later in the bull of 1155 have described the Irish as vicious barbarians ignorant of the Christian faith. Furthermore when Henry II at last went to Ireland in 1171, partly to avoid public obloquy for the murder of Becket, his establishment of royal jurisdiction there was likewise welcomed by the papacy. Pope Alexander III's first sign of favour

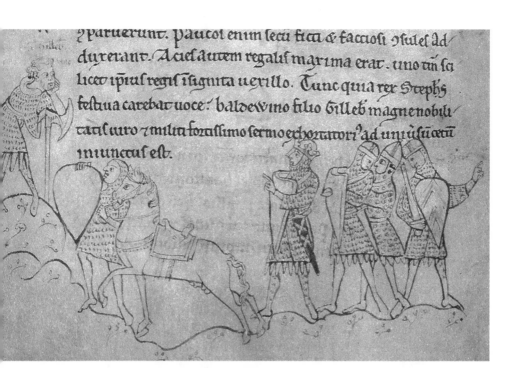

PLATE 2a. An illumination from the *Historia Anglorum* showing Baldwin FitzGilbert rallying troops before the battle of Lincoln of 1141. FitzGilbert spoke for the king, who had lost his voice.

2b. King Stephen, captured by Matilda during this battle, is depicted on the front of a silver penny of *c*. 1135 inscribed STIEFNE RE[X]

after forgiving Becket's murder was to issue letters in 1172 to Henry and to the Irish bishops and nobility, which reiterated papal disapproval of the Irish in unequivocal terms. Henry was described as the pope's dearest son in Christ, a man of majesty and a devoted son of the Church, who through his power would bring peace and tranquillity to Ireland. The Irish, on the other hand, were barbarous and uncouth with bestial sexual practices, and furthermore they all ate meat during Lent. These papal justifications for Anglo-Norman rule in Ireland show the influence of English diplomats in Rome and the need the pope felt to rewin Henry's confidence. The Irish became the scapegoats for Becket's murder.

The dispute with Becket (which lasted from 1163 to 1170) is not only the most dramatic and copiously documented episode of Henry's reign, it is also its crisis point because it concerned both the past and the future. It went back to what Henry claimed were the customs of his grandfather and his Norman ancestors before 1135 and it cast a long shadow forward over the two decades of the reign after 1170. The king had been taken by surprise in 1163 because he had previously worked successfully with Becket in asserting royal authority over churchmen. This is best shown by the case of Hilary bishop of Chichester against Walter abbot of Battle, which was heard in 1157 when Becket was still proud to be the king's chancellor and Theobald was archbishop of Canterbury. Walter claimed that Battle Abbey had been exempted from the authority of its diocesan, the bishop of Chichester, by charters of William the Conqueror and his successors. Hilary replied that this was contrary to canon law and he obtained a letter from Pope Adrian IV ordering Abbot Walter to obey his bishop. When Walter appealed to Henry II, Hilary put forward the papalist argument of there being two powers in the world, spiritual and material, clerical and lay; it was therefore illegal for any layman, even if he were king, to grant ecclesiastical exemptions without the authority of Rome and the pope.

At the mention of Rome, according to the Battle Abbey chronicler, the king grew angry and accused Hilary of betraying his oath of fealty by slandering the majesty of the Crown. Becket as chancellor likewise reminded Hilary of his oath of fealty. The king claimed that Hilary wanted to destroy his prerogatives, which had been handed down to him through God's grace by his royal ancestors in hereditary right. This statement rings true, as it is consistent with Henry's frequent insistence that his mission was to restore the law and order of the Norman kings. That regime was especially symbolised, Battle's advocates argued, by their abbey which was built on the field of Hastings. Once Hilary had angered the king his case lost credibility, despite its basis in canon law, and Becket gave it the *coup de grâce* by revealing that Hilary had a letter from the pope. On hearing this the king's expression changed and Hilary was so frightened that he denied ever having asked for the letter. This case throws more light on the background to the Becket dispute than any other because it shows Henry's power and Becket's loyalty to him. In the face of the king's anger the ecclesiastical arguments were abandoned. Archbishop Theobald could not even persuade Henry to adjourn a decision to the bishops alone. Hilary made his submission to the abbot of Battle before the king and in the presence of bishops and lay magnates, as had been the practice under the Norman kings.

In his dealings with the clergy, as with the lay barons, Henry's authority rested on the alleged good customs of his grandfather, Henry I, which had been justified and reinforced by his own victorious power. If that power were to fail, the justification of these customs was brought into doubt, as they were obscure and inconsistent in themselves. Over the lay barons Henry II had been spectacularly successful in the 1150s in demonstrating the validity of these customs by compelling them to surrender their castles and usurpations of royal authority. He had been equally successful in intimidating churchmen. Shortly before his murder, Becket wrote to the pope citing all the attacks (including that on Hilary of Chichester) which Henry had made in the 1150s on ecclesiastical privileges by virtue of his alleged hereditary right as king. Becket's purpose had been to show that Henry was not taking a new line when he demanded that the clergy acknowledge the Constitutions of Clarendon in 1164. Becket was right; it was he who had changed and not Henry. On being consecrated archbishop in 1162, he transferred his allegiance to God, who was a higher lord than the king. In feudal terms this was not a betrayal of Henry because God was the liege lord of them both. Because Becket actually believed in the superior power of his new lord, he was able to withstand his old one.

Henry therefore found himself resisted from an entirely unexpected quarter: not by a baron with a castle to be assaulted but by the man whom he had created and equipped with the Church's weapons. This was indeed a struggle of material versus spiritual power. Becket proved to be Henry's most formidable opponent because he knew the king well enough to withstand his anger. The conventions of the time made it difficult for the king to use physical force against churchmen. He therefore depended on his capacity to terrify them into submission. With the important exception of the council of Clarendon in 1164, when Becket nearly surrendered without consulting the bishops, he stood up to the king and thus deprived Henry of his power of intimidation. Although a reasoned case can be made in terms of modern political theory for the superiority of the State over the Church, neither Henry nor his defenders like Gilbert Foliot bishop of London were equipped with such arguments. Henry simply reiterated that he stood by the customs of his grandfather and that Becket had betrayed him. As Beryl Smalley concludes, 'It emerged from the muddle of anti-Becket propaganda that Henry II had no coherent theory of royal power to oppose to Becket's defence of the Church, or preferred not to state it, if he had one.'[13] Becket's various biographers tended to idealise him and, like other medieval chroniclers, they use dramatic dialogue to enliven their narrative. Provided allowances are made for these forms of bias, the following exchange between Becket and Henry in 1163 expresses the essence of their different points of view. Becket explains that he has not betrayed his lord because:

> In the dread Judgement day we shall both be judged as servants of one Lord. For temporal lords should be obeyed, but not against God: as St Peter says, 'We ought to obey God rather than men.'[14]

To this Henry replies:

> I don't want a sermon from you. Are you not the son of one of my peasants?

Becket reacts to this attempt at intimidation by striking at the pivot of Henry's policies and propaganda:

> Indeed I am not 'sprung from royal ancestors'; neither was St Peter, prince of the apostles, on whom the Lord deigned to confer the keys of the kingdom of heaven and the primacy of the whole Church.

To this Henry replies that Peter died for his lord, which gives Becket the opportunity to prophesy that he will die likewise. Although this last exchange was perhaps wisdom after the event on the biographer's part, the previous ones have a greater ring of plausibility and are consistent with other reports. Whether or not Henry intended it, it was appropriate that Becket should have been killed at the altar of his own cathedral because the king's anger—and hence his power—could not reach his archbishop in any other way.

Henry II and his sons

Becket's death in 1170 was a greater threat to Henry than his being alive. The king's misfortunes in the next two decades were attributed by hostile critics to divine judgement on Becket's murderer. Stories began to circulate of Henry's descent from a demon countess of Anjou and (according to Gerald of Wales) St Bernard had prophesied, when he had met Henry as a boy, that he came from the devil and would return to the devil. The wheel of Fortune, Gerald adds, began to carry Henry down to his doom. Although the pope pardoned him in 1172, Christendom at large did not. Louis VII of France and Theobald count of Blois demanded unprecedented punishment for what the archbishop of Sens described as the greatest crime in history—exceeding Nero, Julian the Apostate and even Judas. When Henry the Young King (whose coronation in 1170 by the archbishop of York had accelerated the final stage of the Becket crisis) rebelled against his father in 1173, Louis and Theobald supported him because Becket's murder had deprived Henry II of his right to rule. It was also of course a God-given political opportunity.

The rebellion affected all Henry's dominions from the Scottish border to Aquitaine. 'Aquitaine exulted and Poitou was jubilant', wrote a Poitevin chronicler; 'the king of the North' was being judged for the enormity of his crimes.[15] Henry was now compelled to do the public penance from which the pope's legates had excused him in 1172. At Canterbury in 1174 he at last acknowledged Becket's superiority by walking barefoot to the martyr's shrine and submitting to a flogging from the clergy and monks. Much to Henry's surprise this humiliation paid immediate dividends in military victory. William the Lion king of Scots was taken prisoner on the same day at Alnwick in Northumberland and this broke the rebellion. Henry had survived in a trial of strength. If he had been killed, his lands would presumably have been split up among his sons, and the Young King's inheritance of England, Normandy and Anjou might have returned to the chaos of Stephen's reign.

Among the aristocracy war was still a test of manhood rather than an instrument of policy. To the troubadour Bertran de Born it was a pleasure and not an evil: fighting was the greatest joy of the springtime; hearing cries for help and seeing the dead with lances through them was even better than eating, drinking or sleeping: 'Barons, mortgage your castles, towns and cities sooner than not wage war among yourselves!'[16] Against such attitudes (even if Bertran intended his song to be ironical), not even Henry II's combination of power and legalism could make much headway. He pardoned the Young King and gave him and his brothers the opportunity to fight another day, just as Stephen had helped him when he had been his young and inexperienced opponent in 1147. The Young King rebelled again in 1182, in an attempt to win control over Aquitaine from Richard (his brother), and he died in the Dordogne of a fever. Bertran de Born composed a lament in the Young King's honour, describing him as a model of chivalry, and rumours began to circulate of miracles at his tomb in Rouen. But English chroniclers gave the Young King less enthusiastic obituaries: he was Absalom who had betrayed his father and, though he was loved by his knights, he had brought ruin.

An unsympathetic picture of Henry II and his sons is given in the *Anti-claudianus* of Alan of Lille, where they are depicted as sad ghosts from the ancient world. Henry is the emperor Nero, the Young King is Midas, Richard is Ajax, the unmanly Geoffrey of Brittany is Paris and the unfortunate John is Davus. The decadence of the Angevin family is perhaps intended to contrast in this work with the youthful promise of Philip Augustus of France, who succeeded Louis VII in 1180. Although Henry was described as a tyrant by the French and by Gerald of Wales, he was praised by others in equally extravagant terms, even after the murder of Becket, for example by the pope in his letters concerning Ireland in 1172 and by Jordan Fantosme in his verse history of the war with the Scots in 1173–4. Extravagance was appropriate to the heroic genre of Jordan's poem (Henry is described as the best king that ever lived), as it was likewise to the rhetoric of papal letters. Assessments of Henry II's character and intentions tended to be taken to extremes by contemporaries because his rule was on such a huge scale and his actions, particularly the murder of Becket and his wars with his sons, were unusually dramatic.

Gerald of Wales reported that Henry told his intimates that one strong man might rule the world. Gerald associated this with Henry's diplomatic moves against Frederick Barbarossa and his support of Henry the Lion of Saxony (who had married Henry II's daughter, Matilda) against Barbarossa. Henry II extended his influence into Italy by marrying his daughter Joan to William II of Sicily in 1177 and he had proposed in 1173 to marry John to the heiress of Maurienne and Savoy, the controller of the Alpine passes. This proposal came to nothing, although Henry III would take up these strategies in the 1240s. Unlike Henry III, however, Henry II seems to have had a prudent sense of the limitations of his power, despite the flattery of those courtiers who wanted him to act an imperial role. His caution is shown by his refusal to accept the throne of Jerusalem in 1185, even though the crusader kingdom was in desperate straits and there were strong pressures on Henry to go, both to atone for the death of Becket by dying in Jerusalem and because the kingdom was an Angevin inheritance. When he died at Chinon in 1189, Henry was again at war with his sons, this time with Richard. Henry's reputation has increased with the distancing of time and this phenomenon was noticed by William of Newburgh in the 1190s. He records Henry's contradictory qualities and concludes that 'the experience of present evils has revived the memory of his good points, and the man who in his own day was hated by almost everybody is now declared to have been an excellent and useful prince'.[17]

Richard I

By going on crusade only three months after his coronation Richard I tested the resilience of Anglo-Norman government to its uttermost. Since 1066 England's kings with the exception of Stephen had spent less than half their reigns in England. Richard went further and spent only six months of his ten-year reign on this side of the Channel: four months in 1189 for his coronation and preparation for the crusade, and two months in 1194 for a second coronation and preparation for war with Philip Augustus. At first sight neither Richard's government of England, nor his reign as a whole, look successful. He sold offices to raise money and joked that he would have sold London if he could have found a buyer. He failed to take Jerusalem in the Third Crusade, though the crusaders did succeed in re-establishing a base in Palestine at Acre in 1191. But Richard was now on such bad terms with Philip Augustus of France and Count Raymond of Toulouse that he had to make the return journey in disguise through the Alps and was taken prisoner by Duke Leopold of Austria in 1193, who handed him over to the Emperor Henry VI. A ransom of 150,000 marks was demanded, a sum so large that both clerics and laymen were taxed at a quarter of their rents and goods. Furthermore England was surrendered to the emperor as a fief. On his release in 1194 Richard was therefore a vassal of Henry VI for England and a vassal of Philip Augustus for his lands in France. Richard's career at this point is comparable to Stephen's: initial success had been followed by the humiliation of captivity and release on unfavourable terms; in each case the captors admired the chivalry and personal bravery of their prisoner.

Unlike Stephen, however, Richard's captivity had not weakened his government in England. On the contrary, the effort needed to raise his ransom had strengthened the administration. Hubert Walter was chief justiciar from 1193 to 1198 and combined that office with the archbishopric of Canterbury. Richard I had therefore achieved without stress

Henry II's ambition of having the head of his government at the head of the English Church. Hubert was moreover an administrator of exceptional competence. His school had been the Exchequer, as Gerald of Wales contemptuously complained to the pope, and in the five years of his justiciarship the main forms of judicial records took shape: the plea rolls, the coroners' rolls, and the final concords (copies of property agreements). In the ecclesiastical courts of Canterbury likewise Hubert initiated systematic record-keeping. Paradoxically therefore Richard I, who seems to have taken no interest in England except as a source of revenue, did more than any other king to give English government that central capability and continuity through record-keeping which made it such a formidable institution. Hubert was moreover not a desk-bound bureaucrat but a politician and a man of the world who had accompanied Richard on his crusade, negotiated with Saladin, and led the English crusaders without their king back through the diplomatic minefields of Italy and Germany. Richard's reign needs to be seen in the light of the effectiveness of his government in England and of his successes in France in the years between 1194 and his death by the chance bolt of a crossbow at the siege of Chalus in the Limousin in 1199. In these years he tightened the grip of royal government in England, primarily in order to raise revenue for the war against Philip Augustus, and in France he came near to getting the better of Philip militarily. Richard could not know that his efforts would fail and that through forces larger than his own personal bravery and military experience the Capetian monarchy would triumph in thirteenth-century France and the Moslems in Palestine.

Although some contemporaries criticised Richard's war taxation and his character, no one thought that Jerusalem had been lost for ever or that its loss was a matter of no importance. Ralph Niger was unique in voicing objections, and his doubts were not about the rewinning of Jerusalem as such, but about the means of doing so and the motives of true crusaders. More typical is Gerald of Wales who took part in the preaching of the Third Crusade in Wales. Although he wrote of Richard I that he was a tyrant who took pleasure in the spilling of blood, he nevertheless approved of the crusade in principle. When Henry II had remarked that the patriarch of Jerusalem had come to England in 1185 only to seek his own advantage in asking for help, Gerald was shocked: 'I immediately lost all the hope which I had conceived with such great desire; for I had hoped that Israel would be redeemed in our days.'[18] When the True Cross and Jerusalem were captured by Saladin in 1187, neither Henry II nor Philip Augustus could do other than take the cross as crusaders themselves.

Richard I's departure for Jerusalem so shortly after his coronation was therefore not an irresponsible whim on his part but the fulfilment of his sworn duty. He had been the first of Europe's rulers to take the cross and he should therefore be the first to go. In 1185 Henry II's counsellors had advised him to think of his subjects at home and not go in person to Jerusalem. But Richard's position in 1189 was different because Jerusalem had fallen. It was moreover a good opportunity to get the better of Philip Augustus and to settle old scores. The Third Crusade like its predecessors was a mixture of religious inspiration and political calculation. The provisions which Richard made for the government of England in his absence were not neglectful, though they turned out to be ill-judged. His dismissal of his father's officials in 1189 and the fines he levied from them were the usual practice on the accession of a new king and were not unpopular nor necessarily undeserved. The appointment of William Longchamp turned out to be misjudged but Richard recognised his mistake and provided for his replacement by Walter of Coutances, who had been a Chancery officer of Henry II. Similarly Richard could not exclude his brother John from power, particularly not in his absence, and he acquiesced in his being the 'rector' of the kingdom in 1191.

Just as the necessity of raising Richard's ransom reinforced the English governmental machine, so his absence in 1191 had the paradoxical effect of strengthening a common sense of English identity centred on London. Longchamp was removed by the authority of two communal meetings: the first was held in the chapter house of St Paul's Cathedral and the second, which took place in the open air near the Tower, was attended by ten thousand people according to Richard of Devizes. Emphasis was put on Longchamp's being a foreigner, who had insulted the English nation and was ignorant of the English language. All England, wrote the bishop of Coventry in his propaganda letter against him, had to bend its knee to his French pride. Although the meetings in London had been headed by John and the magnates, they were backed by the citizens of London who formed themselves into a commune (as they had done in 1141 against Matilda). As in 1141 and likewise later in the formation of the commune of England in 1258, the magnates and bishops were compelled to become sworn members of this revolutionary association. The removal of Longchamp by an association which claimed to speak for the English people and the Londoners in particular is therefore a significant step towards the articulation of public opinion as a political force. Although the baronial part of the association did not remain in being, London was henceforward a commune with its own elected mayor. The terminology and forms of the new community politics, which were borrowed from France and Italy, took another seventy years or so to establish themselves as norms in England.

Richard I's reign marks the point at which the power of the monarchy and not its weakness becomes the focal point of politics. The king's government with its Chancery and its Exchequer, its sheriffs and its judges, was now the paramount power, whereas in Stephen's reign fifty years earlier its survival had been at stake. Stephen had been unable to restrain the barons even by energetic campaigning up and down England, whereas Richard ruled in absence through Hubert Walter's masterly bureaucracy. Henceforward the question was: 'How should royal power be used?' and no longer 'What could be done to strengthen it in the face of baronial separatism?' Should government be conducted purely for the personal profit of the king and at his whim, as Henry II had assumed, or should it consider the public interest? The barons who imposed Magna Carta on King John in 1215 and the Provisions of Oxford on Henry III in 1258 provided the answers to such questions. Richard I himself looked back in time for his ideals: to the crusade, to the troubadours of the Languedoc, and to international chivalry. These all turned out to be lost causes and so he became a hero of romance. Nevertheless he had also been a man of business and through his choice of officials he proved an able as well as a heroic king.

⁂ VI ⁂

LAW AND ORDER

English law in Henry II's reign was based on two fundamental principles, in civil and criminal cases respectively, which might have surprised a feudal baron in France or Germany. The first principle (as stated in the book attributed to the chief justiciar, Ranulf Glanvill) was that 'no one is bound to answer in his lord's court for any free tenement of his without an order from the king or his chief justiciar'.[1] In other words a vassal's title could only be questioned in his lord's court by the king's authority, because he was the overlord of all freemen and freehold property. The second principle was that in criminal cases the king had sole jurisdiction over everybody, that is, not only over freemen (as in civil cases) but over serfs as well. This principle is not succinctly stated in a single rule by Glanvill, but it is exemplified in the many particulars of the assize of Clarendon of 1166, which gave royal officers like sheriffs and judges exclusive power to hunt down killers and robbers. For example chapter 9 of this assize (an 'assize' is the forerunner of an act of Parliament) warns: 'Let there not be anyone whether within a castle or outside one, not even in the honour of Wallingford, who shall forbid the sheriffs from entering his court or his land.'[2]

These two principles were not novelties. Glanvill states that the first one was a custom of the realm; it was perhaps one of those good old rules which Henry II claimed were the customs of his grandfather. The second principle appears in the *Laws of Henry I* where 'the rights which the king of England has solely and over all men' for keeping the peace are listed.[3] (This is not an official compilation, but its list of crimes is reliable and is based on Anglo-Saxon sources.) Murder, arson, premeditated assault, robbery, rape and other serious offences are included in this list.

The law and feudalism

Neither of these principles was necessarily anti-feudal. The first one recognised the legitimacy of the lord's court while bringing the higher authority of the king to bear upon it. Any feudal society involved a hierarchy of tenants, lords and overlords. Furthermore the king claimed only to be the protector of titles to freehold property; he was not making himself the owner of the land in question. The landlords of medieval England exploited their estates for their own profit as effectively as their counterparts anywhere in Europe. The king granted his protection in property cases only to freemen; serfs had no recourse beyond their lord's court. That 'freemen' essentially still meant the Norman lords in Henry II's reign is suggested by a writ of his protecting the monks of Winchester from being sued 'for any tenement by the claim of an Englishman' unless that Englishman could show possession from the reign of Henry I.[4] An 'Englishman' was a 'native' and hence he was normally a serf.

The second principle might have given a baron in France or Germany more surprise than the first. For example the troubadour Bertran de Born would not have tolerated an officer of the duke of Aquitaine, let alone the king of France, entering his castle of Hautefort in the Dordogne in pursuit of a criminal. Nor would he have accepted that his court had no authority over crimes carrying the death penalty such as murder, robbery and rape. Nevertheless even this principle in English law did not undermine feudal hierarchy as such. It simply stated that the king of England as overlord had greater powers than rulers elsewhere. His jurisdiction over life and death was his inherited right and part of the customs of his kingdom, just as labour services from serfs were the rights of other lords and part of the customs of the manor. Henry II's contemporaries, the Emperor Frederick Barbarossa and Philip Augustus of France, aspired to comparable authority as the heirs of the Ottonian emperors and Charlemagne, but they had fewer means of making monarchical rule a reality. Moreover it was only in England, because of the reinforcement of royal power by the late Anglo-Saxon monarchy and William the Conqueror, that Henry II insisted on such far-reaching powers. In England he believed them to be the customs of his grandfather, Henry I, whereas in Anjou he had a different inheritance and in Aquitaine things differed again. In each place Henry II, like any lord of his time, aimed to rule in accordance with the custom and tradition of the locality.

Most historians now agree that Henry II was not explicitly anti-feudal in his attitude to law. His biographer W. L. Warren writes: 'Henry could not be anti-feudal without destroying the society in which he lived; fief-holding and the mutual obligations of lord and man appear to have seemed to him, as to other men, the natural framework of the social order.'[5] In *The Legal Framework of English Feudalism* and in *Historical Foundations of the Common Law* S. F. C. Milsom has demonstrated how the new forms of writ devised by Henry II's Chancery for civil pleas were directed at the powers of lords, 'not of course in the sense that the king was confronting feudalism, but as additional safeguards for a framework in which all parties believed'.[6] The intention of the new royal writs was to make the seignorial structure work according to its own assumptions. In criminal pleas likewise the king's justices respected the albeit limited rights of lords. In reality, moreover, because the judges and sheriffs were recruited primarily from among the landlords, they favoured their own interests. Although Glanvill insisted on the impartiality of the king's court and its help to the poor, contemporary observers like John of Salisbury were vituperative about its avarice and prejudice. Pessimistically interpreted, the only difference between the English social structure and continental ones was that in England a 'robber baron' exerted his power by royal authority which he had purchased as a sheriff or justice, whereas on the Continent such powers were inherited.

If the struggle between feudalism and monarchy in medieval societies is overemphasised, a third element—the strength of community action and the customs which governed it—gets lost sight of. Without a police force, either royal or seignorial, law enforcement depended upon community action. The most common penalty for crime was outlawry, that is, expulsion from the community. In much of England every adult male was supposed to be in a tithing (a group of ten), which was collectively responsible for its members' behaviour. A hierarchy of communities and courts extended upwards from manor and village through the hundred (a group of villages) to the county court and ultimately to the *curia regis*, where king and barons gave judgements through 'parliament' (meaning 'discussion'). Both Henry II in his enforcement of law and rebel barons in Stephen's reign aimed at using communal powers to the advantage of their cause. Thus Henry's administration largely depended on local juries, both to identify criminals and to decide property cases. Ultimately it was jurors of the neighbourhood, and not royal judges or feudal lords, who decided the fates of men and property by their verdicts of 'Guilty' or 'Not guilty'. Just like the king in his kingdom, lords on their estates had to come to terms with the custom of the manor in order to get their land worked and their tenants disciplined. Nevertheless, collective decisions should not be confused with democracy. Royal officers and landlords herded people into groups in order to control them.

Monarchical authority (the 'tremendous power of the royal majesty' as the *Laws of Henry I* called it; see page 47 above), feudal authority (a hierarchy of lords and tenants), and communal authority (collectivities like tithings and hundreds taking decisions binding on their groups) all interlocked. Whether a particular development or rule is monarchical, feudal or communal in essence is often impossible to say because these three forms of authority overlapped; sometimes they are no more than different ways of looking at the same person or thing. For example the king is the crowned monarch of all his subjects, the feudal overlord of his barons and knights, an immediate lord of serfs on the royal demesne, and the head of the community of the English nation. Similarly a freeman is a member of various communities in his county, hundred and village; he is also the tenant of a lord as well as being, like all freeholders, a privileged subject of the king with the duty to bear arms in his service. Furthermore this tripartite analysis takes no account of other forms of lawful authority, most notably that of the Church. Another important general point is that, because courts were community meetings and legal experts were educated through them and not by book learning, knowledge of the law was more widely diffused than in modern societies. Neither Henry II nor anybody else therefore aimed at sweeping changes because everybody's rights and duties were part of a nexus of custom and dependence.

The system described by Glanvill

The main elements of the legal system need to be described before Henry II's contribution to it can be assessed. This can best be done from the book attributed to Glanvill which was completed in the last years of the reign (1187–9). But Glanvill's warning in his prologue must be borne in mind that it is 'utterly impossible for the laws and legal rules of the realm to be wholly reduced to writing in our time, both because of the ignorance of scribes and because of the confused multiplicity of those same laws and rules'.[7] Glanvill's book overcomes these difficulties by being structured around the forms of royal writs and expounding with clarity the rules of procedure pertaining to each of them. The material is also arranged in a logical order, distinguishing between civil and criminal business, and starting with claims of right to land before proceeding to churches, status, dower and so on.

The great majority of writs cited by Glanvill are in the form of letters by the king to the sheriff of a county. Their tone is peremptory: 'Command N. to render to R. justly and without delay one hide of land in such-and-such a village' or 'Summon N. by good summoners to be before me or my justices at Westminster on the third Sunday after Easter to show why he did not do so-and-so'.[8] The emphasis throughout is on effective enforcement of the law by giving orders that are unambiguous and specific: sheriffs are to be promptly obeyed; recalcitrant defendants will suffer if they make undue delays or excuses; as soon as a decision is reached, it is to be executed by the sheriff's officers. Nowhere does Glanvill suggest that the king is opposed to feudal lordship or ancient custom, but the book does give the impression that royal authority is rigor-

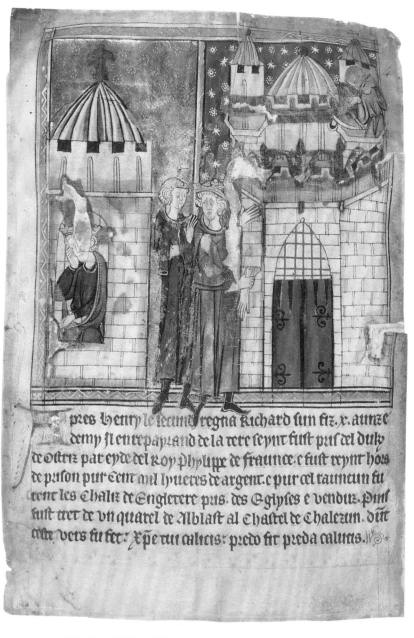

pres henry le secund regna Richard sun fiz. x. aunze
demy si entrepaycand de la tere seynt fuist pris del duk
de Ostriz par eyde del Roy Phylippe de fraunce. e fuist reynt hors
de prison pur cent mil lyueres de argent. e pur cel taunt un tu
rent les chaliz de Englerere pus. des Eglyses e vendiz. Puis
fuist tret de vn quarel de Ablast al chastel de Chalezun. diit
cefte vers fu fet: Xpe tui calicis: predo fit preda caluus.

PLATE IV. King Richard I imprisoned on his return from Jerusalem.
He was released only after a ransom had been paid

ously applied in order to overcome the indecision and confusion caused by conflicting jurisdictions and uncertainties about procedure. In prescribing decisiveness through his writs Henry II was certainly acting in the spirit of his grandfather, Henry I, and evoking the majestic powers of William the Conqueror and the Anglo-Saxon kings.

Glanvill does admit however that there have been some innovations, particularly in the making of 'assizes', which he describes as 'a royal benefit granted to the people by the goodness of the king acting on the advice of his magnates' and as a 'constitution of the realm'.[9] These legislative acts provided trial by jury in various forms of property disputes. Thus the 'grand assize' of twelve knights replaced trial by battle in actions of right, and 'petty assizes' of twelve freemen decided disputes about recent possession, most notably in claims of inheritance ('mort d'ancestor') and unlawful seizure ('novel disseisin'). Jurors acted like witnesses who were expected to know the facts about a case because they were men of standing in their locality. Glanvill is troubled about whether twelve men will always be found who know the facts and whether they will speak the truth, but jury trial is assumed to be better than the doubtful outcome of a duel. The use of juries is a good example of how English law contained monarchical, feudal and communal elements and drew on customary procedures. Juries had been used by William the Conqueror to make Domesday Book, the knights of the 'grand assize' were a feudal element, their collective neighbourhood decisions emphasised the communal element, and their verdicts expressed local custom and belief.

A peculiar feature of Glanvill's book from a modern lawyer's point of view is that although it gives rules of procedure in civil and criminal cases and discusses the effects of Henry II's assizes, it nowhere ascribes this legislation to particular years or places. We depend upon chroniclers of Henry II's reign, particularly Roger of Howden (who was also a royal judge), for texts of the assizes of Clarendon in 1166, Northampton in 1176 and Woodstock in 1184. Glanvill omits these texts for two reasons perhaps. First, he aims to explain current procedural rules and he is not very concerned about how these came into being. Secondly, he cannot include everything (as he explains in his prologue) and he may not have thought piecemeal regulations, which is what these assizes essentially are, had any permanent standing. Roger of Howden rightly recorded them because he was a chronicler concerned with how history came about. Glanvill has rightly omitted them because he was concerned with permanent general rules.

The effect of Henry II's reign on the criminal law, as on civil, was to standardise procedure and make enforcement more likely. The assizes of

Clarendon and Northampton had insisted that jurors in every hundred and every village should name those of their neighbours whom they suspected of murder, robbery or other serious offences and that the accused should be brought to trial before the king's justices. These assizes also indicate Henry II's impatience with some traditional features of the law, as he insisted that persons of ill repute who were acquitted should go into exile nevertheless: 'Within eight days they shall cross the sea unless the wind detains them; and with the first wind they shall have afterwards they shall cross the sea, and they shall not return to England again except by the mercy of the lord king, and they are outlawed both now and if they return.'[10] The realm of England was to be cleared of malefactors at a stroke. Nevertheless these draconian measures were less than successful. Henceforward jurors made many accusations, and trials proceeded before royal judges, but most of the accused were never caught. They became the outlaws and desperadoes of legend and fact in the greenwoods of England.

Henry II's intentions

Henry II has been credited since the nineteenth century at least with being the founder of England's common law. (By 'common law' is meant the royal law that was common to the whole country.) R. C. van Caenegem in *The Birth of the English Common Law* describes him as 'that man of genius—the word is not too strong—who was by instinct a lawyer', and Lady Stenton in her description of what she calls 'The Angevin Leap Forward' in legal development agrees that 'genius was at work'.[11] The problems with this point of view are twofold. First, these modern assessments of Henry II are at variance with contemporaries who emphasise his deliberate dilatoriness in settling lawsuits and the notorious corruption of his judges. Secondly, if he had been a legislative genius, one would have expected to find an 'Angevin Leap Forward' in Anjou and Normandy as well as in England, which is not the case. Another generalisation often made is that Henry II introduced his legal reforms, like the 'grand assize' and the 'petty assizes', in order to restore law and order after Stephen's reign. But the difficulty with this is the chronological gap. There is no evidence that the assize of novel disseisin was introduced as a regular procedure until 1166 at the earliest (twelve years after Stephen's reign) and no evidence of the assize of mort d'ancestor until 1176. If these changes are to be related to political events, the Becket crisis is a better explanation for the year 1166 and the aftermath of the rebellion of Henry's sons for the year 1176.

Henry II's intentions were an enigma to his contemporaries and they must therefore remain an enigma to us. The assize of Clarendon and the procedures in civil pleas described by Glanvill suggest that he wished cases to be resolved speedily and with consistency, even if that meant overriding traditional rights. In this light Henry was 'the subtle discoverer of unusual and hidden judicial procedure', as Walter Map described him.[12] The same point is made in a less complimentary way by Ralph Niger, who says that Henry produced new laws which he called 'assizes' every year. Royal judges were certainly seen by some contemporaries as a public nuisance, rather than as the paragons whom Glanvill describes dispensing equal justice to rich and poor: they were extortioners rather than judges in John of Salisbury's opinion, and the 'wandering judges' (that is, the justices in eyre who went from county to county) 'wandered from the path of equity in order to plunder the people'.[13] Both Ralph Niger and John of Salisbury were partisans of Becket and were therefore prejudiced against Henry II. But even the chronicle belonging to Benedict of Peterborough, which is generally favourable to Henry, criticises his judges when it describes him in 1178 agreeing to reduce their number from eighteen to five because of their oppression.

Although some of this criticism of Henry II arose from prejudice or misunderstanding, the aspect of his rule which is hardest to reconcile with his being a legislative genius is the deliberate way in which he delayed decisions. Gerald of Wales accuses Henry of thinking only of his own advantage in the selling and delaying of justice. Benedict of Peterborough's chronicle describes him postponing things from day to day in accordance with his custom, and Walter Map alleges that Henry was so dilatory that many people died before bringing their suits to a conclusion. Richard of Anstey's graphic account of how it took him seven years, considerable expense (in gifts of gold, silver and horses), and numerous journeys around England and France in order to get possession of his uncle's land suggests that Walter Map may have been right, although Richard survived to tell the tale.

Henry II, or any other king for that matter, was in a difficult position when petitioners asked him for justice because what they usually meant was that the case should be settled in their favour. The king could often not afford to alienate either party in a dispute because both were his loyal subjects. For example, the chronicler of Battle Abbey describes his abbot going to Westminster at dawn to catch the king at Mass. Henry was in the process of granting the abbot's request when the bishop of Chichester came running up to complain. Henry learned from experiences like this to avoid irrevocable decisions. Indeed Walter Map says that Henry's mother, the Empress Matilda, advised him to protract everybody's business: men should be tamed like hawks by giving them a sight of the raw meat and then snatching it away.

The contradiction between Henry's deliberate dilatoriness and the speed and decisiveness of the writ system described by Glanvill is obvious. It suggests that Henry II was speaking the truth when he insisted that he was doing no more than enforcing the customs of his grandfather, as the peremptory tone of Glanvill's writs is that of Henry I and earlier kings (see pages 47 and 52 above). Henry II perhaps remained content with this as a policy until the controversy with Becket compelled him to define in writing what the customs of his grandfather were. The constitutions of Clarendon of 1164 mark the starting point of what a modern lawyer would call 'law reform' or 'legislation', although Henry claimed that they were no more than a 'record' (*recordatio* in Latin) of part of the acknowledged customs and dignities of the kingdom.[14] The canon lawyers whom Henry opposed in the Becket controversy had built up an impressive system of written law. Becket as former royal chancellor knew that the king had nothing to match this and he used his learned counsellors, like John of Salisbury and Herbert of Bosham, to create a coherent clerical ideology. This seems to have been the stimulus for Henry, who was highly educated, to make his court likewise a place where there was school every day (as Peter of Blois described it) and to attempt from 1164 onwards to reinforce the customary law of England by written instructions to judges and other royal officials. Hence the constitutions of Clarendon were followed by the assize of Clarendon of 1166, the inquest of Sheriffs of 1170, the assize of Northampton of 1176, the assize of Arms of 1181 and the assize of Woodstock of 1184. The author of 'Glanvill' likewise aimed (as we have seen) to reduce law to writing in Henry II's last years.

Bureaucracy

Glanvill's book and Henry II's assizes looked greater achievements in retrospect than they did in the twelfth century because the use of writing gave them permanence. Henry II may have done no more to invigorate the law than his grandfather, Henry I, but the difference was that from Henry II's reign onwards the legal system had a fixed identity because of its set procedures. Bureaucracy set in fast and the forms of the possessory assizes and the main elements of the criminal law remained in being until the nineteenth century. Victorian historians of the law, looking back over the centuries, understandably enough credited Henry II with being the founder of the system. In reality, however, more was probably due to the effects of writing as a technology than to Henry himself or any other individual. The impressive legal monument left by Henry II was the product of fossilisation rather than deliberate policy. Writing preserved and hardened the old forms in much the same way as the flora and fauna of the primeval forest were fossilised. Writing proved to be a more powerful and intractable force than anyone had bargained for.

This is best illustrated by considering the effects of the writs in set forms described by Glanvill. The rule that 'no one is bound to answer in his lord's court for any free tenement of his without an *order* from the king or his chief justiciar' was probably customary as Glanvill says. But Glanvill also gives this rule in a significantly different form in another part of his book, where he says that no one can sue for a free tenement 'without a *writ* from the king or his justices'.[15] The crucial difference here is between 'an order' (*precepto*) in the first version and 'a writ' (*brevi*) in the second. Before writs became a routine part of legal procedure a litigant needing 'an order from the king or his chief justiciar' depended on the word of the king or the justiciar, delivered either in person or through an accredited messenger. In these circumstances royal intervention in a lord's court must have been a rare event. Not even a fast-riding king like Henry II could hope to patrol all his dominions in person (even with the aid of his chief justiciar), particularly when they extended from Scotland to the Pyrenees. The use of writs, on the other hand, meant that the king's authority extended as far and as fast as his Chancery officials could write them out, as aggrieved litigants could fetch and carry them, and as sheriffs and bailiffs in the localities were willing and able to enforce them.

Through the technology of writing, therefore, the king's right as overlord of all freemen to redress the wrongs of undertenants could be effectively enforced for the first time. The use of writs as a method of defining and extending royal instructions to remote areas was Anglo-Saxon in origin. The innovation of Henry II's reign lay in providing writs in standardised and replicable forms. Perhaps from the time of King Alfred and certainly since the tenth century the king had given protection to complainants through his writs. But the complainant was expected to draft and sometimes also to write out the complaint for himself, as well as delivering it to his opponent, which might be a hazardous undertaking. Henry II's writs given in Glanvill's book, on the other hand, are in set forms and the great majority of them are addressed to the sheriff and not to the other party in the dispute. The sheriff is to provide a jury, or whatever the writ requires, and he is also to return the writ to the king's justices as evidence of its execution. Where earlier kings had granted petitioners writs against their opponents and then just hoped for the best, the system from Henry II's reign onwards provided well-defined bureaucratic machinery for enforcing royal orders.

The assizes of novel disseisin and mort d'ancestor and similar routine procedures automated the legal system. Complaints were expressed in standard forms, they were written out by Chancery clerks in fast cursive script, the king's will was expressed by impressing his seal on the writs, and his sheriffs enforced them in accordance with their standing orders. The result was that an obscure freeman, provided he could pay the fees and bribes demanded by officials, could obtain a portentous document against his lord announcing the intervention of 'Henry king of the English and duke of the Normans and Aquitainians and count of the Angevins' in his cause. As a consequence the royal courts became flooded with cases and a quantitative change became a qualitative one. Henry II had not probably intended to undermine relations between lords and tenants but this was an inevitable result of making it easier to litigate in the king's court. Without being aware of it, Henry had achieved what Max Weber describes as 'the routinisation of charisma'. The majestic power of the king, symbolised by his seal showing him seated crowned on his throne, was disseminated throughout the kingdom in thousands of royal writs containing his orders.

From the point of view of making society more just and law-abiding this 'routinisation' of royal authority was not necessarily a change for the better. The king's court raised expectations which it could not satisfy; hence the bitterness of contemporary comments against the corruption of judges and officials. Although more grievances were brought into the king's court and a larger proportion of crimes were reported to royal judges, their powers to do justice were vitiated not only by corruption and incompetence but also by the fact that ultimately everything depended on local opinion. In both civil and criminal cases the essential decisions were made by the verdicts of jurors from the neighbourhood and not by the judges from Westminster. English law gave the appearance of being a centralised system emanating from the royal majesty, whereas in reality it was rooted in local opinion. Had it not been acceptable to local interests, and to the landlords in particular, it could not have worked at all.

Why did England develop a system of its own?

The Belgian historian R. C. van Caenegem, from his study of both English and continental medieval law, poses a paradoxical question about the changes of Henry II's reign. Why did English law enter upon its distinctive course in the twelfth century, precisely at the time when cultural and political contacts between England and the Continent were at their closest?

> English scholars studied then in continental universities, John of Salisbury was bishop of Chartres and Nicholas Breakspear became Pope Adrian IV, the English Church was ruled by clerics of continental extraction and very attentive to papal directives. The knightly class that colonised England was of continental extraction and owned land on both sides of the Channel. Kings, prelates and knights spoke French and the kingdom itself was no more than an acquisition first of the Norman and then of the Angevin family.[16]

Van Caenegem discusses various explanations for this paradox. First, English historians of a nationalist temperament cannot see that there is a problem: English law is different because England has always been wonderfully different. But what was so different: the climate; the economy; the tradition of government? Manors and landlords were a commonplace of medieval Europe, and even the English climate was less distinctive in the twelfth century as it was warmer. Van Caenegem concedes that the Anglo-Saxons had built up a unified state, but he puts more emphasis on the Norman conquerors who brought in their own kind of controlled and constructive feudalism. He argues that 'the precision, briskness and sharpness of the common law procedure and its whole atmosphere are quite unlike the traditional qualities of the English of Anglo-Saxon times, who are depicted as warm and gentle . . . If the common law started geographically as an Anglo-Norman phenomenon, its tone in that initial phase was overwhelmingly Norman.'[17]

The 'precision, briskness and sharpness' of the system is accurately characterised here and is borne out both in the arrangement and in the tone of Glanvill's book and the writs it contains. But the contrast van Caenegem makes between Anglo-Saxon and Norman characteristics is overgeneralised. The peremptory tone of Henry II's writs echoes those of Henry I and they in their turn derive from Anglo-Saxon precedents. Briskness and sharpness are arguably Anglo-Saxon characteristics as much as Norman, but there is little point in attributing such general characteristics to whole peoples. Other historians have therefore attributed the briskness and sharpness to Henry II himself, though the difficulty with this is that some contemporaries characterised him as dilatory and evasive, as we have seen. A sufficient explanation for the briskness and sharpness of royal writs is that these qualities result from the use of writing and from the scholastic training of their original drafters.

The distinctive style of English common law derived from many sources and traditions: Anglo-Saxon, Norman, ecclesiastical, Roman and scholastic. The system took the form it did because it developed in the period of the Twelfth-century Renaissance and it retained that form for centuries thereafter because bureaucracy perpetuated it. Hence later lawyers and historians praised as peculiarly English something that was really peculiarly twelfth-century and cosmopolitan. The Latin learning of the schools epitomised by John of Salisbury, the ecclesiastical and canonical world of Nicholas Breakspear and the papacy, the values of French courtly and feudal society, and the eclectic political dominance of Henry II, were all strands in the formation of the common law. Its distinctive form was therefore a product of England's close contacts with the Continent at the time and not in opposition to them. All these strands moreover were woven into an existing fabric of custom and organisation which was Anglo-Saxon in origin. Without the sheriffs, counties and hundreds, and without the habit of thinking of the king as the lord of all freemen (barons and knights, cleric and lay) and of all England, there could have been no common law.

Ultimately the common law system was shaped by the individuals who drafted in Latin the forms of the first returnable writs and the king's instructions to judges and sheriffs. Although we cannot know precisely who these individuals were, there is no reason to think that they were newcomers from Normandy or the Angevin lands. The two most prominent names associated with the law in this formative stage are Ranulf Glanvill, Henry II's chief justiciar from 1180 to 1189, and Hubert Walter, who was Richard I's justiciar from 1193 to 1198 and King John's chancellor from 1199 to 1205. Both Ranulf and Hubert were of East Anglian origin. Although Ranulf claimed Norman ancestors, he was not a newcomer to England. If he were the author of the book attributed to him, he was evidently proud of England's ancient laws, and the best manuscript of Roger of Howden's chronicle states that 'by his wisdom the laws which we call English were established'.[18] Ranulf would have learned law in the first place by attending local courts and listening to debate, rather than by specific instruction. He may have been the author of an account of how his father Hervey Glanvill during Stephen's reign gave evidence in the court at Bury St Edmunds of the wisdom he had gained there by fifty years of attendance.

Both the oral lore of these customary courts and academic learning in Latin were important in the formation of legal experts like Ranulf and Hubert. If Ranulf were the author of 'Glanvill', he was an accomplished Latinist with some knowledge of Roman and canon law. He was also described as the 'master' or tutor of King John when a boy; he may therefore have been a master in the scholastic sense. Hubert likewise, who was brought up in Ranulf's household, knew some Latin as he was archbishop of Canterbury, although Richard I corrected his grammar on one occasion. But Hubert was probably not a graduate of Bologna, as has sometimes been suggested. Gerald of Wales says his school had been the Exchequer; in other words he was educated in administration. Nevertheless that would have required both Latin and intelligence, as the *Dialogue of the Exchequer* demonstrates.

Conflict between book learning and oral learning, and between an academic approach and a practical one, seems to be resolved in the achievements of Ranulf and Hubert. The author of 'Glanvill' explains that the laws and customs of England have their origin in reason and he intends to describe them in a form of Latin which is appropriate to business practice: *in verbis curialibus* is the term he uses, meaning 'in the language of the court'.[19] The court (*curia*) that the author has in mind here is the court of Henry II, which is the hub of political and aristocratic life as well as being a court of justice. The adjective *curialibus* might be translated as 'courtly', but that would be misleading because of its associations with courtly romance. The 'courtiers' (*curiales*) of Henry II were men of business rather than romancers. They were also men of action. Ranulf Glanvill captured the king of Scots at the battle of Alnwick in 1174, and he died accompanying Richard I on crusade. Hubert Walter likewise came to prominence in this crusade as a diplomat and war leader before being appointed chief justiciar.

The careers of Ranulf and Hubert are outstanding, but they are probably also typical of the men who shaped the common law in its formative period. They crossed and intercrossed the conventional divisions of medieval society, combining clerical with lay expertise and the oral traditions of England with the Latin learning of Roman and canon law. Likewise they were men of action as much as being men of ideas, who were as proud of England as of their Norman descent. Such a mixture of talents

and influences best explains why the law was neither exclusively monarchical nor feudal nor communal, but included all these elements; and it
also explains why the law embodied ancient custom and yet looked modern in its logical procedures and dependence on writing. The common
law of England is a monument to a brilliant time in western Europe,
rather than to any single individual (whether Ranulf Glanvill, Hubert
Walter or even Henry II himself) or to any exclusively national characteristics (whether English, Norman or French). And the law became a
monument because it used writing, in the form of Latin writs, as its
special instrument.

✣ VII ✣

THE TWELFTH-CENTURY RENAISSANCE

The idea of the Twelfth-century Renaissance was given currency in the 1920s by the American medievalist C. H. Haskins, in order to draw attention to the achievements of the period and to challenge the assumption that everything stagnated between the fall of the Roman Empire and the Italian Renaissance of the fifteenth century. To keep his arguments as parallel as possible to those of Italian Renaissance historians, Haskins concentrated on the influence of the Latin classics, the development of original Latin prose and verse composition, the awakening interest in Greek science, and the revival of Roman jurisprudence and Aristotelian logic. Seen in this light, the schoolmen of the twelfth century like Abelard and Gratian—and the universities of Paris and Bologna which originated in this time—became, like the humanists of the fifteenth and sixteenth centuries, the harbingers of a new learning instead of obscurantist purveyors of superstition. Drawing on the best of classical tradition and at the same time adapting it to their own needs, the men of the twelfth century created a new art which developed from Romanesque into Gothic, a new literature in both Latin and vernaculars (notably the *Carmina Burana* and the romances of Chrétien de Troyes), and a new system of education centred on the teaching of theology and law at universities.

To carry conviction the term 'renaissance' has to be broadly, and even vaguely, interpreted as a convenient way of describing a renewal of creativity and expertise. Like the 'Angevin Empire', the 'Twelfth-century Renaissance' is not so much a precise reality as a cluster of ideas which cannot be better described in any other way. Strictly speaking there was not a 'rebirth' (*renaissance* in French) of classical learning in the twelfth century because regard for the classics had never died. (The metaphor of 'rebirth' looks like nonsense anyway, as it is impossible in the physical world.) Latin was the dominant language of literacy and literature in the West in the twelfth century just as it had been a thousand years before. John of Salisbury described in *Metalogicon* how the best Latin teaching was done by training boys to imitate the Roman poets and orators and grounding them in grammar. Medieval letters and chronicles are consequently full of quotations and allusions to ancient authors, though their range of emphasis differs from post-Italian Renaissance Latin writing as it includes the Bible and the Church fathers. Considering the paucity of resources, the extent and accuracy of medieval knowledge of Latin is more cause for astonishment than its supposed lapses from classical purity.

The attitude of twelfth-century writers to their classical heritage was ambivalent. Ambivalence is the keynote of the remark of Bernard of Chartres (reported by John of Salisbury) that 'we are like dwarfs perched on the shoulders of giants'.[1] The giants are the pagan philosophers and writers, both Greek and Latin (notably Plato and Aristotle, Cicero and Virgil), and their Christian counterparts (the prophets and evangelists of the Old and New Testaments, and the Church fathers like Jerome and Augustine). The dwarfs are inferior to them, both in intellect and appearance, but they can see further because they stand on their shoulders. This image therefore conveys a theory of progress. Bolder spirits among the schoolmen voiced impatience with the giants and the authority of antiquity. They coined a new Latin word to describe themselves: they were the 'men of now' (the *moderni*) as distinct from the 'ancients' (*antiqui*). In an often quoted passage Chrétien de Troyes in the 1160s or 1170s proudly repudiated the dominance of ancient Greece and Rome:

> Our books have taught us that Greece once had pre-eminence in chivalry and learning. Then chivalry passed to Rome, together with the highest learning which now has come to France. God grant that it remain here, and that it find the place so pleasing that it never departs from France. The honour which stops here, God had but lent to the others. For of the Greeks and Romans no more is said; their word has ceased, their glowing embers are extinguished.[2]

Chrétien is expressing here the idea of a *translatio studii*, of a transfer of culture from the ancient world to the modern one. He claims this inheritance for France whereas at about the same time the Romans, in their revival of the republic under Arnold of Brescia, were claiming it for themselves while the Emperor Frederick Barbarossa replied that he and his Germans had inherited Roman power and now bore the club of Hercules. The Greeks of the twelfth century likewise asserted with equal conviction, notably in the *Alexiad* of Anna Comnena, that 'chivalry' (that is, political and social leadership) and learning had never passed away from Byzantium.

Chrétien de Troyes makes a witty and combative bid for the pre-eminence of French culture in his time. Although he claims that this is God-given, he is aware of the fragility of the flame which has come to rest in France. In saying that 'chivalry' (*chevalerie*) is now French, Chrétien presumably has in mind the knights of epic and romance (in the *Song of Roland* and his own works) as well as the reality of French (including Norman) knights dominating Palestine, southern Italy and the British Isles. The crusades certainly belonged more to France than to any other nation. Learning (*clergie* in Chrétien's terms, that is, clerical knowledge) had likewise taken root in France, in the schools of Paris, Orléans, Chartres and Laon among others, and in the persons of such masters as Abelard and Hugh of St Victor. France likewise dominated in a more strictly clerical sense with its monastic reform movements, above all with the Cistercian order and St Bernard. Although Chrétien may not have been thinking of the visual arts, a comparable French pre-eminence is evident in Abbot Suger's rebuilding of St Denis (consecrated in 1144) and the first Gothic cathedrals which grew up in much the same places as the schools. Like the schoolmen and the composers of romances, the Gothic artists performed subtle variations on the themes of ancient and modern, and in the brilliance of stained glass and manuscript illumination they revived the 'glowing embers' of past greatness.

England's place in this Renaissance

At first sight England's place in all this looks undistinguished. 'Culturally the most obvious thing about England in the twelfth century is its dependence on France,' Sir Richard Southern writes; 'it was a colony of the French intellectual empire, important in its way and quite productive, but still subordinate.'[3] As generalisations these statements are a useful corrective to the chauvinism of some nineteenth-century critics and historians, who wrote of twelfth-century art and literature in England without appreciating its Continental context. The best example of this narrow approach is the use of the term 'Early English' to describe the first phase of Gothic architecture, a term still favoured in descriptions of parish churches. It goes back to Thomas Rickman's *Attempt to Discriminate the Styles of Architecture in England* in 1819. Rickman's analysis of the different styles was excellent, but his naïve nationalism led him to argue that the purest form of Gothic architecture was the 'Early English' type. Foreign examples, he suggested, such as Chartres Cathedral, were spoiled by Italian features. The gradual transition from 'Norman' (Rickman's term for Romanesque) architecture to 'Early English' convinced him that these 'styles were the product of the gradual operation of a general improvement, guided by the hand of genius, and not a foreign importation'.[4]

Rickman stands to the architectural history of the Middle Ages much as Stubbs does to constitutional history. For such nationalists England's

great churches, like her parliament and legal system, had to be purely English. They were the products of native 'improvement' (a favourite Victorian
concept) uncontaminated by Rome or France. There is some truth in such
views, of course. In art and literature, as in law and politics, Anglo-Saxon
traditions influenced the imported forms and produced works which
were distinctively English even though they belong to the mainstream of
medieval culture emanating from France. The choir and stained glass of
Canterbury Cathedral, the illuminated books of the Bible associated with
Henry of Blois bishop of Winchester, and the works of Latinists like
Walter Map and Gerald of Wales are identifiably English (or rather,
British in the cases of Walter and Gerald with their Welsh associations).
Nevertheless these writers and artists worked in the most sophisticated
idioms of their time and they addressed a wider audience than the English.

To describe England as 'a colony of the French intellectual empire' is,
however, a simplification, as Southern points out at the end of his essay.
French culture was indeed pre-eminent but it was not as dominant as the
metaphor of colonisation suggests. Writers and artists in England drew
their inspiration from many sources. Their approach was cosmopolitan
rather than exclusively French, which is not surprising considering the
eclectic nature of Henry II's dominions, the diverse legacies of the Norman Conquest, and the close links between English churchmen and
Rome. After 1066 the educated class in England were distanced from
their own culture and encouraged to prefer Latin and French to their
native English. That this was a largely voluntary process is suggested by
the speed with which the property-owning inhabitants of Winchester and
Canterbury adopted foreign personal names in the twelfth century (see
pages 34–5 above). The bright young men, like John of Salisbury and
Gerald of Wales who were sent to France for their education, were
attracted to a rootless life, searching for the best masters and the most
generous patrons who might employ them as letter writers or even as
entertainers. Many of the wandering scholars were Englishmen whose
education had made them strangers in their own country, although they
were at home at a bishop's court or a scholar's desk in any part of western
Europe. The distinct vein of satire which runs through the works of Walter
Map, Gerald of Wales and even John of Salisbury may have been a product of ambivalence about their identity (which was compounded in the
case of the Welshmen). Experience had made them citizens of the world
and they looked on it with a cynical eye.

A notable work in this cosmopolitan satirical genre is *A Mirror for Fools*
(*Speculum Stultorum*) by Nigel de Longchamp, who was resident in Can-

terbury in the 1190s. He tells the story in Latin elegiac couplets of how Burnel the Ass (echoing the *Golden Ass* of Apuleius) goes to the medical school at Salerno to seek a longer tail, then to Paris where he joins the English students (in the hope of becoming a bishop by mastering theology and law), before deciding in despair to be a monk; but this project also fails because Burnel is dissatisfied with all existing religious orders. The English at Paris are described as clever, charming and elegant, but they drink without restraint: 'Wassail' and 'Drink Hail' are their favourite toasts; Burnel hopes to become an honorary Englishman. In both its style and content this work mirrors the cosmopolitan world of the rootless Englishmen of the time. Polished Latin, invective against religious hypocrisy and the sycophancy of courtiers, moralising anecdotes, and a jumble of incidents symbolising the absurdity of life are features not only of *A Mirror for Fools* but of other works by Latinists in England, notably John of Salisbury's *Policraticus* and Walter Map's *De Nugis Curialium*. In real life moreover John of Salisbury and Gerald of Wales recount going from school to school for many years before ending up as bishops, or only bishop elect in Gerald's case. Burnel the Ass described the ambitions and frustrations of many others:

> To Paris then my way I'll make,
> A ten years' course in Arts to take;
> I'll start at once. Then, if God will,
> I'll come back home, and learning still,
> Become well versed in all the rules,
> By studying in Bologna's schools
> Of civil law: the Sacred Page
> And the Decreta will engage
> My final labours, if I live.
> Then, then at last I shall receive
> The title and reality
> Of Master; Master shall I be,
> And 'Master' shall precede my name.[5]

Curiales and Latinists

Nigel de Longchamp also wrote a tract 'Against Courtiers and Clerical Officials'. The word he uses for 'courtier' is *curialis*, and the *curialis* is the anti-hero of the English Latinists of the twelfth century. John of Salisbury gave to his *Policraticus* ('Statesman's Book') the alternative title 'Courtiers'

Trifles [*De Nugis Curialium*] and Footsteps of Philosophers'. The same title of 'Courtiers' Trifles' was given likewise to Walter Map's book, perhaps because he began with the thought, 'I am in the court and speak of the court but what the court is God alone knows, I do not.'[6] As characterised by these authors, the *curialis* is a cleric who leads a worldly life at court; his is a bewildering life because he is at the beck and call of princes instead of living in the scholarly decorum befitting a university 'Master'. The contrast between the lofty aspirations of the *curialis* and the realities of being a hanger-on at court gave him a taste for the absurd. 'Courtiers' Trifles' were jests both for and about *curiales* and the vanity of human wishes. *Policraticus* was dedicated to Thomas Becket, in his worldly phase when he was Henry II's chancellor, and Walter Map likewise served Henry as an official, as did Peter of Blois who wrote about court life. Like Burnel the Ass these writers were torn between the plain and single-minded life of scholarship and the variegated demands of worldly advancement.

The prominence of the *curialis* theme among Latin writers in England may also be explained by the nature of Henry II's court. Unlike Eleanor of Aquitaine, Henry was no patron of letters or learning for its own sake. He was clever and highly educated (the great master, William of Conches, had been among his tutors), but his interests were in running the monarchy as a day-to-day business. From his court therefore emanated Fitz Nigel's *Dialogue of the Exchequer* and Glanvill's lawbook, containing *utilia* (useful information) and not *subtilia* (see pages 79–80 above). As Southern has emphasised, 'these books were not simply manuals or textbooks for office use like the contemporary collections of decretals [papal and other letters illustrating canon law]: they aspired in some degree to invest the routine of government with an intellectual generality. They were all written in England, and they provide a glittering testimony to the growing claims of secular government such as we could find nowhere else in Europe.'[7] Thus Fitz Nigel composed his work in the form of a classical dialogue, and Glanvill presented English custom in terms of Roman law. They aspired like the other *curiales* to Latin scholarship and an audience larger than English officialdom.

The mastery of Latin displayed by twelfth-century writers in England is remarkable. John of Salisbury is the most eminent of all medieval Latinists and the principal textbook for writing verse, the *Poetria Nova*, was also written by an Englishman, Geoffrey, sometimes surnamed 'de Vinsauf'. Like John, Geoffrey had presumably acquired his advanced knowledge in France and Italy. 'England sent me to Rome as from earth to heaven, it

henricus natus matildis regna tenebat
Sub quo sacratus thomas martire cadebat.

Henricus Rex filius   matildis Imperatris geni̅

henr̅
hauent̅
rege qui
obiit

PLATE Va. An illumination from Peter of Langtoft's chronicle depicting Henry II arguing with Thomas Becket.

Vb. The east end of Canterbury Cathedral was rebuilt as a shrine for Becket and it contains some of the finest and earliest stained glass, like this 'sower' window

sent me to you as from darkness to light,' he wrote when dedicating his work to Innocent III.[8] Like the *curiales*, Geoffrey is both flattering and facetious towards authority, beginning his work with: 'Holy Father, wonder of the world, if I say Pope Nocent I shall give you a name without a head; but if I add the head, your name will be at odds with the metre.'[9] Such word-play is tiresome to a modern reader, and perhaps it was also to the pope, yet it is fundamental to these Latinists because they were writing in a painfully learned foreign language. Hence they delighted in showing off their varied accomplishments. Fine writing was not restricted to professional rhetoricians. Most twelfth-century historical writers display it (for example William of Malmesbury, Ralph Diceto and William of Newburgh) and none has a finer style by the standards of the time than Richard of Devizes in his chronicle of Richard I. He may have learned his exotic Latin in the school of Winchester while Henry of Blois was bishop.

Writing good Latin meant much more than imitating the Romans, as the language had to remain alive. Numerous new words were therefore coined for medieval needs. Walter Map gives a lively example of this process when he describes St Hugh of Lincoln visiting Henry II at a hunting lodge in the 1180s. When the guards barred his entrance, Hugh demanded their identity and received in Latin the answer, 'We are foresters' (*Forestarii sumus*).[10] (They may have answered Hugh in Latin because he was a Frenchman and they perhaps knew only English and some smatterings of Latin.) This answer gave Hugh the opportunity to make a pun: *Forestarii foris stent* ('Foresters should stand outside'). The king heard this and came out to greet Hugh with laughter. This story illustrates not only Henry II's grasp of Latin but the way that a new word, *forestarius*, was received. Particularly at the level of practical business, for composing writs and charters, for example, or keeping accounts, it was essential that Latin vocabulary should be kept up to date. The text of Magna Carta is an excellent example of the clarity and precision of this living Latin.

The legacy of the classics could be a burden, as Walter Map was ready to admit: 'The industriousness of the ancients is in our hands; they even make their past present in our times and we are struck dumb; their memory lives in us and we are without memorials of our own. What a miracle! The dead are alive and the living are buried by them.'[11] Walter does not feel here like a dwarf perched on the shoulders of a giant. Instead the giants are going to bury him and his age in oblivion. Writers of Latin were in a dilemma. They could not hope to better the giants of the ancient world, and yet they wished to excel. Chrétien de Troyes had one answer:

the Greeks and Romans were finished; modern authors should follow his example and write in French. But Walter felt that this solution was humiliating and impermanent. 'Caesar lives in the praises of Lucan, and Aeneas in those of Virgil,' he writes, 'but only the trifling of mummers in vulgar rhymes' celebrates the achievements of Charlemagne.[12] This is presumably Walter's opinion of the *Song of Roland* and other verse in the vernacular. Nevertheless his attitude is ambivalent, as it is so often, because he is credited in medieval manuscripts with composing Arthurian romance (like Chrétien de Troyes) and even with writing in French. Walter's literary achievements are as enigmatic as his view of life, and perhaps that is what he intended. It was difficult to create an acceptable convention of fiction. 'I am not the only one who knows the art of lying,' wrote the romancer Hue de Rotelande; 'Walter Map is very good at it too.'[13]

The Owl and the Nightingale

The most brilliant literary work composed in England in the twelfth century, the debate between the owl and the nightingale, was written in English. Judging from its contents, it is the work of an author who was familiar with Latin and French learning and culture as well as the folklore and natural history of his own country. If the author is the Master Nicholas of Guildford who is described in the poem as a writer of much wisdom, and as good a judge of a song as of right and wrong, he takes shape as a scholastic and a man of the world like the English Latinists. But, unlike John of Salisbury or Walter Map, Nicholas is not alienated from his native environment. *The Owl and the Nightingale* has all the polish and wit of contemporary Latin works without being weighed down by their irrelevance and citations from the classics. It is set not in the hectic and artificial world of the court but in the southern English countryside, in a hidden nook of a summer dale. This is a real environment (the vegetation and the physical characteristics of the owl and the nightingale are precisely described), though it is also the ideal medieval world of the secret garden where birds sing sweetly and maidens are courted.

The owl and the nightingale decide to conduct their debate with courtesy ('with fair words'), with each protagonist pleading her case by reasoning ('with skill') as in a law court or in the disputations of the schools. Because he is a 'master', presumably of the schools and also of canon and secular law, Nicholas is fitted to be their judge and, unlike Burnel the Ass, he has learned wisdom from experience. The owl says that although Nicholas spent an ardent youth delighting in the nightingale, he is not such a fool now and is set on the road of righteousness. The owl stands for seriousness and the nightingale for frivolity, though their positions are more subtle than that. They are worked out in the course of the poem with such sympathy by the author that it is impossible to know which side he prefers. Having reached the high point in the argument when both protagonists are to appear before Master Nicholas, the poem unexpectedly concludes with the author saying: 'How they fared in that judgement I cannot tell, for there is no more of this story.'[14]

The lack of a final decision for one side or the other is in keeping with the ambivalence of much twelfth-century writing. The reader is left poised between truth and falsehood and even uncertain as to which is which. John of Salisbury achieved a comparable effect in *Policraticus* by citing a bogus Roman authority (Plutarch's letter of instruction to the Emperor Trajan) for his image of the body politic with the prince at its head. As John invented this authority, we cannot be sure whether he meant us to take his image seriously, but only a handful of experts in the classics would have been able to recognise this dilemma. *The Owl and the Nightingale* is similarly thought-provoking in its ambivalence and different levels of meaning. The owl is ugly and execrated and yet she is Christ-like and wise. The nightingale is frivolous and yet she can speak seriously and convincingly about love. To the owl's conventional diatribe against lust she replies that the sins of pride and malice, which are sins of the spirit, are worse than bodily sins. Sex cannot be evil in itself and it is usually men who cause the trouble anyway. The nightingale seems familiar with the argument of Abelard's *Ethics* that only an evil intention makes an act sinful. One need not assume however that the author had read this work specifically, as he shows a general familiarity with a range of ideas current in the schools and courts of the time.

The author's most original and inscrutable achievement was to write in English. This was more difficult than composing in Latin or French because he had to adapt the form and diction of his poem from these languages. Master Nicholas, if he were the author, was probably helped by his grounding in grammar and rhetoric in the schools. At about the same time the bishop's clerk and master of the schools in Winchester, Jordan Fantosme, wrote his chronicle of Henry II's war of 1173–4 in French verse instead of Latin prose. Like *The Owl and the Nightingale*, this was a daring and successful experiment. But Jordan at least had Gaimar's *Estoire des Engleis* and other works like Wace's history to follow, whereas Master Nicholas had nothing. Or rather, Nicholas had no model which has survived. He must have written in the hope of pleasing a patron and hence there was evidently some demand for courtly literature in English, as Layamon's version of Arthurian history (the *Brut*) likewise suggests.

Among the rulers of twelfth-century England different languages were appropriate to different occasions and callings. In their written forms, and perhaps in speech too, they all had to be deliberately learned and polished. Thus Jocelin of Brakelond, the biographer of Abbot Samson of Bury St Edmunds (1182–1211), describes his linguistic skills: 'in French and Latin he was eloquent', speaking plainly rather than using ornaments of speech.[15] In other words, at the schools of Paris Samson had learned to speak French correctly, and in Latin he rejected the flowery style of rhetoricians like John of Salisbury. Jocelin similarly distinguishes between different kinds of English: Samson 'knew how to read literature written in English most elegantly and he used to preach in English to the people, but in the speech of Norfolk where he was born and bred'. The distinction here is between written English, which demanded elegance like any literary language, and the colloquial diction of each locality. These distinctions emphasise the complexity of twelfth-century English culture. There was no simple dichotomy between French dominance and English dependence, because French culture was itself part of a larger world of Latin scholarship and cosmopolitan courtly life, and conversely English culture subsumed different regional traditions.

Artists and patrons

The visual arts present a comparable picture of a variety of influences which cannot simply be described as French. This has been specifically demonstrated in the parallels between the full-page painting of the death of the Virgin Mary in the Winchester Psalter and representations of the same scene at Palermo and Mount Sinai. The psalter was probably made for Henry of Blois bishop of Winchester (who died in 1171) and it used to be surmised that he had brought in a Byzantine artist from Sicily to do the painting. An alternative hypothesis is that an artist from England had seen the mosaics of the church of the Matorana in Palermo and copied the scene. English artists might well have visited Palermo, as there were numerous contacts between the Norman kingdoms of England and Sicily. Henry II recalled Thomas Brown from Sicily to a seat at the Exchequer, Robert of Selby had been chancellor of Roger II of Sicily, Englishmen were archbishops of Messina and Palermo, and these contacts were reinforced by the marriage of Henry II's daughter Joan to William II of Sicily in 1177.

Nevertheless it is difficult to see how an artist sketching the mosaics at Palermo would have achieved as close a copy as the painting in the Win-

PLATE 3. The nave of Durham Cathedral, built in the early twelfth century, with its great pillars and ribbed vaulting. It is the earliest example of stone vaulting to span such a large area. The rose window at the end of the nave was added a century later

chester Psalter. Francis Wormald has therefore suggested that the painting in the psalter was done in England from a Byzantine icon, like the one of this scene still extant at Mount Sinai. Such an icon could easily have been acquired on behalf of Henry of Blois in southern Italy, as John of Salisbury describes him transporting antique statues from Rome to Winchester. Alternatively the icon might have been acquired at Constantinople, or even at Mount Sinai itself, as the crusades provided many points of access between east and west. A significant feature noticed by Wormald are some characteristically English details in the painting which echo the conventions of the Bury and Winchester Bibles. The best explanation is therefore that this painting was done by an English artist imitating a Byzantine icon. In the Winchester Bible (like the psalter, this is thought to have been made under the patronage of Henry of Blois) there are other Byzantine-inspired paintings, particularly the figure of Christ the Pantocrator at folio 169 which echoes the mosaic dominating the apse of Roger II of Sicily's cathedral at Cefalù. But in this case the links in the transmission between Sicily and England cannot be traced.

Numerous other examples could be given of the use of imported motifs by twelfth-century English artists. Although it is possible to interpret these as subservience to foreign masters, a deliberate process of absorption and selection makes better sense. In Romanesque art in England a favourite motif is arcading formed by interlaced round arches. This seems to have first been systematically used to ornament the aisle walls of Durham Cathedral (completed by the 1130s), and in the course of the twelfth century it makes its way into country churches; for example, interlaced arches ornament fonts at Alphington (Devonshire), Avebury (Wiltshire) and Foxton (Leicestershire). Such motifs were presumably transmitted by artists' pattern books and manuscript illuminations rather than by direct observation. The motif of interlaced arches is Islamic in origin and appears in Spain and southern Italy. The artists who used it in England may have known nothing of these associations, however; they may merely have thought it to be fashionable.

Country churches were not as remote from cosmopolitan culture as they appear today. They were built by the well-travelled lords who were their patrons, rather than by the parish community. The richness of the imagery of the Herefordshire school of stone carving (especially in the churches at Kilpeck, Brinsop, Stretton Sugwas and the ruins of Shobdon, together with the fonts at Eardisley and Castle Frome) is best explained in this way, as T. S. R. Boase and G. Zarnecki have argued. Celtic, Anglo-Saxon and Viking motifs can be discerned which may be of local and traditional origin (probably transmitted by metalwork), but in addition to them there is imagery associated with the abbey of Cluny, the pilgrimage churches of Poitou, and the baptisteries of Italy. The echoes of Cluny can be explained by the building close by of Leominster Priory, a daughter house of Reading Abbey which had been founded by Henry I in association with Cluny. Poitevin motifs may have been the idea of the builder of Shobdon, Oliver de Merlemond, who made the pilgrimage to Santiago by the land route in the late 1130s. The font at Castle Frome mounted on crouching figures as in Italy is harder to explain, but there were all sorts of contacts with Italy (Zarnecki argues for instance that the west front of Lincoln Cathedral built in the 1140s was inspired by that at Modena).

The mistaken assumption is to think of Herefordshire as a backwater. Among its bishops were the schoolmen Gilbert Foliot (in 1148–63) and Robert of Melun (1163–7). It was the home of Walter Map and Hue de Rotelande, the romancer, and Worcestershire (where Layamon wrote the *Brut*) was its neighbour. A more appropriate metaphor for such regional centres is that of a transmitter or transformer. Herefordshire was a meeting place of languages (Welsh, English, French and Latin) and of cultures (Celtic, Anglo-Saxon, Anglo-Norman and cosmopolitan). The great Jerusalem-centred world map, drawn in the thirteenth century and still kept at Hereford Cathedral, may have had a twelfth-century predecessor. Roger of Hereford compiled a set of astronomical tables for the meridian of the city in 1178. Simon du Fresne, who also wrote in French, composed a polished Latin poem in the 1190s describing Hereford as a centre of the numerate arts in particular. Gerald of Wales called it a place of joy for philosophers. There were a dozen or more such regional centres in England, associated with cathedrals (for example Lincoln, Chichester, Exeter, York) or abbeys (Bury St Edmunds, Malmesbury, Peterborough, St Albans) or both (Canterbury, Winchester, Worcester, Durham).

The variety of achievement round a relatively small centre like Hereford helps explain the brilliance of the best work from twelfth-century England: Durham's great cathedral and its library of manuscripts; the Winchester illuminated books of the Bible associated with Henry of Blois; the choir and stained glass of Canterbury Cathedral. In each case local traditions and expertise were married to the latest ideas from Continental Europe. For example the line drawings in Henry of Blois's books may have been as fundamentally influenced by Anglo-Saxon manuscripts (such as the Benedictional of St Æthelwold) as they were by Byzantine and Sicilian exemplars. The results are works of daunting quality and confidence which nevertheless have an individual feeling of their own, despite

PLATE 4a and 4b. Carvings on the font at Castle Frome in Herefordshire. The details show (*above*) the lion and eagle of St Mark and St John, and (*below*) an angel carrying the word of God

being the product of many hands and diverse influences. The designers of Durham Cathedral cannot be identified, and their work had been completed by the beginning of the period 1135–1200. The Durham style, presumably transmitted by its masons, was carried as far north as Kirkwall Cathedral and also to the south, to Waltham Abbey in Essex. By the latter half of the twelfth century, however, Durham's Romanesque was beginning to look old-fashioned. When the choir of Canterbury Cathedral had to be rebuilt after a fire in 1174, it was done in what we now call 'Gothic' (Rickman's 'Early English').

Canterbury is well documented for a twelfth-century building because the chronicler Gervase recorded its construction, pillar by pillar, and commented on what struck him as novel. He was particularly interested in the new type of vaulting centring on prominent keystones. To describe this effect he used the image of a 'canopy'. Thus William the Englishman, who had taken over as architect when William of Sens fell from the scaffolding, in the summer of 1179 'turned the canopy which is over the high altar' (that is, he completed the great vault over the crossing).[16] Stone vaulting as such was not new, as it had been conspicuously used at Durham. What impressed Gervase was the elegance of the new work with its Sicilian marble double columns, acanthus leaf capitals, and rib vaults forming canopies. Surprisingly Gervase does not describe the stained glass which perfects the design at Canterbury. It too, though, dates from the same time (as M. H. Caviness has demonstrated) and reflects, particularly in the work of the Methuselah master, a classicism that is distinctly English. As Gervase records, the Canterbury monks had consulted French and English architects and brought in William of Sens as their master of works. But the resulting east end at Canterbury is not dominated by any one particular previous building. It draws, like all the best English work of the twelfth century, on many techniques and traditions both native and foreign, new and old. In these ways the masters of art and language of the Twelfth-century Renaissance revived the 'glowing embers' of the past.

PART THREE

The Poitevins
(1199–1272)

IN 1204 Philip Augustus of France took over Normandy and thus brought a formal end to what has misleadingly been called the 'Norman empire' or the 'Anglo-Norman state'. Henceforward, the argument runs, England stood on its own. This argument has been repeated by numerous historians and derives from Stubbs: 'From the year 1203 (*recte* 1204) the king stood before the English people face to face; over them alone he could tyrannise, none but they were amenable to his exactions: and he stood alone against them, no longer the lord of half of France, or of a host of strong knights who would share with him the spoils of England.'[1] Apart from its narrowly English bias (the king could still 'tyrannise' over Ireland, Wales and Scotland, as the thirteenth century demonstrated), Stubbs's statement exaggerates the effects of the loss of Normandy. After 1204 King John remained, in his capacity as count of Poitou and duke of Aquitaine, lord of the area south of the river Loire. Although these lands do not constitute half of modern France, they are at least a quarter and possibly a third of it. More important than size is the fact that John did not accept the events of 1204 as final. He was determined to hold on to Aquitaine and he hoped to restore his influence north of the Loire in Brittany, Anjou and Touraine, if not in Normandy and Maine (see map 1 facing page 2). It had been relatively simple for Philip Augustus to win control of Rouen, the capital of Normandy, which is only 85 miles over easy terrain from Paris; controlling Poitiers (200 miles from Paris) or Bordeaux (350 miles) was much more difficult. Normandy, Maine, Anjou and Poitou were not irrevocably conceded to France until the treaty of Paris in 1259 and even then the king of England remained duke of Aquitaine. The bitterness of Anglo-French relations in the reigns of John and Henry III only makes sense when it is understood that the king of England was still a threat to the king of France and that conversely the kings of England did not accept the loss of their overseas inheritance with equanimity.

Where Stubbs's statement is most misleading is in the assumption that the king of England 'stood alone' and that he could no longer bring in 'strong knights who would share with him the spoils of England'. This is an oversight on Stubbs's part, since in other passages in his *Constitutional History* he is vituperative about John's alien captains like Fawkes de Breauté, who was sheriff of six counties, and the Poitevin favourites of Henry III. The consequence of the loss of Normandy was not to confine the English political system within its own shores but to widen the circle to include the king's vassals south of the Loire. Since 1066 this circle had steadily widened beyond England and Normandy: first with the struggle between Stephen and the Empress Matilda, then with the accession of Henry II count of

Anjou, and now with Richard I and John, counts of Poitou and dukes of Aquitaine. Henry III attempted to widen the circle even further to include the Provençal and Savoyard kinsmen of his wife as well as the Poitevins and Lusignans on his own side of the family. This widening reached bursting point in 1258 with the 'Sicilian business', the attempt by Henry III to win the Hohenstaufen inheritance in Italy for his son Edmund as well as having his brother Richard of Cornwall as emperor in Germany. In this network of alliances extending from Spain to Germany and from Scotland to Sicily the king of England stood very far from alone. That was why the barons rebelled in 1258 and that was also why they were defeated.

The aliens to whom the rebel barons most objected in 1258 were the Poitevins, particularly Henry III's half-brothers, William and Aymer, who had landed at Dover as refugees rather than adventurers in 1247. William had been made lord of Pembroke, and Aymer was given the rich bishopric of Winchester. Resentment against them seems to have been so strong because it was felt that Henry III already relied too much upon Poitevins such as Peter Chaceporc and Peter des Rivaux who managed the king's finances. The appointment of Peter des Rivaux went back to 1232, the year in which Henry dismissed Hubert de Burgh and attempted to restore royal authority to what it had been before Magna Carta. The Poitevins were therefore associated with the growth of royal power and with the king's distrust of the native English. The most prominent of all the Poitevins was Peter des Roches, a sketch of whose career best illustrates the dominant role played by aliens in the governments of John and Henry III and the range of their European experience. Peter probably originated from what is now the little town of Roches-Prémarie-Andillé about eight miles south of Poitiers. He had been a member of Richard I's household, treasurer of the great Romanesque church of St Hilary at Poitiers, dean of Angers and prior of Loches. He came to England in 1200 and was appointed bishop of Winchester in 1205 through the influence of King John. He had experience in war as well as in the administration of the Exchequer, with its pipe and memoranda rolls, and is depicted by an anonymous satirist of the time as:

> *Wintoniensis armiger Presidet ad Scaccarium*
> *Ad computandum impiger Piger ad Evangelium*
> *Regis revolvens rotulum . . .*

> [The warrior of Winchester, up at the Exchequer,
> Sharp at accounting, slack at Scripture,
> Revolving the royal roll . . .][2]

Des Roches remained loyal to John throughout and was temporarily appointed to the highest office in the realm, that of chief justiciar, in 1213 or 1214. When John died, it was Peter and not the archbishop of Canterbury who crowned the young king Henry III in 1216 and who was confirmed in office as the boy's tutor and protector. He was therefore in a position to exercise more personal influence than anyone else over the growing king. Shortly before Henry declared himself of age in 1227 Peter departed for the crusade, where he commanded an army and entered Jerusalem with the Emperor Frederick II in 1229. The next year he was in Italy as one of the negotiators of the peace of Ceperano between Frederick II and Pope Gregory IX. Returning to Winchester, he organised the *coup d'état* in 1232 which removed Hubert de Burgh. But this time Peter had overreached himself and in 1234 he was obliged to withdraw. Nothing daunted, he went back to Italy to command Gregory IX's army and suppressed a rebellion in the papal states. Having won a victory at Viterbo, Peter returned once more to England and died at his castle at Farnham in 1238.

Peter des Roches had exercised more influence over English politics than any other individual of his time apart from King John. Furthermore in the *coup d'état* of 1232 he had made sure that his influence would continue by having his nephew (whom we can assume to be his son), Peter des Rivaux, appointed royal treasurer and titular sheriff of twenty-one counties. The younger Peter's is also an instructive career. He too was treasurer at Poitiers, perhaps in succession to his father, Peter des Roches. The high point of his career were the years 1232–4 when, according to Matthew Paris, 'the whole of England lay under his regulations'.[3] Peter des Rivaux used his authority to reform the Exchequer's system of accounting so that it came under direct royal control. Although he had temporarily to withdraw in 1234 (indeed he was imprisoned), he reappeared as keeper of the Wardrobe in 1236 and thereafter he held various offices concerned with the control of finance until the revolution of 1258 when he was dismissed by the barons. He retained the king's favour, however, until his death in 1262.

The careers of the Poitevins Peter des Roches and Peter des Rivaux span the reigns of John and Henry III. Although Peter des Rivaux was less flamboyant than Peter des Roches, he was as influential as his father behind the scenes. Where the elder Peter had influenced high policy through his wide experience in Poitou, England and Italy the younger Peter concentrated on improving the financial machine. Without the advice of the elder and the expertise of the younger, Henry III might never have successfully re-established a personal monarchy after Magna Carta and the minority. Nor were the two Peters an isolated phenomenon. Aliens dominated much of the royal administration and court life of both John and Henry III because they were not aliens to them but familiar friends; the aliens were the English speakers. The alien character of the court was reinforced in the case of Henry III by his Poitevin mother and his upbringing by Peter des Roches. It is not therefore surprising that Henry preferred Poitevin officials and welcomed his half-brothers in 1247. Poitevins were as prominent and powerful in England in the first half of the thirteenth century as Normans had been in the eleventh century or the Angevin connection was in the twelfth. Partly in reaction to them and partly by assimilating their contribution to government, England developed as a distinctive nation.

❧ VIII ❧

KING JOHN AND THE MINORITY OF HENRY III

(1199–1227)

The Poitevin connection

The critical events of John's reign originated south of the river Loire. Richard I (as we have seen in chapter V) was killed in April 1199 at Chalus in the Limousin, the strategic area controlling access to south-western France. John had to fight for his own succession against the supporters of his nephew Arthur duke of Brittany. The question in law was whether this son of John's deceased elder brother was next in line or whether John himself should succeed (see the genealogical table at page 212). The decision turned in reality on force. Arthur had the support of Philip Augustus and of the area approximately between Normandy and the Loire. John had the support of Eleanor of Aquitaine and the southerners. The crucial points in this struggle were the castles of Chinon and Loches south of the Loire (see map 1 facing page 2). They remained loyal to John and thus by the summer of 1200 he had secured his inheritance—for the time being—from the Cheviots to the Dordogne. That same summer he married Isabella the heiress of Angoulême which lies west of the Limousin. The purpose behind this marriage (apart from John's reported passion for Isabella) was to secure this strategic area, just as Richard I had been trying to do when he was killed. Both kings recognised this southern extremity of Poitou as a key area in which Philip Augustus must be resisted by diplomacy and war.

The risk in John's marriage, which he underestimated, was the offence it caused to another great lord of Poitou, Hugh de Lusignan, to whom Isabella had been betrothed. After being harassed instead of conciliated by John, Hugh appealed to the overlord of them both, Philip Augustus of France. Hugh based his appeal on the principle of judgement by his peers in France (the principle later incorporated into Magna Carta as clause 39) and not by John's court in England. This appeal gave Philip the opportunity in the spring of 1202 to declare John a contumacious vassal and all his lordships in France forfeit. John's nephew Arthur was allocated Aquitaine, Maine and Anjou, and Philip took over Normandy himself.

It is often said that Philip Augustus, unlike John, acted with scrupulous regard for feudal law and won Normandy because he presented himself as the champion of righteousness. This is certainly the impression Philip

wished to give but it is not strictly true. It was not as duke of Normandy
that John had offended but as duke of Aquitaine (Hugh de Lusignan had
nothing to do with Normandy). Even if Philip were entitled to confiscate
Normandy in order to coerce John in Aquitaine, he should have restored
Normandy to the next heir after a year and a day. Pope Innocent III, when
asked by the Norman bishops how they should act, prudently expressed
himself ignorant of the rights and wrongs of the dispute. The takeover of
Normandy illustrates how strict feudal law did not apply to instances of
what would later be called *raison d'état*. Philip Augustus is admired by historians as the founder of the French State precisely because he had the
nerve to override traditional law and ecclesiastical sanctions. His proof of
legitimacy was success. In a way that too was a traditional idea which
Philip turned against John, as it was by conquest that the descendants of
the Normans claimed their lands in England. Success in medieval war
showed that God was on the victor's side.

At the beginning of the struggle, however, it looked as if it might be
John rather than Philip who would succeed. The critical area at first was
Poitou. In the summer of 1202 at Mirebeau (just north of Poitiers) John
overcame all his enemies except Philip: 'We have captured our nephew
Arthur, Geoffrey de Lusignan, Hugh le Brun, Andrew de Chauvigni, the
viscount de Châteleraut . . . and all our other Poitevin enemies who were
there, about 200 knights or more, so that not one of them escaped', John
wrote back to England, asking people to 'give thanks to God and rejoice in
our successes'.[1] But the benefits of this victory soon evaporated because
John was suspected of ordering Arthur's murder in captivity, and that
gave the Bretons a cause for war and Philip a further opportunity to
demonstrate his righteousness. Moreover, Philip directed his main force
in the winter of 1203–4 not at Poitou but at Normandy. John is accused by
the chronicler Roger Wendover of inertia in failing to defend Normandy,
whereas his government records show constant activity. Whatever the
cause, the fact remains that John proved unable to defend Normandy, and
there may be something in Wendover's allegation that he did not consider
it of crucial importance.

Wendover certainly gives a convincing explanation of how Philip used
a combination of persuasion and terror to win over the Normans. He
went in force from town to town and castle to castle on a hearts-and-
minds exercise, telling the Normans that they had been deserted by their
lord John and that he, Philip, was therefore taking over as overlord; he
begged them in friendship to receive him as their lord since they had no
other; anyone who was unwilling would be hanged or flayed alive. This

policy worked and Philip entered Rouen in triumph in 1204. The totality of the English withdrawal was shown by the arrival at Shoreham in May 1204 of Peter de Leon with the Norman government archives, which were transported to London, where they have remained ever since in the Public Record Office. It is often suggested that John lost Normandy because its inhabitants had grown progressively more French in culture and sympathies since 1066. Although a good case can be made for this, the extent of Philip's force was the immediately critical factor at the time. This is shown by the way the Channel Islands (*Iles Anglo-Normandes*, as the French call them) were in a strong enough position to refuse to acknowledge Philip as their duke: they remained loyal to the English crown.

The loss of Normandy did not mean the end of the king of England's involvement in France. Whether wisely or not, John persisted with the strategy he had pursued since the beginning of his reign of concentrating on Poitou and threatening Brittany and France from the south instead of from the English Channel. There was some sense in this, as south of the Loire he commanded more loyalty and he had a secure land base from which to conduct operations. (This was later to be the strategy of the Black Prince in the Hundred Years War.) John therefore conducted two expeditions to Poitou, in 1206 and 1214, each time landing at La Rochelle. It was in pursuit of the same policy, together with family obligations towards his queen, that he brought Poitevins like Peter des Roches and Savari de Mauléon to England. Such men served a dual purpose: they maintained contacts between John and Poitou, and in England itself, because they were dependent on the king, they made useful royal officers, much as they were hated by the English. Similarly the few Englishmen whom John trusted, like the justiciar Hubert de Burgh who was governor of Chinon, had seen service in Poitou.

The Poitevin connection, which by Hugh de Lusignan's appeal to Philip Augustus had occasioned the loss of Normandy, may also be seen as the cause of the greatest crisis of John's reign: the battle of Bouvines in 1214 and the baronial rebellion leading to Magna Carta in 1215. John's expedition to Poitou in 1206 had been a failure, and when in 1213 he demanded a scutage (a tax on knights' fees) for a further expedition, barons in the north of England argued that they were not obliged to serve overseas and certainly not as far south as Poitou. The scutage of Poitou and the other quasi-legal methods, particularly charging excessive sums for inheritances, which John used to raise money for his expedition, were the chief causes of the rebellion against him. Finally, John's concentration on Poitou meant that he was in the wrong place at the wrong time when the decisive opportunity to defeat Philip presented itself. In 1214 John was initially successful in Poitou in defeating the Lusignans and in penetrating north of the Loire by capturing Nantes and Angers. He had written back to England in triumph in May: 'Now by God's grace an opportunity is given us to advance beyond Poitou at our chief enemy, the French king.'[2] The decisive battle in July 1214 was indeed fought 'beyond Poitou'; it took place in Flanders at Bouvines, and John, who was 400 miles away at La Rochelle, had no time nor means to get there. His nephew and ally the Emperor Otto of Brunswick and his general William Longspee earl of Salisbury were routed by Philip. The battle of Bouvines, which ensured the succession of the Hohenstaufen Frederick II as emperor and secured the northern coast of France for Philip, is generally considered one of the few decisive battles in medieval European history.

John's strategy had failed. Instead of rewinning Normandy from Poitou he had weakened his position throughout all his lands. Nevertheless this did not prevent either John or Henry III after him from preferring the company of men who came from south of the Loire. Normandy had been lost, but Peter des Roches and the alien captains remained to impress upon the English that they were still a subject people.

The record of King John

Any person in the public eye acquires a mixed reputation. In the Middle Ages diverse opinions about public figures were conveyed to posterity by monastic chroniclers, whose works developed from mere lists of rulers and public events into comment and narrative. A common practice was for the chronicler to write a succinct obituary notice when recording the death of a well-known person. Thus the so-called Barnwell chronicler writes of King John in elegant Latin antitheses which are difficult to render in English:

> He was indeed a great prince but less than successful; like Marius he met
> with both kinds of luck. He was generous and liberal to outsiders but a
> despoiler of the inhabitants. Since he trusted more in foreigners than in
> them, he had been abandoned before the end by his people, and in his
> own end he was little mourned.[3]

Depending on their experience and knowledge, contemporaries would have differed as to how far they thought this an accurate summary of John's career. By and large, however, the contemporary chroniclers' opinions which have come down to us agree that John was formidable, partial to foreigners and unsuccessful. The disasters of his last years shaped his obituary notices. Not even a partisan could argue that a king was successful who in 1213 had made England a vassal of the pope, in 1214 was defeated by Philip Augustus, in 1215 submitted to Magna Carta, and who died in 1216 with his treasure lost and the French occupying London.

The question arises whether John's failure was due to bad luck (as the Barnwell chronicler suggests) or to some other cause. After his death the belief was given currency by the St Albans chroniclers Roger Wendover and Matthew Paris that John had failed because he was evil and he had therefore received his just deserts: 'Foul as it is, Hell itself is defiled by the foulness of John,' as Matthew Paris expressed it.[4] Victorian historians and their public enjoyed such extravagance, and Matthew's comment (which he had cited not as his own opinion but as that of a reprobate versifier) was stated in J. R. Green's bestselling *Short History of the English People* in 1875 to be the sober judgement of history. In the same year Stubbs published his *Constitutional History*. Although this was a more cautious work than Green's, when Stubbs reached the death of John he let himself go. Like the audience in a court room, his readers had patiently endured many pages of evidence all duly footnoted; now they should have their reward and hear the judge send down the prisoner to exemplary punishment with some fitting words: 'the very worst of all our kings . . . a faithless son, a treacherous brother . . . polluted with every crime . . . false to every obligation . . . not devoid of natural ability . . . in the whole view there is no redeeming trait'.[5]

Because the works of Stubbs, who was Regius Professor of Modern History at Oxford, were prescribed reading for all British history students until well into the twentieth century, his condemnation of John caused a reaction. Furthermore, because Stubbs had purportedly based his work on chronicle evidence, medieval chroniclers began to be suspected by the next generation of historians; they hoped to find a less biased source of information in government records. Partly by coincidence and partly because John was so distrustful of people, the great series of copies of government letters (the charter, close, patent and liberate rolls of the Chancery) begin in his reign. Hence it is possible to compare their circumstantial details of daily life with the reports of the chroniclers.

At first sight records seem more reliable than chronicles, as they are free from prejudice and do not depend on hearsay. The Chancery letters, the pipe rolls of the Exchequer and the plea rolls of the royal courts seem to record events just as they were, intriguingly preserved like flies in amber. On closer acquaintance, however, record sources present as many problems of interpretation as chronicles. What is the significance, for example, of the following entry in the pipe roll for 1209: Peter des Roches is fined a tun of good wine 'because he did not remind the king to give a belt to the countess of Aumale'?[6] What was John's relationship with this lady? Why should Peter have remembered? Was the fine a serious punishment or a joke? These and other questions arising from this single enrolment show how intriguing the records are, but they do not lead to some incontrovertible truth about John's policy or character. Ideally every type of evidence needs to be used up to the limit of its value, whereas the preference of recent historians for records has caused them to exaggerate the shortcomings of chroniclers. It was not the chroniclers who should have been the first target of critical historians but Stubbs who had misrepresented them. His condemnation of John is a product of Victorian culture and has no more in common with medieval realities than a Victorian history painting. The difference in quality and subtlety between the Barnwell chronicler's assessment of John and Stubbs's one is self-evident.

Recent historians have expected too much of chroniclers. Of course chroniclers make mistakes of detail and show bias, just as reporters do today. Moreover the fullest monastic chronicles, like those of Roger Wendover and Matthew Paris, were not written to report mundane events for their own sake but to justify the ways of God to men. Wendover in particular has been the butt of unjustified criticism. The two best works on John's reign (W. L. Warren's *King John* and J. C. Holt's *Magna Carta*) are sometimes overcritical of Wendover. Warren illustrates Wendover's unreliability by considering his report of how John had Geoffrey archdeacon of Norwich crushed to death in prison by starving him and making him wear a cope of lead. Warren states that in no other chronicle is there any hint of the alleged horrific torture. But the annals of Bury St Edmunds report that Geoffrey of Norwich, 'a noble cleric', was arrested at Nottingham and 'dressed in so much iron that he died'.[7] As crushing prisoners with metal weights while starving them, the *peine forte et dure*, was a customary English punishment, these chroniclers may be correct in this respect, although Wendover did misidentify the Geoffrey of Norwich concerned. The chroniclers were probably shocked not by the penalty as such but by 'a noble cleric' being punished in this way.

Holt is overcritical of Wendover's account of how the barons first developed the idea of using the coronation charter of Henry I as the legal form through which to express their grievances. This charter provided the basis for Magna Carta, as has often been pointed out. Wendover ascribes this crucial initiative to Stephen Langton, the archbishop of Canterbury. He reports that in 1213, when Langton attended a meeting at St Paul's about ending the papal interdict, he took 'certain barons on one side and told them in secret' that a charter of Henry I had been found at Winchester (the site of the first royal archives) by which they could recover their liberties.[8] Holt criticises Wendover's report on the grounds that there is no supporting evidence for it and that the text of the public sermon which Langton preached on this occasion gives no indication at all that the archbishop was ready to partake in a baronial conspiracy. This criticism is a good example of how too much is expected of chroniclers. There is no supporting evidence because Langton's remarks were secret and Wendover depended here on hearsay, as he points out. The fact that the sermon does not record Langton's remarks supports Wendover; if it had let out the secret, Wendover's account would be invalid. We know moreover that at least one hearer of this sermon thought Langton to be two-faced, as the Waverley chronicler reports that when Langton opened with the text 'My heart hath trusted in God', someone in the congregation shouted 'You lie, your heart never trusted in God' and temporarily silenced Langton.[9]

Chronicles, like records, provide intriguing details and lead to unanswerable questions. It is the wealth of such material, both in chronicles and records, which gives John's reign its interest. No previous medieval ruler is so well documented anywhere in Europe. This rich material makes it possible for a diversity of opinions about John to coexist. Such diversity, which medieval chroniclers expressed in antithesis and contradiction, is likely to be nearer historical truth than uniformity. A new determination to put things in writing motivated John's Chancery officials with their letters, Peter des Roches 'revolving the royal roll' at the Exchequer, the monastic chroniclers and many others. It was this determination too which made the rebellion against John in 1215 different from its predecessors, as it produced a record of its own in Magna Carta.

Magna Carta

Magna Carta is one of the best known documents in the English-speaking world. Its fame is primarily due, however, not to its intrinsic merits but to the use parliamentarians made of it in their struggle with the Stuarts in the seventeenth century and the export of this myth to New England by the early settlers; Shakespeare's *King John* had made no mention of Magna Carta. Closer acquaintance with the charter is inevitably a disappointment except to specialists. For a start the physical appearance of the earliest copy, preserved in the British Museum, is unimpressive. The actual original sealed by John is lost; nor was any copy kept on the Chancery rolls, because John had no wish to be reminded of it and Pope Innocent III soon annulled it. Although Magna Carta contains at least one eloquent declaration of principle—'no freeman shall be arrested, or imprisoned, or dispossessed, or outlawed, or exiled, or in any way ruined, except by lawful judgment of his peers or by the law of the land' (clause 39)—most of its clauses concern detailed points of law and administration, some of which are of purely local or temporary interest. The removal of fish traps from the Thames and the Medway (clause 33) and the undertaking to dismiss from royal service Gerard d'Athée, Engelard de Cigogné and other named alien officers (clause 50) are extreme examples of how Magna Carta is rooted in its own time and place. Nevertheless the charter is impressive as legislation precisely because it concerns specific grievances, which are clearly defined and systematically listed. From the point of view of legal drafting Magna Carta contains hardly a redundant word or an ambiguous phrase, although it has frequently been misunderstood by later commentators with insufficient knowledge of the administrative practice of the period.

J. C. Holt comments that in the Europe of its time 'Magna Carta was far from unique, either in content or in form'.[10] This is too large a devaluation of its originality. Certainly rulers before John had made concessions to corporations and barons, as the Emperor Frederick Barbarossa did in 1183 when he made peace with the Lombard cities, or as Alfonso VII of León (in northern Spain) did in 1188 when he undertook not to make war without consulting his magnates. The ideas that rulers must make concessions when defeated in war and have the support of their leading men in major decisions were commonplaces of medieval politics. Nevertheless, compared with earlier grants by rulers to their vassals, Magna Carta is original in being so comprehensive and specific in the range of its regulations, which cover the Church, family law, contracts, taxation, legal procedure, penalties, duties of royal officers, weights and measures, merchants, forests and so on. Furthermore Magna Carta is uncompromising in its security provision (clause 61) which entitled a committee of twenty-five barons together 'with the commune of the whole land to distrain and distress us in every way they can', if the king should fail to remedy grievances within forty days. The ideas here expressed, of the country being a 'commune' and of the constituted group being entitled to coerce the king as an individual, may have been implicit in traditional medieval custom but never before had they been given clear expression. Furthermore, like the rest of the common law, Magna Carta applied to all freemen and not only to the little group of barons who had coerced the king.

Pope Innocent III had no doubts about the radical nature of Magna Carta. He based his annulment of it first of all on international principles of feudal law: the barons had made themselves both judges and executors of judgement in their own suit; they were conspirators, rebellious as vassals against their lord and as knights against their king. In addition to this feudal condemnation, which Innocent was entitled to make as John's lord (since England had been surrendered to him as a fief in 1213), he condemned Magna Carta from the plenitude of papal power as a dishonour to the apostolic see, an injury to the king and a reproach to the English people. To emphasise the authority of papal monarchy Innocent cited the text from Jeremiah, 'I have set thee over the nations and over the kingdoms, to root out and to destroy, to build and to plant.' Impressive as all this sounds, the dilemma of the papacy in its dealings with monarchies was the gulf which separated the uncompromising rhetoric of its public letters from the realities of politics. Although Innocent publicly condemned Magna Carta, the fact remained that his personal agent in England, Pandulf, had been one of its signatories. Furthermore when Innocent and John both died in 1216, the legate Guala set his seal to a revised text of Magna Carta within fifteen months of the pope's perpetual annulment of it. The papacy could do this without total loss of credibility because its claim to plenitude of power and its view of events in the light of eternity placed it above mundane considerations of verbal consistency.

The event which assured the future of Magna Carta was John's sudden death in October 1216. Up until April 1216 he looked like winning the civil war which his repudiation of Magna Carta had caused. Then the tide had turned against him with the invasion of England by Louis of France (the son of Philip Augustus), who claimed that John had forfeited the kingdom and that he was the next lawful heir. Louis's claim won the support of the rebel barons who at the time of John's death once more had the upper hand. The future of Magna Carta had therefore lain in the balance. But now that John was dead, his supporters whether from political expediency or genuine commitment reissued the charter in order to win over the rebels. During Henry III's minority Magna Carta was reissued three times in different versions (in 1216, 1217 and 1225), each of the reissues being a concession by the government to its opponents. The contractual nature of the arrangement is made clearest in the reissue of 1225, which states that the king has made this concession of liberties to all the people of his realm in return for a fifteenth part of their movable goods. The 1225 reissue is the version of the charter which became established as the law of the land and constituted the first document in books of statutes. Such books were themselves a product of the struggle for Magna Carta, as they were formed by knights and lawyers in the shires on the basis of the texts of the charter which were issued officially to every shire court.

England was thus – for better or worse – the first country in Europe to have a written constitution, whereby people's rights were enshrined in an official document disseminated and recited throughout the land. Like all written constitutions, however, Magna Carta had severe limitations when it came to practice and it disregarded those who were unfree (apart from clause 20), just as the American Declaration of Independence disregarded slaves. Continuing the American analogy, the weakness of Magna Carta as a basis for civil rights was that there was no Supreme Court to judge violations of it. The clause already cited prohibiting imprisonment without trial and the undertaking appended to it that 'to no one will we sell, to no one will we deny or delay right or justice' (combined as clause 29 in the reissue of 1225) had no enforceable meaning against the Crown because the judges were the king's personal servants. Furthermore, they continued to be corrupt. Justice was bought and sold, denied and delayed as much in England after Magna Carta as it had been before it because winning their cases was more important to litigants than upholding abstract ideals of justice. Nevertheless these ideals persisted in the minds of both judges and litigants and Magna Carta became associated with them. It thus lived on as a myth after its use as a practical remedy for specific grievances had disappeared. This change in Magna Carta's significance dates from the end of Henry III's minority. In the decade 1215–25 the government treated Magna Carta not as a venerable relic but as a living piece of legislation which was amended and updated as required.

The regency of William the Marshal

John's sudden death in 1216 might have brought the end of his dynasty and a second conquest from across the Channel. Louis of France and the rebel barons who supported his claim to be king of England controlled the crucial south-east of the country: the ports of London, Southampton and Portchester and the castles of Guildford, Farnham and Winchester. It is true that access to the midlands was blocked by John's foreign captains, Fawkes de Breauté and Engelard de Cigogné, and that the justiciar Hubert de Burgh was holding out in Dover Castle. But now that John was dead, the French 'were confident' (in Wendover's words) 'that they had the kingdom of England in their power'.[11] Even before John's death

French soldiers had been boasting that England was theirs and that the English had no right in the land. In principle this boast was a riposte to the English claim still to be entitled to Normandy. The French were going to redress the balance: William the Conqueror after all had taken England with a small army in 1066. Because of the power of armed knights a battle involving few troops could have decisive results, as Philip Augustus's victory at Bouvines in 1214 and the Spanish crusaders' victory at Las Navas da Tolosa in 1212 had recently shown. Louis's invasion might even be seen as another Norman conquest. Certainly the Norman branches of families who had lost their English lands in 1204 took part in it, as they were excepted from the peace terms in 1217.

Louis had favourable conditions for victory: control of the centres of government, support of the rebel barons who claimed to be upholding Magna Carta, and a just cause in terms of avenging the disinherited Normans. That 'hammer of kings', Hugh bishop of Lincoln, had supposedly prophesied on his deathbed in 1200 that 'this Frenchman, Philip, will wipe out the English royal stock, just as an ox plucks up grass by its roots, for already three of the sons [Henry the Young King, Geoffrey duke of Brittany, Richard I] have been eliminated and the fourth one [John] will only have a short respite'.[12] Hugh thought this to be appropriate vengeance on the adulterous Eleanor of Aquitaine, who had insulted Louis VII of France by marrying Henry II with such alacrity. Prophecies are not facts, of course, but medieval ones often expressed significant points of view and they were much regarded in a culture which considered divine or devilish intervention a common experience in life.

The answer to the French threat in 1216 was to rely on William the Marshal. He became the hero of the hour, or at least that is the story in his biography which was written in romantic verse (that is, in French) in the 1220s. The Marshal had led an exciting and dangerous life from the time he had been handed over to King Stephen as a hostage in 1152 at the age of five or six. Reality and chivalrous romance blend in his actual life and in his verse biography in a way which it is impossible to disentangle. His recorded career is a model of chivalry: he was trained as a squire in the Tancarville family who were the master chamberlains of Normandy; as a knight he was ransomed by Eleanor of Aquitaine; he himself knighted the Young King (Henry II's son) and fought in France with him against his father. After a pilgrimage to Jerusalem the Marshal returned to the allegiance of Henry II and saved him from defeat by killing a horse under the future Richard I. Yet he won Richard's favour, just as he had won Henry II's. To King John he behaved in a similarly firm way, refusing to give up his homage to Philip Augustus after 1204 and yet supporting John against the rebel barons in 1215. When John died so suddenly the next year, his will named William the Marshal first among his lay executors. The verse biography elaborates this and has John say with his last gasp: 'Sirs, for God's sake beg the Marshal to forgive me, and because I am surer of his loyalty than that of anyone else, I beg you to entrust to him the guardianship of my son, for the land will never be held by anyone except with his help.'[13] The Marshal was reluctant to take on an almost hopeless cause but at last he was persuaded by the sight of the helpless child, the future Henry III, and by his sense of honour.

John's men buried him at Worcester and went to Gloucester where the pathetic dignity of the future king, then aged nine, caused them to burst into tears. The boy seemed, as a poet put it with pardonable exaggeration, a 'tiny spark of minute beauty, the sole hope of the torn kingdom', like the star of Bethlehem.[14] With dubious legality John's men immediately crowned their little king as Henry III in Gloucester Abbey with an improvised gold circlet, for they had no archbishop of Canterbury (Langton was in Rome and had been thought a traitor by John), no Westminster Abbey (Louis held London), and no regalia (some of it had been lost in John's disaster crossing the Wash and the rest was inaccessible in Westminster Abbey). During the coronation dinner a messenger rushed in to say that the Marshal's castle at Goodrich only twelve miles away was being attacked by Louis's partisans.

The Marshal confided to his knights that he seemed to be embarking on a sea without bottom or shore. They replied that even if the worst happened and Louis took the whole of England, there was still an honourable course open to them by seeking refuge in Ireland. Heartened by this, the Marshal told his men that he would carry the little king on his shoulders from island to island and country to country and would not fail him even if he had to beg for his bread. The sentiments expressed here in the verse biography are not so much those of the Dunkirk spirit as of the knights errant in contemporary romances who pledge themselves to superhuman quests. The Marshal's motives in upholding Henry III were presumably more complex than this. Nevertheless, as the verse biography argues, Henry's cause might have foundered at the start if it had not been championed by the Marshal with his reputation as one of the best knights in Europe. This gave the regime prestige, and the Marshal stood as a focus of loyalty in terms of European chivalry as well as of English custom and feudal law.

Support for the boy king, however, did not depend as exclusively on the Marshal as his biography suggests. Like other apparently simple medieval narratives, the biography is a work of art which skilfully presents its author's and hero's point of view. Other elements favouring Henry can readily be cited. First of all, John's death deprived his opponents of the personal cause of their rebellion. Instead of a tyrant they were now resisting a helpless boy, who was as entitled to his inheritance as any other heir. Magna Carta (clauses 2–6) had shown the importance the barons attached to laws of inheritance by specifying the rights of heirs immediately after the claims of the Church. Secondly, the boy had the official backing of the new pope, Honorius III, through the legate Guala. He had added papal authority to the makeshift coronation ceremony at Gloucester by presiding, and furthermore within a month of John's death he set his seal along with the Marshal's to the revised text of Magna Carta, which was issued by the new government to all magnates and royal officials. This reversal of Innocent III's condemnation deprived the rebels of another of their grievances, yet it did not release them from excommunication. On the contrary, Guala made the struggle against Louis into a holy war. The royalist forces wore the white cross of crusaders, they were absolved of all their sins before going into battle, and recruits were described as converts. The precedent for launching a crusade against fellow Christians had been established eight years earlier by Innocent III when he authorised the Albigensian crusade against the Cathar heretics of southern France. That was a frightening precedent, as a crusade meant that the enemy were considered infidels and were therefore given no quarter. Henry III's troops were to show that this is what they too meant by a crusade when they sacked Lincoln and committed other atrocities in 1217.

A third element favouring the royalists in 1216 was the character of the men they had on their side in addition to the Marshal and the papal legate. They were few but formidable. First there were John's foreign captains of whom the two most important—the Norman exile Fawkes de Breauté and the Poitevin aristocrat and troubadour Savari de Mauléon—had been named among John's eight lay executors. Of great experience and the king's personal tutor was the Poitevin bishop of Winchester, Peter des Roches. Then there was the justiciar Hubert de Burgh, who independently of the Marshal had refused to surrender to Louis at Dover when told of John's death. Thirdly, there were loyal English nobles like Ranulf earl of Chester, and John's agents of long standing such as William Brewer. The king's side lacked numbers but not prestige nor experience.

Decisive victory for Henry III came in 1217 in the land battle at Lincoln in May and the sea battle off Dover in August. Battle was joined at Lincoln to prevent the French, who had won control of East Anglia, from penetrating northwards. It was an overwhelming victory for Henry's side despite their inferior numbers: the count de Perche, the French commander, was killed and numerous knights were taken prisoner. The captain responsible for the surprise stratagem of attacking from within Lincoln Castle was Fawkes de Breauté. The sea battle off Dover was thought even more crucial than Lincoln by both Louis and his opponents because it lost the French their access to Kent and London. Matthew Paris has Hubert de Burgh, the justiciar and castellan of Dover, say, 'I beseech you by the blood of Christ to allow me to hang rather than give up the castle to any Frenchmen, for it is the key of England.'[15] Despite the nationalist bias of Matthew Paris (and of his predecessor Roger Wendover), these events should not be seen in simplistic terms as victories of the English over the French. This would be absurd, since the most effective of Henry III's captains, Fawkes de Breauté, was a Norman, and the Marshal himself was Norman by upbringing and remained throughout his life—in his opinion at least—a true vassal of Philip Augustus as well as of the English king. Nevertheless this hard-fought struggle with Louis of France, coming on top of the loss of Normandy, polarised the difference between English and French interests and encouraged a sense of apartness on both sides of the Channel. Such apartness was foreign to the whole life experience of international knights like the Marshal and it was foreign too to the Poitevin and papal influences which shaped the education of the new king, Henry III. He could not have felt that his throne had been saved for him by the English, still less by the French of Paris, but primarily by people of southern (technically Occitan) speech who had come like his mother from south of the Loire or like Guala from Italy.

Although in the autumn of 1217 a formal peace was made with Louis, and another revised issue of Magna Carta (together with a new Charter of the Forest) symbolised settlement at home, the Marshal did not think that anything permanent had been achieved. The only solution he could see when he lay dying in 1219 was to entrust the kingdom to the pope in the person of his new legate, Pandulf:

> Car n'a tele gent en nule terre
> Comment il a dedenz Engleterre
> De divers corages chascuns . . .

> [Because there are no people in any land
> like those in England,
> where each person has his own opinion . . .][16]

That comment came from a man whose memory of strife extended back to Stephen's reign, but it would apply equally well to the next fifty years and the struggles of Henry III with his barons.

Every Christian knight wished to die in Jerusalem. To the Holy Sepulchre the Marshal had borne the cloak of the Young King in accordance with his oath more than thirty years before. He himself was appropriately buried in that evocation of the Holy Land in England, the round church of the London Temple, which had been dedicated by the patriarch Heraclius of Jerusalem in 1185. The Marshal's biographer gives Philip Augustus the last word: 'The Marshal was truly the most loyal man I ever knew in any place where I have been.'[17] Such praise was possible from the king of France because the Marshal, through his conduct as a knight, stood above national rivalries. The Marshal symbolised old-fashioned idealism.

Implications of the minority

Despite the Marshal's pessimism it was evident at the time of his death in 1219 that the beleagured group who had improvised the coronation of Henry III at Gloucester two and a half years earlier had succeeded. Their success was made manifest in the king's second coronation in 1220. This time he was crowned in accordance with tradition: at Westminster by the archbishop of Canterbury with St Edward's crown. Beneath the surface a strong element of improvisation persisted, however, as the loss of the Marshal's authority brought intrigue and rebellion. To counter this Honorius III in 1223, acting in his capacity as overlord of England (in accordance with John's submission to the papacy), declared Henry III to be sufficiently grown up to control the kingdom; he was sixteen years old. Royal letters henceforward bear the significant attestation *Teste me ipso* ('witness, myself'); the word of the king, unlike that of lesser mortals, required no other witnesses' names to uphold it. Nevertheless this formal change did not mean that Henry's tutelage had come to an end in political terms. He was dependent in particular on the justiciar Hubert de Burgh to overcome a rebellion by Fawkes de Breauté in 1224.

Also accredited to Hubert is Henry's proclamation in 1227 that henceforward all charters would be issued under his own seal and that all persons enjoying royal grants must show by what warrant (*quo waranto*) they claimed them. The end of Henry's minority is usually dated from this ominous proclamation, which questioned the validity of all previous acts done in his name or in that of his predecessors. The thinking behind the *quo waranto* proclamation may not have been inspired by Hubert de Burgh, however, to whom it was a potential threat, but by a greater authority. The most recent precedent for resuming grants retrospectively in this way after a minority was that of the Emperor Frederick II in Sicily following his coronation in 1220. He shared with Henry III the experience of being a papal ward, and Henry had written to him in 1226 recommending the services of Peter des Roches. That recommendation bore fruit when Peter organised Henry's *coup d'état* of 1232.

The experience of Henry's minority can be interpreted from opposite points of view. Either it can be seen as a time when the king's incapacity exposed him and his kingdom to foreign influences, notably those of the pope and the Poitevins, which reinforced the Angevin tradition of arbitrary government and in adulthood made Henry III an autocratic ruler repeatedly taking advice from foreigners. Alternatively the king's minority can be seen as a unique opportunity to establish a consensus among the governing class after the excesses of King John. The successive reissues of Magna Carta and the generally moderate terms offered to individual rebels after the civil war of 1216–17 suggest that some reconciliation was achieved. Likewise the re-establishment in 1218 of the justices of the Bench and the procedure of the Exchequer symbolised the restoration of normality and the intention of the government to conduct business as usual. Furthermore the system of justices' circuits or eyres, which was the principal method of enforcing the government's will in the counties and of checking in every village that the law was being obeyed, was re-established in 1218 with unprecedented elaboration. Teams of justices perambulated the counties (half of which had not seen a justice in eyre since 1203) in eight circuits during 1218 and 1219. In 1225 another country-wide visitation was made with the specific purpose of investigating disseisins and clearing gaols, and in 1226–8 a second general eyre was held. Not since the days of Hubert Walter's justiciarship during Richard I's crusade had royal justice been so systematically administered.

The king's absence or incapacity seemed to bring the best out of the judicial system. Indeed from the point of view of legal development the latter years of Henry III's minority are the true age of Bracton, the royal justice to whose authorship the treatise *On the Laws and Customs of England* is attributed. This treatise seems to have been put together in the time of Bracton's predecessor, Martin of Patishall, who was the chief royal judge in the years 1218–29. Patishall and his fellow judges laid down the principles upon which the law was administered for the next fifty years. The treatise attributed to Bracton, which was passed on to him by Patishall's clerk, seems to have been intended as a kind of handbook for the judges which defined the rules systematically and illustrated them by current cases. Despite—or perhaps because of—its creation during Henry III's minority, the law which this treatise expounds is explicitly English: its author starts by pointing out the differences between English custom and Roman or canonical procedure. This tradition of a distinctive English common law was to prove more resilient over time than either royal absolutism or baronial revolution.

Business as usual was not as straightforward or uncontroversial a principle for the royal administration as it looked. Restoration of due process of law inevitably meant restoration of the bureaucracy whose routines extended back fifty years or even a century before Magna Carta. All royal officers were first and foremost executors of the king's will and not the servants of the general public or the common good. 'I notice', says the pupil to the master in the *Dialogue of the Exchequer*, 'that with all your regulations you always stick to the king's advantage.'[18]

As far as the principles behind Magna Carta were concerned, the king's officials had learned nothing and forgotten nothing. This is well illustrated by the Exchequer pipe roll for 1219: debts owed to King John for benevolences were still being collected; lists of the northerners who had refused to pay the scutage of Poitou in 1214 were still noted, together with the names of their heirs if they had died. The enrolment for Yorkshire notes that the scutage of Poitou has 'always been in respite from that time until now', but the clerk wrote it down all the same, just in case presumably the ghost of King John should triumph in the end.[19] This attitude of the administration was to be one of Henry III's greatest and most effortless strengths. The king's officials stood poised to do his will—whatever it was—because he was their lord and they were especially his, as was shown by the liveries they wore and the advantages they received in his service. At the end of Henry III's minority in 1227 the monarchy had revived extraordinarily compared with its position in 1216. As 'King of England, lord of Ireland, duke of Normandy and Aquitaine, and count of Anjou', to quote the royal title, Henry had the opportunity to wield as much power as any ruler in Europe, although he would have to fight very hard if he were to regain what he had been taught to believe was his rightful inheritance in England and abroad.

❧ IX ❧

The Personal Rule of Henry III

(1227–58)

Henry III lived in a time of new risks and new opportunities for kings and, like his father King John, he met with both kinds of luck. From his own point of view his greatest piece of luck was the success of the *coup d'état* in 1232 which removed Hubert de Burgh and put the Poitevins Peter des Roches and Peter des Rivaux in power. Potentially this reversed the effects of John's surrender to Magna Carta in 1215, since Hubert had replaced Peter des Roches as justiciar in that year. In 1232–4 the Exchequer was once more under Poitevin management and Peter des Rivaux undertook a sweeping reform which established Henry as master of the central administration and of the sheriffs in the counties for the next twenty-five years. Understandably enough such radical change produced baronial reaction in the rebellion led by Richard the Marshal in 1233, but Henry overcame this and by 1236 he had established himself firmly in power. From then until 1258 he conducted a highly personal government, successfully resisting repeated demands for the offices of justiciar and chancellor to be public appointments under baronial control.

In one way Henry's style of government was gratuitously provocative, as he favoured Poitevins in his household and after 1236 he added the Savoyard and Provençal kinsmen of his wife. But in another way it was Henry who established the distinctive pattern of the English monarchy, as he named his surviving sons after English royal saints and built Westminster Abbey and palace as the religious and administrative centre of a settled monarchy. Through the justices in eyre, who were nearly all Englishmen, he maintained contact between the centre and the localities. Through them too he reinforced the tradition of a common law before whose majesty all freemen, even if they were barons or bishops, were equal.

The high point of Henry's personal rule came in 1250 when he addressed all the sheriffs of England at the Exchequer, telling them among other things that no peasant should suffer for the debt of his lord and that they should diligently and righteously inquire into how the magnates were treating their men and correct their transgressions. The year 1250 was also the occasion of Henry's ceremonially taking the cross and promising to go on crusade like St Louis. Thenceforward it became increasingly evident that Henry had overreached himself, both in his attitude to the barons and in his ambitious strategies abroad. Thwarted in recovering his inheritance in France, he hoped to establish his family in the even greater inheritance of the Hohenstaufen Frederick II in Italy and Germany. In 1255 Henry's son Edmund became titular king of Sicily and in 1257 Henry's brother Richard of Cornwall was crowned king of the Romans. This looked like Henry's greatest triumph, but in accepting the Sicilian crown for Edmund from the pope Henry had allowed opportunity to blind him to the risks. He could not fulfil the pope's financial conditions and as a consequence he was threatened, like King John before him, with excommunication. This threat at last brought about a successful combination of the barons, who imposed on Henry in 1258 a radical form of control through public officials and standing committees answerable to parliaments. Seen in the short term, from an English viewpoint, Henry's attempt at personal government had failed and the baronial movement symbolised by Magna Carta had successfully reasserted itself.

Contemporary rulers

If Henry's failure in 1258 is viewed in a European context and in the longer term, however, it does not appear so unusual or so exclusively due to his own misjudgement. Other rulers of his time suffered in similar ways. Most spectacular were the disasters which overcame the Emperor Frederick II (1215–50) after the high point of 1231 when he promulgated the *Liber Augustalis*, the most ambitious and overtly monarchist law book of the Middle Ages. In that same year Frederick faced baronial rebellions in the kingdom of Jerusalem as well as in his Italian kingdom. Thereafter his failure to subdue the Lombard communes in the 1230s gave Pope Innocent IV the opportunity to depose him at the council of Lyons in 1245. At that council another king, Sancho II of Portugal, was likewise deposed. His case was similar in some ways to that of Henry III in 1258. A successful conquistador, he had reigned (though first as a minor) since 1223, but he opposed the clergy and gave offices to his wife's family. He was deposed by Innocent IV on the grounds that he had devastated the Church and used evil counsel. Charges similar to those against Henry III were directed also against the conquistador James I of Aragon (1213–76) by his nobility in 1264 and he was forced to make concessions: honours were to be reserved for nobles by birth and the justiciar of Aragon heard complaints against the Crown. Worse happened to Alfonso X of Castile (1252–84), the maker of the *Libro de las Leyes* which is the Spanish equivalent of Frederick II's *Liber Augustalis*. He faced rebellion in 1272 after twenty years of personal rule and in 1282 an association of nobles and cities declared him incapable of governing.

New power and authority was given to these rebellions by the formation of baronial communes, which claimed to speak for the nation as a whole with the backing of the local church and clergy. Whereas in the twelfth century communes had been associated mainly with rebellious citizens and burghers whom the nobility despised, in the thirteenth century barons joined forces with civic and clerical movements in order to elevate rebellion above family conspiracy and feudal defiance. (These ideas are more fully discussed in chapter 11 on the commune of England.) The important point in the present context is that Henry III was not engaged in an isolated dispute. Indeed, Frederick II in the manifestos he issued to the other rulers of Europe claimed that he was neither the first nor the last who would be threatened with deposition and that all rulers suffered from the declared and secret hatred of their peoples and the machinations of the Church. After his excommunication in 1239 Frederick made a personal appeal to Henry III as his good neighbour, his brother-in-law (he had married Henry's sister Isabella in 1235), his friend and his kinsman.

Although Henry judged it expedient to ignore this appeal, it would be a mistake to underestimate the range of contacts and sense of common problems which rulers of the time shared. They were interrelated through generations of alliances and sometimes had common physical peculiarities, like the drooping eye which disfigured both Henry III and Frederick II. Henry's three sisters married Alexander II of Scotland, Frederick II and Simon de Montfort respectively (see the genealogical table at page 212). Henry's wife's sisters married Louis IX of France (St Louis), Richard of Cornwall (Henry's brother), and Charles of Anjou king of Sicily (see the genealogical table at page 212). Although Henry's sense of family solidarity grew excessive in the eyes of his enemies when he lavished favours on his wife's Savoyard uncles in the 1230s and 1240s and on his mother's sons by a second marriage, the Lusignans, in the 1250s, obligations of kinship had strong customary backing in the institution of the bloodfeud and aristocratic vendettas. Louis IX was probably not being purely diplomatic when he is reported to have assured Henry III in 1254 that it grieved him how the opposition of his barons prevented the differences between Henry and himself being amicably resolved, considering that they were such close kinsmen. Similarly Joinville reports in his biography of Louis that he allowed Henry to hold on to Aquitaine because their children were first cousins. As traditionalists, Louis and

Henry were probably both rather mystified by the changes happening in France, where forces of public opinion made articulate by barons and clergy were causing Henry to lose his Angevin inheritance and Louis to gain it by means which could not be adequately justified by the ordinary rules of family and feudal law.

The common interests and problems of thirteenth-century rulers have tended to be ignored because medieval political history has often been written with a nationalist bias. The development of academic history in the latter half of the nineteenth century coincided with the growth of competitive feeling among the European nations. Consequently, instead of examining the similarities between medieval rulers, historians of each nation picked out individual traits in their own kings which they thought revealed incipient national character. Thus Louis IX symbolised French cultural superiority, Alfonso X the Spanish genius for legislating for subject peoples, and Frederick II was the tragic hero of aggrieved German power. By the same token Henry III was the anti-hero against whose futility, 'folly, falseness and foreign proclivities' (in Stubbs's words) the English barons rebelled and thus created parliament.[1] More recently in the Oxford History of England F. M. Powicke indicated a similar narrowness of view by asking, 'How was it that in England alone, among the monarchies of the west, the right of the king to select his own advisers became a subject of such bitter controversy?'[2]

In fact in all the European monarchies, but particularly in the most westerly ones of Portugal, Castile and Aragon, the king's choice of advisers was fiercely debated. New men in government were always resented by baronial families, however short their own pedigrees were. But there was more than prejudice and snobbery at issue in the thirteenth century. The nobility were up against a new type of royal counsellor, who was typically a graduate from a law school and a specialist in finance or record keeping. John of Salisbury and Walter Map had first identified such people as *curiales* in Henry II's reign (see chapter VII). By Henry III's reign there were many more of them and they were more assured. Frederick II had founded the university of Naples in 1225 specifically to produce such men to serve in his administration. They deprived traditional counsellors of their influence because they were the masters of the bureaucracy through which advanced monarchies like Frederick II's and Henry III's operated. Decisions no longer had to be made orally at large meetings of counsellors. Instead, little conclaves of experts executed their orders by written instructions to sheriffs and bailiffs in the localities. The key officials therefore became the keepers of privy seals and the accountants of the king's household. Traditional offices like that of steward, justiciar and even chancellor began to wane in importance not only in England but in France, Sicily, Aragon and Castile.

Furthermore the new type of official tended to do things by the book instead of by oral custom. Consequently new law codes and books of statutes become prominent. The largest such collection is the papal decretals which were formed in the 1230s by Pope Gregory IX into the *Corpus Iuris Canonici*. The most comprehensive of such books are Frederick II's *Liber Augustalis* (1231) and Alfonso X's *Libro de las Leyes* (1256–65) which have already been mentioned. Because these works used Roman law textbooks as their models, they also had the added advantage for rulers of encouraging the Roman imperial idea that the prince himself was above the law because he was its maker. Frederick II's *Liber Augustalis* goes so far as to claim that it is blasphemous to dispute royal decisions. The English equivalent of these books is the treatise ascribed to Henry III's judge, Bracton. Comparable work was being done in most parts of Europe, notably the statutes of Alexander II of Scotland, the German *Sachsenspiegel*, the Norwegian and Icelandic law codes, and the *Etablissements* of Louis IX. Although such works appealed to academics both then and now, they were distrusted by traditionalist barons because written law often claimed that rulers were absolute and knowledge of the law was restricted to experts. This restriction was emphasised in medieval thinking by the similarity in Latin between *lex-legis* meaning 'law' and *legere* meaning 'to read'. Thus the treatise ascribed to Bracton defines 'law' as meaning 'in its broadest sense everything that is read'.[3] Rulers consequently were tending to become readers as much as warriors. Thus Frederick II and Alfonso X, nicknamed *el Sabio* (the Learned), were very highly educated; James I of Aragon was likewise an author in his own right and Louis IX is said to have read devotional works every day. Henry III showed little interest in books except as treasured objects. Nevertheless, because Peter des Roches had been his tutor, he too had a good grasp of administrative procedure.

The return of Peter des Roches

The network of political contacts between England and other European powers is displayed in the *coup d'état* of 1232, which brought the Poitevins Peter des Roches and Peter des Rivaux to power (see page 131 above). Peter des Roches returned to his bishopric at Winchester in 1231 after an absence of nearly four years during which he had entered Jerusalem with Frederick II in 1229, negotiated the peace of Ceperano between

Frederick and Gregory IX in 1230, and on his way back through France in 1231 had participated in the truce between Henry III and Louis IX. Each of these potentates, the Emperor Frederick II, Pope Gregory IX and the French king Louis IX, was involved—directly or indirectly—in Peter's seizure of power in 1232. They are best considered in reverse order, starting with the French. The purpose of the truce of 1231 was to save Henry's face after the failure of his expedition to Brittany in 1230. Henry blamed that failure on the justiciar, Hubert de Burgh, whom he suspected of not wishing to conduct an offensive war in France. Henry is reported to have drawn his sword on Hubert and called him a traitor in 1229, and in 1230 Hubert stopped him accepting an invitation from some of the Norman nobility to invade Normandy. In restraining Henry, Hubert may have been motivated simply by caution and long military experience. Nevertheless Henry's expedition of 1230 seemed to offer the best opportunity ever of rewinning the continental lands, as Louis IX was inexperienced and he faced civil war in France. In replacing Hubert by the Poitevin Peter des Roches, Henry hoped to play a more active and creditable role in French politics.

Hubert was also suspected by Henry of being disloyal to Gregory IX and encouraging an 'England for the English' attitude (in Matthew Paris's words) towards the papacy.[4] In the winter of 1231–2 papal tax collectors in England and religious houses which gave them hospitality received threatening letters, which purported to come from a confederation of knights and magnates dedicated to saving the king and kingdom from Roman oppression. In the name of this confederation masked terrorists held Italian clergy to ransom, burned houses and seized crops. As justiciar Hubert de Burgh was responsible for restoring order but at the same time circumstantial evidence, such as that he was earl of Kent where the trouble started, pointed to his conniving at the confederation if not actually being a member of it. Whatever the truth was, this breakdown of law and order gave the king and Peter des Roches the opportunity in 1232 to demand Hubert's resignation. Furthermore he was charged with a mass of offences ranging from financial peculation to poisoning, witchcraft and treason. The financial and administrative accusations were probably accurate by and large, whereas such charges as that he had poisoned William the Marshal in 1219, or that he had given Llywelyn of Wales a talisman which made him invincible, strained credulity. Nevertheless the king and Peter des Roches successfully used these charges to whip up popular hatred against Hubert so that he ran for sanctuary and was totally humiliated. Royal letters were then addressed to all Christians explaining how Hubert had been discovered attacking the Roman Church and Italians, and how he had surrendered entirely to the king's will, but the king in his mercy had respited judgement against him in return for the confiscation of everything Hubert had acquired since becoming justiciar in 1215. By this clever move Henry avoided having to substantiate the charges against Hubert, while at the same time he acquired Hubert's huge treasure of gold and silver and—more importantly—Henry moved nearer to establishing a government of his own making.

Henry and Peter des Roches used their triumph to restore royal authority to what it had been in the days of King John by tactics of shock and deliberate confrontation. To emphasise the return to John's policies, his captains and clerks were again given offices. Among the captains the Poitevin Peter de Maulay came back in 1232 and Engelard de Cigogné, who had been banned by name in Magna Carta, was back in 1233. Similarly Robert Passelew, who had been Fawkes de Breauté's loyal clerk, was made deputy treasurer. Henry was careful, however, not to repeat John's mistake of making a foreigner chief justiciar, and Stephen of Seagrave, the senior justice of the Bench, was promoted to Hubert de Burgh's office. Along with Hubert nearly all the sheriffs were dismissed and Peter des Rivaux took control by becoming sheriff of twenty-one counties. In addition to that, he was the keeper of all wardships and escheats (the medieval equivalent of death duties), chief justice of the forests, and had charge of the king's property and houses. Of course Peter des Rivaux could not exercise all these offices himself. The purpose of his holding them was to effect a clean sweep in government by centralising financial control at the same time as mastering the localities. To enforce Peter des Rivaux's authority throughout England, Flemish and Breton mercenaries were brought in to garrison castles. Roger Wendover says that Peter des Roches filled England with 'legions of Poitevins'.[5] This is an exaggeration, as many of the foreign mercenaries came from places other than Poitou and there were two thousand of them at the most. Nevertheless, in thinking of them as Poitevins, Wendover probably reflected popular opinion which rightly attributed these changes to the Poitevins Peter des Roches and Peter des Rivaux.

These shock tactics brought about a baronial reaction, which was perhaps what Peter des Roches had been hoping for as a test of strength between the revived monarchy and the champions of Magna Carta. The rebellion was led by Richard the Marshal, a younger son of William the Marshal, who came into his English inheritance on the death of his elder brother in 1231. Richard had earlier inherited the Marshal's Norman lands, had therefore become a liegeman of Philip Augustus and had per-haps commanded a French royal army. Understandably enough Henry III refused at first to allow him his English inheritance, although the two men were reconciled in 1232. However, Richard began to support Hubert de Burgh after his dismissal and he also resented a judgement in a prop-erty dispute, where the claim of the Poitevin Peter de Maulay had been preferred to that of Richard's ally Gilbert Basset. Perhaps it was this dis-pute which turned Richard into a champion of the English baronage against the Poitevins. It is true that Richard, like Simon de Montfort who had also come to England in 1231 to claim his inheritance, was a French-man by prior allegiance, but Frenchmen were as much the enemies of Poitevins as English patriots were. By 1233 Henry and Richard were openly at war on the Welsh border and in 1234 Richard was killed in Ireland, perhaps on the instructions of Peter des Roches.

The differences between Henry and Richard were on fundamental matters of principle, if Wendover's account (which is the only one extant) is reliable. In reply to Richard's first remonstrations Peter des Roches provocatively said that the king was entitled to bring in outsiders to reduce his rebellious men to their proper obedience. Later, in 1233, the rebel barons refused to attend the king at Oxford and threatened to make a new king unless the evil advisers were dismissed. Henry reacted by demanding hostages and special oaths of fealty from the barons. This demand and the barons' threat recall the struggle with King John, when the rebels had made Louis of France king of England. In Henry's mind the rebellion of Richard the Marshal was probably associated with what he and Peter des Roches saw as a revival of French baronial ideology. When Henry was accused of condemning Richard without trial by his peers, Peter des Roches answered that there were no peers in England in the way there were in France and that the king was entitled to condemn anyone by judgement of whatever justices he chose to appoint. At issue here was the meaning of clause 39 of Magna Carta (see page 140 above), stating that no freeman should be condemned except by 'judgement of his peers or [*vel*] by the law of the land'. This clause was ambiguous be-cause the Latin word *vel* could mean both 'or' and 'and'. What Peter des Roches probably meant by stating that there were no peers in England was that, in accordance with the principles of common law established by Henry II, all freemen were equal in the king's court and Richard was not therefore entitled to claim special consideration because he was a baron: judgement by peers meant judgement by other freemen.

English law in Peter des Roches's view was not associated with French aristocratic privilege but with all men being equally humble before the king's majesty. Such a view of English legal development had much to commend it from a historical point of view and it also accorded with the most recent ideas about the powers of rulers emanating from Frederick II's *Liber Augustalis*. This had been promulgated in 1231, shortly after Peter des Roches had left Frederick to return to England. According to Wendover, Richard the Marshal believed that the reason why the Poitevins were so dangerous was that Peter des Roches had given a secret undertaking to Frederick II to make England subject to the emperor. Although Peter had probably never been on such conspiratorial terms with Frederick, it is easy to see how their similar political attitudes gave credence to the idea that Peter was a foreign agent who intended to subdue the barons through Roman law. Ironically enough, Henry III wrote to Frederick II in 1235 that Peter had attributed too much to the plenitude of royal power and he therefore had to dismiss him. Similarly it may not be a coincidence that shortly after Peter's dismissal the teaching of Roman law was prohibited in London. In 1234 Henry was obliged by baronial pressure arising from the killing in Ireland of Richard the Marshal to repudiate Peter des Roches and Peter des Rivaux. But time showed that this was no more than a temporary expedient as Peter des Rivaux, along with Passelew and Seagrave, were given new royal appointments in 1236 and Peter des Rivaux continued to serve Henry until he was removed by the baronial rebellion of 1258.

Henry's style of kingship

The years 1232–4 had established Henry's style and method of government and they also established the lines along which criticism would be repeatedly made for the next twenty-five years. The principal baronial fear continued to be that voiced in 1233 by Richard the Marshal: that the Poitevins were aiming at absolute power. By 1258 this aim had become associated with the second wave of Poitevins, the king's half-brothers, who had come to England in 1247. They were the sons of Isabella of Angoulême's second marriage to Hugh de Lusignan. Of the four younger sons Henry had made William heir by marriage to the Marshal earldom of Pembroke, Aymer bishop of Winchester, and to Guy and Geoffrey de Lusignan he paid large pensions; in addition their sister Alice was married in 1247 to John Warenne earl of Surrey. The rebel barons alleged in 1258 to the pope that the king's brothers 'damnably whispered to him that a prince is not subject to law, thus putting the prince outside the law, and so justice itself was banished beyond the boundaries of the realm'.[6]

To such criticism Henry replied that he was not an unlawful innovator but a restorer of the authority and dignity of the English Crown. 'Up until now', he complained of the barons in 1261, 'the kingdom has been governed by three things in particular: by the law of the land, by the seal and by the Exchequer, or rather by the good and wise men who direct these three things.'[7] By 'the law of the land' Henry meant the common law system established by Henry II. Henry III's claim to have upheld the law is undeniable, insofar as the administration of royal justice through professional judges was intensified and regularised. But it can of course be argued against him that the judges were often corrupt or partial and that insistence on recovering the rights of the Crown conflicted with their duty to be fair to everyone. By 'the seal' Henry meant the Chancery's authority to issue royal letters, which initiated policy of all sorts ranging from international diplomacy to orders to sheriffs to arrest particular individuals. The thousands of copies of such letters of Henry's preserved in the Public Record Office substantiate his claim to have governed by the seal, although as with the law his critics argued that the keepers of the seal were corrupt or incompetent. By 'the Exchequer' Henry meant financial control. Here again the reforms of Peter des Rivaux improved procedure and made fraud more difficult, but there is no doubt that by modern European or North American standards corruption was still common. The overall impression given by the extant records of Henry III's government for the years 1234–58, which are far too large for any individual historian to master entirely, is of consistent attention to detail and of persistent endeavours to supervise localities.

Henry's government was distrusted by many barons and prelates not primarily because it was incompetent but because it was ideologically distasteful. Henry had learned from Peter des Roches not to apologise for royal power, and throughout the period of his personal rule he repeatedly made provocative statements about the nature of his authority and gave them substance by appointing foreigners and relatives to royal offices. Although he was in no way an intellectual like Frederick II or Alfonso X of Castile, Henry articulated more clearly than any of his predecessors the fundamental principles on which the English monarchy rested. His ideas, as befitted a hereditary monarch, were conservative. He believed that he was God's vicar with a duty to look after his people, under the majesty of 'whose protective wings they breathe' as he put it.[8] Likewise he saw himself as the father of a family or head of a great household with total authority within his domain. These were very old ideas, reaching back to Alfred and Charlemagne and imperial Rome, and they gave little room to the developing political theory of the twelfth and thirteenth centuries which saw rulers as the elected heads of communes, and divine authority as the confine of the pope and clergy.

Identifying his chief opponent and meeting him head on in characteristic fashion, Henry got into dispute with Robert Grosseteste, the greatest English prelate and scholar of his time. The principal dispute was occasioned by Grosseteste's refusal in 1245 to approve the appointment of Robert Passelew to a church in Northampton, which came within Grosseteste's jurisdiction as bishop of Lincoln. Passelew, whom Henry had first brought to prominence in the Poitevin coup of 1232 and whom Grosseteste had already prevented from becoming bishop of Chichester, was a justice of the forests. Grosseteste, as a conscientious pastor, rejected Passelew's candidature because he was a royal justice exercising a worldly jurisdiction. But this dispute raised larger questions than that, as Grosseteste wrote to Henry at the same time that the sacrament of anointing a king 'by no means places the royal dignity above or on a level with the priestly' and warned him of the precedent of Uzziah king of Judah who was struck down with leprosy for usurping the priestly office.[9] That text had also been cited by Grosseteste a few years earlier when he had told Archbishop Edmund of Canterbury that the clergy, who are the gods and angels of scripture, should not be judged by kings as they are beasts of burden like all laymen. Whether or not Henry knew the full extent of Grosseteste's commitment to clerical superiority is obscure. Whatever the circumstances, Henry obliged Grosseteste to make an apology in which Henry is addressed as your 'royal excellence', your 'royal magnificence' and your 'royal serenity'.[10] That was the tone Henry liked to hear from the clergy.

Although Grosseteste's claims seem absurdly scholastic to a modern ear, and Henry's victory a shallow one, this dispute was one of many conducted by Henry with Grosseteste and other prelates and the issues involved were very large. Henry was upholding the traditional prerogative of the king to be God's vicar and lord of all men in the realm whether cleric or lay. Grosseteste on the other hand championed the jurisdiction of the clergy, reinforced by the decrees of the Lateran Council of 1215, over the souls of all Christians whether kings or peasants. Ecclesiastical authority had renewed vigour at this time, as the foundation by Innocent III of the Franciscan and Dominican orders of friars and the establishment by Gregory IX of the inquisition against heretics demonstrated. As a progressive churchman and an intellectual, Grosseteste welcomed the friars and set up an inquisition in his diocese to investigate the sins of laymen. This was prohibited by Henry in 1252 in a letter which clarified the differences between them. The letter describes Grosseteste's inquisition as an unprecedented harassment of the poor and defamation of good Christians, as the inquisitors compel people to give evidence on oath about the private sins of others. As a result of this prohibition no clerical inquisition, like that which persecuted the Albigensians in France, was permitted in England. Henry's reason for banning it was not to protect the freedom of the individual but because it was a public nuisance, as the inquisitors interfered with 'the cultivation of the fields and other necessary temporal duties'.[11] Paradoxically Henry's championing of divine kingship defended secularism by humbling the clergy. 'You prelates and religious', he is reported to have told the master of the Hospitallers in 1252, 'have so many liberties and charters that your superfluous possessions make you proud and from pride drive you to insanity.'[12]

Henry had less success intimidating the lay barons than he had had with the prelates, although here too he used traditional arguments and had the support of lesser men who did not benefit from baronial and clerical privileges. He maintained that the barons should extend the principles of Magna Carta to their own men and that it was wrong for the king to be limited in his power whereas they were not. According to Matthew Paris, Henry told the assembly of barons in 1248 that they were trying to deny him the right which every head of a household had to appoint or remove his officers and that it was contrary to feudal law for vassals to bind their lord to conditions and make him an inferior. Henry was referring here to the baronial proposal, which had perhaps first been made in 1238, to elect conservators of liberties who would be with the king constantly to hear complaints and control expenditure, and that the justiciar and chancellor should be similarly elected by the barons. These were the demands which the barons at last realised in 1258.

The argument that the realm of England was different from a private estate or an ordinary family household and that it should therefore be governed in a different way would not have been understood by Henry. He governed not as an exclusively national monarch but in the tradition of his Angevin predecessors who had amassed a conglomeration of lordships by inheritance and war. Landlords in the thirteenth century were replacing customary leases and fixed rents by a system of direct control through bailiffs rendering accounts. Henry aimed to do the same with the land of England through Peter des Rivaux and reformed Exchequer procedure. Ironically enough a code of rules about how to manage an estate, in the form of advice to the countess of Lincoln, was attributed to Robert

Grosseteste. In these rules there is no mention of officials being elected or of open government. On the contrary, the lord commands and the servants obey: 'if any of them complain or grumble, say that you intend to be lord or lady and you intend them to serve you according to your will and pleasure'.[13] The tone of this advice attributed to Grosseteste is identical with that expressed in Henry's speech in 1248, although he put the idea in more legalistic terms as befitted the formality of the occasion. He told the barons that inferiors 'have to be directed at the will of the lord and the wish of the ordinary', who exercises jurisdiction *suo jure*.[14] In Henry's view his critics were simply grumblers, who had to be repeatedly told that he was their lord just as they were lords of their inferiors.

Henry drove home the lesson that he governed according to his own will and pleasure by appointing men of humble origin and foreigners to high office. In doing so he was following the precedents of Henry II and King John, which had been reinforced in Henry III's case by his education by Peter des Roches and the success of the Poitevin *coup d'état* in 1232. Henry made his distrust of the barons even more explicit than John had done and he favoured foreigners on a scale surpassing any of his predecessors. The extent of Henry's distrust is demonstrated by his ordering to be painted in his washroom at Westminster in 1256 a picture of a king being rescued by his faithful hounds 'from the sedition plotted against him by his own men'.[15] Such distrust was of course self-verifying and Henry was correct in thinking that his numerous enemies conspired against him. Although it is possible that his Poitevin upbringing made him distrust all English people, his attitude seems to be more complex than that. Matthew Paris reports him saying, 'You English want to hurl me from my throne as you did my father', but he also reports Henry's interest in the old English kings which is confirmed by Henry's veneration for Edward the Confessor.[16] As well as to Westminster Abbey, Henry was devoted to his birthplace at Winchester and it is probably from there that he learned about the pre-Conquest kings buried in the cathedral. Henry does not seem to have objected to English people as such, but to the barons claiming that they spoke for England and had authority over him. Likewise, although it is true that many foreigners were given high offices, as many if not more powerful and loyal royal officials were Englishmen of obscure origins like Henry's secretary John Mansel and his judge Henry de Bracton.

Henry's blend of English and continental traditions is best seen in the works of art which are his greatest memorial, although what survives is only a shadow of what he achieved. His palaces of Westminster and

Clarendon have been destroyed, but the choir and transepts of Westminster Abbey still stand and the great hall of Winchester Castle is impressive even as a shell. Although the design of the new Westminster Abbey (started in the 1240s) was influenced by the latest French work at Amiens and Reims, for example in the use of flying buttresses and window tracery, it combined this with distinctively English proportions and craftsmanship in sculpture and tile work. To this and his other buildings Henry devoted huge sums of money, using the unique resources of his government to obtain materials and labour. Consequently the work is well documented from an administrative point of view in the public records. In 1250-1, for instance, 800 men were employed on the building of Westminster Abbey and that figure excluded the even larger number servicing and equipping these craftsmen. Henry's delight in buildings is indicated by a French song which has him say that there is a chapel in Paris which he covets so much that he would like to carry it off in a cart to London. This is the Sainte Chapelle which Henry saw, along with Amiens and Chartres, on his visit to Louis IX in 1254.

It would be a mistake to pigeon-hole Henry's building work as an interest in art separated from life and politics. Through buildings and their furnishings he gave visual expression to his conception of monarchy and of his own place as king. In his palace chambers he had paintings done of the Wheel of Fortune, the exploits of Alexander the Great and the combat of Richard I and Saladin. In his churches, and above all in Westminster Abbey, he surrounded his kingship with awe and majesty. He loved liturgical ceremonies, such as processing to Westminster Abbey in 1247 with his newly acquired relic of the Precious Blood, or entering Winchester Cathedral as though he were a bishop to preach in support of his half-brother Aymer's candidature in 1250. Similarly Henry increased in 1233, the year of his struggle with Richard the Marshal, the number of occasions on which the *Laudes Regiae*, the ancient liturgy of praise to the ruler, was chanted. Most importantly, Henry promoted the veneration of Edward the Confessor as a popular cult and he had his own tomb in Westminster Abbey placed in Edward's aura of sanctity and constructed of identical mosaic materials. Henry is responsible for establishing Westminster Abbey as the royal burial place and its palace as the centre of government.

In all these features Henry's style of kingship is comparable with that of his contemporary Louis IX, who like Henry was thought by his critics to spend too long in church and who built the Sainte Chapelle to house relics. Louis and Henry too had similar ideas about the rights of monarchy, as Louis's judgement in Henry's favour in 1264 (the Mise of

Amiens) made clear to the barons. Yet Louis and Henry differ in their historical reputations. Louis is considered a saint and a hero of France, whereas Henry has often been presented as a foolish and extravagant king who should have reached agreement with his barons. These differences of reputation took shape in the lifetimes of the two kings and are a product of different attitudes towards kingship in England and France. In emphasising the sacredness of royal authority Henry was up against English tradition, which had Becket as its favourite saint and knew that Henry was not directly descended from Edward the Confessor and an ancient line of legitimate kings but from William the Bastard, the conqueror of 1066. Louis IX on the other hand benefited from more than two centuries of sympathy and admiration for the Capetian monarchy of France where one king had succeeded another in unbroken male succession, thus proving that the dynasty had God's blessing. Attitudes to the two kings differed in much the same way in nineteenth-century national historiography. English national character was identified with baronial liberty and parliament which Henry had opposed, whereas Louis was admired because his monarchy had united France. If Louis had reigned in England, 'where each person has his own opinion' (as the biographer of William the Marshal wrote), he might not have found it so easy to be the pattern of justice and goodness.[17] In his style of government Henry modelled himself not on the sweet reason of the Capetians but on the wilfulness of his Plantagenet predecessors Henry II, Richard I and John. Henry was as tough, opinionated and mercurial a politician as any of them and, like them, he suffered from pursuing strategies which were becoming too ambitious for a king of England.

Henry's European strategy

As his palaces and churches showed, Henry had extravagant ideas. Yet they were in keeping with the reputation the kings of England enjoyed of being the richest rulers in Europe. That reputation, which went back to the Norman Conquest, had been reinforced in the generation before Henry's by the immense lands of Henry II and the size of the ransom paid for Richard I. Its firm foundation moreover was the power and thoroughness of the English Exchequer. Seen in this light, it is not so surprising that Henry III himself and many of his contemporaries considered the losses of John's reign a temporary misfortune which better luck and better management would overcome. Henry hoped to rewin his inheritance in France and when those hopes faded after his defeats at Taillebourg and Saintes in 1242, he substituted for them even more ambitious projects in Italy.

In France it is difficult to see what the right policy for Henry might have been. If he had been able to foresee the growth of the French state and had conceded to the inevitable by granting Louis IX all his overseas possessions, Henry would have been so discredited that he might have exposed England itself to invasion. He received an intelligence report in 1227 that the French were planning to invade England in order to restore the dispossessed Normans to their English lands; the memory of Louis of France's successes in England in 1216 was still fresh. The best form of defence was attack and consequently Henry made his expedition to Brittany in 1230. The failure of that expedition exposed his main weakness, which was that he could only attack the French with the aid of magnates like the duke of Brittany whose loyalty could not be relied upon. Henry found himself in much the same dubious position in the greater military fiasco of 1242, when he was encouraged by Hugh de Lusignan to make an expedition to recover Poitou and was then betrayed by him. Nevertheless Henry had been obliged by honour and the fear of losing face to make that expedition. Louis IX in 1241 had invested his brother Alphonse as count of Poitou, which was an explicit challenge to Henry, as his own brother Richard of Cornwall had been titular count of Poitou since 1225. Furthermore Henry's mother Isabella of Angoulême, who had returned to Poitou and married Hugh de Lusignan in 1220, claimed that she had been personally insulted by Louis IX. In addition to that, the troubadours of Languedoc were circulating insulting *sirventes*, calling Henry a coward for not coming to defend his people from French domination. So Henry and Richard of Cornwall had duly come to Poitou in 1242 only to be betrayed and defeated.

On the whole Henry hoped to get the better of the French by diplomacy rather than war, and the failure of his military expeditions in 1230 and 1242 convinced him that the best hope of success lay in his network of international alliances. His strategy here was to use English money to buy supporters and to pay other people to do the fighting. This strategy extended beyond the struggle with France itself to Italy and Germany, although it is probable that it was always the French whom Henry had in mind. If he could not defeat Louis IX within France itself, he could block French ambitions elsewhere in Europe. With this aim in view Henry's interests centred on his marriage in 1236 to Eleanor, the second daughter of Raimond-Berenger count of Provence and of Beatrice of Savoy. This was neck-and-neck competition with France, as Louis IX had recently married Eleanor's elder sister; subsequently Richard of Cornwall married the next sister and Charles of Anjou the youngest one (see the genealogical table at page 212). The reason why the royal houses of England and France formed such a close alliance with the relatively minor family of Provence-Savoy was that this prolific family had roots in the most strategic area in western Europe and also acted as international agents linking the papacy and the empire of Frederick II with France and England. The family aimed to control the western Alps and Provence and thus straddle the mountain and coastal routes between what is now France, Switzerland and Italy (see map 2 facing page 3).

Among her uncles Henry III's queen Eleanor had Amadeus count of Savoy, William bishop-elect of Valence, Thomas count of Flanders and Piedmont, Peter who was made lord of Richmond by Henry III, Boniface who was made archbishop of Canterbury, and Philip archbishop of Lyons (see the genealogical table at page 212). Through the experience and contacts of these men Henry hoped to build a network of alliances extending across southern France into Italy and Germany. As he was in competition with Louis IX, who equally had them all as uncles by marriage, Henry outbid Louis in the lavishness of his gifts. At the time of his marriage in 1236 Henry was constructing the Painted Chamber at Westminster and he had written over its great gable the motto *Ke ne dune ke ne tine ne prent ke desire* ('He who does not give what he holds does not receive what he wishes').[18] By playing the traditional lordly role of gift-giving, Henry hoped to win over these new uncles so that he would be at the centre of their diplomatic web in Europe.

Henry also hoped to use the expertise of the Savoyards to govern England in the same way as he had used Peter des Roches. Henry was first impressed by the abilities of William bishop-elect of Valence and his clerk, Peter of Aigueblanche. In 1236, when William accompanied the future queen Eleanor to Henry's court, he was made Henry's chief counsellor according to some monastic sources. But these reports may be exaggerated, as William left England in 1237. Monastic commentators attributed such authority to him because their memories of the Poitevin *coup d'état* of 1232 were still fresh and they now feared a Savoyard one. Thus Matthew Paris complained that the king was permitting aliens, 'now Poitevins, now Germans [i.e. Savoyards], now Provençals, now Romans', to fatten themselves on the goods of the kingdom.[19] It is certainly true that William's clerk, Peter of Aigueblanche, was much favoured by Henry and became bishop of Hereford in 1239. Henry used him on diplomatic missions and as a financial agent involved with the papacy. Another Savoyard clerk who proved useful was Henry of Susa, better known as the canon lawyer Hostiensis, whom Henry made master of St Cross Hospital in

Winchester. He acted as the king's proctor in ecclesiastical cases, before leaving England in 1243 to become a chaplain to the pope.

The Savoyard uncles who were given the most by Henry were Peter, who was made lord of Richmond in 1240, and Boniface, who was nominated archbishop of Canterbury in 1241. These were able but intimidating men who served Henry's interests well, although they frequently differed from him about policy. Peter became known in Savoy as 'little Charlemagne' because he was such an energetic administrator and formidable knight. Boniface was particularly useful at the council of Lyons in 1245 (where the Emperor Frederick II and Sancho II of Portugal were deposed by sentence of the pope), as Boniface's brother Philip was archbishop of Lyons and provided the military force for the council. Boniface became a prelate of the same mould as his elder brother, William bishop-elect of Valence; proceeding backwards and forwards between England and the Alps, fighting (Boniface felled the prior of St Bartholomew in London with one blow of his fist), living well and intriguing. Although Boniface was far from Robert Grosseteste's ideal of a Christian pastor, he upheld the liberties of his Church in the way his contemporaries best understood, that is, by threats and litigiousness.

The characteristic which may have most attracted Henry to the Savoyards was that they had been brought up in a hard country where lordship had constantly to be fought for and power was nakedly displayed. They reminded him perhaps of King John's captains whom he had known in his childhood. Henry even tried to bring English law into line with Savoyard custom, which was a departure from his usual policy of maintaining Englishness in this sphere. When in 1253 the king's baggage train as well as overseas merchants had been robbed by bandits on the Southampton road, Henry attempted to introduce the Savoyard custom whereby the residents of the area in which a robbery takes place would be collectively obliged to pay compensation. Matthew Paris reported the objections to this as being that geographical conditions were different in England from Savoy, that people would be punished without sufficient proof and, above all, that such a great change in the law should only be made with baronial consent. Consequently Henry had to drop this proposal. Nevertheless it illustrates very well the differences between Henry and his barons. He wished to maintain law and order by the strongest means available, whereas his opponents gave greater emphasis to the importance of consent and tradition. The earls and barons would not change the laws of England.

Although Henry used the Savoyards within England, their main function was in international relations. In the land they dominated, the interests of Frederick II as emperor and king of Arles and of Louis IX as over-lord of France converged. Henry aimed to use Provence-Savoy as a wedge between these two great powers and also as a staging post between his lands in southern France and the pope and emperor in Italy. Henry's strategy is illustrated by his sending an expeditionary force in 1238 commanded by Henry de Trubleville, the English governor of Gascony, and William bishop-elect of Valence to aid Frederick II against the Lombard communes. In 1246, following the deposition of Frederick II, Henry made a more ambitious move whereby Amadeus count of Savoy became his vassal and Henry took over responsibility for the Alpine passes. This suggests that Henry was already moving towards the idea of dominating Europe by acquiring the Hohenstaufen inheritance. Although all this seems too much like armchair diplomacy with no grip on reality, Henry's agents like John Mansel and Peter of Aigueblanche went in person on numerous diplomatic missions and Mansel had taken part in the fighting at Milan in 1238 and Saintes in 1242.

The 'Sicilian business'

Henry's ideas grew more ambitious with each decade and by the 1250s they had reached a peak of provocation and stupidity in the opinion of his opponents. The cause of the collapse of Henry's many years of personal rule was the 'Sicilian business' (*negotium regni Siciliae*), the transaction whereby Henry agreed with the pope in 1255 to send money and troops to Italy in exchange for his younger son Edmund being recognised as king of Sicily and Apulia (that is, southern Italy). In itself this was not a stupid idea. The kingdom of Sicily was reputed to be the wealthiest in Europe and the island of Sicily was the key to the Mediterranean just as the Alpine passes were the key to access between northern and southern Europe. After the deposition of Frederick II his kingdom of Sicily might be taken by whoever had the power and formal papal authority to do it. If either the French or the Aragonese got it, they would grow so powerful that Henry's lands in Gascony might be endangered. The best counter move therefore was for Henry to get the kingdom of Sicily for himself.

To nationalist historians like Stubbs, Sicily seemed incredibly remote from England and Henry's plan therefore looked absurd. But to Henry, who viewed Europe through the eyes of the Savoyards and Poitevins, Sicily was not so far away. Matthew Paris in his chronicle included a beautifully illustrated itinerary all the way from London to Apulia. Henry was not the first English king to intervene in Sicily, as Richard I had captured Messina in 1190. In Henry II's reign likewise there had been many

contacts between England and Sicily: Henry II's secretary Thomas
Brown had been a councillor of Roger II of Sicily and another Englishman, Robert of Selby, was Roger's chancellor. England and Sicily were
felt to have close links because they had both been conquered by Normans. In a way, therefore, Henry III was attempting a reconquest by
which Sicily would be wrested from its German overlords and returned to
the heirs of the Normans. Many barons were familiar with Sicily because
of the crusades. Thus Peter des Roches had been there before his return to
England in 1232. Similarly after the defeat and death of Simon de Montfort at Evesham in 1265 his disinherited sons went to make their fortunes
in the Sicilian kingdom and were given large fiefs by Charles of Anjou.
Sicily, like Provence-Savoy, was the kind of multinational lordship which
fascinated Henry III because it seemed similar to his own multinational
status as overlord of the British Isles and of lands in France extending as
far as the Alpine passes.

Henry's mistake was not in buying Sicily for Edmund but in the
unfavourable terms of sale which he agreed with the pope. In addition to
annual tribute the contract of 1255 specified that Henry was to pay the
pope 135,541 marks within eighteen months. If he failed, he personally
would be excommunicated and the kingdom of England would be laid
under an interdict (as it had been in John's reign before Magna Carta). The
huge payment was stated so exactly to the nearest single mark because the
pope claimed that these were the costs already expended by the papacy on
rewinning Sicily, and Henry must reimburse them. This sum was almost as
much as Richard I's ransom, or as a tax on the English clergy for ten successive years. Furthermore this was merely the entrance fee, as Frederick
II's son Manfred controlled much of the kingdom and Henry might have
to fight him all the way. The offer had been made to Henry's brother
Richard of Cornwall before it was accepted for Edmund and (according to
Matthew Paris) Richard had replied to the papal nuncio: 'You might as
well say, I will sell or give you the moon; go up and take it.'[20]

Why did Henry agree to such unfavourable terms? There are many
explanations, though no single one is satisfactory. Henry was used to taking risks and outbidding his rivals: 'He who does not give what he holds
does not receive what he wishes.'[21] The Sicilian business was a gamble,
just as outfacing Richard the Marshal in 1233 and many other angry
prelates and barons since then had been gambles. More than twenty years
of unprecedented power for an English king perhaps blinded Henry to the
danger he was in. Not having the historian's advantage of hindsight, Henry
may have thought that he was still going up on the Wheel of Fortune, that

favourite medieval image like the big wheel in a fairground, which he had had painted in 1247 above the chimney-piece at Clarendon. Indeed events in the short term went in his favour. In 1257 Richard of Cornwall was crowned king of the Romans (emperor designate) at Aachen. The Hohenstaufen inheritance seemed within the grasp of the Plantagenets. In that same year Henry presented the twelve-year-old Edmund, dressed in Apulian costume as king of Sicily, to the English barons. He expected them to be impressed and to see in Edmund the new *puer Apuliae*, as the young Frederick II had been known fifty years earlier, the future lord of Europe. Those other images painted on Henry's palace walls, the exploits of Alexander the Great and the combat of Richard I and Saladin, likewise perhaps played a part in Henry's hopes. The greatness of the Plantagenets was about to be restored and recent humiliations in France forgotten. Or, as Pope Alexander IV put it in 1255, 'the royal family of England which we view with special affection and the distinction of our intimate love, we wish to exalt above the other kings and princes of the world'.[22]

If these were Henry's aspirations, he was entering the realm of fantasy. Yet that too is understandable considering the way high politics were conceived at the time. Frederick II in his *Liber Augustalis* created a fantasy of an all-powerful ruler, laying down the law in books while his people rebelled. Frederick also was responsible for inflating the value of his kingdom of Sicily in the rhetorical letters he sent to other rulers. In one medieval tradition, exemplified above all by the papacy, it was words rather than deeds which mattered in politics. Henry's gain from the contract of 1255 was the pope's word that Edmund was the legitimate king of Sicily; Henry could provide the deeds later, or so he thought. Even the huge sum to be paid to the papacy can be partly explained. Henry had undertaken in 1250 to go on crusade and as a consequence the clergy had been taxed. It was legal to tax the clergy for a crusade because it was an ecclesiastical enterprise. An advantage of the Sicilian contract was that Henry's obligation to go on crusade against Islam was commuted by Alexander IV to crusading against the Hohenstaufen in Italy. The prize for Henry to win was the kingdom of Sicily. This was a more realistic objective than Louis IX's attempts to reconquer the kingdom of Jerusalem; compared with Louis, Henry was a realist.

The sum due to the papacy was indeed huge, but Henry calculated that the clergy would be compelled to pay most of it by papal tax collectors, like the Gascon Rostand whom Henry took into his household. The favour Henry showed to Rostand was consistent with his policy over many years of exploiting papal power to humble the English clergy and promote royal interests: Peter des Roches had taught him that lesson when he brought down Hubert de Burgh, allegedly in the name of an outraged pope, in 1232. In this context Henry's agreeing to the penalty of excommunication and interdict makes sense: the clergy would be impressed by that threat and it would oblige them to pay up. Seen in its most optimistic light from Henry's point of view, the Sicilian contract meant that Henry, in Edmund's name, would win control of the most important kingdom in Europe at the expense of the English clergy. But this time Henry had provoked the prelates and barons too far. They produced a succinct list of objections as seen from England, starting with the distance and going on to the cost and the risks. One point to which they gave emphasis, which Matthew Paris confirms, was the risk of a French invasion of England. The French felt so threatened by the combination of Richard of Cornwall in Germany and Edmund in Italy that Louis IX was patrolling Normandy in 1257. The Sicilian business had therefore had the reverse effect for Henry to the one intended. Instead of perfecting his network of alliances, it united all his enemies at home and abroad and isolated him.

This sense of isolation was reinforced by the barons' tactics in 1258. They were determined to avoid the charge of treason and of plunging England into civil war, as the rebellion against King John had done. They therefore treated Henry as if he were a simpleton who had to be taken into wardship like a child. In this way the rebels could claim that they were acting in the king's own interests and they petitioned the pope to abrogate the Sicilian contract. This was a delicate manoeuvre, as Henry had willingly made the contract and it was consistent with his ambitions over many years. Nevertheless the idea that Henry was a simpleton gained wide currency and it is in this guise that he appears in Dante's *Divina Comedia*, in the valley of unsatisfactory kings in Purgatory, along with other rulers involved in Italian politics:

> *Vedete il re della semplice vita*
> *Seder là solo, Arrigo d'Inghilterra*

> [See the king of the simple life,
> sitting there alone, Henry of England][23]

Henry did not lead a simple life in an ascetic sense, although he might be thought simple in his singlemindedness. Nevertheless Dante has characterised him well in the words '*seder là solo*'. By pursuing sole royal power Henry had come to sit alone by 1258, isolated from people in England.

❈ X ❈
NATIONAL IDENTITY
National feeling in Henry III's reign

The identity of the English as a distinct people had survived the Norman Conquest and been maintained as an ideal by the great Benedictine monasteries with their roots in the Anglo-Saxon past. That identity also existed as a fact of everyday life in the language spoken by the serfs or 'natives', as the landlords called them, of the countryside. There was therefore nothing new in the virulence with which the St Albans chroniclers, Roger Wendover and Matthew Paris, reported Henry III's favours to the Poitevins, Savoyards and other aliens. They were writing in the tradition of English monastic chroniclers. A number of twelfth-century monks had written histories of the English and no one expressed their bitterness more powerfully than William of Malmesbury did in 1125: 'no Englishman today is an earl or bishop or abbot; the newcomers gnaw at the wealth and the guts of England, nor is there any hope of ending this misery'.[1]

The difference between William of Malmesbury's attitude and that of monastic chroniclers a century later is that the latter did see some hope of their humiliation ending. This hope came not from Henry III himself, who pursued the policy of all his predecessors since Edward the Confessor of relying on men from overseas, but from the lay magnates who began to identify themselves with England. In Wendover's report of Richard the Marshal's protest against the Poitevins in 1233 he has Richard complain that they oppress Henry's 'own native men of the kingdom'.[2] The Latin word for 'native' here is *naturalis*, meaning 'true-born'. Wendover avoided the word *nativus* because that described the 'natives' in the sense of 'naïfs' or low-born serfs. The word *naturalis* had the added advantage that it meant 'natural' as well, and hence the king could be accused of dismissing his natural counsellors and appointing unnatural aliens instead. The idea that the barons should counsel the king by right of nature, meaning by birthright and by rightness in the order of things, was thus made explicit. Nor was the concept of 'natural' counsellors a private idea of Wendover's, although it may have been a precocious one in 1233, as the barons themselves use comparable language in their petition in 1258 where they demanded that castles should be entrusted to 'faithful men, natives of the kingdom of England'.[3] The word for 'natives' here is *nati*, meaning 'born', and this is associated with the barons' demand that ladies shall not be married to men 'who are not of the nation [*natione*] of the kingdom of England'.[4] A 'nation' meant a kindred group and hence by extension it was applied to the people of each distinctive country; for example, students at medieval universities were divided into nations for mutual protection.

The barons' opposition to the aliens in 1258 was exacerbated in the civil war which followed. The *Song of Lewes*, which celebrated their victory in 1264, alleges like Wendover that the king intended to supplant the 'native people' (*viros naturales*) by aliens. The song claims too that the rebels fight for England:

> Now England breathes again hoping for liberty; the English were despised like dogs but now they have raised their heads over their van-quished foes . . . Read this, you Englishmen, about the battle of Lewes for if victory had gone to the vanquished, the memory of the English would have been cheap.[5]

National sentiment is often voiced under stress, when the group is threatened by a powerful neighbour or torn by civil war. Thus the war with Louis of France, culminating in the battle of Lincoln in 1217, was seen by one contemporary poet as a struggle for English survival. 'England' (*Anglia*) is personified in this poem (as it is in the *Song of Lewes*) as 'she grasps her conquering swords' and the tears of the English invoke English strength.[6] The 'English people' (*Angligena gens*) have grown degenerate and suffered from the 'belligerent French', the 'black Scots' and the 'feck-less Welsh'. This part of the poem thus identifies the main enemies of England in the later Middle Ages and it also illustrates the tendency of nationalists to associate degeneracy at home with viciousness abroad. Matthew Paris similarly characterises the different nations in abusive terms: the French are proud, the Welsh are faithless, Poitevins are wily, Flemings are filthy, Greeks are insolent and so on. Matthew too makes Hubert de Burgh into a national hero of the war of 1217 as he defended Dover, 'the key of England', and saved England for the English. According to Wendover likewise the king's side at the battle of Lincoln were fighting 'for their country' (*pro patria*).[7] These texts have been cited in a little detail in order to show that the idea of 'England' as a cause to fight for was familiar to thirteenth-century writers. As the biography of William the Marshal makes clear in its rendering of his harangue to the troops before the battle of Lincoln, to defend one's country is a cause justifying war; the troops fight also for themselves and their women and children and to win honour and protect the Church. Such sentiments are not dissimilar from those voiced by military leaders in many later wars.

Familiar elements of later ideology are also evident in a lament for the former greatness of England which was composed in 1265 following the battle of Evesham. The anonymous writer, who is a royalist by contrast with the author of the *Song of Lewes*, reminds England of her qualities starting with her sea power: 'You had the sea for a wall and ports as your gates fortified by strong castles; in you knights, clergy and merchants all flourished.'[8] According to this writer English ships brought spices and treasure from the four quarters of the globe. Furthermore within England there was an abundance of wild and domestic animals, beautiful country-side and numerous birds and fish. Although England is only a small coun-try, the fleeces of its famous sheep warmed the backs of all the nations of the world. But now England has degenerated into civil war because it spurned the heavy yoke of kings. This is an extravagant and tendentious panegyric. Yet it is valuable in showing that the image of England as a sea power, depending on trade and the prosperity of its agriculture, had already been articulated. The baronial wars heightened sentiment for the suffering of England and the English among both royalists and rebels:

Plange plorans Anglia plena iam dolore

[Wail, weeping England, heavy now with woe][9]

The papacy and internationalism

As in the modern world, national pride and exclusiveness existed along-side powerful international organisations. Indeed the growing influence of the papacy encouraged nationalist particularism in reaction to its uni-versal claims. As a consequence of King John's submission to Innocent III and the legations of Guala and Pandulf during Henry III's minority, the papacy had established itself alongside and even inside the English gov-ernmental machine. The aspect of papal power which was most resented was the practice of paying papal officials and nominees out of the rev-enues of English benefices. From the papacy's point of view there were many justifications for this. Its right to appoint to benefices derived from its supervisory authority over all Churches to prevent corruption and uphold Christian values. Rich benefices had often been held by royal or baronial favourites as a reward for secular services. The papacy and the

higher clergy now needed more revenues to provide for the efficient running of the Church. Innocent III had come closer than any of his predecessors to making clerical authority a reality throughout Christendom. To
implement the programme of reforms decreed by the Lateran Council of
1215 required an army of preachers, nuncios, inquisitors, letter writers,
accountants and so on. Good government had to be paid for in the
Church as in the State. The pope, unlike a secular ruler, had few revenues
at his disposal and he therefore began to raise funds by taxing the clergy
and also by obtaining regular incomes for his officials by requiring
churches throughout Christendom to provide benefices for them. In England this was easier than elsewhere because during Henry III's minority
papal officials were on the spot. Furthermore the king's government
was willing to assist the papacy in exchange for a share of the profits both
spiritual and temporal.

The problem for the papacy, as so often in its activities, was the gulf
between theory and practice. The most prominent beneficiaries of papal
provisions to benefices tended not to be high-minded reformers but the
nephews and kinsmen of the pope and cardinals. This was because the
pope was expected like any other great man to reward his followers upon
whom he depended for protection. Robert Grosseteste was so infuriated
by an order from Innocent IV in 1253 to provide for a papal nephew from
the endowments of Lincoln Cathedral that he refused, arguing ingeni-
ously that the papal plenitude of power could not be used to destroy the
Church because that was contrary to its purpose. Although Grosseteste
was not acting here as an English nationalist but as a conscientious
bishop, his resistance fed popular opposition to the papacy just as his
controversies with Henry III were used for the secular purpose of attacking the monarchy.

In 1253, the year of Grosseteste's protest, Italians were receiving at
least 50,000 marks a year from English benefices according to hostile
critics. Moreover Innocent IV himself acknowledged this income to be
above 8,000 marks, as he offered to restrict it to that sum. It has been estimated that 8,000 marks represents about five per cent of the income of
the Church in England and Wales for taxation purposes at the time. From
the papacy's point of view a levy of five per cent on ecclesiastical income
was a reasonable charge for its services. But papal tax collectors were
more conspicuous than their royal and baronial counterparts because
they were foreigners and they had to proceed in accordance with publicly
stated rules of canon law. Furthermore, in order to get the money to Italy
they depended on Lombard and Tuscan bankers and thus built up in the

public mind—and in reality—the connection between the papacy and international finance. The contract with its interest charges, expenses provisions and penalty clauses made in 1255 between Henry III and the pope to promote the Sicilian business shows very well how the pope headed a multinational finance corporation as well as a religious institution.

Resentment against papal provisions in England is best illustrated in the disturbances of 1231–2 which occasioned the fall of Hubert de Burgh (see page 156 above). Threatening letters imitating the tone and style of the papal chancery were sent to prelates in the name of a confederation (*universitas*) 'who would rather die than be oppressed by the Romans'.[10] The letters were sealed with a special seal representing two swords, which traditionally symbolised spiritual and secular authority and for these conspirators symbolised also the use of force. The letters ordered their recipients to pay no more revenues to Roman nominees under penalty of having their produce burned. Italian clergy were held to ransom, papal messengers were attacked and the letters they carried torn up, and houses and crops were seized. The leader of the terrorists was Robert Tweng, a Yorkshire knight who had been deprived of his hereditary right to nominate to a church by a papal provision. He operated under the pseudonym of William Wither ('wither' means 'opponent' in Old English). Tweng alias Wither is a real-life example of a folk hero of the Robin Hood type, who robs fat prelates and fights for English liberties. Instead of being hanged for arson and robbery, Tweng was given a safe-conduct to the pope and subsequently went on crusade. This leniency at the hands of the king and the pope suggests that Tweng had powerful friends in England, as his propaganda maintained. He is last heard of in the baronial wars as an executor of the will of John Mansel, Henry III's secretary.

Tweng's confederation can be interpreted in a number of ways. It was a nationalist movement insofar as the letters it sent out claimed to speak for the laymen and magnates of England against the Romans. The movement also claimed to represent everybody (hence it is a *universitas*) who 'has chosen to resist by common counsel of the magnates'. In these features Tweng's confederation presages the 'commune of England' which was formed to resist Henry III in 1258. But Tweng had a narrower purpose than the rebels of 1258; at his narrowest he is little more than an anticlerical with a specific grievance. The principal significance of Tweng is that his confederation shows that the anti-Roman prejudices of the St Albans chroniclers were not a private eccentricity of their own but voiced wide resentment against the intrusion of foreigners into the English Church. Instead of promoting international understanding and Christian fellowship, the growing power of the papacy from Innocent III onwards united churchmen and laymen in protest and led to the formation of national Churches.

The identity of England

England and the English formed a distinct entity not only in their own opinion but in the view of outsiders. For example Innocent III had condemned Magna Carta as a reproach to the English people. Innocent is also reported to have alluded on another occasion to the English reputation for drunkenness. A dispute between Evesham Abbey and the bishop of Worcester had been taken on appeal to the Roman court in 1206. The bishop's advocate was imprudent enough to show off what he had learned in the schools about one of the points of ecclesiastical law involved. He was caustically rebuked by the pope: 'You and your masters must have drunk a lot of English beer when you learned that.'[11] Medieval England had a reputation for hard drinking which is now more associated with other northern nations. On Richard I's crusade the natives were astonished at the amount the English consumed and at their custom of draining toasts to the sound of horns and trumpets. Similarly Gerald of Wales in his invective against the English at the court of Rome in 1199 emphasised their reputation for drunkenness and double-dealing. The author of the *Dialogue of the Exchequer* blamed the frequency of crime in England on the innumerable riches of the kingdom and the innate drunkenness of the inhabitants.

England's wealth referred to here is another commonly mentioned national characteristic. The French in particular seem to have felt that England was a much richer country than their own. In his life of Louis VI (1108–37) Suger of St Denis contrasted Louis with William Rufus, who enjoyed the profusion of the treasures of the English, and Louis VII (1137–80) similarly contrasted the wealth of Henry II with his own material poverty: 'We in France have nothing except bread and wine and joy.'[12] Louis meant of course that the French had everything worth having. From these and many other comments a consistent picture emerges of England through foreign eyes: the English were drunken, grasping and untrustworthy. In his style of life and diplomacy Henry III was perhaps attempting to correct this unfavourable image, as he was sober (although he enjoyed a glass of wine), generous and consistent in his affection for his kinsmen. A medieval characteristic of the English which has not survived is that they were reputed to have tails. Thus Simon de Montfort showed that he did not think of himself as an Englishman when he remarked that

PLATE VIa. King John with two of his dogs. King John said: 'If I give my peace even to a dog, it must be respected'.

VIb. An illumination from a contemporary manuscript depicts a lawyer's clerk writing out a charter. It is apparent from his red robe and long hair that he is not a monk

the English get you into a tight corner and then turn tail. Simon is also reported to have commented that he had been in many lands and different countries both pagan and Christian but 'in no nation have I found such infidelity and deception as great as that which I have experienced in England'.[13] In retrospective report, treachery of that sort explained his death at the battle of Evesham. These opinions of the English, like all generalised opinions about national character, were no more than prejudice constantly repeated. Nevertheless they show that the English possessed distinct characteristics, in the opinion of their enemies, which made them identifiable as a nation.

The identity of England also became clearer in the thirteenth century in more precise ways. Most importantly England became territorially distinct from Scotland and Wales because they too were developing into nation states. At the time of the Norman Conquest Pope Gregory VII wrote to Archbishop Lanfranc distinguishing the Scots (by whom he meant the Irish) from the 'island of the English' (by which he meant England, Scotland and Wales).[14] Although this was a simplification even at the time, Gregory was right in assuming that Scotland and Wales were not distinct territorial entities and that the Norman conquerors claimed overlordship over the whole island. In the thirteenth century by contrast, both the kingdom of the Scots and the principality of Wales had set locations and names. The Scots were now recognised for international purposes as the people of Scotland and not of Ireland, and similarly the Welsh now acknowledged that name in Latin instead of calling themselves Britons.

In constitutional terms *vis-à-vis* the English, the Scottish position was stronger than the Welsh one. In particular from 1176 at the latest the papacy recognised the Scottish Church as a special daughter of the Holy See, which meant that it was independent of the archbishop of York, whereas Gerald of Wales failed to win similar recognition for the Welsh Church's claim to be independent of Canterbury. Nevertheless the papacy did not support Scottish claims to be free of English secular dominion; for example in 1235 Gregory IX wrote to Alexander II reminding him of the homage and fealty due to the king of England. Even in this letter, however, the Scottish cause received one support as the king is addressed as king of 'Scotland' (*Scotiae*) instead of king of 'Scots' and is thus acknowledged to rule over a specific territory. That territory moreover was defined in the Anglo-Scottish treaty of 1237 which settled the border between England and Scotland. The numerous disputes which followed did not contradict the basic principle that the ancient kingdom of Northumbria had been partitioned and that henceforward

Northumbrians north of the Tweed were Scots, whereas those to the south were English. As on other land frontiers in Europe divisive national identities were thus imposed on people whose language, traditions and way of life were the same.

Welsh status and aspirations were as complex as Scottish ones and they too were most explicit when opposed to the English. In 1212 Llywelyn the Great (1194–1240), describing himself as prince of North Wales and as writing with the assent of all the princes of Wales, made an alliance with Philip Augustus of France to fight their common enemy the English and free the land 'from the yoke of their tyranny'.[15] But Llywelyn's position was not as secure as that of the king of Scots. He was not a king and feudal overlord but a prince in the sense of principal ruler. Nor was Llywelyn prince of the whole of Wales and, even if he had been, he had still to contend with the descendants of the Norman marcher lords who formed a buffer between England proper and Wales. Nevertheless in Wales as in Scotland the thirteenth-century kings of England had to contend with the new force of a sense of national identity (Welshness or Scottishness) being combined with territorial lordship and organisation. Llywelyn the Last took the opportunity offered by the baronial wars to establish himself as 'prince of Wales' and to be recognised as such by Henry III in 1267.

The land of the English, 'England' as distinct from the whole island, was thus defined by its apartness from Scottish or Welsh land. At the same time this sense of apartness fed prejudice between the nations. For example Richard of Devizes puts a racy description of the characteristics of different English towns into the mouth of a French Jew: Worcester, Chester and Hereford are to be avoided 'because of the Welsh who are prodigal of life', while York 'abounds with Scots who are filthy and faithless sub-humans'.[16] Richard's facetious description (composed in the 1190s) has the merit of giving a bird's-eye view of England and its principal towns. From the middle of the thirteenth century there survives a list of more than a hundred centres of population along with a particular characteristic of each, such as 'school of Oxford', 'plains of Salisbury', 'shipping of Southampton' and 'cod of Grimsby'.[17] A more ambitious depiction of England, in the form of a map, appears in four of Matthew Paris's manuscripts made in the 1250s. This map contains more than 250 geographical names and includes the whole island with north at the top and Scotland and Wales described by those names (*Scocia* and *Wallia*). Although this map is crude by modern standards, its cartographer (who was probably Matthew himself) is well aware of the importance of scale and of directional relationships between one place and another. The achievement of mapping England is itself an indication of how the country was beginning to be conceived in territorial terms on the ground instead of in abstract terms, though it must be emphasised that very few thirteenth-century Englishmen would have understood what a map was.

Unlike Scotland and Wales, England did not have to create a new national identity bounded by the authority of its ruler but to restore that idea from the Anglo-Saxon past. The Norman conquerors had to be absorbed and to identify with England instead of France. Generally speaking by the end of the twelfth century the Normans had been absorbed by intermarriage. This is specifically stated in the *Dialogue of the Exchequer* and it is also indicated by the way charters are no longer addressed to both French and English but simply to all faithful persons. Some residual Norman pride remained however; for example at the battle of Lincoln in 1217 the Normans on Henry III's side claimed their traditional right to strike the first blow but they had to concede this to the earl of Chester when he threatened to withdraw altogether unless he commanded the front line. Although a variety of people fought on both sides in 1217, Louis's defeat was seen in retrospect as a victory for England over France: 'Thus the Lord struck his enemies who had come to destroy the English people,' the chronicler Ralph of Coggeshall commented.[18] This nationalist attitude is explicit even in an official document from 1217, which looks forward to the 'English' (*Anglici*) recovering their lands in Normandy.[19]

This form of national cohesion brought with it both advantages and risks. An advantage was that the ruler's authority to enforce law and order within his realm was strengthened. But there was the risk that massive conflict with other rulers was more likely. Under the feudal convention lords with lands in England and Normandy could go back and forth between them and do their best as individuals to keep the peace. But once Norman lands were thought of as English the risk of war between 'England' and 'France' increased. The polarisation of loyalty between England and France also put the English kings in a difficult position because they were the inheritors of lordships on both sides of the Channel. In maintaining his inheritance Henry III inevitably isolated himself from English opinion because he identified with all his lands.

The use of the English language

The point where English national identity seemed weakest was in the way the English language had lost status since the Norman Conquest. A nation does not need to use only one language (for example both English and Gaelic were used in Scotland), nor does the predominant language need to be exclusive to the nation (various modern nations use English or Spanish). Nevertheless one exclusive language is a powerful maker of unity and this is what England had possessed before 1066. Old English was the standard language of government, overcoming differences of English dialect as well as Scandinavian languages. In place of this the Norman conquerors had imposed the standard language of western Europe, Latin. This meant that Latin composition in England improved and that English scholars and clerics could participate in the revival of learning associated with the Twelfth-century Renaissance.

The Normans' effect on the English language is more complex. Old English lost status once it ceased to be the language of government, and by the middle of the twelfth century texts were being written in a variety of English dialects because a common standard was no longer being imposed (see pages 35–6 above). By 1200 original works were being composed in Middle English of which the best known are *The Owl and the Nightingale* (a debate poem; see pages 120–1 above), Layamon's *Brut* (Arthurian history) and the *Ancrene Riwle* (spiritual guidance for ladies). Although such works owed a great deal to Latin and French models, they absorbed these new styles into English idiom and thus re-created English as a literary language. English was also capable once more of expressing in written form the requirements of administration, as the letters in English sent by the baronial government to all counties in 1258 demonstrate. Nevertheless this experiment was an exception, proving the rule that until the fourteenth century English was a language of low status.

Why did English continue to have a low status despite its literary revival by 1200? The chief reason is that all vernacular languages had a low status compared with Latin. Latin had reached a peak of originality and prestige in the twelfth century with its use by great preachers and polemicists like St Bernard, scholastic masters like Abelard, and the innovative poets of the *Carmina Burana*. In addition Latin had shown itself to be an excellent medium for more mundane legal and business documents. Magna Carta was expressed in Latin because it was easiest to achieve precision and economy in that language. English nationalists, like the anonymous authors of the poem on the battle of Lincoln in 1217 and the lament for England in 1265, used Latin as their medium because of its power as the language of rhetoric for more than a thousand years. Furthermore these authors wished to give dignity and permanence to their work and therefore chose Latin. Writers of English were daring eccentrics whereas Latin was the language of the *litterati*, of all those educated in the classics of pagan and Christian Rome. With or without the Norman Conquest it is probable that Latin would have superseded Old English as the language of record in the twelfth century because of the influence of the schools and the Church.

The English language also had to compete with French and, as with Latin, it is probable that French literary language would have been introduced into England whether or not there had been a Norman conquest. The fact that the conquerors of England spoke various forms of French obviously helped to promote it, but the Norman Conquest cannot explain why French begins to be used in England as a language of literature and government from the middle of the thirteenth century onwards, as this occurs two centuries after 1066. Like the growth of Latin in the twelfth century, the flourishing of French in the thirteenth was a European phenomenon and was connected with the dominance of French culture. English knights, like their German or Spanish counterparts, learned French because it was in a special way their language, as it was the language of chivalrous romance. Chrétien de Troyes and other writers in French challenged the cultural dominance of classical Greece and Rome and claimed that France was now the centre of Europe and the arbiter of taste. Furthermore Philip Augustus and St Louis, with Notre Dame de Paris and the Sainte Chapelle, existed to prove it. In addition to the dominance of Parisian France, Henry III and his court of Poitevins, Savoyards and Provençals kept alive the Occitan culture of the south. The cosmopolitan royal court was therefore another force discouraging English, as patronage was extended by Henry to native artists and craftsmen but not to writers.

The English language therefore existed close to the ground under the huge shadows of Latin, both classical and modern, and of French, both *langue d'oc* (south of the Loire) and *langue d'oil* (north). In social terms English was the language of the *nativi*, the serfs bound to the soil. By 1200 it was the mother tongue of nearly everyone except the royal family because the nobility and gentry were brought up by local wet-nurses. Men of ambition were educated in Latin and French by tutors because these were the languages of lordship. Latin led to a career in the Church and French to advancement at court or in a noble household. English was therefore the most common language in every sense of that word: it was the most frequently used (in speech though not in writing) and it was associated with the common people. This ambivalent position of English, being deeply rooted and yet overshadowed, explains why it could flourish so suddenly in the time of Chaucer and Langland when the impediments to its growth had been removed. By the fourteenth century both Latin and French had waned as universal languages of European education and vernaculars could therefore develop.

English as a literary language thus did not contribute to a sense of nationhood among educated people until the fourteenth century. The fiercest nationalists of Henry III's reign, most notably Matthew Paris, wrote in Latin or French. Nevertheless the ordinariness of English speech must have given it a spontaneity which the learned languages of Latin and French lacked and ultimately this brought English out on top. Legal records in Latin and French begin to have pieces of English embedded in them when the clerk is unwilling or unable to abandon his native idiom. An early example of this practice comes from the king's court in 1241 when Henry III's counsellors were so exasperated by his claim for damages of 10,000 marks against Gilbert the Marshal that it is described in the plea roll as *illud nameles fremeles*: something 'nameless' (in the sense of unspecific) and 'pointless'.[20] The English language, like the sense of Englishness, lay just below the surface and it bursts out from time to time when the alien ways of the king and his court become hard to bear. The scarcity of writing in English in this period is misleading, since the language was not declining but growing as it gradually absorbed the literary and scholastic vocabulary of French and Latin and developed through everyday speech into the mother tongue of knights and clergy as well as peasants.

From lordship to nation state

A sense of national consciousness and an awareness of the characteristics of the different nations were not developments confined to England, Scotland and Wales as they occur throughout Europe. For example, when Frederick II wrote in 1241 to the rulers of Europe warning them of the threat of the Mongols, he picked out the qualities of the different powers: Germany 'fervent in arms'; France 'the mother and nurse of chivalry'; Spain 'warlike and bold'; England 'fertile and protected by its fleet'.[21] The lands on the edge of the ocean (that is, at the extremity of the known world) are also distinguished, namely 'bloodstained Ireland, active Wales, watery Scotland and glacial Norway'. The countries named here and the qualities attributed to them have quite a modern ring. Nevertheless they did not exist as sovereign states: Germany was an assortment of principalities; the boundaries of France were undefined; Spain consisted of a variety of kingdoms held together by alliances; England was only beginning to be distinguished in the mind of the king from his overseas lands.

Although medieval nations cannot be equated in terms of political power with the sovereign states of modern Europe, national identity was already in the thirteenth century an important element in a ruler's authority over his own subjects and in the assertion of power over his neighbours. The problem each ruler faced was how to convert his inherited properties and titles into a territorial unit or state. The development of England is a microcosm of Europe in this respect. Henry III had an impressive list of titles as he was king of England, lord of Ireland, duke of Normandy and Aquitaine and count of Anjou. But these titles did not accord with his power. They claimed both too much and too little: too much because Normandy and Anjou had been lost since John's reign; too little because no mention was made of the English claim to overlordship in Wales and Scotland. Henry had either to make these titles into territorial realities or abandon them.

A king could no longer be merely a symbolic overlord, the man on horseback with a conspicuous retinue of nobles and priests who made an appearance from time to time to collect tribute and hear grievances. Instead a king had to have permanent officials on the spot watching over his interests from day to day. To be lord of the land a king had now to act like a landlord. In Normandy Louis IX was now the ruler on the ground and Henry III was duke merely in name. Furthermore Louis gradually used the force of French common feeling and fear of the English to make Normandy part of his territory.

Conversely within what had once been called the 'island of the English' Henry asserted his rights on the ground *vis-à-vis* the Welsh and the Scots. Thus in the 1240s and 1250s he asserted royal authority over the lords of the Welsh march and also over individual Welsh princes. This was a piecemeal process—typical of how territorial units were painstakingly built up over time—of claiming authority in individual disputes as they arose. Gradually the two sides polarised so that the issue became one of English or Welsh dominance, rather than the exercise of royal or feudal authority as such. A similar policy of definition village by village was pursued on the Anglo-Scottish frontier and in the parts of Northumberland and Cumberland which had been granted to the king of Scots in 1237. Scottish lords were not deprived of their lands in England in the way the Normans were because the king of Scots did homage to the king of England. Nevertheless the idea, which was foreign to traditional international feudalism, that a man could owe loyalty to the ruler of one country only was slowly gaining ground. The sons of William the Marshal or the sons of Simon de Montfort (the elder), who inherited lands on each side of the Channel, had to decide whether they were Englishmen or Frenchmen and they found that difficult. For men at the top the demands of nationalism caused a crisis of personal identity.

In a feudal system it had been normal for various individuals at different levels of the hierarchy to have rights over the same land whereas in a territorial state that could not be tolerated. Each ruler therefore tried to make his inheritance into a uniform territory and in doing so inevitably came into conflict with other rulers who had claims in the same territory. Henry III, for instance, could not avoid disputes on the marches of Wales and with the king of Scots because although some boundaries were regulated by treaty they depended in reality on the variable force at each ruler's command. Furthermore each ruler increased that force by appealing beyond his traditional feudal tenants or kinsmen to his men as a whole.

Taxation for purposes of national defence became increasingly common. Unlike feudal taxes these new ones were levied not on knight's fees but on the movable goods of all subjects. Not only vassals, therefore, but every category and rank of society contributed, and in theory consented, to the tax. For example the writs collecting the aid granted to Henry III in 1232 specify that it is granted by the 'archbishops, bishops, abbots, priors and clerics, earls, barons, knights, freemen and serfs of our kingdom'.[22] Although for the great majority, the serfs and poorer freemen, consent meant no more than tacit assent (they did not actively resist when their goods were taken), a tax of this sort overrode the traditional divisions of cleric and layman and lord and vassal and united everyone in adversity. Furthermore, because such taxes were in theory voluntary gifts to the king for specific purposes, matters of royal policy such as Henry III's 'Sicilian business' became the subject of common discussion. More than anything else, perhaps, taxation shaped a forceful public opinion, articulated at every level of society through institutions which had originally been formed to levy the money. Thus a 'national interest', first at the level of barons and higher clergy, then of knights (in the civil war of the 1260s) and ultimately of peasants (in the revolt of 1381), began to emerge in England.

The most powerful rulers of Europe were ambivalent in their attitude towards this concentration of lordship on particular territories and the identification of rulers with specific local groups or nations. The two greatest rulers by tradition, the pope and the emperor, had titles and aspirations which were too large to confine within a single territory and furthermore they both centred on the same territory, Rome and Italy. Nevertheless they could not avoid competing for territory and using the current methods of tax-raising and constant attention to detail in order to consolidate claims of all sorts. Similarly Louis IX was torn between his determination to uphold the international tradition of the crusade and the need to assert himself as king of France with territorial disputes to settle with the kings of England and Aragon. Henry III too, with his claims to half of France, considered himself to belong to this top league of rulers who stood above local prejudices because of the richness of their inheritances. All such heterogeneous rulers came into conflict with their local subjects when they demanded taxes to pursue ambitions which extended beyond the territory concerned. Henry in particular found himself in difficulties because he was so persistent in giving preference to his overseas inheritance and ambitions rather than to England itself. The strength of the reaction against him is the best evidence that the days of symbolic lordship and chance inheritance were waning and that the nation state, formed out of ancient feelings of common kinship and identity reinforced by concentration on territorial units, had taken shape.

The expulsion of the Poitevins

The strength of national feeling among makers of opinion in England is demonstrated by the terms in which monastic chroniclers, up and down the country and not just at St Albans, reported the rebellion of 1258 and the expulsion of Henry III's Poitevin half-brothers. Writing after the war, the chronicler of St Benet of Hulme in Norfolk attributed the troubles solely to the hatred felt for the Lusignan brothers, 'for true-born men [*naturales homines*] were like the disinherited and the magnates of England grieved very much because no Englishman could get his right or obtain a writ against them'.[23] This chronicler is in fact repeating allegations which were frequently made against the Lusignans in 1258. Thus the Waverley Abbey chronicler states that there were so many foreigners of diverse languages in England and they had been so enriched by gifts from the king that they despised the English as inferior beings. This chronicler goes so far as to allege that the foreigners intended to poison the nobility and depose the king and thus bring the whole of England under their sway. He, like other chroniclers, names the Lusignan brothers in particular and reports how they broke the law. 'But at last', the Waverley chronicler concluded, 'the earls and barons, archbishops and bishops, and the rest of the magnates of England, as if miraculously awoken from sleep', united together and expelled the foreigners from England.[24]

Such accounts, like most chronicle reporting, are simplified and exaggerated. The Waverley chronicler borrowed the passage about foreigners of diverse languages from his predecessor who had written of the rebellion against King John in 1215. Foreigners in England in 1258 could not have numbered more than a few hundred and they were not of very diverse languages, as most of them were Poitevins and Provençals speaking Occitan. Nevertheless there is no doubt that Henry III did enrich his four half-brothers when they arrived in 1247. In particular William de Valence, who was made lord of Pembroke, and Aymer, who became bishop of Winchester, were prominent in the king's counsels and received numerous gifts (as the public records testify). It is possible too that they took the law into their own hands, though that cannot be proved as the legal records document only the king's side. Even at their maximum extent, however, the activities of the Lusignan brothers cannot have caused all the havoc which contemporaries attributed to them.

Nevertheless the exaggeration of the chroniclers underlines the importance of national feeling in Henry III's England. In reality the Poitevins were not necessarily above the law, nor did they have the king in their power, and it is unlikely that they conspired to kill the native nobility. Nevertheless these rumours were circulated and constructed by contemporary chroniclers into a recognisably consistent image of a long-suffering England waking miraculously from its sleep. The force of nationalism has always been associated with feeling rather than fact, with prejudice fed by fear and with a sense of identity sharpened by comparison with a minority of aliens. The rebel barons of 1258 expressed to the pope the force of their feeling in a statement of priorities which they claimed Henry III had ignored: 'a prince owes all his duty to God, very much to his country [*patria*], much to his family and neighbours, and nothing whatsoever to aliens'.[25] For better or worse patriotism had become a force in politics.

❧ XI ❧

THE COMMUNE OF ENGLAND

(1258–72)

Henry III's flamboyant regime crashed in 1258 with a suddenness which only the wisdom of hindsight has made look inevitable. For more than twenty years he had withstood criticism and ignored proposals for change. Now that the opportune moment had come (as well as the demands of the pope, record grain prices and famine for the second year in succession caused by harvest failures contributed to unrest), his opponents were well prepared and they proposed a radical constitution in which the king was to be controlled by committees answerable to the community. Although Henry was obliged to swear to these proposals in 1258, he had outmanoeuvred the barons by 1261 and obtained papal absolution from his oath. Furthermore his more determined opponents led by Simon de Montfort were isolated in 1264 by Henry's greatest diplomatic triumph, the Mise of Amiens, whereby Louis IX (whom both sides had accepted as arbiter) came down uncompromisingly in favour of the king.

Henry had brought the weight of European opinion, expressed by the pope and Louis IX, against his opponents in the same way as he and Peter des Roches had discredited Hubert de Burgh in 1232. Instead of running for sanctuary like Hubert, Simon de Montfort decided to stand up and fight and took the king prisoner at the battle of Lewes in 1264. But Simon could not benefit from his victory because the king remained the rightful ruler and retained the loyalty of his family and supporters. In 1265 Simon was defeated and killed by the Lord Edward (the future Edward I) at the battle of Evesham. In the bitter fighting which followed, the king's opponents were hunted down and killed until terms of surrender were published by the king in the Dictum of Kenilworth of 1266. Henry and Edward had won the most total victory in England's history since the Norman Conquest, so total that Edward succeeded as king on his father's death in 1272 although he was away on crusade until 1274.

The confederates of 1258

Henry III was temporarily brought down in 1258 by a confederation of seven magnates. They took a mutual oath in April to stand by each other against all men, saving their fealty to the king and the crown of England.

The document recording this oath, which is preserved only in a copy in the de Montfort archives in France, is careful to avoid the charge of treason and therefore excepts the king and crown from its implications. Nor does the document specify what the confederates propose to do; it simply gives each of them an assurance of the others' loyalty come what may. It was the brief but comprehensive terms of this oath which formed the revolutionary commune of England, as the same formula was sworn to at Oxford in June by everybody present. Those who refused to take the oath and join in the commune, like the Lusignan brothers, fled and were harried out of the kingdom as mortal enemies. This was likewise the oath which Simon de Montfort insisted on upholding for the next seven years, even after it had been declared invalid by the pope and Louis IX. To Simon the backsliders, including Henry III, were traitors.

The seven original confederates formed a powerful and experienced group familiar with European politics. Richard de Clare earl of Gloucester had been on pilgrimages to Pontigny and Santiago and on diplomatic missions to the pope at Lyons, to Alfonso X at Burgos, and to Scotland and Germany; he had also fought in Gascony and frequently on the marches of Wales. John Fitz Geoffrey was a marcher lord like Richard and the son of King John's justiciar, Geoffrey Fitz Peter. Roger Bigod earl of Norfolk had fought in Poitou and Gascony and had headed the English delegation to the council of Lyons in 1245, which aimed to end England's feudal subjection to the papacy. Hugh Bigod, Roger's brother, had taken part in negotiations with France and was chosen as justiciar in 1258. Peter of Savoy, 'little Charlemagne', was the queen's uncle whom he had made lord of Richmond; he was the first of the seven to change sides thereafter. Peter de Montfort (no relation of Simon) had fought in Poitou and Gascony and been on pilgrimages and diplomatic missions to Santiago, Burgos and France; he was keeper of the Welsh march. These six men therefore combined political experience with military power, which was concentrated on the Welsh marches within easy reach of the midlands and south of England.

The seventh man was Simon de Montfort, whom the king with characteristic sharpness identified as his chief opponent: 'I fear thunder and lightning terribly, but by God's head I dread you more than all the thunder and lightning in the world.'[1] These words are reported by Matthew Paris, who had also reported in 1252 that Henry had taunted Simon after complaints about his governorship in Gascony: 'Go back to Gascony, you lover and maker of strife, you will find trouble enough there and reap its fitting reward just as your father did.'[2] Henry was referring here to the ambivalent reputation of Simon de Montfort the elder, who from 1208 until he was killed at Toulouse in 1218 had led the Albigensian crusade, killing and despoiling heretics and innocent alike in southern France. The younger Simon's governorship in Gascony revived his father's arbitrary rule in the opinion of his opponents.

Both the elder and the younger Simon were titular earls of Leicester and both too were chosen as revolutionary rulers of England. The elder Simon had been deprived of his English lands by King John because he remained loyal to Philip Augustus. But his prestige as a crusader was so great that he was rumoured to have been elected king of England by a group of rebel barons at Nottingham in 1210. Whether he or the younger Simon were ever informed of this is unknown. The younger Simon has sometimes been compared with the Poitevins and Savoyards whom Henry favoured, as he (like them) settled in England in the 1230s and he made a profitable marriage in 1238 to Eleanor, the king's sister. Nevertheless Simon felt himself to be in a different class, because he was not a Poitevin but a Frenchman who had come, like Richard the Marshal, to claim his rightful inheritance. Like Richard too, he claimed a hereditary office with wide powers, that of Steward of England, as well as the earldom of Leicester. Simon's coming to England was a family arrangement (again comparable with the Marshal family), whereby his elder brother Amaury took up the French and Norman inheritance and Simon went to England. Although Simon adopted England as his country and in the opinion of his partisans died a martyr for it, he consistently despised the English if the comments of chroniclers are correct.

Because of his father, Simon was unusual among the magnates in being associated with the evangelical Christian movement of his time. As a young knight he had been honoured by being depicted in stained glass in Chartres Cathedral, and when he came to England he associated with Robert Grosseteste and with the Franciscan friar Adam Marsh. Simon saw to it that his sons like himself were educated in Latin and in the scriptures. When he was killed at Evesham, he was found to be wearing a hair shirt like the most ascetic clergy. One myth which should be dispelled, however, is that Grosseteste inspired Simon's political ideas, as distinct from his religious ones. Grosseteste's treatise on royal power, which Adam Marsh may have shown to Simon, concerned ecclesiastical power and not secular.

Although Simon's political ideas were conventional—he was a French aristocrat who assumed the king to be his peer—his determination to keep his oath at all costs must have been motivated by deep conviction. As the *Song of Lewes* put it, 'Simon's wholly singular religion' was the corner-stone of the baronial movement; on his faith depended the security and peace of the whole of England.[3] Already in 1258 Simon had the reputation of being a strong man: a trouble-making and proud fanatic in the opinion of his enemies, a passionate upholder of Christian knighthood in the opinion of his friends. Unlike that earlier model of chivalry, William the Marshal, everything that Simon did went wrong: the king hated him although he had married his sister; he was a divisive governor of Gascony; after 1258 he waited to fight until it was too late; he got no advantage from his victory at Lewes in 1264, as the Lord Edward subsequently escaped and caught him unawares at Evesham. But, unlike the Marshal, Simon was never forgotten because he was England's tragic hero. His story was told in ballads long after his death and the Victorians believed him to be the founder of the House of Commons.

The idea of the commune

The original confederation of seven magnates was expanded by progressive stages into the commune of England. The seven had recorded their oath on 12 April 1258. By 30 April other barons and knights had joined them and on that day they confronted the king in Westminster Hall. They had come armed, although those who entered the hall left their swords at the door. According to an eyewitness the king said: 'What is this, am I your prisoner?'[4] Henry was perhaps suddenly reminded of the days of his minority when he was the ward of the barons. Roger Bigod reassured him that no harm was meant but that he must dismiss the 'intolerable Poitevins'. Bigod added that he and his companions wished to confess their 'secret' to the king: Henry and the Lord Edward must take an oath on the gospels to abide by their rulings. Having no choice, Henry and Edward took the oath and they too therefore became members of the commune. On 2 May the king published letters announcing that he had sworn that the state of the realm would be reformed and that a meeting would be held at Oxford on 9 June for this purpose. At Oxford the delegates again came armed and more oaths were sworn in the name of *le commun de Engleterre*.

A commune was an association bound together by a common oath of loyalty; whereas a vassal swore an oath of homage to his lord alone, the members of a commune swore to serve each other for their mutual benefit. Communes had come to prominence in the twelfth century as revolutionary associations, particularly in cities, opposed to aristocratic and ecclesiastical power. Thus Richard of Devizes describes the formation in

1191 of the commune of London 'into which all the magnates and even the bishops were compelled to swear'; hence it was a conspiracy (*conjuratio*).⁵ Richard then gives a definition of a commune which emphasises its revolutionary associations: 'a commune is a tumult of the people, a terror of the realm, a torpor of the clergy'. By 1258 the communal idea had become more familiar. For example John's government had used it to organise the defence of England after the loss of Normandy. In 1205 a commune was formed throughout the whole realm, to which all men over the age of twelve swore loyalty. This commune like that of 1258 was founded to defend the kingdom against aliens. The communal idea also appears in Magna Carta, where 'the commune of the whole land' is entitled to distrain the king (clause 61).

These precedents show how the conspiratorial nature of a commune as a sworn association could be directed to a public and indeed a national purpose. The king's government increasingly depended on sworn groups of representatives at every level of society, from local jurors speaking for the conduct of each village up to communes defending the realm. In Maitland's words, 'men are drilled and regimented into communities in order that the state may be strong and the land may be at peace'.⁶ Although the term 'commune of England' is not used before 1258, the idea of uniting everyone by a common oath was therefore familiar. Nevertheless the communal idea still retained revolutionary potential in its historical association with popular rebellion and in its mechanism. Whereas Henry III claimed power from above by divine right, the 'commune of England' derived its authority from the mutual oath taken by its members; it assumed that people were entitled to form associations and to use their combined force even to overawe the king. The commune stood for everybody. In French it was described as the *commun*, in Latin as the *communitas*, and in the English-language letters of 1258 it was rendered as the *loandes folk* ('the people of the land'), as English lacked a precise equivalent for 'commune'.⁷ To counter the king's divine authority the commune pointed to the sanction of the oath taken on the gospels by all its members. Both Henry III and Simon de Montfort understood the fundamental importance of this oath. That is why Henry devoted his diplomatic skills to getting it invalidated while Simon insisted that nothing could alter it.

Simon may also have had another precedent in mind when he took his oath in 1258. In 1241 the baronial commune of the crusader kingdom of Jerusalem, which had rebelled against Frederick II ten years earlier, requested Frederick to approve the appointment of Simon de Montfort as guardian of the kingdom. This request does not necessarily imply that

Simon was a partisan of this commune, as his name may have been put forward as a compromise candidate acceptable both to Frederick and the barons. Nevertheless the request does suggest that Simon, who had gone out to Palestine in 1239, was familiar with the issues involved. The historian of the crusader kingdom, Joshua Prawer, points out that the similarities between the communal oath made at Acre in 1231 and that made at Oxford in 1258 are so close that 'one is almost tempted to look for straightforward links between the two events.'[8] Such links are possible, as Simon de Montfort was not the only English baron in 1258 to have been on crusade, and Jerusalem was an attractive precedent since it was the holy land, which (like England) had been conquered by its barons. They claimed, like the descendants of Normans, that the Conquest had been a co-operative enterprise and that the power of the elected king was therefore limited. Two political philosophies, both with deep medieval roots, were therefore in conflict in 1258. On one side stood sacred authoritarian monarchy, championed by Henry III, and on the other communal custom and baronial rights, championed by Simon de Montfort.

The Provisions of Oxford

The rebellion of 1258 was more far-reaching in its proposals than that against John in 1215. Magna Carta had been intended to remedy specific grievances and to establish fundamental principles of legal practice for the future, but it had not provided an effective mechanism for ensuring that justice was administered in accordance with its principles. In the light of this failure the rebels of 1258 drew up a new list of shortcomings in the law (the Petition of the Barons) as well as appointing Hugh Bigod as justiciar to hear complaints against sheriffs and other royal officers in each county. Out of all this activity came the Provisions of Westminster of 1259, which reformed legal procedure on numerous detailed points in a non-partisan way.

Where the rebellion of 1258 differed fundamentally from that of 1215 was in the so-called 'Provisions of Oxford', the reorganisation of the system of government undertaken by the commune at its meeting at Oxford in June 1258. Despite its importance, the details of this reorganisation exist only in an informal memorandum copied into the chronicle of Burton Abbey. The lack of an official record has never been satisfactorily explained. It may be that, as with John's attitude to Magna Carta, Henry III had it excised from the record. Alternatively it is possible that an official statute never was made because Henry soon grew powerful enough to avoid ratifying it. Certainly the details took a long time to settle,

PLATE VII. An illumination of Henry III from the *Chronicle of St Albans*, written about a hundred years after Henry's death. The king is depicted as a venerable old man because he was one of the abbey's benefactors

as the king (prompted by the rebels) wrote to the pope on 12 August 1258 telling him that the barons were working hard on the reform of the kingdom: 'When we have their ordinance, one most fruitful to us and to our heirs, we beg your serenity with all the affection we can to find it not unworthily pleasing and acceptable.'[9] The pope's formal reply came two and a half years later in 1261 when all the ordinances, which 'under the pretext of reforming the state of the realm' had been made by 'some sort of tumult of the magnates', were condemned.[10] But that is to look ahead to Henry's diplomatic victory, whereas in the summer of 1258 he had no option except to go along with the rebels.

The memorandum preserved by the Burton chronicler is of critical importance despite being informal and rather muddled. Under the rubric 'A provision made at Oxford', it gives the Latin text of the arrangements for the justiciar to hear complaints.[11] This is followed by the names of the twenty-four: twelve men from the king's side and twelve from the barons' who are responsible for reform. The king's group actually includes only eleven names, most of whom are his relatives or members of his household, which emphasises how isolated he had become. The barons' group on the other hand includes six of the seven original confederates (Peter of Savoy has dropped out) together with other magnates. The idea of two groups of twelve may have derived from juries or from town councils. After the names of the twenty-four come texts of oaths in French: the oaths of the commune of England, of the twenty-four, and of the justiciar, chancellor and castellans. As already explained, these solemn oaths of loyalty were the ideological basis of the commune. The names of the new council of fifteen persons follows; this was chosen by electors nominated by the opposing group and then confirmed by majority assent. Such an elaborate system of delegation and election would have been familiar to the barons from arbitrations in legal disputes as well as from the constitutional arrangements of city-states in Mediterranean Europe. Indeed the barons intended England to be governed henceforward rather like a city-state with an elected council, officials answerable to the commune, and regular public meetings. 'It is said that the best ordered state [*civitas*]', the barons wrote in their defence (recalling Plato's republic), 'is one in which each person puts aside his own interests and this is proved most conspicuously today in the reformation and ordering of our kingdom.'[12]

The latter half of the Provisions of Oxford consists of a list of proposed reforms starting with the Church, going on to the control of public officials (justiciar, treasurer and chancellor are to be appointed for a year at a time) and concluding with arrangements for parliaments and the powers of the council of fifteen. This is one of the earliest references to 'parliament' by that name (*parlemenz* in French); what it meant is 'discussion'. Parliament is to be held with automatic regularity at Michaelmas, Candlemas and midsummer each year. It is not intended to be a large body, as it consists of the council of fifteen together with twelve reliable men elected by the commune. This provision narrowed down the number of representatives who had customarily agreed to taxation. Nevertheless this may not have been intended as an aristocratic measure excluding the commons who might support the king, but as a practical method of limiting regular parliaments to those who were willing and able to attend.

Taken together, the Provisions of Oxford reduced the authority of the king of England to that of a figurehead, directed by the council which was answerable to the commune. Although such a change was comparable with the way royal power had been reduced in the kingdom of Jerusalem and by the princes and city-states in the Empire, no other kingdom in Europe had gone so far towards a republican constitution. Furthermore the commune in some form was intended to be a permanent part of the constitution. Henry III's incompetence had been the occasion of putting the king in the rebels' power, but the barons of 1258 did not claim (as those against King John had done) that once their grievances were settled the king's power should be restored. On the contrary, in a letter to the pope in August 1258 the ordinance of the barons is described as 'most fruitful to us *and to our heirs*', and in the case put to Louis IX in 1264 the barons explain that castles were to be held by their nominees for a period of twelve years so that their provisions and ordinances 'could pass into law'.[13] The rebels had a well thought out and long-term plan. They proposed such far-reaching changes because they knew that nothing less would prove adequate. An elected justiciar and chancellor had been demanded without effect for twenty years or more. The king had decades of experience of escaping attempts to control his actions, and one or two of the barons could probably remember how King John had repudiated Magna Carta. The Provisions of Oxford were so elaborately devised in order that not even Henry III could slip out of them. He was to be tied down by the council of fifteen, by the public officials at the centre and in the localities, and by the automatic meetings of parliament.

Henry III's recovery

The councillors, Henry complained, 'strive day in and day out to limit and diminish the king's status against his will, although no advantage comes to anyone from this'.[14] He considered it his duty to release himself from these constraints and he vigorously argued his case. Like any head of a medieval family, Henry was obliged to hand on as much of his inheritance as he could to his children. The outlook was bleak in 1258 but, as at the time of the minority, the king had long-term advantages. The force of inertia would favour his servants and established routines. He could expect the backing of the pope because of the 'Sicilian business'. Most importantly Henry was successful in winning the support of Louis IX. Whereas at the time of the minority the French had intervened on the side of the rebels, Henry succeeded—at the heavy price of surrendering his claims in France north of the Loire and in Poitou (the peace of Paris of 1259)—not only in avoiding a French invasion but ultimately in getting Louis to condemn the rebels. By making concessions in France Henry restored his position in England and thus moved one step further towards the formation of a national monarchy, although that had not been his intention.

Henry broke the rebels' unity in the first instance by absenting himself from England. He was in France from November 1259 to April 1260. The communal government could function to a certain extent in his absence, but the idea of controlling the king himself through the council of fifteen foundered. Henry's tactics are best illustrated by a letter he sent the baronial justiciar, Hugh Bigod, in January 1260. The king explained that he had hoped to return to England immediately after Christmas but Louis was pressing him to stay on because of both a marriage and a funeral. Furthermore delicate negotiations were still in progress about Henry's overseas possessions. In addition to these reasons, Henry used the threat of a Welsh invasion to tell Bigod not to waste time with a parliament but to proceed immediately against the Welsh. The point about parliament is then repeated:

> Make no arrangements for a parliament and permit none to be held before our arrival in England. When we return, we shall arrange to hold a parliament with your advice and that of the magnates, as will seem best for us and for our realm.[15]

Henry concludes by telling Bigod that he is proceeding 'by easy stages' from Paris and that he will await a reply on the French coast.

In this letter Henry seems to have been testing the resolve of his opponents. Parliament was due to assemble on 2 February in accordance with the provision that it should be held regularly at Candlemas. Henry's excuse for postponing it (his absence in France and the threat from the

Welsh) could equally well be seen as compelling reasons for holding it. The commune had been formed so that the magnates could look after themselves in such emergencies. Moreover the phrase 'as will seem best for us and for our realm' might be interpreted to mean that Henry should be the judge of when parliaments were to be held. Meanwhile he waited in France to see how Bigod would react. Bigod's submission is best described in the reported words of Simon de Montfort:

> In the common provision made by the king and his council it is provided that three parliaments shall be held every year, of which one is at Candlemas, and so the earl [Simon de Montfort]—to keep his oath—came there, along with the honourable men of the council who were in England, and there in the morning the justiciar came and told them from the king that they should hold no parliament until the king came.[16]

This statement emphasises the clarity of Simon's position: he intended to stand by his oath whatever the circumstances. He appreciated the political consequences of compromise. Regular parliaments were an essential part of the communal constitution. If the least concession were made to the king, he would take advantage of it. Henry was (as Matthew Paris had noted in 1258) like Proteus, the classical Houdini, who needed only one loose knot to escape. Bigod on the other hand had presumably been impressed by Henry's sense of authority and by the apparent reasonableness of his requests. Henry's tactics had succeeded in destroying the unity of the barons.

By slow and painful stages from February 1260 onwards Henry recovered his authority. In doing so he divided his kingdom into partisans of monarchy and opponents until, as a consquence of Louis IX's Mise of Amiens in 1264, open war was declared. Henry concentrated on winning over international opinion, which was a task that suited him. His first public triumph came in 1261 when, through the diplomacy of John Mansel, Pope Alexander IV absolved the king from his oath to the commune. The pope alleged that the oath had been made under pressure and furthermore a religious oath should not be used to uphold 'depravity and perfidy'.[17] He argued, in other words, that the commune as such was an act of treason: a celestial ordinance placed princes, who are lords of laws, above others and they should not be repressed by their subjects. Such statements from the pope were to be expected, both because of Henry's alliance with the papacy and because it was the most monarchical institution in Europe. Even so, this unequivocal invalidation of the communal oaths was of value to Henry as it justified his stand in international law. The hazard of any papal pronouncement, however, was that a new pope might declare its opposite with equal forthrightness on another occasion. This had happened with Magna Carta and, if one chronicler is to be believed, it now happened again. Alexander's successor, Urban IV, in 1262 allegedly ordered the Provisions of Oxford to be observed. But no such letter from Urban is extant, whereas Urban's bull supporting Henry can still be seen in the Public Record Office.

Monarchy versus community

Henry's greatest vindication was Louis IX's Mise of Amiens. Both sides, including Simon de Montfort, had sworn to accept Louis's arbitration and be bound by whatever he ordained. Before his court at Amiens the English monarchy was therefore put on trial. Evidence was given by groups and individuals on both sides and their summarised claims survive. Henry's case, which was presented by his chancellor Walter of Merton (the founder of Merton College, Oxford), concentrated on the way councillors and officials had been elected against the king's will; his subjects had betrayed their oath of fealty; the king asked for a fine from the barons of £300,000 and also claimed damages of 200,000 marks. The barons' case was presented by Thomas Cantilupe (venerated after his death as a saint), a canon lawyer and recent chancellor of Oxford university. It rehearsed the main points in the Provisions of Oxford and emphasised that the king had sworn to observe them; it therefore concluded that 'this provision and ordinance is holy and honest and is made for the king's honour and the common benefit of his kingdom'.[18]

Louis's judgement was uncompromising in its support of the king. It reads as if he had never listened to the barons' case, although he claimed to have fully understood the arguments and counter-arguments of each party. He blamed the rebels for everything which had gone wrong in England since 1258 and then declared all the barons' provisions invalid in the name of the Father and of the Son and of the Holy Spirit, as if he were a priest putting a curse on them. Furthermore he ordered that Henry should have 'complete power and free authority in his kingdom' and that everything should be restored to the state it was in before 1258.[19] The only concession made to the barons was that Louis did not uphold Henry's claims for a fine and damages; instead Henry was to give them a full pardon.

Louis had a reputation as a peacemaker but his judgement started a war. Even the royalist chronicler Wykes thought that Louis had acted with less wisdom and foresight than was necessary. Why did he support Henry so uncompromisingly? Answers can only be speculative, as Louis's reasons are not on record. The barons cannot have thought him to be such an absolute monarchist, otherwise they would not have agreed to the arbitration, although they were being pressed so hard by the royalists that their options were limited. A possible explanation for Louis's conduct is that he only learned the full implications of the barons' commune of England as a consequence of the hearing at Amiens. He might have got the impression from the numerous individual disputes leading up to the arbitration that he was being asked to settle wrangles of a familiar sort about property and offended honour. Not perhaps until the masters from Oxford appeared on the scene to argue the case for each side did Louis realise that monarchy itself was on trial and that Henry faced not a revolt but a revolution. At that point Louis took fright and added his total condemnation of insubordination to the pope's.

The Mise of Amiens had a paradoxical effect. It united the forces against the monarchy and brought about their victory at the battle of Lewes but it also deprived them of legitimacy. After his victory Simon de Montfort could no longer govern in accordance with the Provisions of Oxford because he had insufficient support. Instead a new constitution was devised consisting of three wise men (Simon de Montfort, Gilbert de Clare, Stephen bishop of Chichester) who nominated a council of nine. All this was done in the king's name, as he was Simon's prisoner; the new constitution was uncompromisingly monarchist and authoritarian. The demands of war had narrowed the 'commune of England' down to the 'community of prelates and barons' who might be consulted in certain circumstances.[20] Although the battle of Lewes brought about a narrow dictatorship in the king's name, it nevertheless briefly symbolised in wider estimation a triumph of the community over the monarchy. Or at least that is how it was interpreted in chronicles sympathetic to the barons and also in the *Song of Lewes*.

The song, a long and sophisticated Latin poem, expressed the feelings of Simon's partisans who are identified with the people of England. His steadfastness is contrasted with the duplicity of the Lord Edward who had supported the rebels for a while. The latter half of the song states the arguments for each side, as in a scholastic disputation, or as in the pleadings before Louis IX at Amiens. A significant point is the difficulty the author has in rebutting the royalist arguments which are stated concisely and fairly: the king wishes to be free and to appoint whomsoever he chooses; the command of the prince has the force of law and the barons of England are not to interfere; every freeman in the country has the right to manage his own affairs, why should the king be more servile than they? This question was difficult to answer because the rebel barons were not democrats; they had no intention of allowing all freemen—still less serfs—to elect the stewards of their estates and to manage them for the common good. Like the sorcerer's apprentice and many other rebels, Simon had released forces which he could not control. The commune of England, which he and his fellow magnates in 1258 had envisaged as an aristocratic body, had enlarged into something approaching a community of the people, or at least an association of the lesser knights and burgesses. The *Song of Lewes* voices these wider feelings:

> If one person chooses, he is easily mistaken, as he does not know who will be useful. Therefore the community of the realm [*communitas regni*] should advise and let it be known what everyone [*universitas*] feels, for their own laws are most familiar to them. Nor are all the people of a country such fools as not to know more than others about the customs of the realm which have been passed down from father to son.[21]

Simon's dilemma was that by the time he had triumphed at Lewes in 1264 partisan feelings had grown too fierce to build on this idealism. Despite his summoning of knights and burgesses to parliament, his government was as arbitrary as the king's, indeed it was the king's in name and form. The Wheel of Fortune had turned full circle and brought the king up to the top again.

The king and Westminster Abbey

The king and the cause of monarchy would have triumphed even if Simon had not been defeated and killed at Evesham in 1265 because the seven-year struggle had exhausted the moral and physical resources of the rebels. Henry had won by diplomacy and persistence. His triumph at Evesham was hideously celebrated by the dismembering of Simon's body. The head, arms and feet were cut off and he was castrated. The head was carried on a lance to Wigmore Castle (about fifty miles from Evesham) as a present for Roger de Mortimer's wife. The Mortimers had once been Simon's supporters; the reason for Maud de Mortimer's bitterness against Simon is unknown. One chronicler explains Simon's castration as fitting retribution for his marrying Eleanor, the king's sister, who had been vowed to chastity. The dishonourable treatment of Simon's body explains why Guy de Montfort, who survived the battle and made a new

career with Charles of Anjou in Italy, killed Henry of Almain (Richard of
Cornwall's heir) in revenge in 1271. Ironically it was Simon's son and not
Henry's whom the 'Sicilian business' brought south. Guy de Montfort
died as a prisoner of the Aragonese in Sicily.

The image of Simon's severed head contrasts with the elegant scene
Henry enacted in 1269 when the body of Edward the Confessor was
translated to its new resting place in the choir of Westminster Abbey.
Among the armorial shields carved in stone in the choir is that of Simon
de Montfort. Henry had at least not had that excised, even though the
remains of Simon's body had been denied honourable burial. Henry himself made characteristic arrangements for his own end in 1268. At the
centre of the new choir in Westminster Abbey was placed a mosaic pavement. Its enigmatic inscription establishes Henry's place in space and
time. Here, the reader is told, he will find the end of the *primum mobile*, the
prime mover which encircles the universe: 'King Henry III, the city,
Ordoricus and the abbot have set here these stones of porphyry.'[22] The city
referred to is Rome, Ordoricus is the Roman artist who made the pavement, the abbot is Richard of Westminster, and the stones of porphyry
symbolise Henry's impending death and his high status, for emperors
were buried in sarcophagi of porphyry. The date is given in the curious
form 1000 + 200 + 12 + 60 (= 1272) – 4 (= 1268). By coincidence Henry
had exactly four more years to live (he died in 1272). In this inscription he
had foreseen his own death and placed himself symbolically at the centre
of Europe (in Rome), chronologically in Christian time (AD 1268) and in
the space-time of the *primum mobile*.

This was an ambitious assessment by Henry of his own importance
but it is consistent with his grandiose ideas. Moreover he had come
through such vicissitudes since his accession in 1216 that he had reason to
think that divine providence favoured him. Unlike King John he died at
the height of his power and the monastic obituary writers therefore
treated him kindly. Because of his ultimate success he was identified with
the sharp-sighted lynx in the prophecies of Merlin. Thus the St Albans
chronicler summed Henry up:

> He was strong and vigorous but precipitous in his actions; but because
> he brought them to lucky and happy outcomes, many thought him to be
> the one designated by Merlin as the lynx penetrating all.[23]

The prophecies of Merlin, which had been circulated by Geoffrey of
Monmouth in the 1130s along with his *History of the Kings of Britain*, were

one of the most popular works of the Middle Ages. They evoked a mytho-
logical world of dragons, giants and other ominous creatures whose
struggles unlocked the future, provided a key could be found to interpret
them. Similarly Henry had had set into his mosaic pavement at Westminster a list of creatures (stag, raven, eagle, sea serpent and others) from the
multiple of whose ages the end of the *primum mobile* could be computed.
Like Geoffrey of Monmouth he put his own and his kingdom's destiny in
a wide frame. His dreams of grandeur seem to have shielded him from a
sense of failure and furthermore he had given them reality in Westminster
Abbey and his other buildings.

Henry III created the impressive theatricality of the monarchy which
has lasted until the present day. Fantastic as his sense of destiny was, it
gave him an imaginative grasp of England's past. By naming his first-born
son Edward and making the shrine of Edward the Confessor the focal
point of Westminster Abbey, he acknowledged the Anglo-Saxon roots of
royal authority. On the other hand the Poitevin favourites and the Sicilian
business emphasised equally the foreignness of his family and household.
In these contradictions Henry personified the diversity of England's experience since the Norman Conquest. At Westminster with its great hall,
palace and abbey the monarchy stood at the centre of a strife-torn but
resilient community.

❈ REFERENCES ❈

ABBREVIATIONS

EHD 2 *English Historical Documents 1042–1189* ed. D. C. Douglas and G. W. Greenaway (2nd edn, 1981)
EHD 3 *English Historical Documents 1189–1327* ed. H. Rothwell (1975)
RS Rolls Series (*Chronicles and Memorials of Great Britain*)

I. ENGLAND'S PLACE IN MEDIEVAL EUROPE (PAGES 3–18)

1. *Annales Monastici* (RS 36), vol. 1, p. 339. Cf. ch. 9, n. 22 below.
2. *Historia Ecclesiastica*, ed. M. Chibnall (1969–81), vol. 2, p. 269.
3. Letter to the bishop of Metz, trans. B. Pullan, *Sources for the History of Medieval Europe* (1966), p. 150.
4. Trinity College Cambridge, MS R. 17.1. C. R. Dodwell, *The Canterbury School of Illumination* (1954), p. 36.
5. *De Gestis Pontificum* (RS 52), p. 4.
6. *De Gestis Regum* (RS 90), p. 395.
7. *Lives of the Saints*, vol. 2, pp. 290–1, cited by F. Barlow, *The English Church 1000–1066* (2nd edn, 1979), p. 22.
8. *EHD* 3, p. 998.
9. *Historia Regum Britanniae*, ed. A. Griscom (1929), p. 221.
10. *De Gestis Pontificum*, p. 292.
11. *Vita Lodovici VI*, ed. H. Waquet (1929), p. 8.
12. *Henrici Huntendunensis Historia* (RS 74), p. 231. R. H. C. Davis, *The Normans and their Myth* (1976), p. 121.
13. *De Gestis Regum*, p. 379.
14. *Estoire des Engleis*, ed. A. Bell (Anglo-Norman Text Soc. 1960), lines 5963–8.
15. *Historia Regum Britanniae*, p. 239.
16. *Chronicles* (RS 82), vol. 1, p. 12.
17. *Becket Materials* (RS 67), vol. 3, p. 8. C. Brooke and G. Keir, *London 800–1216* (1975), pp. 258–9.
18. *Henrici Huntendunensis*, p. 262. J. Le Patourel, *The Norman Empire* (1976), p. 353. Davis, *The Normans*, pp. 66–7.
19. *History of Friedrich II of Prussia* (1858), vol. 1, p. 415.
20. *Historical Essays: First Series* (1871), p. 50.
21. *Select Charters* (8th edn, 1895), p. v (preface of 1870).
22. ibid., p. vii.
23. ibid., p. viii.
24. ibid., p. vii.

PART ONE. THE NORMANS (PAGES 19–24)

1. D. C. Douglas, *The Norman Achievement* (1969), p. 65. J. Hermans, 'The Byzantine View of the Normans', *Proceedings of the Battle Conference* 2 (1979), ed. R. Allen Brown, p. 87. *The Alexiad of Anna Comnena* trans. E. R. A. Sewter (1969), p. 422.
2. *Carmen de Hastingae Proelio*, ed. C. Morton and H. Muntz (1972), p. 19.
3. *De Gestis Regum* (RS 90), p. 306.
4. *Carmen*, p. 17.
5. *De Gestis Regum*, p. 306.

II. THE NORMAN CONQUEST (PAGES 25–40)

1. D. C. Douglas, *William the Conqueror* (1964), p. 251, n. 4.
2. *De Gestis Regum* (RS 90), p. 304.
3. *Dialogus de Scaccario*, ed. C. Johnson (1950), p. 52.
4. *EHD* 2, p. 150 (translation adapted).
5. *Historia Ecclesiastica*, ed. M. Chibnall (1969–81), vol. 2, p. 322.
6. *Transactions Royal Historical Soc.* 23 (1973), p. 246.
7. *Governance* (1963), p. 27.
8. *The Norman Conquest and British Historians* (Glasgow University Publications 67, 1946), p. 33.
9. *Historia Ecclesiastica*, vol. 2, p. 190.
10. ibid., p. 279.
11. *De Gestis Regum*, pp. 277–8.
12. *Patrologia Latina*, vol. 195, pp. 773–4. *Vita Edwardi Regis*, ed. F. Barlow (1962), pp. 89–90.
13. *Dialogus de Scaccario*, p. 53.
14. *History of English Law* (1898), vol. 1, p. 81.
15. *Dialogus de Scaccario*, p. 63.
16. 'The Norman Conquest', *History* 51 (1966), p. 283.
17. *Chronicle of Battle Abbey*, ed. E. Searle (1980), p. 310.

III. NORMAN GOVERNMENT (PAGES 41–56)

1. *De Gestis Regum* (RS 90), p. 468.
2. ibid., p. 488.
3. ibid., p. 364.
4. *Chronicle of Battle Abbey*, ed. E. Searle (1980), p. 94.
5. *Anthology of Troubadour Lyric Poetry*, ed. A. R. Press (1971), p. 24.
6. *EHD* 2, p. 195 (translation adapted).
7. R. W. Southern, *Medieval Humanism and Other Studies* (1970), p. 219.
8. *Leges Henrici Primi*, ed. L. J. Downer (1972), p. 97.
9. *Select Charters*, ed. W. Stubbs (9th edn, 1913), p. 122.
10. Southern, *Medieval Humanism*, pp. 184–5.
11. *Dialogus de Scaccario*, ed. C. Johnson (1950), p. 6.
12. *Opera*, ed. J. S. Brewer (RS 21), vol. 3, p. 28.
13. *Dialogus de Scaccario*, p. 15.
14. ibid., p. 2.
15. ibid., p. 14.
16. *Registrum Antiquissimum*, ed. C. W. Foster (Lincoln Record Soc., 27, 1930), p. 26. *EHD* 2, pp. 520–1, nos. 63 and 64.
17. *The Exchequer in the Twelfth Century* (1912), p. 57.
18. *Medieval Humanism*, p. 211.
19. Trans. L. A. Manyon (1961), p. 446 (abbreviated).
20. Stenton (2nd edn, 1961), p. 124, n. 2. Maitland, *Domesday Book* (1897), pp. 305–7. Oswald's memorandum is no. 1368 in P. H. Sawyer, *Anglo-Saxon Charters* (1968).
21. Stenton, p. 130.
22. *EHD* 2, p. 171.

IV. CHURCH REFORM (PAGES 57–72)

1. *Letters of Lanfranc*, ed. H. Clover and M. Gibson (1979), p. 35.
2. ibid., p. 153.
3. *De Gestis Pontificum* (RS 52), p. 69. T. S. R. Boase, *English Art 1100–1216* (1953), p. 1.
4. M. Gibson, *Lanfranc of Bec* (1978), p. 161.

5. *Life of Anselm*, ed. R. W. Southern (1962), pp. 50, 52. 'Novus Anglus', *Letters*, ed. Clover and Gibson, p. 38.

6. *Life of Anselm*, p. 51.

7. 'Acta Lanfranci' in *Two Saxon Chronicles*, ed. J. Earle and C. Plummer (1892), vol. 1, p. 291.

8. *Historia Novorum* (RS 81), p. 23.

9. ibid., p. 83.

10. *S. Bernardi Opera*, ed. J. Leclercq and H. Rochais, vol. 7 (1974), no. 92, p. 241 (abbreviated).

11. *EHD* 2, pp. 207, 208 (translation adapted).

12. *Walter Daniel's Life of Ailred*, ed. F. M. Powicke (1950), p. 11.

13. ibid., p. 11.

14. *Cartulary of the Priory of St Gregory*, ed. A. M. Woodcock (Camden Soc. Third Series, 88, 1956), p. 1.

15. M. L. Coker, 'A Hagiographic Polemic', *Mediaeval Studies* (Toronto) 39 (1977), p. 65.

PART TWO. THE ANGEVINS (PAGES 73–80)

1. *Proceedings of the British Academy* 61 (1975), pp. 239–40.

2. *Chroniques des Comtes d'Anjou*, ed. L. Halphen and R. Poupardin (1913), p. 71.

3. *Gesta Stephani*, ed. K. R. Potter and R. H. C. Davis (1976), p. 224.

4. *EHD* 2, p. 419.

5. *Anthology of Troubadour Lyric Poetry*, ed. A. R. Press (1971), p. 163.

6. 'L'empire angevin était donc conçu comme un état très fort, mais dans le cadre du système féodal', *Le Gouvernement d'Henri II Plantagenêt* (1956), p. 569.

7. *Dialogus de Scaccario*, p. 27. *Glanvill*, ed. G. D. G. Hall (1965), p. 1.

V. STRUGGLES FOR THE KINGDOM (PAGES 81–97)

1. *Gesta Stephani*, ed. K. R. Potter and R. H. C. Davis (1976), p. 2.

2. ibid., p. 222.

3. *Regesta Regum Anglo-Normannorum*, vol. 3, ed. H. A. Cronne and R. H. C. Davis (1967), no. 276, p. 103.

4. *Select Charters*, ed. W. Stubbs (9th edn, 1913), p. 176.

5. *Angevin Kingship* (2nd edn, 1963), p. 87.

6. *Charters*, ed. Stubbs, pp. 137–8.

7. *Gesta Stephani*, p. 198.

8. ibid., p. 206.

9. *Chronicle of Richard of Devizes*, ed. J. T. Appleby (1963), p. 49.

10. *Historia Novella*, ed. K. R. Potter (1955), p. 16.

11. *History* 59 (1974), p. 182.

12. ibid., p. 181.

13. *The Becket Conflict and the Schools* (1973), p. 238.

14. *Becket Materials* (RS 67), vol. 4, p. 28. *EHD* 2, p. 765.

15. *Recueil des Historiens des Gaules*, ed. M. Bouquet, vol. 12, pp. 419–20.

16. *Anthology of Troubadour Lyric Poetry*, ed. A. R. Press (1971), p. 162.

17. *Historia* (RS 82), vol. 1, p. 283.

18. *Giraldi Cambrensis Opera* (RS 21), vol. 8, p. 208.

VI. LAW AND ORDER (PAGES 99–112)

1. *Glanvill*, ed. G. D. G. Hall (1965), p. 148 (my translation).

2. *Select Charters*, ed. W. Stubbs (9th edn, 1913), p. 171.

3. *Leges Henrici Primi*, ed. L. J. Downer (1972), p. 108.

4. *Royal Writs*, ed. R. C. van Caenegem (Selden Soc. 77, 1959), p. 217.

5. *Henry II* (1973), p. 375.
6. *Historical Foundations* (2nd edn, 1981), p. 151. Cf. *Legal Framework* (1976), p. 186.
7. *Glanvill*, p. 3.
8. ibid., pp. 5, 10.
9. ibid., pp. 28, 149.
10. *Charters*, ed. Stubbs, p. 172.
11. Van Caenegem (1973), p. 100. D. M. Stenton, *English Justice* (1965), p. 26.
12. *De Nugis Curialium*, ed. M. R. James (Anecdota Oxoniensa, Medieval and Modern series, 14, 1914), p. 237.
13. *Policraticus*, ed. C. C. J. Webb (1919), vol. 1, pp. 345–6.
14. *Charters*, ed. Stubbs, p. 163.
15. *Glanvill*, p. 137. Cf. ibid., p. 148.
16. *The Birth of the English Common Law*, p. 85.
17. ibid., p. 97, note *e*.
18. *Glanvill*, p. xxxi.
19. ibid., p. 3.

VII. THE TWELFTH-CENTURY RENAISSANCE (PAGES 113–25)

1. *Metalogicon*, ed. C. C. J. Webb (1929), p. 136.
2. *Cligés*, lines 27–42. E. R. Curtius, *European Literature and the Latin Middle Ages*, trans. W. R. Trask (1953), pp. 384–5.
3. *Medieval Humanism* (1970), p. 158.
4. Rickman (6th edn, 1862), p. 45.
5. *A Mirror for Fools*, trans. J. H. Mozley (1963), p. 39.
6. Ed. M. R. James (1914), p. 1.
7. *Medieval Humanism*, p. 176.
8. *Poetria Nova*, trans. M. F. Nims (1967), p. 16.
9. ibid., p. 15.
10. *De Nugis Curialium*, ed. James (1914), p. 5.
11. ibid., p. 203.
12. ibid., p. 203.
13. M. D. Legge, *Anglo-Norman Literature* (1963), p. 94.
14. Ed. E. G. Stanley (1960), p. 101.
15. *Chronicle of Jocelin of Brakelond*, ed. H. E. Butler (1949), p. 40.
16. *Historical Works of Gervase of Canterbury* (RS 73), vol. 1, p. 21.

PART THREE. THE POITEVINS (PAGES 127–32)

1. *Constitutional History*, vol. 1 (1874), p. 519.
2. T. Wright, *Political Songs of England* (Camden Soc. 1839), p. 10.
3. *Chronica Majora* (RS 57), vol. 3, p. 272.

VIII. KING JOHN AND THE MINORITY OF HENRY III (PAGES 133–49)

1. *Radulphi de Coggeshall Chronicon* (RS 66), p. 138. W. L. Warren, *King John* (Penguin edn, 1966), p. 95.
2. *Chronica Rogeri de Wendover* (RS 84), vol. 2, p. 100. Warren, *John*, p. 240.
3. *Memoriale Walteri de Coventria* (RS 58), vol. 2, p. 232. Cf. the translations of J. C. Holt, *King John* (Historical Assoc., 1963), pp. 24–5 and of A. Gransden, *Historical Writing in England* (1974), p. 343.
4. *Chronica Majora* (RS 57), vol. 2, p. 669. Cf. V. H. Galbraith, *Roger Wendover and Matthew Paris* (1944), p. 36 and Warren, *John*, p. 30.
5. *Constitutional History*, vol. 2, p. 17.

6. *Pipe Roll 11 John*, p. 172. Warren, *John*, p. 162.
7. *Memorials of St Edmunds Abbey* (RS 96), vol. 2, p. 25. Warren, *John*, p. 27. Cf. S. Painter, *Reign of King John* (1949), pp. 270–3.
8. *Wendover*, vol. 2, p. 84. *Chronica Majora*, vol. 2, p. 552. J. C. Holt, *Magna Carta* (1965), pp. 137–8.
9. *Annales Monastici* (RS 36), vol. 2, p. 277. F. M. Powicke, *Stephen Langton* (1928), pp. 42–3, 115–16.
10. *Magna Carta* (1965), p. 20.
11. *Wendover*, vol. 2, p. 199.
12. *Life of St Hugh of Lincoln*, ed. D. L. Douie and H. Farmer (1961), vol. 2, p. 185.
13. *Histoire de Guillaume le Maréchal*, ed. M. P. Meyer (1891–1901), vol. 2, lines 15183–8.
14. Wright, *Political Songs*, p. 22.
15. *Chronica Majora*, vol. 3, p. 28.
16. *Guillaume le Maréchal*, vol. 2, lines 18041–3.
17. ibid., vol. 2, lines 19149–52.
18. *Dialogus de Scaccario*, ed. C. Johnson (1950), p. 109.
19. *Pipe Roll 3 Henry III*, pp. xxiii, 205.

IX. The Personal Rule of Henry III (pages 151–72)

1. *Select Charters* (9th edn, 1913), p. 37.
2. *The Thirteenth Century* (1953), p. 130.
3. *Laws and Customs of England*, ed. S. E. Thorne (1968), vol. 2, p. 22.
4. *Chronica Majora* (RS 57), vol. 3, p. 620.
5. *Wendover* (RS 84), vol. 3, p. 51.
6. *Annales Monastici* (RS 36), vol. 1, pp. 463–4.
7. R. F. Treharne and I. J. Sanders, *Documents of the Baronial Movement* (1973), pp. 236–9.
8. Matthew Paris, *Chronica Majora*, vol. 5, p. 52.
9. II *Chronicles*, ch. 26, verse 19. *Letters of Grosseteste* (RS 25), p. 351.
10. *Letters of Grosseteste*, p. 352.
11. *Close Rolls 1251–3*, p. 225.
12. Matthew Paris, *Chronica Majora*, vol. 5, p. 339.
13. *Walter of Henley and other Treatises*, ed. D. Oschinsky (1971), p. 402.
14. Matthew Paris, *Chronica Majora*, vol. 5, p. 20.
15. *Close Rolls 1254–6*, p. 326.
16. *Chronica Majora*, vol. 5, pp. 339, 617.
17. Above, ch. 8, note 16. See page 205 above.
18. *Close Rolls 1234–7*, p. 271.
19. *Chronica Majora*, vol. 3, p. 388.
20. ibid., vol. 5, p. 457.
21. Above, note 18.
22. *Annales Monastici*, vol. 1, p. 339.
23. *Purgatorio* canto 7, lines 130–1.

X. National Identity (pages 173–88)

1. *Gesta Regum* (RS 90), vol. 1, pp. 277–8.
2. *Wendover* (RS 84), vol. 3, p. 49.
3. R. F. Treharne and I. J. Sanders, *Documents of the Baronial Movement* (1973), p. 80.
4. ibid., p. 80.
5. T. Wright, *Political Songs*, p. 72, lines 9, 11–12; p. 92, lines 414, 416.
6. ibid., p. 22.
7. *Wendover*, vol. 2, p. 212.
8. *Flores Historiarum* (RS 95), vol. 3, pp. 266–7.

9. *Chronicon Willelmi de Rishanger*, ed. J. O. Halliwell (Camden Soc. 1840), p. 18.
10. *Wendover*, vol. 3, p. 16.
11. *Chronicon Abbatiae de Evesham* (RS 29), p. 189.
12. Walter Map, *De Nugis Curialium*, ed. M. R. James (1914), p. 225.
13. *Rishanger*, ed. Halliwell, pp. 17–18.
14. *Letters of Lanfranc*, ed. H. Clover and M. Gibson (1979), p. 66.
15. *EHD* 3, p. 307.
16. *Chronicle of Richard of Devizes*, ed. J. T. Appleby (1963), p. 66.
17. *EHD* 3, pp. 881–4.
18. *Radulphi de Coggeshall Chronicon* (RS 66), p. 185.
19. *Rotuli Litterarum Clausarum* (1833), vol. 1, p. 329 (to sheriff of Somerset).
20. *Curia Regis Rolls*, vol. 16, p. 290.
21. Matthew Paris, *Chronica Majora*, vol. 4, p. 118.
22. *Select Charters*, ed. W. Stubbs (9th edn, 1913), p. 356.
23. *Chronica Johannis de Oxenedes* (RS 13), pp. 224–5.
24. *Annales Monastici* (RS 36), vol. 2, pp. 349–50.
25. ibid., vol. 1, p. 463.

XI. The Commune of England (pages 189–203)

1. *Chronica Majora*, vol. 5, p. 706.
2. ibid., vol. 5, p. 313.
3. T. Wright, *Political Songs*, p. 85, lines 265–9.
4. *Annales Monastici* (RS 36), vol. 1, p. 164.
5. *Chronicle*, ed. J. T. Appleby (1963), p. 49. Cf. p. 141 above.
6. F. Pollock and F. W. Maitland, *History of English Law* (1898), p. 688.
7. *EHD* 3, p. 367.
8. *Crusader Institutions* (1980), p. 59.
9. *Close Rolls 1256–9*, p. 328.
10. R. F. Treharne and I. J. Sanders, *Documents of the Baronial Movement* (1973), pp. 238–41.
11. ibid., p. 98.
12. *Close Rolls 1256–9*, p. 328.
13. ibid., p. 328. Treharne and Sanders, p. 258.
14. ibid., p. 216, clause 19 (my translation).
15. ibid., p. 168.
16. ibid., p. 207.
17. ibid., pp. 242–3.
18. ibid., p. 265.
19. ibid., pp. 288–9.
20. ibid., pp. 296–7.
21. Wright, *Political Songs*, pp. 110–11, lines 763–70.
22. S. H. Wander, 'The Westminster Abbey Sanctuary Pavement', *Traditio* 34 (1978), p. 141.
23. *Willelmi Rishanger* (RS 28), vol. 2, p. 75.

✤ GENEALOGICAL TABLES ✤

The following tables do not include all children and connections of the royal family. The tables are designed to show the royal succession and the kings' principal alliances only.

NORMANS and ANGEVINS

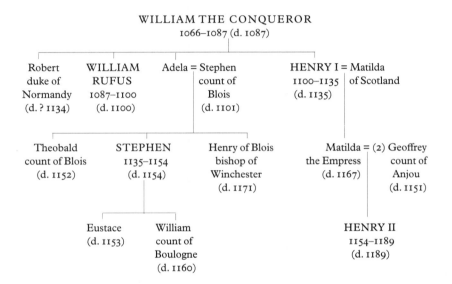

WILLIAM THE CONQUEROR
1066–1087 (d. 1087)

Robert duke of Normandy (d. ? 1134)

WILLIAM RUFUS 1087–1100 (d. 1100)

Adela = Stephen count of Blois (d. 1101)

HENRY I = Matilda 1100–1135 of Scotland (d. 1135)

Theobald count of Blois (d. 1152)

STEPHEN 1135–1154 (d. 1154)

Henry of Blois bishop of Winchester (d. 1171)

Matilda = (2) Geoffrey the Empress count of (d. 1167) Anjou (d. 1151)

Eustace (d. 1153)

William count of Boulogne (d. 1160)

HENRY II 1154–1189 (d. 1189)

ANGEVINS and POITEVINS

HENRY II = Eleanor heiress of
1154–1189 | Aquitaine & Poitou
(d. 1189) | (d. 1204)

| Henry the Young King (d. 1183) | RICHARD I 1189–1199 (d. 1199) | Geoffrey = Constance (d. 1186) of Brittany | JOHN = (2) Isabella 1199–1216 of Angoulême (d. 1216) (d. 1246) |

Arthur
(d. 1204)

| HENRY III 1216–1272 (d. 1272) = Eleanor of Provence | Richard of Cornwall (d. 1272) = Sanchia of Provence | Joan (d. 1238) = Alexander II of Scotland | Isabella (d. 1241) = Emperor Frederick II | Eleanor (d. 1275) = Simon de Montfort |

The SAVOYARDS

Thomas count of Savoy (d. 1233) = Margaret of Geneva (d. ? 1258)

| Amadeus count of Savoy (d. 1253) | William bishop of Valence (d. 1239) | Thomas count of Flanders & Piedmont (d. 1259) | Beatrice = Raimond (d. 1265) Berenger count of Provence (d. 1245) | Peter lord of Richmond (d. 1268) | Boniface archbishop of Canterbury (d. 1270) | Philip archbishop of Lyons (d. 1285) |

| Margaret = Louis IX (d. 1296) King of France (d. 1270) | Eleanor = HENRY III (d. 1291) King of England (d. 1272) | Sanchia = Richard (d. 1261) of Cornwall King of the Romans (d. 1272) | Beatrice = Charles (d. 1267) of Anjou King of Sicily (d. 1285) |

THE WRITTEN
WORD IN THE
MIDDLE AGES

✢ I ✢

THE MAKING OF DOMESDAY BOOK

Once the conquest of 1066 was achieved, King William 'decided to bring the conquered people under the rule of written law'. He therefore had a codification drawn up of Mercian, Dane, and Wessex law and, 'to give the finishing touch to all his forethought', Domesday Book was made so that 'every man might be content with his own rights, and not encroach unpunished on those of others'. This version of events, making William the Conqueror responsible for the transition from memory to written record, is preserved in an oral tradition told by Henry of Blois, King Stephen's brother, to Richard Fitz Nigel, who recorded it in the *Dialogue of the Exchequer* around 1179. As Henry was bishop of Winchester, he may have been transmitting an authentic local tradition emanating from the treasury at Winchester where Domesday Book had originally been kept. Like many legends, Henry's story oversimplifies details and shortens the time-scale in order to convey a fundamental and probably widespread belief. The Norman Conquest did mark a new start in the making of records and Domesday Book was its most awesome precedent.

Having accepted Henry's story, however, as a valuable opinion, it is immediately necessary to add provisos to it. For if the story were taken literally and whole, at least in the form in which Fitz Nigel gives it, it could be misleading. Obviously, for a start, Domesday Book did not succeed in recording everyone's rights between its covers. Nor in the century after it was made was it frequently used to settle questions about such rights, although William the Conqueror may have hoped that it would be. More open to misunderstanding, though less obviously misleading, is the association of Domesday Book with law codes and the proposition that William the Conqueror 'decided to bring the conquered people under the rule of written law'. The Latin phrase for 'written law' here is *juri scripto legibusque*, which recalls the *jus* and *lex* of Roman jurisprudence. Fitz Nigel, rather than the original tradition, may have associated William the Conqueror specifically with Roman law, since it was a fashionable academic subject in Fitz Nigel's time. By presenting William as a maker of literate law, Fitz Nigel was associating him with the emperors of antiquity and bringing England into the international fraternity of jurisprudence. The original tradition may simply have said that William, because he was a conqueror, aimed to put the laws and everyone's rights into writing so that there could be no further dispute about them.

Across a broader time-span, the idea of William the Conqueror replacing the uncertainties of memory and the spoken word by definitive written law is both illuminating and open to misinterpretation at one and the same time. The idea implies that nothing of importance had been written down before 1066 and also that William the Conqueror's records were decisive for the future. Neither implication is acceptable in that form. Important as his achievements were in the development of literate ways of doing business, it would be a misunderstanding of William the Conqueror's administration either to undervalue his debt to the Anglo-Saxon past or to exaggerate his contribution to later forms of medieval government. Like other historical legends, the story of William the Conqueror bringing the people under the rule of written law achieves its dramatic effect by minimising both the past and the future. In historical fact England already had literate traditions extending back for centuries and conversely non-literate habits and methods of proof persisted in unexpected quarters for generations after the Norman Conquest.

A possible misconception to clear away at the outset is any assumption that the Normans had greater expertise in writing than the Anglo-Saxons. On the whole, Norman administrators probably had less experience than Anglo-Saxon ones of written records, and the Normans before 1066 had not shown such a consistent interest as the Anglo-Saxons in recording their history and institutions in literate forms. There was nothing in Normandy comparable with the *Anglo-Saxon Chronicle* and the law codes. The Englishman Orderic Vitalis says that his fellow monks of St Evroul in Normandy 'shrank from bending their minds to the task of composing or writing down their traditions. So in the end I, who came here from the remote parts of Mercia as a ten-year-old boy [in 1085] have endeavoured to commit to writing an account of the deeds of the Normans for Normans to read.'[1] Although Orderic exaggerated his originality, as there already were histories of the Norman dukes, the general idea that Englishmen showed the Normans the usefulness of writing has much to commend it.

Nevertheless a Norman innovation, which may have contributed to the belief that William the Conqueror introduced Roman *jus scriptum*, was the replacement of Old English by Latin as the language of royal writs. This was not an immediate change in 1066, but was probably a consequence of appointing Normans and other foreigners to bishoprics and abbacies. Latin made quick progress because it was the written language with which William's clerks (in both the ecclesiastical and modern sense), from Archbishop Lanfranc of Canterbury downwards, were most familiar. In the eyes of contemporaries on the European continent Latin was the only language of record; a person unfamiliar with it was illiterate. In this frame of mind the foreigners made a fresh start in assembling theological libraries for monasteries and cathedrals, both by gifts of books (like those made by Lanfranc to Canterbury and William of St Carilef to Durham) and by making new manuscripts. 'The century after the Norman Conquest . . . is the greatest in the history of English book production.'[2] In the new books, moreover, less emphasis was put on the illustrations and more on the text than was usual in Anglo-Saxon manuscripts.

In increasing the use of Latin writing, the Norman Conquest brought England into the mainstream of medieval literate communication. At the same time, in the short term, the Conquest may have caused a reduction in literacy (in the modern sense of being able to read and write the language one speaks), because it divorced writing further from everyday speech. Although Old English in its standard written form was itself an archaic and learned language by 1066, it was obviously nearer to the vernacular than Latin. In these paradoxes the difficulties of assessing the effects of the Norman Conquest can be appreciated.

Even greater difficulties arise in estimating how much writing was done in pre-Conquest England and for what purposes. To take the question 'How much?' first of all. An estimate of the extent of writing activity in medieval states is best approached through documents like writs and charters, rather than books, as documents are more widely distributed and they can be attributed to specific persons and times. A disadvantage of estimating by documents, however, is that single sheets of parchment are less likely than books to have survived for a thousand years. Some ephemeral memoranda were probably thrown away as soon as their usefulness was expended. Admitting these disadvantages, the number of writs and charters extant (in either originals or copies) is the best measure of writing activity available, inadequate though it is.

From Anglo-Saxon England rather less than 2,000 writs and charters survive—a small number compared with those extant from the period 1066–1307 and particularly from the thirteenth century. A single collection (which is not the largest) of mainly thirteenth-century charters, the so-called *Registrum Antiquissimum* of Lincoln Cathedral, numbers 2,980 items in the printed edition. A single session of the royal justices in eyre in an average-sized county in Edward I's reign used about 500 membranes of parchment and produced more than 2,000 documents in four or five weeks. Although statistics can mislead—and medieval statistics above all—comparisons of numbers are important because an axiom of this book is that the permanent growth of literacy is related to the growth of documents.

The incalculable question, which becomes progressively harder yet more important to answer the further back one goes in time, is what relation documents now extant bear to the numbers originally made. What proportion of the original whole are the 2,000 or so Anglo-Saxon writs and charters? The conjectures made in answer to this question for late Anglo-Saxon England are necessarily so large that there will never be agreement about them. Examples of such conjectures appear in two lectures given to the Royal Historical Society in 1974. In the first J. Campbell draws attention to miscellaneous memoranda in Old English, such as one concerning levies of men for warships, and suggests that they are 'survivors from a much larger number' and that their existence is one reason for thinking that there was 'a considerable degree of lay literacy' in late Anglo-Saxon England.[3] In the second lecture S. Harvey restates her argument that the Anglo-Saxon government had documents in its treasury upon which Domesday Book was based.[4] The conjecture which both lectures have in common is that many documents in Old English were lost after the Norman Conquest, because the Normans preferred Latin and also because many writs and memoranda may have been ephemeral in purpose in the first place.

The possibility that the Normans dispersed archives of documents and destroyed an extensive literate culture in Old English cannot be excluded, although in some monasteries the Conquest may have had the reverse effect as the English monks laboured to justify their practices and cults to the conquerors. Eadmer of Canterbury describes in the 1090s how he sees 'men of the present age anxiously trying to find out about the actions of their predecessors . . . yet they cannot for all their pains succeed in doing as they would wish because the elusive scarcity of documents [*scriptorum inopia fugax*] has buried them in oblivion'. Even explicit mentions like this of lack of documents could be interpreted as signs of Norman destructiveness, despite William the Conqueror's claim to be the lawful successor of Edward the Confessor.

It is difficult to assess the implications of lost documents. Whereas Campbell argues for 'a considerable degree of lay literacy', C. P. Wormald reasserts that 'the traditional view of restricted literacy is substantially valid for the whole early English period.'[5] Harvey's contention is as controversial. She states that 'chroniclers and cartulary makers have long told us explicitly of the earlier treasury documents and how the Domesday survey using them as its *exemplar* sought additional and extraordinary material.'[6] The chronicle to which she refers is that of Abingdon Abbey and the cartulary is Hemming's. A preliminary difficulty is that the words translated as 'documents' or 'records' in this context are *scriptura* in the Abingdon text and *cartula* in Hemming's. These words are feminine singular forms, not neuter plural ones: the Abingdon chronicler refers not to 'the records [*scriptura*] of the royal treasury' but to an individual 'writing', and Hemming likewise not to 'documents' but to an individual 'little charter' [*cartula*]. The difference between singular and plural is crucial when the quantity of documents is at issue. The texts which the Abingdon chronicler and Hemming cite in this context are connected with the Domesday survey. Whether they are earlier or later than Domesday Book is not explicitly stated.

The Abingdon *scriptura* is a list of the abbot's hundreds and hides in Berkshire, which accord with entries in Domesday Book concerning the time of Edward the Confessor.[7] In origin this *scriptura* might be any one of the following:

* a memorandum extracted from Domesday Book itself;
* one of the records made at the time of the Domesday survey, from which Domesday Book was compiled;
* a record made in Edward the Confessor's reign and subsequently used in the compilation of Domesday Book.

Harvey prefers the third alternative, though the others are also possibilities, as the Domesday survey collected information concerning the time of Edward the Confessor and it kept these preliminary records in royal treasuries. The Abingdon chronicler's reference to 'another book of the royal treasury of the time of King William' does not exclude the possibility that the *scriptura* was extracted from Domesday Book, as the text cited from this other book contains details not included in Domesday.[8] The sense seems to be that both the *scriptura* and the other book were made in the time of King William. Hemming's cartulary likewise refers to records in the treasury of King William *senior* (in other words, William the Conqueror) and not to pre-Conquest documents. In his use of the word *exemplar* Hemming is not referring to a documentary precedent for the Domesday survey, but to an 'exemplification' or confirmatory transcript of some evidence concerning Oswaldslaw hundred. In this purely local context he is explaining that 'as confirmation of this business, an exemplification of it is written down in an authentic charter of the king, which is preserved with the descriptions of the whole of England in the royal treasury'. The 'descriptions' mentioned here are most probably the preliminary records produced by the Domesday survey, from which the book itself was compiled. These alternative interpretations illustrate the difficulties of distinguishing between references to pre- and post-Conquest documents and they also suggest that the case for the existence of earlier treasury documents has been overstated.

Administrative documents were certainly used in late Anglo-Saxon England, since a few copies of them still exist. Whether there were once enough to be kept systematically in archives and to be commonplaces of business are still matters for conjecture. If there had once been many more documents, the forms of those surviving should be stereotyped (as is the case with thirteenth-century charters and writs) because bureaucratic routines would develop. The Anglo-Saxon sealed writ, with its economy of expression, comes closest to such standards. V. H. Galbraith has been the protagonist of the argument that the sealed writ goes back to Alfred's reign or earlier, and that 'long before the Norman Conquest the Saxon kings had a secretariat of their own, and the first great step had been taken towards bureaucratic government'.[9] But P. Chaplais interprets the Alfredian evidence differently and points out that 'no seal impression or trace of sealing of any kind prior to the Confessor's reign has been found', although that is not evidence that none ever existed.[10] The sealed writ is certainly pre-Conquest, but it may have been introduced no earlier than Cnut's reign; whether Anglo-Saxon writs usually carried seals authenticating them before the reign of Edward the Confessor cannot be definitely decided. Chaplais is likewise sceptical about whether the Anglo-Saxon kings had a secretariat of their own; as late as Edward the Confessor's reign the organisation of the secretariat 'is a matter for speculation'.[11] Royal scribes are occasionally named and the consistent wording of writs suggests established drafting rules, yet at least one authentic writ of Edward the Confessor can be shown to have been produced in the *scriptorium* of Westminster Abbey. Nevertheless by that reign sealing probably took place in a royal office; to that extent at least there was a chancery.

Whatever view is taken of the state of the evidence, it cannot warrant Galbraith's assertion that by the tenth century in the administration of England 'the whole structure was articulated by the royal writ'.[12] It is debatable whether bureaucracy had developed as far as that by 1150, let alone 950. Certainly the Anglo-Saxon vernacular writ, as it existed in the reign of Edward the Confessor, was the root from which later varieties of royal charters and letters grew, but the forms had to be changed before the writ could articulate the whole structure of government. From William I's reign, but not earlier (Chaplais argues), writs were used for giving instructions (injunctions) to named individuals.[13] Similarly the practice of keeping sealed writs as title-deeds, 'one of the most important phases in the general change-over from an oral procedure to a written one', was still in the process of happening in William I's reign.[14] Differences of opinion are therefore as large about the purposes for which Anglo-Saxon documents were made as they are about the numbers which once existed. It seems unlikely that England was governed by a bureaucracy using documents in its routine procedures before 1066.

The chief reason for suggesting that Anglo-Saxon government had not already brought the people 'under the rule of written law', in the sense of ruling through a bureaucracy, is that even the Norman conquerors did not succeed in doing this. The effects of Domesday Book are easy to exaggerate because it impressed contemporaries so much. In a well-known passage the *Anglo-Saxon Chronicle* says that King William had the investigation made so narrowly 'that there was no single hide nor virgate of land, nor indeed—it is a shame to relate but it seemed no shame to him to do—one ox or one cow nor one pig which was there left out and not put down in his record'.[15] This description obviously exaggerates in order to emphasise the frightening—and shameful—thoroughness of the Domesday survey. Similarly Fitz Nigel explained a century later that the book had been called *Domesdei* 'by the natives' because it seemed to them like the Last Judgement described in Revelation.[16] The tremendous image of Christ in majesty, seated as a judge holding the book of the Scriptures or laws, would have been familiar to anyone entering a Romanesque church, either sculpted over the doorway or as a mural painting within. An earthly king evoked this image at his ceremonial crown-wearings.

Fitz Nigel is explaining that by his time Domesday Book was of symbolic rather than practical importance: 'That is why we have called the book *The Book of Judgement*, not because it contains decisions on various difficult points, but because its decisions like those of the Last Judgement are unalterable.' For Fitz Nigel Domesday Book was a majestic and unchangeable memorial of the Norman Conquest. The earliest copies of it likewise suggest that its function was symbolic rather than practical. Two multi-coloured editions were made: one in the twelfth century (the manuscript called *Herefordshire Domesday*) and another in the thirteenth (the Exchequer Breviate), the most elegant manuscript ever produced by the royal administration. But the Breviate was of no practical value because it omitted all details of land use. *Herefordshire Domesday* has some marginal notes updating it, making it more useful than the Breviate, yet even here the work is left uncompleted. Embellished like liturgical texts, these manuscripts reinforce the idea that Domesday Book was seen as a sacred book of judgement.

A surprising fact about Domesday Book is that it seems to have been used so rarely in the two centuries after it was made. There are only ten references extant specifically to the use of information connected with Domesday Book between the time it was made and the death of Henry I in 1135. Nor do most of these references unequivocally refer to the book as such, but to writs (*breves*) or charters (*carte*). These writs or charters are probably the same as the 'descriptions of the whole of England in the royal treasury', which Hemming mentions in his cartulary. As a consequence of the Domesday survey the king's government therefore possessed, perhaps for the first time, not only a great book but an archive of writings to which it could refer. Nevertheless this archive was not carefully kept, as it disappears without trace. It is last mentioned by Henry of Huntingdon (writing probably in the early 1130s), who says that the information of the Domesday survey had all been written in 'charters' (*carte*), which were brought to William the Conqueror and 'are kept deposited in treasuries up to the present day'. The disappearance of these treasuries of documents is an argument in favour of the hypothesis that earlier Anglo-Saxon archives had likewise vanished. But it also suggests that even in the middle of the twelfth century government had not yet developed to the point where archives were progressively accumulated.

After Henry I's reign there is no further evidence of Domesday Book being searched for specific information (although fair copies were made of it, as already mentioned) until a plea roll of 1221 notes: 'Remember to search Domesday for the bishop.' Even this reference suggests that it was private litigants, rather than royal officials, who first realised that the book might be used to their advantage. In the 1250s, however, Henry III and his favourites begin to refer to it. In 1256 the king used it to show that the men of Cheshire were obliged to pay for repairing the bridge at Chester. Three years later Peter of Savoy had Domesday Book cited in parliament to prove that Witley in Surrey was not ancient demesne of the Crown from before the Conquest, as his tenants alleged, because it had been held then by Earl Godwin and not by the king; Peter was therefore entitled to increase the rent. Proving ancient demesne became a routine use of Domesday Book in Edward I's reign. For example, in a case in 1306 one counsel asks: 'Are we ancient demesne or not?' and another replies: 'We will send to the Exchequer to search in Domesday.' Two generations earlier counsel's question would have been answered, not by searching Domesday Book, but by asking a jury of twelve knights to give oral testimony; there are numerous instances of the latter procedure in the plea rolls of Henry III's reign. This change in the method of obtaining information—from hearing the testimony of reliable local men to looking up a book kept by the Exchequer—is one indicator of the transition from memory to written record. Once the new procedure has become familiar, that is, from the last quarter of the thirteenth century, relevant extracts from Domesday Book were copied into numerous cartularies and registers.

Two centuries thus elapsed before Domesday Book became a record which was regularly consulted or valued for its contents. Why was this so? One answer is that such a book would have been of only limited use at any time. It was founded on a misconception of how to use writing in administration. The Normans seem to have been so impressed by the way written record, in the form of charters, gave apparent durability to their individual acts that they assumed that a big book would give similar permanence to the government of the whole of England. A document could indeed make time stand still, in the sense that it could pass on a record of an event to remote posterity, but it could not prevent change. In Domesday Book lords and serfs, animals and ploughs, mills and streams, all stand in arrested motion like clockwork automata when the mechanism fails. But historical change has a self-sustaining momentum; not even William the Conqueror could prevent change, and so Domesday Book soon went out of date. Its only practical use was to answer questions about archaisms like ancient demesne. The qualities which make it an unrivalled historical record for us today detracted from its usefulness to medieval administrators.

Another answer to the question why Domesday Book took so long to be consulted is that it was too precocious. In the twelfth century a mythology seems to have grown up around it. The educated believed that it had brought the people under the rule of written law, and 'the natives' compared it with the Last Judgement. Both the educated and the natives were more accustomed to writings in the form of symbolic and sacred books than to business documents for mundane use. Practical questions were answered by oral testimony and not by reference to documents. Only gradually, as documents began to accumulate, did habits of consulting them and ultimately of depending on them become established. Domesday Book began to be consulted regularly in Edward I's reign and no earlier because dependence on records in general only became at all regular at that time. Through this change Domesday Book ultimately became a useful but limited work of reference instead of an awesome relic like a Gospel book.

Although Domesday Book had not brought the people under the rule of written law in any specific sense, it had associated writing with royal power in a novel and unforgettable way. Of course there were precedents for it, from imperial Rome and the Carolingian polyptychs, but there is no firm evidence that anything of the sort had been attempted before in England. The organisation which had made the Domesday survey possible was Anglo-Saxon—the grouping of local communities into shires, hundreds and vills; the practice of juries giving solemn oral testimony which was binding on their communities. The Norman novelty lay in using this organisation to compile a written record which reflected the efficiency of Anglo-Saxon government. The unique event of the Conquest produced a unique document. Nevertheless, because Domesday Book was unique in scale and purpose, it could not itself form the first document in a continuing series. Bureaucracy begins with the pipe rolls of the twelfth-century Exchequer rather than with Domesday Book.

Even in Edward I's reign documentary methods of proof were not as firmly established as his lawyers assumed in the *quo warranto* proceedings. The story of the Earl Warenne exhibiting a sword from the Norman Conquest instead of a charter before Edward's judges, saying 'This is my warrant!' shows that old oral traditions and attitudes persisted despite Domesday Book and the immeasurably greater increase in documentation in the thirteenth century. Some historians have found the Warenne story as unacceptable as Edward's judges may have done, because it seems so primitive and ill-founded by literate standards of proof. Thus it was removed in 1913 from the canon of Bishop Stubbs's *Select Charters*, which used to be the bible of history students. The story is certainly inaccurate in details, but it has a value comparable with the myths Fitz Nigel recorded a century earlier about the Norman Conquest and written law. Myth is not necessarily the 'purely fictitious narrative' of a dictionary definition. In oral tradition it can be a formulation of fundamental belief and experience handed down in a memorable way. The Warenne story recalls a non-literate tradition of the Norman Conquest, and, if examined as an evocation of dying oral culture, it indicates better than more formal records the change of attitudes which had occurred since the coming of the Normans.

The story appears in one version of the chronicle of Walter of Guisborough and runs as follows:

> The king disturbed some of the great men of the land through his judges wanting to know by what warrant [*quo warranto*] they held their lands, and if they did not have a good warrant, he immediately seized their lands. Among the rest, the Earl Warenne was called before the king's judges. Asked by what warrant he held, he produced in their midst an ancient and rusty sword and said: 'Look at this, my lords, this is my warrant! For my ancestors came with William the Bastard and conquered their lands with the sword, and by the sword I will defend them from anyone intending to seize them. The king did not conquer and subject the land by himself, but our forebears were sharers and partners with him.'[17]

Historians have rightly pointed out that the story contains inaccuracies and inconsistencies. Edward I's *quo warranto* prosecutions did not demand warrants for 'lands' but for franchises or privileged jurisdictions. Nor were the magnates' lands seized by the king, as he was not powerful enough to do that. Nor is there evidence from other records that the Earl Warenne protested in these terms, although he was harassed by *quo warranto* prosecutions. Moreover, the story is attributed to a different earl, Gilbert de Clare of Gloucester, in another version of this chronicle, and in the best version it does not appear at all. The story also oversimplifies the conduct of judicial proceedings in Edward I's reign. An earl had learned counsel to advise him and to speak on his behalf. Warenne would have known not to threaten royal judges in open court, and that a rusty sword was not going to help his cause at law, since claims without charters were inadmissible in many *quo warranto* cases.

At first sight so many inaccuracies suggest that the Warenne story is worthless for serious historical purposes. At best it is a popular legend; it is certainly not a precise account of legal proceedings. Nevertheless it is important and useful precisely because it does seem to be a popular legend. At the heart of the story is a memory which allegedly went back to the Norman Conquest and an archaic method of proof, the exhibition of the rusty sword, which had been superseded in Edward I's courts by written evidence and book-learned law. The story seems to be a desperate reassertion of the primacy of oral tradition over recorded history and of non-literate forms of proof over Edward I's lawyers and their demands for charters. Although Warenne's assertions were inadmissible at common law, they had generations of tradition behind them and they probably still commanded wide sympathy. Despite its inaccuracy of detail and the inevitable scarcity of evidence about non-literate beliefs, the heart of the Warenne story can be shown to be credible.

To consider first the memory of the Norman Conquest. The claim that an earl like Warenne was entitled to privileges by right of conquest was certainly circulating at the time of the *quo warranto* proceedings, as it is explicitly contradicted by a royal attorney in 1286 in an action against the earl of Hereford. One justification for this claim was the notion that the earls (*comites*) were the descendants of the companions (*comites*) of William the Conqueror. Similarly the larger idea inherent in the Warenne story, that the descendants of the Norman conquerors were living memorials of that conquest, regardless of whether they had documents to prove it, was certainly a century old. In about 1175 the chief justiciar, Richard de Lucy, recommended Henry II to confirm the charters of Battle Abbey (which were recent forgeries in fact) because 'even if all charters perished, we should all still be its charters, since we are enfeoffed from the conquest made at Battle'.[18] Richard meant that the king's companions should be Battle's testimonials because the abbey had been founded in thanksgiving for the victory at Hastings.

In emphasising conquest the Warenne story may also be recalling a more general and ancient belief among the medieval nobility. That warriors were superior to writers and to all their works seems to have been part of the traditional ideology of the barbarians, who had conquered the Roman empire and replaced the constraining written law of Rome by flexible oral custom. Matthew Paris had recorded one formulation of this idea in a declaration allegedly made by some of the French baronage against the clergy in 1247. They declared that 'all of us, the king's chief men, perceive by applying our minds that the kingdom was not won by written law, nor by the arrogance of clerks, but by the sweat of war'. To the Normans in particular, who were usurpers wherever they triumphed— whether in France, England, Italy or Syria—the righteousness of conquest was part of a mythology.

The most interesting part of the Warenne story is not the justification of conquest, however, for that is quite common in medieval political ideas, but his alleged production of an 'ancient and rusty sword' which purported to be the very sword used by the first Earl Warenne at the Norman Conquest. Whether this relic was authentic and whether it ever was

shown to Edward I's judges are features of the story which cannot be verified. It is possible that such a revered weapon might have been kept and it
is also possible that the earl might have shown it to the judges on some
occasion less formal than a session of the court considering his case.
Although at first sight the story suggests that Warenne was threatening the
court with his sword, closer scrutiny shows that he was enunciating a
familiar theory of conquest and supporting it by the most appropriate
type of evidence, the symbolic instrument of conquest. The sword was
rusty; it was a relic, not a practical weapon. Nevertheless Warenne was
perfectly capable of threatening to fight a royal officer in what he deemed
to be a just cause. The sheriff of Lincolnshire had disarmingly explained
to the king's judges in 1276 that he would have needed a force of 'around
five thousand men' to execute a writ within Warenne's liberty of Stamford.[19] Perhaps it was in reaction to this writ that Warenne had displayed
his sword before the judges.

The use of objects, including swords, as props in the theatre of memory was recommended in medieval academic treatises, since 'the remembrance of things is held by the images, as though they were letters'.[20] At a
less exalted level it had been usual practice, before charters became common, to preserve the memory of a title to property in the object which had
symbolised the conveyance. The earl of the story was producing something different, yet comparable, in the sword which symbolised his family's acquisition of their lands. To emphasise the importance of personal
mementoes in evidence of title, an earlier Earl Warenne in a gift to Lewes
Priory in 1147 had given it possession by the hairs of his head; these,
together with his brother's, were cut off before the altar by Henry of Blois,
bishop of Winchester. Such symbolic objects were retained by the beneficiary, but they have rarely survived because their significance could easily
be lost when it depended on oral transmission only. Among recorded
examples of such objects accompanying gifts of land are a cup given to
Durham Cathedral in c. 1066 by Copsi, earl of Northumberland, which
(according to a Durham author writing in c. 1100) 'is preserved in the
church and retains the memory of that deed for ever'; a gold and ruby ring
given to St Paul's Cathedral in the first half of the twelfth century by
Osbert de Camera, which was affixed to his charter; a staff cut 'from the
land' concerned and given to Ramsey Abbey in 1121–2 by Wulfget,
'which we still have' (according to the Ramsey chronicler writing in
c. 1170). Although specific records like these of such objects are rare, the
practice was presumably commonplace. A comparable practice survives
to the present day in the giving of wedding rings.

There was nothing necessarily unusual, then, in the Earl Warenne possessing a symbolic memento of the Norman Conquest, nor in objects
serving as evidence of title to property. More strange was the form of
the earl's symbol, a sword, and the allegation that he produced it before
the king's judges. At least from the beginning of the thirteenth century,
and probably from Henry II's reign, the king's court had refused to take
cognisance of symbolic mementoes other than seals. Furthermore, it
would certainly not have considered any object to be a sufficient title to
a franchise unless it were supported by a charter. Instances of objects
other than sealed writings being produced as evidence of title in royal
courts are consequently very rare.

One interesting case made its way on to the royal records in 1213,
however, when a litigant objected to the prior of Durham producing a
charter against him, which 'is not made according to the custom of the
realm nor is there a seal on it, but a certain knife which can be put on or
taken off'. This charter (one half of a chirograph in fact, dated 1148) is
still preserved at Durham and from it hangs a knife with a polished haft
of horn and a broken rusty blade. This knife could indeed be easily 'put
on or taken off', as it is attached by a strip of parchment which is
threaded through a hole in the haft and then tied. Judging by the numbers of references to them in charters, knives like this were favourite symbols of conveyances in the Anglo-Norman period, although they have
seldom survived. It is possible that other charters of the twelfth century,
which have empty parchment strips hanging from them, were originally
authenticated by knives rather than seals. Most exceptional is a charter
dated 1151 for St Denys Priory near Southampton with two parallel slits
in it, through which the blade of the donor's symbolic knife was once
fixed to the parchment.

Although knives were common enough, a sword is unusual as a symbol
of title despite its being the most obvious symbol of knightly and secular
power. A knight's oath at his inauguration was made by his placing a
sword on an altar, just as other symbolic objects were placed in conveyances of property. Justifying this practice, John of Salisbury argued
that this symbolic gesture by a knight was valid without any form of words
in writing, such as a bishop or abbot needed at his profession, for 'who
would demand of a non-literate [*illitteratus*], whose duty is to know arms
rather than letters, that he should make a lettered profession?'[21] When
Thomas de Muschamps became a monk at Durham, probably shortly
before his death in *c.* 1130, he invested St Cuthbert and the monks with
the estate of Hetherslaw by his sword offered on an altar. In this instance

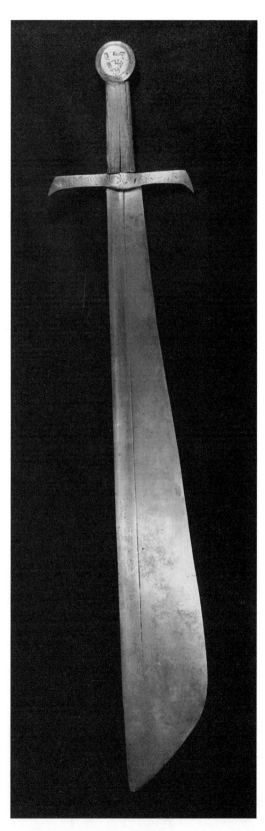

PLATE 5a. A drawing by Matthew
Paris of the justiciar Hubert de Burgh
seeking sanctuary at the altar of
Merton Abbey after he was accused
of corruption by Henry III and a
warrant was issued for his arrest

5b. A medieval falchion from
Durham Cathedral. This thirteenth-
century sword was used like a
document as proof of ownership
of the manor of Sockburn in
Northumberland

investiture by sword was the symbol, not of the beginning of a knightly career, but of its ending.

In presenting his sword to the monks of Durham Priory, Thomas de Muschamps laid down his arms and offered up his worldly goods in one symbolic gesture. Nevertheless this gesture did not prove as memorable as it should have done. Unlike the Earl Warenne, Durham Priory neglected to keep the sword. Record of it survives only because the monks were obliged to get writs from King Stephen and Henry II, when Thomas's heirs repeatedly refused to surrender Hetherslaw. In pursuit of this claim Absalom, the prior from 1154 to 1158, wrote a public letter to the sheriff of Northumberland insisting that he and another monk had actually witnessed the investiture with the sword two or three decades earlier. Ironically the day for settling this claim was fixed by Stephen of Bulmer, whose uniquely inscribed and labelled carving knife (recording an agreement with Lindisfarne) is now preserved as a title-deed at Durham. Although Durham Priory apparently failed in this claim and Thomas's sword was not kept, this dispute at least provides an instance, comparable with the Earl Warenne's, of a title to property depending on the evidence of a sword.

There are, moreover, at least two English examples of early medieval swords being kept as symbolic mementoes. The better-known is the Conyers falchion, which is exhibited in Durham Cathedral treasury. This sword was the symbol by which the head of the Conyers family held the manor of Sockburn from the bishop of Durham. Each head of the family was obliged up to 1860 to show the sword to the bishop as evidence of title. Although this is a parallel with Warenne's sword, a problem is that the falchion does not seem to be the original weapon, as it dates from no earlier than the thirteenth century and has been associated (by the heraldry on its pommel) with Richard of Cornwall, the brother of Henry III. A closer parallel with Warenne is a sword (no longer existing) which was kept in the royal treasury 'to this day' according to the Ramsey chronicler writing in c. 1170. It was preserved 'as evidence of God's bounty and the royal victory' over the Scots by King Athelstan at Brunanburh in 937. St Odo of Canterbury had miraculously provided it, when Athelstan's own sword had slipped from its scabbard. The Ramsey chronicler is careful, however, to report this story with a cautious note, 'as is said'.

Closer in time to the Warenne story and perhaps for that reason a closer parallel is Edward I's use of the symbolism of arms and armour in a letter to the pope in 1301.[22] This letter put forward a battery of arguments, from both myth and recent history, to justify English overlordship in

Scotland. Boniface VIII had argued in 1299 that Scotland belonged to the Roman church from ancient times and he challenged Edward to produce his titles and muniments. Edward was thus obliged in effect to state by what warrant he claimed jurisdiction over Scotland, just as two decades earlier he had required magnates like the Earl Warenne to show warrants for their jurisdictions. Although Edward made it clear at the outset that he did not consider himself bound to answer the pope in this case, his lengthy explanation concedes that an answer was necessary. Placed in a similar situation to his magnates a little earlier, though with many more documents at his disposal, Edward and his advisers resorted to arguments from myth and symbolism almost as readily as the earl in the Warenne story.

Unlike the Earl Warenne, however, Edward did not possess an ancient sword as a symbol of conquest. Athelstan's miraculous sword, which the Ramsey chronicler had mentioned a century earlier, had either got lost or the chronicler may have been mistaken in his original information. Nevertheless Edward did attempt to compensate for not having Athelstan's sword by referring to a fissure in a rock near Dunbar, which had allegedly been made by a miraculous sword blow from Athelstan. This blow had been facilitated by the intervention of St John of Beverley (not St Odo of Canterbury this time) and, according to Edward's letter to the pope, 'may still be seen as an evident sign of this event'. Edward had also a more recent and convincing argument from arms. After King William the Lion was taken prisoner by the English in 1174 he had offered his helmet, lance and saddle on the altar of York Minster as tokens of subjection, 'and they are kept and preserved in that church up to the present day'.

These comparisons between the Warenne story and other sources suggest that it would not have appeared as peculiar or incredible to people in c. 1300 as it has to some twentieth-century historians. The descendants of the Norman conquerors, particularly the earls, probably did believe in a right of conquest. Physical objects, especially knives, were kept as titles to property. Although the use of swords as mementoes is rare in England at least, the sword was the archetypal symbol of knightly as distinct from clerkly authority. Titles to authority or property could not always be proved by producing charters or citing precedents in writing. To justify English claims in Scotland Edward I's government had to resort to myth and physical symbols just as the earl did in the Warenne story. Taken together, these fragmentary details help to reconstruct ways of thinking and remembering which were widespread before the coming of written records. The growth of literacy did not occur in a cultural vacuum. It replaced non-literate ways, which seemed equally natural to those who were accustomed to them. The most difficult initial problem in the history of literacy is appreciating what preceded it.

A paradox of the Warenne story is that, although it is ill-founded by literate standards of proof, it is essentially more truthful than some of the pleadings based on charters which were duly recorded in the official rolls of the *quo warranto* proceedings. In producing an ancient sword instead of a charter as his title from the Norman Conquest, the earl showed greater historical awareness than an abbot who produced a charter of William the Conqueror. Many—perhaps most—charters of Edward the Confessor or William the Conqueror circulating in the thirteenth century were forgeries, including even those of Battle Abbey founded by William himself, because title-deeds had been the exception rather than the rule in the eleventh century (see chapter XII below). If Edward I's lawyers in the *quo warranto* proceedings had persisted in demanding titles in writing from 1066 or even earlier, using the argument that 'time does not run against the king', nearly all owners of property in England would have been disfranchised.[23] In 1290 by the *quo warranto* statute a compromise was made. In subsequent case law the king was understood to have conceded that documentary proof would not be required henceforward from any date earlier than the accession of Richard I in 1189. The last decade of the twelfth century was a realistic date from which to expect written titles, as tenure by charter among the tenants-in-chief at least was beginning to be normal by then.

In the 1290s the earl of the Warenne story could therefore return his 'ancient and rusty sword' to its scabbard for all time, as it was now a mere historical oddity instead of being a living relic transmitting memory to future generations. 'Legal memory', that artificial memory which depended primarily on documentary proof and not on mementoes or mortal oral testimony, had been arbitrarily set at 1189 and remained there for the rest of the Middle Ages. William the Conqueror had not brought the people under the rule of written law. Nor was Domesday Book the last judgement; rather, it was a symbolic new start. By contrast two centuries later, in the last decades of Edward I's reign, when the Earl Warenne allegedly produced his ancestral sword as testimony of the Norman Conquest, his claim (assuming that something like it was made) went unrecorded in the official rolls of the king's court because it was irrelevant. By then the province of myth and hearsay was the only appropriate place for a story which claimed priority for memory over written record in the king's court.

The growth of reliance on writing has been a continuing process without a precise beginning or end. In England it had started long before 1066 with Roman inscriptions and Anglo-Saxon charters, and would go on for centuries after 1307. In the twelfth century, when charters were still uncommon and bureaucracy had scarcely begun, William the Conqueror was credited with the impossible and therefore heroic feat of having made a definitive book of judgement by which to govern the conquered people. A century or more later the idea of bringing the people under written law had come closer to reality, with the expansion of royal and seignorial bureaucracies and the use of charters even by some serfs. Popular legend reacted then with the story of the Earl Warenne, who is committed to the equally heroic task of halting the *quo warranto* proceedings with his rusty sword. The Norman Conquest, which was identified with the threat of written record in the twelfth century, had become by 1307 in the Warenne story a symbol of the good old days of simple and forceful memory. Magnates like Warenne could indeed curtail the king's political power and they maintained a tradition of doing so from Magna Carta onwards, but they could not stop the advance of writing into more and more areas of ordinary life because that was caused by the massing of documents in archives and the spread of literate skills over the country.

❧ II ❧

THE PROLIFERATION OF DOCUMENTS

In 1170 Master David of London wrote from France to an unnamed agent in England, giving him directions about the safekeeping of his correspondence. The year before, David had been a representative at the papal *curia* of Henry II and Gilbert Foliot, bishop of London, against Thomas Becket. As a consequence he had earned an annuity of £20 (paid partly by the king and partly by Foliot) and the enmity of Becket. The controversy had become so fierce in the last few months of Becket's life that David took steps to safeguard this new pension. He explained to his agent in England that he had obtained from Henry II two charters, one confirming the king's portion and the other Foliot's obligation. As Henry II's eldest son, Henry the Young King, had just been crowned, David also obtained a letter close from Henry II, commanding the Young King to issue similar charters for him.

The two royal charters, and the letter close promising two more, only safeguarded the principle of David's pension. In addition he needed writs detailing how the payments were to be made. The king's bailiff in Godalming, Ranulf de Broc, was therefore ordered in another royal letter close to pay David £15 a year at specified intervals. This letter, David explained, was intended to save him having to apply for a new royal writ to the bailiff every time he required payment. A similar letter was sent to the bishop of London concerning the remaining £5 of the pension. To ensure that the bishop was not charged twice, another royal writ had to be issued ordering the sheriffs of Middlesex not to exact the £5 from the bishop in future. Likewise the Exchequer (which accounted with the sheriffs) was instructed to allow the £15 from Ranulf de Broc and the £5 from the bishop, so that Ranulf and the bishop would not have to apply for writs acquitting them each time. Settling how David's pension was to be paid had therefore necessitated letters to various levels of the king's bureaucratic hierarchy ranging from the bailiff, Ranulf, up to the barons of the Exchequer. By these means David had acquired a series of 'standing orders' so that the payments due to him would be authorised automatically in future.

David was still not satisfied. 'To be on the safe side,' he wrote, 'so that they cannot malign me, I have had sealed [by the Chancery] a transcript of that [writ to the Exchequer] and a transcript of the one which is to be sent to Ranulf.' David told his agent 'to keep these with my charters'; he was evidently rapidly acquiring an archive of his own. Even so, neither the king's letters nor the transcripts allayed his anxieties entirely. As an added precaution, he got two of the king's confidential ministers, Richard of Ilchester and Geoffrey Ridel, to write on his behalf to William St John and Thomas the Sealer (who were probably officers of the chief justiciar in England) 'so that things may be made to run expeditiously'. After all these letters, David had the temerity to conclude his instructions to the agent by telling him that he had not been able to obtain the one writ which the agent wanted for himself, because he did not wish to trouble the king with trifles when Henry was so worried about Becket.

To sum up, the documents which David needed to safeguard his pension comprised two charters from Henry II, two charters from the Young King and a letter close to the Young King; writs to Ranulf de Broc, the bishop of London, the sheriffs of Middlesex and the barons of the Exchequer; official transcripts of two of these writs; two letters from ministers to officials in England. Altogether eleven royal documents were to be produced and two letters from ministers. These letters would in their turn have created other correspondence. David had also, of course, to get the letter written to his agent and to keep the copy of it, which was preserved in his register and hence retained for posterity.

Master David's letter explains better than many generalisations how records proliferated, and it suggests the point this process had reached at the time of Becket's death, a century after the Norman Conquest. In England, with its extraordinarily centralised monarchy, the principal producer of documents was the king's government. Many, perhaps most, of the letters produced were written within the organisation to other royal officials. The letters to the bailiff, the sheriffs and the Exchequer, and those from Richard of Ilchester and Geoffrey Ridel, illustrate this in Master David's case. Behind any solemn royal charter now extant there once existed numerous ancillary documents—petitions, drafts, transcripts, writs to officials, letters to other interested parties, and correspondence among the officials themselves 'so that things may be made to run expeditiously'. As the king moved continually from place to place within England, and often across the Channel as well (particularly in Henry II's case), he communicated with many of his officials by letters. Almost any royal order required some sort of writ to, or from, the Exchequer in London; the purpose of Master David's 'standing orders' was to reduce the repetitious issue of writs of this sort.

Moreover, all these officials had to be cajoled and encouraged by offerings and fees to produce the necessary documents. One advantage enjoyed by royal clerks was that they were not expected to make such offerings to each other and could therefore get the documents they needed free of charge, thus further enlarging the number of documents produced. On one occasion at Henry II's court, Thurstan, the king's steward, complained to Henry that Adam of Yarmouth, the spigurnel (the sealer of writs), had refused to seal a writ for him for nothing. It emerged that Adam felt aggrieved because Thurstan had not let him have two cakes when he was entertaining guests; Adam had refused to seal the writ in retaliation. The king resolved the dispute by making Adam sit down, with the writ and his seal, while Thurstan offered him two cakes on bended knee. This little piece of gossip, from Walter Map's *Courtiers' Trifles*, illustrates how the king himself could get involved in the pettiest disputes within his household and the discretion his bureaucrats had to dispense or withold favours. The proliferation of documents meant that government became more dependent on literates; it did not make it any less arbitrary or capricious.

In Walter Map's story and Master David's letter it is evident that the initiative for obtaining the writs came from the beneficiaries and not from the bureaucracy itself. David was anxious to provide against every conceivable mishap; so he took the trouble to obtain transcripts for himself, writs to other officials, and letters from persons of influence to expedite his business. Once the bureaucratic machine had taken shape, overanxious users encouraged it to grow progressively more complex and extensive. On the other hand, neither Thurstan, the king's steward, nor David are entirely typical in their attitudes, as both were connected with the royal court and would consequently have had a special knowledge of, and interest in, forms of documentary proof. David had also attended the schools of Paris and Bologna, which would have made him literate in every sense of the word. By 1170 the king's government was much more dependent on documents than a century earlier, but it was still relatively primitive. It would be wrong to assume that the whole of England was bureaucratically controlled in Henry II's reign.

A century later, however, by Edward I's reign, the use of documents had extended down to village level. The English *Song of the Husbandman* (probably dating from the early fourteenth century) depicts the beadles collecting taxes from the peasants, 'the men on the earth' (*men utho mold*), by the authority of an Exchequer writ. The beadles say: 'You are written in my list, as you know very well' (*Thou art written y my writ that thou wel wost*). The beadles may not have been exaggerating. The statute of Exeter of 1285 had required local bailiffs to supply the king's commissioners with the names, written down in a roll, of every village, half-village and hamlet within franchises as well as in the kingdom as a whole. Furthermore, from at least the 1270s, seignorial stewards and bailiffs were meant to have written on rolls the names of all males (excluding clerics) over the age of twelve; these lists were read out twice a year when the sheriff or the franchise-holder visited the locality for the view of frankpledge. In theory at least, Edward I's government thus had access to lists of every place of habitation, however small, and every man, however lowly his status.

By 1300 beadles and their like were accustomed to making lists; or rather, that was the practice recommended by writers of treatises on estate management in Edward I's reign. The book called *Husbandry* recommends the bailiff in the autumn to list everything that remains on the manor, such as tools and horseshoes, great and small, so that he will know what to buy for the coming year. The same book mentions in passing, as if it were a commonplace, *la respounse del issue de let*—the record of yields of milk from the cows. Such a record may have been a notched wooden tally, and not a parchment. Even so, it shows that some manorial bailiffs and reeves used records, other than their memories, for day-to-day management. The editor of these treatises, D. Oschinsky, argues that 'it was probably within their power to write symbolic signs and figures', but she does not think that a reeve or his agents could read or write Latin.[1] P. D. A. Harvey likewise rejects the proposition that 'the peasant farmers who normally became reeves were able to read, let alone write their own annual accounts'.[2] Nevertheless one of the treatises, *Seneschaucy*, assumes that the bailiff or reeve can read (in French, if not in Latin), as it warns him to admit no one and hand over nothing from the manor to any person whatsoever 'without the warrant of a writ' under pain of repaying the loss from his own purse. If the bailiff or reeve were unable to read such warrants when they were delivered to him, he would soon have been out of pocket. It is impossible to know how many farms in England in 1300 were administered with the degree of bureaucratic efficiency laid down in the rule books. At the least, however, the leading men in villages must have considered wooden tallies a commonplace and been familiar with written warrants in Edward I's reign.

The fact that many—perhaps most—people in thirteenth-century England had to read from time to time does not mean that they also wrote. In manuscript culture reading and writing were separate skills. Writing documents required clerical training and special equipment; parchment, ink and quill pens were not on sale at the village shop. Reeves and bailiffs employed clerks to draw up accounts and send letters to their superiors. In many villages, in addition to the priest, there would have been other peasants (both men and women) who had received some clerical training when young, either by serving in the parish church or in a lord's domestic chaplaincy. But writing was not required as often as reading. It may have been harder in a village to get ink and parchment than to find a clerk to use them. Like buying a ribbon or a needle, writing something down might mean waiting until an itinerant specialist appeared in the neighbourhood. Documents of one sort and another can have been no rarer in villages than ribbons and needles, but they were as ephemeral. Only very special ones have survived.

Even the lowest class in society, vagrants, were expected to carry certificates of good character. In Essex in 1248 five men from as far afield as Barnard Castle and Canterbury, after being acquitted of theft, were forbidden to return to the county unless they brought with them 'their testimonial of trustworthiness'. That a written document is referred to here, rather than oral testimony, is suggested by two cases from Sussex in 1261–2. In one Robert de Parys of Battle, who had been arrested as a horse thief, obtained the bailiff of East Grinstead's permission to go away and fetch a testimonial of his trustworthiness, but he never returned.

The other case from Sussex is more explicit about the testimonial being in writing. William of Badgeworth (in Gloucestershire) sued Peter de Turvill, the bailiff of the honour of Bramber (in Sussex), for wrongful imprisonment and grievous bodily harm. William's story, which was upheld by a special jury, was that he had come to Sussex to visit a relative when he was arrested by Peter on suspicion of theft. He asked Peter's permission to return to Badgeworth to obtain 'letters testifying to his trustworthiness' from his lord's court. William was duly issued at his manorial court with a letter, sealed by the bailiff and suitors of Badgeworth, testifying that he was a trustworthy man. He then returned to Sussex and presented his letter to Peter in the honorial court at Bramber, but Peter reacted by imprisoning him in a dungeon and only released him because he was at death's door. Although this case shows that William's letter failed to protect him (initially at least), it also suggests that the sending of such letters between seignorial courts was a routine procedure. The bailiffs who had the letters written, the suitors or members of the court who sealed them, and the recipients who benefited from them, must all have been sufficiently familiar with writing to understand the import of a letter. Indeed William—mistakenly as it turned out—had such confidence in his letter that he thought it would save him from a dungeon when he returned to Sussex.

Comparable with testimonials of trustworthiness are the warrants of lawful purchase which accompanied sales of livestock. In Kent in 1241 John le Keche and others were acquitted of stealing oxen, but the jury noted that they had bought the animals foolishly and 'without the warrant that they could have had'. That a written warrant was meant is made clear by a case from Oxford in 1258 in which a receipt (in the form of a letter patent) for the purchase of a horse is mentioned. Similarly in 1292 a plaintiff told the king's justices that he had been deprived of a letter issued in the name of Hereford corporation, stating that he was searching for a stolen horse. The conclusion to draw from such evidence is that by the second half of the thirteenth century it was imprudent for anybody to wander far from his own village without some form of identification in writing, both for himself and for anything in his possession. Medieval society's savage laws against strangers and vagrants must have been a forceful promoter of literacy in the countryside.

Given these facts, it comes as no surprise to find that by 1300 serfs and villeins used documents. If they wished to advance themselves or provide for younger sons or daughters, they had to imitate their betters and exploit written procedures. A Latin poem written in *c.* 1276 describes, from a hostile point of view, the efforts of the people of Stoughton to sue their lord, the abbot of Leicester. One of the rustics says: 'I will go to the king, I will bow to the king, I will hand him the case in writing' (*Ad regem vadam, coram rege cadam, causam scriptam sibi tradam*).[3] But these wretches, who had hoped to be *magistri* ('masters' in both the academic and the social sense), were quickly overawed by a smooth advocate at the king's court and returned weeping and empty-handed. In this case the serfs had achieved nothing with their document and were treated almost as a band of rebels. Occasionally, however, individuals were more successful. An action in the King's Bench twenty years later concerned a certain John son of Robert of Estgate, whose grandmother had been a serf of Robert de Mortimer.[4] Robert of Estgate had (according to the plea roll) 'subsequently increased in goods and by his trading improved himself so much' that he acquired lands by charters from the Mortimers. Robert is thus a real instance of that stereotype, the peasant of servile origins who bettered himself by trade. The charters from the Mortimers were intended to give documentary reinforcement to his eminent status.

The legality of serfs acquiring or conveying property by charters is complex. In the case just mentioned Robert had been obliged to surrender his charters to William de Mortimer, his lord, who argued on those grounds that Robert was his villein; but John, Robert's son, claimed to be a freeman and was adjudged to be so. Similarly the Peterborough Abbey cartulary, entitled *Cartae Nativorum*, can be interpreted in contrary senses. 'Natives' ' or 'serfs' charters' might imply that these were illegal documents, which had consequently been surrendered to the lord, the abbot of Peterborough, just as Robert had surrendered his charters to William de Mortimer; if that is so, Peterborough Abbey made a record of the charters because they concerned its own property. Conversely the title *Cartae Nativorum* might suggest that charters made by serfs were a legal commonplace; they were recorded in the cartulary to reinforce their validity, just as private charters of greater men were sometimes enrolled in the royal archives for further security. The former hypothesis, that the documents had been surrendered to Peterborough because serfs had no legal title by charter, is the more likely.

Whether or not the serfs who made these charters had a legal right to do so, the existence of the Peterborough documents (even in cartulary copies) demonstrates that in the latter half of the thirteenth century small properties were being conveyed by peasants using writing. Whether the persons and properties concerned were technically free or unfree, these charters are a landmark in the development of written record. There are, for example, fifteen *cartae nativorum* from the village of Tinwell in Rutland; seven of these charters concern half-acres of land, another five one acre each, and the remaining three the rent and sale of some houses. If in many parts of England, as is probable, and not just on the Peterborough Abbey estates, single acres and half-acres were being conveyed by charter by 1300, the number of peasants' charters produced amounts to hundreds of thousands or even millions. Supposing that on average one charter was produced for each acre of arable once in the thirteenth century, the number of charters made would total at least eight million. It is very unlikely of course that a charter was made for every acre, even of arable. On the other hand, the *Cartae Nativorum* show that numerous documents concerned less than one acre, and the same land might be rented or conveyed more than once in the century. Attempted partitions and short-term conveyances must have been common, because the population and hence the pressure on land had reached a peak by 1300. It seems reasonable to conclude that at least hundreds of thousands, and perhaps millions, of peasants' charters were made, although those who made them were the more prosperous smallholders and in that sense were not typical serfs.

Unlike papal or royal letters for the great monastic houses, peasants' charters would not have been kept when they went out of date; because the legal status of the charters was dubious, peasants did not make

cartularies, and such small and fragile documents would have been difficult to preserve anyway. Nevertheless a few actual charters (as distinct
from copies like those in the *Cartae Nativorum*), undoubtedly concerning
unfree tenures, have been found and more are likely to come to light.
R. H. Hilton describes a lease (dating from *c.* 1230) between Gloucester
Abbey and a widow, Emma, who was to perform ploughing and other
duties in addition to paying a money rent.[5] Even if she were not of servile
status herself, some of the services prescribed are those of an unfree tenement. Her charter is in the form of a bipartite chirograph, which implies
theoretical equality between the contracting parties, Emma and the
abbot. The abbey's half of the chirograph (the extant half) is authenticated, as was required, by Emma's seal, which bears her name and a cross
as a central device.

The possessor of a seal was necessarily a person familiar with documents and entitled to participate in their use. The metal matrix of a seal
like Emma's would not have been made to use once only. Even if it were
mass-produced by casting and sold ready-made with a blank space
around the border, as is possible, the owner's name had still to be
engraved by hand. The name made the seal unique and hence legally
valid. Possession of a seal thus implied that its owner could read his own
name, as well as being prepared to authenticate documents with the
impress of his 'signature'. Emma's chirograph therefore demonstrates
that a holder of unfree land, even a woman (albeit a widow), might 'sign' a
document as early as 1230. From the same date or earlier there survives a
chirograph, made by the earl of Chester and Lincoln with the men of
Freiston and Butterwick in Lincolnshire, which bears the seals of at least
fifty of the men. Most of these men were probably not technically serfs,
but they were certainly smallholders.

In Henry II's reign his chief justiciar, Richard de Lucy, had smiled contemptuously when Gilbert de Balliol had mentioned a seal, saying: 'It was
not formerly the custom for every petty knight to have a seal, which befits
only kings and important people.'[6] Yet a century later not only knights,
but some of the smallest property-owners had seals. So far from opposing
this development, the statute of Exeter of 1285 actually required 'bondsmen' to have seals to authenticate their written evidence, when they served
on inquests for which there were insufficient freemen. The government
was prepared to overlook the distinction between freeman and serf when
it found it inconvenient. On the other hand, as with the surrender of serfs'
charters, some lords attempted to enforce that distinction rigidly. In 1295
the customary tenants of Bromham in Wiltshire were fined 100 shillings

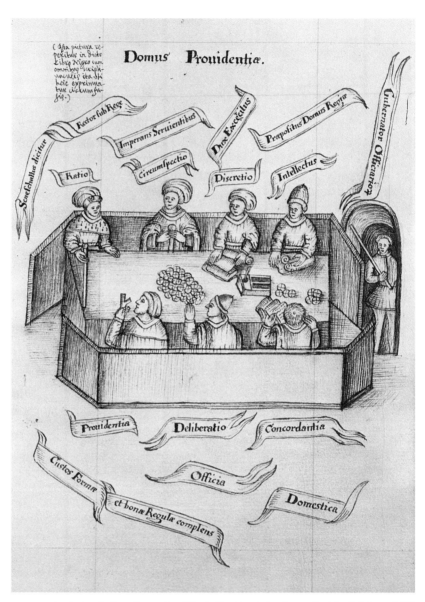

PLATE 6. A depiction from the Black Book of the household of Edward IV showing members of the household including the chancellor of the Exchequer seated around a table doing their accounts. Above them are captions listing the qualities they need for their posts: reason, caution, discretion and intelligence

'because they made a common seal in contempt of the lord', the abbot of Battle.[7] Seals for individuals may have been tolerated more readily; a communal seal suggested an organised association against the lord. Perhaps too Battle Abbey pursued a consistent policy against seals, as it was an abbot of Battle, Richard de Lucy's brother, whom Gilbert de Balliol had been opposing a century earlier. Despite the objections of some lords, seals like charters were probably possessed by the majority of landowners, however small their holdings, by 1300. The possession of any type of seal implied that its owner considered himself to be of sufficient status to use and understand documents, even if this were an aspiration rather than a reality.

By and large, the evidence suggests that the number of documents increased progressively, only being temporarily affected by political crises. During the civil war of Stephen's reign there was a small recession, yet the numbers of letters are more than double those of William Rufus's time.

The increasing mass of royal documents tended to enlarge and stratify the bureaucracy which produced them. There was obviously a close connection between the growth in numbers of documents and of the functionaries who made them. This is best illustrated by a story, told by Fitz Nigel in the *Dialogue of the Exchequer*, which can be taken to stand as typical.[8] Fitz Nigel describes how Henry II employed Master Thomas Brown, who had been the secretary of Roger II of Sicily, to keep a watching brief in the king's interests over the administration. In this capacity Brown made a roll 'of the laws of the realm and the secrets of the king'. To make this roll Brown needed a scribe to sit at the Exchequer table. But his scribe could not be fitted on to the writers' bench at the Exchequer because it was already occupied (from right to left) by the treasurer, the treasurer's scribe (who wrote the pipe roll), the chancellor's scribe (who copied from the treasurer's scribe and made the chancellor's roll), the chancellor's clerk (who supervised the chancellor's scribe) and the clerk of the constabulary. Brown's scribe was therefore given a place higher up, where he could make his copy over the treasurer's scribe's shoulder. As the pupil in the *Dialogue* comments, the scribe must have been 'lynx-eyed to avoid mistakes'.

This story gives the impression that the proliferation of documents and functionaries was inexorable and almost subject to some mathematical law. Nevertheless there are significant exceptions to the rule that documents steadily multiplied. Even Fitz Nigel's story about Thomas Brown's

scribe can be interpreted in a contrary sense. After Brown's death or re-
tiral in *c.* 1180 the copy of the pipe roll which he had kept was discon-
tinued, though his scribe may have stayed at the Exchequer as the earliest
king's remembrancer.

A clearer instance of the bureaucracy being first enlarged and then
curtailed appears in Fitz Nigel's remarks about another of Henry II's con-
fidants, Richard of Ilchester, archdeacon of Poitiers, who sat on another
side of the Exchequer table. Richard's duties were to supervise the making of the rolls and to stop the treasurer from falling asleep. As we have
seen, Master David of London had hoped to expedite his business by getting a letter addressed to him. Richard introduced a system of keeping a
copy of every summons sent to a sheriff in order to prevent him from
altering it: 'so, when the sheriff was sitting at his account and the chancellor's clerk was reading the summons, the archdeacon's clerk, with his eye
on the copy, watched him to see that he made no mistake.' By this means a
check was kept on both the chancellor's clerk and the sheriff. 'But', Fitz
Nigel continues, 'as time went on, and the number of debtors enormously
increased, so that a whole skin of parchment was scarcely long enough for
a single summons, the number of names and the labour involved proved
overpowering.' The roll of summonses was therefore abolished. As Fitz
Nigel points out, it had not really been necessary in the first place, as all
the debts summoned were already recorded on the pipe roll. This anecdote illustrates the speed at which record-making increased: the lists of
debtors had become enormous within a decade or so; but it also shows
that the advance of bureaucracy could, occasionally at least, be stopped.
The formation of the royal bureaucracy was thus a complex process of
experiment and makeshift; although the net result, when averaged over
decades, was a constant increase in the production of documents.

❧ III ❧

The Work of Hubert Walter

From the point of view of posterity—by looking, that is, at documents which have survived—the most decisive increase in production occurred within a decade or so on either side of 1200. The earliest extant series of plea rolls, feet of fines, and Chancery enrolments of outgoing letters begin at this time. These are the years in which Archbishop Hubert Walter held office, first as chief justiciar (1193–8) of Richard I and then as chancellor (1199–1205) of King John. Whether Hubert invented all these types of record, or whether some had existed earlier but did not survive, are matters for conjecture. An explicit instance of deliberate record-making by Hubert is the earliest tripartite final concord, dated 15 July 1195. The document is endorsed:

> This is the first chirograph that was made in the king's court in the form of three chirographs, according to the command of his lordship of Canterbury [Hubert Walter] and other barons of the king, to the end that by this form a record can be made to be passed to the treasurer to put in the treasury.

The reference to Hubert's responsibility for the innovation is reinforced by his brother, Theobald, being the plaintiff whom this chirograph concerns. The purpose of the third copy (which was the novelty), or 'foot of the fine', is explicitly stated to be 'to the end that by this form (*per illam formam*) a record' might be deposited in the treasury. Keeping a third copy was not entirely novel, however, as the practice had Anglo-Saxon precedents and within living memory Henry II had personally insisted in 1164 that a third copy of the chirograph recording the controversial Constitutions of Clarendon should be put 'in the royal archives'.

Although there were precedents for Hubert Walter's action, the importance of the feet of fines should not be underestimated. For the first time, a form of record had been deliberately inaugurated as a continuing series for archival purposes. Furthermore the feet of fines gave private individuals the opportunity to have transactions kept on permanent record in the royal treasury. What had in the past been exceptional practice now became the rule; that is the principle underlying many of Hubert's bureaucratic reforms. Although the king's government already made regular records for its own purposes, it had not normally extended its archival facilities to private individuals. A few non-royal conveyances of property were enrolled in the pipe rolls and the *Cartae Antiquae* before 1195; but, unlike the feet of fines, this practice was neither systematic nor regular. The use of feet of fines was of course confined to the more prosperous landowners, who were able to pay the fees and take the risks of litigating in the king's court. Hubert Walter could not, and probably did not intend to, benefit everybody. Nevertheless the extent to which these documents became widespread among landowners within a few years is indicated by a concord made at Westminster on 29 October 1198 between William de Bruce of Annandale and Adam of Carlisle concerning eight ploughgates in Lockerbie. Lockerbie was (and is) in Scotland, though the fine was filed with those from Northumberland.

The success of the feet of fines archive may have been the cause which encouraged the government to enrol copies of royal letters during Hubert Walter's chancellorship. These rolls form three main series—the charter, close and patent rolls, extant from the first, second, and third years of John's reign respectively. Like the feet of fines, the Chancery rolls bene-fited private individuals, who paid fees to have their royal grants recorded in them. Had such rolls existed in Henry II's time, for example, Master David of London would have been able to have the various royal letters he obtained recorded there. These rolls also served the government as an official register. In 1201 (the second year of the extant charter rolls) Jocelin of Brakelond records that King John ordered an inquiry to be made 'through his register about what sort of charter' he had given the monks of Ely because the monks of Bury disputed its terms.[1] The con-tentious passage was duly found, as it still can be in the charter rolls, and letters protecting Bury were issued. The immediate consequence of this, however, was an armed raid by Bury on Ely and not a peaceful settlement. Similarly, many years later, Henry III wrote to Pope Gregory X in 1272 assuring him that some letters patent, which the prior of Christ Church Canterbury was exhibiting in a lawsuit at the Roman *curia*, were a forgery because 'no such letters can issue from our court unless they have first been registered [and] we have had our register searched about this case with the utmost care and diligence, and nothing whatsoever is to be found in it about the aforesaid letters'.[2] In fact the king was mistaken, as these letters had been enrolled in the patent rolls in November 1265. It was easier to make records than to use them efficiently.

The twelfth century had been a great period of making documents, the thirteenth was the century of keeping them. From the viewpoint of the historian today, the formation of an archive seems an obvious and essential step, once documents were produced in any quantity. To medieval governments, however, neither the urgency nor the usefulness of archives would have appeared as compelling. Copying outgoing letters on to rolls was an immense labour, as Fitz Nigel's anecdote about the fate of Richard of Ilchester's attempt to enrol the Exchequer summonses illustrates. Hubert Walter was not necessarily the inventor of the principle of enrolling outgoing charters or of filing incoming documents (returned writs, feet or fines and so on) on leather thongs, but he did create the principles of organisation which made continuous royal archives possible. The French royal archive of the letters which it received begins in 1194, with the retention of a treaty between Philip Augustus and the future King John of England. There may be more than coincidence in the development of royal archives in England and France in the same decade, as the two kingdoms were in almost daily contact because of the struggle between the Angevin and Capetian monarchies.

It would be rash to assume that such archives brought a return of information to the government which balanced the worry and expense of making them. Like Domesday Book, the Chancery and judicial rolls and writ files benefited remote posterity rather than contemporaries, since they provide minutely detailed information about the countryside and people of England as viewed by the king's government. The making of such records is an indicator of the efficiency of the government rather than its cause. They are a notable step in the transition from memory to written record because documents created more documents in their own image, not because they made for more effective government in themselves. The two examples cited in the preceding paragraph, of King John consulting his 'register' in 1201 and Henry III in 1272, suggest that the information provided, even when it was correct, did not help to keep the peace. The royal archives constituted a vast potential source of information, which could not be thoroughly consulted in the medieval period itself. Historians today are better equipped to search the rolls than the king's clerks were in the thirteenth century.

The creation of these central government archives (still extant in the Public Record Office) during Hubert Walter's years of office has been frequently described and has therefore been summarily treated here. Just as important in the proliferation of documents at the time was Hubert's effect on local government, although very few local records survive from this early period. Within his first year of office as chief justiciar, in the instructions for the justices' visitation in September 1194, he instituted coroners in each county including a clerk; from this order stemmed the coroners' rolls. From 1202 and 1203 comes the earliest evidence of the coroner's rolls being used to check oral testimony in county courts. In the Lincolnshire justices' visitation of 1202 the county was fined £200 because their oral 'record' differed from that of the coroners' rolls. Likewise in Staffordshire in 1203 the county court and the coroners 'recorded' that Simon Pring had not been outlawed, whereas the rolls of the coroners (as distinct from their persons) and of the sheriff showed that he had. In the judgment against the county court and the coroners, preference was accorded to the written records.

Hubert Walter's instructions for the justices' visitation in September 1194 also provided the first public local archives and official writers. The purpose of this legislation was to regulate loans made by the Jews. Neither moneylenders' bonds nor royal intervention in Jewish business were novelties in themselves; what was new was the establishment of archives and supervised writing facilities on a regular basis. It was ruled that *all* debts and pledges of the Jews were to be put in writing: loans were to be made in designated places only, where two scribes (financed by fees) would be provided and supervised by a clerk appointed by the king's commissioners, William of Sainte-Mère-Eglise and William of Chimillé. The documents recording the loans were to be written in the form of bipartite chirographs: one part would be kept by the Jews, and the other deposited in a communal archive (*in arca communi*) or public chest, with three sealed locks, whose keys were kept by the Jews, the Christians and the royal commissioners respectively. As if this were not sufficient security, the commissioners' clerk was also to keep in a roll up-to-date transcripts of all the chirographs in the chest; furthermore a roll of receipts of money by the Jews was to be kept in triplicate. These regulations were not all immediately enforced, but within two decades seventeen towns (mainly county towns) had archives of this sort.

By these means the principles of producing authenticated documents, retaining them in archives and transcribing copies on to rolls for ready reference spread from the royal Chancery and Exchequer to provincial centres. It may not be a coincidence that the earliest extant borough records, the Leicester guild rolls of 1196, survive from this period, although Leicester itself was not a Jewish centre. The king's government was not in this instance primarily concerned with promoting record-making as such, but with taxing the Jews and their transactions as thoroughly as possible. Taxation had been the king's main motive for making records, certainly since the institution of the Exchequer at the beginning of the twelfth century and probably since Domesday Book.

PLATE 7a. An anti-Semitic cartoon at the head of a thirteenth-century tallage roll of Isaac Jurnet of Norwich. The document records Jewish payments to the Crown

7b. An axeman depicted in the margin of an Exchequer document from the thirteenth century

The same principles, of making multiple records in the localities for taxation purposes, received their greatest extension in the plans for the carucage of 1198, which was required to finance Richard I's war against Philip Augustus in Normandy. This tax on every plough team necessitated making a survey of how many teams there were in each village. Such a survey was not novel in itself; as in the Domesday inquest, 'all these things were to be reduced to writing' (*in scriptum redigebantur*).[3] The innovation lay in requiring rolls to be made in quadruplicate. In each county a clerk and a knight were to act as collectors. Each was to have a copy of the carucage roll; a third copy was to be kept by the sheriff and a fourth by the baronial steward, whose lord's land was involved. Thus of these four rolls, only one was to be kept by a clerk; the three others were in the hands of laymen.

If these regulations had been enforced, every baronial steward would have possessed a list of his lord's plough teams, which comprised his basic resources in men and animals. Familiarity with documents, if not literacy itself, would have been compulsorily extended to knights and barons and their officers by legislation. It is doubtful, however, whether all these rolls were made, as Hubert Walter resigned from the chief justiciarship in the summer of 1198 at his own insistence (according to Richard I) because of 'the intolerable burden of work and his own incapacity'. Perhaps the difficulties in making England a more documented kingdom had temporarily overwhelmed him. Yet he returned to record-making within a year as King John's chancellor.

There is every reason to think that the king was by far the largest producer of documents at the time, as well as having the best archives to transmit them to posterity. In England, from the time of William the Conqueror's Domesday Book and Henry I's Exchequer onwards, it was not the Church or churchmen as such who were the principal promoters of the documentary habit but the king's clerks. Although such men were technically clerics, they usually put the interests of the king before those of the Church as an institution. Thomas Becket, chancellor and archbishop, is the most notable exception to this rule. More typical is Hubert Walter. 'Where did the archbishop come from?' asked Gerald of Wales in his denunciation of Hubert at the papal *curia* in 1199. 'From the Exchequer . . . This was the academy, this was the school, in which he had already grown old, from which he was called to all the grades of his [ecclesiastical] dignities, like nearly all the English bishops.'[4]

Hubert was no theologian, nor probably even a canon lawyer; there is no real evidence that he was a graduate of Bologna. *Illitteratus* (in the opinion of an unfriendly chronicler), or 'only indifferently endowed with book-learning' according to a more charitable estimate,[5] he had been brought up in the household of his kinsman, Ranulf de Glanvill, who became the chief justiciar. Both Hubert and Ranulf have been credited with the authorship of the lawbook ascribed to Glanvill, whose prologue regrets the impossibility of reducing the laws of England entirely to writing because of the ignorance of scribes and the confusion of the sources. If either Hubert or Ranulf were accepted as the author, it would be possible to see where Hubert derived an ambition to put so much into documentary form. In that case the Jewish archives of 1194, the feet of fines of 1195, the rolls of plough teams of 1198, and the Chancery rolls of 1200 were all products of a consistent purpose in making records, pursued by Hubert throughout his years of office.

The Exchequer may well have been Hubert's school, as Gerald of Wales alleged, although he probably came to it only when he was grown up. As a member of the chief justiciar's household, Hubert could have learned about making records from the acknowledged experts, Richard of Ilchester and Richard Fitz Nigel. The earliest known reference to Hubert 'surnamed Walter' is as a witness to a charter in *c.* 1181, where his name accompanies those of the two Richards and of Glanvill. Richard of Ilchester's innovations in record-making have already been mentioned. Richard Fitz Nigel, as author of the *Dialogue of the Exchequer*, had shown his aptitude for instruction by question and answer and his delight in the technicalities of documents. 'Master,' asks his pupil, 'why do you not teach others that knowledge of the Exchequer for which you are famous, and put it into writing lest it should die with you?'[6] Even in that question the concern for putting as much as possible into writing is evident. The making of records was a difficult and technical business, not requiring book-learning nor academic training as such, but instruction by those with practical experience. Fitz Nigel claimed to teach 'useful things' (*utilia*), not the 'clever things' (*subtilia*) of the scholastic masters. Hubert became the legatee of all this expertise and put it to more ambitious uses. The proliferation of documents was a European and a continuing phenomenon, yet if it were to be associated in England with one man, he would be Hubert Walter.

❧ IV ❧
Types of Written Record

An educated Englishman in the thirteenth century would have become familiar with a variety of writings over his lifetime—charters to safeguard his landed property, royal writs for litigation, homilies for devotion, romances for entertainment, and so on. Among the forty or so volumes which Guy de Beauchamp, earl of Warwick, gave by charter to Bordesley Abbey in 1306 are books of the Bible, meditations and saints' lives, romances and histories, a book of physic and one of surgery, a child's primer, an encyclopaedia, and 'a little red book in which are contained many diverse things'.[1] All the books are described as 'romances', meaning that they are in French and not Latin. A step down the social scale, the Northamptonshire gentleman, Henry de Bray of Harlestone, copied out with his own hand in Latin at the age of fifty-two (in 1322) a compilation for the instruction of his heirs containing a general description of the world, a more detailed description of England (its counties, bishoprics, kings and Cinque Ports), extracts from Domesday Book and other royal records, information about Northamptonshire feudal and local government, a list of his own tenants, the dimensions of Harlestone common field and the village, a table of measures, records of his expenses, and numerous copies of documents concerning his property. Both Guy's charter listing books and Henry's estate book are exceptional survivals. Most of the nobility and gentry were not so careful with their documents; but they would all have come across, even if they did not possess, a comparable variety of written records during their lives.

The experience of medieval writers and makers of records cuts across the lines dividing knowledge which scholars draw today. Although writers became gradually more specialised as the demand for documents increased, in the twelfth century and earlier they tended to perform a variety of functions. One of Thomas Becket's biographers, William Fitz Stephen, describes how he was a draftsman in his chancery, a subdeacon in his chapel, a reader in his law court, and on occasions a judge. In the chancery he would have been familiar with letters and literary style, in the chapel with liturgical books, and in the law court with records of pleas. Becket himself had started his career as an accountant to a London merchant and was also described as a 'clerk and accountant' of the sheriffs of London. He thus had experience of financial and civic record-making before he went into Archbishop Theobald's service and thence into the king's. In the thirteenth century Matthew Paris, who was the scribe and illustrator of most of his own works, wrote the chronicles for which he is famous in Latin prose and he is associated with the making of lives of English saints in French verse for aristocratic ladies. In addition he had a very competent knowledge of charters and royal writs (which he cites verbatim), Latin verse, heraldry, cartography, and an interest in natural science. His exceptionally varied activities emphasise the difficulty of classifying medieval writings too strictly into types.

Even single works of Matthew's defy exclusive classification. His best-known book, the *Chronica Majora*, is in part a history copied from other sources (Matthew performed here the role of editor and scribe) and in part a contemporary monastic chronicle composed by himself. It is also an illustrated book of lively caricatures probably intended to entertain, a cartulary of documents (in the *Liber Additamentorum*), an atlas (each volume was originally prefaced with maps and itineraries), and a heraldic reference book. Matthew included in it, moreover, his famous drawing from life of the elephant given by St Louis to Henry III in 1255 (together with a discourse on elephants) and the beautiful painting of the Virgin and Child, with himself kneeling at her feet, which prefaces the final part of the chronicle. In Matthew's mind history, literature, art and science were not separate realms of knowledge.

The works of Matthew Paris are an exceptional instance of a typical characteristic of medieval writings. Documents and books in manuscript tend to depart from standard forms and to contain a diversity of subject matter because there is no printing press automatically imposing uniformity. In the layout and content of their works writers and scribes aimed at the elegance which results from regularity and consistency, but personal idiosyncrasies and interests inevitably remained prominent in writings produced entirely by hand. Moreover, it is often impossible with medieval books to give an adequate single classification to an individual volume, as a modern librarian does, because a variety of works are frequently bound between the same covers. Guy de Beauchamp's 'little red book' containing many diverse things is an example of the problem. Miscellanies of this sort often reflected the interests of the compiler or owner of the book. The diverse contents had unity in his own experience and needs, rather than in any external scheme of things. An excellent introduction to the variety of works bound together into books in the thirteenth century is Oschinsky's descriptive list of the manuscripts containing treatises on accountancy and estate management.[2] For example, MS 17 includes (among other items) parliamentary statutes, cooking recipes, a lapidary (a discourse on precious stones), a glossary of measures, and treatises on management. Similarly MS 68 contains Walter of Henley's treatise on husbandry, together with Walter of Bibbesworth's poem to aid learning French, a moral poem (*La desputaisen du cors et de l'âme*), proverbs, a brief encyclopaedia called *L'image du monde*, and other works. Diverse as these subjects might appear to a modern scholar, they could all have been of interest or use to a country gentleman like Henry de Bray.

Even illuminated manuscripts, which look as if they were made exclusively for their magnificent paintings, might be seen in other ways. When in the 1180s Henry II arbitrarily gave the Winchester Bible to the ascetic St Hugh for his Charterhouse at Witham, the Carthusians were delighted because 'the correctness of the text pleased them especially, even more than the delicacy of the penmanship and the general beauty of the work'. There is likewise the remarkable case of the Sherborne Abbey manuscript which is partly a cartulary of documents concerning a lawsuit in 1145 and partly an illuminated missal for use at the altar in Holy Week.

The most fundamental distinction to make is between primary and secondary records. A charter extant in its original form as a single piece of parchment (preferably with the seal still attached) is a primary record, whereas a copy of that charter in a monastic cartulary or in the royal Charter rolls is a secondary record. By this classification original charters, writs, chirographs, wills, court rolls, ministers' accounts and so on are primary records; whereas chronicles, cartularies, the Chancery rolls, Domesday Book and similar surveys are secondary records because they are compiled from other sources. In this sense too most medieval books, from copies of the Bible downwards, are secondary because they were made from exemplars. This distinction between primary and secondary does not readily apply in all cases. Thus the parts of Matthew Paris's chronicles which he himself composed and wrote are essentially primary records, whereas many original charters and court rolls may have been compiled from drafts which were thrown away and in that sense they too are secondary records. If this latter assumption is universally applied, however, all extant medieval documents become secondary records, which is absurd.

Taken generally, the distinction between primary and secondary is applicable and useful, because it emphasises the difference between documents in their original form and copies or edited versions of them, whether medieval or modern. Primary and secondary records usually differ too in their format. Primary records are most often single sheets of parchment or a small stitched gathering, whereas secondary records are made up into rolls or bound books. The format of the records has affected their chance of survival over the centuries. The great majority of primary documents have been lost, because they consisted of single sheets of parchment, whereas registers and books survive in relative abundance. One purpose of copying documents into registers in the Middle Ages was to ensure that their texts did survive.

The following examples are of records made on parchment; but there are also writings on paper, wood, fabric and metal, and—most common among English non-parchment records—the tally-stick.

The primary records most commonly met with are letters of one sort or another. They are here collectively described as 'statements issued by individuals' because the generic term 'letters' is ambiguous and can mis-lead. A variety of descriptive terms for such written statements were used in the Middle Ages, such as *breve*, *carta*, *chirographum* and *litterae* itself. These terms were not used with strict consistency or uniformity, nor are they mutually exclusive. Nevertheless they can be adapted to create definitions which distinguish documents by their function with a fair degree of precision.

Working on this principle, a charter is a public letter issued by a donor recording a title to property. Charters are frequently therefore addressed to the general public—to 'those whom the present writing shall reach' or to 'all who shall hear and see this charter'. As the general public was the same as the Christian community, the donor sometimes addressed 'all the sons of Holy Church' or 'all the faithful in Christ' or 'cleric and lay'. Addi-tionally or alternatively, he might particularise and address 'his constables and stewards and barons and all his men and friends, French and English, of Yorkshire'. All the above examples are taken from the charters of Roger de Mowbray, who died in 1188.[3] What the donor did not do in a charter was to address the beneficiary exclusively, because the charter itself was given to the beneficiary (and sometimes written by him) and served as a kind of open testimonial. Addresses have such a variety of forms primarily because standardisation became usual only in the thirteenth century, when charters were issued in tens of thousands. The charter form is much older than the Norman Conquest; the main change which occurred thereafter is that their texts and format at last became stereotyped owing primarily to the increase in numbers.

In practice a charter might concern any form of property, although rights over land were by far the most common conveyances in a primarily

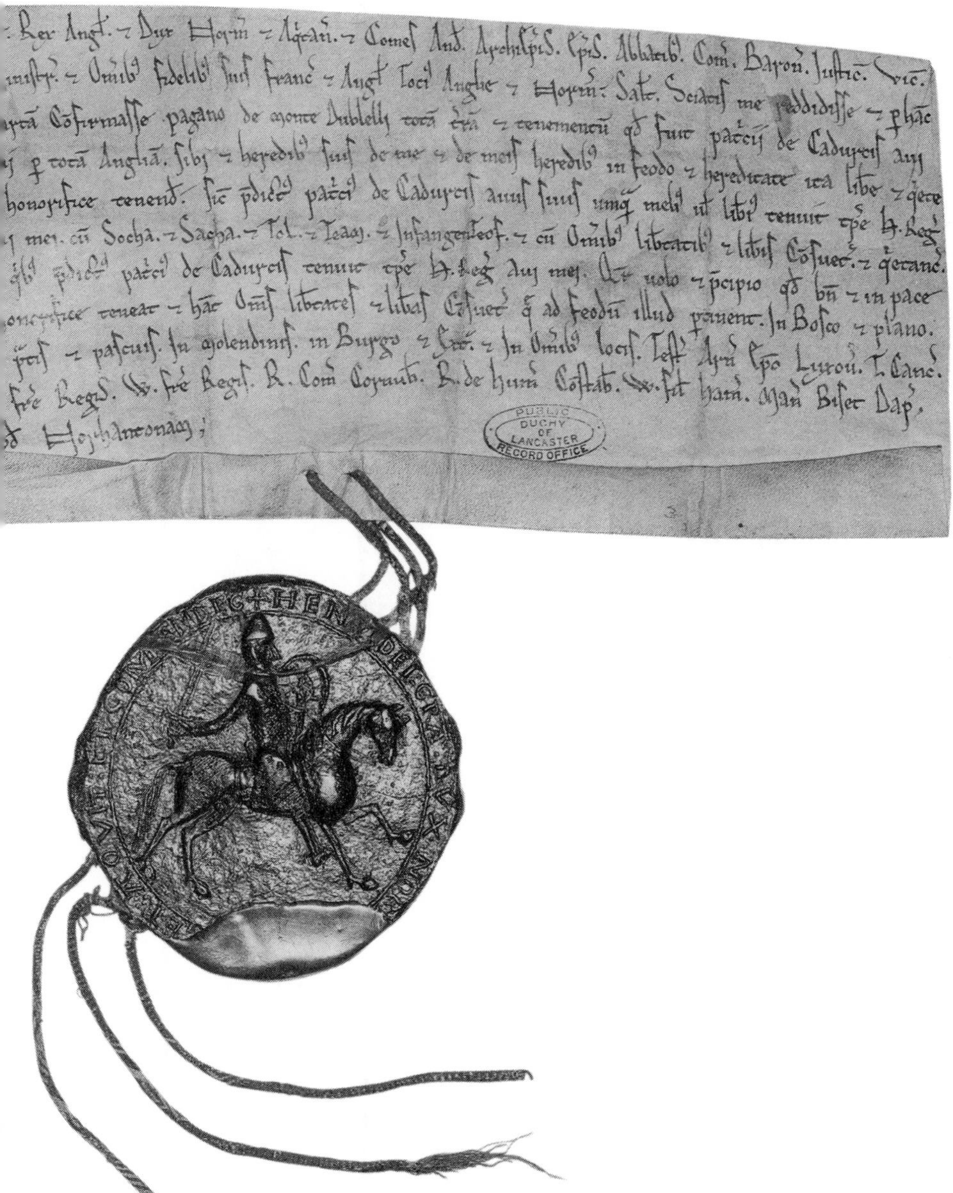

PLATE 8. A charter and seal of Henry II, 1155, showing the king as a mounted knight. On this letter patent the seal is attached to the document by a cord enabling the letter to be opened and closed repeatedly

agricultural community. Of other gifts, we have already seen that Guy de Beauchamp listed books in a charter in 1306. A few years earlier John de Camoys had conveyed his wife, Margaret, with her goods and chattels to Sir William Paynel by a charter, insisting that he did this of his own free will. The ordinary formulas for conveying land, 'I have given and granted, released and quitclaimed', are used in this charter. The details survive because Margaret and William attempted to claim dower from John's lands and the case came before parliament in 1300–2. In 1267 or earlier Peter of Pecham wrote (in French verse) a parody of a compact with the Devil, in the form of a charter: 'Be it known to all my servants present and future that I, Prince of Greed, Pride and Envy, have given and granted to the rich, who are my retinue in chief, that they can do all that they want: by force and deceitful covetousness, by all wrong and ransom, by seizure and by false pretences, by pawn and by tallage, by privilege and by outrage, or by anything else they can think of to destroy the common people.'[4]

The amount of detail in which a conveyance is described varies according to the nature of the property, the date it was made, and the mutual trust between the parties. A later charter describing the same property might be more specific. For example, in 1209 or earlier William Blanch granted (among other lands in Ewell near Epsom) half an acre in Dunfurlong. When Gilbert son of Osbert obtained a confirmation of this grant from William Blanch's heir, John, in the 1230s, the new charter defined the half-acre in Dunfurlong more exactly as that lying 'between the land of John Skinner and of William Cupping'.[5] In this more precise description may be seen the influence of Gilbert's brother-in-law, Walter of Merton, the future chancellor who was already a royal clerk. Some attempts at definition were more amateur. A crudely written charter of the late twelfth century, issued by Jordan of Cheadle, describes the land he is giving as extending 'in length from a certain oak towards Hedilis-lethe, which has been uprooted there' up to another point.[6] Jordan's contemporaries in the village would have known where the remains of this oak might be seen, but not the general public, present and future, to whom this charter is addressed. Occasionally the specifications in a charter can evoke a whole landscape, as they had done so strikingly in some Anglo-Saxon charters. This is an extract from a grant of land at Lambrigg (near Kendal) in the Lake District, describing the boundaries in c. 1210:

> then by Sti Coleman up to the nearest pile of stones which is towards the north under the head of Langescaghe, and then rising beyond

Langescaghe up to the little valley which is next to the upper head of Lickegile, then out across the head of Lickegile by the middle of the moor . . . [and so on].[7]

In charters there is often a contrast between the dignity and portentous language of their issuers and the pettyness of the matters they concern. In 1219 the monks of Abbey Dore obtained a confirmation in Rome of their title to a piece of land only twenty feet in width heading their millstream. Anyone 'infringing this page', Pope Honorius III warned, 'would incur the indignation of Almighty God and the Blessed Apostles Peter and Paul'.[8] This illustrates very well what Max Weber meant by the 'routinisation of charisma': through bureaucracy, the pope's voice as God's mouthpiece on earth was multiplied into tens of thousands of trivial pronouncements.

Rather similar in function to charters, though different in format, are chirographs. A chirograph recorded an agreement between two parties. The agreement might concern almost anything—matters of state, a conveyance of land, a marriage settlement, or the repayment of a loan of money to a Jew. Unlike a charter, each of the parties received a copy of the agreement, usually authenticated by the seal of the other party. The method is described in detail, probably because it was still relatively unfamiliar, in an agreement made before papal judges delegate between the prior of Luffield and John, vicar of Towcester, in *c.* 1215:

> This composition is reduced into a duplicate writing, made in the form
> of a chirograph, of which writing [*scriptura*] the prior of Luffield is to
> have one document [*scriptum*] sealed with the seals of the judges and of
> John, while John is to have the other document sealed with the seals of
> the judges and of the prior.[9]

The document was thus written out in duplicate and then cut in half. Across the line of the cut, before it was made, was written in capital letters a formula such as JUSTUS DOMINUS ET JUSTICIAS (an extract from Psalms XI, 7) or the word CHIROGRAPHUM. Forgery of one part could thus be checked by aligning the severed formula with its counterpart. As a further precaution, the cut was often made by a wavy or indented line, instead of a straight one. This practice grew so common in the latter Middle Ages that chirographs became generally known as 'indentures'.

The text of a chirograph might be drafted in the form of a letter to all and sundry (like a charter), or it might be a memorandum recording that this is the covenant or final concord which has been made, at such and such a court or place, in the presence of certain persons who are named. The making of a chirograph might conclude an actual dispute between the parties, or alternatively the chirographic form was often used for amicable conveyances, because it had the advantage over an ordinary charter that both donor and beneficiary received a copy and these copies could be checked against each other. The first official records of proceedings in the king's court, extant as originals, are halves of chirographs recording agreements made in 1176 and 1182, the former cut straight and the latter indented. Moreover, some chirographs were made in triplicate: the two parties each received a copy and the third copy was deposited in an archive for safekeeping. This had been an Anglo-Saxon practice, which was revived (using a different format) by Hubert Walter when he introduced royal feet of fines in 1195. Most exceptionally, all three parts of chirographs made before royal justices survive from 1232 and 1272. The practice was extended to ecclesiastical records by an interpretation of canon 38 of the Fourth Lateran Council in 1215.

Like other documentary forms, the chirograph made its way down the social scale. At the top it was the standard form for international treaties, of which the earliest extant exemplars are four Anglo-Flemish alliances made in the twelfth century. Likewise in times of civil war magnates used chirographs to record alliances. Extant examples are two treaties made in Stephen's reign, one between the earls of Chester and Leicester and the other between the earls of Gloucester and Hereford. Similarly the war between King John and his barons was concluded by a chirograph beginning, 'This is the covenant made between Lord John, king of England, for the one part, and Robert Fitz Walter, marshal of the army of God and of the holy Church in England [and other named barons] on the other.'[10] This treaty immediately preceded Magna Carta itself, which was issued in the form of an ordinary charter, presumably in order to emphasise that it was a free gift by the king and not a compromised agreement. Nevertheless when Magna Carta was reissued in 1217 by the regent, William Marshal, it too was drawn up *in modum chirographi*, according to the Waverley Abbey chronicler at least. At the other end of the political and social scale, we have already discussed the chirograph which the widow, Emma, made with the abbot of Gloucester in *c.* 1230 concerning ploughing and other servile duties (see page 240). The chirograph was a most versatile, and therefore a very common, type of document; but it is unusual for more than one of the original parts to survive to the present day.

In addition to charters and chirographs, public statements by individuals were issued in the form of recognisances, testimonials, notifications, wills, sealed memoranda and similar records. For convenience these miscellaneous documents are here called certificates. They are often similar in form to charters, but they do not exclusively concern gifts of property. The following extract from a testimonial by Miles earl of Hereford, probably issued shortly before he died in 1143, is exceptional in its subject matter but typical in its form:

> Miles earl of Hereford to all his friends, French and English, of England and of Wales, greeting. You are to know that this Folebarba is my jester and my man. So I entreat all my friends that they look after him, lest harm happen to him. And if anyone does him good for love of me, I will know how to thank him.[11]

Folebarba (? Funny Beard) was perhaps apprehensive of being parted from his master and hoped that this certificate of the earl's affection would help him; whether it did or not is unknown—jesters inevitably made enemies.

By far the commonest form of certificates were recognisances concerning the payment of money debts. The earliest moneylender's bonds extant in England are eight documents from the coffers of the financier, William Cade, whose archives came into the possession of the Crown on his death in c. 1166. The documents are brief and take the form of undertakings by persons named to stand surety for others, or themselves make payments to Cade or his son, Ernulf, at specified dates. Documents classed here as certificates are so varied that it would be impossible to describe all types. Sometimes there is no convincing explanation as to why a particular record was ever made or preserved. Richard of Anstey's account of the protracted delays he experienced in the lawsuit he prosecuted between 1158 and 1163 has been described in numerous general histories of the period. Yet why Richard made this memorandum is unclear. It begins like a solemn charter or prayer by invoking the Trinity, but it is not addressed to anyone, nor does it ask for anything or give it; it simply records his expenses and how and when they were incurred. Another form of certificate which must have been common by Edward I's reign were the testimonials which served as warrants identifying persons or their goods when moving about the country.

The documents considered so far are not 'letters' in the modern sense of missives. Charters, chirographs and certificates were not usually sent by the writer to a recipient who is addressed in the document; instead they were addressed to the public and handed to the beneficiary at the time they were written. They were primarily intended to be records rather than communications. The habit of sending missives, conveying ephemeral information about day-to-day matters, developed slowly because writing in Latin was too formal a medium. 'Letters' (*litterae*) were appropriate for 'literature' to pass on to posterity; the spoken word of messengers sufficed for conveying the ordinary business of the day. The finest letters were composed and kept as examples of style and were not necessarily sent to their addresses. In the first half of the twelfth century the art of writing such elaborate yet intimate letters reached a peak in the collections of St Bernard, Peter the Venerable, and Abelard and Heloise. This type of correspondence was exemplified in England in the latter half of the century in the letter collections of John of Salisbury and Gilbert Foliot. The best single example is John's letter to Peter abbot of Celle in *c.* 1159 recalling their friendship. It is often impossible to establish whether letters in anthologies like these are authentic missives; they may be literary essays, propaganda pieces, or even forgeries, as has been alleged of the correspondence between Abelard and Heloise.

In the thirteenth century more mundane letters begin to survive, which are actual missives although they are less intimate. An example are the letters written to Ralf Nevill, bishop of Chichester (1224–44), by his steward in Sussex, Simon of Senlis. These concern the management of the farms, the doings of the local clergy, arrangements for visits, request for favours, and so on. They evoke without effort a picture of country life which a rhetorician could not have bettered, yet they have survived only because Ralf was the chancellor and Simon's letters became mixed in with the royal archives.

Letters first become common in England, not in the form of correspondence between individuals, but as 'writs' (*brevia*). Writs have a brevity and directness of style which contrasts with the elaboration of explicitly personal letters; as a result they can sometimes reveal more of individual attitudes. 'If we have given our peace even to a dog, it should be inviolably preserved,' King John wrote in 1203 to the Londoners when reproving them for molesting the Jews. The term 'writ' is used in this classification exclusively to mean a written command given by one person to another. The most frequent issuer of writs was the king, as in this example by Henry I: 'Henry, king of the English, to the abbot of Ramsey, greeting. I forbid you to do Hugh Oilard anything but right, no matter what writ might be produced. Witness: the chancellor. At Gloucester.'[12]

It is debatable whether a writ in this form is a real missive directed by the sender to the addressee. The surviving writs of Henry I are letters patent; this means that they were open documents, which were handed to the beneficiaries at the time they were made, like charters. In the writ cited above, it was up to Hugh Oilard, the beneficiary, to show the document to the abbot of Ramsey as evidence of the king's intervention in his case. The king took no further steps to ensure that the writ reached the abbot unchanged, nor did he require the abbot to reply to him directly. The phrase, 'no matter what writ might be produced', demonstrates that writs were already being issued in some numbers, but it also suggests that the king had no knowledge of what happened to them. If he were not ordinarily responsible for dispatching them, his ignorance is understandable.

Real missives were sent in the form of letters close. Closing up letters for confidential purposes must have been common practice for centuries, though actual examples are rare because the recipient ordinarily opened the letter up and destroyed it. Letters written on almost paper-thin slivers of wood, which closed up, have been discovered on Hadrian's Wall dating from AD 100. The next example of a letter close in England comes from AD 700; this is a confidential letter written by the bishop of London to the archbishop of Canterbury. By Henry II's reign, it can be shown that a letter close was sealed and addressed on the tie that kept it rolled up, though no such letter has been found unopened until the reign of Henry VIII. Opened letters close, with their seals and ties cut off, begin to be kept from Henry II's reign because he made some categories of writ 'returnable'. This meant that the addressee, usually a sheriff, was instructed to produce the writ at a subsequent time and place, most often before a royal justice. A method had therefore been devised of sending confidential instructions in writing and of checking on whether these writs were obeyed. Likewise in Henry II's reign writs begin to take common forms, both for administration (for instance the writs of summons used by the Exchequer) and for litigation. Writs in common form, available for purchase, were the framework of Henry II's legal reforms, based on the principle that no one need answer for his freehold without a royal writ. Henry II had thus created a system which could potentially mass-produce documents from a few stereotypes.

This discussion has concentrated on royal writs because they set the pattern and are by far the most common. Royal practice was imitated by the magnates and by officials in the counties: an early example of this is the letter sent in *c.* 1130 by Richard Fitz Gilbert of Clare to one of his tenants, ordering him to restore a tithe to Stoke Priory in Suffolk. The letter

PLATE 9a and 9b. Writs of King Stephen and Henry I. The writ of King Stephen (*above*) is an unusually early English example of the cursive script, indicating that this document was one that needed to be written quickly, unlike the more painstaking script of the writ below. Like the previous illustration, Stephen's writ is a letter patent with two tags used as ribbons to reseal the document. The seal was attached to the parchment itself. *Below*: the writ of Henry I was probably written by a monk of Canterbury. The text is in Latin and English, although as much of the Latin text consists of English formulas (*on strande & streame, on wudu & felde*, etc., line 3) the bilingualism is largely superfluous

concludes with a warning: 'And if you do not so, Adam, my steward, is swiftly going to do it, so that I hear no plaint for want of right.' The phraseology echoes that of royal writs of right, as in a letter of Henry I protecting Ramsey Abbey:[13] 'And if you do not do so, Ralf Basset is going to have it done, so that I hear no plaint about it for want or right.'

In due course, writs generated other letters and memoranda in the form of replies to their demands and written plaints and petitions to the king for redress; replies to royal writs (returns of inquests) are extant in originals from Henry III's reign and petitions are extant from Edward I's.

Most of the documents so far described, particularly charters and chirographs, could serve as memoranda and were kept as such by the persons they benefited. Such documents differ, however, from the type of memoranda which were systematically compiled, usually by institutions, as a record of past practice for their own future guidance. Court rolls, financial accounts, cartularies and chronicles cannot be classed as single 'statements issued by individuals', because they usually form part of an accumulating series of records compiled by an authority. Although in the light of hindsight compiling memoranda seems an obvious step once the idea of writing for posterity in charters had become familiar, there is a time-lag of a century or more between the two activities. It is probable that the only type of cumulative written record used at all widely by the Anglo-Saxons was the chronicle. A century after the Norman Conquest the one continuous series of memoranda kept by the Crown were the Exchequer pipe rolls; numerous additional types of Exchequer record were, however, created in Henry II's reign, for instance rolls of receipts and the rolls made by Richard of Ilchester and Thomas Brown. Judging by documents extant, cumulative non-financial record-keeping by the Crown began during Hubert Walter's years of office between 1193 and 1205; the plea rolls of the royal courts, the coroners' and sheriffs' rolls in the counties, feet of fines, the Chancery rolls of outgoing letters, all start or are first unequivocally referred to at this time (see pages 243–8 above).

Outside the king's court, making cumulative memoranda got under way in the thirteenth century. Seignorial accounts belatedly followed the lead of the Exchequer, the earliest extant series being the pipe rolls of the bishops of Winchester starting in 1208. These rolls record receipts (in money, crops, and livestock) and expenditure on the bishop's manors in detail. They are so orderly that they must have been based on drafts or preliminary accounts in writing submitted by each bailiff. Although the earliest Winchester rolls draw up balances of receipts and expenditure, they do not aim to show profit and loss as such, but to act as a check against the bishop being cheated by his ministers. The king's Exchequer provided a model for collecting revenues rather than for running a business. The earliest records calculating the profits of manors are the Christ Church Canterbury accounts of 1224–5. Manorial accounts of any sort remain very rare until the latter half of the thirteenth century and the majority of those extant were produced by the greater monasteries. Lay lords undoubtedly also possessed ministers' accounts, as some survive by chance in the Public Record Office when estates were forfeited to the Crown; an example are the records of Adam of Stratton, an Exchequer official and financier, who was put on trial for corruption in 1289. In addition to manorial accounts, accounts of the separate departmental heads in the great religious houses, the obedientaries, begin to be extant from the 1260s; among these are the earliest non-royal household accounts. Similarly Merton College at Oxford has accounts of its administrative officers from 1277. The accounts of towns follow a similar pattern to manors; the earliest continuous series are the Shrewsbury rolls of accounts of 1256 which were cast at weekly intervals.

The most remarkable early accounts are the household rolls made in 1265 for Eleanor, countess of Leicester, the sister of Henry III and wife of Simon de Montfort. These record her expenditure, mainly for the supply of food and drink, under different departmental headings such as the kitchen and the marshalcy of the stables. The entries are made in a variety of cursive hands, which suggests that they were compiled by the week or fortnight. Furthermore they specify the expenditure of each day separately and thus comprise a kind of diary of expenditure. The rolls cover the period 19 February to 29 August, the latter date being nearly a month after Simon's death at the battle of Evesham. As the accounts are set out in a regular form, these rolls are evidently not the first of their kind, although they are the earliest to survive. Perhaps Eleanor retained these ones because they concerned the last weeks of Simon's life. Their chance survival suggests that by the middle of the thirteenth century many magnates' households, both clerical and lay, were keeping daily accounts of expenditure in writing on parchment. But because such records concerned petty expenditure only, they must usually have been treated as ephemeral and thrown away. The most commonplace records are the least likely to survive.

In 1293 Edward I's treasurer, William March, introduced into the Exchequer *jornalia* or 'journal' rolls. These were diaries ('day-books' in modern accounting terms), which showed the amount of cash in the

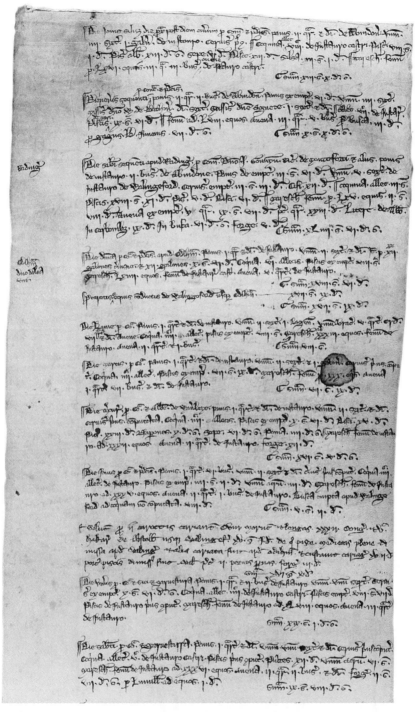

PLATE 10. Household roll of Eleanor de Montfort. This roll records Eleanor's daily expenditure and itinerary during the last months of Simon de Montfort's life. The portion illustrated concerns the week of 19–26 February 1265, and each day is enrolled separately, sometimes by a different clerk, thus the first three entries appear to be in different hands

treasury at the start of each day's business and the disbursements made during the day. As with household rolls like Eleanor de Montfort's, the purpose of the daily record was to balance income against expenditure week by week. But, in the case of an organisation as complex as the royal government, 'this merely created a false sense of security, for the *jornalia* rolls took no account of the total number of wardrobe bills in circulation, or of the considerable sums paid out at source after 1298 from the county farms and taxes.'[14] Like Edward I's other attempts in the 1290s to increase royal control by doubling up on documentation, the *jornalia* rolls were a failure in practical terms, although they provide a fascinating record for posterity.

Extant financial accounts of the thirteenth century raise the question of what type of records preceded them. Obviously the great monastic estates made some financial records before 1200. Payments (both made and received) were probably recorded on tally sticks from early in the twelfth century, although there was no conception at that time of keeping a continuous series of financial memoranda to guide the steward of an estate. A landlord in the twelfth century obtained an overall view of his property, not from account rolls, but from a survey. The typical survey was not part of an accumulating series of records, as it was made *ab initio* by the incoming lord. Jocelin of Brakelond describes how Abbot Samson conducted such a survey:

> At his order a general description [*descriptio generalis*] was made in each hundred of leets and suits, hidages and corn dues, renders of hens, and of other customs, rents and issues, which had always been largely concealed by the farmers; and he had all these reduced to writing, so that, within four years of his election [in 1182] there was no one who could deceive him even about a single pennyworth from the abbey's revenues, whereas he had received nothing in writing from his predecessors about the management of the abbey, except a little schedule containing the names of the knights of St Edmund, the names of the manors, and the rent which each farm should yield. [Abbot Samson] called this book his *kalendarium*, as individual debts which he had acquitted were also inscribed in it. He consulted this book almost daily, as if he contemplated in it the physiognomy of his own probity as in a mirror.[15]

Samson called his survey a *kalendarium* because in classical Latin that word had meant a list of debts due at the kalends of each month. Surveys and rentals of this sort, summarising in writing the revenues due to a lord, became increasingly common. Jocelin refers in the citation above to an earlier list made at Bury St Edmunds, whose size he minimises, as Abbot Baldwin's *Book of Feoffments* (dating from early in the twelfth century), is still extant.

The precedent for all such surveys, great and small, was Domesday Book, which had likewise been called a *descriptio*. Judging by surveys known, the decade 1180–90, when Samson made his *kalendarium*, was the most productive period: from these years came the royal Assize of Arms and the *rotuli de dominabus* (lists of marriageable ladies), and inquiries conducted by Durham and St Paul's Cathedrals, Glastonbury Abbey, and the Knights Templar; likewise the earliest known bishop's *matricula* or *scrutinium*, that of Baldwin of Worcester, dates from this decade. A remarkably detailed survey was made by Christ Church Priory at Canterbury in *c.* 1200. Set out in four columns, it lists each tenant, the amount of his annual rent, the date when payment is due, and the whereabouts and dimensions of the tenements. For example, the first entry describes the land of the sister of Roger son of Hamel as lying 'behind the wall of our almonry; its breadth northwards 26 feet; length from the street westwards 110 feet'.[16] In recording the dimensions of individual tenements the priory hoped perhaps to settle boundary disputes by referring to the precise evidence of writing instead of the partial recollections of neighbours.

In the thirteenth century the practice of making surveys in writing extended beyond the royal government and great religious houses to landlords in general. In the rules for estate management composed for the countess of Lincoln in the 1230s or 1240s, Robert Grosseteste recommends an incoming landlord to make a survey of his revenues in triplicate; just as Abbot Samson had consulted his *kalendarium* almost every day, Grosseteste recommends the countess to 'keep this roll by you and often look at it'.[17] In addition to serving as rentals for estates, such surveys were the basis of systematic taxation: notable early examples are the royal subsidy assessments of 1225, Wallingford's rolls of tradesmen of 1227 and 1230, and the well-documented valuation of the English Church (diocese by diocese) for the papal tenth of 1254. Impressive though surveys are as pioneers of written record and as historical documents, they cannot have been as useful to landlords as annual accounts because they soon went out of date. All surveys shared with Domesday Book the characteristic of being symbols of efficiency and authority rather than its reality.

In courts, lists and books of rules are generally earlier than systematic memoranda of particular cases, just as surveys and rentals precede financial accounts. Thus in boroughs the oldest records, apart from the charters constituting them, are lists of guildsmen forming the corporation and custumals summarising municipal by-laws. Leicester's guild rolls begin in 1196; they are the oldest series of memoranda now extant made outside the king's court or a monastery. Northampton has a custumal of similar date, although it is not in its original form. The most remarkable early custumal is a roll in French made for Exeter, which was probably compiled in the 1230s by the town clerk, John Baubi. The borough court's rolls of pleas are usually of later date: 'the court's official memory still reposed in the heads of its *probi homines* [responsible men] when the guild began to commit its lists of names, fines, and vats of ale to parchment';[18] exceptionally early are the rolls of the Wallingford burghmoot which begin in 1231–2.

The records of the king's court follow a comparable pattern, with lists and books of rules preceding enrolments of actual litigation. Notes of pecuniary penalties (oblations, fines, amercements) are listed in the pipe rolls of the Exchequer from Henry I's reign and separate rolls of amercements were kept in Henry II's reign. Likewise from late in Henry II's reign comes Glanvill's treatise 'on the laws and customs of England', which is essentially a custumal for the king's court summarising its most common rules in writing, as the author explains in his prologue. Rolls of pleas, on the other hand, are not extant until 1194; their retention was perhaps due to Hubert Walter, who had been appointed chief justiciar in 1193. The making of such rolls may date back to Henry II's appointment of itinerant justices twenty or so years earlier. A Lincolnshire litigant in 1219 appealed to 'the record of the rolls of the justices itinerant' there during Henry II's reign.[19] But there is no record of these rolls being produced, and the defendant denied that this plea had ever been in Henry II's court. Court records of proceedings are essential in any modern judicial system and it is difficult to understand how Henry II's judges could have operated effectively without them. Nevertheless the judges may not have been 'modern' in this respect but traditionalist, like many lawyers. Pleas had been heard in royal courts for generations without official records of proceedings being kept, because—ideally—each case was to be judged on its merits, unrestricted by precedents in writing.

Ecclesiastical courts might be expected to have been more advanced than their royal counterparts in keeping records, since the clergy were *ex officio* experts in literacy. Yet the pattern and chronology of development here is much the same as in the king's court. The classic textbook of canon law, Gratian's, was composed in around 1140. But 'the earliest records of an English church court (as opposed to records of ecclesiastical litigation preserved by a party to the case)' do not appear until 1200.[20] Again it is Hubert Walter who is responsible for this development, this time in his capacity as archbishop of Canterbury. After his death in 1205, church court records become spasmodic until rolls of suits and act books appear with regularity in the fourteenth century. But in this instance extant records are misleading, as ecclesiastical cases were usually recorded in chirographs in triplicate (for the judge and the two parties), instead of being enrolled, and consequently they have not survived as well as rolls.

The pattern of making memoranda in local courts other than boroughs—hundred and manor courts for example—is less clear. Their records are more scattered and relatively few are extant, because local lordships have not had such a continuous institutional life as boroughs or the king's government. As in other courts, keeping lists of names seems to have preceded making records of proceedings. Thus Jocelin of Brakelond describes the bailiffs of the sacrist and cellarer of Bury St Edmunds enrolling men in frankpledge each year as early as 1200, whereas the first hundred court rolls date from the 1260s and they survive from no more than a dozen places before 1300. Similarly the earliest manor court rolls come from the 1240s and it is unlikely that any earlier ones will be found. Even plea rolls from county courts are extraordinarily rare, considering the court's importance as the principal and regular assembly of each shire. The only county court rolls extant from the thirteenth century are some from Cheshire (beginning in 1259), which are exceptional anyway because the earldom of Chester was a privileged jurisdiction. As in the development of the king's court, lists of fines from county courts are more common at first than records of pleas.

Local court rolls become more common towards the end of the thirteenth century, but they remain rare compared with the plea rolls of the king's court, which exist in multiple copies in Edward I's reign. Similarly among cities and boroughs, only eleven possess extant records of any type earlier than Edward I's accession, although that figure doubles by the time of his death. On the other hand, treatises written for baronial stewards in the 1260s and 1270s assume that court rolls are kept: the *Court Baron* has the bailiff say to the steward, 'By my faith, see here all that for which you ask written down in this roll' and John of Oxford's treatise advises the bailiff's clerk 'to note down everything that is done in the court as it occurs'. Even if every clerk made a roll, he certainly did not note down everything. Local court rolls are usually laconic. Their main purpose was to record the names of litigants and suitors attending the court and of persons who had been fined; occasional individual items do get recorded in detail, however, when the clerk did not know how to abbreviate them. Such rolls derived their form from lists and often they are little more than that.

Contrasting with the rigorously summarised local court rolls are the Year Books, which merit attention because they are the largest and most detailed collection of dialogue made in the Middle Ages. They are reports of court cases, beginning in the reign of Edward I, which purport to record the actual words (translated into French or Latin) of litigants, their counsel and the judges for the benefit of law students and practitioners. The Year Books' practice of recording dialogue seems to have emanated from law reporters in London and not from the king's clerks. The earliest instance of such reporting occurs in London's Latin record of the royal justices' visitation of the City in 1244. Certain cases are recorded twice, first in reported speech, as is usual in plea rolls, and then again in dialogue form using the first person. For example, Alfred de Pinchbeck sued John de Coudres, a former sheriff, for wrongful imprisonment. The plea roll records in formal and general terms Alfred's complaint and John's defence that Alfred had resisted arrest and refused to find a pledge for good behaviour. In the alternative version of this case, however, more circumstantial details are given: it explains that Alfred's family had been imprisoned at Newgate because a Jew had accused him of killing the Jew's wife; when Alfred returned from King's Lynn fair, John, the sheriff, had demanded a pledge from him because of this charge. The alternative version then records John's cross-examination by the justices in direct speech:

> The justices said: 'For what cause did you exact a pledge from Alfred, whereas he was not in the City when the Jewess was allegedly killed?'
> John said: 'I asked him for a pledge and when he drew his knife, I seized his hand with the knife, for which cause I imprisoned him.'
> The justices said: 'You had no cause to exact a pledge from Alfred.'[21]

This version thus explains the facts of the case and the points of law involved by recording the justices' questions and comments, whereas the official plea roll is concerned only to note the procedural stages of the case in due form. This comparison between alternative versions of the same case illustrates the paradox, familiar to historians, that unofficial records are often more informative and factual than the formal texts made by professional clerks. Although formal legal records are the largest group of medieval documents extant, they are not as reliable as their orderly appearance suggests.

This description of memoranda-making has proceeded mainly by referring to the earliest extant exemplars of various types of record, and it leads to the general conclusion that outside the king's court the main series of memoranda started in the thirteenth century. Although great monastic houses had made surveys and rentals in the twelfth century and the royal Exchequer kept pipe rolls from the reign of Henry I, communal and seignorial court rolls and financial accounts are products of the thirteenth century; they were almost certainly not made before the 1190s. There are, however, two obvious objections to generalising in this way. Firstly, the earliest records extant are not necessarily the earliest records made. For example, a Cheshire chirograph of 1228 refers to 'the authentic roll of our lord the earl' (of Chester) which preserves memory and record, whereas the earliest roll of any sort now extant from Cheshire is a plea roll from 1259. The roll referred to in 1228, the 'Domesday' roll which registered covenants, existed as late as 1580 when extracts were copied from it. It was probably the first of its kind, however, as it started with a poem explaining that its 'holy page' would ensure that the agreements enrolled in it were kept. Secondly and conversely, a record surviving from an early date may have always been unique and did not necessarily form part of a cumulative series of memoranda; estate surveys from the twelfth century for example, like Abbot Samson's *kalendarium*, were intended to be unique.

To sum up, the general impression left by the evidence, taking account of references to documents now lost as well as those that survive, is that the habit of making and keeping records of proceedings in continuous series stemmed from the king's court at the end of the twelfth century and took another century to spread across the country. Hazarding a guess, manors which did not belong to the king or to ecclesiastical magnates probably only began, as a rule, to have financial accounts and court rolls in Edward I's reign.

One type of cumulative memorial, the chronicle, had far older origins. Not all chroniclers were monks: Ralf de Diceto and Roger of Howden were secular clerics, and Arnold Fitz Thedmar, the probable author of the London chronicle, was a layman. Nevertheless the typical chronicle was monastic and had its origins in the Benedictine preoccupation with the careful regulation of time. The typical monastic chronicler distinguished his function from that of the historian: 'The historian proceeds diffusely and elegantly, whereas the chronicler proceeds simply, gradually and briefly,' Gervase of Canterbury explained in *c.* 1188. 'The chronicler computes years *Anno Domini* and the months and kalends and briefly describes the actions of kings and princes which occurred at those times; he also commemorates events, portents and wonders. There are many, however, writing chronicles or annals who exceed their limits.' Because Gervase intended to remain a humble chronicler, he insists that he wants 'to compile rather than to write' and explains that he does not write for a public library, but for his own monastic family at Christ Church Canterbury. The typical chronicle was thus a dated series of events recorded for the guidance of a monastic house; it was not an interpretation of the past presented to the public by a historian. Paradoxically, but understandably, the greatest monastic chroniclers, like Matthew Paris or Gervase himself, went far beyond these narrow limits.

The chronicle is thus an unstylish production, concerned with the matter rather than the manner of presentation, and 'added to year by year and therefore composed by various people'. The writer of this description, an anonymous monastic annalist of the thirteenth century associated with Winchester, advises the composer of a chronicle to see that there is always a sheet attached to the book, on which may be noted in pencil the deaths of illustrious men and other memoranda whenever the news comes to hand. At the end of each year the monk 'who has been appointed to the task, and not just anyone who so wishes, should write out briefly and succinctly in the body of the book what he thinks truest and best to be passed down to the notice of posterity'. That such notes were commonly kept is suggested by John of Salisbury's statement about sixty years earlier that he had seen in the archives of churches 'notes of memorable things', which would help future writers even where chronicles were unavailable.

Twentieth-century historians have often distinguished between chronicle sources, which they consider biased and unreliable, and official records (such as the Chancery rolls) which they prefer. Yet the best chronicles were the official records of the monastic houses which produced them and were treated as such on occasions by the royal government. When Matthew Paris attended the ceremonies in 1247 for the Feast of Edward the Confessor, Henry III ordered him from the throne in Westminster Hall 'to write an accurate and full account of all these things and commit them indelibly to notable writing in a book, so that their memory shall in no way be lost to posterity'. The king evidently knew that Matthew was writing a chronicle and invited him to dinner. Similarly when Edward I looked for historical precedents to support his claims in Scotland in 1291, he turned first to monastic chronicles and not to the royal archives. At the same time he sent monasteries information about his claims and ordered them 'to be noted in your chronicles as a perpetual memorial of the business'. In

Edward's time the monastic chronicle was the most ancient, but still the most secure and productive form of record in existence.

Like chronicles, cartularies are monastic in origin. Hemming, a monk of Worcester who composed much of the earliest cartulary extant, describes his purpose:

> I, Hemming, monk and priest have composed this little book concerning the possessions of this our monastery, so that it may be clear to our posterity which and how many possessions in land pertain to the endowment of this monastery for the sustenance of the monks, the servants of God; or rather which [possessions] ought by right [to be ours], although we have been unjustly dispossessed of them by force and fraud.[22]

A cartulary was thus a collection of title-deeds copied into a register for greater security. Unlike chronicles, cartularies do not have ancient origins in England. They were products of the insecurity brought about by the Norman Conquest and the civil war of Stephen's reign, combined with greater competition between monastic houses to acquire and retain lands, which resulted from the increase in the number of monasteries in the twelfth and thirteenth centuries. Thus the compiler of Ramsey Abbey's *Book of Benefactors* explains in *c.* 1170 that the abbey had lost almost everything in the 'dark and gloomy days' of King Stephen, both from attacks from enemies and domestic disputes, 'and so we have collected together in one volume our chirographs and the charters of our privileges . . . as a warning for future ages and to instruct our readers'. This compiler also translated the abbey's pre-Conquest documents from English into Latin to make them more acceptable. Apart from convenience and greater security, another advantage of copying records into a cartulary was that they could be modernised and improved, or even forged.

The first portion of Hemming's cartulary was not composed by him, but dates from a generation before the Norman Conquest; Hemming made his portion towards the end of the eleventh century. The only other cartulary extant from the eleventh century, the Oswald cartulary, also emanates from Worcester. It is therefore probable that the cartulary form in England was created at Worcester in the generation before the Norman Conquest and brought to fruition by Hemming as a consequence of the Conquest. English monks in the great Benedictine houses aimed to justify and explain their heritage to their Norman masters. There may even be a direct connection between Hemming's cartulary and the Normans, as V. H. Galbraith has suggested that Samson of Bayeux, the bishop of

Worcester in Hemming's time, had been the compiler of Domesday Book. The next oldest cartulary extant is the Rochester book *Textus Roffensis*, again from an ancient monastic house, which dates from *c.* 1125. No more than half a dozen cartularies are earlier than 1150 and fewer than thirty earlier than 1200. Like other series of memoranda (excepting chronicles and royal Exchequer records), cartulary-making became firmly established, not in the twelfth century, but in the thirteenth. In this century the practice spread from monasteries to laymen, although lay cartularies from the thirteenth century are very rare. They seem to have been particularly prevalent in Northamptonshire; from there come Richard Hotot's estate book, Ralf Basset's roll, and the Braybrooke cartulary. Richard Hotot was a younger brother of William Hotot, abbot of Peterborough (1246–9); so he could have learned about the importance of keeping documents from the abbot, or he may have learned from his father, Thomas Hotot. In 1322 another Northamptonshire gentleman, Henry de Bray, actually wrote his own cartulary, as we have already seen (page 249).

In the medieval period the commonest term for a cartulary was a *registrum*. The rolls of the Chancery were likewise described as a *registrum* and so was Domesday Book on one occasion. This wide definition of 'register' is useful, as all these records shared the common characteristic of being edited collections, in books or rolls, which had been compiled from primary sources from separate pieces of parchment. Moreover, some of the works described as cartularies in the preceding paragraphs do not exclusively concern charters: the estate books of Richard Hotot and Henry de Bray were intended as general reference books for their families and are not narrowly legalistic. Once the idea of copying documents into books for greater security and convenience became familiar, the practice took many forms. For instance, the royal Exchequer made registers in books, like a monastic house, to provide fair copies and guides to its records and to note down miscellanea. The oldest of these Exchequer remembrance books (Domesday Book excepted) are the Red Book and the Black Book, which were compiled in the 1230s. The one most commonly used by scholars today is *The Book of Fees*, containing surveys of feudal tenures between 1198 and 1293. A note on its flyleaf, probably written at the time it was compiled in 1302, reminds the user that the book is a register and not a primary source: 'Remember that this book was composed and compiled from several official inquests . . . and therefore the contents of this book is to be used for evidence here in the Exchequer and not for the record.' Registers like this were guides; they did not have the authority of the original documents themselves, which were the authentic official records.

On the other hand, another class of registers were treated as official records. These were the registers which recorded copies of outgoing documents, as distinct from monastic cartularies and Exchequer remembrance books which recorded documents in the compiler's possession. The greatest series of registers of outgoing documents are the Chancery rolls of royal letters, beginning in the first three years of John's reign; the Charter roll is described as a register as early as 1201. Also well known are the bishops' registers (starting in 1217 or a little earlier), which were modelled on the Chancery rolls. Even earlier than the Chancery rolls are the provisions Hubert Walter had made in 1194 for registering Jewish chirographs of loans and receipts on rolls in designated centres throughout England. The earliest local register of recognisances of debt which is extant, however, is London's *Liber A* beginning in 1276. London also has early rolls of registered wills (beginning in 1258), and some title-deeds are enrolled in the court of Husting rolls (beginning in 1252).

The practice of registering deeds of title in towns probably followed the lead of the Chancery rolls, although it could have derived from monastic practice. The earl of Chester's Domesday roll 'which preserves memory and record' is the earliest known of such registers, but it is now lost. The oldest municipal register extant is a roll from Wallingford, made in 1231–2. This roll is of particular interest because it appears to be a record of conveyances of small properties (houses, rents, market stalls and so on), which had been made orally in the borough court without charters. The next oldest Wallingford register, made in 1252–3, seems by contrast to be a summary of charters. It looks as if in the twenty years between 1232 and 1252 the habit of conveying property in writing had become established among the Wallingford burghers.

The increasing number of documents issued and memoranda compiled in the twelfth and thirteenth centuries is matched by a substantial upsurge in the production of 'books', in the general modern sense of learned and literary works. Yet medieval books were essentially different from modern ones because they were manuscripts. Consequently the total numbers are small by modern standards and counting them is of useful but only limited value, since individual manuscript volumes are not uniform objects like printed books. Making approximate estimates from contemporary catalogues, Durham Cathedral library had about 490 volumes in the twelfth century, Rochester Cathedral about 241 in 1201, and Christ Church Canterbury about 1,300 volumes in the catalogue of Prior Henry of Eastry (1285–1311). These estimates are subject to every kind of qualification, because

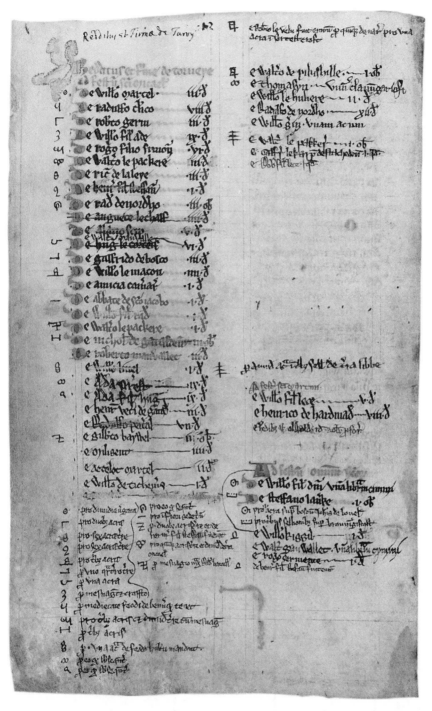

PLATE 11. Estate book of Richard Hotot, *c.* 1240s. The book lists the rents due from Richard's tenants; the marginal symbols are cross-references to further details below, one of the earliest known examples of footnotes

the makers of medieval library catalogues were not primarily concerned with counting their stock. The earliest Durham catalogue (from which the estimate of 490 volumes has been derived) illustrates the difficulties of counting, as various items are described as being in a certain number of 'books' (*libri*) or 'sets' (*paria*) or 'parts' (*particuli*) or 'quires' (*quaterniones*). Furthermore, books varied so much in size and in the layout of each page that the number of volumes gives little indication of the amount of reading material available. In general, however, library catalogues show that many more books were acquired in the twelfth and thirteenth centuries, as they often list new acquisitions from particular persons.

Individuals likewise possessed few books by modern standards. Robert Grosseteste, the greatest English scholar and bishop of the thirteenth century, perhaps had about ninety; John of Foxton, who gave his books on Scripture to Lincoln Cathedral library in *c.* 1240, possessed about thirty-four volumes on that subject; Master Peter of Peckham, a lawyer, had eighteen books in a coffer when he died in 1293; Guy de Beauchamp, earl of Warwick, gave away about forty books in 1306. The limitations of such fragmentary information are obvious. An inexplicable exception to the rule that neither individuals nor institutions had many books is a court case from Worcestershire in 1221, in which the toll collector of Wychbold was alleged to have impounded 'two carts which bore the books of Richard, dean of Worcester'. Two carts suggests a large number of books, but whether they all belonged to Richard and where they were being taken is not specified.

Library catalogues are more informative about the types of books kept than about numbers; but there are difficulties here too, as some catalogues list only some of their books (those kept in particular places for example) and items specified can be difficult to identify because many books had no uniform titles. The library of Bury St Edmunds, which can be reconstructed with confidence for the twelfth century, indicates the main categories of books. It was largely built up—by gift and purchase and by copying in the *scriptorium*—by one abbot, Anselm, between 1121 and 1148. By the end of the twelfth century Bury possessed Bibles and liturgical books, texts of the main Church Fathers (largely added by Abbot Anselm), pagan Latin classics, histories both English (for example, Bede and the *Anglo-Saxon Chronicle*) and European (for example, Paul the Deacon and the *Gesta Francorum*), 'modern' (that is, twelfth-century) scholastic textbooks in divinity and law, and some 'modern' Latin literature such as the poems of Walter of Châtillon.

It would not be profitable to list in greater detail here the various books used and made in England between 1066 and 1307, as that would involve an extended essay on medieval learning and literature in Latin, Hebrew, French and English. Instead, a few main types will be alluded to briefly. Unlike some of the forms of documents and memoranda already discussed, books were not a novelty at the time of the Norman Conquest, nor is the format of the book unfamiliar to the modern reader. Although books were no novelty, they do seem to have been a rarity in late Anglo-Saxon England. Or at least the prelates appointed by the Normans considered the libraries they found to be so inadequate that they restocked them on an unprecedented scale. Abbot Anselm's work at Bury is an example of what was done in the main cathedrals and abbeys. Nor were the principal texts which were acquired or made in the century after the Norman Conquest new in themselves: they were the Bible, the Church Fathers, the pagan Latin classics, all works hallowed by antiquity. Scribes and illuminators wrote more accurate texts and embellished them in new ways, but they did not alter their essentials. These classics continued to be the foundation of any medieval library.

Alongside these relatively few perennials, planted by the sages of antiquity (whether Jewish, Christian or pagan), there were growing up numerous recent books by lesser men. These latter works were lesser in dignity, but not necessarily in length; the *Ormulum*, a series of homilies on the Gospels in the Missal composed in *c.* 1170, numbers 20,512 short lines in Middle English in its extant form, which is perhaps one eighth of the original. Furthermore, as John of Salisbury commented in *c.* 1150 (quoting Bernard of Chartres), 'modern' authors are dwarfs, but they stand on the shoulders of the giant sages of antiquity and so see more and further than their predecessors. This confident attitude, combined with widening literacy caused by the dissemination of documents of all kinds in the twelfth century, produced a growing number of newly composed writings as well as further copies of the classics, both pagan and Christian. These new works are of two principal sorts. Firstly, there are the productions of the schoolmen, which aimed to cope with the increasing mass of written material by providing guides to it (in Latin) in logically organised treatises: the *Summa Theologiae* of Thomas Aquinas (composed in *c.* 1260) is the best-known of such texts. Secondly, there are the very varied works composed for the book-reading or book-using public, both cleric and lay, in Latin, French and English—poems, songs, histories, romances, saints' lives, sermons, and so on.

Taking the writings of the schoolmen first, the typical scholastic book is in the form either of a *glossa* or of a *summa*; both took definite shape in the twelfth century and aimed to cope with the increasing number of documents. The *glossa*, the 'gloss' around a text, is discussed with reference to the layout of the page in the next chapter. The *summa* is explained here. Robert of Melun, an Englishman by birth and bishop of Hereford (1163–7), defined a *summa* both as 'a concise encyclopedia of instances' and 'a compendious collection of instances'.[23] The prototype was Abelard's *Sic et Non* (composed in the 1130s), which aimed to cut through the 'mass of words' presented to divinity students by bringing together selected apparently contradictory quotations under headings and subheadings. Although many *summae* juxtaposed contradictory texts in this way, the essence of the genre was that it comprised a selection of texts organised in accordance with a logical scheme. Likewise although many *summae* contained explanatory commentaries, at the basis of the *summa* form were the quotations cited from authorities; Abelard's *Sic et Non* had no commentary apart from a prologue.

Long before the twelfth century rhetoricians had collected quotations, particularly from classical authors, into anthologies called *florilegia* (bunches of flowers), and this practice continued. As well as using such anthologies himself, Gerald of Wales presented his *Gemma Ecclesiastica* (written in *c.* 1197) as a kind of *florilegium* selected from the 'mass of words': 'I am like one who with much labour extracts precious gems from the innumerable sands of the seashore, or one who, walking through spacious gardens, plucks the useful and virtuous from among the worthless and fruitless plants, separating the lilies and roses from the nettles and brambles.' Such an anthology differed from a *summa* in its function: the *florilegium* provided verbal ornament to garnish a composition, whereas the *summa* invited its readers to examine the citations critically. The *florilegium* stemmed from the ancient arts of grammar and rhetoric, whereas the *summa* stemmed from 'modern' logic and dialectic.

Within the general class of *summae* there were numerous species, theological and legal textbooks being the most common. Bracton presented his treatise on English law, which was contemporary with Aquinas's *Summa Theologiae*, as a *summa*:

I, Henry de Bracton, to instruct the lesser judges, if no one else, have turned my mind to the former judgments of just men, examining diligently their decisions . . . and have compiled whatever I found therein worthy of note into one *summa*, organised by titles and paragraphs, without prejudice to any other opinion, and committed to memory forever by the aid of writing.[24]

Bracton's description epitomises the main elements of a *summa*: it is compiled for instruction; it is a selection of authoritative statements; it is organised systematically.

Like other writers of textbooks, Bracton can be accused of plagiarism, as the treatise to which he gave his name had been put together a generation earlier by his own masters in English law. But in manuscript culture, without a distinction between hand-written and printed copy, it was harder for an author to distinguish between his own text and his notes from various sources. As a conscientious compiler and publisher, it may never have occurred to Bracton that he was guilty of theft of intellectual property. A generation later his treatise was in its turn superseded by Fleta, who made similarly bold claims:

> To many who are in a hurry and many who are unlearned, a compendium in a brief volume of the justices' judgments may be very necessary, so that an inquirer does not have to turn over a mass of books and chapters, when he will find what he is looking for without trouble, brought together here in a brief space.

A *summa* was a sort of highly organised and selective register, which aimed to instruct a wider public than one monastic house like a cartulary, or one government department like an Exchequer remembrance book. If a *summa* is defined as broadly as that, the genre includes a variety of formularies and treatises which instruct by citing examples in how to conduct law courts, draft charters, cast financial accounts, manage estates, and so on. In a sense too the collections of papal decretals and parliamentary statutes which lawyers used were *summae*. Compiling *summae* was a reaction to the proliferation of documents and books in the twelfth and thirteenth centuries; they were intended as a guide through the maze, although sometimes they added to the confusion.

The very varied works written for, or used by, the general reader in this period are not characterised by a single dominant type like the *summa*. Old works continued to be read, particularly the pagan Latin classics, and new ones were created, in Latin and Hebrew verse and prose, and in the vernacular languages of French and English. Ideally, from the point of view of making and using documents, all works available in England in whatever language and whatever their provenance are relevant. But generalisation about what was read is made difficult by the emphasis of modern scholarship, which usually concentrates on one of the languages only and is concerned primarily with linguistic development or critical assessment

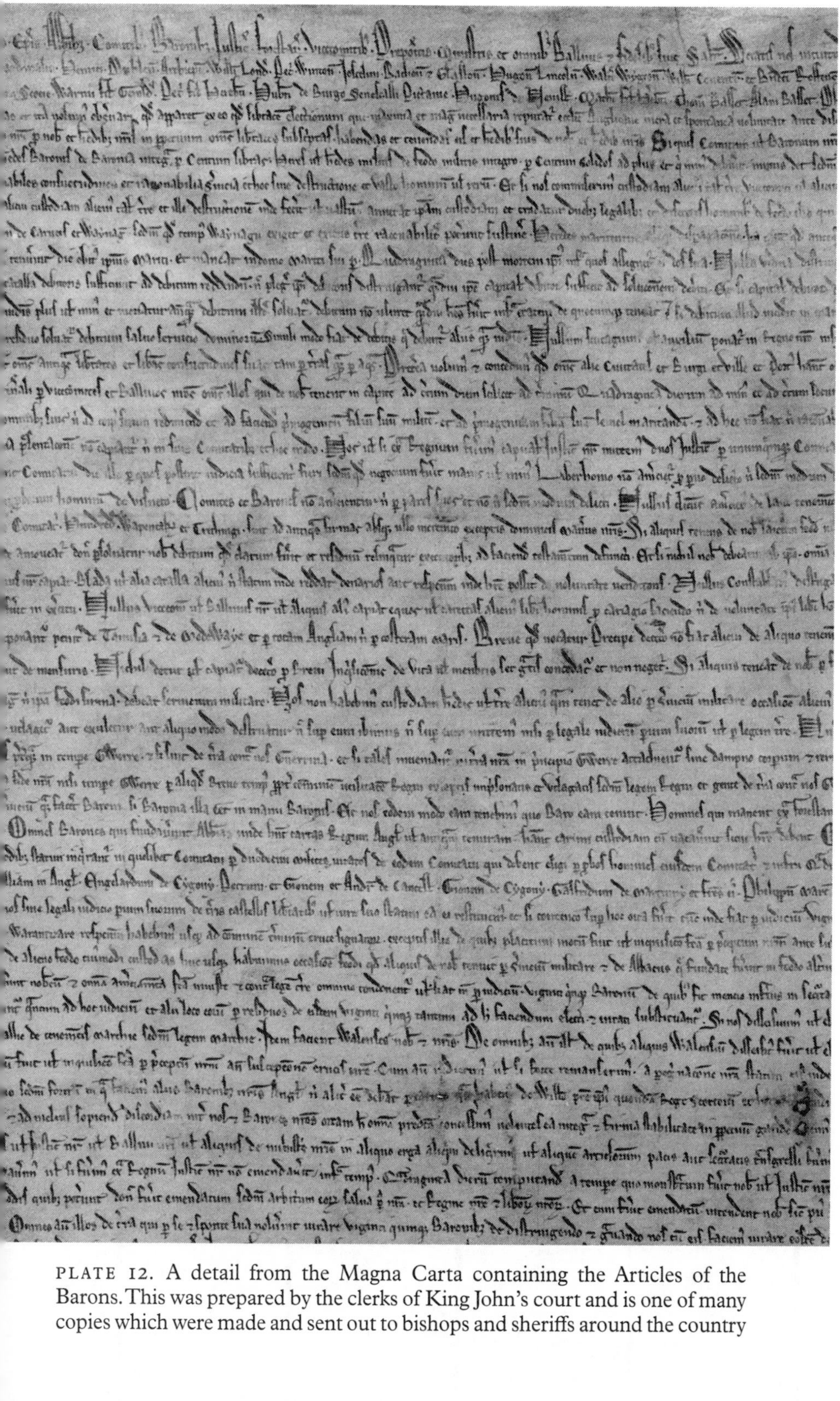

PLATE 12. A detail from the Magna Carta containing the Articles of the Barons. This was prepared by the clerks of King John's court and is one of many copies which were made and sent out to bishops and sheriffs around the country

of newly created literature. An educated layman in 1300, by contrast, like Henry de Bray, was probably familiar with some writing in three literary languages (Latin, French, and English) and did not necessarily care whether the sermons, songs and tales he heard or read were new or old.

Scholarship in England has tended to concentrate on medieval literary works in inverse proportion to their frequency. Latin was the commonest literary language in the period 1066–1307, yet the use of Latin in England had not been surveyed until recently. English, on the other hand, which was the least used literary language (apart from Hebrew), has been intensively studied. French has fared much better than Latin, but not as well as English. Consequently the use of Latin works in medieval England is too large and unstudied a subject to summarise in a few pages, whereas summaries of writings in English and French are unnecessary, as excellent introductions to them already exist. The foundations have now been laid, however, for renewed study of Latin writing in England by George Rigg's encyclopedic chronological survey of authors (religious and secular, whether writing in prose or verse) and Tony Hunt's provision of authoritative texts, particularly of didactic works.[25] Most importantly, the basic materials for what was read have been listed in N. R. Ker's *Medieval Libraries of Great Britain: A List of Surviving Books*.[26]

Books made for the church's liturgical chant and readings look at first sight an odd category of text to include in a survey of records. But to medieval Christians these were the most important records of all, because they enshrined the very words of God in script. 'Writing' (*scriptura*) essentially meant holy 'Scripture'. Throughout the Middle Ages the Four Evangelists were depicted at the opening of each Gospel as scribes, seated at their desks with pens and blank parchment at the ready, poised to record whatever the Holy Spirit dictated to them. To write or read out the words of Scripture was an act of worship in itself, because it replicated and renewed what the Evangelists themselves were believed to have done. No expenditure of effort and precious materials was therefore too great for the making of the 'sacred page'. As a consequence, illuminated Gospel Books and liturgical manuscripts are the most impressive of all medieval records. Typically they take the form of huge volumes, designed to rest on lecterns at eye level and display their texts in bold lettering (and musical notation where appropriate) enhanced by lavish illumination.

These books are described in medieval inventories by a variety of names, which reflect their contents or functions: 'psalters' (texts of the Psalms), 'missals' (texts of the service of the Mass), and many others. Because they formed part of the service of the altar, liturgical books had to compete in magnificence with the gold and silver, jewellery, and silk amassed there. Since they embodied the most ancient and revered texts of Latin Christendom, liturgical books might be expected to undergo little development over the centuries. But this is not the case. Very old books, directly associated for example with St Augustine at Canterbury or St Cuthbert at Durham, were indeed kept as relics on the altar; but they were not used for ordinary church services. Liturgical manuscripts, like other textbooks, had to take account of frequent minor changes in regulations by producing numerous new editions. Furthermore, because these were in the texts most highly valued by the most literate persons, the monks and clergy, they had to exemplify the latest fashions in book production. Every bishop and abbot wanted the shiniest and most advanced model of liturgical book, just as every ambitious executive today wants the most luxurious limousine.

Such wants help explain why Paul of Caen, the first new abbot of St Albans after the Norman Conquest, replaced so many of the abbey's books. According to Matthew Paris, he gave 'twenty-eight notable volumes' to the abbey, as well as 'eight Psalters, a Collect, an Epistolary, a book containing the Gospel readings throughout the year, two Texts (i.e. Gospel Books) ornamented with gold, silver and gems; and other Ordinals, Custumals, Missals, Tropers and Collects'. These books were kept in 'little cupboards' in the first half of the thirteenth century, when Matthew Paris wrote this description. By that time, however, they were largely obsolete, as Abbots Geoffrey and Ralph in the mid-twelfth century had replaced them, again on a grand scale, with more up-to-date books incorporating innovations in the liturgy like the feast of the Immaculate Conception of the Virgin Mary. Like other medieval churches, St Albans Abbey proved its vitality by renewing its books.

Liturgical manuscripts are the prime form in which the habit of using and possessing books reached the laity from the thirteenth century onwards. Everyone needed a prayer-book, their own interactive record of Scripture, whether or not they could read. Liturgical books did not make high demands on reading ability anyway, as their texts were familiar from constant repetition and they were written out in the largest lettering. Although they had originally been made for clerical and church use, liturgical books were attractive to the laity as well. Men and women who had close relatives among the clergy must have asked themselves why such covetable objects as the Psalter of Robert of Lindsey (abbot of Peterborough, 1214–22), or the Missal (dating from 1250) made for Henry of Chichester, should be the monopoly of their clerical brethren.

Anyone—cleric or lay, male or female, rich or poor, saint or sinner—
who saw the full-page portrait of Henry in his Missal, showing him in his
best vestments offering a prayer to the enthroned Virgin and Child, might
have desired such a book and such a portrait for himself or herself.

An example of a liturgical book made for an identified lay person in
England is the so-called 'Grey–FitzPayn Hours', which was probably presented by Richard de Grey to Joan FitzPayn as a bridal gift in 1301. Husband and wife are depicted in it, in their coats of arms, kneeling beneath
an image of the Annunciation of the Virgin. On another page Joan is portrayed, within an initial of the text, being individually blessed by Christ in
Majesty; a few lines below a young man, probably her husband, looks out
from the initial 'V' of *Venite exultemus* ('Come let us rejoice', Psalm 94).
This portrait page may be intended to celebrate and bless their marriage.
Prayer-books like this, designed for aristocrats to hold in their hands and
treasure in the privacy of their chambers, retained the magnificence of
ecclesiastical manuscripts while leavening the traditional recipe with witty
drawings and naturalistic colour. Many of these books were made for
young ladies, and it is not too fanciful to see a feminine and domestic taste
in the miniatures in their borders of playful furry animals and languid
damsels. In the case of the FitzPayn marriage portrait, there is potential
sexual symbolism in the squirrel and the rampant goat on the borders of
the page and in the beaks and tails of song-birds penetrating the body of
the text.

From the aristocratic prayer-books of the thirteenth century derive the
Books of Hours of the later Middle Ages. Potentially these were 'books for
everybody', as C. de Hamel has characterised them. 'To the great majority
of the medieval population of Europe, the first book they knew—and
often the only one—must have been the Book of Hours.'[27] This form of
manuscript took shape, as a portable manual of prayer for lay people—
and for ladies in their private chambers in particular—in England. It
looks as if it was invented in *c.* 1240, possibly by William de Brailes, the
Oxford illuminator, who made the first such book now extant (British
Library Additional Manuscript 49,999) for the lady who is depicted in it.
C. Donovan has identified half a dozen portable books of this sort, mostly
having an Oxford provenance and made between *c.* 1240 and *c.* 1270
(dates can be no more than approximate because they depend on stylistic
comparisons of the artwork).[28] These books were all made for women,
and their owners are sometimes portrayed, within the illuminated initials,
at their devotions. The dimensions of these books are the same as those of
small modern paperbacks.

Through Books of Hours, ladies introduced their families and children to prayer—and hence to literacy—in their own homes. This domestication of the liturgical book was the foundation on which the growing literacy of the later Middle Ages was built; but that is another story.[29] Medieval lay people became functionally literate through prayer because the clergy had insisted for centuries that prayer was everyone's most important function. In liturgical books prayer was writ large: first for God and the clergy, then for ladies in their homes, and ultimately for everybody.

Many of the documentary forms developed in England between 1066 and 1307 were ancient in origin. The charter, the chirograph and the rhetorician's letter had been used by the Anglo-Saxons and derived from the traditions of the late Roman empire. Similarly, skills in writing and illuminating books and ensuring that posterity had a record of the past had been the preoccupation of monks for half a millenium before the Norman Conquest. What was new after 1066 was the increase in the number of documents made and the gradual extension of literate modes to more people and diverse activities. As a result old forms, like the charter and the chirograph, became stereotyped in the thirteenth century because numbers imposed standardisation. The form of the letter itself, which had been used hitherto mostly as an open declaration or a literary device, became with Henry II's letters close an actual missive sent from one person to another.

The increase in the number of documents in circulation encouraged institutions to organise and record those which most concerned them in cartularies and registers, both of documents received and of documents sent out. The habit of making an accumulating series of memoranda year by year, of which the chronicle had been the forerunner, was extended first to financial accounting and then to the proceedings of law courts, from the king's court downwards. Memoranda as such were not new; the novelty consisted in annually accumulating series.

Likewise books as such were not new: the Bible, the Church Fathers, and the pagan classics were the heritage of antiquity, preserved and lovingly illuminated by monks. Innovation came from the schoolmen of the twelfth century, who provided in the *summa* a tool for cutting through the increasing mass of written words. Contrasting with the uniformity and order which the schoolmen attempted to impose on documents are the variety of literary works produced in Latin, particularly during the twelfth-century Renaissance, and in French and English from the latter half of the twelfth century onwards. In the eleventh century and earlier, making documents in England had been largely the prerogative of monks. In the twelfth and thirteenth centuries schoolmen and secular clerics successfully challenged this tradition. Monks and schoolmen between them created and wrote nearly all the types of document described in this chapter. Thereafter, however, the initiative lay neither with monks nor with schoolmen, who wrote in Latin, but with those who wrote in vernacular languages for a gradually enlarging public. Even so, old traditions proved resilient and the most treasured and popular of all manuscripts were those enshrining the Latin prayers in Books of Hours. Upon them the future of literacy in Western culture largely rested.

✣ V ✣

THE MAKING OF MANUSCRIPTS

The scribe sitting at his desk is depicted in numerous manuscripts in the guise of the author writing the book which is being copied. In place of the venerable author, most commonly one of the Four Evangelists, some scribes and illuminators of the twelfth century began to have themselves depicted in this way. The most remarkable example of the practice is the full-page portrait of Eadwine, monk of Christ Church Canterbury, whose picture has an inscription round the frame declaring him to be 'the prince of writers' whose praise and fame will not die. Eadwine sits in the conventional pose (apart from facing to the left instead of to the right), with a quill pen in his right hand and a penknife in his left, on an elaborately carved upright chair, leaning towards a high writing desk draped with a cloth, on which is a book open at a blank page. In another unusual full-page portrait, contemporary with Eadwine's but this time of the author, Laurence prior of Durham (1149–54) sits at a desk which is shown as a folding extension of the chair, projecting out from its arms.

Verbal portraits of the scribe indicate much the same features. These are found in lexicons, like Alexander Neckham's *De Nominibus Utensilium* (composed at the end of the twelfth century), which describe everyday things. A work derived from Neckham begins its picture of the scribe as follows: 'A writer of books (*librarius*), who is commonly called a scribe (*scriptor*), should have a chair with projecting arms for holding the board upon which the quire of parchment is to be placed.' This work then describes the tools required for preparing the parchment—the knife or razor for scraping it, the pumice for cleaning and smoothing it, and the boar or goat's tooth for polishing the surface to stop the ink running. Then there are the tools for ruling the lines—the stylus, the pencil, the straight ruler, the plumb line, and the awl for pricking holes to mark the beginnings of the lines. Finally there is the writing equipment itself—the quill pens and penknife, the inkhorn, and the various coloured inks. This description also includes the importance of adequate heat and good light for writing, although the hot coals recommended seem mainly intended for drying the ink on damp days rather than keeping the scribe himself warm. There are some indications that in monasteries writing was a seasonal activity. Orderic Vitalis, the English historian of the Normans, says at the end of one of his books (which he penned himself) that he is so numbed by the winter cold that he is going to finish his book at this point and will relate what he has omitted when the spring returns.

Writing was certainly seen as an act of endurance in which 'the whole body labours'. As such, it was an appropriate theme for sermons and homilies in monasteries. A twelfth-century sermon copied into a Durham manuscript exhorts its hearers to consider how they may become scribes of the Lord, writing with the pen of memory on the parchment of a pure conscience, which has been scraped by the knife of divine fear, smoothed by the pumice of heavenly desires, and whitened by the chalk of holy thoughts (the chalk is a detail which Neckham's lexicon omits). The metaphors extend the theme still further: the ruler is the will of God, the bifurcated knib of the quill pen is the joint love of God and our neighbour, the different coloured inks are heavenly grace, and the exemplar is the life of our Redeemer. Although the Durham sermon eulogises monks as scribes, we should not conclude either that all monks were scribes or that all monastic books were written by the monks themselves. When Abbot Paul of St Albans (1077–93) had books made for his church, he sought out the choicest scribes 'from afar' and gave them regular ready-cooked meals so that they would not have to stop working. Income was specially assigned to pay for them, their materials, and the new scriptorium in which they worked. Abbot Faricius of Abingdon (1100–17) likewise 'instituted scribes, in addition to the cloister monks' for the writing of missals and other fine liturgical books.

Obviously neither visual nor verbal portraits of the scribe are drawn directly from life in all their details, as they formed part of a conventional repertoire. Since one of the functions of a lexicon like the *De Nominibus Utensilium* was to enlarge the reader's vocabulary, it tends to exaggerate the amount of equipment the scribe requires in order to present as many unfamiliar words as possible. The average scribe did not presumably sit in an elaborate chair at an elegantly draped desk; nor did he normally write on the blank pages of a bound book, as in Eadwine's portrait, but on a folded quire of parchment. Moreover, the classic portraits of the scribe are monastic in origin. They describe the traditional copyist, who wrote beautiful liturgical books from an exemplar at an even pace. In the twelfth century a new type of scribe, less worthy of a dignified portrait, came to the fore. He was the secular clerk, who rapidly wrote letters and official records from dictation. The 'scribbler' and 'petty clerk', who fawned around the king's Chancery in the thirteenth century (the description is Henry III's), had little in common with Eadwine, 'the prince of writers'.

Medieval books are made up of gatherings of parchment, folded into bifolios (two large leaves, making four pages), quires (four leaves half the size, making eight pages), and so on, depending on the required size of the page. The gatherings in a medieval book can therefore be of diverse character and provenance, forming distinct 'booklets' within the binding. In manuscript culture the coherence of the bound book was established not by the publisher's mass-production of identical units for sale but by the individual requirements of each owner or maker; each medieval book was unique. One Durham manuscript from the twelfth century, discovered in a drawer in the cathedral library in 1935, is preserved in its gatherings still unbound. The great majority of medieval books have been rebound in later centuries. Nevertheless a few bindings from the twelfth century survive, in whole or in part. Winchester's 'Domesday' book retains elaborate leather work on its boards, done with metal punches. In the case of the Knights Templars' survey of their property made in the 1180s, the stitching, headbands, pegs and clasps of the bound book largely remain, as well as the ornamental leather work. Ornamented bindings were expensive. More typical probably are the plain boards and spines on Cirencester Abbey's twelfth-century books, now preserved at Jesus College, Oxford.

Gathering writings up into books, instead of into rolls as in the ancient world, is associated with the Bible and the official reception of Christianity in Constantine's Roman Empire. Books guarded, preserved and enshrined their contents between their boards more effectively and visibly than rolls. The scribe-Evangelist writing in a bound book became a medieval stereotype because he embodied this ideal of the durability of holy Scripture; such an image does not aim to portray ordinary writers in their mundane workplaces. Everything to do with writing in medieval Christendom had potential transcendent significance, and this creates difficulties for the modern historian asking utilitarian questions and looking for representations of actual daily life in medieval images.

The most important equipment of the twelfth-century writer who composed for himself or wrote from dictation, as distinct from the copyist, was not the parchment book depicted in conventional portraits of scribes, but the writing tablets on which he noted down his drafts. The tablets were ordinarily made of wood, overlaid with coloured wax, and often folded into a diptych which could be worn on a belt. When something needed noting down, the diptych was opened, thus exposing the waxed surfaces, which were written on with a stylus. In two manuscripts of Boethius's *Consolation of Philosophy*, dating from the 1140s, he is depicted holding writing tablets open on his knees, a single tablet in one picture and a diptych in the other. In both pictures the wooden frames around the wax surfaces are clearly drawn. In one of the pictures Boethius writes with a stylus considerably taller than his hand; it tapers to a point at its writing end and is topped by a crossbar or handle. Whether this was a form of stylus in use in the twelfth century, or whether the artist intended it to appear pagan or archaic (and therefore appropriate to Boethius), awaits archaeological investigation. A story by Orderic Vitalis illustrates the use of wax tablets. He was visited by Anthony, a monk of Winchester, who showed him a copy of a life of St William. Orderic wished to have a copy too, 'but in truth, since the bearer was in haste to depart, and the winter cold prevented me from writing, I made a full and accurate abbreviation on tablets, and now I shall endeavour to entrust it summarily to parchment'. This story incidentally illustrates again how writing with a pen on parchment, as distinct from making notes with a stylus on wax, was a seasonal activity for Orderic.

It seems to have been common practice for monastic authors to write on wax and then have a fair copy made on parchment. Eadmer describes the difficulties St Anselm had in writing the *Proslogion*, because the tablets on which it was written were first lost and then shattered, perhaps by diabolical intervention. That wax was the normal medium for writing in the twelfth century is also indicated by other saints' biographies. The author of the life of Christina of Markyate remarks how he could not pollute 'the wax by writing' how scandalously the cleric had behaved who had been commended to Christina as her companion by Thurstan, archbishop of York. On his deathbed in 1200 St Hugh dreamed that the great pear tree in his garden at Lincoln had fallen to the ground and he was worried about the waste of its timber, 'for so many diptychs could be cut from it that there would be more than enough for the scholastic studies of the whole of England and France'.[1] The tablets of Moses, on which God wrote the Ten Commandments, were likewise envisaged as a diptych: they are drawn as a pair of framed wax surfaces, in a case concerning a Jew, in an Exchequer memoranda roll of 1270.

In the thirteenth century pieces of parchment were used for notes, either as a substitute for wax tablets or in addition to them. Such notes are occasionally referred to in the royal plea rolls. Making notes on parchment had also been a practice of Robert Grosseteste. This is known because dispute arose about which of his works were authentic. The regent-master of the Franciscans stated that Grosseteste had made some marginal notes in manuscripts because 'when some noteworthy thought occurred to him, he wrote it down there so that it should not escape his memory, just as he also wrote many slips of parchment [*cedulas*] which are not all authoritative'. This statement suggests that Grosseteste was not accustomed to using wax tablets for his notes and drafts, although undue reliance should not be put on an argument from silence. The practice of making memoranda, whether on wax or parchment, contradicts the common assumption that medieval people had such good memories that they required no notes. Once they were literate, they had the same needs as a modern writer. Drafts on wax or slips of parchment are the equivalent of a modern author's original manuscript, while the parchment text is comparable to a fair copy produced by a word processor.

Before discussing parchment, a few words need to be said about paper. The earliest paper documents extant in an English medieval archive are the letters sent from Italy to the Riccardi, Edward I's bankers, dating from 1296–1303. The earliest records made in England on paper come most appropriately from major seaports: a register from King's Lynn beginning in 1307 and another from Lyme Regis in 1309. London described its registers of apprentices, citizens, and debts as the 'paper' or 'papers' of the Chamber of Guildhall in 1300 (and perhaps as early as 1275), but its extant records from this period are in fact made of parchment. Paper occurs first in seaports because it was imported. In the long term its principal advantages over parchment were that it was easier to write on and potentially cheaper. The most significant fact about paper in England in the period up to 1307 is that it was scarcely known. Consequently parchment became established for centuries to come as the appropriate material for all the most formal records, because they took shape in the twelfth and thirteenth centuries.

The commonest word for parchment was *membrana*, simply meaning animal skin. In northern Europe the skins normally used were those of cattle and sheep; goat, rabbit, and squirrel were also used. The finest parchment was vellum, made of calf skin. Thus to make the great Bury Bible in the time of Abbot Anselm (1121–48), Harvey the sacrist obtained parchment from Scotland (perhaps meaning Ireland) because he could not find calf skins locally which suited the illuminator, Master Hugh. For the equally magnificent Winchester Bible it has been estimated that about 250 calf skins must have been required. These 250 skins must have been selected from ten times that number, in order to find ones from healthy young animals without blemishes. Sheepskin was the usual material for royal records, both because it was cheaper and because (according to the *Dialogue of the Exchequer*) it is not easy to make an erasure on sheepskin without it showing plainly. Once parchment has been scraped and prepared for writing on, it is usually impossible to tell what species of animal skin is being used.

It is frequently assumed that parchment was rare and expensive, and that its high cost obstructed the spread of literacy. Such an assumption fails to distinguish between the finest parchments, required for illuminated manuscripts like the Bury Bible, and cheaper varieties. It is also necessary to take into account the relative cost of other items, such as the scribe's time, the cost of ink and binding materials, and (in the case of letter-writing) the cost of sealing wax and delivery. These costs in their turn need to be related to the general cost of living. As no detailed study has been made along these lines, only a few indicative facts will be cited here. When Henry II asked St Hugh how much money he needed to build up a library for the new Charterhouse at Witham, Hugh replied that one silver mark would be enough for a long time. The king smiled at this, saying, 'What heavy demands you make on us', and gave him 10 marks. As Adam of Eynsham, Hugh's biographer, wished to emphasise the saint's modesty, he may have minimised his requirements; even so, Adam's story assumes that 10 marks ($£6$ 13s. 4d.) would have bought a large amount of parchment.

At the time Adam wrote this biography, the Exchequer was keeping accounts of its running costs. Although these records do not survive in complete series and some of the sums are fixed charges, which went back to Henry II's time or earlier, they do supply sufficient information to sample the relative costs of different stages in the production of documents in the 1220s and 1230s. Parchment was charged for at a fixed rate of 10 shillings a year. As this sum was already customary when Fitz Nigel wrote the *Dialogue of the Exchequer*, it does not indicate the real cost; but in some terms varying supplementary charges, ranging between 20 and 40 shillings a year, are recorded which presumably do indicate actual expenditure on parchment. Compared with these sums, one scribe in 1222, Robert of Bassingbourn, was paid 3s. 2d. for ten days' work 'while he wrote summonses', and the customary charge for scribes was 5 pence per day each. Similarly in Easter term of the same year the nightwatchman and lighting cost the customary 12 shillings (1½d. per night) and the rushes on the floor 3s. 5d. Ink was also a notable expense, which increased in a constant ratio with the expenditure on parchment. In Fitz Nigel's time 2 shillings a year had been allowed for it, that is, one fifth of the cost of parchment; by the 1220s 3 shillings a year was being allowed, and by the 1230s 40 pence for the half year. The cost of sealing the writs was likewise high (about 12d. for thirty writs on average), although this sum may include the sealer's charge as well as the cost of the wax (about 7*d.* per pound). An even greater expense was delivering writs to their destinations (more than 2*d.* per writ in the 1220s); on 11 July 1226 the charge for carrying six writs to sheriffs in various counties was 3*s.* 6*d.*

These figures are not presented as statistics of real expenditure, but as an indication of relative costs. As far as materials were concerned, parchment seems to have been rather cheap. Ink and sealing wax were surprisingly expensive, although all materials were relatively cheap compared with the customary charges for labour of both the unskilled, like the nightwatchman, and the skilled scribes at 5 pence per day. If parchment cost the Exchequer at the most about 50 shillings a year in the 1220s and 1230s, that is the equivalent of 4 silver marks, a negligible sum considering that the standard rate for a single fine or oblation in the king's court was half a mark. Like Henry II, Henry III might have smiled at the suggestion that a few marks for parchment was a heavy burden on his revenues.

It does not follow from the proposition that parchment was relatively cheap that the finished product, the manuscript, was commensurately so; but the high cost of manuscripts arose primarily from their being produced by hand and not from the initial cost of animal skins. In the last decades of the thirteenth century the obedientiaries' accounts of some monasteries are sufficiently detailed to distinguish between the cost of writing materials and labour costs. Like the Exchequer records, these accounts suggest that even the finest parchment was cheaper than the scribe's time.

Apart from parchment, the most important material for making records, as distinct from ephemeral drafts written on wax, was wood. In Michaelmas term 1224 the Exchequer spent 5 shillings on rods for tallies at the same time as it spent 4 shillings on parchment. Tallies were used as receipts for money or other items rendered, such as bags of corn at a mill, and also as records of obligations to make payments. The appropriate sums were shown on the tally by notches of differing widths, depths, and intervals. Like a chirograph, the English tally was a bipartite record. When the notches had been cut on the stick, to the satisfaction of both renderer and receiver, the tally was split down its length so that each party had the same record. The interlocking halves were intended to act as a check against forgery. Although the numbers on the tally were cut with a knife, the names and business of the parties it concerned were written in script in ink. Some tallies also bore seals like charters. Tallies were not a primitive survival from the preliterate past, but a sophisticated and practical record of numbers. They were more convenient to keep and store than parchments, less complex to make, and harder to forge. They were the foundation and origin of the royal financial system of the twelfth century and were widely adopted by private accountants in the thirteenth, who described in detail how they should be cut, just as Fitz Nigel had done in the *Dialogue of the Exchequer*.

Of the millions of medieval tallies made, only a few hundred survive. In 1834 the Exchequer tallies stored at Westminster were burned after the passing of the statute abolishing the Receipt of the Exchequer. The fire accidentally spread to the Houses of Parliament and thus brilliantly symbolised the abolition of the *anciens régime* and the triumph of 'reform'. The burning of the tally sticks has further ironies for the historian, because at the same time the Record Commissioners were publishing in lavish volumes with spurious Latin titles the earliest medieval records in parchment, like the Chancery rolls of King John. The Commissioners would not have dreamed of burning Domesday Book or the Chancery rolls, yet these records of the Exchequer were deliberately destroyed because they were in a medium, wood, which was too uncouth for scholars to appreciate. The fire of 1834 entered the mythology of English history. In reality the only tallies burned were the most recent ones, probably dating from after 1800. But people at the time believed them to be medieval because doing accounting with sticks looked so primitive, and even shameful, to nineteenth-century reformers. Charles Dickens for example demanded: 'What was to be done with such worn-out, worm-eaten rotten old bits of wood', which 'ages ago a savage mode of keeping accounts' had introduced into the Exchequer?

Wax, parchment, and wood were the commonest documentary materials in medieval England. In addition to them, inscriptions were of course made on other materials, notably on stone, metal, bone, and fabric. Such inscriptions are too varied and scattered to discuss in detail here. The lettering of those that were cut and painted on stone monumental slabs and sculptures, or engraved and enamelled on brasses, seals, swords, rings, cups, and so on were probably designed by scribes. Their users presumably understood the significance of the Latin inscriptions, even if that were the limit of their literacy. Everyone would have seen inscriptions, or at least symbolic letters, on vestments and sacred images and utensils in churches. Similarly the Bayeux Tapestry, with its summary captions in Latin (HIC HAROLD REX INTERFECTUS EST, for example), assumes an audience in which someone could read. Coins are a special case. Because they were the medium in which lettering circulated most extensively among the population as a whole, their inscriptions were

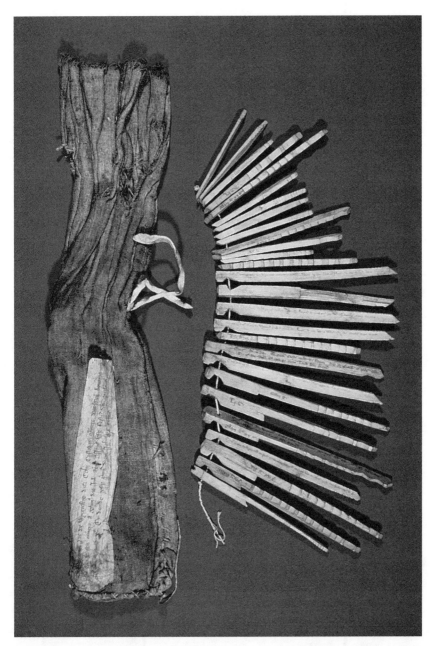

PLATE 13. Tallies and the original canvas bag belonging to Richard of Worcester, keeper of the king's mines in Devon, 1316–17. There are fourteen foils (the shorter pieces of wood) and thirteen stocks (the longer pieces), the equivalent of modern-day cheques and stubs

made by a form of mass-production. The lettering was not individually engraved on to the dies in accordance with a scribe's design; instead the letters were formed in sections by moneyers using punches of different shapes. Coins were the only form of writing which remained unaffected by the Norman Conquest; even a century later in Henry II's reign archaic lettering was still in evidence.

The most far-reaching change in the making of royal records was the use of rolls instead of books. Rolls are so familiar to any medievalist who has worked in the Public Record Office that their existence tends to be taken for granted. Yet there is no evidence that rolls were made by the royal government before the twelfth century and, in the forms they took, they are peculiar to England. Continental governments, from the papacy downwards, kept their most important records in the form of books not rolls. Consequently when William the Conqueror undertook his *descriptio* of the conquered land, the results were compiled for posterity in volumes, 'Domesday Book', not in rolls. Although some of the preliminary drafts for Domesday Book may possibly have been stitched together into rolls, they were described vaguely as *breves* or *carte* and not as rolls. A special Latin word for the record in roll format came into vogue in the twelfth century at the earliest: it was a *rotulus*.

This word seems to have been brought into general use by Fitz Nigel's *Dialogue of the Exchequer*.[2] He describes a variety of types of roll—'rolls of the treasury' or 'great annual rolls of accounts' (that is, the pipe rolls), 'rolls of the chancery', 'rolls of receipts', the 'lesser rolls of the itinerant justices', and others. To Fitz Nigel and his colleagues working in the Exchequer in the 1170s the roll or *rotulus* was evidently a commonplace. Nevertheless the general public were probably unfamiliar both with the name and the thing until Fitz Nigel's book made the secrets of the Exchequer plain to his readers. His purpose, he explained in his prologue, was to reveal hidden treasure or the treasury (the Latin *thesaurus* means both 'treasure' and 'treasury') in ordinary language, 'even though it is permissible to invent new terms'. Fitz Nigel may not have been aware that *rotulus* was a new term, as it could have been part of the jargon of the Exchequer since his boyhood when his father had been the treasurer of Henry I. Rolls had certainly been made then, as Fitz Nigel refers to 'the old annual rolls of that king' and furthermore much of the pipe roll for the fiscal year ending Michaelmas 1130 is still extant.

The novelty of the roll in the twelfth century, outside the Exchequer that is, is suggested by the variety of forms the word takes. Fitz Nigel's form, *rotulus*, took time to establish itself as the norm. A certificate confirming acquittance from paying Danegeld, dated the eighth year of Henry II's reign (1162), states that the acquittance was written down at the Exchequer 'in the roll' (*in rollo*). As this statement can be checked with the extant pipe roll and as the acquittance is one of a series of written privileges obtained by Ralf of Caen, who is described by Henry II as 'my clerk', the form *rollus* must have been acceptable in official circles in the 1160s. Early in the thirteenth century, on the other hand, Jocelin of Brakelond uses a feminine form, *rolla*, to describe a bailiff's roll and also to describe 'the great roll of Winchester'. The latter description is strange, as the context shows that this 'great roll' is Domesday Book. Perhaps Jocelin did not know that Domesday was in the form of a book, or alternatively *rolla* may have meant for him any sort of formal record. Some years earlier, in the 1180s, Alan prior of Christ Church Canterbury had likewise referred to the 'roll of Winchester', using another variant, *rotula*. Although the context is obscure, this reference may also be to Domesday Book, since Alan was arguing that the muniments and privileges of the whole English Church would be subverted if they had to accord with 'that roll' (*rotulam illam*). An alternative possibility is that Alan was referring to a pipe roll or some other form of Exchequer record kept at Winchester.

These rare and scattered references suggest that until the thirteenth century writers were uncertain about how a roll should be described in Latin and some of them may also have been unclear about what a roll really was in the royal bureaucratic sense. The royal records were not available for public inspection then as they are now. A sheriff answering at the Exchequer would certainly have seen the clerks writing things down, but he would not necessarily have understood how the rolls were compiled until Fitz Nigel revealed these 'holy mysteries' in his book. Fitz Nigel implies moreover that confusion about the nomenclature of the rolls had existed even in the Exchequer itself, as he remarks at one point that the 'so-called exaction roll' (*rotulus qui exactorius dicitur*) is also named *breve de firmis*. The word *breve* (originally associated with 'abbreviation') came to mean a writ or short letter, as distinct from a roll, in the course of the twelfth century. It is possible that the 'exaction roll', which listed the sheriffs' farms, may have been the oldest written record used in the Exchequer and had been called a *breve* before the word *rotulus* came into vogue. Monastic obituary rolls in the late eleventh and early twelfth centuries were likewise sometimes described as *brevia* or *breves*.[3]

An apparent exception to the rule that the word *rotulus* only came into general use in Fitz Nigel's time is a writ of Henry I's dating from as early as 1110. It instructs Richard de Monte to allow the abbot of Westminster 10 shillings of the royal alms, 'as it is in my rolls' (*in rotulis meis*). If this writ were entirely genuine, it would suggest that the word *rotulus* and the habit of referring to the royal rolls were already established in the second decade of the twelfth century. However, the text of the writ is suspect for a number of reasons. First it is in favour of Westminster Abbey which was a centre of forgery. Secondly it has a postscript saying, allow 'this also every year', whereas an authentic writ would probably have made this conces- sion an integral part of the text. By the same token the phrase, 'as it is in my rolls', may be a later interpolation. The comparable certificate of acquittance for Ralf of Caen states that it is written *in rollo*, that is, in the roll of a specified year, and not *in rotulis* in general. It would have been tempting for a copyist—and this Westminster writ exists only in a copy— to insert the phrase 'as it is in my rolls' and the postscript into the text of a genuine writ of Henry I. Westminster Abbey's dilemma may well have been that Henry I had indeed made this grant, but in subsequent reigns a writ of this sort would have required the supporting evidence of the pipe rolls. A Westminster monk therefore supplied this evidence as best he could by inserting a vague reference to 'my rolls', even though Henry I may not have had any rolls at the time the writ was issued.

To summarise the argument so far, the pipe rolls of the Exchequer, which were created at some unknown time by Henry I's government, seem to be the prototype for royal records in roll form in England. Whether they were started in the decade 1100–10 (as the Westminster writ implies if it is genuine) or in the decade 1120–30 (as the extant roll for 1130 might suggest) is an unresolvable problem. Either way there is no evidence of royal records in roll form before the reign of Henry I. At what- ever date the Exchequer rolls were started moreover, we should not assume that their form and purpose was generally understood until Fitz Nigel revealed the 'holy mysteries' of the Exchequer in Henry II's reign.

Nevertheless records in roll form were not entirely unknown in Eng- land before 1100. The earliest roll now extant was begun in the decade preceding 1088; it records professions of obedience by suffragan bishops to the archbishop of Canterbury. Likewise another Canterbury roll, in- forming the archbishop of elections to bishoprics, contains some mem- branes from the 1090s. As the former of these rolls dates from Archbishop Lanfranc's pontificate, it may have originated from his interest in the reform of books and records. Until they grew in length over the years, rolls like the Canterbury ones would not have been seen as startling innova- tions. Rolling up a membrane of parchment was the easiest and most obvious way of storing it. Moreover, the roll had ancient origins, as it had been the usual format of writings in the Graeco-Roman world. But the layout and material of ancient and medieval rolls differed, as the text was written in ancient rolls in columns on the longer way of the papyrus, whereas in medieval rolls it was written from the head to the tail of the parchment.

The roll was also the most convenient format for conveying a message or letter in parchment. It was customary for monasteries to send a messenger from house to house, collecting an accumulating series of obituaries forming a roll when an abbot died. A long roll of this sort, commemorating Matilda, first abbess of William the Conqueror's nunnery at Caen, was taken on an extensive tour of England soon after her death in 1113. Although this roll disappeared at the French Revolution, that of Abbot Vitalis of Savigny (who died in 1122) survives and bears over seventy inscriptions from English monasteries. It was perhaps an obituary roll of a comparable type that St Dunstan's biographer had in mind a century earlier when he described the saint having a vision, presaging King Edgar's death, of a man carrying a great *prolixe cartule rotella* covered all over with letters. This is the earliest example of the use of the word 'roll' (*rotella* in this instance) in England. But this example also suggests that the word was unfamiliar to the biographer's readers, since he explains that the *rotella* was of *prolixe cartule*, literally meaning 'a roll of prolix little charter'. If rolls had already been common for writing purposes, it would not have been necessary to add that this one was covered with letters like a charter.

Despite the use of rolls for monastic obituaries, there was a prejudice against them which makes it surprising that the roll was adopted as the format for the most important royal records. The parchment roll was the characteristic format for the copies of the Jewish law read in synagogues and had been so since antiquity. In twelfth-century legal procedure in England the Jew was distinguished from the Christian by the fact that he took an oath 'on his roll', whereas the Christian swore on the book of the Gospel. Similarly the prophets of the Old Testament were depicted in painting and sculpture holding rolls. This was not an insignificant distinction, as the Bible had been written in the form of a book almost since the historical beginnings of Christianity, probably deliberately in order to distinguish it from both Jewish and pagan works in rolls. In the rare instances where Christ is depicted holding a roll instead of a book in medieval manuscripts, he is usually intended to represent the God of the Old Testament. Thus the miniature in the Winchester Bible of the Christ of the Gothic Majesty, holding a rolled-up scroll in his left hand and an opened one in his right, depicts God calling the prophet Isaiah; Isaiah is appropriately shown as a Jew both by his hat and by the scroll. In the Bury Bible similarly the distinction between the new dispensation and the old is made in Ezechiel's vision by depicting Christ in majesty bearing a book, while Ezechiel is placed at his feet holding up a scroll. Rolls bore the old law and books the new.

The faithful were reminded of the image of Christ in majesty bearing the Book of Judgement whenever they went to church, as that was how Christ was most commonly depicted in Romanesque art. William the Conqueror's book was appropriately called 'Domesday' because it reminded people of that Last Judgement. Had Domesday Book been in the form of a roll, it might not have been so readily compared with holy writ. This suggestion should not be exaggerated, however, as royal rolls were themselves being compared with Scripture before the end of the twelfth century. When Fitz Nigel explains that not even the king's justices may alter their rolls, once they have been delivered to the treasurer, he recalls the Gospel's warning that not one iota of the law shall pass away. The Exchequer may have had the odd effect of hallowing the roll format in England.

The idea of making the pipe rolls probably originated not directly from the Jews, though that is a possibility, but from cosmopolitan arithmeticians who were familiar with Arabic practice. One suggestion is that Adelard of Bath, who introduced Arabic works on astronomy and geometry to the west, may have been an official in Henry I's Exchequer. Another candidate is the royal clerk, Thurkil, who knew Hugh de Bocland, the sheriff of Essex from 1101 and perhaps earlier. Thurkil's treatise on the abacus is addressed to his colleague, Simon de Rotol. 'Rotol' might either be extended to 'Rotolanda', meaning 'of Rutland', or to 'Rotolis', meaning 'of the Rolls'. If the latter extension is accepted, Simon may have been the first maker or keeper of the pipe rolls. Thurkil and Simon had a common master, described only as Guillelmus R., the greatest living arithmetician; he may have been William, bishop of Syracuse in Sicily, which had just been conquered from the Arabs. These scraps of information cannot satisfactorily explain the origin of the pipe rolls, but they are consistent with the hypothesis that their format was non-Christian.

The problem of origins has further complexities because the pipe rolls are in a unique format. The term *rotulus* does not describe a continuous series of membranes of parchment, which are stitched head to tail to form a length of four metres or more, like the Chancery rolls. Instead an Exchequer *rotulus* consists of two membranes only, stitched together to form a length of less than two metres. Each *rotulus* comprised the account of a different county or bailiwick. When all the accounts for the year had been written, the different *rotuli* were piled one on top of another and secured at their heads with cords. As the lower ends are left free, referring from the face to the dorse of a particular *rotulus* is easier than on a continuous roll. Although the Exchequer had thus adopted a form of record which was easier to consult than a continuous roll, its style did not become the norm. A simplification of it, using one membrane instead of two per *rotulus* was adopted by the law courts for their plea rolls in the 1190s, but not by the Chancery in the next decade. Furthermore, when receipt rolls were introduced at the Exchequer in Henry II's reign, they were made into continuous rolls at first, as is evident from the fragments extant for Michaelmas term in 1185. The consequence of these haphazard developments is that in the thirteenth century the royal government made rolls in two principal formats—Exchequer style (the membranes piled on top of each other) and Chancery style (the membranes stitched head to tail in a continuous length).

These technicalities suggest that the reason why medieval England, alone in Europe, kept its records predominantly in rolls remains largely a mystery. Convenience is not a good explanation, as continuous rolls are not convenient to consult. The folded parchment forming a quire, which was the basic component of a medieval book, was as convenient as any form of roll. Nor is economy in parchment a sufficient explanation, as the pieces from which the pipe rolls were made were of exceptional size. Economy in binding costs is a possibility, but that has to be balanced against the cost of making protective covers for the rolls. Rolls had short-term advantages, which might originally have made them attractive: the separate membranes of which they were composed could be of slightly differing sizes, and they could be compiled separately by different clerks and then stitched together in appropriate order, whereas the scribe of a book had to proceed from one page of his quire to the next. As various formats of roll were used by different departments of the royal government by the time of King John, habit and precedent seem the best general explanations, although they do not explain why certain decisions were taken in the first place. Once these distinctive formats had been established, bureaucracy ensured that they remained unchanged for centuries.

In the thirteenth century other authorities followed the lead of the royal government in keeping records on rolls. Sometimes they were evidently unsure about which form of royal roll to imitate. Thus among borough records the earliest guild rolls, those of Leicester (starting in

1196), are made up in Chancery style, whereas the second earliest, those of Shrewsbury (starting in 1209), are in Exchequer style; the custumal of Exeter (dating from the 1230s) combines both styles. Similarly the earliest part of the first bishop's register (starting between 1214 and 1217), that of Hugh of Wells, bishop of Lincoln, is in Chancery style, but one subsequent part is in Exchequer style and the *Liber Antiquus* is in book format; contemporaries probably did not think of these diverse records as forming one register. By the end of the century the book format had become usual for bishops' registers, probably in order to bring them into line with continental and papal practice. Likewise the royal government itself seemed to acknowledge in the thirteenth century that rolls were not necessarily the best way to keep records. Material from rolls was copied into books, such as the remembrance books of the Exchequer, to make consultation easier. Moreover, new classes of record were made into books instead of rolls; the best examples are the Wardrobe books of Edward I, which contain the sort of financial details which might have gone on to the pipe rolls in Henry I's reign.

Roll formats were also used for types of record other than accounts and memoranda of proceedings. A few cartularies, both monastic and lay, are in rolls, as are some monastic chronicles and narratives. This practice is understandable, as such documents are akin to records. Equally understandable are those texts for which the roll format was more suitable than the book. For example, histories of the kings of England were produced in the thirteenth century in long rolls. They were perhaps intended for laymen of restricted literacy, as they depict the kings in a series of roundels with a brief commentary alongside each picture. When the roll is fully unfurled, the whole history of England, from its mythical foundation by the Trojans down to the reign of Edward I, is displayed as a continuous line. The most spectacular example of pictorial narrative in a roll is the life of St Guthlac of Crowland, which depicts the life of the saint in a series of roundels without a commentary; its precise purpose is unknown.

Occasionally ordinary texts appear in roll format. One pictorial history of England has on its dorse the Anglo-Norman romance, *Amadas et Ydoine*. This combination is not really strange, as history and romance were closely connected in the mind of the lay reader. More bizarre are legal and managerial textbooks in the form of continuous rolls: the Harvard Law School has a mid-thirteenth-century text of Glanvill 293 cm long, and St John's College, Cambridge, has Walter of Henley's *Husbandry* 223 cm long. Here again perhaps lay landowners, who were more familiar with records than with traditional books, did not consider it strange or inconvenient to have texts in this form. Thus one copy (dating from early in the fourteenth century) of Walter of Bibbesworth's rhyming French vocabulary, which was intended to improve the French of the gentry, is in the form of a roll 268 cm long. It is unusually narrow (10 cm wide) and the tail is slotted into a length of wood, with knobs at each end, which serves as a winder. When tightly wound up, this roll can be held in the palm of the hand.

An even smaller and earlier roll (less than 8 cm wide and 56 cm long) has written on one side of it *The Song of the Barons* in French (composed in *c.* 1263) and on the other side the oldest secular play extant in English, the *Interludium de Clerico et Puella*. Very probably this roll was made so small so that it could be carried by a wandering minstrel in his pouch as part of his repertoire. Its chance survival (until 1971 when it went missing from the British Museum) is a reminder of the thousands of little rolls of parchment, containing memoranda of all sorts, which supplied the material for more formal books. On the threshold of literacy, among knights and minstrels as distinct from monks and clerks, writings were perhaps at first more familiar and inviting in the form of rolls containing short vernacular texts than in the form of weighty Latin books. The contents of a little roll could be seen at a glance and readily grasped in the hand, whereas traditional liturgical books had been kept on lecterns or locked up in monastic sacristies.

In Spenser's *Faerie Queene* Eumnestes, the sage of infinite remembrance, inhabits a ruined chamber which

> . . . all was hanged about with rolls,
> And old records from ancient times derivd,
> Some made in books, some in long parchment scrolls,
> That were all worm-eaten and full of canker holes.

Spenser wrote when the Middle Ages were just beginning to be gothicised and made picturesque. To the Elizabethans the twin format of English parchment documents, rolls and books, seemed as old as time itself. In fact these records took their distinctive shapes in the twelfth century. A pedantic historian or archivist might also comment that, on the whole, the real records of medieval England have been preserved in better condition than Eumnestes kept his.

Although some medieval records have been attacked by vermin, and many more have been lost or damaged by neglect, parchment has proved a remarkably durable material. This particular characteristic of it was

PLATE 14. Adam and Eve, from a biblical genealogy and history by Peter of Poitiers. This is in the form of a roll which, when unrolled, displays the entire genealogical tree from Adam down to Christ

recognised from the start by medieval scribes, whose illuminated manuscripts, like the *Book of Kells* and the *Lindisfarne Gospels*, became a talisman of Christian endurance in the Dark Ages. The initial difficulty of applying script to parchment combined with the circumstances of the time to make writing the special art of monks in Anglo-Saxon England, as elsewhere in western Europe. When documents began to be required on an unprecedented scale after the Norman Conquest, the skills of monastic scribes were adapted and extended to meet these new needs.

Surprisingly perhaps, both the traditional methods of writing and the materials, in particular parchment, showed themselves to be flexible as well as durable. It proved possible to produce parchment in varying qualities relatively cheaply and also to cut, stitch, and fold it into shapes ranging from the great Winchester Bible and the pipe rolls to pocket-sized manuals for lawyers or preachers and tightly rolled royal writs no larger than a man's little finger. Similarly the cursive script, essential to secular clerks who had to write fast from dictation, was adapted from traditional book hand and not consciously invented. The price of adaptation, as contrasted with planned innovation, was a variety of styles of writing and formats of document, which were perpetuated when they settled down into bureaucratic routine. There is more history than logic in the miscellany of styles of document preserved in the Public Record Office.

On the other hand, an advantage of adapting existing practice was that the makers of medieval records had in parchment a writing medium which was better suited to long texts than the clay bricks and stone tablets of the ancient world, yet was stronger than papyrus. Moreover, the new secular documents, from Domesday Book onwards, inherited much of the respect and even awe which had been accorded to liturgical books in the monastic tradition. Some charters at first were laid out like pages of Gospel books and the finest secular legal and literary texts continued to be indistinguishable in physical appearance from other illuminated manuscripts. The growth, from the monastic *scriptorium*, of new branches and styles of writing was probably the chief reason why documents became acceptable to the laity, and upon that acceptance the future extension of literacy depended.

It is a facile speculation to assume that paper or printing, had they been readily available in 1100, would have automatically accelerated the growth of literacy faster than parchment. The initial and most difficult task was to make the laity, knights in the countryside typically, accustomed to writing. Traditionally such men respected monks, though they did not aspire to be like them, and gave them lands on their deathbeds or in time of peril. Traditionally too the monks symbolised these gifts with Gospel books and recorded them in charters. When documents produced by the king's government began to proliferate in the twelfth century, they also were accepted because, by and large, they used traditional materials and skills. The changes which were made in the technology of writing in the twelfth and thirteenth centuries went largely unnoticed by contemporaries. They were subtle and technical; but because they were adapted and extended, rather than revolutionised, fundamental changes in this most conservative area of human skills were set in motion. Techniques of writing records tended to be conservative because conservation was their main purpose.

❧ VI ❧

WRITING FOR POSTERITY

Documents do not automatically become records. Writing may be done for ephemeral purposes without any intention of keeping the documents permanently. In modern societies, where mass literacy is normal, most writings are made for purposes of immediate communication or short-term administrative convenience; when the message has been received or the obligation discharged, the piece of paper recording it is generally thrown away. Most people are literate, to a minimal standard, but relatively few documents are kept for long. The situation in the Middle Ages was the reverse of the modern one: there were fewer literates, but a larger proportion of their writings were intended to be preserved for posterity.

Medieval writing materials themselves made the scribe conscious of time. Because he was presented with the alternatives of wax or parchment as a medium, he made an initial choice between the ephemeral and the permanent. Notes written on wax tablets were necessarily transitory, whereas the fair copy on parchment was obviously durable. To write on parchment was therefore to make a lasting memorial: to commit 'bare and transient words' to script with its 'tenacious letters', as Adam of Eynsham says in the prologue to his life of St Hugh of Lincoln. Modern paper, on the other hand, which is used for both notes and fair copies and is constantly disposed of, does not make the writer feel that he is producing a permanent record. Even when printing gives a modern work a physical permanence comparable with that of parchment manuscripts, the modern writer is more concerned with printing's ability to reach a wide audience in the present than with the transmission of his work, in a unique copy like a medieval manuscript, to posterity. Because parchment manuscripts were rare and special in the eleventh century and earlier, they were valued in a way which no modern literate can fully appreciate.

The presupposition that documents were primarily records to be transmitted to posterity depended not only on the durability of parchment as a material, but on writing skills being so closely connected with monasticism. Before the Norman Conquest, and for a century after it, the majority of writers (in every sense of that word) were monks. In monasteries scribes had not been much concerned with using their skills for day-to-day business, the things of this world, but with making liturgical books for worship and with keeping in charters and chronicles a record, for future generations of monks, of the working of God's providence as revealed in gifts and portents. Documents were more often dedicated or addressed to God or to posterity than to individual contemporaries. Monasticism gave writers the humility or the arrogance, depending on one's point of view, to care about posterity. Their acute awareness of the passage of time is expressed in numerous chronicles. 'With the loss of books', says Orderic Vitalis, 'the deeds of the ancients pass into oblivion . . . with the changing world, as hail or snow melt in the waters of a swift river swept away by the current never to return.' Although these phrases are variations on a theme appropriate to a chronicler's *apologia*, they probably express a point of view which was as deeply felt as it was familiar.

As most early charters concerned gifts to monasteries, they were drafted by monks in similar terms, sometimes at length, as in this notification by William de Braose of a grant to Sele priory in the mid-twelfth century: 'Since memory is frail, and as the sage has said "old age runs in from the first", it is necessary that things which are said or done be reinforced by the evidence of letters, so that neither length of time nor the ingenuity of posterity can obscure the notice of past events.'[1] A century later charters had become sufficiently commonplace for Bracton, the lawyer, to express the same idea more succinctly: 'Gifts are sometimes made in writings, that is in charters, for perpetual remembrance, because the life of man is but brief and in order that the gift may be more easily proved.'[2]

The fact that most monastic charters and chronicles are exclusively concerned with property rights and worldly events does not invalidate the rule that their makers had a religious purpose. Even Matthew Paris, whose work combines a broad and fascinated interest in English and European politics with a narrow and acquisitive concern for the aggrandisement of his house and his order, thought of his chronicle as an instrument of divine providence. In 1250 he decided to stop writing because twenty-five half-centuries had passed since the Incarnation. So he wrote an endpiece to the *Chronica Majora*, which typically combines a concern for posterity with a dedication to God and his saints: 'Here end the chronicles of Brother Matthew Paris, monk of St Albans, which he has committed to writing for the use of succeeding generations, for the love of God and the honour of St Alban, protomartyr of the English, lest age or oblivion destroy the memory of modern events.' Although Matthew started writing again almost immediately, there is no reason to think that his attempted ending in 1250 was insincere. He, like other chroniclers, wrote in the face of God and was motivated by the wish to give himself and his fellow monks, who lived under the protection of St Alban, a place in the divine unfolding of events.

Monks were so worldly because they considered themselves and the property of their houses to belong to God, who would support them in their battle with the 'world', which consisted of everyone else. Writings served as a memorial of their triumphs or as a warning of their difficulties: 'Because it is certain that man's memory is frail, it is a valuable labour to put some things in writing, which can be profitable and useful to our church, so that our brethren, present and future, may be assisted in their difficulties by looking at this little book.' This explanation comes from the prologue to Barnwell Priory's *Liber Memorandorum*, which was compiled in the 1290s to serve as a precedent book for litigation (see pages 325–6 below). No monastic book could be more worldly. Yet its author, like Matthew Paris, declares his place in time—the sun is setting, the world is declining into senility, charity grows cold—and proposes to help God's servants, by which he means the canons of Barnwell, in their struggle against their neighbours. For monks, writing had an ulterior motive; it was a providential instrument, rather than a merely convenient form of communication.

Monks would not have understood the modern demand for mass literacy. There was no point in teaching writing to people who would never have anything worth committing to the permanence of script. What was written down was carefully selected. The annalist should write 'what he thinks truest and best to be passed down to the notice of posterity', one monastic chronicle advised. Similarly Gervase of Canterbury distinguished between memorable events (*memorabilia*) and those worth remembering (*memoranda*); only the latter which are really worthy of memory should be recorded. So far from advocating the mass-production of literates or documents, the monastic writer aimed to use records to convey to posterity a deliberately created and rigorously selected version of events. Thus Eadmer, who believed it 'to be a great thing to commit to the memory of letters the events of our times for the use of students in the future', deliberately omitted many business letters from his life of St Anselm because he considered them unworthy of more than a mention. Likewise Anselm himself would not send copies of all his letters to Theodoric, the monk of Christ Church Canterbury who was collecting them, 'because I do not think it useful for them to be preserved'.[3] Awareness of posterity made monks destroyers as well as preservers of writings.

The same preoccupation with posterity led to the forgery or alteration of documents. If a monastic house required a writing to support its title to some property in a lawsuit, an appropriate charter would be created. A historian today will say that such a charter is a forgery, as indeed it is, but its makers probably felt that it had been written just like their other charters and chronicles to justify the ways of God to men. As God and the patron saint wished the particular monastic house to flourish, they also wished to provide the means to fight the world with the world's weapons. Thus Eadmer was an accessory to forging papal bulls which supported Canterbury's claims to primacy over York. The monks of Canterbury were very worried by the challenge from York, Eadmer explains, so they put their trust in God and discovered by divine revelation in some ancient Gospel books (which were sacred objects in themselves) about a dozen papal bulls, ranging in date from the seventh century to the tenth, which supported their cause. These Eadmer cites verbatim, because what had been found in the archives of the church was well worth commending to the memory of posterity. He adds that some even older documents had also been discovered but, as some of these were of papyrus and had grown illegible with age or were written in a script which he could not understand, he reluctantly refrained from citing them. Eadmer probably did not forge the papal bulls himself, but he added these corroborative details which made the story credible.

Monasteries experienced fortunate losses of documents as well as fortunate finds. The Crowland chronicle ascribed to Abbot Ingulf, which is itself a complex tissue of fact and forgery, records that a fire in 1091 destroyed the abbey's Anglo-Saxon royal charters and other muniments numbering nearly 400 documents. Fortunately, however, Ingulf had removed several duplicates of these charters from the archive some years earlier in order to instruct the younger monks in Old English. These duplicates had therefore been preserved and upon them Crowland based its claims. This is an ingenious story, as there was indeed a fire at Crowland in 1091 which destroyed many books (as Orderic Vitalis attested at the time), and it is probable that Crowland, like other great abbeys, made an effort to keep Old English alive after the Norman Conquest. Moreover, Crowland Abbey did not claim that these charters were originals, but duplicates, and that explained any deficiencies in them. Similarly in its dispute with York, Canterbury claimed that it had only been left with duplicates of some documents because ancient papal bulls had been destroyed in a fire in 1067.

The least credible story of a document's disappearance comes from Matthew Paris. He reports that in the time of Abbot Eadmer (in c. 1012) a cache of books and rolls, written in an unfamiliar language, was discovered in a cavity in a wall among some Roman foundations at St Albans. Fortunately an old priest, named Unwona, was found who could read this ancient British language. All the texts except one contained invocations to pagan Gods, such as Phoebus and Mercury, and they were therefore burned. The remaining one turned out to be the story of St Alban himself, which the old priest translated from British into Latin for Eadmer and his brethren. But once the Latin translation had been noted down, 'the original and primitive exemplar—strange to relate—was suddenly and irretrievably reduced to dust and collapsed annihilated.' It is entirely credible that Roman remains were found at St Albans, and even possible that documents may have been preserved in a wall cavity. On the other hand, the finding of an old priest with unique knowledge of a lost language, and the initial survival of the finds when first exposed to air, strain credulity too far. Perhaps the story started with the discovery of some Roman remains which disintegrated when exposed to the air.

Monks' propensity to forgery does not imply that they are unreliable in all their statements, but only in those which particularly concern the honour of their patron saint or the status of their house. Where there was doubt, they were determined to establish the truth for posterity. By truth about the past they meant what really should have happened. For a monastic house there was a providential truth, which was higher than the random facts from which a twentieth-century historian, motivated by mere worldly curiosity, attempts to piece together what happened in the past. Essentially there is no inconsistency between Eadmer of Canterbury's or Matthew Paris's religious concern for posterity and their readiness to be accessories to forgery. The problem of forging documents is more fully discussed in Chapter XII below. The fact it illustrates in the present context is that for monks the primary purpose of writing was to inform, or misinform, posterity. Thus the monastic approach to records was ambivalent: documents were created and carefully conserved so that posterity might know about the past, but they were not necessarily allowed to accumulate by natural accretion over time nor to speak for themselves, because the truth was too important to leave to chance.

Documents such as taxation lists or injunctions to officials, which were primarily intended for administrative use at the time they were made rather than being directed to posterity, obviously have a different function from monastic writings. The early development of such documents in medieval England is hard to trace, partly because writing had been used in such a different way in the monastic tradition. Administrative documents may have been in circulation long before they were kept, since they would not have been thought worthy of preserving like monastic charters. Alternatively administrative documents may have developed only with the greatest difficulty, because writing was not considered an appropriate medium for mere secular ephemera. The skills and traditions of monastic scribes could not automatically be transferred to build up a bureaucracy, although they were successfully adapted and extended in our period. Neither monks nor laymen were literate, in the modern sense of using writing for day-to-day communication, at the time of the Norman Conquest.

The Domesday survey provides the first explicit evidence for a royal archive of administrative documents, as a writ of William Rufus refers to land 'which was written down in my writs, which are in my treasury at Winchester'. But even this evidence is ambiguous, because these 'writs' (that is, the circuit returns upon which Domesday Book was based) no longer exist and some historians have argued that references to them, like the one cited above, refer to the volumes of Domesday Book and not to a separate archive of writings. Moreover, the making of Domesday Book itself, as distinct from the Domesday survey, suggests that William the Conqueror had no intention of using an archive of administrative documents. Like scribes making monastic cartularies, the compilers of Domesday Book selected information from the circuit returns and other drafts to make a fair copy for the perpetual use of posterity. Whatever his intentions, William the Conqueror had created in Domesday Book a unique record in the old monastic tradition, the *Book of Judgement* of Revelation, rather than a document of administrative value.

The principal objection to this interpretation of Domesday Book is Fitz Nigel's statement that it was kept in the treasury, along with the pipe rolls and many charters and writs, because such documents were required 'for daily use' in the Exchequer.[4] But the use of Domesday Book seems to have been principally symbolic, like the regalia, since it cannot be shown that it was frequently consulted at the time Fitz Nigel was writing in *c.* 1179. He himself was unfamiliar with its contents, as he insists that it makes no mention of 'blanch farm' (payments in assayed silver from certain counties), whereas references to such payments are quite common in Domesday Book. His ignorance has puzzled editors of the *Dialogue of the Exchequer*, who have suggested as a solution that this passage about Domesday Book is an interpolation, although there is no textual evidence for that. A sufficient explanation of Fitz Nigel's mistake is that neither he, nor his colleagues at the Exchequer, consulted Domesday Book at all frequently because there was scarcely any documentary continuity in administration between William the Conqueror's reign and Henry II's.

For Fitz Nigel and his colleagues the pipe rolls of Henry I, rather than the Domesday survey, marked the beginning of an archive of documents which they understood and regularly consulted. One story of Fitz Nigel's shows a pipe roll of Henry I being used to overrule a writ of Henry II, and another remark about what is frequently to be found 'in the old annual rolls' of Henry I suggests that a number of early pipe rolls were still extant in Fitz Nigel's time. The whole tone of the *Dialogue of the Exchequer*, with its meticulous regard for precedent and correct form, shows how the Exchequer was dominated by bureaucratic routines by the 1170s. Yet the writings it produced were still not systematically kept as records, as many of the types of document mentioned by Fitz Nigel are not extant today, nor can they be traced in the thirteenth century. The pipe rolls of Henry I themselves have been lost, apart from the roll for 1130. That roll demonstrates, moreover, that hundreds of writs were issued each year, for such ephemeral purposes as authorising expenditure, of which no record was kept. The sparse evidence available suggests that administrative documents first came into routine use in Henry I's Exchequer, rather than at the time of the Domesday survey or earlier. Turning such documents into records for posterity took even longer to develop and was far from thorough in Fitz Nigel's time.

As we have seen, Hubert Walter seems to have been principally responsible for making the royal government as a whole, and not just the Exchequer, begin keeping records as well as issuing documents. He laid the foundations of an accumulating archival memory, first in the law courts (in the form of the feet of fines and the plea rolls) while he was chief justiciar (1193–8), and then in the Chancery (in the form of the various rolls of outgoing letters) while he was chancellor (1199–1205). Thenceforward the Chancery rolls are extant for almost every year. Similarly the feet of fines were successfully kept in the treasury from the start, though the plea rolls proved harder to recover from the judges because they treated them as their personal property for reference purposes. To compile Bracton's *De Legibus*, for example, judges and their clerks in the 1220s and 1230s (possibly including Bracton himself as a junior) made extracts from their plea rolls and notebooks of cases. Nevertheless, by the latter half of the thirteenth century, the plea rolls too were being surrendered to the treasury for preservation, as the almost complete series extant from Edward I's reign attests.

In Edward I's reign, the era of Hubert Walter began to be recognised as a turning-point in the history of keeping records. By statutes in 1275 and

1293 the date of Richard I's coronation (3 September 1189) was fixed as the legal limit of memory. This meant that a litigant was not required to go any further back into the past than that date when proving a claim. Fixing an arbitrary limit for claims based on precedents was not a new device, as the date of Richard I's coronation replaced Henry II's coronation and that date had replaced Henry I's death. Up until the reign of Edward I the assumption seems to have been that memory extended back for a century at the most, that is, to the earliest time which could be remembered by the oldest living persons; any period before that was considered to be 'time out of mind'. The novelty of establishing Richard I's coronation as the new legal limit only became apparent by the end of Edward I's reign, when it was left to stand instead of being updated. In retrospect the fixed limit of 3 September 1189, which continued for the rest of the Middle Ages, marked the formal beginning of the era of artificial memory. Repeated updating was no longer urgently required, because remembrance in litigation now depended primarily on documentary evidence and not on mortal memory. It was appropriate, though at first a coincidence, that Richard I's reign was acknowledged as the point in time from which it was reasonable to require proof, as Hubert Walter's reforms had made such proof possible.

Although Hubert Walter had laid the foundation of an extensive royal archive, another century elapsed before its potential was tested. In 1291, when Edward I required historical evidence to support his claims to over-lordship in Scotland, he made no attempt at first to use the royal records. Instead monasteries were ordered at short notice to search their 'chronicles, registers, and other archives, both ancient and modern, of whatever shape or date'. The evidence adduced by this method turned out to be scrappy and unsatisfactory. For example, the treaty of Falaise of 1174 (by which King William the Lion submitted to Henry II) was cited from a monastic chronicle, whereas more accurate transcripts were to be found in both the Red Book and the Little Black Book of the Exchequer.

Belatedly in the summer of 1291, after the monasteries had submitted their evidence, Edward I wrote in haste from Scotland, ordering a chest of Chancery rolls at the New Temple to be broken open and searched. Two rolls of Henry III were taken out of this chest and sent to the king—the patent roll for 1254–5 and the charter roll for 1237–8. What Edward expected to find in these rolls is not specified. As they are still extant today, however, the historian can point out that in the former roll are details of Henry III's treaty with Alexander III of Scotland in 1255 and in the latter is Henry's treaty with Alexander II in 1237. Since neither of these treaties would have helped Edward's case, this preliminary attempt to use the archives for historical purposes may have temporarily discouraged further research.

Nevertheless a precedent had been established and when evidence was again required in 1300 in order to justify the English case to Pope Boniface VIII and international opinion, the royal records were ordered to be searched as well as monastic sources. The instruction was vague but comprehensive—to search all the remembrances concerning the business of Scotland—and it was coupled with a similar order 'to search all the rolls and remembrances', including all the rolls of the Exchequer and Chancery, concerning the king's forest rights. Whoever ordered all the rolls to be searched, 'so that nothing is left unsearched', can have had little conception of how numerous they were, or of how inadequately they were stored and filed. This search seems to have produced no new information, presumably because it proved impossible to search the archives effectively at such short notice. But despite the ineffective nature of the searches, Edward I's claims in Scotland and the need to document them had at last made the government aware of the large historical archive it had accumulated. It is probably not a coincidence that plea rolls and other legal records likewise began to be systematically listed in detail in the 1290s. In 1302 a similar attempt was made to bring together the archives of the Wardrobe, 'so that we can be advised of things at all times that we want, and these books and rolls are to remain in the Wardrobe in perpetual remembrance'.[5] To keep documents for perpetual remembrance had been the purpose of archives for centuries; what was new was the demand that records should be readily available 'at all times'.

The aim of making the royal archives accessible for reference, initiated by Edward I in his last years, reached maturity in 1320 in Bishop Stapledon's great survey of the records. The prologue to Stapledon's commission deplores the way records had been carried about from place to place and from person to person, and frequently mislaid, whereas the frailty of the human condition requires the acts of princes and rulers to be reduced to writings as memorials, so that kings can rule their subject people justly. Although Stapledon's extensive survey of the records had little immediate effect on the conduct of government, his commission marks the point at which the Crown formally recognised that its administrative documents were records for posterity. The writings of kings were a bastion against human frailty and a warning or encouragement to their successors, just as their deeds had been when recorded in monastic chronicles. The gulf between records specifically made for posterity and secular documents for mundane use had been bridged. As a consequence the English government was set on the course which has produced the largest archive to survive from medieval Europe.

To sum up, administrative documents had been in routine use since Henry I's reign, they had been extensively kept since Hubert Walter's reforms around 1200, and now in the 1300s the government subjected them to comprehensive inspection. Perhaps documents had to accumulate in considerable numbers before they could be seen as an archive with a historical purpose. Searching Domesday Book, for evidence of whether land was ancient demesne of the Crown or not, had followed a similar pattern; searches had started in the 1250s and only became an established routine in Edward I's reign or later, although Domesday Book had been available for two centuries. Making documents for administrative use, keeping them as records, and using them again for reference were three distinct stages of development which did not automatically and immediately follow from each other.

⚜ VII ⚜

ARCHIVES AND LIBRARIES

At the time of the Norman Conquest documents and books had a place among the precious objects, the hoard of treasure and relics, which a ruler or the head of a religious house aimed to pass on to his successors. Documents, books, relics of the saints, and jewellery were not usually kept in places distinct from each other, because they were often physically joined together, and the difference between writings and other precious objects was not as obvious as it is to a modern literate. Books of the Bible—illuminated with gold leaf and precious paints, their bindings studded with gems or even with relics—were obviously treasure, both heavenly and terrestrial, rather than mere reading matter. A book as special as the *Lindisfarne Gospels*, for example, was itself a relic and a shrine, hallowed by its age and by its alleged association with St Cuthbert. Single documents like charters were sometimes bound or copied into such liturgical books for safekeeping. This practice has already been illustrated by Eadmer's story of finding in Gospel books ancient papal bulls which upheld Canterbury's claims over York. Although these bulls were forged, the practice of keeping documents in books was evidently commonplace enough to sound convincing to Eadmer's readers. In the Sherborne cartulary of the mid-twelfth century liturgical texts and charters (probably forged) were made into an integrated book. 'All the secular portions were placed under the protection, as it were, of the book's sacred contents and its connection with the altar. If anyone in the future was to be so unwise as to question the validity of any of the documents, the protection and wrath of heaven could be invoked.'[1] Similarly C. R. Cheney has argued that the massive isolated pages of the so-called *Domesday Monachorum* of Christ Church Canterbury, recording estate documents of various dates in the twelfth century, originally formed part of a 'great Gospel book' (*textus magnus*), so that future violators would (in the words of Archbishop Hubert Walter) come under the 'curse of God and the saints of the church of Canterbury'.[2]

Like family bibles in later generations, liturgical books were the most obvious place in the Middle Ages to record items of importance, as they were made of the most durable materials and were likely to be solemnly handed down from one generation to the next. Where written materials were rare, these were also the texts which most readily came to hand. In *c.* 1200 a Jew used the last leaves of his prayer-book to jot down (in Arabic written down in Hebrew characters) a memorandum of 'all that I have since being here in England'; his list comprises debts due from the bishops of Exeter, Bath and Winchester, from an unnamed earl, and from some lesser clerks and knights. What happened to him, or them, is unknown, as only his sacred book survives.[3] Recording items in liturgical books was made a rule by the Salisbury diocesan statutes of *c.* 1217: parish priests are enjoined to 'write in missals and other books the properties and rents of the church and lists of the books, vestments and furnishing'.[4] This was the first step in the long process of making parish priests the registrars of their villages.

As some charters were placed for safekeeping in sacred books, it comes as no surprise to find that others were put in shrines. The best-known instance of this practice is the use of the Anglo-Saxon royal *haligdom* as a place for depositing charters. The *haligdom* was probably the sanctuary associated with the chapel royal. Thus a Ramsey charter (dating from the 1050s) was deposited 'by the king's order in his chapel with the relics of the saints which he has there'. This chapel was probably a stone building rather than a portable altar; in that case its most likely location was either at Westminster Abbey or in the ancient palace of the West Saxon kings at Winchester. It has been argued that charters had been kept at Winchester, systematically filed, since the ninth century. Wherever it was situated, the *haligdom* was a depository of sacred documents for posterity and not an administrative archive.

Churches and reliquaries were the obvious place to keep documents not just because they were relatively secure, being protected by stone and iron as well as by anathemas, but also because charters were themselves relics of past gifts. Moreover, since gifts to monasteries were often made to the patron saint of the church rather than to the monks themselves, it was appropriate that the charters recording the gifts should be placed as close to the relics of the saint as possible, because they belonged to him. It was common practice to offer charters at an altar; thus the Guthlac roll depicts the benefactors of Crowland Abbey presenting their charters at St Guthlac's shrine. Similarly one of the seals of Bury St Edmunds Abbey hung from the shrine of St Edmund, presumably because it was a secure place and because the seal belonged to St Edmund in a personal sense.

Together with sacred books and relics of the saints, documents came to be mixed in with cups, rings, wooden staffs, knives, and any other symbolic objects which retained the memory of past events. For example in 1096 Tavistock Abbey deposited in the shrine of St Rumon the ivory knife

PLATE 15. A roll depicting benefactors of Crowland Abbey. They are laying charters recording their gifts on the altar at the shrine of St Guthlac, while at the side of the picture an epileptic with bound hands is having a fit so forceful as to raise him from the ground and to eject the devil from his mouth

(with an explanatory note attached) by which William Rufus had given the abbot seisin of a manor; likewise Spalding Priory fifty years later put Thomas of Moulton's knife into its archive or *secretarium*. As long as it remained customary to symbolise a conveyance of property by an object laid upon an altar, it was natural for such objects, whatever their form, to be kept with the sacred vessels and liturgical books which were similarly associated with the altar. To the modern eye an early medieval archive would have looked more like a magpie's nest than a filing system for documents. Yet however bizarre such objects might look at first sight, the sacristan could no doubt have explained the significance as a memento of each individual object. The best modern comparison might be with an old lady's handbag, which likewise might contain symbolic rings, jewellery, miscellaneous mementoes, and a few letters and papers.

Each document or book had a special place of safekeeping, appropriate to its associations and function, but not all the documents or books were kept in one place. Liturgical books were often kept in the church, because that is where they were used, whereas other books were kept in the refectory for reading aloud, or in a chest or cupboard in the cloister for individual study. At Lincoln Cathedral in the thirteenth century the chancellor had charge of the scholastic books and saints' lives, the precentor kept the music books, the treasurer had the other liturgical books like breviaries and missals, and the provost looked after the charters and muniments. There were good reasons for the arrangement, as the chancellor was associated with the school, the precentor with the choir, the treasurer with the safekeeping of sacred utensils, and the provost with the correspondence of the dean and chapter. The need for a centralised library or archive only became apparent if the number of books or documents increased to unmanageable proportions.

Furthermore, documents were scattered about on principle and not just from negligence. The Anglo-Saxon practice of depositing two or three copies of an agreement in different places for greater security continued after the Norman Conquest. For example, sealed copies of Henry II's will were deposited in 1182 at Canterbury, in the Winchester treasury, and in his coffers; likewise Gerald of Wales proposed in 1202 to deposit copies of his evidence concerning the bishopric of St David's in the archives of the pope, the archbishop of Canterbury, and the bishop of St David's. Similarly one reason given in 1221 for having more than one justice on the bench at a time was that each justice kept his own copy of the plea roll, whereas one roll on its own was not sufficiently secure as a record. Only gradually did the Crown move from the traditional notion of safety in numbers as a way to preserve its legal records to the idea of a central archive at the treasury.

To sum up, the tradition at the time of the Norman Conquest had been that documents and books were kept with other precious objects. Writings were too few and too diverse in their functions and physical formats to be treated as a special class of memento. Books and documents were not neglected, but they were kept in ways which made consultation difficult and their dispersal among various repositories meant that books belonging to an institution were not usually seen as a whole as a library, still less were documents seen as an archive.

Gradually in the twelfth and thirteenth centuries, as the number of writings increased, more specific and uniform regulations were made for their safekeeping. The initiative in this movement seems to have come from ecclesiastics and not from the royal government. The Norman Conquest encouraged monastic houses to examine their heritage in order to justify the existence of themselves and their saints to the conquerors. Moreover, the reforming prelates appointed by Archbishop Lanfranc aimed to bring their churches into line with the best continental practice, and that meant reviewing and renewing their books and muniments. The Latin word *archiva* (neuter plural), meaning 'archives' in something like its modern sense of a safe and secret place for documents, was first used in England by Lanfranc in the early 1070s when ordering some letters concerning the bishop of the Orkneys to be preserved as a memorial for the future 'in the archives' of the churches of Worcester and Chester. Examples of monasteries reviewing their muniments are numerous and relate to the beginnings of cartulary making, which has already been discussed (see pages 268–9 above). V. H. Galbraith has pointed out that Hemming, who completed the first cartulary, also has claims to be the earliest English archivist, as he had a new lock put on Worcester's muniment chest and repaired original documents which were torn or damaged. Repairing charters was closely associated with replacing them, and hence with forgery. In the monastic community archivists and forgers shared a common aim in documenting a house's titles to its property.

Archives and archivists did not originate from the requirements of disinterested historical research, but from the immediate necessity to produce documents even where none existed. This monastic movement to review and modernise records continued in the twelfth and thirteenth centuries. Thus the compiler of Ramsey Abbey's *Book of Benefactors* in *c.* 1170 describes the 'very ancient' charters and chirographs 'which we have found in our archives', which he claims to have translated from 'barbarous' Anglo-Saxon into Latin. A decade or so later the dean of St Paul's, Ralf de Diceto, made a survey of the churches owned by the cathedral and combined this with an examination of their charters; he devised a system of cross-references between his survey and the charters by using special identification symbols.

The preoccupation with making lists and surveys, which had originated with the *descriptiones* of monastic estates like Abbot Samson's *kalendarium*, also produced the first monastic book catalogues in the twelfth century. Strictly speaking perhaps these lists of books owned by particular houses should not be described as library catalogues, as most of them are simply inventories of possessions which do not indicate to the user where he will find a particular book. Such lists were not intended for the reader's use anyway, but for the librarian's. Nevertheless among the earliest half-dozen or so English library lists extant is one from Christ Church Canterbury (dating from *c.* 1170) in which a series of small letters and symbols correspond with symbols on the first leaf of each book. The librarian had thus marked his books in much the same way as Ralf de Diceto marked the charters of St Paul's. Such marks did not indicate where the books or charters were placed, but they did at least show which description in a list corresponded with which document in a cupboard or chest.

A good example of an early book list is the inventory, on the fly-leaves of a work of St Augustine's, made at Rochester Cathedral in 1202. It begins, unusually, with a precise date and description: 'In the year AD 1202 this is the survey of our library.' The use of the term 'survey' (*scrutinium*) suggests that a comprehensive review was intended. The books are listed partly under the names of authors (Augustine, Gregory, Ambrose, Jerome, Bede) which are not in alphabetical order, partly by where certain books are placed, such as those which are 'in the precentor's chest [*archa*]', and partly under special collections comprising gifts or acquisitions from named individuals. The list comprises 241 items (according to the edited text) and is evidently more complete than an earlier fragment of a list on the fly-leaves of the mid-twelfth century *Textus Roffensis*.

On the fly-leaf of a copy of the sermons of St Bernard, Lincoln Cathedral library has a borrowers' list (as distinct from an inventory or catalogue) dating from *c.* 1220. The entries are jotted down in an informal script, without ruled lines, which contrasts with the regular bookhand of the text. For example William of Avallon, the bishop's nephew, is recorded as having Bede's commentary on St Luke's gospel, the 'canonical epistles', and a *mappa mundi*. Another title has been added below these, in lighter ink: *& Ysidor'*, that is, a book by Isidore of Seville, perhaps his

'Etymologies'. None of the total of fourteen titles noted on this fly-leaf are recorded as having been returned by their borrowers. To obviate loss, some Lincoln books have *Liber Sancte Marie Linc*' ('a book of St Mary's Lincoln') written on them in a bold hand. A few St Albans Abbey books retain a more forceful inscription of ownership: 'This is a book of St Alban's; anyone who removes it, or deletes the title, or alienates it from the church by any kind of art, fraud, or ingenuity is anathema.'[5] These inscriptions invoke the curse of the patron saint, to whom everything in the institution was deemed to belong in a personal sense. Many of 'St Mary's' books are still housed in Lincoln Cathedral library, but St Alban's ones were dispersed at the Dissolution of the Monasteries. St Alban's books had been additionally protected by their physical proximity to the saints. Thus Abbot Simon (1167–83) ordered that the fine books he had made should be kept 'in the painted chest which is up against (or "opposite", *contra*) the tomb of St Roger the hermit'.

Modern libraries really started with the friars. The Dominican rule of Humbert de Romanis (dating from *c.* 1260) lays down all the principal duties of a modern librarian. The librarian should choose a good site for the library, secure, waterproof and well ventilated; there should be ample shelving in the book cupboard, the shelves being designated to different subjects and having explanatory notices on them; there should be a catalogue (*charta*) of the books, which should have their titles written on the spines and an inscription inside each stating the house to which the book belongs and who gifted it; the stock should be kept up to date by replacing old books and selling duplicates; the librarian should have the key of the library and open it at specified times. Books in common use, such as the Bible, papal decretals, sermons and chronicles were to be kept in a chained reference section, whereas less used books might be borrowed by readers provided loans were recorded in writing. A general inspection of the library was to be made once or twice a year.

If these Dominician regulations are compared with those made by Archbishop Lanfranc in his constitutions for Christ Church Canterbury two centuries earlier, the change in the use of books is striking. There is a librarian (*custos librorum*) in Lanfranc's constitutions and he keeps a written list of books on loan, like his Dominican counterpart; but there the similarity ceases, as the principal duty of Lanfranc's librarian is to supervise the borrowing of books once a year on the first Monday in Lent. The books were to be laid out on a carpet and each monk was issued with one book and given the year to read it. Many books of the Church Fathers were of course long and difficult; a monk who read with attention and understanding every word of St Augustine's *City of God*, for example, had achieved a great deal in a year. Nevertheless Lanfranc's constitutions indicate a different approach to reading from the Dominican rules.

The Dominicans, like modern academics, required extensive libraries in which they could glance rapidly over a whole series of books, many of very recent authorship, in order to construct a wide-ranging argument. The purpose of the library was to ensure 'that the community of friars can have ready to hand (*in promptu*)' whatever works they required.[6] Lanfranc's monks, on the other hand, were expected to ruminate on a text which had been designated to them as a sacred task. For monks in the old Benedictine tradition, books, with their precious and brightly illuminated words, were images which produced a state of mystical contemplation and understanding. The difference in approach towards writing of Lanfranc's Benedictines and Humbert's Dominicans is so fundamental that to use the same term 'literate' to describe them both is misleading. The parallel with the change of attitudes towards records is evident: at the time of the Norman Conquest documents were special objects which were treasured in shrines; whereas by 1300 Edward I, like the friars, expected them all to be available for scrutiny and comparison whenever he wanted.

In fact, however, the king's books and records were less well regulated for a long period than those either of an average Benedictine house or of the friars. John is the first king since the Norman Conquest who can be shown to have owned and used books. This is surprising, as Henry I was *litteratus* and Henry II was the most educated king of his time; at his court there was 'school every day'. Evidence about John's books comes from incidental references in the public records. An entry in the pipe roll of 1203, recording the cost of supplying 'chests and carts to take the king's books overseas' suggests that John had a library as large as any monastic house. About the contents of this library, or where it was kept, there is only the sparsest information. In 1205 the king had 'a romance of the history of England' (that is, a text in French) sent him at Windsor by one of his stewards. In 1208 'our book called *Plinius*' (that is, a Latin text of Pliny) was sent him from Reading Abbey, where it had been deposited for safekeeping. A few days earlier he had obtained from Reading Abbey a copy of the Old Testament, a work by Hugh of St Victor, the Sentences of Peter Lombard, and some other scholastic texts. This last reference is the most interesting evidence about John's use of books, as all educated laymen of his time enjoyed history in 'romance' (in other words, in the form of vernacular stories or poems) and most *litterati* read the more obvious Latin classics like Pliny; but King John is the first king in Europe to have been interested in the theological works of the 'modern' schoolmen of the twelfth century. It is likely, however, that he required these books for a particular purpose, namely his dispute with Stephen Langton over clerical privileges; moreover, these scholastic texts probably belonged to Reading Abbey rather than to the king himself.

This episode showed that the king's government required a reference library, particularly for ecclesiastical business. Yet the only books possessed by John's successor, Henry III, were liturgical texts and a few romances. Henry, as a patron of artists and craftsmen rather than writers, had missals made for his and the queen's numerous chapels up and down England. Queen Eleanor also used in 1250 a 'great book' in French, 'in which are contained the deeds of Antioch and of the kings', which was kept by the Knights Templar probably as part of the royal wardrobe. This may be the same as Henry's 'great book of romances', garnished with silver clasps and nails, which is mentioned in 1237. Such books were evidently treasured objects, rather than a library of information, and it is therefore appropriate that they should have been kept by sacristans or by the Templars.

Similarly there is no evidence of Edward I having a library. When he wished to justify his claims to overlordship in Scotland in 1291, he had to ask monasteries to consult their chronicles (as we have already seen), presumably because he had no histories of his own, even allowing for ready access to the library of Westminster Abbey. Few books are to be found in Bishop Stapledon's survey of documents in 1320. In one chest a few texts were deposited along with some seals—a book called *De Regimine Principum* (On Royal Rule) bound in red leather, a 'little book' of the rules of the Knights Templar, a quire (that is, part of an unbound book) of the life of St Patrick, another quire 'in an unknown language' (Welsh), and a book of the chronicles of Roderick archbishop of Toledo. These books may have belonged to Edward I. Even if they did, they have the air of miscellaneous gifts and acquisitions rather than the foundations of a library or of a personal collection. In having no library and in leaving little evidence of possessing books, the English kings were no different from other contemporary rulers. The first pope of the period who can be shown to have had a library is Edward I's contemporary, Boniface VIII, and that was dispersed after his death. The explanation for the dearth of libraries is not primarily that kings were ignorant laymen, more interested in fighting and hunting than in study. Rather it is that the business of government, whether ecclesiastical or secular, only gradually became associated with book-learning and written precedents.

The development of the royal archives after the Norman Conquest requires special discussion because it is inconsistent and perplexing. The proliferation of documents beginning in the twelfth century, combined with the erratic movements of the kings back and forth across the Channel, caused records to be dispersed and frequently moved about, whereas they had been more safely preserved in the eleventh century. There is no clear line of progress from dispersal to centralisation. As we have already seen, some charters which served as title-deeds before the Norman Conquest were deposited in the king's *haligdom* or sanctuary, which may have had a permanent location at either Westminster or Winchester. The returns of the Domesday survey were likewise kept at Winchester in the reign of William Rufus 'in my treasury'. Whether this *thesaurus*, the 'treasure' or 'treasury' of William Rufus, was the same place as the *haligdom* of the West Saxon kings is a matter for conjecture. Certainly in the twelfth century the *thesaurus* at Winchester was developing into a permanent central archive for the government, perhaps because Winchester with its access to Southampton was a good location for the capital of the Anglo-Norman lordship. Henry I's coronation charter was deposited at Winchester by his order. Similarly in 1155 Henry II ordered the bull of Adrian IV giving him jurisdiction over Ireland, together with the gold and emerald ring which the pope had sent as a symbol of investiture, to be deposited 'in the archives of Winchester', according to Gerald of Wales. John of Salisbury, who had brought the papal bull and ring to Henry, confirms this story by noting that the ring was deposited *in cimiliarchio publico* for safekeeping. *Cimiliarchium* had been the term used by Justinian to describe the imperial archive. John had probably therefore derived the idea of a public archive from his interest in Roman law and history, rather than from English realities. Nevertheless he was at least one influential Englishman who considered that England had a public archive in a fixed place in the middle of the twelfth century.

Later in Henry II's reign, however, as the government expanded, the use of a fixed treasury and archive at Winchester was abandoned. Instead, treasure chests were constantly moved to and fro between Winchester, London, and other royal palaces, hunting lodges and fortresses. The assumption has been frequently made that the treasury at Winchester was simply replaced by a similar fixed and central treasury at Westminster, but that is contradicted by the evidence. Fitz Nigel's *Dialogue of the Exchequer* indicates the ambivalence of official attitudes towards the idea of one fixed place for a treasury, and hence for an archive, by the 1170s.[7] The Pupil prompts the Master to describe the king's seal and the Book of

Judgement (Domesday Book), 'the former of which, if I remember correctly, is kept in the *thesauro* and not taken out'. The Master replies that the seal, Domesday Book and many other things are not taken out either. Before enlarging on this statement, he explains to the Pupil the ambiguity of the word *thesaurus*, which means both 'treasure' (such as coins, gold, silver and vestments) and 'treasury' (a place where treasure is deposited). In reply to the Pupil's implied question, 'Where is the treasury?' the Master cites chapter VI, verse 21 of St Matthew's Gospel, 'Where your treasure is, there will your heart be also.'

Speaking through the Master, Fitz Nigel thus refuses to give one geographical location to the treasury, because the king's treasure was dispersed in a number of repositories and some of it was taken about with him on his travels. In the Master's words, '*plura sunt in repositoriis archis thesauri que circumferuntur.*' In the English version of the *Dialogus* this passage is translated, 'There are several things in the vaults of the Treasury which are taken about.' However, *repositoriis archis thesauri* does not mean 'the vaults of the Treasury', but 'storage chests of treasure'. *Archa* is used by Fitz Nigel in the sense of a 'chest' or 'archive', not in the sense of an 'arch' or 'vault': thus the *arche* containing the Exchequer rolls are mentioned earlier in his book. The Master is simply informing the Pupil that 'several things'—among which are Domesday Book, the Exchequer rolls and numerous writs and charters—are locked up in treasure chests, which are taken about the country in accordance with the wishes of the king. For Fitz Nigel there is no contradiction between his statement that Domesday Book is kept in the treasury and not taken out and his statement that it is taken about the country, because the treasury is in the king's heart; in other words, it is wherever he wants it to be.

Once it is understood that *thesaurus* by the late twelfth century usually meant treasure kept in portable chests, rather than a government department or a fixed place, it becomes clear why relatively few royal records of Henry II's reign (with the exception of the pipe rolls) or earlier were successfully preserved. King John likewise had no single place for his treasure. In 1215 some of his treasure chests are known to have been deposited at Reading Abbey, as he recovered from there jewels, relics and 'all our rolls of our Chamber, together with our seal, and our rolls of our Exchequer'. The archives in *thesauro* were evidently being 'taken about', as they had been in Fitz Nigel's time a generation earlier. In addition to the records of the household and the Exchequer referred to by King John, the Chancery rolls were likewise transported from place to place by the 'portejoye' or 'serjeant of the rolls of Chancery'. Some Cistercian abbeys were required in rotation to provide a strong horse to carry the rolls and books of the Chancery in the mid-thirteenth century and later.

Because the royal archives had no permanent home, their safekeeping initially depended on the reliability of archivists rather than repositories. The earliest of such officials on record are William Cucuel, who had charge of the close rolls (the copies of the king's confidential letters) in 1215, Roger of Whitchester, who was appointed keeper of the rolls and writs of the justices' Bench at an annual salary of £10 in 1246, and John Kirkby, who held the 'office of the rolls of Chancery' at an annual salary of twenty marks in 1265 and was subsequently described as 'keeper'. Unlike the 'portejoye', who was probably a mere porter, these men were royal clerks of education and status. They were archivists in the sense that they were in charge of *arche* of documents, but their archives were portable chests not permanent repositories.

Obviously, however, once documents accumulated, permanent repositories had to be found. Once a series of records like the Exchequer or Chancery rolls had piled up for fifty years or more, it became impractical and unnecessary to keep carting them all about in chests. Where the older royal records were kept in the thirteenth century has not been fully elucidated. In Henry III's reign London and Westminster replaced Winchester as the centre for storing royal treasure, but the repositories were scattered. Judging from later evidence, the Tower of London, the New Temple in London, and stores off the cloister of Westminster Abbey were the chief repositories. The New Temple and Westminster Abbey locations suggest that religious houses were still considered the most appropriate places to keep documents. Orders like one in 1257 to deposit plea rolls and chirographs 'in the king's treasury' throw no light on the location of this archive, although Westminster Abbey is likely in this instance as legal records were subsequently kept in its chapter house.

In Edward I's reign the largest archive in the kingdom was probably the New Temple in London. In 1279 Roger of Seaton, chief justice of the Bench, kept his plea rolls there and other memoranda show that the Chancery rolls were kept there: in 1289 a charter granting land to the king is described as being 'in a box in the chest in which the rolls of Chancery are kept at the New Temple'; in the summer of 1291, as we have already seen, Edward I ordered a chest at the New Temple to be broken open and a charter roll and a patent roll of Henry III were taken out of it. The New Temple had also been a repository for books and documents of the Wardrobe, like the 'great book' which Queen Eleanor had brought from there in 1250, although in 1300 many recent books and rolls of the Wardrobe were deposited at St Leonard's hospital in York.

The dissolution of the Knights Templar by papal decree in 1312 may have been an ancillary reason for reviewing the royal archives, as it deprived the king of the chief custodians of his documents. Certainly in that year new cupboards for keeping the older records were installed in the Tower of London. When Bishop Stapledon began his survey of the records in 1320, the White Chapel in the Tower was selected as the central repository to which all the records were brought. The idea of having a central royal archive in a fixed place under the king's direct control had at last been realised, but the government let the opportunity slip and many of the records were returned to their former repositories. The records were not again brought under a single custody until the Public Records Act of 1838.

Ideally the king's government needed archives in the localities as well as a central repository. In Anglo-Saxon England cathedrals and monasteries, which were under the king's particular protection, acted as keepers of his valuables including documents. Monks preserved royal charters because they were frequently the beneficiaries, as well as often being the writers of them. In Alfred's reign, for example, the Canterbury monks had written not only 'documents of interest to the archbishops and community, but also royal diplomas granting lands to lay nobles, private agreements between laymen, and the solemn decisions of royal councils'.[8] These practices continued intermittently after the Norman Conquest. Thus copies of Henry I's coronation charter were deposited in abbeys in each county, as well as being put in the Winchester treasury, according to later chronicle evidence. One of the early copies of the reissue of Magna Carta was deposited at Lacock Abbey by the knights of Wiltshire, presumably for safekeeping. By the time of Magna Carta, however, sheriffs kept rolls themselves and must have been beginning to develop archives of their own. The earliest evidence of this arises from exceptional cases in which documents were mislaid. In 1212 a clerk of the sheriff of Gloucestershire explained to the king's justices that he had been obliged to go to London on the county's business and had left the sheriff's roll with 'Richard the priest of the castle'; when he returned, he found that the text of the roll had been altered. In this instance Richard the priest was evidently acting as an unofficial, and inefficient or dishonest, archivist in the sheriff's castle. Past experience of documents in the sheriff's care being lost may have led the barons in 1258 to insist that copies of the letter, whereby Henry III undertook to submit to their council, should 'remain in the treasury' of each county. Likewise in 1265 the letter publishing the terms of Henry III's peace with the barons was sent to every county, together with an order to keep it and accompanying documents safely as 'a memorial of the business' in the custody of trustworthy men chosen for the purpose.

The precedent for regulating local archives and appointing commissioners to supervise them had been established in 1194 by Hubert Walter's statute for the safekeeping of Jewish bonds. It is possible that such bonds had been kept in chests in great churches before the statute; in the anti-Jewish riot at York in 1190 the mob broke into York Minster, seized the 'muniments of debts' deposited there by the Jews and burned 'these instruments of profane avarice' in the middle of the church. By the statute of 1194 the bonds were to be stored in future in designated centres in a communal archive (*in arca communi*) or public chest, fitted with three locks. The keys were to be kept by two Jews, two Christians, and the clerk of the royal commissioners. The Jewish and Christian key-holders are the first recorded local public archivists in England and became known as 'chirographers'. Instances can readily be found in the thirteenth century of the appointment of both Jewish and Christian chirographers and of the keys being delivered to them. A chirographer was usually chosen by a jury, appointed before the justices of the Jews, and took an oath to perform his duties faithfully. As an additional precaution, the contents of these archives were surveyed and enrolled from time to time.

As public royal archives with official archivists and writers had thus been established in the principal towns in England by Henry III's reign, it is surprising at first sight that greater general use was not made of them. An exceptional instance from Oxford in 1227–8 shows a third copy of an agreement, made by the hospital of St John the Baptist with Geoffrey Malin and his wife, being deposited 'in the king's archive [*archa*] in Oxford'. The archive meant is presumably the chest of Jewish bonds; yet neither of the parties is a Jew, nor does the business concern moneylending but a conveyance of land. From 1195 third copies of agreements (feet of fines) made before royal justices were deposited in the royal 'treasury'; likewise third copies of Jewish bonds were deposited in the local *arche* from at least 1205. It is possible that William, the Oxford town clerk, who was the writer of this agreement in 1227–8, may also have been one of the keepers of the Jewish *archa* and recommended his archive as a safe place for retaining a third copy of this conveyance.

Had the procedure used in this Oxford conveyance become widespread, the archives of the main towns of England would have developed into centres for registering conveyances of property under the supervision of official writers and archivists. Local royal archives thus had the potential of notarial centres in imperial cities on the Italian model. The potential was not realised, however, probably because the *arche* were too closely associated with the Jews and usury. In the eyes of Christians, depositing a Christian charter in a Jewish archive would have had the reverse effect of putting it in the shrine of a saint, as the charter would have been contaminated by the 'instruments of profane avarice' all around it. Furthermore, local *arche* may have been considered insufficiently secure despite their public supervision. In times of riots Jewish archives were burned, as happened at York in 1190 and at Bedford in the civil war between Henry III and the barons.

This discussion has concentrated on the royal archives in their various forms because the king's government had the largest problems and also because, although evidence is sparse, there is sufficient to discern the outline of development. For magnates, whether ecclesiastical or lay, fewer details are available and most are of an incidental or an anecdotal type. After the king, the bishops might have been expected to accumulate business archives the fastest. Yet, just as bishops were slower than the king to make registers, their records suffered more than the king's from being carried around and having no single place of deposit in each diocese. At Rochester it was reported early in the fourteenth century that 'there never was any certain safe place appointed as a repository of muniments, but they were left about, sometimes in the cathedral church or in the manor of Halling'. Some lay lords followed the king's lead and deposited documents with the Templars or at Westminster Abbey. Charters were also handed over to other religious persons or houses or to the village parson.

Some landowners preferred to keep their own muniments, in which case they were sometimes lost or stolen. One of the earliest chirographs made before royal justices (in 1182) concerns the loss of a charter for Rochester Cathedral priory by William son of Ralf of Wye. The most spectacular story of a theft of charters comes from Babington in Somerset in 1201. An unnamed lord was allegedly attacked in his house by a gang of eight conspirators who pulled out his tongue, broke open his chests, took out charters of Henry II, Richard I and an archbishop of Canterbury, and burned them in his face before beheading him. Whether this allegation is entirely truthful, however, is doubtful, as the accused were allowed to make a compromise and the king did not prosecute.

Making documents, keeping them in archives, and subsequently using them again for reference were three distinct stages of development, as has already been argued. Even when documents were successfully preserved and kept in safe yet accessible places, it might still prove difficult to find a particular item of information within a book or roll. An example has already been given of Henry III insisting to the pope in 1272 that letters patent of his being exhibited by the prior of Christ Church Canterbury at the Roman *curia* were forgeries because they could not be found in his register (see page 244 above). In fact these letters had been enrolled in the patent rolls in 1265, but the Chancery clerks were unable to find them because they thought the letters had been issued in 1270. Without an alphabetical index of names, the clerks could not search their records thoroughly.

Searches of the rolls for particular documents were usually successful only when the record was of recent origin and its date of issue was known. For example in 1250 Walter Bloweberme, a robber who had abjured the realm after triumphing in trial by combat at Winchester in 1249, was recaptured and reconvicted by referring to the Hampshire plea roll of 1249 in which his trial had been recorded. Or in the London justices' visitation of 1276 the prior of Holy Trinity at Aldgate claimed from the 'record of the Chancery rolls' that he had been authorised by Henry III to close a road; the rolls were duly searched and the record found. Although it was possible to find particular cases or charters in the rolls when the exact circumstances were already known, royal records could not be effectively searched in a more general way. Thus Edward I's attempt in 1300 to search all the rolls for information about Scotland produced no new information because royal records had no indexes. Similarly the pioneering attempt of baronial commissioners in 1259 to assess from the records of the Exchequer how much money had been raised by tallages during Henry III's reign was not brought to a specific conclusion, although some information may have been gathered.

The government's inability to use its archives for general guidance or for precedents in making policy decisions meant in the long term that its records were of more benefit to the governed than to the Crown itself. An individual property owner or the head of a monastic house who possessed a royal charter or a transcript of litigation in the king's court could use the Chancery and plea rolls to prove his title by referring to a particular enrolment. Without systemised guides to their records the king's clerks on their side had no means of finding out whether other royal documents existed which might modify or even contradict such a claim.

A good example of the king being caught in his own bureaucratic net by insisting on written proof occurred in the *quo warranto* proceedings of Edward I. The rule had been established in 1282 that the privilege of excluding royal officers from executing writs within franchises (the franchise of 'return of writs') could be upheld only by a royal charter which made specific mention of the privilege. This rule was reinforced by a statute in 1285 which proposed that the treasurer should make a roll of those entitled to 'return of writs'; thenceforward any sheriff who made a return to an unenrolled franchise would be punished as a disinheritor of the Crown. The government's insistence on recording privileges in writing is exemplified in this dispute, both in the rule that a claimant must have a royal charter and in the proposal to make an official treasury list of franchise-holders. In the real world of practical politics, however, as contrasted with the theoretical world of Edward I's legal advisers and Chancery clerks, these rules threatened the great majority of magnates because their privileges rested on unwritten acceptance and custom rather than on royal charters or treasury lists. The roll of those entitled to 'return of writs' was consequently never made.

The story did not end there, however, as a handful of ecclesiastics, who were more concerned than lay magnates to ensure that their privileges were precisely expressed in writing, obtained new charters. Among them was the abbot of Chertsey, who appeared to comply promptly with the new rules by having a charter of Richard I, which had granted 'return of writs' to his predecessor, inspected by the Chancery and enrolled on the charter rolls in 1285. What the Chancery clerks did not notice was that this charter was a daring forgery, as it was a conflation of two genuine charters of Richard I for Chertsey supplemented by interpolations. The facts can be simply proved today by looking up the Chertsey charters in the index to the printed edition of the *Cartae Antiquae* rolls which were published in 1939. These rolls date from Richard I's reign and should have been known to the king's clerks in 1285. But even if they were known, they would have been difficult to search without an alphabetical index. The abbot of Chertsey had presumably taken a calculated risk that the royal archives would not, or could not, be searched for a grant which was earlier than the Chancery rolls of King John.

The Chertsey case illustrates the way powerful individuals or institutions successfully used the king's bureaucratic apparatus to benefit themselves to the detriment of the Crown. Ancient monasteries like Chertsey had traditionally forged charters when they required title-deeds in writing. Now that the king was keeping copies of charters on his Chancery rolls, abbots ensured that their forged documents were reinforced by inspection in the Chancery and enrolment among the royal records. The Chancery rolls, which were intended to prevent fraud, thus became a means of making forgeries official. Once the abbot of Chertsey had got the forged charter of Richard I enrolled in 1285, his title depended on that enrolment rather than on the *Cartae Antiquae* rolls or his original charters of Richard I, which had presumably been destroyed in the process of making the forgery. Chertsey had acted in a similar way in 1256, when a forged charter of Edward the Confessor had been enrolled on the charter rolls of Henry III; the abbey had paid 100 marks for this 'confirmation'.

Potentially the archives recording the acts of successive kings should have been a bastion against human forgetfulness and an assurance of just and efficient government, as Bishop Stapledon's commission claimed. If there had been an efficient filing system and indexes, royal clerks could have kept a check on fraudulent claims. In practice, however, the king's records had become so unwieldy by Edward I's reign that they constituted a largely unmapped territory. Particular monastic houses used them to their advantage by paying fees to have documents enrolled in much the same way as a modern company buys advertising space in a newspaper. As monasteries often kept careful records of these enrolments, they had better 'maps' of those parts of the royal archives which concerned them than any royal official had of the whole. For example, Bury St Edmunds Abbey in 1281 paid 1000 marks to Edward I and made a gift of gold to the queen as well to have a new royal charter enrolled, which settled the division of property between the abbot and convent. This enrolment was noted in the Bury chronicle to be 'at the end of the Charter roll for the ninth year' of Edward I, where it can be duly found.[9]

The makers of monastic chronicles and cartularies had kept a watchful eye on the royal records since they had begun to expand in the 1200s. Many chroniclers cite official documents: the best example is Matthew Paris, who obtained transcripts of records through Alexander Swereford of the Exchequer and perhaps also through John Mansel of the Chancery. Some of these documents may have been 'leaked' to Matthew by these officials so that he could give them wider currency and record them for posterity. In a sense a monastic chronicle like Matthew Paris's was an official record which was useful to the Crown. Some monasteries claimed that they had a right to make extracts of royal records which concerned them. Thus Dunstable Priory submitted in 1276 that the prior was entitled to sit with the royal justices on the bench, and his 'enrolling clerk' with the justices' clerks, in order to copy the plea roll.

The most remarkable collection of extracts from the royal records is Barnwell Priory's *Liber Memorandorum*, which was composed in the

1290s, the most appropriate time to be compiling documents systematically as Edward I was beginning to do the same. The book contains the texts of nearly ninety official documents, ranging from citations from Domesday Book and the pipe rolls of John's reign to writs and plea rolls of Edward I. The compiler makes his purpose explicit in his extracts from a sheriff's roll at Cambridge Castle: 'It will not be necessary in future to go to the castle to see the sheriff's roll, but rather the facts can be seen and learned from this book.'[10] The book was a kind of cartulary of other institutions' records concerning Barnwell. In one citation from a Bench roll of 1288 the compiler notes that 'this record is to be found in a certain roll on the white part [that is, on the top side of the parchment] at the end of the roll where this sign [*signum*] is depicted'. The *signum* is a hand with outstretched index finger, which is indeed to be found in the roll in question in the Public Record Office. In this instance Barnwell Priory had evidently been allowed to mark the official roll itself, as well as obtain a transcript of it. The Barnwell book is exceptional in containing so many extracts from royal records, but typical in its desire to keep pace with and master the methods of the royal bureaucracy in order to maintain the privileges gained by monks in the past. Monks had been the specialists in written record before the king's clerks appeared on the scene. Although they had lost this initiative by 1300, they fastened on the royal records like leeches and drew from them the information to sustain their privileges.

The use of a sign, like Barnwell's hand with outstretched index finger, to mark a particular item in a document was a simple way of facilitating the retrieval of information. Such signs are not essentially different from the rubrics, capital letters, running titles, introductory paragraph flourishes, and other aids to the reader which are usual in medieval manuscripts. The royal records, from Domesday Book and the pipe rolls onwards, are particularly notable for their clear and orderly layout. Marginal abbreviations and symbols were systematically used to extract payments due to the Crown from a roll and to distinguish the business of one county or jurisdiction from another. It is usually easy to identify a particular item on a membrane or page of a royal document. The medieval archivist's problem lay in not knowing which page or roll to search in the first place.

Medieval writers were so good at layout because they were taught that ordering things on the page was directly related to ordering them in the mind.

To fix something in the memory, it is of great value when we are reading to take pains to imprint (*imprimere*) on the memory through the imagination not only the number and order of the verses or sections in books, but also at the same time the colour, shape, position and placement of the letters: where we saw this written down and where that; in what part (of the book) and in which place (on the page) we saw it positioned—whether at the top, in the middle, or near the bottom; in what colour we discerned the shape of a particular letter or the ornament on the surface of the parchment. I think there is nothing so effective for exciting the memory as meticulously paying attention to the surroundings of things (*circumstantias rerum*), to those features which can occur accidentally and externally.[11]

Master Hugh of St Victor, the most influential teacher of biblical studies in Paris in the twelfth century (he died in 1142), is explaining here how to remember a text by placing it in the mind's eye and associating its abstract contents with something visible and circumstantial. In the process, he explains why scholastic books can be ornamented and illuminated as elaborately as liturgical books; the distinctive colour and shape of the words on the page helped remind the reader of where they occurred in the book. Hugh calls his memorising techniques elementary ('puerile' is his term) and he claims no originality for them, as they derived from Greek and Roman practice. Although Hugh and his contemporaries considered training the memory to be commonplace, it was none the less important because it structured the way medieval writers set out their thoughts.

'My son,' Hugh of St Victor says, 'knowledge is a treasury (*thesaurus*) and your heart is its strong-box (*archa*).' This is the same image and the same biblical reference ('Where your treasure is, there will your heart be also,' Matthew VI, 21), as the Master recommends to the Pupil in the *Dialogue of the Exchequer* to explain the meaning of 'treasury' (see page 318 above). Because the heart is a treasury of precious information, remembering is the process of extracting a particular item from it by recalling its 'colour, shape, position and placement' in the archive of the mind. Learning by heart according to Hugh's method did not mean the oral repetition of phrases until their sounds became a recording, but the visual scanning of a page until its images were imprinted in the mind's eye like a photograph. The medieval schoolmen 'printed' books, before the invention of the mechanical process of printing, by scanning texts and accessing 'through the imagination' the pages imprinted on their minds.

Because memorising was done by associating words with their circumstantial surroundings, which 'occur accidentally and externally', medieval systems of recording and filing information can look arbitrary and strange at first sight. In *The Book of Memory* M. J. Carruthers illustrates some marginal notes drawing attention to particular passages in a text of St Augustine, such as: 'Mark (*Signa*) human benevolence!' and 'Mark (*Signa*) a most useful and brief statement!'[12] The reader's attention is drawn to the first of these notes by its being ringed by a drawing, in coloured inks, of a hound's head linked with a hare's head to form a clasp. The second note is similarly ringed, by a dragon encircling the words with its sinuous tail. The book containing these notes was made for the Cistercian abbey of Holme Cultram, probably late in the twelfth century. The embellishment of the notes does not appear to form part of a coherent iconographical sequence, nor does it illustrate or echo the text. Like much embellishment in medieval manuscripts, these Holme Cultram marginalia look as if they have no purpose other than entertainment.

Cistercian monks, according to St Bernard at least, were not meant to look at images of mythical beasts, like the Holme Cultram dragon, nor admire such sports as hare coursing with hounds. The monks then and art historians since have struggled to reconcile St Bernard's strictures with actual practice. Hugh of St Victor was a contemporary of St Bernard and he too was a monk, but of the Augustinian order which was less austere than the Cistercians. Hugh's remarks on memory training provide an answer to St Bernard: images in monastic manuscripts 'serve the basic function of all page decoration, to make each page memorable'; 'they also serve to remind readers of the purpose of books as a whole—that they contain matter to be laid away in their memorial storehouse.'[13] In the case of the Holme Cultram marginalia, the embellishments help to highlight and tag them, so that the reader may more readily file them away in the archive (*archa*) of his heart.

The Holme Cultram marginalia are 'signs': *signa*, as the Latin text describes them. They probably functioned in much the same way as medieval heraldry functioned, or as advertising symbols function in the twentieth century. A symbol of this sort does not necessarily illustrate the subject-matter it highlights, because memorability has to be its overriding quality. The symbol must imprint itself on the mind. In heraldry a golden circle, or a fiery dragon, on a knight's shield proved memorable primarily because it was mysterious and striking. Twentieth-century advertising uses a comparable technique in imprinting on the mind's eye the symbolic shell of Shell Oil or the tiger associated with Esso. Because the symbolic image is memorable in itself, it cues the memory, which then recalls the information required about the particular knight or brand of oil. This is the process which Hugh of St Victor describes as 'exciting the memory' (*ad memoriam excitandum*).

Rationalising the symbol—by thinking of the knight as rich in gold or fiery in temper, or of the oil as spouting from the seabed or burning bright—may help reinforce the image, but it is not essential. Effective symbols are memorable regardless of whether they make sense of the subject matter which the mind associates with them. In the Holme Cultram marginalia, the hound and hare heads clasped together may symbolise the process of hunting something down in the text, as this metaphor had been used for recollection since the time of Aristotle. Even if the medieval reader knew this, however, the memorability of the image primarily depends on its strangeness: in nature, hare and hound heads do not stem from clasps. The dragon image works through a similar piece of whimsy, as its sinuous tail is the reverse of 'brief' (in contrast with the 'statement' which it encircles) and no one has seen a real dragon. It is the peculiarity of the Holme Cultram images which makes them effective as *signa*. Images from medieval heraldry and manuscript illumination can still be seen today in England acting as *signa*, when they cue the memory on public-house signs such as the 'Hare and Hounds' or the 'Green Dragon'.

Attempts were made from the end of the twelfth century to convert the use of visual signs into a system for classifying subject matter. Ralf de Diceto, dean of St Paul's, who marked charters with *signa* (as we have already seen), seems to have been the pioneer of such systems. His elaborate explanation of the *signa* used in his chronicle suggests that he had invented them himself and wished them to be appreciated. He warns the reader: 'You will find certain *signa* placed in the margin. Do not immediately conclude that this is in any way superfluous, for they are there to jog the memory more easily and are very convenient.' He then explains that, because the making of a chronicle 'always runs on infinitely', the reader needs some guide to its contents. So he has devised twelve symbols (some are pictorial and some use letters of the alphabet) to indicate different subject matter, such as a sword for information about Normandy and 'PS' for persecutions of the Church. The phrase Ralf uses for 'jog the memory' is *ad memoriam excitandum*, the same term as Hugh of St Victor used. Furthermore Ralf cites the beginning of Hugh's treatise on memory verbatim in his chronicle and he cites Hugh also in his preamble to the statutes of St Paul's Cathedral. Ralf had studied at Paris and he may have 'heard with his own ears the teaching of Hugh of St Victor, which directly or indirectly impressed him so deeply'. Hugh's advice to 'imprint on the memory through the imagination' (*per imaginationem*, that is, by image building) was converted by Ralf into a visible system. 'Here begin', he writes, 'the images of histories (*ymagines historiarum*), which Ralf de Diceto dean of London has put into order.'

A manuscript of Ralf's work, displaying his twelve *signa* highlighted in gold, silver and colours, has annotations and drawings by the St Albans chronicler, Matthew Paris. He developed Ralf's 'rudimentary system into a complex sequence of tinted narrative drawings, painted shields and pictographic symbols'.[14] For example, Matthew used reversed shields in the margin of his chronicle to indicate the deaths of knights and reversed mitres for the deaths of bishops. For Matthew, these *signa* became an artistic device in themselves: thus the reversed and broken shield and shattered sword and banner of William Marsh, who was executed for treason in 1242, epitomise his dishonourable end.

Matthew Paris understood that *signa* are memorable because they are rooted in feeling rather than logic. Through the sensitivity of his drawing, he made heraldry into a visual language capable of expressing emotion. As striking as the shattered insignia of William Marsh are Matthew's obituary notices for Gilbert the Marshal in 1241 and the Emperor Frederick II in 1250. The Marshal died in a tournament accident. Matthew uses his lance, drawn in the margin of the text, as a pointer to his picture at the foot of the page, where the Marshal in full armour is shown at the moment when his neck breaks as he is dragged by his horse. To commemorate the portentous death of Frederick II, 'the greatest prince on earth and the wonder of the world', Matthew shows the double-headed black imperial eagle on a reversed shield hurtling down the page, while a fragile pointer makes a cross-reference to the 'Book of Additions' where Frederick's will is recorded.

Ralf de Diceto and Matthew Paris shared a common inspiration for the pictographic indexing of their chronicles in the teaching of the school of St Victor. For Ralf this is explicit in the citations he makes from Hugh's treatise on memory, for Matthew the evidence is conjectural. One link with Paris is contained in Matthew's surname: he is 'the Parisian' (*Parisiensis*). Another link is the unusual number of references Matthew makes to the schools of Paris. Schooling in Paris also helps explain the common features, in imagery and handwriting, which Matthew's work shares with the sketchbook of his contemporary, the Picard architect Villard de Honnecourt. Both men may have been at the school of St Victor, where drawing, painting, and penmanship were integral parts of the curriculum. Hugh of St Victor had taught geometrical and figurative drawing, and the use of colours, because he believed that training the outward eye developed spiritual insight. By meticulous draughtmanship, rather than abstract intellectualising, students imprinted the meanings of things on their memories.

'Thinking (*cogitatio*)', declared one of Hugh's successors, Richard prior of St Victor, 'is without labour or fruit': understanding comes through the immediate insight of contemplation. In training this faculty in his students, Hugh of St Victor explained that 'the Church is the body of Christ and—to make this concept clear for you—I have depicted in visible shape (*in forma visibili depinxi*) the whole person of Christ, that is, the head and the members'. In this spirit Matthew Paris treasured, and made for himself, realistic drawings of the human person of Christ. Into his 'Book of Additions' he inserted Brother William's full-page drawing of Christ; in another manuscript Matthew drew Christ enthroned, and he is likewise the painter of a striking icon of Christ (the Veronica). For Matthew, as for Hugh of St Victor, artistic image, memory image, and spiritual image were a single continuum advancing towards understanding.

Matthew Paris's intellectual and spiritual concerns—as much as his range of linguistic and artistic skills—exemplify at St Albans the teaching of the school of St Victor, just as Ralf de Diceto had exemplified that teaching at St Paul's in London. St Albans Abbey is known to have sent monks to the school of St Victor and it took pains to obtain all Hugh's works, including the manuscript (now in the Bodleian Library) celebrating in a full-page portrait Hugh teaching some monks. These contacts are documented for the period when Richard was prior of St Victor (1162–73), which may be before Matthew's lifetime (he died at an unknown age in 1259). Even so, contacts between the two houses could have continued long enough to provide Matthew with a Victorine education. He records that he took the religious habit at St Albans in 1217. How old he was in that year, how long he had been connected with the abbey, where he was born, and why he was called *Parisiensis* are details of his biography which he does not provide.

From the 1290s there is evidence of a system of *signa*, similar to those devised by Ralf and Matthew, being used in the royal archives to mark particular storage chests or rolls. Thus Exchequer *Liber A*, which was completed in 1294–5, used a pictogram of a man with a lance and broadsword to indicate material which was in coffer 'T' under the title 'Scotland'. Likewise, when in 1296 chests of documents and treasure were sent by Edward I from Scotland to London, the chests bore identification *signa*; and in 1298 a record of a serjeanty tenure in Essex is said to be 'contained in the roll *Teste de Nevill*'. This is the earliest instance of the rolls of knights' fees being identified by the 'Head of Nevill', which was probably the symbol painted on the chest containing them. As there is no evidence for the use of pictorial *signa* of this type in the royal archives before the 1290s, it is likely that they were introduced when Edward I's claims to overlordship in Scotland at last made the government aware that it needed some such system. As the king's clerks inspected chronicles for the Scottish business, they may have borrowed the idea directly from Ralf de Diceto and Matthew Paris.

Why did schoolmen as educated as Ralf de Diceto and Matthew Paris, or Edward I's clerks handling important business, use such peculiar and clumsy methods of retrieving information? Why not make an alphabetical index corresponding to numbered sections in the text? W. J. Ong provides some answers in his discussion of *Orality and Literacy* (1982). The word 'index' is a shortened form of *index locorum*. The *loci* ('places') in such an index were the 'commonplaces' or headings, under which a thinker organised various subjects for recall. These 'places' were located in the mind's eye and not in the book being read. Memorising information by indexing it in the mind's eye was well known to Ciceronian rhetoric: 'if we want to remember a large number of items, we should equip ourselves with a large number of places (*locos*), so that we can use them to locate a large number of images (*imagines*).'[15] The remembrancer visualises a landscape, for example, or a chequer-board or some other pattern; then he places different images, signifying different subjects, in particular squares, rather like locating points on a map by latitude and longitude.

To learn all 150 psalms in the Psalter, Hugh of St Victor recommended making a mental grid of 150 sections. This is how the schoolmen learn to quote any part of any psalm, he explains:

> For surely you don't think that, whenever they wanted to cite one of the psalms by its number, they turned over the pages (*paginas replicasse*) starting from the beginning and counting in order until they recognised the one they wanted? That would have been far too laborious a way of going about the business. Instead, they had an indexing scheme (*noticiam*) off by heart, which they retained in the memory as they learned the number and order of the individual items.[16]

As well as being quicker than thumbing through the pages, mental indexing overcame the difficulty in manuscripts that pagination might differ in a book from one copy to the next. A schoolman who knew the Psalter by heart could apply the indexing scheme he had already learned to any copy he came across. In this way he might readily find his place in an unfamiliar manuscript, or quote a psalm in an oral disputation without having to look it up. Matthew Paris describes how Abbot John of St Albans (1195–1214), who had excelled as a master in the Paris schools, could recite the psalms backwards or forwards in any order, an exercise which Hugh of St Victor recommends.

Because readers indexed texts in their minds, medieval copies of the most widely studied books often have no contents tables, either at the front or the back, and no key-words or chapter numbers at the heads of the pages. To a modern eye a block of blackletter text in a medieval manuscript, differentiated only by coloured ornament and lettering in a variety of sizes from huge to minute, is bewildering and distracting. An inexperienced researcher finds his place in it by checking a passage he can recognise against a modern printed and indexed edition. A medieval reader, on the other hand, recollected an appropriate indexing scheme, his *noticiam*, and then he found his place in the manuscript by relating the images in his mind's eye to the texture of lettering and ornament on the page confronting him. Such a reader might have found a typical modern printed page, lacking colour, ornament and different letter sizes, equally bewildering because it would not cue his memory.

A change occurs in the thirteenth century, when indexing schemes make their way from the hearts and minds of their creators, their *arche* in Hugh of St Victor's terms, on to the pages of books and documents. The *signa* of Ralf de Diceto and Matthew Paris are examples of this. These authors were not original in using *signa*, since mental indexing was routine, but in making their schemes visible to the reader. Ralf and Matthew gave the shapes in their imaginations, their 'images of histories', a local habitation and a name. R. H. and M. A. Rouse remark that indexing tools 'emerge with striking suddenness in the West, to the point that one may say that, probably before 1220, certainly before 1190, no such tools existed; and that, after the 1280s, the dissemination and new creation of such aids to study were commonplace'.[17] Essentially, this was a change in the medium rather than the message. Indexing tools had existed before 1190, as the works of Hugh of St Victor demonstrate, but they were held in the mind's eye. In the thirteenth century, *signa* make the move from memory to written record.

The proliferation of writings of all sorts, in government as much as in the schools, made reliance on identifying material solely by mental indexing less effective. The psalms might be learned by heart, but the accumulating mass of glosses on them could not. Similarly no archivist could find his way through the hundreds of membranes in the royal pipe rolls, plea rolls or memoranda rolls. To help him in his philosophical reading at Oxford around 1230, Robert Grosseteste devised a system of about 400 symbols, which he placed in the margins of texts to indicate different subject matter. An upturned 'V', for example, indicated references to 'God's wisdom' and a crescent moon pointing to the left indicates 'the dignity of man'.[18] Unlike the croziers, mitres and other illustrative symbols used by Ralf de Diceto and Matthew Paris, Grosseteste's *signa* are abstract in form: intersecting lines, patterns of dots, and the like. They are comparable in appearance with masons' marks and other tradesmen's signs. In terms of Ciceronian memorising techniques, however, Grosseteste's *signa* are 'images' as much as those of Ralf and Matthew: Grosseteste located them on the pages he read in order to map his path through the thicket of scholastic texts.

Comparable in appearance and date with Grosseteste's *signa* are those used in Richard Hotot's estate book. Their palaeography has still to be fully worked out. Three points are noteworthy: Hotot, a literate layman, may have written these *signa* himself; their form may derive directly from Grosseteste's *signa*; Hotot's *signa* function as actual footnotes on the page, whereas Grosseteste's do not. That Hotot, a minor Northamptonshire landowner, might have borrowed a scholastic procedure from Robert Grosseteste, chancellor of Oxford University and bishop of Lincoln, is not as surprising as it looks. Hotot belonged to one of those families of middle rank and independent resources, which Sir Richard Southern has described in his reconstruction of Grosseteste's educational milieu. Richard Hotot's elder brother was abbot of Peterborough. Their father, Thomas, was literate; Richard being a younger son, may have been educated as a cleric and personally known to Grosseteste. Richard is named quite often in the plea rolls of the king's courts and he may have got a living as a lawyer. In that case, written records would have been very familiar to him, as would the plea roll clerks' practice of making annotations in the margins and cross-referencing entries.

Ingenious as these various systems of symbols are, the question remains: why not make an alphabetical index instead? Medieval *signa*, whether held in the mind or depicted on the page, were inevitably idiosyncratic because each person's imagination differed, as Hugh of St Victor had recognised. The alphabet, on the other hand, provided a uniform and ready-made sequence of notation. The principle of using it to classify words for reference was of great antiquity. Lists of words in Old English giving their Latin equivalents are arranged in alphabetical order in manuscripts as early as the eighth century. The commonest medieval occurrence of alphabetical arrangement is St Jerome's dictionary of Hebrew names, which is appended to biblical texts. In a Rochester manuscript dating from *c.* 1120 the connection between alphabetical indexing and elementary schooling is made explicit: within the initial 'A' of St Jerome's dictionary is drawn a man frantically trying to teach a performing bear the ABC by beating it with a stick to make it cry out 'A'. In English Bibles of the thirteenth century, the list of Hebrew names is arranged in strict alphabetical order to the third or fourth letter of each word.

By the end of Edward I's reign alphabetical indexes had been made to parliamentary statutes and other law books. An index at Harvard shows just how elaborate these could be. The layout is magnificent, the alphabetical order quite good, and the references elaborate (they use a system of roman and arabic numerals combined with letters of the alphabet). Nevertheless this index does not work properly, although the occasional reference in roman numerals accords by chance with a folio number in the book. The index seems to have been made for another manuscript of similar contents but different pagination. The person who went to the trouble of appending this index to a book to which it does not refer precisely cannot have understood that indexes need to be exact in every detail if they are to work at all. Thus even when the principles of indexing by alphabetical order and numerical sequence had been laid down, it was still difficult to apply them widely in practice because the average reader did not expect to use a medieval manuscript as a source of ready reference. The owner of the law book at Harvard, probably Worcester Cathedral Priory, was perhaps well pleased with the index as it stood. For the monks of Worcester it was valuable as an object of beauty and mystery rather than utility. Medieval intellectuals were ambivalent towards alphabetical order because it militated against their sense of hierarchy. A Franciscan *Book of Examples for the Use of Preachers* dating from *c.* 1270 lists the troubles of human kind alphabetically, starting with *accidia* (sloth); nevertheless its section on the heavenly beings (Christ, the Virgin Mary, angels, saints) is arranged hierarchically. Of similar date is Peter of Pecham's parody of a charter, involving a compact with the devil, which lists the names of the evil spirits witnessing the deed alphabetically except for Beelzebub at their head.

Instead of borrowing a primarily pictorial system of classification from traditionalist monks and their chronicles, the king's government would have done better to consult the friars, as they had the most recent experience of coping successfully with the large number of books required for their libraries, as we have already seen. Because they were the latest religious order, the friars were the most up-to-date experts in the problems posed by the proliferation of literature and documents. As early as 1239 the Dominicans in Paris had compiled an alphabetical concordance of the Bible, which was the first of its kind. It was elaborated into the dictionary entitled *Concordancie Anglicane* by a group of English Dominicans, each of whom took responsibility for a separate letter of the alphabet. Probably among them was John of Darlington, who became Henry III's confessor and counsellor in the 1250s. Edward I's first archbishop of Canterbury was another Dominican friar, Robert Kilwardby (1273–8), who when teaching at Oxford had compiled an alphabetically indexed summary (a kind of *Readers Digest* guide) to the works of the Church Fathers. By the end of the thirteenth century the English Franciscans were constructing a union catalogue of books in more than 180 ecclesiastical libraries. Each institution was allocated a reference number in arabic numerals: Christ Church Canterbury is number 1, for example, and St Albans Abbey is number 15. The catalogue is arranged by authors' names and, following the title of each work, is the series of reference numbers indicating which English libraries possess the work. To make this catalogue, the Franciscans gained access to the most exclusive and ancient cathedral and monastic libraries and treated the books they found in them as so many units of information. The contrast between the old Benedictine rule of mulling over a single book for a year and the friars' demand for immediate information is clear.

The Dominicans and Franciscans thus showed that they had between them the experience required to construct alphabetical indexes to particular documents and to list works scattered in numerous repositories. Moreover, some of the authors of these systems were personally known to Henry III and Edward I. To ask why these kings made no use of such expertise, when it was readily available, is to expect too much too soon of the shift from memory to written record. The friars devised new guides to ancient works, like the Bible and the Church Fathers. The only equivalent document of ancient scripture for the king's government was Domesday Book and that was being consulted regularly and systematically by Edward I's reign; it had been so beautifully designed in the first place that an index was not essential. The royal records of the twelfth and thirteenth centuries, on the other hand, were too recent and too large and diverse to be seen as a whole. Their potential was not appreciated until the last years of Edward I's reign, when the dispute over Scotland compelled the king

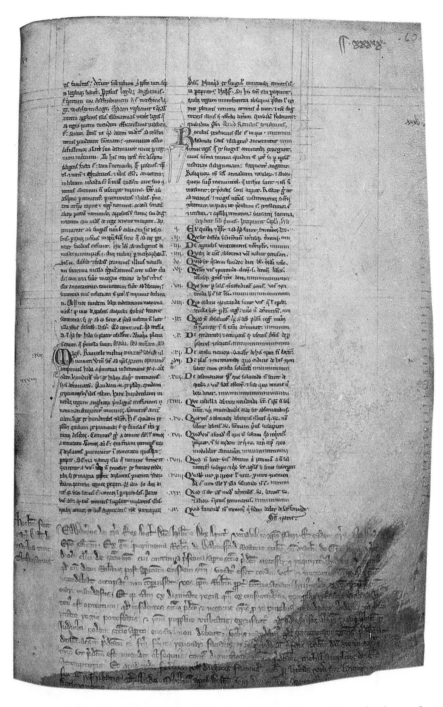

PLATE 16. A page from the Red Book, a lawbook containing the laws of Henry I and lists of knights' fees, and the text of the *Dialogue of the Exchequer*. This book was kept in the office of the Exchequer and referred to daily

to consider events from a historical point of view. Even then, he relied primarily on the evidence of monastic chronicles in preference to the royal archives. Although the difficulty of consulting his own records is a sufficient explanation for this procedure, there was probably political wisdom in it as well. If monasteries were asked to give evidence from their chronicles which had been compiled in the face of God, the king's case would be strengthened by this public process of consultation, whereas evidence which came exclusively from the royal archives could be said to be one-sided and clandestine.

Professional historians are bound to approach medieval archives in an anachronistic way. Their business is to hunt among documents for information and then rely on the evidence they find to construct an argument. Historians assume too readily that their medieval predecessors would have acted likewise. But in the world of thirteenth-century politics, where literate modes were relatively novel, written records were of limited value to governments. In Edward I's last years a terrible warning of what might happen to those who put their trust in written law and precedent was presented to Europe by the attack on Boniface VIII at Anagni in 1303. In a campaign of words, the pope had attempted to enforce his claims of overlordship over Philip IV of France. From the point of view of traditional ecclesiastical law Boniface's various bulls, particularly *Unam Sanctam*, were well founded. Yet in the *Dispute between a Cleric and a Knight*, which was composed as counter-propaganda, the Knight says:

> I had to laugh when I heard that Lord Boniface VIII had just decreed that he is and ought to be over all governments and kingdoms. That way he can easily acquire a right for himself over anything whatever: since all he has to do is to write, and everything will be his as soon as he has written.[19]

The Knight implies that the pope could not distinguish between the theories of his chancery and *curia* and the realities of power. In reality authority depended on country-keeping knights like himself, who did not believe in the creed of writing everything down. In the *quo warranto* proceedings against the magnates, and perhaps also in his claim to overlordship in Scotland, Edward I showed that he too had been occasionally beguiled by the advice of academic lawyers with their confidence in written precedents, although by and large Edward relied on the sword rather than the pen.

Nor was it only knights and laymen who distrusted documents. In the

1180s some Parisian clerics who were going to litigate at the Roman curia were advised by the archbishop of Lyons: 'Do not confide in your decretals, for whether the pope decides for or against you, it will be said that he has decided justly.' That was realistic advice, as Pope Lucius III himself admitted in 1184: 'Because of the mass of business which is referred to the Apostolic See, we cannot possibly remember the tenor of our letters and other decisions. For this reason we may be tricked into contradicting what we have written earlier.' This naïve and honest revelation of helplessness in the face of the mass of records, 'the inextricable wood of decretal letters',[20] would no doubt have been shared by the clerks of Edward I's Chancery vis-à-vis their letters, if they had dared to confess to such incompetence. A comparable statement, though it differs in being weary and cynical rather than naïve, was made in 1279 about English official records by Roger of Seaton, who had recently retired from being chief justice of the Bench. When asked about the whereabouts of his plea rolls, he replied that they were deposited at the New Temple, but he added: 'Yet I cannot vouch for them for a number of reasons: because one thing is done and something else—more or less—is written in the rolls by the clerks, who are always failing to understand the litigants and disputants correctly.' Thus in Seaton's opinion the plea rolls, which were the most formal and solemn records of the king's court, were fundamentally unreliable because the clerks who wrote them were too stupid or too careless to understand the business of the court.

The wheel had come full circle. Records had been made first of all by monasteries as an act of worship and to inform posterity of selected historical portents. Then in the twelfth century the king's government had begun to use documents in its daily business; intermittently these documents accumulated into an archive of potential written precedents. They were a treasure like the crown jewels. In the last decade of Edward I's reign ambitious, but largely unsuccessful, attempts were made to search among the royal records for precedents. 'Search all the rolls and remembrances,' Edward ordered in 1300, 'search Domesday at the Exchequer at York and all the other rolls of the Exchequer and Chancery, so that nothing is left unsearched, then go to London to search all the other rolls there.'[21] In reality the authority of Edward I, or of any other king, depended more on his armies and castles than on his archives. The incalculable investment of time and skill in making records may not have been a benefit to the king's government. Or rather, lists of debts and the like were obviously useful for a year or two, but thereafter their only interest was historical. The government needed documents, but it did not necessarily require records. 'In fact, the sudden increase in documentation during the early 1290s seems to have been largely redundant.'[22]

Records had not originally been made for utilitarian purposes, measurable in cost-benefit terms. Rather they had been pledges to posterity and an assurance of the continuity of institutions under God's providence. Over the passage of centuries medieval royal documents have taken on the same qualities as monastic records: they have become a monument for posterity to the power and organisation of the kings who persisted in making and keeping them. Whether they were profitable in the twelfth and thirteenth centuries is a question asked only by professional historians. At the time courtiers and armies, castles and palaces, gold and silk, were doubtless more potent and immediate manifestations of royal wealth and power than parchments. But now that the king's men are buried, his buildings in ruins and his treasures dispersed, the hundreds of thousands of documents survive as the best memorial to past greatness. Ironically, in attempting to make an archive for daily and practical use, the English monarchy had created one of the greatest historical monuments of all time.

❧ VIII ❧
The Growth of Literacy

Literacy is unique among technologies in penetrating and structuring the intellect itself, which makes it hard for scholars, whose own skills are shaped by literacy, to reconstruct the mental changes which it brings about. This difficulty has often been noticed and is most clearly put, with reference to medieval England in particular, by Maitland:

> The habit of preserving some written record of all affairs of importance is a modern one in the north and west of Europe. But it is so prevalent and so much bound up with our daily habits that we have almost forgotten how much of the world's business, even in communities by no means barbarous, has been carried on without it.[1]

Having described how and when 'the habit of preserving some written record of all affairs of importance' grew up, it is important now to analyse developments in literate ways of thought. Because the formation of literate habits was relatively slow in England, documents from different dates can be used to pinpoint various aspects of the development. Some of these aspects are peculiar to medieval England, whereas others are common to all societies which have experienced the transition from memory to written record. Although it is difficult to reconstruct pre-literate ways of thought from historical documents, there is sufficient evidence over the two and a half centuries 1066–1307 to discern the main outlines. What is most evident is that literate habits and assumptions, comprising a literate mentality, had to take root in diverse social groups and areas of activity before literacy could grow or spread beyond a small class of clerical writers.

In medieval England all kinds of problems and prejudices had to be overcome before literate modes became acceptable to the rulers, and particularly to the knights in the counties upon whose lead further change depended. It was not, for example, a simple matter of writing down the language which was spoken, as a variety of languages and dialects were used, and Latin had a special status as the traditional language of literacy. To be *litteratus* meant to know Latin and not specifically to have the ability to read and write. The literacy of the laity is the most frequently discussed aspect of medieval literacy, yet that cannot be understood until the terms are defined in their medieval contexts.

The problems just described are peculiarly medieval. Added to them are the psychological differences between learning by ear and learning by looking at script. Medieval writing was mediated to the non-literate by the persistence of the habit of reading aloud and by the preference, even among the educated, for listening to a statement rather than scrutinising it in script. Writing had the profoundest effects on the nature of proof, as it seemed to be more durable and reliable than the spoken word. On the other hand, those who valued the traditional wisdom of remembrancers within their communities had reason to distrust it. In England at least, in matters of legal proof, compromises were made which helped written modes to become more acceptable. The growth of literacy was not a simple matter of providing more clerks and better schooling, as it penetrated the mind and demanded changes in the way people articulated their thoughts, both individually and collectively in society. The shift from memory to written record, then, was a cultural one, taking place in the imaginations and assumptions of numerous individuals. The unquantifiable sum total of these varied experiences—or rather, of those that are recorded in some form—constitute what may be described as the medieval 'literate mentality'.

Jacques Le Goff describes how in the Middle Ages 'between heaven and earth there was an incessant coming and going. The watchful choir of angels was drawn up against the cohort of demons who swooped on men whose sins called out to them. Jacob's ladder was erected between heaven and earth and on it the heavenly creatures climbed and descended ceaselessly in two columns.'[2] In one of his sermons Jacques de Vitry (who died in 1240) told the story of how a cleric in choir saw a devil weighed down with a sack. The devil explained that the sack was full of 'syllables and slurred utterances (*dictiones syncopate*) and verses of the psalms' which the clergy had stolen from God when enunciating their prayers incorrectly. This devil was described in sermons across England, France and Germany and was sometimes named 'Tutivillus'. The Oxford master and Franciscan friar, John of Wales, described in the 1280s how Tutivillus appeared in choir collecting up 'minutiae and little bits of the Psalms'.[3] Judging from his concern with correct diction in choir, this devil was a product of the monastic culture of the twelfth century and earlier. Although he had an exacting ear for Latin quantities, his skills were oral rather than literate; he simply stuffed the sounds he collected into his sack, weighing himself down the more he laboured.

In addition to the sack-carrying devil (or perhaps as a metamorphosis of him), another demon makes his appearance in the thirteenth century who specialised in written record. He sat in churches like the sack-carrier, but he was equipped with pen and parchment, with which he recorded the words not of the clergy but of the laity and gossiping women in particular. In *Handlyng Synne* Robert Manning described him, sitting unseen between two women, 'with penne and parchemen yn honde' writing down everything they said. V. Sekules has published a carving in the nave of Sleaford church depicting this scene: above the heads of two women squats a bat-like demon writing intently on a roll of parchment.[4] Sleaford is less than fifteen miles from Bourne in Lincolnshire, where Robert Manning came from, and the carving is contemporary with him (he claims to have started writing in 1303). M. Camille has discussed the little scribe who sits at the foot of the demon king's throne in the Lambeth Apocalypse (painted before 1281).[5] He is tonsured like a clerk and writes on an oblong piece of parchment, shaped like a royal writ, in incomprehensible devilish script. In a contemporary picture of Edward I doing justice three little tonsured clerks sit at the foot of his throne; two of them are shown writing. The scene which the scribe in the Lambeth Apocalypse is witnessing is the moment when Theophilus, the medieval Dr Faustus, shakes hands with the demon king and gives him his sealed charter, written in his own blood.

The Lambeth Apocalypse shows two types of written record in use at the court of the demon king: there is the charter which Theophilus hands over and also the writ in devilish script. This doubling-up of record-keeping accurately reflects the English royal court of Henry III or Edward I, where the charter which a litigant proffered might be copied by a royal clerk into a plea roll or Chancery record. The devil not only became literate in the thirteenth century, therefore, he also established a hellish bureaucracy to match that of the king or the pope. The bat-like demon who writes down what gossips say may not look as sinister as the scribes of the demon king, were it not that he emerges into the light of medieval art and literature at the same time as the inquisition. Ecclesiastical inquisitors, whose business was proving mortal sins, depended on written depositions of people's conversations. Although the Roman Inquisition against heresy was banned in England, conscientious bishops like Grosseteste did nevertheless investigate the laity's sins (particularly fornication) in their courts.

In the Lambeth Apocalypse the scene of record-making at the court of the demon king was most probably painted for Lady Eleanor de Quincy, who kneels in an accompanying picture at the feet of the Virgin Mary.[6] In the Theophilus story it is the Virgin who rescues him and his charter from

Hell. A Book of Hours illuminated by William de Brailes some thirty years before the Lambeth Apocalypse shows the Virgin wresting Theophilus's charter from a devil, who grasps its seal-tag with both hands.[7] The Virgin restores the charter to Theophilus by giving this devil a blow to the forehead with her enlarged fist. A caption in French alongside this scene confirms that the Virgin succeeded in recovering the complete document: *tout la chartre*. In the Lambeth Apocalypse the Virgin is similarly shown wresting the charter from a devil's grip, this time with the assistance of an angel who spears him through the throat. The Lambeth Apocalypse and the de Brailes Hours were made for ladies; indeed most of the first illustrated Apocalypses and Books of Hours in England were made for ladies. They may have liked the Theophilus story because it showed the Virgin triumphing over men, in the guise of devils, including their husbands and fathers. The story's concern with written record would also have appealed, particularly to those ladies whose happiness depended on the enforcement or cancellation of written contracts. In 1302 John de Camoys conveyed his wife Margaret to William Paynel by charter. In the scene in the de Brailes Hours where Theophilus does homage to the devil, his charter is labelled *Carta Theofoli* to emphasise its importance; the caption to this miniature reiterates in French that this is an *escrit chartre*.

In the Lambeth Apocalypse and the de Brailes Hours, as in other books of this sort, the mixture of Latin and French on the pages raises questions about what languages their lady users understood. The practice of using French to caption illustrations goes back to the monastic books of the twelfth century; it is a convention of presentation rather than a comment on the patron's linguistic acumen. Captions are written in French in order to indicate that they are not integral parts of the Latin scriptural text. In the Becket story-book (made for Isabel de Warenne under the direction of Matthew Paris), where the text is in French, the picture captions are put in Latin. In the de Brailes Hours they are written in rubrics, in a smaller informal script, to distinguish them further from the blackletter Latin text. In most Books of Hours and Apocalypses the main text (whether in French or Latin) is the easiest part to read, as the lettering is large and the passages are mainly familiar prayers or liturgical readings. Even though no lady owner of a prayer-book could have learned Latin in a grammar school (because schools became male preserves in the twelfth century or earlier), constant repetition and reading aloud would have made the contents of scriptural texts familiar. Furthermore women may have received some formal instruction at home, as the households of great ladies had chaplains, books and private chambers.

The difficulty for Lady Eleanor de Quincy probably did not lie in reading (in the sense of voicing or articulating) the Latin text or the French captions in her book, but in comprehending the pictures. The Apocalypse or 'Book of Revelation' contained mysteries. Ladies like Eleanor, who imitated their chaplains by possessing sacred books, had to learn to read the scripture, as the clergy did, at four or more levels of meaning: historical, allegorical, tropological, and anagogical. Literal construing of the Latin gave the reader no more than the 'historical' or contextual meaning of the text, which was merely the first step. 'The letter killeth, but the spirit giveth life' (2 Corinthians III, 6) was well understood by medieval readers. The letters of scripture were illuminated and embellished in medieval books in order to give them greater significance and memorability. From embellishing initial letters and the margins of pages, it was a relatively short step to presenting half pages, or even whole pages, in pictures as in Eleanor's book. Precedents for making picture-pages existed from the earliest Romano-Christian and Irish books.

In a de luxe book like the Lambeth Apocalypse the pictures are undeniably ornate; they glow with gold-leaf and expensive pigments. At the same time they are functional, as they illustrate the scriptural text page by page. For the pious user of a book like the Lambeth Apocalypse, moreover, beyond ornament and illustration lay the inviting realm of contemplation, where the reader sought for visionary meanings, which transcended the literal interpretation of the text and the representations in the illustrations. The Apocalypse was peculiarly well suited to this sort of reading, as it announced in its first chapter:

> *Beatus qui legit et audit verba prophetiae hujus*: Blessed is he that readeth and they that hear the words of this prophecy, and keep those things which are written therein; for the time is at hand.

Whereas the prophets of the Old Testament were extinct volcanoes now that Christ had come, the Apocalypse still held its promise of imminent doom for some and salvation for others. It had been much resorted to in the eleventh and twelfth centuries, judging by the use of its imagery in Romanesque art. What is new in the thirteenth century is lay people, and ladies in particular, getting Apocalypses for their own private use. The pictures in them vividly portray the scenes described by the author: earthquake and massacre, the seven-headed dragon, the beast, the great harlot and so on. In their sensationalism these 'Doomsday Books' are the equivalent of the tabloid press of the twentieth century. Eleanor de Quincy was countess of Winchester; English aristocratic ladies still enjoy the same sort of reading material, much of it pictorial, in daily newspapers.

Pope Gregory the Great had justified the use of images in worship by arguing that pictures let the illiterate 'read by seeing (*videndo legant*) on walls in churches what they are unable to read in books'.[8] This idea soon became a commonplace, which allowed the literate clergy to patronise the laity and justified the veneration of images, though Pope Gregory himself—by using the word *legere* of pictures—had been hinting at something more profound about the relationship between images and writing. As a commonplace, Gregory's words were recalled in another de luxe book made for an English lady, Christina of Markyate, a century and more before the Lambeth Apocalypse. In addition to over 200 picture initials, Christina's Psalter has forty full-page pictures showing the progress of the Christian dispensation from the Garden of Eden to Pentecost. Following these pictures is a page citing Pope Gregory's justification of images, written in both Latin and French. The editors of Christina's Psalter thought its scribe was responsible for this citation, but the decision to provide such a large number of picture pages and to justify their use by papal authority probably came from a more exalted source in the ecclesiastical hierarchy. The most likely candidate is Geoffrey, abbot of St Albans (1119–46), who was an entrepreneur of book production as well as being Christina's patron. Christina, who was a visionary like her contemporary Hildegard of Bingen, presumably 'read' the pictures by meditating on them. The translation of Pope Gregory's words into French suggests that Christina read French rather than Latin, though her biographer says nothing about her literacy or linguistic abilities. (Hildegard came to understand Latin by divine inspiration at the age of 43 in 1141.) Christina had been born into the Anglo-Danish patriciate of Huntingdon, and English was presumably her mother tongue.

The full-page Annunciation scene in Christina's Psalter is the earliest representation to show the Virgin Mary unequivocally as a reader meditating on a text. (There are Carolingian and Anglo-Saxon representations of the Virgin Annunciate with an open book on a lectern, and eleventh-century ones of her with a closed book on her lap, but Christina's Psalter is the first representation to combine the open book with the lap.) The language of the text is unspecified, as the pages are blank, though late medieval representations of the Virgin had no hesitation in showing her with a Latin or vernacular text. In Annunciation scenes before the thirteenth century, the Virgin is ordinarily shown spinning, without a book in sight, whereas in the fourteenth and fifteenth centuries she is often depicted as a pious reader in an oratory with up to half a dozen books. In keeping with the shift from memory to written record, the clergy made the Virgin into a reader in their own image, much as they made the devil into a writer. Both ideas were disseminated to the laity by sermons. A sermon by Ailred, abbot of Rievaulx (1147–67), describes how, at the moment of the Annunciation, the Virgin held the book of Isaiah in her hands and read the verse: 'Behold a virgin shall conceive.'[9] This may be what the Virgin is doing in Christina's Psalter: the book is open on her lap and she raises her eyes from it to the Angel Gabriel at the door, as if she had been interrupted in her reading. This representation of the Virgin absorbed in her studies provided a role model for Christina herself, as she sat in her busy hermitage (by Watling Street on the London road) interrupted by her own visions and passing visitors. Abbot Geoffrey of St Albans, who had been a master in the schools before becoming a monk, may have designed this studious image of the Virgin for her. It became, in the Books of Hours of the later Middle Ages, the most popular of all images of the Virgin.

Pope Gregory's 'read by seeing' is rendered into English in an early fourteenth-century prologue to an Apocalypse, addressed to *Who redes this boke of ymagerie*—'Whoever reads this book of imagery'.[10] In the Lambeth Apocalypse one full-page picture specifies by numerous captions in French how it should be 'read'. In the bottom left-hand corner of this page sits a lady, a younger and prettier version of Eleanor de Quincy, on a wooden chair carved with the elaboration of a royal or episcopal throne. A caption at her head explains: *par la Dame est signifie repentant*—'by the Lady is signified the penitent'. On the finial on the back of her chair perches a dove symbolising the Holy Spirit, who expounds the scripture to the Lady. The Lady defends her front with the shield of faith, which has three bosses at its corners, spelling out the persons of the Trinity and meeting in a central boss marked *deu*—'God'. Her shield is directed at a devil, who shoots arrows of evil suggestions at her; in appearance he is like the demons who beguile Theophilus in the same book. Above the Lady's head circle large bluish flies, signifying those empty thoughts which disturb the penitent at prayer. Many other features in this picture of the Lady Penitent are similarly explained by captions, and on other folios in the Lambeth Apocalypse there are pictures with explanations almost as elaborate. Their interest in the present context lies in the questions they raise about the medieval literate mentality.

Was Lady Eleanor de Quincy *alias* the Lady Penitent literate? In the Lambeth Apocalypse she is depicted holding it, or another prayer-book, open while she prays to the Virgin and Child. Was a lady's ability to recite daily prayers, in Latin or French, literacy? There is no evidence that Lady Eleanor, or Christina of Markyate, could write. Nor is the Virgin Mary ever depicted in an Annunciation scene making a note of the Angel Gabriel's message, though in Virgin and Child scenes the Child is sometimes shown writing. The Virgin was expected to remember the angelic message by taking it into her innermost being: 'Mary kept all these words and pondered them in her heart' (Luke 11, 19). In his treatise on memory Hugh of St Victor explained how knowledge is a treasury and 'your heart is its strong-box' (see page 327 above). He recommended remembering what one read, rather than depending on the written text. This was prudent in manuscript culture, when no two books were exactly alike and books were hard to come by anyway. But, in emphasising the priority of memory, Hugh's concern was probably religious and ideological rather than utilitarian.

The danger with writing was that it implanted forgetfulness in the soul, as Socrates had said, preventing people from recalling the truth from within themselves. Writing anything down externalised it and—in that process—changed it and falsified it to some extent. 'Writing restructures consciousness,' as W. J. Ong has put it.[11] Throughout twelfth-century Europe charters and title-deeds were frequently forged by monks, the experts in writing. They understood very well, from their experience in expounding and copying holy scripture, that a document which stated something untrue or unverifiable would continue to state it—and make it look authentic and proven—as long as that document existed. In all societies literates face problems about whether writing is true or not. In modern western culture the primary meaning of 'writer' is a creator of fiction. Unaccustomed to the convention of the fictitious narrator in the modern novel, twelfth-century readers were unsure whether Geoffrey of Monmouth or Walter Map was a historian or a liar. Writing was untrustworthy in itself, and furthermore its use implied distrust, if not chicanery, on the part of the writer. An honest person held to his word and did not demand written proof. It was appropriate that the devil should become a writer. The recording demon consumed rolls of parchment noting down people's sins and made himself ridiculous, according to the preachers, by trying to stretch the parchment with his teeth to accommodate his screeds. (The skin is stretched in the process of manufacturing parchment, but the finished product has little elasticity.) Likewise the ugly little clerk in the Lambeth Apocalypse, who sat at the foot of the demon king's throne writing in his devilish script, was no more to be admired by noble people than the scriveners of the king's Chancery or the law clerks in Westminster Hall.

Writing was a very necessary activity, but it was not to be done by great ladies like the Virgin Mary, Christina of Markyate and Eleanor de Quincy. They were its beneficiaries, not its makers. They understood the significance of writing and enjoyed its fruits, in the form of their splendid books and of documents (whether true or false) entitling them to their material privileges. The illuminated and gem-encrusted books of the Middle Ages were indeed made for the glory of God and his saints, but equally they were made to glorify their owners and donors. Christina's and Eleanor's books were designed for conspicuous display as much as any piece of jewellery. They are akin to the large enamelled brooches and golden torques, which in the Celtic world had distinguished aristocrats from their social inferiors for a millennium. Abbot Geoffrey of St Albans headed one of the richest and most exclusive corporations in medieval England; in the name of piety and learning he conferred the distinction of its wealth, in the form of a Psalter, on Christina of Markyate. Her Psalter and the Lambeth Apocalypse show that lady readers might enjoy both a heavenly and an earthly reward.

The reading ability of these ladies was not the equivalent of modern reading. In many ways it was more demanding. It was not sufficient simply to read the mother tongue. Ideally ladies (and gentlemen) in twelfth- and thirteenth-century England should be able to read in three languages at least: Latin, French and English. In their religious devotions they had also 'to read the book of imagery', that is, to understand through the labour of meditation the forms and signs of divine revelation. In the Lambeth Apocalypse one picture-page illustrates the story of the monk who kept the face of the Virgin Mary so successfully in his mind's eye that the Virgin appeared to come alive and the holy Child gestured towards him. This was a model for the level of concentration that Lady Eleanor should have in her study of the book. People who succeeded in doing this and who became visionaries, like Christina of Markyate, won prestige and wealth. Christina's Psalter is one of the most expensive artefacts made in twelfth-century England. Another very rich manuscript, originating from St Albans and identified with the Winchester Bible, was arbitrarily given by Henry II to Hugh of Lincoln; the king believed that Hugh's power of prayer had saved him from shipwreck when crossing the Channel.

The profits of literacy, in terms of both heavenly and earthly advantage, were therefore best sought in religious reading. Skill in writing (which was taught separately from reading) could be rewarding for scribes working in rich monasteries and professional ateliers, like Eadwine 'the prince of writers', but such men were the exceptions. Most

writing involved repetitive manual labour of the type done by the recording demons and the king's clerks. Neither for reading nor for writing
were materials readily available in domestic settings. Consequently the
relatively few books that there were, of which Christina's Psalter and
Eleanor's Apocalypse are outstanding examples (by and large only the
finest manuscripts have been preserved), were studied by their owners
intensively and repeatedly, over years or decades, in order to seek out their
deeper levels of meaning. This involved a variety of reading strategies:
hearing the text read aloud while looking at the lettering and images on
the pages; repeating the text aloud with one or more companions, until it
was learned by heart; construing the grammar and vocabulary of the languages of the text silently in private; translating or transposing the text,
aloud or silently, into Latin, French or English; examining the pictures
and their captions, together with the illuminated letters, as a preparation
for reading the imagery.

The ultimate stage of reading was contemplation, when the reader
'saw with his heart', like St John the author of the Apocalypse, the truth of
hidden things. In this stage, text and image combined with the reader's
own perceptions and feelings to produce enlightenment. Richard, prior of
St Victor, who is contemporary with Christina of Markyate and had contacts with St Albans, described how 'contemplation endures (*permanet*)
without labour but with fruit', whereas thinking on its own was fruitless.
Such a non-utilitarian approach to reading is alien to modern western
culture. Richard of St Victor would be more at home now in a Buddhist
community than in his native Scotland or in the University of Paris. Similar reading strategies were applied to secular romances and other forms
of vernacular literature, which were rendered into fine manuscripts from
the thirteenth century onwards. Often they were bound into books alongside religious texts. For many medieval readers, tales of King Arthur or
Alexander the Great were not essentially different in their structure and
content from tales of King David or Jesus Christ.

Medieval texts were designed to be read in a variety of ways—orally or
silently, by one person or in a group—and at different levels of meaning,
taking account of word and image and a variety of linguistic registers. Even
common law writs, the most mundane of business documents, were
embellished in that they bore on them the great seal of the king, with its
two-sided image signifying laws (the king enthroned in majesty) and arms
(the king riding as a knight). Most exceptionally, the text of a charter of
Edward I's, granting hunting rights to Roger of Pilkington in 1291, is surrounded on all four sides with good coloured drawings of animals, birds

and trees, as if to embody the privileges it grants. The charter may have been granted in this form as a sign of royal favour, as the realistic depiction of birds in particular is characteristic of the finest illuminated manuscripts associated with Edward I's family, like the Alphonso Psalter and the Ashridge *Historia Scholastica*. Medieval users of books understood very well that picturing and writing are connected. 'Writing stands at the basis of the picture just as much as the picture stands at the basis of writing.'[12]

Enough has been said by way of introduction to show that medieval attitudes to literacy differed in a variety of ways from our own. Our modern literate mentality makes it difficult to understand theirs. Ideally and traditionally, medieval readers were concerned with quality in their literacy rather than quantity. Similar criteria applied to writing. Soon after the invention of printing in the fifteenth century, the abbot of Sponheim commented contemptuously that paper books would only survive a couple of centuries, whereas parchment manuscripts had been made to last for a thousand years. Medieval owners of books like Christina of Markyate and Eleanor de Quincy may not have known how to write, but they did know what good writing should be like: it should be magnificent and awe-inspiring. How much responsibility these ladies had for the design of the books they owned is unknown. Any medieval book owner, however, had a more personal relationship with his books than a modern literate who buys a mass-produced item in a bookstore.

Although the modern literate receives his books in mass-produced and stereotyped forms, he has a more individualistic approach to handwriting than his medieval predecessor. Literates reacted to the mechanisation of writing, after the invention of printing, by cultivating their own distinctive and idiosyncratic writing styles. In the form of personal signatures on credit cards, these are accepted in modern societies as warrants of authenticity. Medieval people, on the other hand, warranted documents with their seals or by a notary's mark; handwriting was the business of professionals, who aimed to make it as uniform and impersonal as possible. The ability to write well, in the sense in which Eadwine 'the prince of writers' wrote well, is as alien to the average modern literate as the ability to read a text at different levels of meaning. Our twentieth-century western form of literacy is not an invariable norm; it is as culture-bound and shaped by available technologies as medieval manuscript literacy was. Comparing medieval norms with modern ones puts current questions about literacy in perspective. The best way of understanding the modern western literate mentality is to see where it came from. The abbot of Sponheim looked back on a tradition of manuscript writing which had lasted for a thousand years (over the medieval millennium AD 500–1500) and repeatedly renewed itself. Twentieth-century planners and educators, on the other hand, have found it difficult to provide even for a decade in advance.

❧ IX ❧

LITERATE AND ILLITERATE

In the summer of 1297 some jurors from Norfolk came to the court of King's Bench to attest that Robert de Tony was twenty-one years of age and was therefore entitled to have his wardship terminated. Proving the age of feudal heirs by sworn testimony was a routine procedure at the time, in which each juror attempted to recollect some memorable event which coincided with the birth of the child in question. Jurors might recall, for example, specific gifts or public events or accidents to themselves or their neighbours.[1] Thus in a case in 1304 at Skipton in Yorkshire Robert Buck, aged forty-one, remembered being at school at Clitheroe where he had been so badly beaten that he ran away and that was twenty-one years ago. Such a cumbersome system was required because births were only rarely recorded in registers. This customary method of establishing the age of individuals by collective oral testimony is a good example of the medieval reliance on memory rather than written record.

The case from Norfolk in 1297 is exceptional in that the proof primarily depended not on the usual personal recollections, but on a record of the date of Robert de Tony's birth (4 April 1276), which had been written down in the chronicles of West Acre Priory. This record had not been made at the time of Robert's birth, as he was born in Scotland, but a year or more later when he was brought down to West Acre Priory, of which the de Tony family were the founders, by his mother. She seems to have been seeking the protection of the priory on her son's behalf and had his date of birth written down there to establish that he was the lawful de Tony heir. Because the circumstances of Robert's birth could not have been known to the Norfolk jurors from personal experience in the customary way, resort had to be made to the West Acre chronicle.

The first juror, William de la Sale of Swaffham, therefore gave evidence that he had seen the chronicle and read it and was thereby certain of Robert's age. Six other jurors agreed with William without exception or addition, that is, they too claimed to have read the chronicle and understood its significance. Three more likewise agreed and added ancillary recollections: Robert Corlu said his younger brother was born in the same year who was now twenty-one; John Kempe said his father had died five years after Robert had been brought down from Scotland. The eleventh juror, John Laurence, agreed with William 'with this exception, that he had not read the aforesaid chronicles because he is *laycus*'. The twelfth, Roger of Creston, attested the same. A thirteenth juror (why evidence was taken from thirteen men instead of twelve is not explained), Thomas of Weasenham, said that he had neither seen nor read the chronicle, but he had learned of its contents from the prior. Thomas was not necessarily incapable of reading like John and Roger. He may have presented his evidence in this form simply because he had not been present on the day his fellow jurors saw the chronicle.

Thus, of the thirteen men examined, ten swore that they could read the entry in the chronicle, an eleventh may have been able to read, and two were unable to do so. The latter two were described as *layci* (laymen) presumably because they had no 'clergy' in the sense of a reading knowledge of Latin. In his book which aimed to help the English gentry improve their French, Walter of Bibbesworth took it for granted in the 1250s or 1260s, the time when these Norfolk jurors were growing up, that the gentry usually had experience from childhood of the 'book which teaches us *clergie*'.² Those without this knowledge were 'laymen' in the modern sense of being inexpert. The other jurors were 'clergy' only in the sense of knowing some Latin. William de la Sale and his fellows were no churchmen. They were knights and freemen of the neighbourhood, approximately the social equals of the heir in question, as required in jury trial procedure.

This case therefore shows that from a random sample of thirteen gentlemen of Norfolk at the end of the thirteenth century, ten could read an entry in a chronicle, two could not, and one's ability is unrecorded. Those who swore that they had read the chronicle were presumably telling the truth, as they risked being cross-examined in the King's Bench, and they had no apparent motive for perjuring themselves since they were not claiming benefit of clergy. The statement that two of the jurors were incapable of reading, together with the unspecific testimony about Thomas of Weasenham, adds credibility to the contrasting testimony of the rest. Although evidence of proof of age was sometimes falsified, there is no reason to reject the essential facts of this testimony. Obviously no generalisations about levels of literacy can be made from a unique case. On the other hand, the evidence of this case, that the great majority of the jurors examined were capable of reading one line of Latin in a chronicle, need cause no surprise. The procedure for giving juries' verdicts in royal courts, which depended on documents written in Latin and perhaps also in French and English, demanded a higher level of literacy among jurors than that. By 1297 the two who were unable to read at this elementary level are more surprising than the ten who could do so.

The fact that most of these Norfolk gentlemen could read conflicts in appearance only with the medieval axiom that laymen are illiterate and its converse that clergy are literate. The terms cleric and lay, literate and illiterate, were used in ways which preserved intact the appearances of these fundamental axioms while acknowledging the realities of daily experience, where some clergy were ignorant and some knights knew more of books than brave deeds. Traditional roles had become confused, as Nigel de Longchamp of Canterbury observed with regret in *c.* 1192: 'In the church today there are clergy without knowledge of letters, just as there are many knights without skill and practice in arms, who for that reason are called "Holy Mary's knights" by the others.'[3] This discrepancy between theory and practice, between literature and life, did not of course mean that the ideals were immediately altered to fit the facts. On the contrary, the ideals of the learned cleric and the valorous knight became reinforced as fantasies, which had three or four centuries of vigorous life before them in literature and academic treatises.

The axiom that laymen are illiterate and its converse had originated by combining two distinct antitheses:

clericus: laicus
litteratus: illitteratus

The latter antithesis derived from classical Latin, where *litteratus* meant 'literate' in something like its modern sense and also (in the most classical usage of Cicero) described a person with *scientia litterarum*, meaning a 'knowledge of letters' in the sense of 'literature'. The former antithesis derived from the Greek *kleros*, meaning a 'selection by lot' and hence subsequently the 'elect' of God in terms of Christian salvation, whereas *laos* meant the 'people' or crowd. Gradually in the process of Christian conversion those who were specially consecrated to the service of God, the *clerici* or 'clergy', became distinct from the mass of the people, the *laici* or 'laity'. The antithesis *clericus: laicus* was thus a medieval creation, while *litteratus: illitteratus* was of Roman origin. In the half-millennium AD 500 – 1000 the reduction of the number of learned men in the west coincided with the expansion of Christianity by the conversion of the barbarians. As a consequence *clerici* began to be associated with *litterati*, although the two concepts had originally nothing in common. This association of ideas reflected the fact that outside the Mediterranean area nearly all Latinists were churchmen and most were monks. As academic standards declined, *litteratus*, which had meant 'lettered' or 'learned' for Cicero, more often came to mean 'literate' in the sense of having a minimal ability to read Latin. Such *litterati* were still learned compared with the great majority, who had no Latin or book learning at all.

These first clerical *litterati*, whose sparse knowledge had scarcely anything in common with the Latin scholars either of ancient Rome or of the twelfth-century Renaissance, established a privileged status for themselves in society by despising non-Latinists as an ignorant crowd of *laici*. In reality the *clerici* were unsure of their status, as Europe was dominated not by them but by warriors with a non-literate sense of values. Charlemagne and Alfred were exceptional in wanting the nobility to be better Latinists; their examples were lauded by the clergy to encourage the others. Dark-Age Europe was far from unique in creating an élite of priests who monopolised writing, yet who were constantly aware of their impotence *vis-à-vis* the dominant war-lords. The supposed gulf between cleric and lay, between the elect and damned, was some compensation to the clergy, although not even Pope Gregory VII could make it a reality for long in the terrestrial world.

Thus by constant repetition the pairs of antitheses, *clericus: laicus* and *litteratus: illitteratus*, were coupled in the mind. The terms of each antithesis became interchangeable and ultimately synonymous. By the twelfth century *clericus* meant *litteratus*, *laicus* meant *illitteratus*, and vice versa. The case from Norfolk has already illustrated *laicus* being used to mean *illitteratus*. The converse (*clericus* meaning *litteratus*) was discussed in detail in the 1170s by Philip of Harvengt, who observed that a person was not called a cleric unless he was 'imbued with letters', and hence:

> A usage of speech has taken hold whereby when we see someone *litteratus*, immediately we call him *clericus*. Because he acts the part that is a cleric's, we assign him the name *ex officio*. Thus if anyone is comparing a knight who is *litteratus* with a priest who is ignorant, he will exclaim with confidence and affirm with an oath that the knight is a better *clericus* than the priest . . . This improper usage has become so prevalent that whoever gives attention to letters, which is clerkly, is named *clericus*.

Philip, like Nigel de Longchamp and other writers on the state of the clergy, deplored the way real knights and clergy no longer fitted the traditional roles assigned to them. More important in the present context is his observation that a learned knight would be called a *clericus*, because that implies that a person described as *clericus* in a document was not necessarily a member of the clergy. Such a person is just as likely to have been an educated layman.

Philip of Harvengt's comments are best illustrated in England by Matthew Paris's obituary of Paulin Peyver or Piper, a steward of Henry III who died in 1251. He is described as *miles litteratus sive clericus militaris*, 'a literate knight or knightly clerk'. Matthew thus emphasised that these terms were interchangeable in Paulin's case. Paulin was a cleric only in the learned sense, as he had numerous knights' fees and a wife and legitimate children. Similarly the Northamptonshire knight, Henry de Bray, who was born in 1269 and wrote his own cartulary, noted that his maternal grandfather, Richard lord of Harlestone, 'was called Ricardus Clericus because he was *litteratus*'. The most familiar example of this usage is the nickname 'Clerk' or 'Beauclerk' given to Henry I. How learned Henry really was is a separate and controversial question; certainly he was described by Orderic Vitalis as *litteratus* and 'nurtured in natural and doctrinal science'.[4] A *clericus* in common parlance was therefore a person of some scholarly attainments, regardless of whether he was a churchman. As early as the third decade of the twelfth century a polemic of English origin, commenting on the large number of schoolmasters, asked rhetorically: 'Are there not everywhere on earth masters of the liberal arts, who are also called *clerici*?'[5] Peter the Chanter summarised the situation in around 1200: 'There are two kinds of *clerici* and in both there are good and bad, namely those who are ecclesiastics and those who are scholastics.'[6]

The use of *clericus* and *litteratus* as interchangeable terms, both meaning 'learned' or 'scholarly', is clearest in Jocelin of Brakelond's descriptions of the debates within Bury St Edmunds Abbey over the election of Abbot Samson in 1182 and Prior Herbert in 1200. On each occasion the more scholarly monks argued that they must be governed by *litterati* and not by the ignorant. Their opponents teased them with a new litany. '*A bonis clericis, libera nos, Domine!*' (From good clerics, good Lord, deliver us), and with puns about learning Latin grammar, 'Our good *clerici* have declined so often in the cloister that now they themselves have declined.'[7] *Clericus* was a relative term. Thus Jocelin has one monk say: 'That brother is something of a cleric [*aliquantulum clericus*], although much learning [*littere*] doth not make him mad.' On another occasion Jocelin told of how Hubert Walter, the archbishop of Canterbury, had to admit that Abbot Samson was a better *clericus* than he was, meaning that Samson was the better scholar. The way Jocelin uses *clericus* is explained by Philip of Harvengt, who notes that when we meet a monk of humanity and charity,

We ask him whether he is a *clericus*. We don't want to know whether he has been ordained to perform the office of the altar, but only whether he is *litteratus*. The monk will therefore reply to the question by saying that he is a *clericus* if he is *litteratus*, or conversely a *laicus* if he is *illitteratus*.

It might be added that a monk who aspired to Christian humility would not call himself *litteratus*, even if he were of scholarly inclinations. Thus Adam of Eynsham, in his life of St Hugh of Lincoln, claims not to know how to satisfy the *litterati*, who will cavil at his style and simple narrative. Adam is using here the hagiographer's common device of making his story appear more truthful by being naïve.

As *clericus* and *litteratus* both meant learned, it followed that a person of no great book learning was a *laicus*, a 'layman', even if he were a monk or a priest. Thus Archbishop Hubert Walter was described by the chronicler of St Augustine's Abbey at Canterbury as *laicus et illitteratus*. Hubert was not of course a layman in the ecclesiastical sense, nor was he illiterate in any modern sense, as he was the chief justiciar and chancellor who did more than any other individual to create the royal archives. The St Augustine's Abbey chronicler was using *laicus* and *illitteratus* as terms of abuse—he also called Hubert a legal *ignoramus*—but he was not using these terms inaccurately. Hubert was a *laicus* in Philip of Harvengt's sense and *illitteratus* in Jocelin's, as he lacked the academic learning of Bologna or Paris. That academic snob, Gerald of Wales, alleged that Hubert's Latin was shaky and that his only school had been the Exchequer.

Like *clericus*, *litteratus* was a relative term. Whether a particular individual was appropriately described as *litteratus* was a matter of opinion, since essentially it meant 'learned'. The same man might be *litteratus* in one assessment and *illitteratus* in another. Thus Ralf Nevill, Henry III's chancellor and bishop of Chichester, was certified by a papal legate as *litteratus* when elected dean of Lichfield in 1214, but *illitteratus* by another papal adviser in 1231 when his candidature for the archbishopric of Canterbury was rejected. Conscientious churchmen considered Ralf to be a worldly administrator. Like Hubert Walter, he was no *clericus* or *litteratus* in the ideal sense of being either the elect of God or a scholar. On this occasion in 1231 the successful candidate for Canterbury, St Edmund of Abingdon, was both. Hubert and Ralf were not the only distinguished churchmen and administrators to be described as *illitteratus*. To their company should be added Roger, bishop of Salisbury, Henry I's chief justiciar, and the controversial Abbot Ording of Bury St Edmunds. In the exalted view of John of Salisbury, who aspired to Ciceronian standards, all those who are ignorant of the Latin poets, historians, orators, and math-ematicians should be called *illitterati* 'even if they know letters'.

John's contention is taken for granted by Walter Map when he described a boy he had known, who was a paragon and was 'educated among us and by us'; yet 'he was not *litteratus*, which I regret, although he knew how to transcribe any series of letters whatever.'[8] Walter would have liked to have described this boy as *litteratus*, since he was one of his kins-men, but he had to admit that nice penmanship was no substitute for scholarship. He adds that the boy left England and became a knight of Philip of Flanders (1168–91). At his learned court, where many of 'the order of laymen' knew 'letters' (according to Philip of Harvengt), this boy would presumably not have been numbered among the *milites litterati*. The ability to write well comprised the technical skill of an artist and was not an integral part of the science of letters. Writing is not included among the skills which cause Philip of Harvengt's knight who is *litteratus* to be described as a *clericus*. In Philip's opinion the essential abilities are to read, understand, compose by dictation, make verse, and express oneself in the Latin language. The medieval *miles litteratus* was thus a gentleman edu-cated in the classics; he embodied a recurrent ideal in European culture.

The way the words *clericus* and *litteratus* were used has been discussed in detail here because such examples demonstrate that neither word, when applied to an individual, can be accurately translated by its modern equivalent. A *clericus* was not necessarily either a 'cleric' or a 'clerk', although he was someone with a reputation for erudition. Likewise a per-son described as *litteratus* was much more than 'literate' in the modern sense. Counting the number of persons called *clericus*, or making lists of knights described as *litteratus*, provides examples of persistent and char-acteristic medieval ways of thinking, but it throws no light on whether such persons, whether designated cleric or lay by ecclesiastical law, were 'literate' in a twentieth-century sense of that word.

Discussions of medieval literacy have been bedevilled by the difficulty of distinguishing between the modern 'literate' and the medieval *litteratus*. When a knight is described as *litteratus* in a medieval source, his excep-tional erudition is usually being referred to, not his capacity to read and write. Such knights were rare because good Latin scholars have always been rare among country gentry and government officials in England. A few existed even in this period. Thus shortly after the Conquest a Norman called Robert, *miles ille litteratus*, endowed St Albans Abbey with an income to provide books for the church. He probably had a greater inter-est in books than most of the monks. About a century later Gerald of

Wales tells how a *miles litteratus* appeared as a ghost, demanding to play a game of capping Latin verses with a learned master, for that had been his 'social recreation' when he was alive. Similarly Matthew Paris is recording his admiration for the learning and not the elementary schooling of John of Lexington, when he describes him as *miles elegans* (refined) *et facundus* (eloquent) *et litteratus*, or of Roger de Thurkelby, *miles et litteratus*. John was the keeper of the royal seal, whose obituary Matthew was writing in 1257, while Roger was one of the few royal judges who possessed legal wisdom in Matthew's opinion.

The historian's initial difficulty, when discussing the literacy of the laity, is to avoid anachronisms. Medieval ideas of literacy were so different from those of today that some modern questions are meaningless. To ask, 'Were laymen illiterate?' is a tautology: of course *laici* were *illitterati* because these terms were synonyms. Faced with the question another way round, 'Were laymen literate?' a medieval schoolman might have thought that he was being invited to take part in an exercise in elementary dialectic. Asking whether laymen were literates was like asking whether evil was good or black was white. Every bachelor of arts knew that the validity of axioms such as these was not affected by individual cases of moral imperfection or greyness in this imperfect world. The axiom that *clerici* were *litterati* and its converse belonged to the same order of thinking. Contemporaries, like Philip of Harvengt or Jocelin of Brakelond, knew of numerous exceptions in their daily experience, but they saved the appearances of the rules by calling learned knights *clerici* and ignorant monks *laici*. Such axioms cannot be equated with twentieth-century historians' generalisations, which derive from an assessment of a multitude of individual cases. Scholastic axioms derived their validity not from individual experience but from universal rules, which were superior and prior to particular cases because they were part of a divine order of things. When explaining medieval ways of thought it is correct to say that all laymen were considered illiterate, yet it would be mistaken to conclude from that proposition that in any particular time or place all non-churchmen were unable to read or write. Scholastic axioms differ from real cases.

Another anachronism is the assumption that the capacity to read and write is a simple and constant measure which readily applies to medieval cases. The automatic coupling of reading with writing and the close association of literacy with the language one speaks are not universal norms, but products of modern European culture. Literacy in this modern sense is so deeply implanted from childhood in every twentieth-century scholar that it is difficult to liberate oneself from its preconceptions, or to avoid thinking of it as an automatic measure of progress. Over the last two centuries medievalists have painfully learned to overcome anachronisms when discussing feudal society or scholastic philosophy. Yet, when they reach elementary education and literate skills, they tend to assume that these problems can be readily understood by applying modern criteria and experience to the medieval past. Past ideas must be analysed in their own terms before they are addressed in modern ones.

As the citations from Walter Map and Philip of Harvengt have already illustrated, reading and writing were not automatically coupled at the end of the twelfth century, nor was a minimal ability to perform these actions described as literacy. Writing was a skill distinct from reading because the use of parchment and quills made it difficult. Likewise the traditional emphasis on the spoken word caused reading to be coupled more often with speaking aloud than with eyeing script. Although the average medieval reader may have been taught to form the letters of the alphabet with a stylus on a writing tablet, he would not necessarily have felt confident about penning a letter or a charter on parchment. Scholars and officials employed scribes, particularly for drafting formal legal documents, just as typists and word processors are employed today. To this rule there are exceptions, of which the most spectacular is the beautifully written will of Simon de Montfort, as it states in its text that it is written in the hand of his eldest son, Henry. Wills were unusually personal documents, intimately associated with the family circle, because their main purpose was to ensure the testator's state of grace at death rather than the worldly disposition of his property; hence Henry was performing a special act of filial devotion in writing his father's will.

Another fundamental difference between medieval and modern approaches to literacy is that medieval assessments concentrate on cases of maximum ability, the skills of the most learned scholars (*litterati*) and the most elegant scribes, whereas modern assessors measure the diffusion of minimal skills among the masses. Consequently modern assessments of literacy have been primarily concerned with the minimal ability of persons to sign their own names and the development of elementary schools in which this ability is taught as the basic educational skill. In twelfth- and thirteenth-century England the ability to sign one's name was likewise considered important, but it was not directly associated either with writing or with schools. The personal signature or sign manual was not accepted by itself as a lawful symbol of authentication on a document unless the signatory were a Jew. A Christian was required either to sign with a cross, indicating that he was making a promise in the sight of Christ crucified, or more commonly he affixed to the document his *signum* in the form of a seal.

In medieval England possession of a seal bearing the owner's name comes closest to the modern criterion of making the ability to sign one's own name the touchstone of literacy. Although the possessor of a seal might not be able to write, he or she was a person familiar with documents and entitled to participate in their use. Neither the medieval seal nor the modern sign manual on a document indicates that the signatory has anything more than a minimal competence in the skills of literacy. Such a person need not be *litteratus* in a medieval sense nor 'educated' in a modern one. If possession of a seal is taken as the medieval equivalent of the modern sign manual as a measure of minimal literacy, the growth of literacy (in this modern sense) can be approximately assessed. Scarcely anyone apart from rulers and bishops possessed seals in 1100, whereas by 1300 all freemen and even some serfs probably had them. Thus the statute of Exeter of 1285 expected 'bondsmen' to use them when they authenticated written evidence. How far the expectations of this statute reflected actual practice is a matter for conjecture, although instances can be readily cited as early as the 1230s of smallholders and tenants owing labour services affixing their personal seals to charters. The extent of minimal literacy in this sense among the peasantry by 1300 has been underestimated because historians have been reluctant to allow such competence even to the gentry.

The discrepancies between modern and medieval conceptions of what constituted literacy go deeper than differences in minimal requirements. The variety of languages in which spoken and written thoughts were formulated in medieval England made any capacity to read or write an intellectual achievement. This variety also obstructed the rapid spread of literacy, in the modern sense of the majority of people acquiring a minimal ability to read and write the language they spoke. Elementary instruction in reading and writing started from Latin because that was the traditional language of literacy and sacred Scripture. Those who wrote in vernaculars, whether in Middle English or French, were building novel and complex structures on a foundation of Latin. Neither Middle English nor French was sufficiently standardised, or well enough established as a literary language, to become the basis of elementary instruction in reading and writing until well after 1300. If a person in Edward I's reign or earlier had learned to read in English or French but not in Latin, he could never have become *litteratus*, nor could he have understood the majority of writings circulating in his own lifetime because these were in Latin.

English and French had to have become common business and literary languages before it was practical or desirable to initiate literate skills with them.

Nevertheless by 1300 the supremacy of Latin, and the privileges of the *clerici* and *litterati* who upheld it, was increasingly being challenged, both by writings in vernaculars and by anti-clericalism. Boniface VIII introduced his bull *Clericis Laicos* in 1296, directed primarily at Edward I and Philip IV of France, with the provocative words: 'That laymen are notoriously hostile to clerics antiquity relates and recent experience manifestly demonstrates.' Yet English non-churchmen were slower than their French counterparts to abandon Latin as the basis of literate skills, probably because of the competition between English and French as alternative literary languages. In general from *c.* 1300, lawyers and government officials preferred French, while creative writers favoured English. Moreover, in the later Middle Ages an elementary reading knowledge of Latin became a matter of life and death for Englishmen. Any person charged with felony, who could read a prescribed verse from the Psalter, was theoretically entitled to benefit of clergy and hence escaped the death penalty. Now that middle-class laymen were beginning to assert themselves, they took over the old association of *clericus* with *litteratus* and turned it to their own advantage in order to save themselves from hanging. *Litteratus* was thus reduced from meaning a person of erudition to meaning a person with a minimal ability to read, albeit in Latin. A *clericus* was still a *litteratus*, but he was now neither a churchman nor a scholar: he was anyone who was literate in this minimal sense. By the middle of the fifteenth century London tradesmen are being described as *litterati*. Consequently after 1300 it became relatively common to be literate. What had changed, however, was not necessarily the proportion of persons in the population who had mastered reading and writing, but the meanings of words. A *clericus* was now a common clerk and a *litteratus* was a minimal literate. The literacy of the laity had been achieved, perhaps not so much by the efforts of schoolmasters and the mysterious forces of progress, as is sometimes alleged, as by the method which Humpty Dumpty explained to Alice in *Through the Looking-Glass*: 'When *I* use a word, it means just what I choose it to mean—neither more nor less . . . The question is which is to be master—that's all.' Verbally at least, the *laici* had mastered the *clerici* and *litterati*; and from that mastery the modern concept of literacy, meaning a minimal ability to read, was born.

To avoid ambiguities the question, 'Were laymen literate?' needs recasting. A more productive question to ask is, 'Did non-churchmen know any Latin?' since Latin was the foundation of literacy in England in this period. The latter question has been progressively answered in the affirmative by scholars over the past fifty years. Starting at the top of the social hierarchy, historians have demonstrated that at least an acquaintance with Latin became increasingly widespread over the two centuries 1100–1300.

Independently of each other in the 1930s, V. H. Galbraith in Britain and J. W. Thompson in California demonstrated that the kings of England from Henry I onwards were instructed in Latin and that Henry I and Henry II were even considered *litterati* by some contemporaries.[9] More importantly, Henry II showed his mastery of written instruments in a series of judgements concerning the charters of the abbeys of St Albans in 1155, Battle in 1157 and 1175, and Bury St Edmunds in 1187. He evidently enjoyed presiding over legal wrangles between abbots and bishops in his court, as it gave him an opportunity to scrutinise their charters and demonstrate that he was their master in intellect and legal wisdom as well as in material power. Peter of Blois was probably not exaggerating when he states that among Henry's commonest forms of relaxation were private reading and working with a group of *clerici* to unravel some knotty question: at his court there was 'school every day'. By 'school' Peter did not mean an elementary school, but a circle of learned schoolmen discussing *questiones* as they did at Paris or Oxford. From King John's reign onwards elementary instruction in Latin was taken for granted: 'Henceforth all our kings were taught letters in their youth, and their literacy, as distinct from their culture, has no particular importance.'[10]

The example set by the kings inevitably gave the baronage and gentry a motivation to learn some Latin, both to avoid looking foolish at court (where there was school every day), and to have sufficient understanding of the written demands, expressed in Latin, which began to pour from the royal Chancery and Exchequer. For these reasons H. G. Richardson and G. O. Sayles in 1963[11] widened the range of those who had 'a limited knowledge of Latin, a knowledge to be easily and rapidly acquired by any intelligent youth', from kings to the baronage and gentry of twelfth-century England. Their conclusion concerning the baronage is cautious and unexceptionable: 'Without rashly generalising from what may perhaps be called a handful of cases, it may fairly be said that they create a presumption that a man of noble birth will in his youth have had the opportunity of learning something of Latin letters.' Richardson and Sayles also suggested that even some of the lesser knights read and wrote Latin. This suggestion is based on the written replies to Henry II's inquest into knights' fees in 1166 and his Inquest of Sheriffs in 1170. The argument is that 'the more informal documents, those that have no marks of clerkly skill' were written by the knights themselves. Although the assumption that such men would or could write on parchment is contentious, the lesser conjecture that many knights read the royal writs themselves and drafted their own replies is possible.

The strongest argument of Richardson and Sayles for a relatively wide acquaintance with Latin is that royal officials like sheriffs and judges, most of whom were non-churchmen, had to have a working knowledge of Latin because they performed offices 'demanding the use of written instruments'. Although such officials usually employed clerks to do their writing, and to read letters aloud to them, they had to understand enough Latin to master the business in hand and not be misled by their clerks or by the litigants' lawyers. At least one of Henry II's lay sheriffs, Richard, sheriff of Hampshire, wrote as well as read in Latin, as his holograph acknowledgement of a debt to William Cade is extant.

The presumption that officials knew some Latin, which applies to officers of the central government by 1200, extends to manorial and village stewards, bailiffs, beadles and reeves by 1300. On the basis of this evidence M. B. Parkes, in his contribution to the literacy of the laity question, argues that historians should allow for an 'extent of pragmatic literacy among the peasantry'.[12] His arguments are strengthened by the instances of peasants using seals and charters which have already been discussed. Parkes cites Walter Map, who took it for granted that 'serfs [servi], whom we call peasants [rustici], are eager to educate their ignominious and degenerate children in the [liberal] arts'. Walter deplored this because a liberal education was appropriate only for freedom. The question had arisen one day when he and the chief justiciar, Ranulf de Glanvill, were discussing why it was that the clerical judges of Henry II were harsher than the lay ones. Walter's explanation was that the clerics did not behave like gentlemen because they were serfs in origin. Although Walter was only expressing a personal opinion, and his opinions were often perverse and ironical (Walter was a clerical justice himself), his remarks had some basis in fact.

Starting at the top of the hierarchy with kings and descending through barons and knights, historians of medieval literacy have reached the peasants at the bottom and are suggesting that even some of them were acquainted with Latin. N. Orme has surveyed literacy (mainly in the later Middle Ages) from the top of society to the bottom as an introduction to his study of medieval schools.[13] He divides people into seven classes—

clergy; kings and princes; nobility and gentry; administrators and lawyers; merchants, craftsmen, artisans; villeins; women. For the twelfth and thirteenth centuries a fourfold classification into kings and princes, nobility or baronage, gentry or knights, and peasantry (both free and unfree) is more appropriate. Neither the clergy nor women were separate social classes, as they derived their place in society from their families. Nor were administrators and lawyers yet a distinct class, as the legal profession (in a literate sense) emerged only in the late thirteenth century.

It might be thought that merchants are worth distinguishing as a group, as their families were at the forefront of education in the city states of Flanders and northern Italy. In England, however, merchant dynasties like those of London took on the social colouring of the landed gentry and were not, in the thirteenth century anyway, a distinct 'bourgeoisie'. Knightly merchants were as educated as other knights. With lesser merchants, it is doubtful whether literacy in Latin was yet an essential skill, as they worked from memory and tally sticks. Book learning and book keeping became crucial to lesser merchants only when they ceased to travel with their wares and sat in offices instead. On the whole, that is a development of the fourteenth century rather than the twelfth, as far as England is concerned. St Godric, who mastered the *mercatoris studium* without any formal education, is probably typical of eleventh- or twelfth-century experience. Financiers, on the other hand, like Osbert Huitdeniers (Eightpence) of London, who employed the young Thomas Becket as a clerk and accountant, needed as much Latin as the judicial side of their business (writing and enforcing bonds for loans) required. But financiers are not a sufficiently homogeneous group to constitute a social class, as many of them were Jews; they were literate in Hebrew and often in Latin as well.

The knowledge of the peasantry (both free and unfree), at the bottom of the social pyramid, remains to be discussed. The suggestion that some peasants were acquainted with Latin is not implausible when the role of the church in village life is considered. Theoretically at least every adult in England should have known some Latin because of its use in the liturgy. The attitude of the western Church towards Latin was ambivalent. The identification of *clerici* with *litterati*, which implied that only Latinists were the elect of God, was counterbalanced by the perennial message of the Gospels insisting that Christian teaching should be conveyed to everybody, and therefore to the crowd of *laici*. Various attempts had consequently been made to translate prayers, Scripture and the Church's teaching into vernacular languages. The works of Alfred and Ælfric are obvious examples of such attempts in pre-Conquest England.

By the eleventh century an uneasy compromise seems to have been reached whereby, for the people at large, the irreducible minimum of Christian teaching—namely the Lord's Prayer and the Creed—was to be recited in Latin, while sermons, homilies and the like were expressed in the vernacular. Thus a law of Cnut enjoined every Christian to apply himself until he could at least 'understand aright and learn the *Pater Noster* and the *Credo*'. Although this law does not mean that everybody is to read Latin, they are to recite these two Latin texts by heart. Hence one of the glosses accompanying this law adds that Christ himself first recited the *Pater Noster*. That Latin texts are meant and not English translations is suggested by the use of the Latin names for the texts and also by the glosses which describe the penalties for failing to learn them. If the texts had been in the vernacular, there would presumably have been no problem about learning them.

As it was, most people probably did not find this minimal amount of Latin overwhelmingly difficult because they were accustomed to using their ears to learn and furthermore they heard these texts recited whenever they went to church. Assuming that most of the population were minimally conscientious about their religious duties, we are led to the conclusion that most people could recite a little Latin. They had thus taken the first step towards literacy, as paradoxically they could speak *litteraliter*. Those who reached slightly greater competence, in other words, those who understood what they recited and could perhaps also distinguish the letters of the alphabet, would not have been altogether at a loss if they were required to sign their names with seals on Latin charters.

A conjecture of this sort, concerning the level of education of the mass of medieval people, is impossible to prove because evidence of any sort about elementary instruction, and particularly about that of ordinary people, is rare. The biographies of saints sometimes provide glimpses of childhood, but the only detailed description of an English saint of this period of undoubted peasant origins is the life of St Godric, which was written (in various versions) from his own recollections. Although he features in numerous social histories, because he is the first English example of the Dick Whittington type who made his fortune as a merchant, Godric's story is worth examining again from the point of view of what sort of education he acquired.

Godric was born in Norfolk in *c.* 1065 of parents who were good, though poor and ignorant. Since he had no wish to remain a peasant, but to exercise his mind, he exerted himself to study. So he strove to learn to be a merchant (*mercatoris studium*), first by selling things locally, then by joining travelling chapmen and ultimately by becoming an international shipman. As merchants travelled with their wares, he mastered navigation and practical maritime astronomy. Business combined well with religion, as he journeyed to the shrines at Lindisfarne and St Andrews, and beyond Britain to Rome, Santiago and Jerusalem. For a while he returned to Norfolk and became steward and general manager to a certain rich man. Godric was a pious but not yet a bookish man, although he had known the Lord's Prayer and the Creed 'from the cradle' and he often pondered them on his journeys. At about the age of forty a kinsman in Carlisle gave him a Psalter, from which he learned the Psalms most diligently, retaining them in his memory. This was an abbreviated version of the Psalter, commonly called 'St Jerome's Psalter'. The book must have been quite large, as Godric permanently distorted his little finger by carrying it around, even to bed. After further travels he came to Durham, where he learned more Psalms 'and afterwards he learned the whole Psalter'. By staying around St Mary's Church at Durham, where 'boys were learning the first elements of letters', he tenaciously applied his memory to 'hearing, reading and chanting' and thus became 'firm and certain' in the liturgy. Finally he settled at Finchale, near Durham, as a hermit.

Because Godric was self-educated, both the devil and the monks of Durham adopted a patronising attitude towards him. The twelfth-century devil shared Walter Map's opinion of serfs who had advanced in the world and called Godric a 'stinking old peasant', while his chief biographer, Reginald of Durham, quite often describes him without malice as *laicus*, *illitteratus* and *idiota*. Technically Reginald was correct, as Godric was not a *clericus* and *litteratus*. Nevertheless Reginald revealed his own ignorance of the effects of travel on an intelligent man, when he considered it miraculous that Godric understood 'French or Romance', even though his mother tongue was English. Reginald likewise considered that it was the Holy Spirit, rather than his native wit, which enabled Godric to understand the Latin conversation of four monks from Durham, who had been sent to cross-examine him. By these means Godric was able to give an impressive exposition of the Scriptures to them (in English), 'as if he were an outstanding *litteratus*'. The information provided by Godric's biographers about his knowledge was not recorded for its own sake, as it was intended as evidence of his religious devotion and of those miraculous powers which were the indispensable sign of a saint. Nevertheless the various versions of the life are sufficiently circumstantial and consistent to provide a historical record of one man's self-education and rise from the mass.

Godric's life story provides numerous correctives to the modern tendency to assume that schools are the beginning and end of education. He received his instruction in the Lord's Prayer and the Creed 'from the cradle', presumably meaning from his parents. He is therefore an example of Christian law being applied in practice, as it was the duty of every parent to teach his child the *Pater Noster* and the *Credo*. Thereafter Godric was self-taught. He learned numeracy and navigation, the *mercatoris studium*, by experience. Literacy obviously presented greater problems. Godric may never have learned to write and his knowledge of Latin depended primarily on hearing and memorising. Although he could never become *litteratus* by this method, he could evidently cope with the normal uses of Latin in ecclesiastical circles. Gerald of Wales gives an example of another hermit and traveller, Wecheleu, who had likewise miraculously learned Latin by ear. The fact that such knowledge was considered miraculous suggests, however, that Latin was thought difficult to learn without formal instruction in grammar. Nevertheless even Latin was in its rudimentary stages primarily a spoken language, to which children were introduced by the Church's liturgy and prayers in the home.

Although a man like Godric, who had memorised whole portions of the liturgy, could not pass as a Latinist among the *litterati*, he could probably make as good a show of Latin as some clergy. His self-taught Latin became a problem only when he wanted to be accepted as a conscientious churchman and monk. In lay society Godric's lack of a formal education had not prevented him from mastering the *mercatoris studium*, or from becoming a rich man's steward. In the latter capacity tally sticks and a trained memory were more useful than parchments, although if Godric had lived a century later, he might have found it more difficult to conduct business without writing. Yet before deciding that Godric could not have succeeded a century later, it is worth recalling that the greatest of all medieval stewards and business managers, Hubert Walter, was likewise described as *laicus et illitteratus*. Like Godric, he had little or no formal schooling and was ignorant of elementary Latin grammar, if Gerald of Wales is to believed. A little Latin, like a little literacy in more recent times, could get a man a long way in ordinary business, deplorable as that was in the eyes of scholars.

Godric's life shows that a little Latin, and a great deal of education in the broader sense of understanding and mastering one's environment, could be acquired by a determined peasant without any formal schooling. Nevertheless those children of serfs whom Walter Map had in mind who became royal justices had probably risen through some clerical training in childhood, as Latin could only be superficially acquired by self-education. The commonness of such instruction has probably been underestimated, both in terms of the number of children involved and of the social classes from which they came. A polemicist of the early twelfth century argued that there were numerous *clerici*, just as there were numerous royal tax collectors and officials, since highly expert schoolmasters existed 'not only in cities and boroughs, but even in little villages [*in villulis*]'. Even if this were not exaggerated, however, the problems for a serf's family were paying for instruction and doing without the labour of the child concerned.

As a solution of these problems, the role of the Church in disseminating free instruction in villages through its priests may have been as underestimated as its role in familiarising people with Latin through the liturgy. Village priests became increasingly common from the eleventh century onwards, as a network of parish churches gradually replaced and supplemented the centralised minster churches of the missionary period. Henceforward priests and their books were more widely and permanently distributed over the countryside. 'By 1154 the existence of elementary education was taken for granted: that is to say, there was basic education available for everyone who wanted and could afford it; and the clever poor would often be educated free.'[14] Isolation in villages and local recruitment, compounded after 1066 by the alienation of the Normanised prelates from the Anglo-Saxon lower clergy, may in the short term have caused the educational standards of some priests to deteriorate. Nevertheless most scholars agree that by the thirteenth century, when information becomes sufficiently abundant to make generalisations, parish priests were often of peasant, even servile, origins and also that the standard of learning of the priesthood was on the whole quite high. The latter generalisation is the more controversial, as a handful of cases of priestly ignorance have been repeatedly cited against it. The most frequently quoted report is from the dean of Salisbury's visitation of Sonning in 1222, where some of the vicar's chaplains' ignorance of Latin grammar was exposed. Yet this case does not suggest that such ignorance was normal, as the incompetent chaplains were suspended or dismissed as a consequence of this visitation.

Cases of priestly ignorance, when recorded in detail in bishop's registers, indicate not that priests were generally ignorant but that reformers were requiring higher standards. Thus it has been calculated from the earliest bishop's register, that of Hugh of Wells, concerning the largest diocese, Lincoln, over a period of a quarter of a century (1209–35) that out of 1,958 institutions to benefices only 101 candidates were recorded as deficient in learning and most of these cases arose from candidates not having completed their education; only four deficient candidates were already priests. If most parish priests were of peasant origins, and if by 1230 many were sufficiently instructed, it follows that a number of persons of peasant origins had been efficiently instructed in Latin, with a view to becoming priests, even in the twelfth century.

How was the initial instruction of peasants achieved? Not often presumably through schools in towns because of the expense, either of travel or of lodging. Certainly would-be clergy lodged in town schools after they had shown sufficient ability to learn reading and elementary Latin grammar, but their initial instruction and selection must have taken place in the villages themselves. If, as has been argued, parish priests were themselves sufficiently instructed, they could perform this function. Indeed it was required of them by canon law, reiterated in numerous manuscripts. Thus the ninth-century provision of Theodulf, bishop of Orléans, that 'priests should have schools throughout the villages [*per villas*] and teach children free of charge' was translated into English and copied into ecclesiastical compilations of the eleventh century. Of course the repetition of such rules implies that some priests failed to comply. Moreover, a village priest, who was relatively poor and ignorant himself, could not have instructed many children at a time, nor have got them much beyond the ABC and the bare elements of reading Latin. Many priests probably performed these duties to a minimal level at least, as incidental references to them can be found. Thus in one of the fables attributed to Marie de France, which may be of English origin, a priest is pictured teaching a wolf the ABC. The wolf is the rarity and not the priest. Among the miracles of St Edmund, recorded by Hermann in *c.* 1095, is the cure of a man who had been so ill that the parish priest named Goding, immediately 'coming with his scholars', rushed to give him the last rites. The elementary teaching duties of priests were so commonplace that they seem only to be mentioned in exceptional circumstances like these.

Even if the average parish priest taught only one poor boy a year, a boy for example who served him at the altar, and if only one such boy in ten proceeded beyond the ABC, nine sons of peasants in the village had acquired a little familiarity with letters and one had advanced into the lowest ranks of the clergy. Perhaps only one in ten of these boys rose to be a parish priest, and only one in a hundred became a *litteratus*, because the course grew progressively more difficult. Such speculations—and they are no more than that—suggest that each prelate and *litteratus* of humble origin whose name has come down to history (Robert Grosseteste is the obvious example, though medieval hagiographers may have exaggerated his humble birth) was the one in a thousand who achieved his objective.[15] Although it was difficult, therefore, for a poor boy to rise through the Church, some succeeded, and the difficulties ensured that many who were disappointed in their expectations had at least learned the ABC. Famous prelates of humble origin stood at the visible apex of a pyramid of peasant education extending deep into the villages.

More specific information about peasants' sons rising through a clerical education is difficult to find, however, because childhood is rarely described and the social origins of particular persons are often a matter of subjective judgement. Either poverty or gentility may be misleadingly reported by a biographer wishing to demonstrate his subject's sanctity or success. Autobiographical information is even rarer and no easier to assess. Thus John of Salisbury, who may have been a peasant as his parentage is very obscure, remarks that he learned Psalms from a priest, and he was presumably first taught to read in this way. Yet this instance does not indicate John's confidence in such instruction, as he only mentions it because the priest had tried to teach him sorcery as well. A clearer case of a country boy rising to be a *litteratus* is Jocelin's account of Abbot Samson, although that also illustrates the difficulties of assessing social class. Samson may even have been the model for Walter Map's remarks about Henry II's clerical judges of servile origins being harsher than the lay ones, as he 'exalted justice over mercy' according to Jocelin.[16]

Jocelin reports that, although he had heard Samson say that he had kinsmen of noble blood, 'he had no kin within a third degree, or at any rate pretended that this was so'. It is possible that Samson's reticence concealed servile origins. He seems to have been brought up by his mother, who introduced him to the shrine of St Edmund at the age of nine. Instead of kinsmen, Samson rewarded those 'who had treated him as their kinsmen when he was a poor cloister monk'. Thus he gave benefices to the sons of the man 'of no high birth' who had preserved his patrimony, to the chaplain who sold holy water to maintain him as a student at Paris, and to the son of Master William of Diss who let him enter his school out of pure charity. Whatever Samson's origins, he is certainly an example of a promising country boy who was picked out for training as a *clericus* and owed his rise primarily to ecclesiastical charity.

Samson's career also illustrates another important aspect of clerical education. He once confided to Jocelin that he would never have become a monk if he had possessed sufficient money to remain at the schools. It was therefore only chance which confirmed him in his ecclesiastical vocation. Some *clerici* abandoned ecclesiastical life and traded their skills in the world, even becoming knights. This was another way in which literate education was integrated into lay society. Among the miracles of St Godric is one in which he identified one of the household knights of Bertram of Bulmer (in the middle of the twelfth century) as a *clericus* and *litteratus*, even though the knight had grown his hair to conceal his tonsure. This young knight had been sent to Godric on his lord's business on a Sunday. Godric made him reveal his clerical upbringing by compelling him to read the lesson at Mass, which he did 'not at all like a *laicus*, but rather as a *litteratus*'. So Godric gave him a good talking to, telling him that he was making unworthy use of his education in not going on to be a priest. A century later John of Gaddesden, a cleric with numerous benefices who had been the queen's chamberlain, renounced his ecclesiastical status with more ceremony. He was belted as a knight by Henry III on Christmas Day 1244 and married a lady's daughter. Matthew Paris reported that this gave rise to envious gossip, which he thought misplaced, as John had willingly given up all his benefices. More scandalous presumably in Matthew's view were those clerics who, instead of acknowledging their lay status, maintained spouses and illegitimate children from their benefices.

The rule of clerical celibacy, which had long been an ideal of the Church, was given new force by the Gregorian reformers of the eleventh century and had come near to being the norm among the higher clergy by the thirteenth. Ironically, this rule may have been the chief cause of the dissemination of clerical skills in literacy among all classes of the laity. If the Gregorian reformers had not intervened, the *clerici–litterati* might well have become a hereditary caste, like priestly scholars in some other cultures. Knowledge of Latin would then have been restricted to a self-perpetuating élite. Instead, clerical celibacy drove trained men who could not accept it back into lay society, thus disseminating literate skills, and it also made the production of future clergy depend initially and primarily on the laity. Priests found it increasingly difficult to hand on their benefices to their sons, as they were deemed illegitimate. Opportunities consequently increased for non-clerical families to get a clerical training.

A text of the mid-twelfth century, extant only in England though connected with the school of Abelard, comments that Christian families unlike Jewish ones educate one son only, 'not for God but for gain, in order that the one brother, if he be a cleric, may help his father and mother and his other brothers'; because a cleric has no heir, any acquisitions will return to the family. That this selective attitude prevailed in the twelfth century, even among the nobility, is suggested by the childhood of Gerald of Wales. He was the youngest (born in *c.* 1147) of four brothers and showed his suitability for the clergy at an early age by building sand churches and monasteries at the seaside while his brothers built castles. His father was pleased and called the boy his 'bishop'. So Gerald was put in the charge of his uncle, David, who was the real bishop of St David's. In due course Gerald was himself twice a candidate for the bishopric of St David's, though his election was quashed. Gerald's family had a hereditary interest in the bishopric of St David's. Clerical celibacy at least ensured that offices now passed from uncle to nephew instead of father to son, and hence initial recruitment depended on laymen like Gerald's father.

Before Gregorian reform became effective, many future *clerici* must have been introduced to Latin and formal education by their own parents. Thus Orderic Vitalis's father, who was a priest, knew that Latin should be started young and had him instructed by another priest from the age of five. As hereditary priests grew rarer, the responsibility for inaugurating children in Latin became the duty of parents who were technically *laici* and *illitterati*. They thus became familiar with the problems of learning, even if they remained uninstructed themselves. As clergy were required at all social levels, ranging from a noble bishop like Gerald's uncle to peasant parish priests, an increasing number of families began to have experience of education. *Clerici* and *laici* were united in the closest kinship by celibacy, not set apart. Literacy ceased to be a high arcane mystery when a younger brother was obliged to acquire it because he had no patrimony.

Among the nobility, pious mothers who read the Psalter and lives of the saints often perhaps took an active role in educating their children, as in the uniquely documented case of Guibert de Nogent. At a humbler social level in England, it may have been Samson's mother who arranged for his schooling, when she showed off her precocious son of nine at the shrine of St Edmund. A century later Walter of Bibbesworth assumes that it will be the mother, albeit a widow, Denise de Montchensy, who improves her children's French. 'Woman teacheth child on book' is put forward as a statement commanding general assent in an English poem (dating from *c.* 1300) associated with Walter of Bibbesworth. Walter assumes furthermore that both mother and children are familiar with the Latin primer, the 'book which teaches us *clergie*', because by the thirteenth century, among the nobility at least, all children both male and female were usually taught a little formal Latin and hence initiated into 'clergy'. A little *clergie* had the advantage of keeping children's options open. From inclination or necessity, boys or girls could subsequently join the 'religious', provided they had a grounding in Latin and some local influence. From the fourteenth century, moreover, a little Latin, 'benefit of clergy', was also an insurance against being hanged. Thus by 1300 conscientious or ambitious parents of all social classes had strong motives for seeing that their children were *clerici* and *litterati* in the new minimal sense of being capable of reading a verse from the Bible.

Real *litterati*, in the old sense of 'scholars', of course remained rare. Those who were totally ignorant, that is, those who could not pass a Latin reading test, were perhaps as rare. Detailed cases of failure to read are thought amusing, particularly by academics, and have therefore been repeatedly cited. Repetition gives the false impression that such cases were typical and commonplace. The numerous lively descriptions of clerical ignorance by Gerald of Wales are difficult to generalise from, as he even alleged that Hubert Walter was ignorant of elementary grammar. Possibly that was so, yet it did not prevent Hubert mastering the royal archives. Gerald's anecdotes, like other detailed reports of illiteracy among churchmen, suggest that normal expectations were relatively high.

Total inability to read was likewise the exception and not the rule among knights by 1300. Examples of such knights are as difficult to find as their converse, the *milites litterati*. Certainly there were some, like the two jurors in the de Tony case who were described as *laici*, though the use of the word 'layman' in this context implies that *clerici* were now the norm. One example of a really ignorant and boorish knight is a certain Hugh, who was charged with rape in 1293. He had pleaded benefit of clergy and, when this plea was disallowed, he wished to challenge some of the jurors, which required reading out their names. At this point he had to admit that he was unable to read. But Hugh's predicament does not suggest that he was typical in being unable to read. On the contrary, it emphasises how important it was by 1300 for a man in trouble to have sufficient *clergie* to get himself out of it. Even a century earlier in 1198 an illiterate landlord in Oxfordshire, Alan Fitz Roland, had found himself arraigned before the king's justices when he had failed to act on a writ brought against him in his court by his serfs; Alan's excuse was that he had no clerk who could read the document. Thus sometimes by 1200 and invariably by 1300 a landlord, on however small a scale, needed sufficient *clergie*, in the sense of a personal knowledge of Latin, to assess, if not fully to understand, the written demands made upon him.

Knights who were able to read a little Latin, sufficient to get the gist of a royal writ or to understand a line in the Bible or in a chronicle, were literate in something like a modern minimal sense. By 1300, such an ability was common among the gentry and may not have been rare among peasants. The conclusions to be drawn from this extension of minimal literacy are more problematical, however. In the modern world a little literacy enables a person to begin to cope with the mass of written instructions and bureaucratic demands which are a commonplace of daily experience. Further ability opens to the private reader, for recreation or self-improvement, the thousands of printed books available in his own language. A person who cannot read and write is therefore at a disadvantage in the mastery of daily life and he is also excluded from those areas of culture which depend on the printed word. These truisms are stated here only because they did not apply with equal force in the Middle Ages. A knight of the eleventh century who learned the rudiments of Latin in childhood would not have found this skill had much application in daily life, nor did it open to him the cultural heritage of his people, because Latin was a foreign language and books were not generally available.

By 1300 the situation had changed, though not radically. Bureaucratic demands in Latin were now sufficiently common to make it useful for any landowner to be able to understand them. 'Pragmatic' literacy, defined by Parkes as 'the literacy of one who has to read or write in the course of transacting any kind of business',[17] thus became usual. Literacy for purposes of recreation or self-improvement, the literacy of 'the cultivated reader', was still not very useful, although that too was beginning to change as more was being written down in vernacular languages. The books given by the earl of Warwick to Bordesley Abbey in 1306, or the various late thirteenth-century manuscripts containing treatises on accountancy and estate management, indicate the kind of literature which might be found in a nobleman's, or even a gentleman's, household by 1300. On the whole, however, private reading must still have been a luxury, largely confined to retiring ladies and scholars. Books were scarce and it was ordinary good manners to share their contents among a group by reading aloud.

The increase in the number of persons who could read, at a minimal level, over the period 1066–1307 was thus a consequence of the demands of the 'pragmatic' rather than the 'cultivated' reader. That is why I have approached literacy from record-making, instead of from the usual standpoint of an advance in culture and education. Documents had to precede widening literacy. The gentry were not going to learn to read until documents were available and necessary. Although a little Latin had become an essential of business and a commonplace of gentlemanly education by Walter of Bibbesworth's time, it was still something alien, and even contrary, to traditional knightly culture. Hence Latin was learned from the 'book which teaches us *clergie*'. An aspiring knight of the thirteenth century did not become a cultivated gentleman primarily by being a reader, necessary as that now was. He had to master the skills of combat, hunting, hawking and chess, and know the vernacular languages, law, traditional oral 'literature' and music of his people. Such knowledge was not primarily to be found in Latin books, but in speech, gesture, and memory.

The biography of William Marshal (who died at an advanced age in 1219) is a unique recollection of knightly life in this period. It was written not in Latin but in French rhyming couplets (19,254 lines survive in the manuscript), so that it could be readily understood and remembered by the Marshal's family and retinue. His senior knight, John of Earley, supplied the information and he too may have been the composer of the verse. The biography says nothing about the Marshal's abilities in literacy. 'His accomplishments in Latin were probably no more than the basics required of a layman: the Lord's Prayer, the Ave Maria, and the Creed, which he would have learned, as like as not, from his mother or the household chaplains.'[18] Nevertheless it can be shown from the Marshal's charters that he, like other great men, had a clerical staff of three or more persons to keep accounts and do correspondence, together with household chaplains to look after his travelling chapel and its furnishings including prayer-books. When he became regent of England after the death of King John, the Marshal headed a bureaucratic administration which differed in scale rather than in substance from what he was already used to as an earl and a courtier. It was not reading and writing that made the life of knights like the Marshal so challenging, as he had his own clerks, but the unpredictability of his lay peers, particularly the Angevin royal family. Judging from the Marshal's biography, understanding what a horse and its rider might do under stress was a more precious form of knowledge than *clergie*.

Clerici and *litterati* might claim that book learning was the only intellectual and noble pursuit. Yet the slighest consideration of the languages an English knight needed to know, or any knowledge of the subtleties of heraldry or hawking, suggests that knightly education was equally demanding intellectually though in a different way. This suggestion cannot be incontrovertibly proved, however, because knightly culture before the fourteenth century has been largely lost to posterity, as it was primarily oral. Lack of written record did not of course make knightly culture any less real or less demanding for contemporaries. Indeed it may have been more lively than later literate culture, because knightly culture depended on the immediacy of speech. Judging from the romances, intellect and wit were prized among knights. A knight of advanced oral education was expected to contribute towards the knowledge and entertainment of his fellows instead of being a passive and silent recipient of book learning. The *clerici* might claim to be the elect of God, but the knights or warriors (*bellatores*) were as powerful and as venerable an élite. In the extension of medieval literacy the *clerici* did not impose their culture on ignorant and passive *laici*. Rather, clerical skills were gradually absorbed, in so far as they were useful, and an amalgam was formed over generations of literate and pre-literate habits of thought.

To give substance to generalisations which may seem vague and romanticised, this chapter will conclude with a look at two small incidents concerning knights recorded by Jocelin of Brakelond.[19] Samson's first action after being inaugurated as abbot in 1182 was to turn away all suitors except one man. This was a knight (Jocelin does not record his name), 'eloquent and expert in law' (*juris peritus*), who was retained because Samson had no experience of business in secular courts. After a while Samson began to master secular law, just as he mastered canon law, and the services of this knight presumably then became less essential. According to Jocelin, everyone marvelled at Samson's new expertise and the under-sheriff, Osbert Fitz Hervey, said: 'This abbot is a debater [*disputator*]; if he goes on as he has begun, he will dazzle us all, every one of us.' Soon, 'having proved himself in cases', Samson's competence in secular law was officially recognised by his being appointed a royal justice in eyre.

In these two incidents (first Samson's initial appointment of the anonymous knight and then the remark of Osbert Fitz Hervey on Samson's progress) Jocelin introduces his hero and his readers to an uncharted intellectual world, for which Samson's training as a *clericus* and *litteratus* had not explicitly prepared him. As it turned out, Samson mastered this world of secular law in due course, as he mastered everyone and everything in Jocelin's opinion. Yet this was a cause for surprise. Fitz Hervey had evidently not assumed that Samson's clerical education would make him a good debater in the county court. Knights like Fitz Hervey, who mastered county business, had learned their skills which were predominantly oral by years of attendance at the court, first by listening and then by speaking. About thirty years earlier in the same county court (again in a case concerning Bury St Edmunds) one of its 'proved and prudent men', Hervey de Glanvill, recalled how he had attended county and hundred courts first with his father and then as a householder in his own right for over fifty years.[20] His ancient wisdom had been duly heeded on that occasion.

From knights like Osbert Fitz Hervey, who learned their business orally, the king chose most of his justices and sheriffs, and litigants chose their advocates. Such expert knights were those 'greater men of the county, who are called *buzones*, on whose nod the views of the others depend', according to Bracton.[21] The *buzones judiciorum* are recorded giving judgement in a case in 1212. Samson was not the only abbot to take legal advice from knights. In 1201 the abbot of Crowland had relied on the counsel of 'the wise and discreet knight, Reynold surnamed de Argento', in his litigation with the prior of Spalding.[22] Reynold in the 1190s had been a sheriff, a justice in eyre and an attorney of the bishop of Ely among others. Osbert Fitz Hervey himself served as a justice in eyre in Richard I's reign and also on the Bench at Westminster between 1192 and 1206. As a judge he achieved exceptional distinction, since he is one of only seven judges (including three chief justiciars) whose opinions on points of law are referred to in manuscripts of *Glanvill*.[23]

Although knights like Fitz Hervey were experts in law (*juris periti*), their expertise was not in book learning but in oral advocacy. Skilful pleading in courts, the mastery of the spoken word, has been admired in many non-literate societies and is best exemplified in medieval Europe from those two extreme geographical points of medieval culture, the Iceland of the sagas and the crusader Kingdom of Jerusalem. From Iceland the best-known example is the story in *Njal's Saga* of how Gunnar tricked the expert, Hrut, into summoning himself. In the Kingdom of Jerusalem its knightly jurists (Ralf of Tiberias, John of Beirut, and Balian of Sidon) were the contemporaries of Osbert Fitz Hervey and Reynold de Argento. Although their opinions were subsequently written into the law books of the Kingdom, there is no doubt that they themselves learned their art, like the English jurists of the county court, from vernacular practice and not from ecclesiastical Latin schools.

It is a mistake to regard knightly jurists as amateurs and clerical ones as professionals. Both knights and clergy contributed skills which shaped the legal profession. Pleading had been developed by knights as an alternative to private warfare, both as an honourable profession and as an intellectual pastime. When Henry the Young King and his companions spent a year in England in 1175 under the guardianship of that model of chivalry, William

Marshal, they did nothing 'except pleading, hunting and fighting in tournaments'. Clerics were trained in a comparable, though more book-centred, form of intellectual warfare by the disputations of the schools. Peter Abelard, the prototype of scholastic masters, in his autobiography saw his whole life in terms of warfare with other masters. The schools of Paris had probably taught Abbot Samson more than Osbert Fitz Hervey realised about how to be a *disputator*. In the twelfth century, when literate and pre-literate ways of thought were beginning to penetrate each other and interact, strong and novel institutions were formed by drawing on both traditions. Thus English common law benefited from the clerical training of scholastics like Samson and the oral lore of knights like Osbert. Whether royal judges were technically clergy or laymen seems to have had no bearing either way on their professional competence, although Walter Map thought it affected their severity. Once the judiciary becomes sufficiently documented in John's reign, it can be shown that of his fifteen regular judges (that is, those who served for ten or more terms) only four were clergy. Similarly in Henry III's reign some judges, like Bracton, were clergy whereas others of equal distinction at the time, like Thurkelby, were knights.

The knights of English county courts, like knights all over Europe, were educated and cultured men regardless of whether they were literate. Perhaps by 1200, and certainly by 1300, they had usually learned enough Latin to cope with the documents which came their way. But this restricted knowledge of literacy was a pragmatic convenience, rather than a positive contribution to their intellectual education. A little Latin, learned from a relatively ignorant priest, did not educate a man in the culture of Imperial or of Christian Rome, and hence it did not make him a *litteratus* in the traditional sense. Literacy became something more positive for non-churchmen only when writing recorded a substantial part of their own heritage in vernacular languages. That is a development of the later Middle Ages and not of the period 1066–1307.

Yet the twelfth and thirteenth centuries are crucially important because these are the years in which the traditional division between cleric and lay, literate and illiterate, was broken down. Gradually, by all sorts of avenues, a little literacy, in the sense of minimal Latin or *clergie*, became commonplace until 'benefit of clergy' came to mean the ability to read a few words of Latin. Because literacy had been identified with Latin for a thousand years, it had first to be learned by the laity in this clerical and alien form. Those old rivals, the *clerici-litterati* and the *laici-illitterati*, had to come to terms and absorb each other's thought processes before literacy could become a common vernacular habit. The extension of literacy was therefore a complex social problem in the Middle Ages and not a simple matter of providing more educational facilities. Knights absorbed clerical culture and clergy lived alongside knights. That archetypal *clericus*, Gerald of Wales, recounts how in 1188 his nephew, William de Barri, was committed at the age of twelve to Gerald's care for his education. This accorded with the custom whereby aristocratic boys were educated in a household other than their own. The boy was set 'continually to riding' in the retinue of Baldwin archbishop of Canterbury, whom Gerald was accompanying in the preaching of the Third Crusade in Wales and England. William grew up to become a knight and not a cleric, a knight who had acquired both book learning ('doctrine') and 'courtliness' under Gerald's direction.[24]

A fundamental question which has not been addressed here is the role of women in the dynamics of medieval literacy. The subject is too large and complex to be discussed in detail here, not least because it requires a different approach, using the evidence of imagery as much as written sources: explicit references to women's literacy are rare. The best-documented literate women are nuns and anchoresses, like Christina of Markyate, but they are the least significant as far as female literacy is concerned because their rules and way of life were modelled on male monasticism. Nuns can be classified either as honorary males or as of neuter gender like all clergy. More significant in the history of literacy are the ways in which clerical habits and values were absorbed into the households of the aristocracy through ladies acquiring prayer-books for their own use and commissioning or owning other works (see pages 343–8 above). It has already been shown, moreover, that liturgical books, in the form of Books of Hours, began to be made for lay people in the thirteenth century and that the earliest English examples were made for women rather than men (see pages 277–8 above).

Ladies with their own households and withdrawing chambers could conduct themselves like groups of male clergy: reciting prayers, reading silently, and looking at and listening to—and perhaps even writing—their own books, whether religious or secular. Within such female households, too, children acquired familiarity with books at an early age, and habits of literacy were thus transmitted from one generation to the next. By these means literate skills were extended beyond the caste of *clerici*. The 'domestication' of ecclesiastical books by great ladies, together with the ambitions of mothers of all social classes for their children, were the foundations on which the growth of literacy in fourteenth- and fifteenth-century Europe were constructed. This shift in the focus of literacy from monastic church to noble household was perhaps as significant a cultural change as the shift from memory to the written record, but it lies beyond the scope and period of this book.

X

HEARING, SEEING AND MAGNA CARTA

Numerous charters of the twelfth century are addressed to 'all those seeing and hearing these letters, in the future as in the present' or to 'all who
shall hear and see this charter'; these two examples come from the charters of Roger de Mowbray who died in 1188.[1] The grantor of another charter, Richard de Rollos, actually harangues his audience, 'Oh! all ye who
shall have heard this and have seen!'[2] Early charters likewise quite often
conclude with 'Goodbye' (*Valete*), as if the donor had just finished speaking with his audience. Documents made it possible for the grantor to
address posterity ('all who shall hear and see') as well as his contemporaries. In the opening words of the Winchcombe Abbey cartulary, 'when
the voice has perished with the man, writing still enlightens posterity'.
Writing shifted the spotlight away from the transitory actors witnessing a
conveyance and on to the perpetual parchment recording it. By the thirteenth century, when charters had become more familiar to landowners,
donors ceased addressing their readers, as Richard de Rollos did, and
likewise they no longer concluded with *Valete*. Once it was understood
that charters were directed to posterity, it must have seemed foolish to say
'Goodbye' to people who had not yet been born. In place of such conver-
sational expressions, thirteenth-century charters are more stereotyped;
they are often impersonally addressed in some such form as 'Let all
persons, present and future, know that I, A of B, have given X with its
appurtenances to C of D'.

A comparable change occurs in wills. Until the thirteenth century the
will was an essentially oral act, even when it was recorded in writing. The
persons present witnessed the testator making his bequests 'with his own
mouth'; they 'saw, were present, and heard' the transaction.[3] By the end of
the thirteenth century a man's final will no longer usually meant his
wishes spoken on his deathbed, but a closed and sealed document. The
witnesses no longer heard him; instead they saw his seal being placed on
the document. When wills were first enrolled, as they were in London
from 1258, the formula of probate still put emphasis on the witnesses who
had seen and heard. But a generation later, by the 1290s, the London roll
often omits the names of the witnesses, presumably because the written
will was the preferred evidence. The validity of the will now depended
primarily upon its being in a correct documentary form and not on the

verbal assurances of the witnesses. This is another illustration of the shift from memory to written record between 1100 and 1300. Wills had been made in writing by the Anglo-Saxons; the novelty lay in their being closed and sealed documents.

Before conveyances were made with documents, the witnesses 'heard' the donor utter the words of the grant and 'saw' him make the transfer by a symbolic object, such as a knife or a turf from the land. William the Conqueror went one better and jokingly threatened to make one donee 'feel' the conveyance by dashing the symbolic knife through the recipient abbot's hand saying, 'That's the way land ought to be given.' Such a gesture was intended to impress the event on the memory of all those present. If there were dispute subsequently, resort was had to the recollection of the witnesses. Similar rules applied to the oral 'records' of courts, which were retained (in theory at least) in the memory of those present. For example, if the record of the county court were disputed, the aggrieved litigant brought forward two witnesses who each gave evidence of what they had heard and seen. In such a case in 1212 the prior of Ware (in Hertfordshire) defended himself by 'one hearing and one understanding', namely Jordan of Warew and Robert of Clopton; Robert also offered to prove the prior's allegation by battle, 'as he was present and heard this'. In this case some distinction is evidently being made between the knowledge of the two witnesses: Jordan had heard, or at least understood, less of the proceedings than Robert. Likewise at Cheshunt (in Hertfordshire) in a seignorial court in 1220 a litigant challenged the record by 'one person hearing and another seeing'. Which testimony was thought preferable in this instance, that of the person who heard or of the other who saw, is unclear. These cases suggest that the legal commonplace of making a record by 'hearing and seeing' was not a mere formula made meaningless by repetition.

Documents changed the significance of bearing witness by hearing and seeing legal procedures, because written evidence could be heard by reading aloud or seen by inspecting the document. John of Salisbury defined letters as indicating voices and bringing things to mind 'through the windows of the eyes'. Once charters were used for conveyances, 'hearing' applied to anyone hearing the charter read out loud at any time, instead of referring only to the witnesses of the original conveyance. From there it was a short step to substitute 'reading' for 'seeing', as one of Roger de Mowbray's charters does, which is addressed to 'all his own men and to the rest, *reading* or hearing these letters'.[4] This phrase plays also with the ambiguity of the word 'letters', which in Latin (as in English) means both alphabetic symbols and missives.

A curiously worded grant for St Mary's Priory at Monmouth is addressed to the donors, Richard de Cormeilles and Beatrice his wife, instead of to the recipients. The charter rewards Richard and Beatrice with divine bliss because they have given the tithes of Norton-Giffard to Mary the mother of God. She is the ostensible grantor of the charter, though the document itself was presumably written by a monk of St Mary's Priory which was the terrestrial beneficiary. The writer's Latin is eccentric—for example he spells *uxor* (wife) as *hucxor*—but revealing in its phraseology. He includes the phrase *sicut presens breve loquitur* (as the present writing speaks), whereas ordinary usage would have *dicitur* (says) or *testatur* (attests) in place of *loquitur*. The writer also makes it clear that the named witnesses, who 'saw and heard the gift solemnly exhibited by the book upon the altar', are 'subsequent' and therefore secondary to the evidence of the writing itself. In making the writing 'speak' and in putting the pre-literate witnessing ceremony of seeing and hearing into a subsidiary role, the naïve writer of this charter has exemplified John of Salisbury's scholastic definition (which is contemporary with the charter) that letters 'speak voicelessly the utterances of the absent', the absent in this instance being the grantor, Mary the mother of God.

Once property was conveyed in writing, it would have seemed logical for the charter to supersede the symbolic object, such as the knife or turf, which had formerly been used in the witnessing ceremony. As the grant to Monmouth Priory shows, that object had sometimes itself been a writing—a book solemnly exhibited upon an altar. Traditionally the book used for this purpose was the text of the Gospels. For example a gift of a saltpan was made to St Peter's Priory at Sele in Sussex in 1153 'by the text of the Holy Gospel upon the altar of St Peter, many persons hearing and seeing'. The Gospel book was used because it was customary to reinforce oaths with it (as is still the practice in law courts); thus in Edward I's wardrobe there was kept 'a book, which is called *textus*, upon which the magnates were accustomed to swear'.[5] To replace a Gospel book by a charter in a conveyancing ceremony was a relatively small change in appearance (it was simply substituting one document for another), but a large one in substance. The charter in its text actually 'represented' in a durable record the terms of the conveyance, whereas the Gospel book merely symbolised the solemnity of the occasion for the witnesses. The Monmouth Priory charter therefore distinguishes the written grant (*breve*), which 'speaks' to the hearers, from the symbolic book (*liber*) which is 'exhibited' to the viewers. Nevertheless, although it seemed logical to dispense with symbols and make full use of the potentialities of writing, contemporaries continued with their pre-literate habits long after charters had become common. In the rare instances where the conveyance appears to be made by the written document itself (as in the Monmouth Priory charter), we should probably assume that the document is serving the ancient function of a symbolic object, rather than being considered primarily for its contents in a modern literate way.

The increasing use of documents created tension between the old methods and the new. Which was the better evidence, for example, seeing a parchment or hearing a man's word? How was the one to be evaluated if it conflicted with the other? A good illustration of this particular dilemma is Eadmer's account of the investiture controversy between St Anselm, archbishop of Canterbury, and Henry I. Both Anselm and the king had sent envoys to Pope Paschal II; Anselm sent two monks of Canterbury, while the king sent the archbishop of York and two other bishops. The envoys returned to England in September 1101 with papal letters addressed to the king and to Anselm, prohibiting royal investiture of churches and exhorting resistance to them. When the pope's letter to Anselm had been publicly read out, Henry's envoys objected. They claimed that Paschal had given them a purely verbal message that he would treat the king leniently on the investiture question and would not excommunicate him; the pope had added that he did not wish this concession to be put in written form (*per carte inscriptionem*) because other rulers would use it as a precedent. Anselm's envoys replied that the pope had given no verbal message which conflicted in any way with his letters. To this Henry's bishops answered that Paschal had acted in one way in secret and another in public. Baldwin of Bec, Anselm's chief envoy, was outraged at this allegation and said that it was a calumny on the Holy See.

Dissension then arose in the audience. Those favouring Anselm maintained that credence should be given to 'documents signed with the pope's seal' (*scriptis sigillo pape signatis*) and not to 'the uncertainty of mere words'. The king's side replied that they preferred to rely on the word of three bishops than on 'the skins of wethers blackened with ink and weighted with a little lump of lead'. They added further venom to the argument by alleging that monks were unreliable anyway, as they should not be engaged in worldly business. Eadmer puts the controversy into dialogue form:

Anselm's monks: 'But what about the evidence of the letters?'
Henry's bishops: 'As we don't accept the evidence of monks against bishops, why should we accept that of a sheepskin?'

Anselm's monks: 'Shame on you! Are not the Gospels written down on
      sheepskins?'

Obviously the conflict could not be quickly resolved. In Lent 1102 Anselm
set out for Rome and opened on his way another letter from the pope, in
which Paschal denied that he had ever given contradictory verbal instructions to the bishops or said that he was reluctant to set a precedent in writing. Who was telling the truth is of course impossible to resolve. Paschal
was attempting to make peace and settle the investiture controversy by
diplomacy. He may well therefore have said something off the record to
the bishops which they had possibly exaggerated. Like all statesmen, the
pope obviously had to make a formal denial of such secret negotiations
once they became public.

    The substance of the story is not our concern here, but the attitudes it
reveals towards documentary evidence. Papal letters, sealed with the
leaden bull and bearing the symbols and monograms of curial officials,
were the most impressive documents produced in medieval Europe, their
only rival being Byzantine imperial letters. Yet in Eadmer's story the papal
bull is disparagingly described as a sheepskin blackened with ink with a
bit of lead attached to it, an extreme example of a document being treated
simply as a physical object rather than for its contents. Anselm's supporters were entitled to riposte that the Gospels too were written on
parchment—in other words, that Christianity was essentially the religion
of a book. At Orléans in 1022 a group of heretics had been burned for
disparaging the book learning of the clergy cross-examining them, which
they had called human fabrications 'written on the skins of animals',
whereas the heretics claimed to believe 'in the law written in the inner
man by the Holy Spirit'. The heretics had therefore been arguing that the
true written law (*lex scripta*) was not canon law nor Justinian's code, but
inspiration retained in the mind alone; real writing was not man-made
script on animal parchment. Such an idea may well have derived from the
Scripture itself, most probably from St Paul's Second Epistle to the
Corinthians, 'written not with ink, but with the spirit of the living God . . .
for the letter killeth, but the spirit giveth life'. Early in the thirteenth century St Francis was to take up this theme as part of his revolt against the
spiritually empty book learning of some monks: 'Those religious have
been killed by the letter who are not willing to follow the spirit of the
divine letter, but only desire to know words and interpret them for other
men.'[6] As so often in his work, Francis blended orthodox and heretical
viewpoints in an insight of his own. Literacy was not a virtue in itself.

Emphasis on the word inscribed spiritually on the minds of men, as contrasted with letters written on parchment, retained its strength in the Christian message as it did in secular conveyancing ceremonies.

The argument of Henry I's envoys, that their word was better evidence than a papal bull, would not in fact have appeared as outrageous or surprising to contemporaries as Eadmer suggests in his account of the controversy with Anselm. The principle that 'oral witness deserves more credence than written evidence' was a legal commonplace. It was cited, for example, by Hubert Walter, archbishop of Canterbury, in a letter to Innocent III in 1200 controverting Gerald of Wales's well-documented claim to be bishop-elect of St David's. Gerald conceded the point in his reply to the pope, but added that he had brought both documents and witnesses. Behind this principle lay the correct assumption that numerous documents used in legal claims, from the Donation of Constantine downwards, were forgeries. Not all those who relied on the traditional use of the spoken word, rather than parchments, were necessarily therefore obscurantist conservatives. The technology of written record was insufficiently advanced to be efficient or reliable. As a consequence, documents and the spoken word are frequently both used in a way which appears superfluous to a modern literate. To make a record often meant to bear oral witness, not to produce a document. For example, in the civil war of Stephen's reign Robert earl of Gloucester and Miles earl of Hereford made a treaty of friendship in writing, in the form of a sealed letter; yet both parties in this document also name witnesses, who are 'to make legal record of this agreement in court if necessary'.

The rule that oral witness is preferable to documents, like the rule that seisin is superior to a charter, shows how cautiously—and perhaps reluctantly—written evidence was accepted. Much important business continued to be done by word of mouth. Bearers of letters were often given instructions which were to be conveyed *viva voce*, either because that was convenient and traditional or because the information was too secret to write down. Twice, for instance, in March 1229 Henry III sent messengers to the count of Toulouse. In their mouths, the king wrote, he had put matters which they would disclose more fully to the count, since the business (presumably concerning a truce with Louis IX) could not be committed to writing because of the dangers of the roads. Similarly in the period of the baronial rebellion, when Henry was in France in 1260, he wrote to the earl of Gloucester instructing him to report on the state of the kingdom by Gilbert Fitz Hugh, the king's serjeant, who would tell the earl more fully *viva voce* about the king's situation. In such negotiations the letter itself did not convey essential information but, like a modern ambassador's letter of credence, was a symbolic object replacing the messenger's ring or other *signum* which had formerly identified him as a confidential agent of his master.

Oral messages were also used to give instructions which later generations would have put in writing. For example, in 1234 John le Franceis and John Mansel were authorised by royal letters of credence to conduct inquiries concerning Jews in certain counties and give instructions to sheriffs *viva voce*. An interesting but non-English case of oral delivery is the poem which the troubadour, Jaufre Rudel, lord of Blaye in the Gironde, sent to the Comte de Marche in *c.* 1150 'without a parchment document' (*senes breu de parguamina*) by the mouth of the jongleur, Filhol.[7] The jongleur is thus being used as a kind of living letter. There is, however, a paradox in all such evidence, since historians can only know of the survival of oral ways of conveying information by extant written evidence. Jaufre Rudel's poem, once sent without a script, is written down none the less.

Much business was still done by word of mouth for the obvious reason that documents were bound to be relatively rare until printing made their automatic reproduction possible. The usual way of publishing new laws and regulations was by proclamation. The following instances from the Chancery records of Henry III for 1234 are typical. On 28 August the sheriff of Northumberland and some others were ordered to have it proclaimed (*clamari facias*) that pleas were to be adjourned until the coming of the eyre justices. On 29 August all sheriffs were to proclaim the regulations for supervising hundred courts in accordance with the revision of Magna Carta in 1234. On 1 September the sheriff of Norfolk and Suffolk was to proclaim throughout the two counties that no Jew was to lend money to any Christian in the king's demesne. Matthew Paris suggests that Henry III pursued a policy of legislating by proclamation: in 1248 the people were harassed by diverse precepts promulgated 'by the voice of a crier' (*voce preconia*) throughout the cities of England; the king established a new fair at Westminster, for example, in this way. The proclamation to which Matthew gives most attention likewise occurred in 1248, when the king 'ordered it to be proclaimed as law by the voice of a crier' that henceforward no man might castrate another for fornication except a husband in the case of his wife's adulterer. The reason for this was that John le Bretun had castrated the Norfolk knight, Godfrey de Millers, for lying with his daughter.

How extensively or frequently proclamations of this sort were made is not clear. Proclamations were a quick and effective way of conveying information in crowded cities like London, but were obviously less practical in the countryside. Most references to proclamations concern cities. For example, in 1252 Henry III had it proclaimed throughout London that no one should lend money to the abbot of Westminster; or in the preceding year a proclamation had been made against the royal judge, Henry of Bath, in London and in the king's court. One consequence for the historian of Henry III's government's use of the spoken word for legislation is that all trace of it is lost, unless a chronicler happened to record it or the Chancery rolls refer to it incidentally. Edward I is considered a great lawgiver partly because the legislation of his time is preserved in the statute rolls. In Henry III's reign less was written down, though a comparable amount of legislative activity probably took place.

Magna Carta became the great precedent for putting legislation into writing. Yet even it was not officially enrolled in the royal archives, although it was proclaimed extensively and repeatedly. Within a few days of King John's assent to it letters were sent to all his sheriffs, foresters, gamekeepers, watermen, and other bailiffs informing them of the agreement between the king and the barons, 'as you can hear and see by our charter which we have had made thereon', which they were ordered to have read publicly throughout their bailiwicks.[8] As a result, in theory at least, everyone in England should have heard Magna Carta read out, although it is unlikely that a sufficient number of copies were available. Similarly when the barons again had the upper hand in 1265, they ordered the terms of Henry III's oath to keep peace with them to be published in the full county court at least twice every year, at Easter and Michaelmas. In 1300 transcripts of Magna Carta and the Charter of the Forest were delivered to every sheriff to read out 'before the people' four times a year, at Christmas and Midsummer as well as at Easter and Michaelmas. Nevertheless by 1300 there had been a significant change, as considerable emphasis was now being put on seeing the document as well as hearing it. Sealed transcripts of Magna Carta were sent to all judges, sheriffs, and civic officials and also to all cathedral churches. A precedent for the latter had been made in 1279 when Archbishop Pecham's council at Reading had ordered a copy of Magna Carta to be posted up in every cathedral and collegiate church in a public place 'so that it can be clearly seen by the eyes of everyone entering'; in the spring of each year the old copy was to be taken down and a new fair copy substituted for it.[9] The royal government was sufficiently alarmed to make Pecham have all these copies removed from church doors shortly afterwards.

By 1300 there should have been hundreds of copies of Magna Carta in existence, some transcribed into books of statutes and others circulating in individual exemplars. Not all those who saw them were able to read Latin, but they could be assured of Magna Carta's main points by oral explanations and be confident that the document existed. In modern society similarly it is only lawyers who understand the full texts of legislation; the literate public are generally satisfied with newscasts and press summaries. The copies of Magna Carta which have survived from the thirteenth century are not all identical in their texts, even those of the same redaction, which they would be if they had been printed or photocopied like modern statutes. Not only did scribes make mistakes which were overlooked, they also inserted emendations which in their judgement made better sense of the text. They wrote the words *in capite*, for example, into Clause 34 of Magna Carta in order to update it, even though there was no textual warrant for this. 'Most scribes were not tremendously concerned to follow their exemplars exactly. The charter mattered, but what mattered to both compilers of statute books and writers of chronicles was its gist, not its exact words.'[10] Manuscript culture put the emphasis in any text on its current presentation rather than its archaeological correctness. This was because reading aloud compelled both reader and listener to make immediate sense of the text. Insistence on absolute literal accuracy is a consequence of printing, compounded by photocopying and computing. As Ong points out, the mechanisation of letter formation disengages words entirely from speech and living thought; writing takes on an independent existence in typographic space.[11] Operatives of printers and photocopiers can produce texts which have not passed through their minds at all, which was impossible in manuscript culture.

Public readings of documents were done in the vernacular as well as in Latin and might reach a wider audience that way. Thus in 1300, according to the chronicler Rishanger, Magna Carta was read out at Westminster 'first in Latin (*litteraliter*) and then in the native tongue (*patriae lingua*)'. Similarly a year earlier letters of Pope Boniface VIII about the peace between England and France had been read out in Parliament 'in Latin for the literate and in the native tongue for the illiterate'. Also in 1299, according to the Worcester annals, royal letters concerning a new perambulation of the forests were 'proclaimed in the city of Worcester in the mother tongue (*materna lingua*)'. The 'paternal' or 'maternal' language might mean either English or French. Thus in 1254 the papal excommunication of infringers of Magna Carta was ordered to be published 'in the English (*Anglicana*) and French (*Gallicana*) tongues' whenever and wherever appropriate. The use of English and French in this instance was probably a reiteration of existing practice, rather than an innovation, as it is likely that Magna Carta itself had been proclaimed throughout the land in both English and French in 1215.

The distinction the chroniclers wished to emphasise in the citations above was between the language of literacy (Latin) and spoken language; they were less concerned with which vernacular was used. To pedantic Latinists vernacular simply meant the spoken language. Gerald of Wales hoped that someone would translate his work into French and claimed that Walter Map used to tell him that he (Gerald) had written much, whereas Walter had said much. Although Gerald's writings (*scripta*) were more praiseworthy and durable than Walter's speeches (*dicta*), Walter had the greater profit because his *dicta* were accessible, since they were expressed in the common idiom, while Gerald's *scripta* were appreciated only by the declining few who knew Latin. In fact the distinction Gerald drew here between himself and Walter Map was misleading, as Walter also was a precocious Latinist. Possibly Gerald felt that Walter had been a more successful preacher and *raconteur* in the vernacular than he was. The point of the story from our angle, regardless of whether it is true or not, is that Gerald felt that the spoken vernacular brought greater prestige than written Latin.

Whatever the language, and whether the record was held solely in the bearer's memory or was committed to parchment, the medieval recipient prepared himself to listen to an utterance rather than to scrutinise a document visually as a modern literate would. This was due to a different habit of mind; it was not because the recipient was illiterate in any sense of that word. Literary works, especially vernacular ones, were frequently explicitly addressed by the author to an audience, rather than to readers as such. Thus the nun of Barking in her French version of Ailred's life of Edward the Confessor in *c.* 1163 requests 'all who hear, or will ever hear, this romance of hers' not to despise it because the translation is done by a woman.[12] In the *Romance of Horn* by Master Thomas the author begins by addressing his audience: 'Lords, you have heard the lines of parchment' (*Seignurs, oi avez le vers del parchemin*). The parchment is evidently thought of here as a direct substitute for a jongleur; it speaks and is heard, like the charter of Richard de Cormeilles for St Mary's Priory at Monmouth. Likewise in the *Estoire de Waldef* (dating from *c.* 1190) the author refers to the *Brut* story:

> If anyone wants to know this history
> Let him read the *Brut*, he will hear it there

(Qui l'estoire savoir voldra
Lise le Brut, illoc l'orra)[13]

A modern literate would not say 'he will *hear* it there', but 'he will *find* it'
or 'see it there'. The emphasis in such works on hearing does not necessarily mean that their contents stem directly from oral tradition, but that
reading continued to be conceived in terms of hearing rather than seeing.
Until cheap printing supplied every 'reader' with his own book, this
emphasis on hearing was understandable.

Latin works too were generally intended to be read aloud—hence the
speeches and frequent use of dramatic dialogue in monastic chronicles.
Eadmer concludes the first book of his *Life of St Anselm* with an interval, as in a play: 'But here, lest our unpolished speech (*oratio*) weary our
readers or hearers by being too long drawn-out, we shall make our first
halt in the work.'[14] Traditional monastic reading in particular bore little
relation to a modern literate's approach to a book. *Lectio* was 'more a
process of rumination than reading, directed towards savouring the divine
wisdom within a book rather than finding new ideas or novel information'.[15] The process is well illustrated by St Anselm's *Meditation on Human
Redemption*: 'Taste the goodness of your redeemer . . . chew the honey-
comb of his words, suck their flavour which is sweeter than honey, swallow
their wholesome sweetness. Chew by thinking, suck by understanding,
swallow by loving and rejoicing.'[16] Reading was a physical exertion, demanding the use not only of the eyes, but of tongue, mouth and throat.
Writing was a similar act of endurance, requiring three fingers to hold the
pen, two eyes to see the words, one tongue to speak them, and the whole
body to labour. For these reasons some monks argued that work in the
scriptorium was an adequate substitute for manual labour.

Ideally a 'reader' was expected to look at the text as well as listen to it,
but that was the exception and not the rule. In the *Life of St Margaret* of
Scotland the author considered it a point worth remarking that Margaret's daughter, Matilda (Henry I's queen), 'desired not only to hear, but
also to inspect continually the impress of the letters' of her mother's life.[17]
A school manual, not English and later than our period, sums up in a
dialogue the medieval meaning of 'reading' (*lectio*):

'Are you a scholar, what do you read?'
'I do not read, I listen.'
'What do you hear?'
'Donatus or Alexander, or logic or music.'[18]

Donatus's *Ars Minor* and Alexander's *Doctrinale* were Latin textbooks. The term 'reading' a subject has been preserved at Oxford and Cambridge; whereas some undergraduates think that 'reading' implies studying books instead of hearing lectures, medieval students understood *lectio* primarily to mean that the master read while they listened. Whole books were published by being read aloud. Gerald of Wales says that he published his *Topography of Ireland* in this way in *c.* 1188 by reading it at Oxford to different audiences on three successive days. But Gerald's action was not typical, as he boasts that 'neither has the present age seen, nor does any past age bear record of, the like in England'. The normal way of disseminating scholarly works, as distinct from popular romances, was by the modern method of circulating copies. For instance Herbert of Bosham assumed in his life of Becket that his readers will be able to study Becket's correspondence, which he omits for the sake of brevity, 'because that book of letters is already in the possession of many persons and churches'. If Becket is thought too exceptional an example because of his extraordinary popularity, Eadmer mentions in his appendix to St Anselm's *Life* that he intends to make a new start, because the *Life* has already 'been transcribed by many and distributed to various churches'. Distributing copies did not of course rule out public readings; on the contrary, as more books became available, the practice may have grown even more widespread.

Just as reading was linked in the medieval mind with hearing rather than seeing, writing (in its modern sense of composition) was associated with dictating rather than manipulating a pen. Reading and writing were not inseparably coupled with each other, as they are today. A person might be able to write, yet not be considered literate. As we have seen, Walter Map mentions a boy 'who was not *litteratus*, although he knew how to transcribe any series of letters whatever'. Literacy involved being learned in Latin, whereas writing was the process of making a fair copy on parchment, which was the art of the scribe. Some authors (notably the great monastic historians Orderic Vitalis, William of Malmesbury, and Matthew Paris) did their own writing, but they are the exceptions and they distinguished that activity from composition.

Medieval distinctions are well illustrated by Eadmer. He explains that he had to conceal from St Anselm that he was 'writing' his biography. When he had begun the work 'and had had already transcribed on to parchment a great part of what I had composed (*dictaveram*) in wax', Anselm asked 'what it was I was composing and copying' (*quid dictitarem, quid scriptitarem*). The process of composing on wax tablets is thus

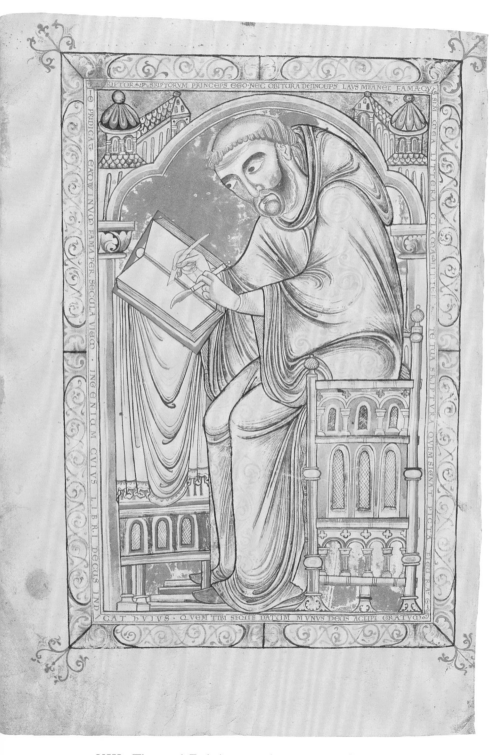

PLATE VIII. The monk Eadwine at work on a manuscript *c.* 1150.
The inscription round the frame declares him to be 'the prince of writers'

described in Latin by the word *dictitare* (literally, 'to dictate'), even though in Eadmer's case he was dictating to himself. The use of 'writing' (*scriptitare*) is confined to making the fair copy on parchment. Similarly when Orderic Vitalis wishes to say that before the time of William the Conqueror the Normans had concentrated on war rather than reading and writing, the phrase he uses is *legere vel dictare*, not *legere vel scribere*.[19] Numerous other examples of using 'dictate' where a modern literate would use 'write' could be given. Dictating was the usual form of literary composition and the *ars dictaminis*, taught in the schools as part of rhetoric, was the skill governing it. Letter writing was thus an intellecutal skill using the mouth rather than the hand. Peter of Blois, a busy secretary of state like John of Salisbury, boasted that the archbishop of Canterbury had seen him dictating to three different scribes on diverse subjects, while he dictated and wrote a fourth letter all at the one time.

Reading aloud and dictating permit the non-literate to participate in the use of documents, whereas reading and writing silently exclude the illiterate. When the voice is used, the clerk or scribe becomes no more than a medium between the speaker or hearer and the document. Neither the hearer of a book nor the *dictator* of a letter needs to be a master of every detail of the scribal technique himself, just as modern managers are not required to type or to programme computers. Obviously it is helpful if the manager understands how these things are done and has some experience of them, but this experience is not indispensable. For these reasons medieval kings and their officials, such as sheriffs in the counties, did not need to be literate in the modern sense. Lack of literacy did not mean that they were ignorant or incapable of coping with business; they were as literate as the tasks required. As the number of documents increased and habits of silent visual reading became more common, levels of literacy (in the modern sense) presumably increased also; but there is no evidence of a crisis suddenly demanding numerous literates. Because the pre-literate emphasis on the spoken word persisted, the change from oral to literate modes could occur slowly and almost imperceptibly over many generations.

The text usually quoted to show that medieval attitudes towards literacy were similar to modern ones is John of Salisbury's quotation in *Policraticus* that '*Rex illitteratus est quasi asinus coronatus*' (an illiterate king is like a crowned ass).[20] In this passage John is primarily concerned that the prince should have wisdom, which is gained by reading the law of God daily. For that reason, and not for administrative requirements, the prince needs skill in letters. John concedes moreover that it is not absolutely necessary for the prince to be *litteratus*, provided he takes advice from *litterati*, that is, from priests who, like Old Testament prophets, will remind the prince of the law of God. 'Thus the mind of the prince may read in the tongue of the priest. For the life and tongue of priests are like the book of life before the face of the peoples.' John is obviously thinking here of the spiritual, and not the worldly, value of reading. His discussion emphasises that an illiterate prince can participate in wisdom through the medium of the priest's voice. The prince is not excluded by being illiterate: 'nor is he altogether destitute of reading (*lectionis*) who, even though he does not read himself, hears faithfully what is read to him by others'. John thus shows that in his day non-literates could participate in literate culture; he is not arguing for the absolute necessity of rulers being literate in either the medieval sense of being learned in Latin or the modern sense of having a minimal ability to read and write. Ironically the king of England at the time, Henry II, was literate in every sense of the word; yet he was not a good king by John's definition, as he refused to listen to the lectures of priests and was responsible for the murder of Becket.

XI

WRITINGS AS WORKS OF ART

Writing has the power to change the way words are perceived by the senses, because it shifts the emphasis in communicating language from hearing to seeing. The language of script can be received 'through the windows of the eyes' by silent reading, or it can be transmitted 'voicelessly', even to people not yet born, by shaping letters with the hand. In non-literate cultures the skills of eye and hand are associated primarily with craftsmanship and the visual arts, while the skills of language which depend on the transmission of sound are identified with mouth and ear. Although writing had the potential, in medieval England as elsewhere, to change the perception of language by making it visual as well as auditory, it is also true that pre-literate habits of mind persisted long after documents became common. Books and letters continued to be read aloud and listened to, instead of being silently scrutinised by the eye, and authors went on thinking of composition in terms of dictation rather than of manipulating a pen. The skills of reading and writing therefore remained separate, because reading was part of the mastery of speech whereas writing was one of the manual and visual arts.

Early medieval civilisation shared with other ancient cultures of the world an approach to writing which was non-utilitarian. The skills of the scribe were primarily devoted not to transmitting mundane information in an economical and straightforward way, but to making illuminated manuscripts which were masterpieces of calligraphy, painting, jewellery, and metalwork. In such works as the *Book of Kells* or the *Lindisfarne Gospels* the text was of secondary importance. It was there to remind the chanter of the familiar phrases of the liturgy, if he did not immediately recall them, and to serve as an act of worship in itself by catching the words of God in sacred script and displaying them on the page like butterflies in a showcase. Writing was aimed at God's eye more often than at communicating information to fellow human beings. For that reason books were kept on the altar or in a sacristy rather than in a library. Because illuminated manuscripts appealed primarily to the eye, like pictures, they could be understood almost as well by the non-literate as by the literate. To appreciate their finer points required expertise, but the knowledge needed was that of the artist and craftsman rather than that of the linguistically educated. Walter Map distinguished the good scribe, who 'knew how to transcribe any series of letters whatever', from the *litteratus*. The scribe was expert in calligraphy, whereas the *litteratus* was expert in Latin.

The separation of the skills of reading and writing continued up until the invention of printing and was not immediately affected by the proliferation of documents in the twelfth and thirteenth centuries. Gutenberg himself, the putative inventor of printing, had not aimed to supersede the illuminated book, but to improve it and make it more readily available. The earliest book to come from his press, the 42-line Bible, is indistinguishable at first sight from an illuminated manuscript. Similarly the first dated book (18 November 1477) printed by Caxton, *The Dictes and Sayengs of the Philosophers*, was copied and illuminated by hand from the printed text for presentation to Edward IV and his family, presumably because the printed version was thought too poor-quality a product to present at court. Caxton states proudly that the book had been 'sette in forme and emprynted in this manere as ye maye here in this booke see', but the king might not have been so pleased by an untried technology which produced inferior goods.[1] He and his kind were not going to benefit from mass-production anyway. Writings continued to be works of art, embellished in a variety of ways, as long as they were produced by hand. However humble a scrivener he was, the medieval scribe was an individual artist, who had to discipline himself to achieve anonymity and uniformity, whereas printing imposes uniformity automatically and excludes ornamentation except when it has been deliberately planned in advance.

At the very time that documents were beginning to be used in greater numbers for business purposes, in the middle of the twelfth century, some of the most elaborately written and illuminated manuscripts were produced. In pride of place stand the glossed texts of Scripture, such as the Psalter inscribed *Johannes me fecit Rogerio* ('John made me for Roger'), the double-glossed Epistles of St Paul, and the Eadwine Psalter. Eadwine's work is clearly in the old tradition of emphasising form in writing rather than literal meaning, as elegant design takes precedence over textual accuracy. His Anglo-Saxon text is peculiarly corrupt and his Latin has unnecessary errors. The scribe and the *litteratus* were not invariably at odds, however, as the Winchester Bible (which is contemporary with Eadwine's Psalter) has a good text as well as magnificent calligraphy and illuminations. In the unusually purist opinion of St Hugh's Carthusians, the correctness of the text was its best feature. A rigid distinction between an artistic and a practical manuscript is often impossible to make, because a synthesis of the beautiful and the functional is a general characteristic of medieval art, as churches and castles make abundantly evident.

Even the most businesslike manuscripts required some embellishment, in the form of rubrics and enlarged initials, to enable the user to find his place in the book. Thus the larger volume of Domesday Book uses vermilion paint for three distinct types of rubrication—capital letters for the names of shires and other headings; shading for the initial letter of each paragraph and certain abbreviations; underlining for the names of places and tenants. The rubrication contributes to making Domesday Book a masterpiece of functional layout, which is a form of abstract art in itself. Subsequently, however, the embellishment of the Domesday text was taken much further when multi-coloured copies were made from it: one in the twelfth century (*Herefordshire Domesday*) and another in the thirteenth (the Exchequer Breviate). Unlike the original, these manuscripts are primarily ornamental. They show that Domesday Book had achieved the status of a revered text, which was worthy to be beautified and embellished like a Gospel book. The name 'Domesday', recalling the book of Revelation, had already associated it with Holy Writ.

Most manuscript books show a similar mixture of the pictorial and the functional. A representative small collection are the dozen English lawyers' manuals, containing parliamentary statutes and other texts for ready reference (dating from a decade or so on either side of 1300), which are now preserved at the Harvard Law School. Lawyers' textbooks might be expected to be severely practical and economical in format. A few are, notably MS 36 in the Harvard collection, which uses rubrics sparingly and is written rather untidily, like a plea roll, in a rapid business hand. By contrast, MS 173 has initials illuminated in blue, green and gold leaf, in addition to the usual rubrics; while MS 12 has broad margins, pictorial initials, and other drawings illustrating the subject matter of the statutes; for example, a boar and a deer in a wood and a man shooting a deer with a longbow accompany the text of the charter of the Forest. English canon lawyers' books of decretals of a century earlier show similar contrasts between plain working copies, presumably used by practitioners and teachers, and illuminated fair copies intended for presentation or as show pieces.

At the opposite poles of writings intended to catch the eye of God with their illuminations and writings intended for mundane consultation are liturgical manuscripts on the one hand and the public records (particularly legal and financial documents) on the other. Yet here also some exceptions can be found. The Sherborne cartulary of the mid-twelfth century integrates royal charters and illuminated liturgical texts into one book intended for the altar. Conversely the most mundane public records are occasionally illustrated. Thus an Exchequer receipt roll for 1233 has at its head an elaborate drawing caricaturing prominent Jews of Norwich, and a plea roll for 1249 depicts trial by combat and the hanging of the loser. Much more common throughout the royal records are amateurly foliated initials and caricatured heads in profile, which seem to be doodles made by bored enrolling clerks. In a plea roll from 1249, which has a friendly-looking devil at the foot of one membrane, the clerk admitted his boredom by cancelling an enrolment and replacing it with what may have been a snatch from a French popular song, which in translation reads: 'It's my little loves that keep me cheerful and give me fun.'[2] Traditional scribal habits made rigorous formality and a total lack of personal embellishment difficult to impose. In private business documents minor embellishments are even more common, as scribes were less constrained by bureaucratic standards. For example, the earliest account roll of Crowland Abbey (dating from 1258–9) is ornamented with foliations, animal heads and what seem to be facetious portraits. Although to a modern eye such amateur ornament detracts from a document's dignity, the monastic writer even of an account roll may have felt obliged to give his work some embellishment to make it look authoritative.

The continuing emphasis on the visual aspects of writing, despite the increasing number of business documents (which grew more uniform and economical of materials and time in the thirteenth century), helped to bridge the gap between non-literate and literate, just as the persistence of reading aloud and listening did. As we have seen, before writing became common, people were accustomed to use knives, or even Gospel books, as symbolic objects which could be transferred in the presence of witnesses as a sign that property had been duly conveyed. Conveyances by charter may have been made acceptable to non-literates by the seals attached to them. Like illuminated manuscripts embellished with precious stones and relics, seals were visible and tangible symbols of a donor's wishes. Neither clergy nor laity would have trusted or admired documents which were writings pure and unadorned, because they would have been inadequate as symbols of a person's wishes. It is true, however, that the modern belief that medieval books were invariably magnificently illuminated is a misconception, which has grown up because—generally—only the most lavish manuscripts are exhibited or made into facsimiles.

To knights, who were on the threshold of literacy in the twelfth century, writings may have appeared attractive as another system of signs. Their capacity to devise and understand a complex system of pictorial signs is shown by the development of heraldry, which is contemporary with the shift from memory to written record. The first recorded rolls of arms were illustrated and written in the language of blazon in the middle of the thirteenth century, although heraldry had been developing visually and orally for more than a century before that. Whether the growth of recorded heraldry and the contemporaneous spread of literacy among knights are coincidental or connected developments is a matter for conjecture. Inauguration into literate ways of thought through pictorial manuscripts and visual symbols like seals may have caused knights to create an alternative system of 'shapes indicating voices' in heraldry. Traditionally 'letters' were the clergy's symbolic way of indicating their superior status, since a *clericus* was a *litteratus*. Heraldry originated as an alternative language of signs. Clerics intoning the Latin liturgy at the altar from great illuminated manuscripts wore embroidered vestments bearing sacred scenes and insignia: the Holy Cross, the Lamb of God, Alpha and Omega, and many others. The knights, who were their brothers both spiritually and in fact, responded with a liturgy and learned language of their own. Their silken coats of arms displayed the insignia of their calling and their families in the form of stylised animals, birds, plants and geometric shapes.

In England heraldic shields are first found depicted in a series on the pages of a Psalter, which may date from the 1230s and contains work by the illuminator William de Brailes. The shields were probably included on the instructions of the knightly family who commissioned this book. Shields are first found massed on the page in order of rank of the persons concerned, as if recorded by a herald, in Matthew Paris's 'Book of Additions' to his chronicles. The heraldic drawing on these shields is very similar in style to the shields in the margins of Matthew's chronicles, which he devised as a finding system (see pages 330–1 above). Thus the traitor William Marsh's broken shield and Frederick II's reversed imperial eagle stand in the margins of the page alongside the notices of their deaths. Matthew was the greatest all-round writer in the monastic tradition in thirteenth-century Europe. Throughout his work he shows that the ideal of making a synthesis of the visual and the intellectual in writing was still alive, as he composed and penned his own works and illustrated them with line drawings, maps, diagrams and more formal paintings. Nor did he ignore the need for accurate texts, although like other scribal artists he considered himself entitled to make variations and embellishments of his own. Matthew Paris is exceptional in his abilities, but not in his approach to his art, which treats writing as a visual skill inseparable from pictorial values.

In Matthew Paris's history of Edward the Confessor, which he wrote in French rhyming couplets probably in the 1240s for the royal family, he provided illustrations (*portraiture figurée* is his term). 'For I desire and wish', he explained, 'that what the ear hears the eye may see.' In writing in French for the aristocratic laity Matthew was in line with current fashion. Another schoolman and contemporary of Matthew's, Richard de Fournival, wrote in northern France a popularising work which he entitled *Li Bestiare d'Amours*, 'The Bestiary of Love'. Bestiaries, describing animals real and imaginary, were a familiar genre of picture-book which introduced the laity to natural history and mythology. Among the earliest writings in French is Philip de Thaon's bestiary, composed for Henry I's queen Adeliza in the 1120s.

One of the pictures which Richard de Fournival designed for his bestiary is an image of Lady Memory, standing in a niche like the statue of a saint, flanked on her right by a gigantic disembodied eye and on her left by an ear. He explains the symbolism: 'Memory has two doors, sight and hearing'; the paths to these doors are imagery (*painture*) and speech (*parole*); imagery serves the eye and speech the ear. 'When I am not present', he adds, 'this writing—by its *painture* and by its *parole*—will bring me back to your memory as though I were present.'[3] The supposedly ignorant vernacular reader thus has the commonplaces of medieval psychological theory presented to him, or rather her, in dramatic form. Like Matthew Paris, Richard de Fournival thinks of the text (his 'writing'— *escrit*) entering the intellect primarily through the ear. 'All writing', he comments, 'is done to signify *parole* so that one may read it; and when one reads it, it reverts to its nature as *parole*.' The typical medieval reader therefore reconstituted the script before his eyes as speech (*parole*) by spelling it out, either silently in his mind or pronouncing it aloud. Richard does concede, however, that writing is not purely auditory; it also has the quality of *painture* 'because a letter does not exist unless one depicts it'.[4]

Comments of this sort by medieval authors suggest that they questioned the value of writing and that neither they nor their readers took its significance for granted. Did writing exist independently of speech? Was it heard or seen? Was it a record or a picture? The paradoxes of writing are pointed up in the portrait of Eadwine of Canterbury 'the prince of writers' in the Eadwine Psalter. This portrait may have been made as an obituary for him in the 1160s. The inscription round its frame takes the form of a dialogue in Latin rhyme between the 'writer' and the 'letter'. The 'writer' poses a riddle: 'Ask my letter who I am.' The 'letter' answers: 'You whom the painted image shows, your writing declares to be Eadwine, living by your fame through the ages.'

★

However many explanations and versions of a text a scribe as expert as Eadwine could fit on to a single page, difficulties remained with any statement in writing even for the most expert reader. Writing, like all language, has the capacity to mislead, either unintentionally (when the reader misunderstands it) or by the author's design. Doubt remains, moreover, even when the tone of an author's statement can be established and his sources verified. Writing is so attractive a medium for the artist precisely because of its disjuncture from speech. The writer (in the modern sense of a creator of fiction) makes imagined voices ring true; he takes the word from 'its natural, oral habitat' (in Ong's metaphor) and sounds it out in the solitude of his study.[5] No 'notarial art', in John of Salisbury's sense, could ever have distinguished the certain from the dubious in the writings of such contemporaries of his as Geoffrey of Monmouth and Walter Map. They divided and fascinated readers then, just as they perplex medievalists now. John of Salisbury himself produced doubt and ambiguity in his own writings, deliberately 'manufacturing pseudo-antiques' in the opinion of one modern critic.[6] Even the tone of his description of the lost 'notarial art' is difficult to gauge, as his references to Seneca and Cicero are flawed. Whether John misquoted classical texts because he could not get better copies of them, or whether he did it deliberately, remains a matter of opinion. Before the Italian Renaissance, even scholars as learned as John had a less literal attitude towards texts. They were not going to let 'the industry of the ancients', as Walter Map called it (perhaps facetiously), bury their own creations.

Before John of Salisbury, Gilbert Crispin abbot of Westminster (c. 1085–c. 1117) had taken up the same subject of 'notations' (using Isidore of Seville's *Etymologies*, as John had done), in order to argue that 'just as letters stand in one way as images and notations of words, so also pictures exist as likenesses and notations of things written.'[7] Gilbert did not mean this was invariably the case, but that it applied in the particular context he was discussing, which was the controversy about images in Christian worship. The passage occurs in Gilbert's *Dispute of a Jew with a Christian*, where the Christian argues that a sculpture of Christ in Majesty surrounded by the four Evangelist symbols (a recurrent theme in Romanesque art) is justifiable because this image occurs in the Old Testament itself. 'Therefore what Isaiah saw, said and wrote, what Ezechiel saw, said and wrote, may after them be said and written and signified by some pictorial notation.'[8] Gilbert traces an unbroken line from seeing through saying to writing, because medieval readers of the Bible believed that the sacred page of scripture was literally what the prophets themselves had written down. As Gilbert's Christian explains in the passage above, there are three stages in approaching Isaiah or Ezechiel: first there is 'saying' (that is, reading the text aloud), secondly there is 'writing' (as in the penning of the sacred page in a monastic scriptorium), and finally there is 'signifying' pictorially (by painting or otherwise giving visible shape to the text in question). As the starting point of Isaiah or Ezechiel had been a vision, not a text, the reader's ultimate aim must be to reconstruct that vision.

But Gilbert Crispin was being disingenuous, as it cannot have escaped his notice that a great deal of imagery in Romanesque art, in sacred manuscripts as much as in churches, did not explicitly signify or illustrate things in Scripture. Gilbert might have replied that illustrating the mysteries of Scripture was best done implicitly, through symbolism, rather than explicitly. In the example he gives of the four Evangelist symbols described in the prophecy of Ezechiel, the reader has to know that the man's face in Ezechiel's vision prefigures the Evangelist Matthew, the lion prefigures Mark, the ox Luke, and the eagle John. The image of the eagle, for example, can therefore be read as the name of the Evangelist John, like a pictogram in a non-alphabetic script. This accords with Pope Gregory the Great's justification of 'reading by seeing' and it accords too with Gilbert's description of pictures as 'notations' (*note*), just as letters are 'notations'. Once the symbolism is understood, such grotesque images as the Evangelist Luke seated with pen and parchment facing backwards on an ox, or Mark seated with a portable writing-frame but having the head of a lion, make sense (these examples are taken from English books of Gilbert's time). Since symbolic imagery was drawn from a mass of Christian and pagan sources, what looks like monstrous ornamentation in manuscripts can sometimes be due to a modern reader's ignorance of its meaning rather than to its maker's lack of religious fervour. 'Few habits of the medieval mind are as foreign to the modern Western world as the impulse to take symbolism seriously.'[9]

When prayer-books begin to be made for the laity—mainly for aristocratic ladies—in the middle of the thirteenth century, they too often have what looks like monstrous ornamentation. This appears peculiarly irreligious when grotesque figures are detached from the text and begin to enjoy a life of their own, as it were, on the border bars and margins of the page. The earliest and best example of an English book of this sort is the Rutland Psalter. As it records the death of Edmund de Lacy, earl of Lincoln, in May 1258, it was presumably made before this date, possibly for his wife or mother. Prominent in the borders of its pages are a brilliant repertoire of grotesques, of the sort that will be repeated and varied in prayer-books made for the aristocracy during the next hundred years, most famously in the Luttrell Psalter. Some idea of what the Rutland Psalter's grotesques are like is conveyed by N. J. Morgan's summary description of a few of them in his analysis of the artists involved. 'Artist A', for example, produced the following series of figures: 'hybrid musician, semi-nude man dancing, Marvel of the East with pickaxe, shepherd with dog, rabbit in landscape, female centaur suckling her child, griffin holding head of man, dragon, cat approaching mouse on sheaf of wheat, man pointing to woman crawling with devil on back'.[10] Explanations may be found for some of these subjects in classical mythology or medieval folklore, and perhaps they can also be related to Christian symbolism. Even then, however, it is difficult to show what relevance they have to the text of the psalm on each page.

Like any form of notation, the grotesques in the borders of a manuscript provide some sort of commentary on its text, even if they do no more than distract the reader. As 'likenesses of things written', it might be possible to read them like glosses. But what they signify is a perplexing problem, to which there is no single answer. As far as the relationship of hearing and seeing is concerned, grotesques are *painture* in Richard de Fournival's terms, though they do not necessarily accord with Matthew Paris's wish 'that what the ear hears the eye may see'. The difficulty of interpreting them is well illustrated by an example from the Egerton Hours, a little prayer-book (contemporary with the Rutland Psalter) made for an unknown lady. She is depicted in a miniature, kneeling beneath the enthroned Virgin and Child. She holds her prayer-book up with both hands, so that she can read the text (this is a mirror image: an open book within an open book). But her prayer may be disturbed by a monkey with a gittern and a hare, standing on his hindlegs, equipped with a pipe. This pair are tuning up, to a handbell held by the hare, on the border-bar a little to the left of the Virgin's head. Even if the lady depicted in the miniature cannot see them from beneath the Virgin's throne, they are distractingly visible to the actual user of the Egerton Hours. Possibly they are contributing to the prayer set out on the page, 'My mouth will announce thy praise' (the opening response in the Matins of the Virgin), as the hare blows his pipe while the monkey prepares to sing. Further along the border-bar a crane or stork is feeding something (quite a common motif) to a hybrid creature with a dog-like body and human face. The prayers for Matins begin with the words 'Lord, open my lips', and this is precisely what the crane is encouraging the hybrid to do.

Grotesques like this appear in the margins of books made for scholastics, as well as in prayer-books for the laity. The fashion originated in Paris, possibly in the schools, and it appears first in England in manuscripts associated with Oxford. Margins were an 'extra-textual realm, where both artist and reader sought evocative escape from the wearisome codification of the *logos* and its illustration'.[11] Grotesques also served as memorising images, whether pictured in the mind or painted on the page. The scholastic reader used the grotesques, in the margins and at the head and foot of the page, to find his place in the book. The Oxford philosopher Thomas Bradwardine described memorising images more bizarre than anything on the pages of manuscripts, such as a bright red bull with bleeding and swollen testicles confronting a woman in labour with her womb ripped open. Bradwardine was not intending to be obscene or sadistic, but to create unforgettable images to which his students could attach abstract propositions for memorising purposes. Even when grotesques in scholastic texts are explained as aids to relaxation or memorising, their presence in prayer-books remains disturbing. Perhaps the monkey and the hare in the Egerton Hours, and even the crane and the hybrid, are reverencing the text as best they can. Nevertheless these creatures have lascivious associations in medieval symbolism. The monkey and the hare may be about to start such a cacophony that the lady in the miniature will be unable to hear herself pray.

On this interpretation, grotesques are jesters who make a nonsense of the text. They do indeed provide a commentary, as they demonstrate through their antics the difference between the chaos on the edge of the page and the stability at the centre. Where grotesques penetrate the body of the text (which they do often), they challenge writing's function as a system of controls. In John of Salisbury's or Isidore of Seville's terms, they undermine the grammar of the Latin letters. Occasionally grotesques mock writing explicitly, like the monkeys in a French manuscript who tease the scribe by imitating his gestures. By drawing the eye away from the body of the text to the surrounding pictorial forms of penmanship, grotesques remind the reader that letters themselves are not the truth. Primarily the letters, like the grotesques, are 'shapes' (*figure*, as John of Salisbury called them); they are 'indicators of voices' and not their reality. In that case, what are the grotesques indicators of? The short answer is: equivocation. The hybrids in particular make a nonsense of John's hopes for an art which will distinguish the clear from the obscure and the certain from the dubious. The realism of much grotesque ornament compounds the problem of ambiguity. In the Egerton Hours the hare musician, standing on his hindlegs, is as life-like a figure (though miniaturised) as Tenniel's March Hare in *Alice in Wonderland*. Through skilful penmanship the scribe artist, whether painter or writer, created the illusion on the page that 'the fiction is not a fiction'.[12] Like Alice, the lady kneeling in the Egerton Hours is in wonderland: letters metamorphose into mythical creatures, animals change size and act like human beings, sacred words become the playthings of equivocators and blasphemers.

The way manuscripts were made as splendid visual objects, rather than mundane communications, ensured that there was no irreconcilable division between writers and non-writers when documents began to be used more widely in the twelfth and thirteenth centuries. Many manuscripts continued to be lavishly embellished and all were read aloud so that the non-literate could participate in their use. There was no conscious or deliberate attempt to integrate literate and non-literate—indeed the clergy wanted to remain a class apart—but change was sufficiently slow to make gradual adaptation possible. As long as all writings were manuscripts, that is, as long as they were made exclusively by hand, old habits of mind persisted. Throughout the Middle Ages the writer remained a visual artist and the reader a specialist in the spoken word. Medieval reading (*lectio*) was primarily something heard rather than seen until the invention of printing, and writing (*scriptura*) often continued to be admired for its calligraphy rather than its textual accuracy. The laity were gradually coaxed towards literacy by ensuring that it changed the old ways of hearing and seeing as little as possible.

❧ XII ☙

TRUSTING WRITING AND THE ART OF FORGERY

Documents did not immediately inspire trust. As with other innovations in technology, there was a long and complex period of evolution, particularly in the twelfth century in England, before methods of production were developed which proved acceptable both to traditionalists and to experts in literacy. There was no straight and simple line of progress from memory to written record. People had to be persuaded—and it was difficult to do—that documentary proof was a sufficient improvement on existing methods to merit the extra expense and mastery of novel techniques which it demanded.

A modern literate tends to assume that statements in writing, especially if they are in print, are more reliable than spoken words. This assumption is the result of schooling in reading and writing from an early age and the constant use of documents, such as bills, for even the smallest transactions. The obvious advantage to a modern literate of documentary proof is that it cannot be as easily or as readily changed as a person's word. But this advantage of writing was less obvious in medieval England, since even literates did not use documents in ways which assured their effectiveness as proof. Most charters of the twelfth century were neither dated nor autographed, nor were they copied into registers for future reference. In the earliest private charters draftsmen and scribes give the impression that, instead of sharing a common training in the drawing up of instruments, they are each making a personal and individual but necessarily amateur effort to master the complexities of documentary proof for the first time.

A charter whereby Ralf of St Audoen gave a saltpan to Sele Priory in Sussex illustrates the work of an amateur draftsman very well, even though it is dated (1153 *Anno Domini*) and autographed, which is unusual. The draftsman or scribe, who was probably one of the monks of Sele, begins with a justification for written record: 'Because, it is appropriate that this should be brought to reach the notice of many, it is committed to the muniments of letters by provident deliberation, lest in the process of time it be destroyed by ruinous oblivion.' The gift itself was publicly symbolised not by this charter, however, but by a more traditional form of writing—a Gospel book which was laid on the beneficiary's altar. The monks of Sele seem to have been determined to ratify the gift in as many ways as possible, both traditional and novel. Ralf's lord, William de Braose, made his autograph sign of the cross on the charter twice, once in the priory and again when the document was exhibited and ratified at his court in Bramber Castle. Ralf also put his seal on the charter. Those who trusted the sign of the cross and those who favoured the more modern wax seal, which with its device of a knight on horseback was a symbol of feudal lordship, could therefore both be satisfied. For those who trusted neither, lists of witnesses were specified for both transactions.

Objectors to written record had a case which was strong in substance as well as in sentiment, since numerous medieval charters were forged and the authenticity of the genuine ones was difficult to prove. Such a bewildering variety of 'external marks' had been used in idiosyncratic attempts to demonstrate the authenticity of charters that written record was highly suspicious. There were thousands of authentic charters without dates or places of issue, some of them written by scribes who seem never to have wielded a pen before. Although most English charters had seals attached to them, a few were authenticated by inked crosses (some autographs and others not), or by other symbolic objects signifying the donor's wishes such as rings or knives. Nearly all charters listed witnesses to the transaction, ranging in numbers from the king's unique *Teste me ipso* (witness, myself) to the 123 individuals named in an agreement in Kent in 1176. It was common for a scribe to conclude his list of witnesses with some such phrase as 'and many others who would take too long to enumerate', a description which was useless for future identification, although it recorded the impressiveness of the occasion at the time. The scribe of an Oxfordshire charter dismissed the witnesses to the deed with the phrase: 'whose names we have been prevented by tedium from writing'.[1] Witnesses soon died anyway and some, like the saints who witness a Christ Church charter of *c.* 1200, may never have lived. Sometimes the scribe of the charter identifies himself as the last witness, offering a test of authenticity, but more often he does not.

In these circumstances, where practice was so varied and even eccentric, both literate and illiterate were entitled to distrust charters. Authentic-looking documents might well be forged, or conversely amateur scrawls might turn out to be genuine. In addition to inconsistencies and lack of uniform scribal training, the principal difficulty was that monks, who were the traditional experts in writing, were also the greatest forgers. The more powerful and ancient the house, the more likely it was that its documents would be forged in a professional manner. Of the seals used by Christ Church Canterbury, Archdeacon Simon Langton wrote to

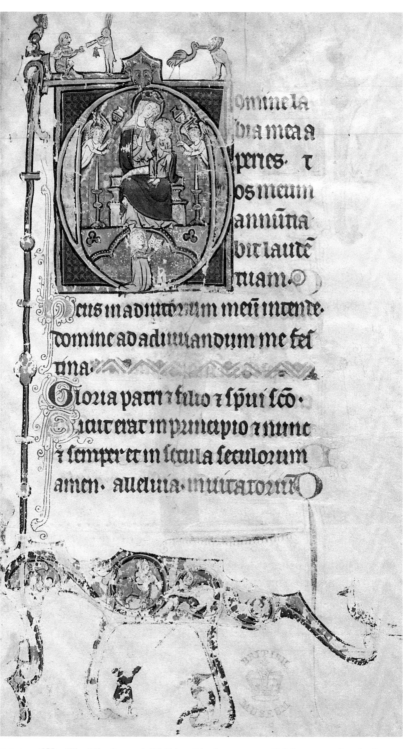

PLATE IX. The Virgin and Child, with the owner of this prayer-book shown kneeling at her feet, distracted by the mischievous hare and monkey above, playing their musical instruments. Luxurious books like this began to be made in the thirteenth century for ladies to use in their homes. The manuscript is damaged towards the foot of the page, probably natural wear and tear due to frequent handling

Gregory IX in 1238; 'Holy Father, there is not a single sort of forgery that is not perpetrated in the church of Canterbury. For they have forged in gold, in lead, in wax, and in every kind of metal.'[2] Much the same, of course, could be said of the papal *curia* in an earlier period, when it had used the Donation of Constantine and other forged decretals.

In England the greatest period for forging documents was the century after the Norman Conquest, when the old houses of Black monks had to convince the incomers of their ancient dignities and privileges. 'No document coming from such centres of proved fabrication as Westminster, Evesham, Winchester Cathedral, Chertsey and Malmesbury should be accepted at its face value without close examination.'[3] This list of monasteries is cited by F. M. Stenton in his summary of the critical work of W. H. Stevenson at the beginning of this century. Many more centres of proved fabrication could now be added to this list, such as Christ Church and St Augustine's Abbey at Canterbury and Gloucester and Ramsey Abbeys. Nor was the Norman Conquest the root cause of the problem, since houses founded after the Conquest, notably Battle Abbey, likewise forged audacious title-deeds. Even the estimate made by C. N. L. Brooke, that about seventeen out of thirty pre-Conquest monastic houses 'tolerated forgery on a fair scale', may be an under-assessment.[4] Recent research may ultimately lead to the conclusion that in England in the century after the Norman Conquest forgery of charters was the rule rather than the exception.

The extent of forgeries can be gauged by looking at the estimated number of documents extant in the name of Edward the Confessor (1042–66). Out of a total of 164, only sixty-four are thought to be authentic, with forty-four spurious and a further fifty-six dubious. In the greatest monastic houses documents of his were specially valued because William the Conqueror claimed to be his lawful successor. The figures are subject to every kind of qualification because opinions will always differ about what makes a document authentic. Many of the problematical charters about which scholars are undecided may never be satisfactorily resolved. Allowing, however, for all such qualifications and for the possibility that Edward the Confessor's writs were forged more than those of any other king, the conclusion to draw is that most documents extant in his name are of doubtful authenticity. Medieval forgeries are extraordinarily difficult to evaluate because a document like a charter of Edward the Confessor may be spurious, in the sense that it was written after his death, and yet be accurate in the essentials of the information it records. Forged charters were often based on earlier authentic documents or on good oral traditions. The purpose of forgery was to produce a record in a form which was acceptable, particularly in courts of law, at the time it was made. Forgery was necessary because contemporaries had no historical sense. A good oral tradition or an authentic charter of an early Anglo-Saxon king might be rejected by a court of law because it seemed strange, whereas a forged charter would be acceptable because it suited contemporary notions of what an ancient charter should be like.

Forgers re-created the past in an acceptable literate form. They are best understood not as occasional deviants on the peripheries of legal practice, but as experts entrenched at the centre of literary and intellectual culture in the twelfth century. The most influential historical writer of the century, Geoffrey of Monmouth, probably invented most of the *History of the Kings of Britain* (written in *c*. 1136), although scholarly opinion will always differ about that. Similarly, in order to give verisimilitude to the Arthurian legend which Geoffrey had made popular, Glastonbury Abbey in 1191 exhumed the bodies of King Arthur and Queen Guinevere. Here again, scholars differ as to whether this was a deliberately staged forgery or a genuine discovery of ancient tombs. Judging by some other forgeries of the time, the Glastonbury monks would certainly have been capable of creating such an ambitious deception. Forgery succeeded because it was ordered or condoned by the greatest scholars, prelates and administrators. Walter abbot of Battle, who was responsible for the Battle forgeries, was the brother of Richard de Lucy, Henry II's chief justiciar, and Walter presumably acted with his brother's knowledge. The former head of Henry I's writing-office, Robert de Sigillo, seems to have been responsible for forging a royal charter for Reading Abbey after he became a monk there. Among scholars responsible for forgeries were Osbert de Clare, prior of Westminster, who created charters of Edward the Confessor in Stephen's reign, and Gilbert Foliot, who was an accessory to forgery when abbot of Gloucester.

Those monastic writers who are most insistent in the prologues to their works on the importance of telling the truth are often those who were involved in fabricating charters. Thus Eadmer of Canterbury, who affirmed 'that it is a shocking thing for anyone knowingly to write what is false in sacred histories, for the soul of the writer is slain every time they are read or listened to', was an accessory to the Canterbury forgeries in 1121–2. Similarly 'it is hard to exonerate William of Malmesbury from the charge of knowingly including forged material in his history', despite his precocious concern with evaluating evidence.[5] In general, twelfth-century writers protest too much about their veracity to inspire confidence. For example, the compiler of Ramsey Abbey's *Book of Benefactors* insists that his purpose is to translate charters from Old English into Latin, so that the Normans will understand them, and also to retain the record of oral gifts in the memory of writing 'so that all falsehood and controversy may be removed'. Yet two of the royal charters he cites were certainly forged, although it is possible that the compiler himself was ignorant of this.

The distinction between fact and fiction was sometimes so finely drawn by twelfth-century writers as to be impossible to see. Occasionally authors may have misled themselves as well as their readers. Not only monastic chroniclers but literary historians, like Geoffrey of Monmouth, and composers of vernacular romances insisted that their works derived from ancient books. Thus the Anglo-Norman poet, Hue de Rotelande (writing in *c.* 1180), assures his audience that his story of *Ipomedon* comes from a Latin text, although he is surprised that 'those wise clerks who understand many languages have not put it in memory'. Hue's audience were presumably intended to appreciate the irony of referring to the authority of a Latin text which probably did not exist. Likewise in *Ipomedon* Hue is able to describe for his secular audience the writer's craft with greater frankness than a self-righteous monk like Eadmer can:

> Now understand this very well, my lords,
> Hue says that he never tells a lie in it,
> Well, hardly ever, and then not much;
> No one can keep himself entirely from it.

To a modern reader Hue de Rotlande is a composer of creative literature, a writer of fiction or romance, who therefore has no need to excuse himself for telling untruths to his audience. Hue himself, however, apparently felt that some explanation was required, perhaps because poetic licence or unadorned fiction was difficult for his 'lords' to accept, particularly when authors were just developing into writers on their own account instead of being reciters of traditional tales. Unlike Hue, a monastic chronicler or composer of charters is expected by a modern reader to record the literal truth, and furthermore the chronicler will often assure the reader in his prologue that this is precisely what he intends to do. Nevertheless the distinction between fact and fiction in writing, which leads the modern reader to think of Walter, abbot of Battle, or Osbert de Clare as forgers and Hue de Rotelande as an entertaining romancer, would not have been as sharp to medieval people, although they were very conscious of the moral difference between truth and falsehood and of the penalties, both material and spiritual, for fabricating seals or documents.

The fundamental difficulty was that literate criteria for making or criticising documents had not usually been applied in the first place. Even the English royal government, which was a pioneer of chancery procedure, did not consistently date its charters until Richard I's reign and began to keep regular copies of them only in John's reign. Nor was keeping registers of documents much use unless they could readily be referred to. We have already seen that neither Henry III's government nor Edward I's had foolproof means of searching their own rolls; Edward I's Chancery was deceived by a forged charter of Richard I even though an authentic copy was in the government's possession. Up to Henry II's reign the practice had continued of the royal seal being affixed to documents written by the beneficiaries' scribes, although gradually this practice became the exception rather than the rule. From the king's point of view, the procedure whereby a royal officer fixed the royal *signum* to a writing made by the beneficiary was essentially oral and manual rather than literate. The document was presumably read out aloud to the king or his delegate, perhaps only in a translated and summarised form, and then authenticated by the touch of the seal. In these circumstances the difference between a document which had received the royal touch and one which had not, between 'authentic' and 'forged' by modern criteria, was a fine one.

Often documents were produced in duplicate or triplicate for greater security, and occasionally alternative texts seem to have been prepared by the beneficiary, probably in the hope that the seal would be affixed to the more advantageous one. This hypothesis seems the most plausible explanation for the existence of two parallel charters in King Stephen's name, both dated Christmas Day (1139) and written by the same scribe, who had probably been a clerk of Roger, bishop of Salisbury, the chief justiciar. As Roger had just died, the purpose of the charters was presumably to ensure that Salisbury Cathedral retained the property they concerned. Both charters quitclaim royal rights in lands and churches, which Roger had given to Salisbury, but the second charter adds that King Stephen had given 10 pounds' worth of his own demesne lands as well; the place in which this demesne lies is left blank. H. A. Cronne, who published these two charters (though with a different explanation), has drawn attention also to a charter in King Stephen's name for Reading Abbey, which is written by a known royal scribe although it bears a forged seal. He suggests that Robert de Sigillo, who had been the master of Henry I's writing-office and had become a monk at Reading, may have been behind this forgery. These instances show that documents might be unauthentic even when they were written by official scribes. Indeed, to think of writs produced by the royal Chancery as official and other documents bearing the royal seal as unofficial is an anachronism until the last decade of the twelfth century. Without defined standards of authenticity, there could be no definite criteria for distinguishing forgeries from authentic documents.

The apparently careless attitude of even the king's government towards its written *acta* was not a product merely of incompetent administration, nor of the special circumstances of Stephen's reign when so many forgeries seem to have been made. Stricter procedures were not followed because written record itself was unfamiliar and abnormal outside a small circle of royal officers and old monastic houses. Despite the growth of the Exchequer and the proliferation of writs, the emphasis in royal government remained largely oral until Henry II's reign at least. Henry himself was an energetic legislator, yet even his decrees were not written down in authoritative and officially authentic statutes. They seem to have been promulgated orally and then noted haphazardly by chroniclers. There was no *Liber Augustalis* of the common law. This lack of a *jus scriptum* so troubled the author of *Glanvill* (writing at the very end of Henry II's reign), who wished to harmonise his knowledge of English and Roman law, that he felt obliged to begin by arguing that it is not absurd to speak of English 'laws' even though they are unwritten because 'what pleases the prince has the force of law'. With this nod towards Roman principle, the author then hopes that it will not be considered presumptuous on his part, 'but rather very useful for most people and highly necessary to aid the memory', if he commits at least the commonest rules of the king's court to writing.[6]

Like the author of *Glanvill*, monastic charter makers and chroniclers had to set about filling the gaps and correcting the anomalies in written record which kings and other past benefactors appeared to have negligently left. It was the responsibility of the beneficiaries and not of the donor to see that adequate documents were supplied. In the non-literate past, people had been accustomed to the flexibility of speech and memory and they applied similar criteria at first to written record. A charter was inaccurate and should be corrected if it failed to give the beneficiary a privilege which the donor had obviously intended it to have, had he still been alive to express his wishes. Writing, or the lack of it, should not be allowed to annul or invalidate previous pious gifts. From this point of view 'forgery' is an inappropriate term to apply to renewals of evidence which were intended to ensure that a monastic house was adequately provided with charters to defend its patrons and saints against rivals. Even a charter which a modern critic would consider perfectly genuine did not record the complete and precise wishes of the donor himself, as these had been expressed orally and physically by oaths and symbolic gestures at a public ceremony in the presence of witnesses and not by any form of writing. The charter could not record the donor's exact words, because it was written in Latin, and furthermore it was often expressed in the past tense— 'Know that I, A of B, have given . . .'—which made it clear that it was an afterthought.

In these circumstances the distinction between a 'genuine' and a 'forged' charter depended on what interval of time between giving and writing, and what mark of approval by the donor, was generally considered allowable. To a modern critic a charter of Edward the Confessor, if written by Osbert de Clare seventy years or more after the king's death and sealed with a new seal, is a forgery. To Osbert, on the other hand, who composed a life of the Confessor and was pressing for his recognition as a saint, Edward was immortalised by his sanctity and still lived in the church where his relics were preserved. In his capacity as prior of Westminster, Osbert may have thought that writing a charter in the dead king's name was essentially no different from writing on behalf of a contemporary ruler. Osbert was fulfilling Edward's pious intentions and assuring him his place in heaven by restoring the evidence of his endowments. Discussing Osbert's work, Brooke comments:

> There had been forgery in England before the Conquest, and it may even be the accidents of survival which lead us to suppose the twelfth century to be its golden age. Yet there is clearly a sense in which the spread of literacy and of written instruments of land tenure made the eleventh and twelfth centuries, in a special sense, *the period of the shift from oral to written testimony*. The opportunities, the temptations, and the urgent calls of duty in such a period were quite exceptional.[7]

Galbraith, referring to 'this slow evolution from oral to written government', made a comparable observation twenty years earlier: 'Written evidence was still the exception rather than the rule, and, as a novelty, was apt to be accepted without very close scrutiny. It is scarcely surprising, then, to find that the twelfth century was the golden age of forgery.'[8] The forgery or renewal of documents was essentially a product of the movement from memory to written record and is best understood in that context.

In theory it would have been as easy to eliminate forgeries as to produce charters which were uniformly dated and signed. Reliable criteria for detecting forgeries had been developed by canon lawyers in Italy, just as Roman law prescribed rules for the production of notarially authenticated instruments. The *summa* (dating from the last quarter of the twelfth century) of the best canonical authority on forgeries, Huguccio, was known in England. He recommended that, where there was doubt about the authenticity of a decretal, resort should be had first of all to the papal registers. If the document were not found there, other tests should be applied regarding the style and substance of the text and the physical characteristics of the parchment, the *bulla* and its attaching thread. In short, the document should be examined as a whole from as many aspects as possible. These were sound rules, which were subsequently promulgated generally by Innocent III, who had been Huguccio's pupil at Bologna.

Nevertheless the gulf between theory and practice was enormous, because these rules were as difficult to enforce as those governing the drawing up of written instruments. When discussing forgery, the English canonist glossators were obliged to ignore Huguccio's advice to resort first of all to registers, presumably because there were no systematic registers of English ecclesiastical documents. Instead, they recommended testing forgeries by the customary oral method of swearing oaths and producing witnesses. In other words, the validity of documents was primarily assessed by the pre-literate wager of law and not by tests using writing.

Similarly Innocent III himself, when he came to practice as distinct from laying down rules, could be as easily deceived by a forged papal bull as anyone else. Thomas of Marlborough, abbot of Evesham (1229–36), gives a first-hand account of how Evesham forgers deceived Innocent and his cardinals in a case in the Roman *curia* in 1205. Thomas was at that time Evesham's principal advocate in its claim to be exempt from the jurisdiction of the bishop of Worcester. Among other documents adduced as evidence by Thomas were two bulls in the name of Constantine I, who had been pope from 708 to 715. Worcester counter-claimed that these documents were forgeries 'in parchment and script, thread and *bulla*', and stated that privileges of Constantine I were entirely unknown in England. So the bulls were handed to the pope, who 'felt them with his own hands and pulled on the *bulla* and the parchment to see if he could separate the *bulla* from the thread, and he examined them most diligently'. He then passed them round the circle of cardinals, while Thomas admits to being worried about the outcome. However, when the bulls were passed back to the pope, he held the documents up and magisterially pronounced: 'Privileges of this sort, which are unknown to you, are well known to us, and they cannot be forged. These are genuine.' Although Thomas perhaps exaggerated the forthrightness of Innocent's opinion, there is no reason to doubt the substance of this story. The papal judgment in Evesham's favour encouraged Thomas to copy the bulls of Constantine I, which had released Evesham from the 'Egyptian slavery' of Worcester, into his chronicle for future reference. The copies demonstrate that the bulls were undoubtedly forged and, as Thomas 'improved' Evesham's chronicle as well to suit the dispute with Worcester, it is likely that he had played a major part in deceiving the pope.

This case suggests that, although by 1200 the papal *curia* had developed rules for detecting forgeries of recent decretals, it had no effective means of checking documents which claimed to be hundreds of years old. By fingering the parchment and pulling the thread, Innocent III was applying elementary physical tests and not the canons of careful textual criticism which would have revealed the bulls to be forgeries. But it would be anachronistic to expect even Innocent III to have shown a sharper awareness or a deeper understanding of the development of papal documents than he did in this case. Scientific historical criticism was first applied to early papal documents by Renaissance humanists of the fifteenth century, and it revealed that the pope's own title-deeds, the Donation of Constantine, were themselves forgeries. Of course Innocent III was highly educated and learned in law, yet he and his cardinals were not accustomed to the careful scrutiny of documents. Their training in the schools had been predominantly oral in character and caused them to prefer touch, speech, and hearing to intensive literate study.

Moreover, neither the papal *curia* nor lesser courts had anything to gain by scrutinising forged charters with strict regularity. Decisions had to be reached in cases even when both parties produced forged documents. Conventions seem to have existed among the higher clergy within which forgery, while not being openly approved of or acknowledged, was at least tolerated. Every ruler in Europe, from the pope downwards, had suspect title-deeds if historically authentic writings were to become the yardstick of authority. Medieval criticism of charters was quite sophisticated compared with general standards of historical criticism. The fictions or half-truths of Geoffrey of Monmouth and other creators of political myths were often accepted as historically reliable. Thus Geoffrey's *History of the Kings of Britain* was used by Edward I (though admittedly as an afterthought) in his letter to Boniface VIII in 1301, setting out the precedents for English overlordship in Scotland going back to the days of the prophets, Eli and Samuel, and the fall of Troy. Nor in their reply did the Scots deny the historicity of such myths, but only the English interpretation of the evidence. Although by 1300 governments and owners of property had begun to use documents on a scale unprecedented since the fall of the Roman empire, they still approached the past through hearsay and myth.

This is not to suggest that literate standards of documentation were unknown, but rather that they could not be uniformly or readily applied to particular cases, because literate ways of doing business were still too novel. In exceptional cases, where the opposing parties were unequally matched and unprotected by clerical conventions, forgery could be systematically revealed. Thus Galbraith has described a case in 1220 in the Jewish Exchequer where a bond attributed to the prior of Dunstable was shown to be a forgery on numerous counts—its unusual form of date, ungrammatical Latin, unauthorised handwriting, false chronology and peculiar physical condition (it had been washed and whitened).[9] Nevertheless it is a mistake to conclude that this case shows how skilful the English courts had become in the detection of forgery, as these points of criticism were made not by the court but by the plaintiff, Master Richard de Morins, the prior of Dunstable, who was a canonist and a graduate of Bologna. He was able for once to put legal theory into practice because his opponent was a Jew and the bond was evidently an amateur forgery. Had Richard been facing an opponent of his own expertise and status, like Thomas of Marlborough, he might have found that his allegations of forgery received no more sympathetic a hearing than Innocent III had given to Worcester in its plea against Evesham. Successful forgery was the business of monks and *magistri*; amateurs, still less Jews, were ill-advised to try it.

The Dunstable case, like the exceptional instances (which have already been discussed) of documents being dated with simplicity and consistency or of English scribes authenticating charters with the precision of Roman notaries, shows that principles of good documentary procedure were known to experts. The problem lay in putting academic theory into general practice. Landowners, whether cleric or lay, were just as likely to distrust genuine charters as to be suspicious of forged ones. Not even the greatest experts, like Innocent III or Edward I's Chancery officials, could be relied upon to detect forgeries. The monks who had the temerity or desperation to deceive them must have learned that forgery was the best course, provided it was competently done.

Cases of simple deception with a document, as distinct from the complex forgeries done by monks, are rarely recorded. One came up in the justiciar's visitation of Surrey during the baronial revolution of 1258. Peter le Templer showed that Walter Kardun had altered the amount of a payment from 2 shillings a year to one clove of garlic (a peppercorn rent). Walter had 'confected' the charter and read its terms out to Peter as a rent of 2 shillings. Peter 'being ignorant' failed to check the text before sealing it. Whether Peter was unable to read or merely ignorant of the law is impossible to know. He had legal experience as a bailiff in Kingston-on-Thames and he had been involved in litigation before. Furthermore, he allowed Walter to deceive him a second time. Walter had him summoned into the ecclesiastical court of Master Rostand, the papal nuncio, a hundred miles away in Suffolk. The sting took the form of Walter getting the vicar of Kingston to tell Peter that he no longer intended to prosecute. Walter then went ahead with the prosecution, so that Peter was excommunicated in his absence and had to pay Walter 40 shillings. Possibly Walter was something of a scoundrel and an expert in legal procedure, like Chaucer's Summoner who was also partial to garlic and knew how to punish a man through his purse.

In this bewildering world, where holy men forged documents and writers of fiction were concerned to tell the literal truth, it may seem surprising that written record ever got a good name at all or established itself as a reliable form of communication. Perhaps it did so not for the practical and progressive reasons which a modern literate would expect, but because of the prestige which writing had acquired in the centuries before the Norman Conquest from its use by monks in liturgical books. The Gospel book placed on the altar had been used as a symbol of conveyance by laymen long before they became accustomed to charters. Although it is true that monks were commonly forgers, they compensated for this by imbuing script with sacred associations. All writers of the twelfth century—whether forgers, romancers, or simple scribes—drew on this rich reserve of awe and faith.

Faith was needed because most twelfth-century documents, whether forged or not, were not trustworthy in the strict sense of that word, as they did not state precisely when they had been written, nor were they penned by authorised and professionally trained scribes. Effective precautions against fraud were not taken, because they demanded extensive professionalism and because writings seemed to have been thought of at first as subsidiary aids to traditional memorising procedures and not as replacements of them. A new technology usually adapts itself at first to an existing one, camouflaging itself in the old forms and not immediately realising its potential. By the thirteenth century documentary proof had become more familiar and routine. Nevertheless throughout the Middle Ages many common forms of document, particularly charters for conveyances of property, retained in their physical format and set phraseology numerous reminders that they had been developed in an earlier period when more reliance had been put on living memory than on parchment.

✤ XIII ✤
CONCLUSION

The theme of the second part of this book has been the growth of literacy for practical purposes. Laymen became more literate in order to cope with written business, initially in England with writs from the royal government demanding information or money. Knights involved in county business, and even peasants who acted as manorial reeves, needed to be able to read the warrants presented to them and to keep records themselves in order to make adequate answers. According to the *Anglo-Saxon Chronicle* William the Conqueror in the Domesday survey had made a list of every ox and cow and pig in the land; two centuries later bailiffs were recommended to record in writing in the autumn of the year each tool and horseshoe and everything that remained on the manor, great and small. Although these schemes were too ambitious and can never have reached the point of listing every person, animal and thing in up-to-date inventories, the idea of such lists was a continuing aspiration between William the Conqueror's Domesday Book and the series of inquests undertaken by Edward I's government which culminated—and collapsed under their own weight—in the *quo warranto* proceedings.

During the years 1193–1205 when Hubert Walter dominated the royal administration, written record was effectively extended to nearly every sphere of government, both central and local. Hubert Walter's achievement was to put theory into practice. It is possible that Chancery rolls, plea rolls, feet of fines, Jewish *arche* and the rest had been thought of before he appeared on the scene; but he first gave them continuing life. His influence on county and village record-making was as important as his effectiveness at the centre, although local records took another century before they were established as a norm. By Edward I's reign serfs possessed seals to sign their names and they recorded their property transactions in writing. Thus the *nativi*—the natives, naifs, villeins or serfs—who had thought Domesday Book to be the Last Judgement (according to Fitz Nigel in the twelfth century) had charters of their own (the *Cartae Nativorum*) by the 1300s.

The types of writing which were done became increasingly more practical. The sacred Scriptures, which had dominated literate culture before 1066, still stood in pride of place of course, but they were surrounded and overlaid from the twelfth century onwards by the glosses and summaries of the schoolmen. The scholastic *summa*, 'a concise encyclopedia of instances', was intended as a short cut through the mass of words for the 'many who are in a hurry and the many who are unlearned'. The written statements of individuals likewise became more immediately practical in purpose and format. Although solemn charters (which had often been written by monastic beneficiaries after the event) were still produced, less portentous and more sophisticated forms of document increased in numbers. Sealed chirographs in particular emphasised the equal status of the two contracting parties and required both of them, together with their witnesses, to participate with their seals in the making of the written instrument. Similarly in the late twelfth century letters, in the modern sense of missives sent by one individual to convey confidential information to another, came into more general use. Previously letters had usually been either writs patent, which were open declarations or title-deeds, or 'literature' composed by rhetoricians and preachers.

Gradually too the idea of accumulating memoranda for future reference became established, first with the pipe and plea rolls of the king's court and then with comparable documents produced by bishops, barons and boroughs. By the 1260s the countess of Leicester, and presumably other great housekeepers also, were keeping diaries of their daily expenditure. At a similar date records begin in the Year Books which purport to record every word spoken by learned counsel and judges in royal courts. Even the art of speech itself was taught in books of hypothetical dialogues for students of law and estate management.

The traditions and techniques of monastic writing, which had been created to produce illuminated liturgical manuscripts, had to be adapted to the utilitarian demands made on them by secular writs and rolls. It was relatively easy to economise on materials by omitting coloured inks and using thinner and smaller pieces of parchment. Although most business documents continued to have enlarged initial letters and some still had rubrics and even illustrations, they were generally on a far less lavish scale than Gospel books. Even the Scriptures themselves were presented in cheaper and more accessible formats. Orm, who wrote his Gospel homilies or *Ormulum* probably with his own hand in *c.* 1170, seems to have cared little about its untidy and unprofessional appearance. As an Augustinian canon he exemplified the new ideal of simplicity in spreading the Gospel, instead of treasuring it in precious manuscripts as the Black monks did. Illuminated manuscripts themselves began to be produced in more economical formats so that they could be put in the pocket or held in the hands while at prayer. Likewise students' and lawyers' textbooks of the thirteenth century use smaller and more economical formats.

Even more pressing than the need to economise on parchment and pigments was the need to save the scribe's time, as the application of his skill was the most expensive element in the production of documents. To meet this need, secular scribes learned to write faster in cursive hands instead of the traditional monastic book hands. Contrary to former palaeographical teaching, cursive script is not evidence of special training in chanceries but of 'a common pressure of urgent business'. Hence in the thirteenth century cursive scripts began to be used for writing books as well as writs and rolls. The royal administration even automated writing, at least to the point of producing stereotyped documents (like common law writs) and of authenticating them with a seal instead of with the king's sign manual. The seal was the forerunner of printing as it reproduced script from a metal exemplar in a repeatable series.

Speeding up the production of documents was easier than organising archives and reference systems to make good use of them. There was nothing new about keeping precious writings in treasuries or reliquaries. The novelty lay in getting into the habit of referring to a book or archive for information instead of seeking oral testimony. Domesday Book seems rarely to have been consulted in the century after it was made; only in Edward I's reign did regular consultation begin. Gradually Edward I's government began to realise that it possessed an archive of information which could be used in disputes with opponents. As late as 1290 when the king first called for historical information about the claims of the English Crown in Scotland, resort was made to the monasteries, as the traditional remembrances and chroniclers, and not the royal archives. A year later, however, Edward I hurriedly sent a message from Scotland, ordering a chest of Chancery rolls to be broken open and searched, and thus inaugurated systematic searches of the archives.

The reasons for not regularly consulting records hitherto had been mixed. Even when officials had learned that documentary evidence could be more advantageous than oral testimony (which was not invariably the case of course), archives and the collections of documents within them had to be arranged in ways which made consultation possible. Edward I's instructions in 1300 to search all the rolls and remembrances 'so that nothing is left unsearched' was absurd, when chests of documents were scattered in a variety of repositories and their contents unlisted. The surveys of the records in Edward I's last years, which culminated in Bishop Stapledon's array in 1320, mark the point at which the royal government at last recognised the usefulness of its archives. Archives had become a department of government instead of a treasury of relics. Libraries

likewise, owing to the initiative of the friars, began to be arranged systematically so that readers could have books 'ready to hand' (*in promptu*),
just as Edward I wanted his archives available 'at all times'. Hurriedly extracting information from quantities of books was a different kind of literate activity from meditating on a single text for a year, as the Black
monks had done in the old Benedictine tradition.

In establishing literacy as a practical convenience, much in the inheritance of the past had to be overcome. Most fundamental was the problem of language itself. After the Norman Conquest written Old English
became an archaic language like Latin, with which it had competed for so
long. Neither English nor Norman administrators could use the language
of everyday speech in business documents, because they did not share a
common language and also because written English and French were still
in a fluid stage of development. Both languages, moreover, were for long
overshadowed and beguiled by the ancient dignity of Latin. In these circumstances the linguistic skill required of a local man doing a practical
task, like a foreman of a jury or a knight collecting testimony for the
county court, was unusually demanding. In the thirteenth century such a
man needed to speak English and French and to read in English, French,
and Latin. In this multilingual society people switched languages often
probably without comment. The practice of writing documents in a particular language for the record, usually Latin (or French by 1300), does
not mean that Latin (or French) was necessarily the language in which the
business was done. By and large the knights of thirteenth-century England, and their families too, probably had a wider and deeper knowledge
of language than those historians who have adopted a patronising tone
towards them because they were not highly literate.

The question, 'Were laymen literate?' cannot be answered directly
from contemporary sources because it is a contradiction in medieval
terms. A layman (*laicus*) was unclerkly by definition, whereas a literate
(*litteratus*) was clerkly even if he were a knight. Leaving these scholastic
subtleties to one side, it is probable that a minimal knowledge of Latin
among the population at large has been underestimated. A little Latin
was the broad but shallow foundation from which men of peasant origin
rose to be clerics, and it was also indispensable for literacy in vernacular
forms. Gradually 'clergy' in common parlance came to mean a little Latin
instead of meaning an estate of the church. From the fourteenth century a
person who knew a little Latin had 'benefit of clergy'.

This minimal knowledge of Latin did not make a person educated in
any real sense, but it was of practical use. It could save a man accused of

felony from being hanged and it gave him sufficient knowledge to cope with government business. Thus in a case in 1297 ten jurors were able to read the entry of Robert de Tony's birth in a monastic chronicle and those who were unable to do so were described as *laici*, meaning that they were non-readers rather than 'laymen' in a more general sense. Such minimal skill did not make a man either *litteratus* or educated in the traditional sense. Knights had been educated in the skills of language long before they were required by the growth of documentation to learn a little Latin or 'clergy'. Traditionally they had learned to speak well and to give counsel to clergy as much as to kings. Thus the judges who shaped the English common law in the twelfth and thirteenth centuries were drawn indifferently from knights and clergy. For laymen, literacy was a practical convenience long before it became an education. Although the Scriptures might teach religion, wisdom in the worldly sense did not depend on writings.

Because writing was only an ancillary aid at first for laymen, it did not immediately sweep away traditional non-literate ways of doing business. Reliance upon symbolic objects and 'livery or seisin' in conveyances of property persisted. Writing was converted into the spoken word by the habitual practice of reading aloud and of listening to or making an 'audit' of a statement, rather than scrutinising its text on parchment. Clerks and scribes themselves were slow to comprehend the full potentialities of documentary proof, as their inconsistencies in dating and signing documents demonstrate. Writing was distrusted and for good reason, as numerous charters of the twelfth century in particular were forgeries. Paradoxically the continuance of non-utilitarian and primarily visual forms of writing, especially in liturgical manuscripts, may have helped to persuade the laity that literacy was valuable because of its long association with sacred Scripture. Writers of the twelfth and thirteenth centuries— whether they were composers or copyists of texts, or clerks making business documents—drew on the reserves of awe and faith with which monks had imbued writing in the half millennium before 1066.

The growth of literacy for practical purposes, therefore, was not necessarily an inevitable process. Emphasis on practical literacy is a commonplace of twentieth-century culture because we have inherited the values of the utilitarians. In nineteenth-century Europe and North America mass literacy was promoted by governments for the first time in the history of the world in order to ensure that populations could cope with the growing written demands of daily life—in railway trains, factories, conscript armies and so on. Opponents of government policy were worried that schools might succeed in educating people to a point where there would be a surplus of scholars and critics who might undermine the social hierarchy. Such fears were allayed by reformers emphasising elementary practical literacy and numeracy (the three Rs of reading, writing and arithmetic) rather than a liberal education in the classical tradition, which remained as much the preserve of an élite of *litterati* in 1900 as it had been in 1200. The twentieth-century assumption that literacy is primarily utilitarian in purpose and character is a product of recent history and not an invariable norm.

Although practical or utilitarian literacy only became a mass movement in Europe in the nineteenth century, this book has argued that it had its origins in the twelfth and thirteenth centuries in the shift from memory to written record. That change might alternatively be described as a shift from sacred script to practical literacy. In Anglo-Saxon England, and generally in early medieval Europe, writing had been primarily associated with monasticism, sacred Scripture, and the liberal arts of antiquity. Only in the twelfth century did the number of documents, and the number of persons who understood them, begin to increase at a fast rate under the pressures of emerging bureaucracy. Practical business was the foundation of this new literacy.

The recording of disputes, collection of village statistics, transmission of government orders to villagers are essentially the uses to which literacy was applied in England by William the Conqueror in his Domesday survey. Thereafter his successors, because they were foreigners ruling in a tradition of conquest, bombarded local officials with one inquest after another. Landlords, clerical and lay, followed suit. From that momentous new start—*Doomsday* to the 'natives' and a Roman triumph of *jus scriptum* to court functionaries like Fitz Nigel—documents proliferated and accumulated in archives until lay literacy became the basis of the culture which produced our own.

Writing takes many forms and has been used for diverse purposes in different societies. Ashanti warriors covered their war-coats with written charms to ward off bullets. Likewise medieval knights had their swords inscribed with prayers or mysterious letters and Richard the Engineer (who may have been one of the architects of Durham Cathedral in the twelfth century) carried around with him numerous names of Christ and extracts from the Gospels on slips of parchment, which he kept in a small silken bag with some relics of St Cuthbert. Warriors and builders were in perilous professions where they needed charmed lives. Technologies are created or adapted to suit the requirements of different societies. The

Tibetans used rotary motion solely for prayer wheels, and their monks used block printing to make charms and to write invocations on the surface of the water to acquire merit. In early medieval Europe the skills of scribes were likewise primarily applied to acts of worship through the production of liturgical manuscripts like the *Lindisfarne Gospels*. Gradually, however, despite Christianity being a religion of a book and medieval culture being shaped by monks, writing on parchment was adapted and applied to mundane purposes of government, property-owning and commerce.

Most appropriately, the long continuity of England's history from the Middle Ages to the present has become enshrined in its great documents of government. Domesday Book and Magna Carta have been familiar names in the English-speaking world since the thirteenth century. The former symbolised the awesome ordering capacity of William the Conqueror and his Normans, while the latter spelled out the determination of the rebel barons to define the meaning of their victory over King John: they claimed to speak for England and for justice. Whereas Domesday Book used writing to attribute overriding power to William the Conqueror as king, Magna Carta compelled King John to acknowledge that written law was his superior. Over the centuries that followed, the significance of both these documents extended beyond the mundane details recorded in them, as they came to symbolise the rule of law itself. England's rulers believed that Domesday Book guaranteed all lawful titles to property and Magna Carta gave universal entitlement to justice. In reality, of course, these or any other writings could only be as good as the people who used them. All writing is *scriptura* or 'scripture' and its meaning depends on its interpreters. England's medieval documentary heritage does not look as relevant to law and justice today as it did to the Victorians and their predecessors who had so carefully preserved it. Even so, the hundreds of thousands of parchments still stand as formidable records of their makers and of the power of writing.

REFERENCES

I. The Making of Domesday Book (pages 215–32)

1. Orderic Vitalis, *Historia Ecclesiastica* ed. M. Chibnall (1969–80), Bk V, ch. 1, vol. iii, p. 4.
2. N. R. Ker, *English Manuscripts in the Century after the Norman Conquest* (1960), p. 1.
3. 'Observations on English Government from the Tenth Century to the Twelfth Century', *Transactions of the Royal Historical Society*, 5th series XXV (1975), p. 42.
4. 'Domesday Book and Anglo-Norman Governance', *TRHS* (1975), p. 175.
5. 'The Uses of Literacy in Anglo-Saxon England and its Neighbours', *THRS*, 5th series XXVII (1977), p. 113.
6. Harvey, 'Domesday Book', p. 176.
7. Text ed. D. C. Douglas, 'Some Early Surveys from the Abbey of Abingdon', *English Historical Review* XLIV (1929), p. 623.
8. D. C. Douglas (ibid., p. 619, n. 2) notes differences between this text and Domesday's, whereas Dr Harvey ('Domesday Book', p. 176) suggests that it is an extract 'from Domesday itself'.
9. V. H. Galbraith, *Studies in the Public Records* (1948), p. 36. Galbraith's case has been sustained in the 1980s by S. Keynes. Keynes's work is brought together in his 'Royal Government and the Written Word in Late Anglo-Saxon England' in *The Uses of Literacy in Early Medieval Europe*, ed. R. McKitterick (1990).
10. *Facsimiles of English Royal Writs Presented to V. H. Galbraith*, ed. T. A. M. Bishop and P. Chaplais (1957), p. xii.
11. ibid.
12. Galbraith, p. 36.
13. P. Chaplais, *English Royal Documents: King John–Henry VI* (1971), p. 5, n. 4.
14. *Facsimiles of English Royal Writs*, p. xi.
15. *The Anglo-Saxon Chronicle: A Revised Translation*, ed. D. Whitelock et al. (1961).
16. *Dialogus de Scaccario*, ed. C. Johnson (1950), p. 64; Revelation, XIII, 8.
17. *The Chronicle of Walter of Guisborough*, ed. H. Rothwell, Camden S., 3rd series LXXXIX (1957).
18. *The Chronicle of Battle Abbey*, ed. E. Searle (1980), p. 310.
19. R. C. Palmer, *The County Courts of Medieval England* (1982), p. 265, n. 10.
20. F. Yates, *The Art of Memory* (1966), p. 64 (citing Martianus Capella).
21. *Policraticus*, Bk 6, ch. 10, ed. C. C. J. Webb (1919).
22. *Anglo-Scottish Relations: Some Selected Documents*, ed. E. L. G. Stones, reprint (1970), pp. 96–117.
23. D. W. Sutherland, *Quo Warranto Proceedings in the Reign of Edward I* (1963), p. 14.

II. The Proliferation of Documents (pages 233–42)

1. *Walter of Henley and Other Treatises on Estate Management and Accounting* (1971), p. 223.
2. *Manorial Rolls of Cuxham*, Oxfordshire Record S. 50 (1976), p. 42.
3. R. H. Hilton, 'A Thirteenth-Century Poem on Disputed Villein Services', *English Historical Review* LVI (1941), p. 95.
4. *Select Cases in the Court of King's Bench under Edward I*, ed. G. O. Sayles, Selden Society III, pp. 47–9.
5. *The English Peasantry in the Later Middle Ages* (1975), p. 153.
6. *The Chronicle of Battle Abbey*, ed. E. Searle (1980), p. 214.
7. G. C. Homans, *English Villages of the Thirteenth Century* (1941), p. 332.
8. *Dialogus de Scaccario*, ed. C. Johnson (1950), p. 35.

III. THE WORK OF HUBERT WALTER (PAGES 243–8)

1. *The Chronicle of Jocelin of Brakelond*, ed. H. E. Butler (1949), p. 133.
2. *Diplomatic Documents*, ed. P. Chaplais, HMSO (1964), p. 304, no. 434.
3. *Select Charters*, ed. W. Stubbs, 9th edn, ed. H. W. C. Davis (1913).
4. *Giraldi Cambrensis Opera*, ed. J. S. Brewer et al., Rolls Series XXI (1861–91).
5. C. R. Cheney, 'Hubert Walter and Bologna', *Bulletin of Medieval Canon Law*, new series II (1972), pp. 81–4.
6. *Dialogus de Scaccario*, ed. C. Johnson (1950), p. 5.

IV. TYPES OF WRITTEN RECORD (PAGES 249–79)

1. M. Blaess, 'L'abbaye de Bordesley et les livres de Guy de Beauchamp', *Romania* LXXVIII (1957), pp. 511–18.
2. *Walter of Henley and Other Treatises on Estate Management and Accounting* (1971), pp. 11–50.
3. *Charters of the Honour of Mowbray*, ed. D. E. Greenway (1972), nos 31, 347, 20, 167, 166, 380.
4. D. L. Jeffry and B. J. Levy, *Anglo-Norman Lyric* (1990), p. 137 (my translation).
5. *Fitznell's Cartulary*, ed. C. A. F. Meekings, Surrey Record S. XXXVI (1968), nos 57, 62.
6. *Facsimiles of Early Cheshire Charters*, ed. G. Barraclough, Lancashire and Cheshire Record Society (1957), no. 14.
7. *Facsimiles of Early Charters from Northamptonshire Collections*, ed. F. M. Stenton, Northamptonshire Record Society, IV (1930), no. 53.
8. J. E. Sayers, *Papal Government and England* (1984), pp. 220–1.
9. *Luffield Priory Charters*, ed. G. R. Elvey (1968).
10. J. C. Holt, *Magna Carta* (1965), p. 342, plate v.
11. 'Earldom of Hereford Charters', ed. D. Walker, *Camden Miscellany*, Camden S. 4th series XXII (1964), p. 15, no. 7.
12. Van Caenegem, *Writs*, p. 420, no. 17.
13. ibid., p. 418, no. 12.
14. W. M. Ormrod, 'State Building and State Finance under Edward I', in W. M. Ormrod ed., *England in the Thirteenth Century*, Harlaxton (1991), p. 24.
15. *The Chronicle of Jocelin of Brakelond*, ed. H. E. Butler (1949), p. 29 (my translation).
16. W. Urry, *Canterbury under the Angevin Kings* (1967), p. 249 and map 26, sheet 3.
17. *Walter of Henley and Other Treatises*, p. 388.
18. G. H. Martin, 'The Origins of Borough Records', *Journal of the Society of Archivists* II (1960–4), pp. 153, 149.
19. *Rolls of the Justices in Eyre*, ed. D. M. Stenton, Selden S. LIII (1934), p. 411.
20. *Select Canterbury Cases*, ed. N. Adams and C. Donahue, SS XCV (1979), p. 3.
21. *The London Eyre of 1244*, London Record S. VI (1970), p. 134, no. 345.
22. N. R. Ker, *Books, Collectors and Libraries* (1983), p. 47.
23. M. D. Chenu, *Nature, Man and Society in the Twelfth Century*, trans. J. Taylor and L. K. Little (1968), p. 298.
24. Henry de Bracton, *De Legibus et Consuetudinibus Angliae*, ed. G. E. Woodbine (1915), reissued with translations and revisions by S. E. Thorne (1968–77), vol. 2, p. 19.
25. A. G. Rigg, *A History of Anglo-Latin Literature 1066–1422* (1992); T. Hunt, *Teaching and Learning Latin in Thirteenth-Century England*, 3 vols (1991).
26. 2nd edn (1964); *Supplement* (1987) by A. G. Watson.
27. C. de Hamel, *A History of Illuminated Manuscripts* (1986), p. 164.
28. C. Donovan, *The de Brailes Hours* (1991), p. 183, MSS nos. 1–5.
29. See my 'The Medieval Experience of Learning to Read' in my *Literacy and Law in Medieval England* (Hambledon, 1998), and my *Woman and the Book in the Middle Ages* (Blackwell, 1998).

V. The Making of Manuscripts (pages 281–98)

1. *The Life of St Hugh of Lincoln*, ed. D. L. Douie and H. Farmer (1961) II, p. 209.
2. *Dialogus de Scaccario*, ed. C. Johnson (1950).
3. *Dictionary of Medieval Latin from British Sources*, ed. R. E. Latham (1975) I, p. 216.

VI. Writing for Posterity (pages 299–308)

1. *Facsimiles of Early Charters in Oxford Muniment Rooms*, ed. H. E. Salter (1929), no. 11.
2. Henry de Bracton, *De Legibus et Consuetudinibus Angliae*, ed. G. E. Woodbine (1915), reissued with translation and revisions by S. E. Thorne (1968–77).
3. N. F. Cantor, *Church, Kingship and Lay Investiture in England* (1958), p. 169.
4. *Dialogus de Scaccario*, ed. C. Johnson (1950).
5. *Book of Prests*, ed. E. B. Fryde (1962), pp. 229–30.

VII. Archives and Libraries (pages 310–39)

1. F. Wormald, 'The Sherborne Chartulary' in *Fritz Saxl Memorial Essays*, ed. D. J. Gordon (1957), p. 109.
2. 'Service-Books and Records', *Bulletin of the Institute of Historical Research* LVI (1983), pp. 7–15.
3. M. Beit-Arié and Z. E. Rokeah, *The Only Dated Hebrew MS Written in England* (1985), pp. 33–56, plates 6, 7.
4. F. M. Powicke and C. R. Cheney, *Councils and Synods* II (1964), p. 82, no. 67.
5. R. M. Thomas, *MSS from St Albans Abbey 1066–1235* (1982) II, plate 258.
6. K. W. Humphreys, *The Book Provisions of the Medieval Friars* (1964), p. 136.
7. *Dialogus de Scaccario*, ed. C. Johnson (1950).
8. N. Brooks, *The Early History of the Church of Canterbury* (1984), p. 168.
9. *The Chronicle of Bury St Edmunds*, ed. A. Gransden (1964), p. 73.
10. *Liber Memorandum*, ed. J. W. Clark (1907).
11. 'Liber Magistri Hugonis Sancti Victoris', ed. W. M. Green, in *Speculum* XVIII (1943) (my translation).
12. M. J. Carruthers, *The Book of Memory* (1990), plates 18, 19, comment at pp. 243–5.
13. ibid., p. 247.
14. S. Lewis, *The Art of Matthew Paris in the 'Chronica Majora'* (1987), p. 48.
15. *Ad Herennium*, ed. H. Caplan, Loeb Classical Library 403 (1954), p. 208. This text was not composed by Cicero, but medieval scholars believed that it was.
16. 'Liber', ed. Green, p. 489, lines 42–6 (my translation).
17. *Preachers, Florilegia and Sermons* (1979), p. 4.
18. R. W. Southern, *Robert Grosseteste* (1986), pp. 188–9.
19. B. Tierney, *The Crisis of Church and State* (1964), p. 201.
20. C. Duggan, *Twelfth-Century Decretal Collections and their Importance in English History*, University of London Historical Studies XII (1963), p. 26 (citing Stephen of Tournai).
21. *Calendar of Chancery Warrants*, HMSO (1927) I, p. 120.
22. W. M. Ormrod ed., *England in the Thirteenth Century*, Harlaxton Medieval Studies I (1991), pp. 24–5.

VIII. The Growth of Literacy (pages 341–52)

1. F. Pollock and F. W. Maitland, *The History of English Law before the Time of Edward I*, 2nd edn (1898).
2. *Medieval Civilization*, trans. J. Barrow (1988), p. 163.
3. M. Jennings, 'Tutivillus: The Literary Career of the Recording Demon', *Studies in Philology* LXXIV (1977), no. 5, p. 16.
4. 'Women and Art in the 13th and 14th Centuries', in *Age of Chivalry: Art in Plantagenet England 1200–1400*, ed. J. Alexander and P. Binski, Exhibition Catalogue (1987).

5. M. Camille, 'The Devil's Writing: Diabolic Literacy in Medieval Art', *World Art* (Acts of the 26th Annual Congress of the History of Art), ed. I. Levin (1989).

6. N. J. Morgan, *The Lambeth Apocalypse* (1990), pp. 72–82.

7. C. Donovan, *The de Brailes Hours* (1991), p. 75, fig. 44.

8. C. M. Chazelle, 'Pictures, Books, and the Illiterate: Pope Gregory I's Letters to Serenus of Marseilles', *Word and Image* VI (1990), p. 139.

9. O. Pächt, C. R. Dodwell and F. Wormald, *The St Albans Psalter* (1960), p. 64.

10. R. H. Robbins ed. *Secular Lyrics of the 14th and 15th Centuries* 2nd edn (1955), p. 93, no. 100.

11. *Orality and Literacy* (1982), pp. 78–80.

12. Roy Harris, *The Origin of Writing* (1986), p. 156.

IX. Literate and Illiterate (pages 353–82)

1. S. S. Walker, 'Proof of Age of Feudal Heirs in Medieval England', *Medieval Studies* (Toronto) XXXV (1973), pp. 316–20.

2. *Le Traité de Walter de Bibbesworth*, ed. A. Owen (Paris, 1929).

3. Nigellus de Longchamp dit Wireker, *Tractatus Contra Curiales et Officiales Clericos*, ed. A. Boutemy (1959), I, p. 204.

4. J. W. Thompson, *The Literacy of the Laity in the Middle Ages*, University of California Publications in Education IX (1939).

5. R. W. Southern, 'Master Vacarius and the Beginning of an English Academic Tradition', in *Medieval Learning and Literature: Essays Presented to R. W. Hunt* (1976), p. 268, n. 1.

6. J. W. Baldwin, *Masters, Princes and Merchants* (1970), II, p. 51, n. 57.

7. *The Chronicle of Jocelin of Brakelond*, ed. H. E. Butler (1949).

8. *De Nugis Curialium*, ed. M. R. James, C. N. L. Brooke, R. A. B. Mynors (1983), Bk IV, ch. 1, p. 278.

9. Galbraith's lecture to the British Academy ('The Literacy of the Medieval English Kings', *Proceedings of the British Academy* XXI (1935), pp. 201–38) was published in 1936. Thompson's *The Literacy of the Laity in the Middle Ages* was completed in the same year but was not published until 1939 (University of California Publications in Education).

10. Galbraith, 'Literacy', p. 215.

11. *The Governance of Medieval England from the Conquest to Magna Carta* (1963), pp. 269–83.

12. 'The Literacy of the Laity', in *The Medieval World*, ed. D. Daiches and A. Thorlby (1973), p. 560.

13. *English Schools in the Middle Ages* (1973), ch. 1.

14. F. Barlow, *The English Church 1066–1154* (1979), p. 229.

15. R. W. Southern, *Robert Grosseteste* (1986), p. 63.

16. *Jocelin*, ed. Butler, pp. 34–44.

17. 'The Literacy of the Laity', p. 555.

18. D. Crouch, *William Marshal* (1990), p. 23.

19. *Jocelin*, ed. Butler, pp. 24 and 34.

20. *English Lawsuits from William I to Richard I*, ed. R. C. van Caenegem, i, Selden S. CVI (1990), p. 290.

21. Henry de Bracton, *De Legibus et Consuetudinibus Angliae*, fo. 115b, vol. ii, p. 326.

22. D. M. Stenton, *English Justice between the Norman Conquest and the Great Charter* (1965), p. 192.

23. *The Treatise on the Laws and Customs of the Realm of England Commonly called Glanvill*, ed. G. D. G. Hall (1965), pp. xliv–xlv.

24. *Speculum Duorum*, ed. Y. Lefèvre and R. B. C. Huygens (1974), p. 52.

X. Hearing, Seeing and Magna Carta (pages 383–96)

1. *Charters of the Honour of Mowbray*, ed. D. E. Greenway (1972), nos. 92, 347.
2. F. M. Stenton, *The First Century of English Feudalism 1066–1166*, 2nd edn (1961), pp. 111, 273, no. 27.
3. M. M. Sheehan, *The Will in Medieval England*, Pontifical Institute of Medieval Studies: Studies & Texts VI (1963), pp. 186–7.
4. *Charters of the Honour of Mowbray*, no. 98.
5. *Facsimiles of Early Charters in Oxford Muniment Rooms*, ed. H. E. Salter (1929), no. 9.
6. R. B. Brooke, *The Coming of the Friars* (1975), p. 126.
7. A. E. van Vleck, *Memory and Re-Creation in Troubadour Lyric* (1991), p. 41.
8. J. C. Holt, *Magna Carta* (1965), p. 345.
9. D. L. Douie, *Archbishop Pecham* (1952), p. 113, n. 2.
10. S. Reynolds, 'Magna Carta 1297 and the Legal Use of Literacy', *Bulletin of the Institute of Historical Research* LXII (1989), p. 241.
11. *Orality and Literacy* (1982), ch. 5.
12. M. D. Legge, *Anglo-Norman Literature and its Background* (1963), p. 65.
13. ibid., p. 143.
14. *The Life of St Anselm by Eadmer*, ed. R. W. Southern (1962), p. 62.
15. C. J. Holdsworth, 'John of Ford and English Cistercian Writing', *Transactions of the Royal Historical Society* 5th series XI (1961), p. 124.
16. *Opera Omnia*, ed. F. S. Schmidt (1938–61) III, p. 84.
17. J. W. Thompson, *The Literacy of the Laity in the Middle Ages*, University of California Publications in Education IX (1939), p. 171, n. 46.
18. F. M. Powicke, *The Christian Life in the Middle Ages* (1935), p. 88.
19. Orderic Vitalis, *Historia Ecclesiastica*, ed. M. Chibnall (1969–80), Bk III, vol. ii, p. 2.
20. Bk IV, ch. 6, C. J. Webb (1909) I, p. 255.

XI. Writings as Works of Art (pages 397–407)

1. L. Hellinga, *Caxton in Focus* (1982), p. 77, colour plates I, III.
2. *Crown Pleas of the Wiltshire Eyre*, ed. C. A. F. Meekings, Wilts RS XVI (1961), p. 25.
3. M. J. Carruthers, *The Book of Memory* (1990), pp. 223–4, 341, n. 12.
4. ibid., pp. 223, 341, n. 11.
5. *Orality and Literacy* (1982), p. 101.
6. J. Martin, 'John of Salisbury as a Classical Scholar', in *The World of John of Salisbury*, ed. Wilks, p. 194.
7. *The Works of Gilbert Crispin Abbot of Westminster*, ed. A. S. Abulafia and G. R. Evans (1986), p. 52.
8. ibid.
9. T. A. Heslop, 'Brief in Words but Heavy in the Weight of its Mysteries', *Art History* IX (1986), p. 2.
10. 'The Artists of the Rutland Psalter', *British Library Journal* XIII (1987), pp. 176–7.
11. M. Camille, 'The Book of Signs', *Word and Image* I (1985), p. 142.
12. F. H. Bäuml, 'Varieties and Consequences of Medieval Literacy and Illiteracy', *Speculum* LV (1980), p. 262.

XII. Trusting Writing and the Art of Forgery (pages 409–21)

1. *The Sandford Cartulary*, II, Oxfordshire Record S. XXII (1941), p. 181.
2. C. R. Cheney, *Medieval Texts and Studies* (1973), p. 104.
3. F. M. Stenton, *The Latin Charters of the Anglo-Saxon Period* (1955), p. 11.
4. *Gilbert Foliot and his Letters* (1965), pp. 128–9.

5. A. Gransden, *Historical Writing in England* c. *550–1307* (1974), pp. 177–8.
6. *The Treatise on the Laws and Customs of the Realm of England Commonly Called Glanvill*, ed. G. D. G. Hall (1965), pp. 2–3.
7. 'Approaches to Medieval Forgery', *Medieval Church and Society* (1971), p. 115 (my emphasis).
8. *Studies in the Public Records* (1948), pp. 48–9.
9. ibid., pp. 51–2.

SUGGESTIONS FOR FURTHER
❋READING❋

INTRODUCTORY

F. Barlow, *The Feudal Kingdom of England 1042–1216*, 4th edn (1987).

R. Bartlett, *The Making of Europe: Conquest, Colonization and Cultural Change 950–1350* (1993).

M. Chibnall, *Anglo-Norman England 1066–1166* (1986).

R. R. Davies, *Domination and Conquest: the Experience of Ireland, Scotland and Wales 1100–1300* (1990).

D. C. Douglas and G. W. Greenaway, eds, *English Historical Documents 1042–1189*, 2nd edn (1981).

R. Frame, *The Political Development of the British Isles 1100–1400* (1990).

E. Hallam, ed., *The Plantagenet Chronicles [1128–1216]* (1984).

E. Hallam, ed., *Chronicles of the Age of Chivalry 1216–1377* (1987).

E. King, *Medieval England 1066–1485* (1988).

J. Le Goff, trans. J. Barrow, *Medieval Civilization 400–1500* (1988).

R. Mortimer, *Angevin England 1154–1258* (1994).

H. Rothwell, ed., *English Historical Documents 1189–1327* (1975).

C. Tyerman, *Who's Who in Early Medieval England 1066–1272* (1996).

W. L. Warren, *The Governance of Norman and Angevin England 1086–1272* (1987).

WILLIAM THE CONQUEROR, WILLIAM RUFUS AND HENRY I

Anglo-Norman Studies, vols 1–19 (Proceedings of the Battle Conference 1978-96), ed. R. Allen Brown, M. Chibnall, C. Harper-Bill.

F. Barlow, *William Rufus* (1983).

M. Chibnall, *The World of Orderic Vitalis: Norman Monks and Norman Knights* (1996).

H. Clover and M. Gibson, eds, *The Letters of Lanfranc Archbishop of Canterbury* (1979).

R. H. C. Davis, *The Normans and their Myth* (1976).

D. C. Douglas, *William the Conqueror* (1964).

R. Fleming, *Kings and Lords in Conquest England* (1991).

R. Gameson, ed., *The Study of the Bayeux Tapestry* (1997).

J. A. Green, *The Government of England under Henry I* (1986).

E. M. Hallam, *Domesday Book Through Nine Centuries* (1986).

J. C. Holt, ed., *Domesday Studies* (1987).

E. Mason, *St Wulfstan of Worcester* c. *1008–1095* (1990).

S. Morillo, *Warfare under the Anglo-Norman Kings 1066–1135* (1996).

P. Stafford, *Unification and Conquest: A Political and Social History of England in the Tenth and Eleventh Centuries* (1989).

E. Van Houts, 'The Norman Conquest through European Eyes', *English Historical Review* 110 (1995), pp. 832–53.

A. Williams, *The English and the Norman Conquest* (1995).

M. Wood, *Domesday: a Search for the Roots of England* (1987).

STEPHEN, MATILDA AND HENRY II

E. Amt, *The Accession of Henry II: Royal Government Restored 1149–1159* (1993).

F. Barlow, *Thomas Becket* (1986).

M. Chibnall, *The Empress Matilda* (1991).

D. Crouch, *The Beaumont Twins* (1987).

P. Dalton, *Conquest, Anarchy and Lordship: Yorkshire 1066–1154* (1994).
R. H. C. Davis, *King Stephen*, 3rd edn (1990).
Gesta Stephani, ed. K. R. Potter and R. H. C. Davis (1976).
J. Gillingham, 'Henry of Huntingdon and the Revival of the English Nation', *Concepts of National Identity in the Middle Ages*, ed. S. Forde, L. Johnson, A. V. Murray (1995).
T. K. Keefe, *Feudal Assessments and the Political Community under Henry II and his Sons* (1983).
E. King, ed., *The Anarchy of King Stephen's Reign* (1994).
D. D. R. Owen, *Eleanor of Aquitaine: Queen and Legend* (1993).
B. Smalley, *The Becket Conflict and the Schools* (1973).
The Chronicle of Battle Abbey, ed. E. Searle (1980).
The Historia Novella by William of Malmesbury, ed. K. R. Potter (1955).
W. L. Warren, *Henry II* (1973).

RICHARD I AND JOHN

R. Bartlett, *Gerald of Wales 1146–1223* (1982).
D. Crouch, *William Marshal 1147–1219* (1990).
J. Gillingham, *Richard Coeur de Lion* [includes his 'The Angevin Empire'] (1994).
J. Gillingham, *Richard the Lion Heart*, 2nd edn (1989).
J. C. Holt, *Magna Carta*, 2nd edn (1992).
J. C. Holt, *Magna Carta and Medieval Government* (1985).
Selected Letters of Pope Innocent III Concerning England 1198–1216, ed. C. R. Cheney and W. H. Semple (1953).
The Chronicle of Richard of Devizes, ed. J. T. Appleby (1963).
R. V. Turner, *King John* (1994).
W. L. Warren, *King John* (1961).

HENRY III AND EDWARD I

G. J. Brault, ed., *Rolls of Arms of Edward I* (1997).
D. A. Carpenter, *The Reign of Henry III* (1996).
P. R. Coss, ed., *Thomas Wright's Political Songs of England* (1996).
S. D. Lloyd, *English Society and the Crusade 1216–1307* (1988).
J. R. Maddicott, *Simon de Montfort* (1994).
D. Parsons, ed., *Eleanor of Castile* (1991).
M. Prestwich, *Edward I* (1988).
M. Prestwich, *English Politics in the Thirteenth Century* (1990).
R. Stacey, *Politics, Policy and Finance under Henry III 1216–1245* (1987).
Thirteenth-Century England vols 1–5, ed. P. R. Coss and S. D. Lloyd (1986–95).
M. Vale, *The Angevin Legacy and the Hundred Years War* (1990).
R. Vaughan, *Chronicles of Matthew Paris* (1984).
N. Vincent, *Peter des Roches: an Alien in English Politics* (1996).
S. L. Waugh, *The Lordship of England: Royal Wardships and Marriages in Society and Politics 1217–1327* (1988).

ARCHAEOLOGY AND ARCHITECTURE

J. Alexander and P. Binski, eds, *Age of Chivalry: Art in Plantagenet England 1200–1400* (1987).
M. W. Beresford and M. K. St Joseph, *Medieval England: an Aerial Survey*, 2nd edn (1979).
P. Binski, *Westminster Abbey and the Plantagenets 1200–1400* (1995).
J. Blair and N. Ramsey, eds, *English Medieval Industries* (1991).
H. Clarke, *The Archaeology of Medieval England* (1984).
N. Coldstream, *The Decorated Style* (1994).
T. A. Heslop, 'Orford Castle: Nostalgia and Sophisticated Living', *Architectural History* 34 (1991), pp. 36–58.

C. Platt, *Medieval England: a Social History and Archaeology from the Conquest to 1600 A.D.* (1978).

C. Platt, *The Architecture of Medieval Britain* (1990).

T. Rowley, *The Norman Heritage 1066–1200* (1983).

J. M. Steane, *The Archaeology of Medieval England and Wales* (1985).

C. Wilson, *The Gothic Cathedral* (1990).

F. Woodman, *The Architectural History of Canterbury Cathedral* (1981).

Books and Documents

M. P. Brown, *A Guide to Western Historical Scripts from Antiquity to 1600* (1990).

P. Chaplais, *English Royal Documents 1199–1461* (1971).

C. de Hamel, *A History of Illuminated Manuscripts* (1986).

C. Donovan, *The De Brailes Hours: Shaping the Book of Hours in Thirteenth-Century Oxford* (1991).

M. Gibson, T. A. Heslop, R. W. Pfaff, eds, *The Eadwine Psalter* (1992).

A. Gransden, *Historical Writing in England 550–1307* (1974).

S. Lewis, *The Art of Matthew Paris in the Chronica Majora* (1987).

M. B. Parkes, *Scribes, Scripts and Readers* (1991).

R. A. Skelton and P. D. A. Harvey, *Local Maps and Plans from Medieval England* (1986).

R. M. Thomson, *William of Malmesbury* (1987).

Church, Religion and Learning

F. Barlow, *The English Church 1066–1154* (1979).

R. C. Finucane, *Miracles and Pilgrims: Popular Beliefs in Medieval England* (1977).

D. Knowles, *The Monastic Order in England 940–1216*, 2nd edition (1963).

H. Mayr-Harting, ed., *St Hugh of Lincoln* (1987).

B. Harvey, *Living and Dying in England 1100–1540: the Monastic Experience* (1993).

Jocelin of Brakelond, *Chronicle of the Abbey of Bury St Edmunds*, trans. D. Greenway and J. Sayers (1989).

B. Millett and J. Wogan-Browne, eds, *Medieval English Prose for Women* (1990).

R. W. Southern, *St Anselm: a Portrait in a Landscape* (1990).

R. W. Southern, *Robert Grosseteste: the Growth of an English Mind in Medieval Europe* (1986).

R. N. Swanson, *Religion and Devotion in Europe 1215–1515* (1995).

The Book of St Gilbert, ed. R. Foreville and G. Keir (1987).

The Life of Christina of Markyate, ed. C. H. Talbot (1959).

The Letters of John of Salisbury, 2 vols, ed. W. J. Millor, H. E. Butler, C. N. L. Brooke (1979, 1986).

S. Thompson, *Women Religious: the Founding of English Nunneries after the Norman Conquest* (1991).

B. Ward, *Miracles and the Medieval Mind* (1982).

Economy and Society

G. Astill and A. Grant, *The Countryside of Medieval England* (1988).

J. M. Bennett, *Women in the Medieval English Countryside* (1987).

J. L. Bolton, *The Medieval English Economy 1150–1500* (1980).

R. H. Britnell, *The Commercialisation of English Society 1000–1500* (1993).

D. Crouch, *The Image of Aristocracy in Britain 1000–1300* (1992).

C. Dyer, *Standards of Living in the Later Middle Ages: Social Change in England 1200–1520* (1989).

C. Dyer, *Everyday Life in Medieval England* (1994).

B. Hanawalt, *The Ties that Bound: Peasant Families in Medieval England* (1986).

A. Harding, *England in the Thirteenth Century* (1993).

A. Haverkamp and H. Vollrath, eds, *England and Germany in the High Middle Ages* (1996):
N. Orme on lay literacy, D. A. Carpenter on law and order, M. Prestwich on armies,
P. R. Hyams on Jews, S. Reynolds on towns, C. Dyer on the development of the manor,
J. Gillingham on social mobility.

E. Miller and John Hatcher, *Medieval England: Rural Society and Economic Change 1086–1348*
(1978).

E. Miller and John Hatcher, *Medieval England: Towns, Commerce and Crafts 1086–1348* (1995).

LANGUAGE, LITERATURE AND EDUCATION

N. Blake, ed., *The Cambridge History of the English Language*, vol. 2, *1066–1476* (1992).

J. I. Catto, ed., *The Early Oxford Schools*, vol. 1 of *The History of the University of Oxford*,
ed. T. H. Aston (1984).

S. Crane, *Insular Romance: Politics, Faith and Culture in Anglo-Norman and Middle English Literature* (1986).

E. J. Gardner, 'The English Nobility and Monastic Education', *The Cloister and the World:
Essays in Honour of B. Harvey*, ed. J. Blair and B. Golding (1996), pp. 80–94.

Lawman (Layamon), *Brut*, trans. R. Allen (1992).

C. M. Meale, ed., *Women and Literature in Britain 1150–1500* (1993).

N. Orme, *From Childhood to Chivalry: the Education of the English Kings and Aristocracy
1066–1530* (1984).

A. G. Rigg, *A History of Anglo-Latin Literature 1066–1422* (1992).

Two Medieval Outlaws: the Romances of Eustace the Monk and Fouke Fitz Waryn, trans. G. S.
Burgess (1997).

T. Turville-Petre, *England the Nation: Language, Literature and National Identity* (1996).

Walter Map, *Courtiers' Trifles – De Nugis Curialium*, ed. M. R. James, C. N. L. Brooke, R. A. B.
Mynors (1983).

LAW AND ORDER

R. Bartlett, *Trial by Fire and Water: the Medieval Judicial Ordeal* (1986).

P. A. Brand, *The Origins of the English Legal Profession* (1992).

M. T. Clanchy, 'Highway Robbery and Trial by Battle in the Hampshire Eyre of 1249',
Medieval Legal Records Edited in Honour of C. A. F. Meekings, ed. R. F. Hunnisett and J. B.
Post (1978), pp. 25–61.

J. Hudson, *The Formation of the English Common Law* (1996).

J. M. Stenton, *English Justice Between the Norman Conquest and the Great Charter* (1965).

The Course of the Exchequer by Richard Son of Nigel, ed. C. Johnson, revised edn (1983).

The Treatise on the Laws of England Commonly Called Glanvill, ed. G. D. G. Hall, revised edn
(1993).

R. V. Turner, *Judges, Administrators and the Common Law in Angevin England* (1994).

R. C. van Caenegem, ed., *English Lawsuits from William I to Richard I*, 2 vols, (Selden Society,
1990, 1991).

WARFARE AND CHIVALRY

R. Barber, *The Knight and Chivalry*, 2nd edn (1996).

P. Coss, *The Knight in Medieval England 1000–1400* (1993).

R. H. C. Davis, *The Medieval Warhorse* (1989).

J. Gillingham, '1066 and the Introduction of Chivalry into England', *Law and Government in
Medieval England and Normandy: Essays in Honour of Sir James Holt* (1994), pp. 31–55.

J. Gillingham and J. C. Holt, eds, *War and Government in the Middle Ages: Essays in Honour of J. O.
Prestwich* (1984).

C. Harper-Bill, R. Harvey, S. Church, eds, *The Ideals and Practice of Medieval Knighthood*, vols 1–5
(1981–1995).

C. Harper-Bill, C. Holdsworth, J. L. Nelson, eds, *Studies in Medieval History Presented to R. Allen Brown* (1989).

Jordan Fantosme's Chronicle, ed. R. C. Johnston (1981).

M. Keen, *Chivalry* (1984).

S. Reynolds, *Fiefs and Vassals* (1994).

M. Strickland, ed., *Anglo-Norman Warfare* (1990).

❋ INDEX ❋

Note: Medieval persons are indexed by forename and modern persons by surname